Wild Flowers

of Britain & Ireland

MARJORIE BLAMEY

RICHARD FITTER

ALASTAIR FITTER

A & C Black · London

First published in 2003 by A & C Black Publishers Ltd.,
37 Soho Square, London W1D 3QZ

www.acblack.com

ISBN 0-7136-5944-0

A CIP catalogue record for this book is available from the British Library

The authors gratefully acknowledge help with cartography from
David Fitter and Robert Fitter

Reproduction by Digitronix Ltd., Bradford, England
Printed in Great Britain by Butler and Tanner Ltd., Frome, England

CONTENTS

Soils formed on chalk, limestone and some volcanic rocks are not acid and so have a richer flora. The map's reddish area shows where those rocks, and hence those soils, are found. But in the north and west, where rainfall is high, the rocks are sometimes covered by acid peats, and there lime-rich soils are only found where the rocks outcrop through the peat.

INTRODUCTION

This is a mapped and illustrated guide to all the wild flowers that the reader is likely to find growing wild in England, Scotland, Wales and Ireland. It includes all species that grow here naturally, and also many that have been introduced by humans, whether as garden plants or accidentally as weeds of farming. It does not include plants that are only ever seen planted, or which occur briefly after they are discarded by humans or accidentally sown.

The **area covered** is that between the Shetlands and the Scilly Isles, including the Isle of Man. The Channel Isles, however, are botanically French, part of the European Continent, and we shall treat them in a separate guide. The range of habitats represented by our area is immense: the tops of the highest Scottish mountains are true tundra, and have some plants elsewhere found only in the Arctic and the Alps. On the western fringes of our islands, especially in the south, there are plants whose main home is Spain and Portugal. In contrast, East Anglia has a climate more like that of central Europe – hot and dry in summer, cold in winter – and it has plants characteristic of that part of the continent. The botanist at large in Britain, therefore, has an exciting diversity of plants and habitats to explore.

Arrangement. The plants are arranged in systematic order, reflecting their evolution, except that we have put groups such as waterweeds, trees and grasses separately at the back for ease of reference. Plants early in the book tend to have open, saucer-shaped flowers with many parts (petals, anthers etc.). Later on come plants with more distinctively-shaped flowers, often two-lipped, or with small flowers gathered into heads. Getting to know the pattern and sequence of families greatly helps in locating a new species.

Coverage. As well as all the plants with obvious and conspicuous flowers, some groups of plants superficially look as if they have no flowers – usually because they are pollinated by wind rather than insects and so have no need for their flowers to be conspicuous. These include grasses, sedges and rushes; waterweeds which grow completely under water (plants that float on water usually have conspicuous flowers); and many trees and tall shrubs, including conifers (see below) which have cones rather than flowers. We also cover those that genuinely have no flowers – ferns and horsetails which, though not flowering plants at all, are conspicuous, beautiful and intriguing when encountered – as they are in many habitats.

Flowering plants. Most of the plants in this guide are Seed Plants or spermato-phytes; the majority of them true Flowering Plants or Angiosperms, but 15 spe-cies are Conifers or Gymnosperms – all trees or shrubs, nearly all evergreen, with narrow, usually needle-like leaves, and most producing their seeds in cones. The true Flowering Plants comprise Dicotyledons, with two seed-leaves (cotyledons), broad, net-veined leaves, and petals and sepals usually in fours and fives; and Monocotyledons with one seed-leaf, unstalked, parallel-sided and parallel-veined leaves, and 3 or 6 petals or sepals.

monocotyledon seedling   dicotyledon seedling

The ferns, horsetails and their allies that we see are called sporophytes be-cause they produce spores, usually in tiny pouches under their leaves. The spores germinate and grow into a tiny but distinct plant, called the gametophyte, which then itself reproduces to form the sporophyte again. Seed plants also have these two generations, but their gametophyte grows inside the sporophyte and so does not exist as a separate plant. The only plants we have left out of the book altogether are mosses and liverworts.

English names are from the list approved by the Botanical Society of the Brit-ish Isles; in a few cases we have simplified those or used indigenous names for introduced plants (e.g. the Maori names of some introduced New Zealand shrubs). For **scientific names** we have followed Clive Stace's authoritative *New Flora of the British Isles*, Second Edition, 1997.

The **systematic order** is hierarchical: within the major groups (angiosperms, gymnosperms, ferns) are groups called families, which in turn are composed of genera (plural of genus), and genera of species. All the genera in a family share the diagnostic features of the family, and all the species in a genus share its key characters. Each species is described by two names: first the genus with a capi-tal initial, then the species, with a small initial, and both in italic type. Hence the Common or Meadow Buttercup is *Ranunculus acris*.

This system, devised by the great Swedish naturalist Linnaeus 250 years ago, is used internationally for all organisms, and avoids problems of communica-tion as well as the idiosyncrasies of English names. The Burnet Saxifrage (p. 184), for example, is neither a burnet (p. 134) nor a saxifrage (p. 116-20)! The family names (which are not italicised) all end in –aceae, and usually start with the name of some typical genus; so the buttercup family is the Ranunculaceae because buttercups are *Ranunculus*. There are categories within species (subspecies and varieties); we have only used these where there are very obvious differences within a species.

Group introductions. Introductions in the text to families and other groupings of plants summarize the range of plants within each and characteristics they share or in which they may differ. This both saves the need for much repetition in the species descriptions and is important when learning to recognize and name plants within the group. These introductions must therefore always be read and borne in mind as the background to the descriptive texts within each group.

Keys in this book are of two kinds. First, the whole arrangement of the plants is, wherever helpful, in the form of a key. Rather than simply list the plants in their approved scientific order, we have arranged them, particularly in the large or complex groups, in different sub-groups by recognizable characters they share. This is summarized at the head of each such group in the form of numbered and coloured headings, with page references to the start of each section where the key covers many pages of the book. The same numbered and coloured heading appears at the start of each such section's text descriptions. Note that the numbering used for these key headings is quite separate from the plant numbers used on each page for connecting illustrations, descriptions and maps.

For the start of a key to a large and complex group, see for example that of the Pea Family on page 140:

1. Flowers in loose heads or short spikes: (below)
    1a. Leaves with many leaflet pairs, ending with a leaflet (below)
    1b. Leaves with many leaflet pairs, ending with a tendril (p. 142)
    1c. Leaves with many leaflet pairs, ending with neither leaflet nor tendril (p. 144)
    1d. Leaves with 3-5 leaflets (p. 146)
    1e. Leaves with 1-2 leaflet pairs (p. 148)
    1f. Leaves undivided (p. 148)
2. Flowers in tight heads: (p. 148)
    2a. Yellow (p. 150)
    2b. Pink or pink-purple (p. 150)
    2c. White (p. 152)
3. Flowers in long spikes: (p. 154)
4. Flowers solitary or paired: (p. 158)

1.   2.   3.   4.

Nobody can master the Pea Family in 20 minutes, but by reading its introduction, following the choices and finally confirming the diagnosis, the reader will we hope arrive at his or her plant rather than give up in despair.

A further type of quick visual key is found in the **key boxes**. These we provide wherever relevant and helpful in the course of text descriptions, at the start of a group or in the course of a main key.

An example of the last is on p. 294 where in the Daisy Family we have reached yellow flowers of the dandelion type:

3a. Dandelion-type: Flowers yellow

Stems with milky juice:		Dandelion, Goatsbeard, Viper's Grass, Sow-thistles, Lettuces
Flowering stems leafless:		Dandelion, Catsears, Hawkbits, some Hawkweeds, Mouse-ear Hawkweeds
Runners:		Mouse-ear Hawkweeds, Fox-and-Cubs
Leaves	grass-like:	Goatsbeard
	pimply:	Bristly Ox-tongue
	prickly:	Prickly/Great Lettuces
Flowers	orange:	Fox-and-Cubs

At this point, the reader can quickly narrow the choice of likely plant by observing whether or not it has milky juice, flowering stems with leaves, or the other aspects considered. If it has runners and distinctly orange flowers, it is probably the attractive Fox-and-Cubs, or perhaps one of its two close relatives sometimes found as chance escapes – as the pictures, text and maps should then confirm.

The **text** for each plant gives at least three key identification clues, if possible visible to the naked eye; the most important ones are printed in *italics*. The picture opposite gives a general impression of the plant and illustrates the clues. Facts not readily illustrated, such as height, habitat and flowering time, are given in the description of each species. Each plant has a number corresponding to the numbers below its map and/or illustration.

For very similar species, the descriptions of some are often given briefly following that of a commoner one. They keep its number but are distinguished by an added letter – e.g. **3a**. These subordinate or "**sunk**" species descriptions show only where they differ from the main one, so you need to bear its characteristics in mind.

Rarity. For the rarest native plants in Britain (but not for those found only in Ireland), we use a system of asterisks after each plant's number to give a more precise idea of their rarity, based on recording the distribution of the plants in fine detail within areas of 1 kilometre (1 km) square:

* * = scarce, found in less than 100 1 km squares

* ** = endangered, found in less than 15 1 km squares

* *** = very rare, found in no more than 3 localities in Britain

Some plants are easy to identify from the picture alone, but even then you need to check the description in the text. Plants can be quite variable in some features, so the most critical things are the shape and structure of the flowers, because these are what decide the position of a species in the evolutionary order. If your plant does not match those features, you need to look elsewhere.

Very often, a group of plants, perhaps those in a single genus, will look similar and be hard to separate just by studying pictures. In these cases, the diagnostic features in the text are critical. All the plants in a genus will share the obvious characters such as flower shape. In such cases, you will have to examine other features, for example the shape of the leaves and whether they are hairy or not, and sometimes habitat, flowering time or distribution. However, no two species differ only in ecology or geography: there has to be some physical difference for botanists to accept a plant as a separate species.

Form. Unless the text specifies otherwise, plants are assumed to be upright but not woody. The **height** stated is the maximum typical height of the plant. This is indicated as:

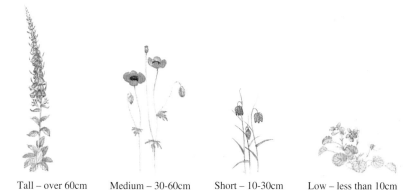

Tall – over 60cm   Medium – 30-60cm   Short – 10-30cm   Low – less than 10cm

Some features can be very variable. For example, height varies greatly according to altitude, climate and soil, and for woody plants, age as well. A 2cm high flowering specimen of Broad-leaved Willowherb (p. 160) has been found in a pavement crack, though it normally grows to 50-60cm, while docks (p. 60-4) and goosefoots (p. 38) can grow much taller than normal on manure heaps.

The flowering parts provide a wealth of identification factors. In addition to obvious features such as size and colour, and the fundamental aspects of structure, there are many more subtle clues. The relative length of sepals and petals is often important, as are the presence and size of spurs (as in orchids and honeysuckle), or of the leaf-like bracts that often surround the flowers; and how the flowers are grouped together, which may be in long spikes, branched or not, in clusters or singly. The shapes and arrangement of flowers are shown in the Glossary (p. 16-19).

Flowers are open and their sizes are diameters except where stated. Flower colour refers to petals or to sepals when there are no petals. Most red, pink, mauve, purple and blue flowers may produce white forms, and some white flowers can be tinged pink, but there will usually be a normally coloured flower nearby.

Flowering times are given for southern England for widespread plants, and will often be earlier in the south-west, near the sea and in early springs, and later further north, on mountains and after severe winters. For plants with a wide geographical range, the first flowering date can be a full two months difference between the south and the north. It is also common to find occasional plants that flower before most of the population, so an isolated plant may not be typical.

Some plants have very fixed flowering times, determined by an internal clock set by the length of the day. Others are more flexible and may flower a second time in autumn. Weeds such as Groundsel (p. 280) and White Dead-nettle (p. 216) regularly flower through normal winters, and others, such as Cow Parsley (p. 182) will do so through mild winters. Plants that are cut just before they flower, for example on road verges, may try again later in the year and so produce a confusing late flowering.

Leaves are stalked except where stated. Their characteristics are only given where they are diagnostic, but the pictures always show leaves. It is very common for all the members of a genus to have a common leaf-shape, so it is important to check the genus (or even family) descriptions.

Leaves are the plants' food factories: their different shades of colour, shapes and sizes reflect habitat. It is common to find large, untoothed leaves in woodland plants and narrow or deeply toothed leaves in dry places. Underwater leaves are often feathery, creating a huge surface area for absorbing carbon dioxide from the water. Leaves are what most plant-eating animals eat, so they and the stems which carry them are often well defended, by prickles, spines, thorns or stinging hairs. These are nearly always good identification features.

Fruits are usually only described when important for identification, and (except for sedges, p. 416-38) when a lens is not needed to see the important features.

The fruit is the structure that protects and usually helps to disperse the seed. Some fruits (berries and apples, for example) are conspicuous to both birds and botanists, while other plants increase the surface area of the fruit, so making it easily carried by wind, as in sycamores and dandelions. These features too are valuable identification aids.

Habitat is one of the most important aids to identifying plants. A key to understanding plant distribution is to recognise geology: the acidity of the soil is, after climate and wetness, the main reason why plants grow in some places, not others. Soils formed on chalk and limestone and on sand-dunes where the sand is shell-sand all have large amounts of limestone (calcium carbonate) in them, and this neutralises the natural acidity of soil. Some species are restricted to such calcareous (lime-rich or base-rich) soils; others avoid them. Their distributions on the maps distinctively mirror the distribution of chalk and limestone rocks.

The **maps** show where each species occurs in this area, distinguishing where it is commonest (in darker green) from where it is more scattered (pale green). Islands do not show up well on such small maps, so the letters **s** (Scilly), **o** (Orkney) and **z** (Shetland) indicate that the plant grows there.

Increase and **decrease**. A map is a snapshot in time, and many species are either becoming commoner or rarer, shown by:

↑ for expanding species –   ↑↑ dramatically so
↓ for declining species –   ↓↓ dramatically so

Local abundance (how it grows, when found at all) is shown by a symbol:

■   – dominant species that cover large areas with dense populations.
▨   – species that are frequent where they are found, but rarely dominant.
⊡   – species that grow as isolated individuals among other species; many are also rare geographically.

Plants vary hugely in abundance. The commonest plants are found almost everywhere and are common wherever they are found; others may be equally widespread but even so have to be looked for, usually because they grow in more specialised habitats. The different colours on each map refer to the varying abundance of that plant only: you are more likely to find Sticky Mouse-ear (p. 52) in the areas where it is shown as less common (pale green), than you are to find Thyme-leaved Sandwort (p. 54) in its main (darker green) area.

The **distribution** of a plant is a great help towards its identification. If you are in the Lake District or Ireland, you are extremely unlikely to be looking at a plant only known to occur in south-east England – or vice versa. However, plants do get found outside their known areas, and some of the plants in this book, especially those that have been recently introduced, are rapidly expanding their range. Others, less happily, are getting rarer and some may have become extinct in these islands. Plants that are decreasing are usually those of natural habitats that cope badly with disturbance or enrichment of the soil with nutrients – two things that we as a species are especially fond of doing.

In any habitat, some species are dominant because they can compete strongly, either by rapid growth in good soils or by being able to survive on soils so miserable that almost nothing else can grow there. Other species survive in a subordinate role, for example by exploiting micro-habitats that are favourable to them. Many plants have long underground stems that throw up shoots at intervals; these will almost always appear above ground as scattered individuals.

The maps for rare species do not attempt to show precise localities, since many of these plants cannot withstand accidental trampling by visitors, let alone picking. Indeed plants should never be picked unless they are very obviously common and widespread; if in doubt, and if you don't have the book to hand, make notes of the plant's appearance, using the hints given here as to what are likely to be the most important features. A photograph is always helpful. In no circumstances should a plant ever be dug up: indeed it is illegal to do so without the permission of the landowner. For certain rare plants it is always illegal to dig up, pick or remove any part (including the seeds); 110 species are protected in this way at present.

GLOSSARY

achene

alternate

anther

appressed

auricle

berry

bipinnate

↑ bracteole
bract

bulb

bulbil

calyx

Achene: a small dry fruit.

Acid soils contain very few alkaline minerals and are formed above rocks such as sandstone. Peaty soils are usually acid since plant humus is often acid.

Aggregate: group of closely related species.

Alternate: neither opposite not whorled.

Anther: the tip of the stamen, producing the pollen,

Annual plants live for a year or less; cf. biennial, perennial.

Appressed: flattened against the stem or leaf.

Auricle: small ear-like outgrowth at base of leaf.

Berry: fleshy fruit.

Biennial plants produce flowers in the second year and then usually die; cf. Annual, Perennial.

Bipinnate: a double-pinnate leaf – one whose primary divisions are themselves pinnate.

Bog: a mire on acid peat; cf. Fen.

Bract: a modified, usually small and often scale-like, leaf just beneath a flower. At the base of flowers in compound flowerheads it is a **Bracteole**.

Bulb: underground storage organ, composed of modified fleshy leaves.

Bulbil: small bulb-like organ at base of a leaf or instead of a flower, breaking off to form a new plant.

Calyx: the sepals when joined.

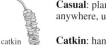
catkin

composite

corm

corolla

corymb

crucifer

Capsule: a dry fruit that breaks open to liberate seeds.

Carr: a fen wood, usually of alder or willow.

Casual: plant which may turn up anywhere, usually on bare ground.

Catkin: hanging spike of small flowers.

Chalk: a soft white limestone.

Cluster: a more or less loose spreading group of flowers at the top of a stem.

Composite: a member of the Daisy Family – Asteraceae, p. 264 (formerly Compositae).

Conifers: see p. 398.

Corm: an swollen underground stem, forming a storage organ.

Coppice: trees or shrubs, most often Ash or Hazel, cut nearly to the ground and growing again from the old stools. Not to be confused with a copse, which is a small patch of woodland.

Corolla: the petals when joined.

Corymb: a flat-headed raceme, the pedicels progressively shorter to bear flowers all at the same level.

Crests (Irises): see p. 322.

Crucifer: a member of the Cabbage Family – Brassicaceae, p. 82 (formerly Cruciferae).

Cultivar: a variety produced in cultivation.

Deciduous: with leaves falling in autumn.

Decurrent: running down on to.

Deflexed: bent downwards.

dicotyledon

disc floret

epicalyx

female flowers

floret

hip

Dicotyledons: see Introduction.

Disc florets (Composites): see p. 264.

Dunes: areas of sand, usually lime-rich, almost always by the sea, and often with damp hollows called *slacks*.

Epicalyx: a ring of extra sepals just below the true sepals, especially in the Mallow and Rose Families.

Falls (Irises): see p. 322.

Female (♀) flowers contain styles, not stamens.

Fen: a mire on lime-rich peat; cf. Bog.

Floret: a small flower, part of a compound head, especially in the Daisy Family.

Flower: the reproductive element of a plant, usually brightly coloured to attract pollinators. It comprises petals, sepals, stamens and styles.

Fruit: the seeds and their covering.

Glaucous: dull greyish blue or green.

Head: more or less compact clusters of flowers.

Heath: lowland area of acid, usually sandy soil, often dominated by Heather (p. 104); cf. Moor.

Hemiparasite: plant with green leaves which derives part of its nutriment from the roots of other plants, e.g. Yellow Rattle (p. 234). Cf. Parasite, Saprophyte.

Hip: the usually brightly coloured outer covering of a Rose fruit.

Hoary: greyish with short hairs.

Honey-leaf: Nectary, the organ in the flower producing nectar.

Humus: partly decomposed vegetable or animal matter in the soil.

Introduced plants have been brought in by man, either aliens from abroad or natives from some other part of Britain or Ireland.

keel

lanceolate

linear

lobed

male flowers

monocotyledon

net-veined

node ↗

ochrea

Jizz: characteristic appearance.

Keel (Peaflowers): see p. 140.

Labiate: a member of the Dead-Nettle Family – Lamiaceae, p. 216 (formerly Labiatae), mostly with 2-lipped flowers and square stems.

Lanceolate (of leaves): narrowly oval and pointed.

Lazy-bed: a cultivated plot in the Hebrides, fertilised by seaweed.

Lime: Calcium in the soil derived from the calcium carbonate in chalk and limestone rocks.

Linear: almost parallel-sided.

Lobed: of leaves deeply toothed but without separate leaflets.

Male (♂) flowers contain stamens only, no styles.

Marsh: mire not on peat.

Microspecies: closely related species, biologically distinct, but often hard to distinguish, except by a powerful lens or a microscope.

Midrib: central leaf-vein, usually raised and thick.

Mire: waterlogged ground, cf. Bog, Fen and Marsh.

Monocots, Monocotyledons: see Introduction.

Moor: an upland Heath (q.v.) typically on peaty soil.

Nectar: sugary substance secreted by plants to attract insects, and the chief ingredient of honey. Nectary, see Honey-leaf.

Net-veined: of a leaf with net-like smaller veins.

Node: where leaves join the stem.

Ochrea (Dock Family): see p. 60.

opposite

ovary

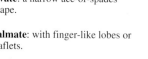
ovate

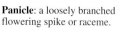
palmate

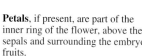
panicle

peaflower

pedicel

petals ↑ ↗

pinnate

pinnatifid

pod

pollen

raceme

ray　　ray floret

Opposite: on opposite sides of the stem.

Ovary: the base of pistils containing ovules (immature seeds).

Ovate: a narrow ace-of-spades shape.

Palmate: with finger-like lobes or leaflets.

Panicle: a loosely branched flowering spike or raceme.

Parasite: plant, usually without green colouring, which obtains its nutriment from other plants, e.g. Broomrapes, p. 244.

Peaflower: member of the Pea Family – Fabaceae, p. 140.

Peat: Soil composed of undecayed plant matter, often acid; cf. Bog, Fen, Humus.

Pedicel: the stalk of an individual flower.

Perennial plants survive for more than two years, are usually stouter than annuals and more likely to be seen in winter; cf. Biennial.

Petals, if present, are part of the inner ring of the flower, above the sepals and surrounding the embryo fruits.

Pinnate: leaf-shape with opposite leaflets; pinnatifid if leaflets are joined at base.

Pod: fruit, usually long and more or less cylindrical, as in garden peas.

Pollen: powdery grains produced on anthers which must be transferred to a stigma to fertilise the future seeds.

Raceme: an unbranched flower-head in which the flowers are borne on individual stalks (pedicels).

Ray (Umbellifers): see p. 180, and **Ray floret** (Composites): see p. 264.

rhizome

rosette

runner

samara

↑
sepal

silicula

siliqua

spadix　spathe

spike

spine

Rhizome: horizontal underground stem.

Rosette: ring of flattened leaves at the base of the stem.

Runner: horizontal above-ground stem, leafy and often rooting at the nodes.

Samara: a key-shaped winged fruit.

Saprophyte: a plant which feeds on decaying plant matter, e.g Birdsnest Orchid (p. 336).

Scale: unleaflike outgrowth, usually small, papery and brownish or colourless.

Seed-plants: plants which reproduce by seeds, not spores, comprising the Dicotyledons, Monocotyledons and Conifers.

Sepal: part of the outer ring of the flower, below the petals, around the embryo fruit.

Shoddy: wool waste used as manure.

Shrub: much branched woody plant, with no single trunk.

Shy flowerer: perennial sometimes passing whole years without flowering.

Silicula and **Siliqua** (Crucifers): see p. 82.

Sinus: A bay or hollow between two adjacent leaf-lobes or teeth.

Slack: damp hollow in dunes.

Spadix and **Spathe** (Arums): see p. 340.

Species: the basic unit of plant and animal classification.

Spike: flowerhead with the flowers, stalked or unstalked, up the stem.

Spine: straight, sharp-tipped appendage; cf. Thorn.

stalk ↗

stamen

staminode

standard

gma ↗

stipule ↑

olon

style →

tendril

Spreading: standing out horizontally or at a wide angle from the stem.

Stalk: a subsidiary stem (q.v.), bearing a flower or leaf.

Stamen: the male organ in a flower, comprising an anther (q.v.), bearing pollen, at the tip of a stem, the filament. Usually in a ring around the female organs (styles).

Staminode: an infertile stamen, often reduced.

Stem: the main axis of a plant and its branches; cf. Stalk.

Standard (Peaflowers), p. 140; (Irises), p. 322.

Stigma: the surface receptive to pollen at the tip of the style (q.v.)

Stipule: scale-like or leaf-like organ at the base of the leaf- stalk.

Stolon: a short-lived creeping stem, below or above ground.

Style: the upper part of the female organ of a flower, a filament bearing the stigma (q.v.). Usually lying within the ring of stamens.

Subspecies: a category within a species, with various small distinctions from each other but able to interbreed.

Tendril: a twisted filament arising from a leaf or stem, and used for climbing.

Tepal: a term used when petals and sepals are indistinguishable from each other.

Thallus: plant body not differentiated into stems and leaves.

thorns

trefoil

umbel

whorl

wings

winged

Thorn: sharp-tipped woody appendage, straight or curved.

Tree: tall woody plant, arising from a single woody stem; cf. Shrub.

Trefoil, Trifoliate: with three leaflets.

Turlough: a deep flooded hollow on limestone in W Ireland, often drying out and grassy in summer.

Umbel: compound flowerhead with its lower branches longer than the upper, so that all flowerheads are level. **Umbellifers** are members of the Carrot Family – Apiaceae, p. 180, (formerly Umbelliferae) and mostly have flowers in umbels.

Undershrub: low, often creeping woody perennial.

Variety: a naturally occurring distinct form of a plant, of lower rank than a subspecies. Cf. Cultivar.

Vascular plants: Higher plants which have a vascular system (i.e. containing channels for conducting liquids) of plant tissue, and comprising the seed-plants (q.v.) and the ferns, the horsetails and their allies.

Waste places: uncultivated areas much disturbed by man.

Whorl: a group of stems or leaves arising at the same point on a stem; cf. Opposite.

Wing (Peaflowers), see p. 140.

Winged: with a flange running down the stem or stalk, or occasionally a seed.

FURTHER READING

GENERAL

New Flora of the British Isles, by Clive Stace (Cambridge University Press, 2nd edition, 1997). The standard British flora for serious workers, with numerous keys and illustrations. The essential reference.

Field Flora of the British Isles, by Clive Stace (Cambridge University Press, 1999), is a shortened version of the *New Flora* above.

The New Atlas of the British and Irish Flora, by C.D. Preston, D.A. Pearman and T.D. Dines (Oxford University Press, 2002), is a *tour-de-force* providing maps of all plant species on a 10-km grid.

Wild Flowers of Britain and Northern Europe, by Richard Fitter, Alastair Fitter and Marjorie Blamey (HarperCollins, 5th edition, 1996). Pocketable. Covers the whole of north-west Europe from the Loire and the Alps to the Arctic.

The Illustrated Flora of Britain and Northern Europe, by Marjorie Blamey and Christopher Grey-Wilson (Cassell). A very handsome larger illustrated book, covering the same area as the above.

Wild Flowers of Britain by Roger Phillips (Pan Books, 1977) was the first of Roger Phillips' magnificently photographed series in collaboration with Martyn Rix.

The Wild Flowers of the British Isles, by Ian Garrard and David Streater (Macmillan, 1983), had good paintings rather too softly reproduced.

Flora Britannica, by Richard Mabey. A personal survey, illustrated with fine photographs and excellent background reading.

List of Vascular Plants of the British Isles, by D.H. Kent, lists all species growing in the region.

Scarce Plants in Britain, by A. Stewart, D.A. Pearman and C.D. Preston (Joint Committee for Nature Conservation, 1994), surveys plants found in between 16 and 100 10-km squares in Great Britain, while British Red Data Books (Vol.1 Vascular Plants) by M.J. Wigginton do the same for the rarer plants.

Local Floras. These have now been published for most counties, and are invaluable for finding plants in one's neighbourhood. The B.S.B.I. sells most of them to members, and their list is far the best, if there is one for your area. This is available from BSBI Publications, c/o Summerfield Books, Main Street, Brough, Cumbria CA17 4AX, email bsbipubs@beeb.net.

Alien Plants of the British Isles, by E.J. Clement and M.C. Foster (Botanical Society of the British Isles, 1994). Lists far more introduced plants than can be covered in this book.

English Names of Wild Flowers, by J.G. Dony, C.M. Rob and F.H. Perring (Butterworth, 1974). The Botanical Society's recommended list, which we have largely followed for this book.

Botanical Latin, by William T. Stearn (David & Charles, 3rd edition, 1983) will help those to whom scientific names of plants are apparently meaningless.

PLANT GROUPS

The Botanical Society of the British Isles has published a series of Handbooks covering *Docks and Sorrels, Willows and Poplars, Crucifers, Roses, Umbellifers, Dandelions,*

Pondweeds and Sedges. These provide detailed keys for the identification of plants in these difficult groups, including hybrids and microspecies.

The Grasses, Sedges, Rushes and Ferns of Britain and Northern Europe, by Richard Fitter, Alastair Fitter and Ann Farrer (HarperCollins), is an illustrated guide to these groups, with maps.

Aquatic Plants in Britain and Ireland, by C.D. Preston and J.M. Croft (Harley Books, 1997) is not an identification guide but an atlas, with maps and ecological information.

The Trees of Britain and Northern Europe, by Alan Mitchell and John Wilkinson (HarperCollins) is a very attractive identification guide to all our native and widely planted trees.

Trees of Britain and Europe, by Keith Rushworth is an impressive photo-illustrated guide.

Cassell's Trees of Britain and Northern Europe, by David More and John White (Cassell, 2003) is a new, much larger and more comprehensive manual.

Grasses, by C.E. Hubbard (Penguin, 3rd edition, 1984) is a favourite of grass aficionados, with line-drawings, keys and a detailed text.

Alien Grasses of the British Isles, by T.B. Ryves, E.J. Clement and M.C. Foster (Botanical Society of the British Isles, 1996) is a catalogue for the specialist.

The Ferns of Britain and Ireland, by C.N. Page (Cambridge University Press, 2nd edition, 1998) is a very comprehensive handbook, whereas *The Fern Guide*, by J. Merryweather and M. Hill (Field Studies Council, 1992) is key-based and intended specifically for identification.

Illustrations of British and Irish Orchids, by D.M. Turner-Ettlinger (1998), a comprehensive set of pictures.

SOCIETIES TO JOIN

Botanical Society of the British Isles, or "B.S.B.I." Membership Secretary, 68 Outwards Road, Loughborough, Leics. LE11 3LY. The leading national society for those seriously interested in the British flora, both amateur and professional. Runs field meetings. Web site: www.bsbi.org.uk

Plantlife, c/o Natural History Museum, Cromwell Road, London SW7 5BD, is the leading plant conservation charity. Runs field meetings. e-mail: Plantlife@nhm.ac.uk

Wild Flower Society, c/o 68 Outwoods Road, Loughborough LE11 3LY, caters for amateur lovers of wild flowers, who enjoy keeping annual diaries, enter for flower-hunting and recording competitions and attend field meetings.

Many local *Natural History Societies* have botanical sections and run field meetings, which beginners will find useful for learning to recognise their local wild flowers. Most local libraries can supply their addresses. All lovers of British wild flowers ought to join their local County Wildlife Trust, whose address can be supplied by the Wildlife Trusts Partnership, The Kiln, Waterside, Mather Road, Newark, NG24 1WT.

DICOTYLEDONS: flowering plants with two seed-leaves

BUTTERCUP FAMILY Ranunculaceae

Flowers with many stamens, usually five petals (or no petals but petal-like sepals, here referred to as petals), and at their base often small honey-guides, which secrete nectar. Fruits with many separate nutlets or tiny pods.

Yellow-flowered *Ranunculus*: **Buttercups** have palmate leaves; usually drier places. **Spearworts** have usually narrow untoothed leaves; wet places. **Lesser Celandine** has many petals and heart-shaped leaves.

Flowers	imperfect:	Goldilocks
Sepals erect/spreading:		Meadow, Creeping, (Rough-fruited), Corn, Goldilocks, Spearworts
	down-turned:	Bulbous, Hairy, Rough-fruited, Small-flowered, Celery-leaved
Flower-stalks furrowed:		Creeping, Bulbous, Hairy, Small-flowered, Celery-leaved, Lesser Spearwort. Adderstongue Spearwort
	not furrowed:	Meadow, Corn, Goldilocks, Creeping Spearwort
By fresh water:		(Creeping), Celery-leaved, Spearworts

1 Meadow Buttercup *Ranunculus acris*. The tallest and most graceful of our common yellow buttercups; a variable hairy perennial, to 80-100cm. Flowers glossy yellow, 15-25mm, with *erect or spreading* sepals and *unfurrowed* stalks; April-Oct. Leaves palmate, deeply cut, the end lobe unstalked. Damper grassland.

2 Creeping Buttercup *Ranunculus repens*. Our only common yellow buttercup with creeping and rooting *runners*; a low/medium hairy perennial, to 40-60cm but usually shorter. Flowers glossy yellow, 20-30mm, with *erect or spreading* sepals and *furrowed* stalks; May-Oct and sporadically through mild winters. Leaves triangular with three deeply cut lobes, the end one long-stalked. Damp, rather bare places in woods, mires, grassland and an invasive weed in gardens; on waysides and waste ground and by fresh water.

3 Bulbous Buttercup *Ranunculus bulbosus*. The commonest yellow buttercup that has *down-turned* sepals when the flowers are fully open; a hairy perennial, to 40cm, with a markedly swollen stem-base. Flowers glossy yellow, 15-30mm; Late March-May. Leaves with three deeply cut lobes, the end one usually stalked. Drier grassland, especially on lime.

4 Hairy Buttercup *Ranunculus sardous*. Annual and hairier than Bulbous Buttercup (**3**), with paler yellow flowers (May-Oct), stem-base not swollen and *paler green*, often shining leaves. Damp grassy and arable places, usually *near the coast*.

5 Small-flowered Buttercup *Ranunculus parviflorus*. Pale green downy annual, sprawling, to 40cm. Flowers unbuttercup-like, pale yellow, *3-5mm*, the petals no longer than the down-turned sepals; April-Dec. Root-leaves rounded, lobed, well toothed. Fruits with tubercles and very short hooked spines. Bare dry places on lime, often near coast, also among crops.

6 Corn Buttercup *Ranunculus arvensis*. Another unbuttercup-like buttercup, differing from Small-flowered Buttercup (**5**) mainly in its usually larger (4-12mm) flowers, the *sepals erect*, narrower, much more deeply cut leaf-lobes and fruits with longer straight spines. A much decreased cornfield weed.

Rough-fruited Buttercup *Ranunculus muricatus* and **St. Martin's Buttercup** *Ranunculus marginatus* are Scilly specialities, see p. 456.

7 Goldilocks Buttercup *Ranunculus auricomus*. Our only non-acrid buttercup, usually with distinctively *imperfect flowers*, with 0-5 usually deformed petals. Medium hairless or downy perennial, to 40cm. Flowers glossy yellow, 15-25mm; sepals tipped purple; April-May. Root-leaves kidney-shaped, deeply lobed. Woods, hedges, occasionally on rocks.

Buttercups

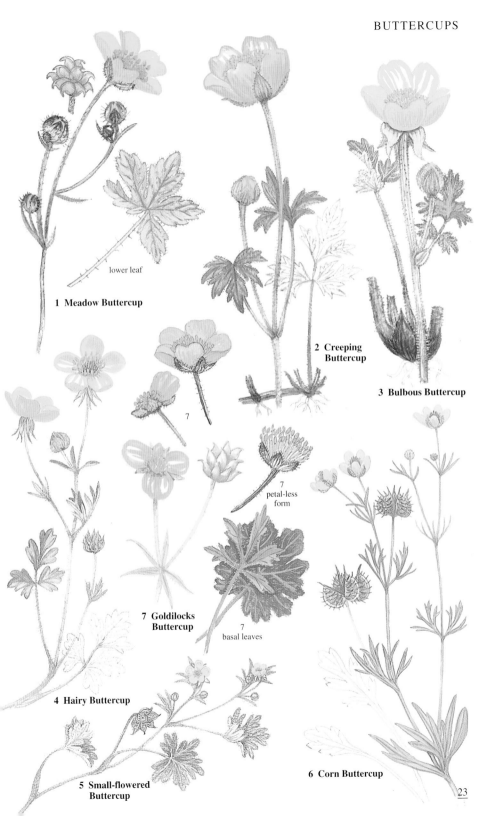

lower leaf

1 Meadow Buttercup

2 Creeping Buttercup

3 Bulbous Buttercup

7

7
petal-less
form

7 Goldilocks Buttercup

7
basal leaves

4 Hairy Buttercup

5 Small-flowered Buttercup

6 Corn Buttercup

1 Celery-leaved Buttercup *Ranunculus sceleratus.* Medium, pale green, usually hairless, often bushy annual, to 60cm. Flowers pale yellow, *5-10mm*; May-Sept. Leaves *shiny*, palmately lobed, narrower on the hollow stems. Fruits in an elongated head. By fresh water, marshy places, often on mud.

2 Greater Spearwort *Ranunculus lingua.* Our tallest and largest-flowered buttercup, to a stately 120cm; a hairless perennial with long creeping runners. Flowers glossy yellow, *20-50mm*, with *unfurrowed* stalks; June-Aug. Leaves lanceolate, toothed, to 25cm long. Fruits winged, with a curved beak. Marshes, fens and by fresh water.

3 Lesser Spearwort *Ranunculus flammula.* A very variable, common, short/medium hairless perennial buttercup of wet places, erect or spreading, to 50cm, the runners sometimes rooting at the leaf-nodes near the base. Flowers glossy yellow, *7-20mm*; June-Oct. Leaves, especially in Scotland, vary from ovate through lanceolate to linear. May overlap in size with Greater Spearwort (**2**), when the *slightly furrowed* flower-stalks and short blunt beak of the unwinged fruits help to separate them. Wet mires and by fresh water. **3a** *****Creeping Spearwort** *R. reptans* is much shorter and slenderer, *rooting at all leaf-nodes*, with solitary flowers (June-Sept) *c.* 5mm and leaves only 1.2mm wide. Currently known only from two Scottish loch shores. **Hybrid Spearwort** *R.* × *levenensis*, the hybrid between **3** and **3a**, differs from the much rarer **3a** mainly in not rooting at all nodes and having flowers and leaves intermediate between the two. May occur away from **3a**.

4 *****Adderstongue Spearwort** *Ranunculus ophioglossifolius.* Hairless annual, to 40cm. Flowers yellow, 5-9mm, sepals spreading; May-August. Lower leaves *ovate*, untoothed; stem-leaves narrower, obscurely toothed. By two ponds in Gloucestershire.

5 Lesser Celandine *Ranunculus ficaria.* One of the first heralds of spring; low hairless perennial, to 30cm. Flowers solitary, 10-30mm, with 7-12 rather narrow, glossy yellow petals, often fading whitish; *February*-May. Leaves long-stalked, heart-shaped, dark green, often with dark or light patches. Grassland, woods, hedges, waysides, bare ground, by fresh water. Ssp. *bulbilifer* has bulbils at the base of the leaf-stalks and fewer flowers; usually in the shade.

~

6 Marsh Marigold *Caltha palustris.* Medium hairless perennial, to 60cm, like a thick-set buttercup, making a brilliant splash of gold in spring. Flowers petalless with 5-8 glossy yellow sepals, *10-50mm*; March-June. Leaves long-stalked, *kidney-shaped*, dark green, glossy and often mottled paler above. Wet grassland, marshes, by fresh water. In the hills var. *radicans* is slenderer, creeping and rooting at the nodes, with smaller flowers and narrower sepals; May-July.

7 Globe Flower *Trollius europaeus.* Our only wild flower that looks like 'orbed moons of pale yellow', the 10 yellow sepals *curving inwards* to make a globe, 30-50mm; May-August. Medium hairless perennial, to 70cm, leaves palmate, deeply cut, very like Meadow Buttercup (p. 22) or Meadow Cranesbill (p. 174), but not downy. Damp pastures and gullies, mainly in the hills.

8 Winter Aconite *Eranthis hyemalis.* Our only yellow spring (January-March) flower with a *green frill*; chalice-shaped, 30mm. A low unbranched hairless perennial, to 15cm, with glossy palmate root-leaves appearing after the flowers until May. Widely naturalised in woods, parks and copses.

3a Creeping Spearwort   **5 Lesser Celandine**

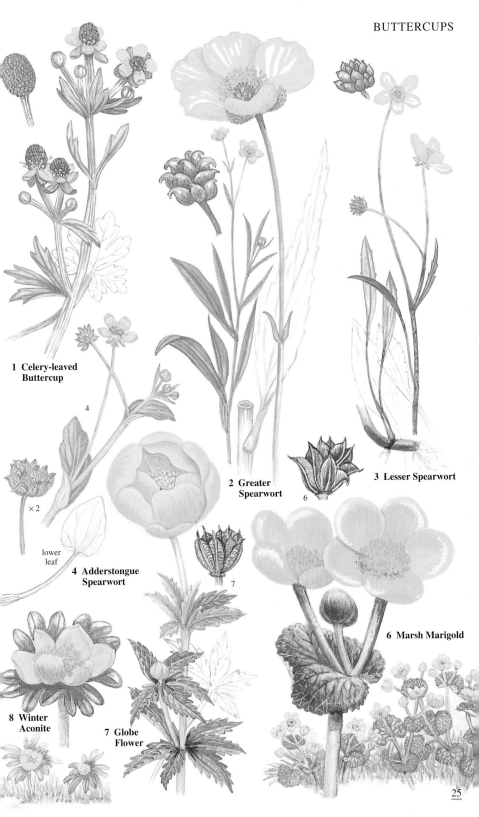

1 Celery-leaved
  Buttercup

4

×2

lower
leaf

4 Adderstongue
  Spearwort

2 Greater
  Spearwort

6

7

3 Lesser Spearwort

6 Marsh Marigold

8 Winter
  Aconite

7 Globe
  Flower

Water Crowfoots *Ranunculus* subgenus *Batrachium*. Very variable hairless aquatic annuals or perennials, with white buttercup flowers, floating or above the surface, sometimes in glorious masses; at the base of each petal is a honey-guide (usually half-moon-shaped) and a yellow claw; sepals usually erect or spreading; April-Sept, at their best May-June. Stems numerous and trailing in the water or short and creeping on mud. Leaves floating or terrestrial (smallish, kidney-shaped or lobed) and/or submerged (more numerous, hairlike, in long tresses or stiffly curled bunches). Stems and leaves may vary according to the depth or speed of the water.

No submerged leaves:	Ivy-leaved, Round-leaved, Three-lobed, New Forest, (Brackish)
Some submerged leaves:	Brackish, Common, Pond, (Chalk-stream)
All leaves submerged:	Thread-leaved, Fan-leaved, Chalk-stream, River, Hybrid

1 Ivy-leaved Crowfoot *Ranunculus hederaceus* has flowers 4-8mm with gaps between the petals, which equal the sepals; March-Oct. Leaves shiny and *ivy-shaped*, the 3-5 lobes widest at the base, usually terrestrial or floating. Usually on mud, when stems root at intervals. **1a Round-leaved Crowfoot** *R. omiophyllus* has larger flowers (10-12mm) with down-turned sepals shorter than the petals and larger leaves, the lobes widest above the base. **1b **Three-lobed Crowfoot** *R. tripartitus* has more variable flowers (March-May), 3-10mm, the sepals *blue-tipped* and down-turned, the usually three leaf lobes being widest above the base, and growing only in still water. **New Forest Crowfoot** *R.* × *novae-forestae*, the hybrid between **1a** and **1b**, with often five leaf lobes, is confined to the New Forest, Hants, where **1b** no longer occurs.

2 Brackish Water Crowfoot *Ranunculus baudotii*. The only water crowfoot of *brackish water*, with flowers 11-20mm and down-turned, usually blue-tipped sepals, Leaves usually both floating and submerged, but may be submerged only, and more rarely floating only; segments stiff.

3 Common Water Crowfoot *Ranunculus aquatilis*. Flowers 10-20cm, with honey-guides *rounded*. Leaves either both floating (usually 5-lobed, the sinus between the lobes pointed) and submerged, or submerged only. **3a Pond Water Crowfoot** *R. peltatus* has larger flowers, 24-30mm, with pear-shaped honey-guides; leaf-sinuses obtuse.

4 Chalk-stream Water Crowfoot *Ranunculus penicillatus*. Prefers *fast-flowing* streams, especially with limy water. Flowers 20-30mm, the honey-guides pear-shaped. Leaves usually submerged only, with long trailing tresses of either loose parallel or stiff divergent segments, usually forked 6-8 times; sometimes also 5-lobed and floating. **4a River Water Crowfoot** *R. fluitans* has sometimes smaller flowers 14-26mm, and submerged leaves only, the segments always parallel, usually not forked more than four times. Usually in larger rivers, avoiding limy water. **Hybrid Water Crowfoot** *R.* × *bachii*, the hybrid between the two, is most like **4**, but often replaces **4a** in larger rivers.

5 Thread-leaved Water Crowfoot *Ranunculus trichophyllus*. Flowers 7-12mm, with *half-moon-shaped* honey-guides. All leaves submerged, with tassels of usually *stiff segments*, repeatedly branching into three. **5a Fan-leaved Water Crowfoot** *R. circinatus* has leaf-segments distinctively lying all in one plane and branching into two; flowers 8-20mm.

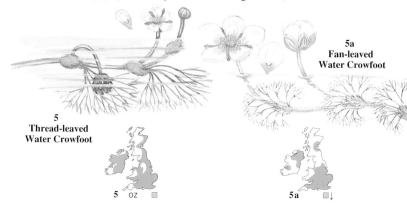

5a
**Fan-leaved
Water Crowfoot**

5
**Thread-leaved
Water Crowfoot**

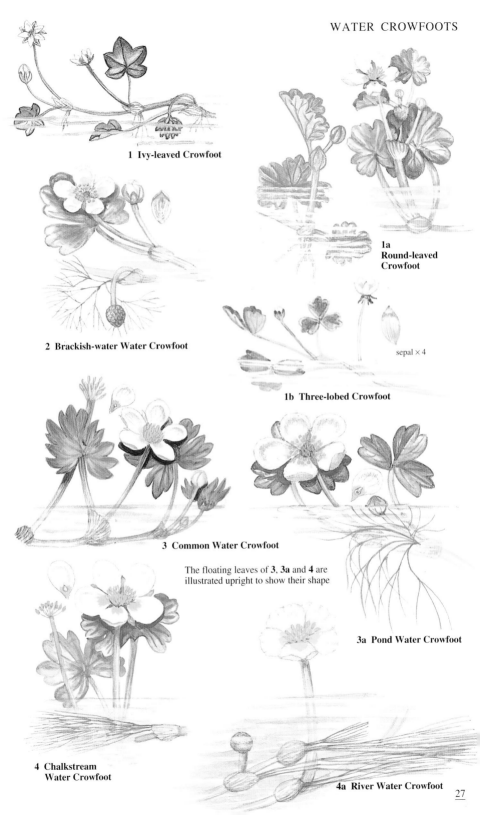

1 Ivy-leaved Crowfoot

1a
Round-leaved
Crowfoot

2 Brackish-water Water Crowfoot

1b Three-lobed Crowfoot

sepal × 4

3 Common Water Crowfoot

The floating leaves of 3, 3a and 4 are
illustrated upright to show their shape

3a Pond Water Crowfoot

4 Chalkstream
   Water Crowfoot

4a River Water Crowfoot

1 Stinking Hellebore *Helleborus foetidus*. Stout foetid perennial, to 80cm. Flowers *bell-shaped*, bright yellow-green, purple-edged, in clusters, 10-30mm; February-April. Leaves *all on the stem*, dark green, palmate, the leaflets lanceolate and toothed. Woods and scrub on lime; widely naturalised elsewhere.

2 Green Hellebore *Helleborus viridis*. Short perennial, to 40cm. The 40-50mm *open* Christmas-rose-like flowers much the same mid-green colour as the palmate or undivided leaves, *all basal*, which appear just after the flowers in February and grow steadily larger till summer. Woods on lime, often with same-coloured Dog's Mercury (p. 168); widely naturalised elsewhere.

3 Common Meadow-rue *Thalictrum flavum*. Tall stout perennial, to 1m or more. Flowers small, in conspicuous dense clusters, coloured by their yellow stamens, which last longer than the obscure whitish petals. Leaves 2-3-pinnate, the leaflets *wedge-shaped*, the end one longer than broad. Wet meadows, fens and by fresh water.

4 Lesser Meadow-rue *Thalictrum minus*. Very variable medium/tall perennial, 25mm to more than 1m, the rather wiry stems often zigzag. Flowers in open clusters, 4-petalled, yellowish, often tinged purple, with long yellowish stamens. Leaves 3-4 pinnate or 3-4-trefoil, with most leaflets about *as broad as long*, often glaucous on coastal dunes. Limestone rocks and grassland, mountain ledges, coastal dunes and gravelly or shingly freshwater shores; widely naturalised.

5 Alpine Meadow-rue *Thalictrum alpinum*. Slender low perennial, to 15cm, hard to detect among the grass. Flowers tiny, in a 7cm spike, with four purplish petals and long yellow stamens. Leaves 2-trefoil with rounded leaflets. *Mountain* turf and ledges.

6 Columbine *Aquilegia vulgaris*. Medium/tall native perennial, to 1m, also well known in gardens; easily told by its conspicuous blue flowers the five tubular petals with short hooked spurs. Escaped garden forms, often with violet, pink or white flowers and straighter spurs, are more frequent than the wild native. Root-leaves trifoliate. Woods, fens and damp limy grassland; elsewhere probably an escape.

7 *Monkshood *Aconitum napellus*. Tall perennial, to 1.5m, hairless except for downy flower-stalks, flowers in conspicuous spikes, *helmeted*, blue-violet; May-Sept. Leaves dark green, palmate, cut almost to midrib. Shady stream-sides, also garden escape. Three other escapes are: **Hybrid Monkshood** *A. × cammarum*, with flowers sometimes blue and white, their stalks sometimes hairless; **7a Wolfsbane** *A. lycoctonum*, with yellow flowers; and **7b Larkspur** *Consolida ajacis*, a shorter garden annual and cornfield weed with flowers spurred and blue, pink or white.

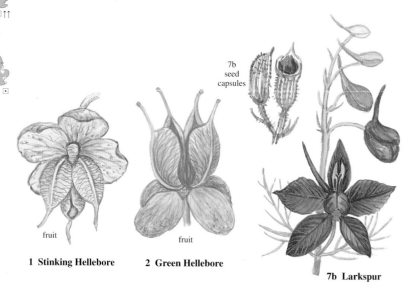

7b
seed
capsules

fruit

fruit

1 Stinking Hellebore   **2 Green Hellebore**

7b Larkspur

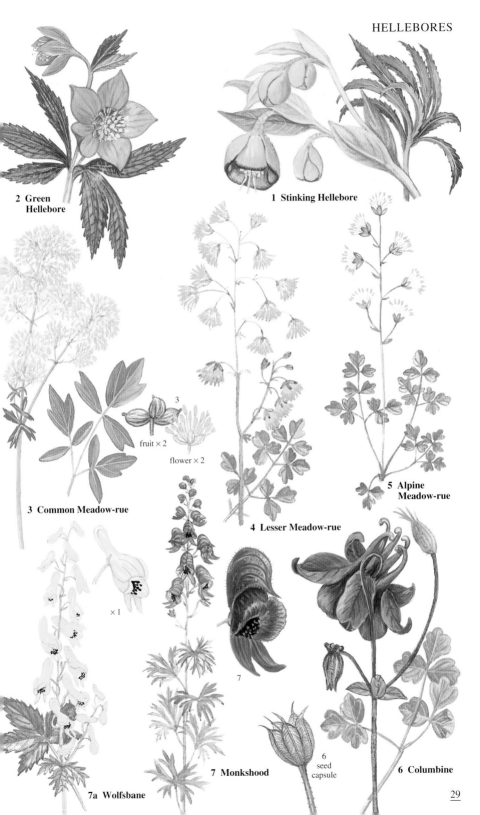

2 Green
Hellebore

1 Stinking Hellebore

3

fruit × 2

flower × 2

3 Common Meadow-rue

5 Alpine
Meadow-rue

4 Lesser Meadow-rue

× 1

7

6
seed
capsule

6 Columbine

7 Monkshood

7a Wolfsbane

1 S ■

2 ■

3 ▫↓

4 ▫↓

5 ■

6 ▫↓↓

1 Traveller's Joy *Clematis vitalba*. Deciduous *woody climber* with trusses of faintly fragrant, 4-petalled creamy to greenish-white flowers; July-Sept. More conspicuous with its autumnal 'old man's beard' formed by the *woolly greyish-white plumes* on the fruits, which last through the winter. Our only climber with opposite pinnate leaves, their stalks often twining and the leaflets often toothed. Scrub and hedges on lime, often reaching up to 30m into trees and hanging down like lianas; also creeps along the ground. **1a Virgin's Bower** *C. flammula* with flowers white and leaves 2-pinnate is established on some coastal cliffs and dunes.

2 Wood Anemone *Anemone nemorosa*. Low/short hairless perennial, to 30cm, carpeting the spring (March-May) woodlands with its graceful *solitary* white (sometimes tinged purple) flowers, 1cm, above leaflike bracts. Leaves trifoliate, much divided. Deciduous woods, hedge-banks, occasionally in grassland and on mountains. Three fairly frequent garden escapes in shady places and on rough ground: **2a Yellow Anemone** *A. ranunculoides* with smaller yellow flowers; **2b Blue Anemone** *A. apennina* whose larger blue (or white or pink) flowers have more numerous narrower petals, downy beneath; and the less frequent **2c Balkan Anemone** *A. blanda*, which is like **2b** but with narrower petals hairless beneath.

3 *Pasque Flower *Pulsatilla vulgaris*. One of our most gorgeous wild flowers, its rich violet petals with silky hairs on the back offset by a boss of golden anthers; April-May. Low, hairy perennial, to 30cm, with silky 2-pinnate leaves. The long silky plumes on the seeds may persist in the lengthened dead flowerheads well into summer. *Short turf on lime.*

4 *Mousetail *Myosurus minimus*. Low annual, to 10cm, with a basal tuft of grasslike leaves. The tiny greenish-yellow flowers, 6-8mm, solitary on long (to 7cm) leafless stalks (April-July), produce an elongated *plantain-like* (p. 248) fruiting head, fancifully like a mouse's tail. Bare, often arable and usually damp ground.

5 *Baneberry *Actaea spicata*. A strong-smelling hairless medium perennial, 30-60cm. Flowers in a stalked spike, white, with conspicuous stamens, turning to shiny *black berries*. Leaves 2-pinnate or 2-trifoliate, the leaflets well toothed. Ashwoods, limestone pavements.

6 **Pheasant's Eye *Adonis annua*. A long-established arable weed, now virtually extinct except as a rare casual; hairless annual, to 40cm. Flowers deep scarlet, the petals *black-based*, 15-25mm, not unlike a diminutive garden De Caen Anemone. Leaves feathery, 3-pinnate. Fruits in an elongated head.

7 Love-in-a-Mist *Nigella damascena*. Short annual, to 50cm. Flowers with five *pale blue* petal-like spurred sepals, often solitary, surrounded by leaf-like bracts, the 'mist'; June-August. Leaves thread-like, pinnate. Fruits inflated. A frequent garden escape, sometimes persisting.

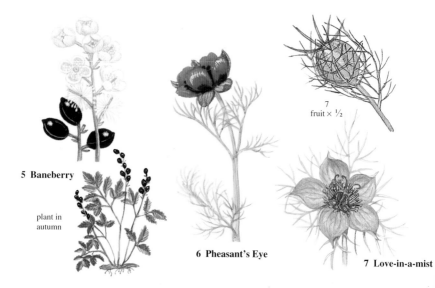

7
fruit × ½

5 Baneberry

plant in
autumn

6 Pheasant's Eye

7 Love-in-a-mist

1

1a Virgin's Bower

1 Traveller's Joy

2 Wood Anemone

2a Yellow Anemone

2b Blue Anemone

colour forms

2c Balkan Anemone

3 fruit

3 Pasque Flower

fruiting head

4 Mousetail

POPPY FAMILY Papaveraceae

Flowers usually solitary, with usually four, often rather large and floppy, petals, crumpled in bud, numerous stamens and two sepals which soon fall. Stems with white or yellow juice. Leaves pinnate or pinnately lobed. Fruit a capsule.

Poppies *Papaver* are hairy annuals, mostly with red flowers, often with a blackish centre, blue-black anthers and (the red species) 1-2-pinnate leaves. Arable and other disturbed ground.

1 Common Poppy *Papaver rhoeas.* Medium, to 70cm, with usually spreading hairs and juice rarely yellow. Flowers 50-100mm, *bright scarlet*; June-Oct, sometimes reddening unsprayed arable fields. Our only red poppy with *rounded, flat-topped, hairless* capsules. The origin of garden Shirley Poppies, which may escape in various colours and sometimes yellow anthers. An outsize red poppy, with flowers 100-150mm across is likely to be the **Oriental Poppy** *P. pseudoorientale*, often established from gardens.

2 Long-headed Poppy *Papaver dubium.* Medium, to 60cm, with hairs closely appressed; juice yellow in **2a** ssp. *lecoqii*. Flowers smaller (30-70mm) and a *pinker red* than Common Poppy (**1**), much less often dark-centred; May-August. Our only red poppy with *long hairless* capsules.

3 *Rough Poppy *Papaver hybridum.* Medium, to 50cm, with both spreading and appressed hairs. Flowers the smallest of our red poppies, 20-50mm, of a quite different red, *deep crimson*; June-August. Leaves neat, rather stiff. Our only red poppy with *egg-shaped* capsules covered with *straw-coloured bristles*. Mainly on lime.

4 *Prickly Poppy *Papaver argemone.* Short/medium, to 45cm, with appressed hairs. Flowers 50-65mm, *pale scarlet*, the petals rather narrow and spaced out; May-July. Our only poppy with *long, narrow, sparsely bristled* capsules.

5 Opium Poppy *Papaver somniferum.* Short/tall, to 30-120cm, *greyish* and almost hairless; its white juice yields opium. Flowers 100-180mm, usually *lilac* with purple centre, but escaping cultivars can often be red or white; June-August. Leaves wavy, *coarsely toothed*, clasping the stem. Capsule rounded, hairless.

~

6 *Welsh Poppy *Meconopsis cambrica.* A dainty and attractive, tufted, slightly hairy medium perennial, to 60cm; juice yellow. Flowers *yellow*, 50-75mm; May-August. Leaves pale green, pinnate, the leaflets pinnately lobed. Capsule narrowly egg-shaped, beaked. Rocky places in hill districts; much more widespread as a frequent garden escape. **6a Atlantic Poppy** *Papaver atlanticum*, an increasing garden escape, has *orange* or reddish flowers, white juice and pinnately lobed leaves.

7 Yellow Horned-poppy *Glaucium flavum.* A conspicuous sprawling seaside biennial/perennial, to 80cm; juice yellow. Flowers yellow, 60-90cm; June-Sept. Leaves silvery grey, the root ones pinnate. Capsules *curved, 15-30cm*, the longest of any British plant. Coastal shingle.

8 Greater Celandine *Chelidonium majus.* A rather greyish, sparsely hairy, medium, bushy perennial, to 85cm, resembling Lesser Celandine (p. 24) only in name and flower colour; juice orange. Flowers rich yellow, *15-25mm*; April-Oct. Leaves pinnate with lobed leaflets. Capsule thinly cylindrical. Walls, disturbed ground, usually near buildings.

1 soz □

2 soz □

2a □

3 □↓

4 □↓↓

5 soz □↑↑

6 oz □↑↑

7 s □

8 □↓

2a Papaver dubium ssp. *lecoqii*

6a
Atlantic Poppy

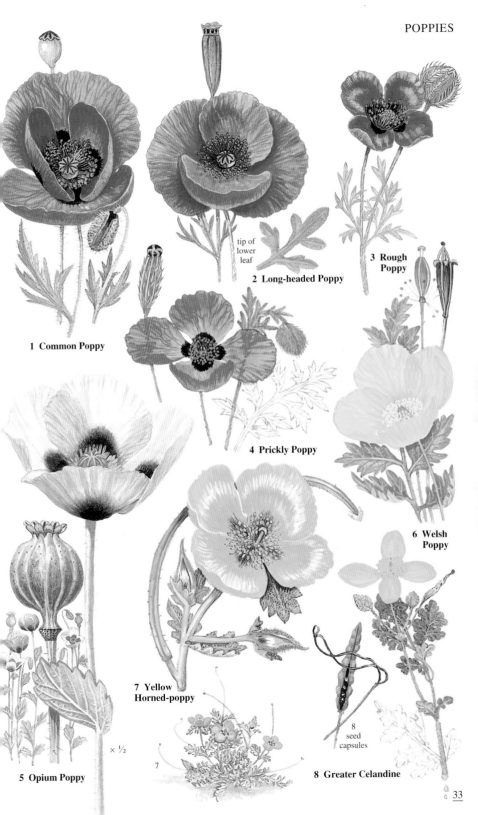

1 Common Poppy

tip of lower leaf

2 Long-headed Poppy

3 Rough Poppy

4 Prickly Poppy

6 Welsh Poppy

7 Yellow Horned-poppy

7

× ½

5 Opium Poppy

8 seed capsules

8 Greater Celandine

FUMITORY FAMILY Fumariaceae

Hairless; distinctive tubular, 2-lipped, spurred flowers, leaves usually pinnate.

Fumitories *Fumaria* are rather floppy annual weeds of disturbed ground to 20cm, or scramblers on hedge-banks or walls to 1m. Flowers in stalked spikes, elongating in fruit, which is globular; April-Nov. Leaves 1-3-pinnate, greyish. One widespread and common species; the rest with flowers either larger or smaller.

1 Common Fumitory *Fumaria officinalis*. Much the commonest of our 10 species; when it grows in mass its leaves are grey enough to look smoky at a distance, hence the name. Flowers pink, tipped darker, *7-8mm long*, the sepals more than quarter the length of the stalks, usually more than 20 in the spike, which is longer than its stalk.

Species robuster and with flowers *larger* than Common Fumitory, often scrambling over other plants; often on hedge-banks and walls.

2 Common Ramping Fumitory *Fumaria muralis*. Our second commonest fumitory; flowers pink, *9-11mm long*, lower petal slightly broader at tip, toothed near base, and spikes equalling their stalk; April-Oct. **2a Tall Ramping Fumitory** *F. bastardii* has flowers pink or pale pink, 9-11mm, sepals *sharply toothed all round*, spikes longer than their stalks. **2b ***Martin's Ramping Fumitory** *F. reuteri* has flowers pink, 11-13mm, with sepals *scarcely toothed* and spike much longer than its stalk; two sites only. **2c *Purple Ramping Fumitory** *F. purpurea* has purplish-pink flowers, 10-13mm, upper petal with erect margins, sepals sometimes toothed; fruiting stalks recurved.

3 White Ramping Fumitory *Fumaria capreolata*. Flowers *creamy-white*, often tinged pink, tipped blackish-pink, 10-13mm, petals with narrow margins, sepals toothed, usually near base. Fruiting stalks recurved. **3a **Western Ramping Fumitory** *F. occidentalis* has flowers whitish, turning pink, wings of upper petal purple and white-edged, and lower petals with broad margins, 12-14mm.

Species slenderer and with flowers *smaller* than Common Fumitory; arable weeds, mainly on lime.

4 *Dense-flowered Fumitory *Fumaria densiflora*. Flowers pink, 6-7mm, spike *much longer* than its stalk and bracts no shorter than fruiting stalks. Leaf-lobes channelled. **4a *Fine-leaved Fumitory** *F. parviflora* has flowers white or pale pink, 5-6mm, spike scarcely stalked. **4b *Few-flowered Fumitory** *F. vaillantii* has flowers pale pink, 5-6mm, and spike loose and much longer than stalk and bracts shorter than fruiting stalks. Leaf-lobes flat.

~

5 Climbing Corydalis *Ceratocapnos claviculata*. A delicate annual *scrambler*, to 75cm. Flowers *pale creamy yellow*, in clusters opposite leaves, 4-6mm long; May-Sept. Leaves greyish, pinnate, ending in *tendrils*, unlike the Fumitories (above). Woods, rocks, avoiding lime.

6 Bird-in-a-Bush *Corydalis solida*. Low/short perennial, to 20cm. Flowers in loose spikes, purple, 15-25mm long, with an *almost straight* spur and lobed bracts; April-May, Leaves greyish, 3-4-ternate with wedge-shaped segments, almost all from roots, with a large scale beneath the lowest. Widely naturalised, sometimes in quantity. **6a Hollowroot** *C. cava* has a hollow (not solid) root, *curved* spur, unlobed bracts and no scale beneath lowest leaf. Less often naturalised. **6b Bleeding Heart** *Dicentra formosa* has 2-spurred pink flowers on always leafless stems. Naturalised mainly by streams.

7 Yellow Corydalis *Pseudofumaria lutea*. Short, tufted perennial, to 30cm. Flowers rich yellow, in dense spikes opposite upper leaves; May-Oct. Leaves greyish, 2-pinnate. Well naturalised on *walls*.

sepals × 3

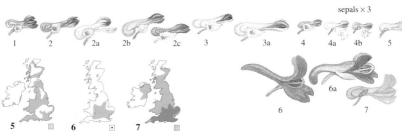

1   2   2a   2b   2c   3   3a   4   4a   4b   5

6a

6   7

1 soz
2 so
2a so
2b
2c so
3 so
3a s
4 o
4a
4b   5   6   7

34

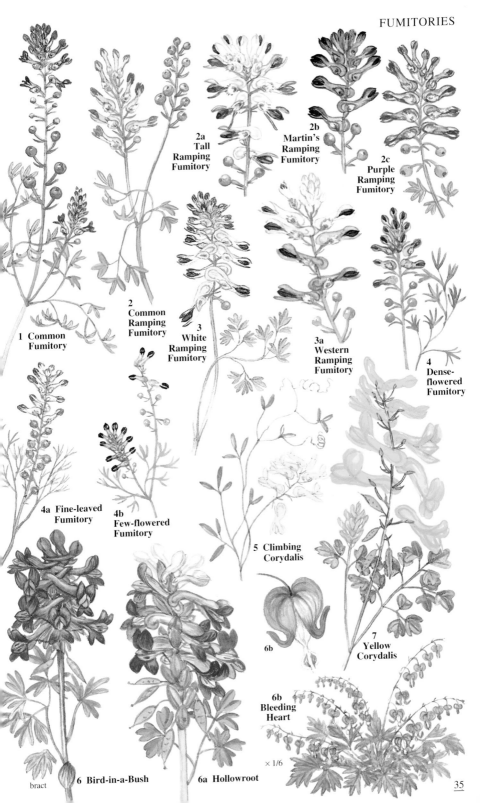

2a Tall Ramping Fumitory

2b Martin's Ramping Fumitory

2c Purple Ramping Fumitory

1 Common Fumitory

2 Common Ramping Fumitory

3 White Ramping Fumitory

3a Western Ramping Fumitory

4 Dense-flowered Fumitory

4a Fine-leaved Fumitory

4b Few-flowered Fumitory

5 Climbing Corydalis

6b

7 Yellow Corydalis

6b Bleeding Heart

× 1/6

bract **6 Bird-in-a-Bush**

6a Hollowroot

35

HEMP FAMILY Cannabaceae

Flowers greenish, male and female on separate plants.

1 Hop *Humulus lupulus*. Roughly hairy perennial *climber*, the 4-angled stems twining clockwise to 8m. Flowers greenish-yellow, the male in branched catkins and the female in short globular heads, which enlarge to become the fruiting cones used to make beer bitter and so are commoner. Leaves palmately lobed, coarsely toothed. Hedges, scrub, fens.

2 Hemp *Cannabis sativa*. Medium/tall strong-smelling annual, to 2.5m. Flowers green, male in a branching cluster, female in stalked spikes; July-Sept. Leaves palmately *3-9-lobed almost to base*. Casual of disturbed ground; cultivated for fibre and (illegally) as a drug.

NETTLE FAMILY Urticaceae

3 Common or **Stinging Nettle** *Urtica dioica*. A tall tenacious patch-forming perennial to 2m; avoided for its *coarse stinging hairs*, but relished by the caterpillars of peacock and small tortoiseshell butterflies. Flowers tiny, greenish (rarely tinged purple) with yellow anthers, male and female on separate plants, in thin catkins at the base of the lanceolate/oval leaves; *May*-Sept. Shady places, including woods, river banks, road verges, and around towns, villages and farm buildings wherever the soil is rich in nitrogen. ***Fen Nettle** *U. galeopsifolia*, with somewhat narrower leaves, is almost stingless and does not flower until July. Fens, especially at Wicken, Cambs, and by fresh water. Aka Stingless Nettle.

4 Small Nettle *Urtica urens*. Low/short annual, smaller, greener and less hairy than Common Nettle (**3**), to 60cm. Flowers similar but in much shorter catkins, male and female on the same plant; April onwards and through mild winters. Leaves *rounder*, with less strongly stinging hairs. A frequent weed of disturbed, mainly cultivated ground.

5 Pellitory of the Wall *Parietaria judaica*. Spreading hairy perennial to 50cm; *stems reddish*. Flowers tiny, green, becoming red-brown in fruit, anthers creamy white; in clusters at base of slightly glossy oval/lanceolate leaves; May-Oct. Mainly on walls.

6 Mind-your-own-business *Soleirolia soleirolii*. Prostrate, mat-forming perennial with thread-like stems to 20cm. Flowers tiny, bright pink, male and female separate, solitary at the base of the *roundish* evergreen 4-5mm leaves; May-August. An increasing garden escape, especially on walls in relatively frost-free areas.

AMARANTH FAMILY Amaranthaceae

Mostly casual annuals with leafless spikes or tight clusters of usually small brownish-green petalless flowers (goosefoots, p. 38 and oraches, p. 40 have green flowers) with 3-5 bracteoles; male and female separate. Leaves untoothed. Bare or cultivated ground. Besides the three most frequent species below, some 30 amaranths have been recorded as casuals, including the well known **7c Love-lies-bleeding** *A. caudatus* of gardens, with its long tassel-like flowerhead, variously red, yellow, green or white.

7 Common Amaranth *Amaranthus retroflexus*. Erect, to 1m; stems grey-downy. Flowers in erect terminal spike-like tassels, mixed with *shining, bristle-like* bracteoles with a green midrib and twice as long as the five sepals; female sepals blunt; July-Sept. Leaves pointed oval. Aka Pigweed. **7a Green Amaranth** *A. hybridus* is almost hairless, yellowish-green, with shorter, looser, sometimes nodding tassels and female sepals pointed. Aka Green Pigweed. **7b White Pigweed** *A. albus* has often prostrate, *whitish* stems, 3-sepalled flowers in clusters along the stem, bracteoles with a spiny tip and small, pale green, wavy-edged, minutely pointed, rounded leaves. *A. bouchonii*, very similar to Green Amaranth but with fruits not opening naturally, is the most frequent of three amaranths more or less established locally in E Anglia. The others are *A. blitoides* and *A. deflexus*.

6 Mind-your-own-business

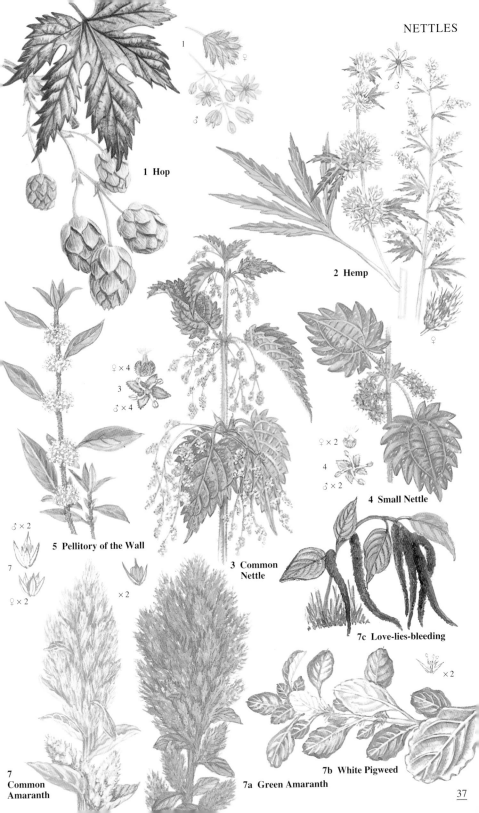

1 Hop

2 Hemp

♀ × 4
3
♂ × 4

♀ × 2
4
♂ × 2

4 Small Nettle

♂ × 2
7
♀ × 2

× 2

5 Pellitory of the Wall

3 Common
Nettle

7c Love-lies-bleeding

× 2

7
Common
Amaranth

7a Green Amaranth

7b White Pigweed

GOOSEFOOT FAMILY Chenopodiaceae

Most **Goosefoots** *Chenopodium* and **Oraches** *Atriplex* are unattractive mealy annual weeds, prostrate or erect to 50cm or in rich soils to 1.5m. Their tiny petalless flowers, with joined green sepals and yellow stamens, are in spikes; leaves toothed and alternate. They are often hard to tell apart, though goosefoots have stamens and styles in the same flower and fruits surrounded by a ring of 3-5 small sepals, while oraches have separate male and female flowers on the same plant and fruits enclosed in two triangular bracts. These swell as the fruits ripen and become much larger and more obvious than goosefoot fruits, making the spike irregular. There are 16 other rare goosefoot casuals, some very hard to tell from commoner species.

flower   fruit   ♀ flower   ♂ flower   fruit bract

GOOSEFOOT   ORACHE

Inland only:	Fat-Hen, Fig-leaved G, Nettle-leaved G, Upright G, Many-seeded G, Good King Henry; cf. Amaranths, p. 36
Inland & seashore:	Red G, Oak-leaved G, Stinking G, Common O, Spear-leaved O
Seashore only:	Saltmarsh G, Babington's O, Long-stalked O, Early O, Grass-leaved O, Frosted O, Sea Purslane, Annual Sea Purslane

1 Fat Hen *Chenopodium album.* Much the commonest and most variable goosefoot, well branched, erect to 1.5m; stems sometimes purplish, especially at leaf junctions. Flowerspike usually leafy; late June-Oct. Leaves *lanceolate to diamond-shaped*, the lower toothed, mealy especially when young. Cultivated and other disturbed ground. **1a Fig-leaved Goosefoot** *C. ficifolium* has no purple on stems and lower leaves *deeply 3-lobed*, the upper linear; flowering July-August.

2 Red Goosefoot *Chenopodium rubrum.* Fleshy, not mealy; prostrate or erect to 80cm. Flower spike leafy; August-Oct. Leaves diamond-shaped, *well but irregularly toothed*, often reddening in fruit. Sepals surrounding fruits fused to half-way. Manure heaps and other disturbed soils rich in nitrogen, also drier saltmarshes, dune slacks. **2a **Saltmarsh Goosefoot** *C. chenopodioides* is shorter, to 30cm, and more often prostrate, with smaller, more triangular, *untoothed* or less well toothed leaves; sepals surrounding fruits fused to near the tip. Not inland.

3 Maple-leaved Goosefoot *Chenopodium hybridum.* Erect to 1m, rarely mealy. Flowers in loose leafless clusters; July-Oct. Leaves *triangular*, heart-shaped, with a few large teeth. Aka Sowbane. Disturbed ground. **3a Nettle-leaved Goosefoot** *C. murale* is more often mealy, with leaves not heart-shaped and sepals minutely toothed. **3b Upright Goosefoot** *C. urbicum* also has leaves not heart-shaped but sepals untoothed. (The native status of the above three casuals is much debated.)

4 Oak-leaved Goosefoot *Chenopodium glaucum.* Prostrate to erect, to 50cm, Flowers in leafy spikes; June-Sept. Leaves *oak-like*, irregularly lobed, mealy white or grey beneath. Disturbed ground, rarely on sea-shore.

5 Many-seeded Goosefoot *Chenopodium polyspermum.* Erect or sprawling, to 1m; stems usually square. Flowers in leafy spikes; July-Sept. Leaves *pointed oval* to elliptic, scarcely toothed, reddening in autumn. Cultivated and other disturbed soils.

6 ***Stinking Goosefoot *Chenopodium vulvaria.* Aptly named for its *rotting-fish stench*, erect or sprawling to 40cm, mealy grey. Flowers in almost leafless spikes; July-Sept. Leaves oval, scarcely toothed. Bare ground, usually near the sea.

7 Good King Henry *Chenopodium bonus-henricus.* Our only perennial goosefoot, medium to 50cm; stems often mealy when young and reddish when old. Flowers in *almost leafless spikes*; May-August. Leaves large, broadly triangular, otherwise untoothed and scarcely lobed. Bare and grassy places near rural buildings.

1   soz   ▣

1a   ▣↑↑

2   s   ▣↑

2a   ▣

3   s   ▣

3a   s   ▣↓↓

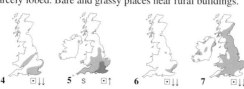

4   ▣↓↓   5   s   ▣↑   6   ▣↓↓   7   ▣↓↓

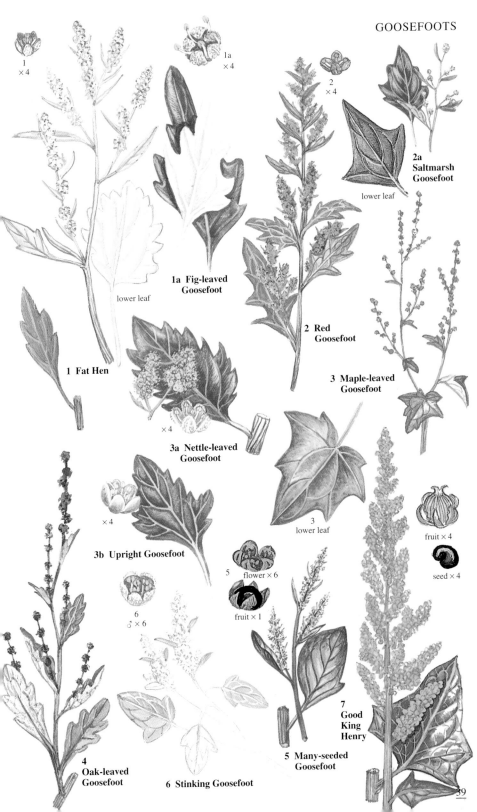

1
×4

1a
×4

1a Fig-leaved
Goosefoot

lower leaf

1 Fat Hen

3a Nettle-leaved
Goosefoot

×4

3b Upright Goosefoot

×4

6
♂ ×6

4
Oak-leaved
Goosefoot

6 Stinking Goosefoot

2
×4

2a
Saltmarsh
Goosefoot

lower leaf

2 Red
Goosefoot

3 Maple-leaved
Goosefoot

3
lower leaf

5
flower ×6

fruit ×1

5 Many-seeded
Goosefoot

fruit ×4

seed ×4

7
Good
King
Henry

Oraches *Atriplex.* For differences from *Chenopodium* see p. 38. Most species have bracteoles toothed or not and fused only at the base. Flowers in slender open leafy spikes; July-Sept. Many hybrids occur, often without one or both parents.

1 Common Orache *Atriplex patula.* Generally the commonest orache, very variable, often mealy, sometimes reddish, erect or sprawling to 1m. Leaves lanceolate to triangular, the lower ones with basal lobes *pointing forwards* and narrowing into the stalk. Fruits with bracteoles triangular, sometimes stalked, fused below halfway. Bare and disturbed ground, including sea-shores.

2 Spear-leaved Orache *Atriplex prostrata.* Differs from Common Orache (**1**) especially in having the lower leaves more triangular, the basal lobes pointing sideways at right angles to the stalk and bracteoles unstalked, sometimes spongy at base and fused only at base. Less frequent inland. **2a Babington's Orache** *A. glabriuscula* is usually prostrate and mealier, with bracteoles always spongy at base and fused to halfway. *Seashores only.*

3 *Long-stalked Orache *Atriplex longipes.* Erect, to 80cm; not mealy. Leaves *narrowly triangular*, often toothed, and basal lobes pointing either forwards or sideways. Bracteoles untoothed. *Saltmarshes*, among reeds and other tall plants. The hybrid with Babington's Orache (**2a**) may be more frequent than Long-stalked Orache itself.

4 *Early Orache *Atriplex praecox.* Erect or sprawling, to 10cm; not mealy. Flowers June-July. Leaves narrowly triangular, with basal lobes variously directed; *reddening* in late summer. Sandy or shingly *shores*, especially of sea lochs.

5 Grass-leaved Orache *Atriplex littoralis.* Medium/tall annual, with upright branches, to 1.5m. Leaves *linear* to linear lanceolate, toothed or not. Bracteoles unstalked. May resemble narrow-leaved forms of Common Orache (**1**), which, however, have spreading branches and translucent, not opaque, leaf-veins. Bracteoles spongy at base. Sandier edges of *saltmarshes*, increasing on salted road verges inland.

6 Frosted Orache *Atriplex laciniata.* Sprawling, to 30cm; much more *silvery-white* than our other oraches, the buff or pinkish stems and the neat diamond-shaped toothed leaves being both very mealy. Bracteoles fused to halfway, sometimes short-stalked. *Sandy beaches.*

7 Sea Purslane *Atriplex portulacoides.* Short *undershrub*, to 1m, mealy grey, often fringing saltmarsh creeks and pools. Flowers small, with conspicuous yellow stamens in slender leafless spikes; July-Sept. Leaves elliptical, evergreen. Bracteoles 3-lobed. *Saltmarshes.*

8 ***Annual Sea Purslane *Atriplex pedunculata.* Low mealy *annual*, to 30cm. Flowers in a leafless branched spike; August-Sept. Leaves elliptic, untoothed. Bracteoles long-stalked, 3-lobed, fused to tip. Drier saltmarshes. Believed extinct, but refound in Essex in 1987.

1   SOZ

2   SO

2a SOZ

3

4   Z

5   OZ

6   SO

7

8

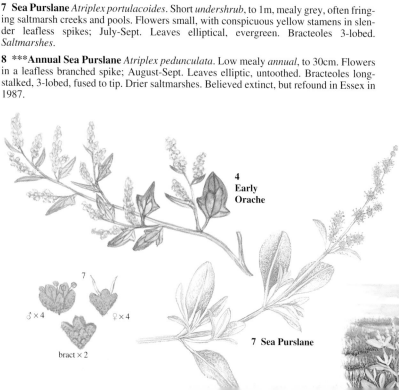

**4
Early
Orache**

7

♂ × 4   ♀ × 4

bract × 2

7 Sea Purslane

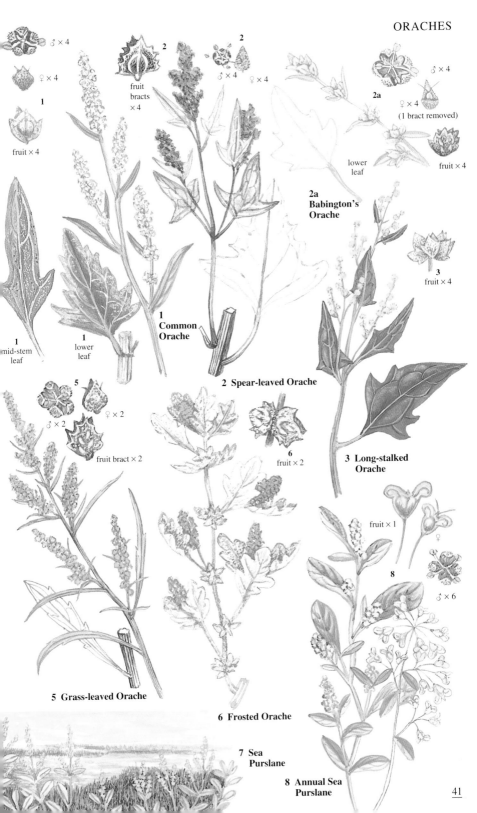

$\male \times 4$

$\female \times 4$

1

fruit $\times 4$

2
fruit
bracts
$\times 4$

2

$\male \times 4$ $\female \times 4$

$\male \times 4$

2a

$\female \times 4$
(1 bract removed)

fruit $\times 4$

lower
leaf

**2a
Babington's
Orache**

3
fruit $\times 4$

1
mid-stem
leaf

1
lower
leaf

**1
Common
Orache**

2 Spear-leaved Orache

**3 Long-stalked
Orache**

5

$\female \times 2$

$\male \times 2$

fruit bract $\times 2$

6
fruit $\times 2$

fruit $\times 1$

$\female$

8

$\male \times 6$

5 Grass-leaved Orache

6 Frosted Orache

**7 Sea
Purslane**

**8 Annual Sea
Purslane**

1 Summer Cypress *Bassia scoparia*. Medium, *densely bushy* annual, to 1m; grown for foliage reddening in autumn. Flowers tiny, green/red, petalless; July-August. Leaves linear to linear/lanceolate, numerous. Disturbed ground, now colonising motorway system in E England.

2 Sea Beet *Beta vulgaris* ssp. *maritima*. A dull-looking, often sprawling perennial, to 80cm. Flowers tiny, green, sometimes reddening, petalless, in long, narrow leafy spikes; June-Sept. Leaves dark green, *shiny, leathery*, the lower roughly triangular and wavy, the upper narrow. Bare ground by the sea. Other subspecies, the cultivated beets, occur as casuals.

3 Prickly Saltwort *Salsola kali*. A stiff, prickly, sometimes hairy, often half-prostrate, grey/blue-green annual, to 50cm; stems often pink-striped. Flowers tiny, white or tinged pink, usually singly in a tuft of leaf-like bracts at the base of the leaves; July-Oct. Leaves short, linear, fleshy, *spine-tipped*. Sandy shores, usually on the drift-line.

4 Annual Seablite *Suaeda maritima*. An erect or prostrate glaucous *annual*, to 30cm. Flowers tiny, green or purplish-red, petalless, 1-3 together at base of upper leaves; July-Oct. Leaves short, fleshy, *cylindrical*, pointed, green, turning dull purple then red. Salt-marshes, tidal mud.

5 *Shrubby Seablite *Suaeda vera*. A greyish *evergreen bush*, with stout woody stems to *c.* 1m; young shoots tinged red. Flowers as Annual Seablite (**4**), but yellowish-green; June-Oct. Leaves short, cylindrical, rounded at base and tip. Coastal shingle and sand.

Glassworts *Salicornia*. Succulent (edible) annuals, erect or spreading, to 50cm, sometimes unbranched, often reddening or yellowing in fruit. Flowers tiny, green with yellow anthers, usually in groups of three in the leaf-nodes up the stem; August-Sept. Leaves scale-like, translucent, fused to envelop the stem. Muddy saltmarshes.

6 Common Glasswort *Salicornia europaea*. Usually erect; branches straight, often numerous. Has the central flower the *largest of the three*. Fertile segments with convex sides. Becomes yellow-green tinged red or pink. May include **6a Purple Glasswort** *S. ramosissima*; often sprawling, tinged purple. **6b Glaucous Glasswort** *S. obscura* has branches (if any) curved; glaucous, becoming dull yellow-green.

7 Long-spiked Glasswort *Salicornia dolichostachya*. Often sprawling, usually much branched. Has all three flowers *the same size*. Fertile segments cylindrical. Becoming dull green, dull yellow or yellow-brown, sometimes tinged purple. Mainly lower saltmarshes, aka Marsh Samphire. **7a Shiny Glasswort** *S. nitens* is usually erect and little branched, with fertile segments variable. Becoming brownish, tinged purple, red or orange. Mainly upper and middle saltmarshes. **7b Yellow Glasswort** *S. fragilis* is usually erect and variably branched, becoming yellow or yellow-green, sometimes tinged purple.

8 *One-flowered Glasswort *Salicornia pusilla*. Differs from all other annual Glassworts in having only *one flower* at each node. Becomes pink, tinged purple or orange. Fertile stem segments disintegrate when ripe. Drier saltmarshes.

9 *Perennial Glasswort *Sarcocornia perennis*. Our only shrubby glasswort, forming *tussocks* up to 30cm tall and 1m across. Flowers as annual Glassworts, in same-sized groups of three. Dark green, becoming yellowish to reddish. Mainly middle and upper salt-marshes.

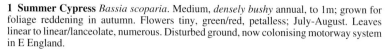

6 Common Glasswort

2 Sea Beet

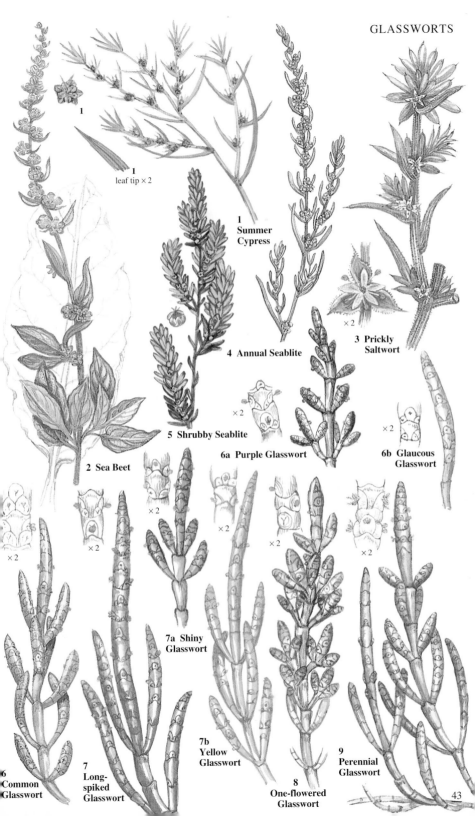

1 leaf tip × 2

1 Summer Cypress

4 Annual Seablite

3 Prickly Saltwort

× 2

5 Shrubby Seablite

× 2

6a Purple Glasswort

× 2

6b Glaucous Glasswort

2 Sea Beet

× 2

× 2

× 2

× 2

× 2

7a Shiny Glasswort

7b Yellow Glasswort

9 Perennial Glasswort

6 Common Glasswort

7 Long-spiked Glasswort

8 One-flowered Glasswort

43

PINK FAMILY Caryophyllaceae

Stems usually swollen at the nodes of the opposite pairs of usually untoothed and unstalked leaves, with stipules only in spurreys and their allies (p. 56). Flowering shoots repeatedly forked; flowers with 4-5 petals or none and 4-5 sepals, often joined at the base, in the campions and pinks (below) forming a tube or more or less inflated bladder. Stitchworts (p. 50), chickweeds (p. 50) and mouse-ears (p. 52) have *notched petals*; those of sandworts (p. 54), pearlworts (p. 58) and spurreys (p. 56) are *not notched*.

Campions, **Catchflies** and **Pinks**. Sepals fused to form a more or less inflated tube. Petals 5.

1 SOZ ■

1 Red Campion *Silene dioica*. Medium/tall perennial, to 1m; stems downy, densely so in Shetland, rarely hairless. Flowers *bright rosy-pink*, 18-25mm, unscented, petals cleft; male and female (styles 3) on separate plants; March-Nov and throughout the winter in the far SW. Flower colour ranges from deep red in Shetland through the normal bright rosy-pink and the paler pink of the frequent hybrid with White Campion (**2**) to the occasional albino sport, which has purer white flowers than White Campion and triangular calyx-teeth. Leaves lanceolate with long winged stalks, the upper pointed oval. Fruit with 10 rolled-back teeth when ripe. Rich soils in light shade in woods and hedge-banks, also on river banks, mountains and sea cliffs.

2 White Campion *Silene latifolia*. The white-flowered counterpart of Red Campion (**1**), from which it also differs in being sometimes annual, with flowers slightly larger, 25-30mm, the teeth of the greener calyx narrower and twice as long, and slightly fragrant at night; May-Oct; lower leaves with unwinged stalks and ripe fruits with more or less erect teeth. For hybrid with Red Campion, see above. Arable fields and other disturbed ground.

2 SOZ ▫

3 ▫↓↓

3 Night-flowering Catchfly *Silene noctiflora*. Not unlike a rather starved, stickily hairy White Campion (**2**), but annual only, and has flowers *c.* 18mm, the deeply cleft, very pale pink petals *usually rolled up* and showing only their yellowish undersides by day, at night opening and becoming fragrant to attract moths; styles 3; July-Sept. Leaves broad lanceolate. Ripe fruits with six recurved teeth. Arable fields, especially on lime.

4 ▫↓↓

4 Bladder Campion *Silene vulgaris*. A much-branched medium grey-green perennial, erect or half-sprawling to 1m. Flowers white, 17-19mm, petals deeply cleft, the calyx *bladder-like*, purplish or yellowish; May-August. Leaves narrowly pointed oval, often wavy-edged. Fruits with erect to spreading teeth. Bare and thinly grassy, more or less disturbed places. The Mediterranean ssp. *macrocarpa* with pink or greenish flowers has for many years been naturalised on Plymouth Hoe, Devon. **4a Berry Catchfly** *Cucubalus baccifer*, with less deeply cut greenish-white petals and fruit a black berry, is naturalised in at least six woods in Norfolk.

4a ▫

5 Sea Campion *Silene uniflora*. The coastal counterpart of Bladder Campion (**4**), but with a mat of non-flowering shoots to 30cm, and large flowers, 20-25mm, often *solitary* and with broader sepals; March-Oct; also fruits with spreading to down-turned teeth; and fleshier and narrower leaves. Cliffs, rocks, shingle *by the sea*, also by fresh water on mountains.

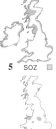

5 SOZ ▫

6 *Nottingham Catchfly *Silene nutans*. A variable, medium/tall, often stickily hairy perennial, to 80cm. Flowers 17-19mm, often drooping, in very open clusters, all usually pointing one way; the petals white above, greenish or pinkish beneath, *deeply* cleft into very narrow lobes, rolled-back by day and with a small rounded scale at the base; opening and fragrant at night; May-July. Leaves narrow, broadest at tip, the lower long-stalked. Rocks, cliffs, shingle and other dry, undisturbed, bare or sparsely grassy places. **6a Italian Catchfly** *S. italica* has larger flowers, *c.* 30mm, with the scales at the base of the petals very pointed. Naturalised in and near quarries at Greenhithe, Kent, since 1863.

6 ▫

5 Sea Campion

44

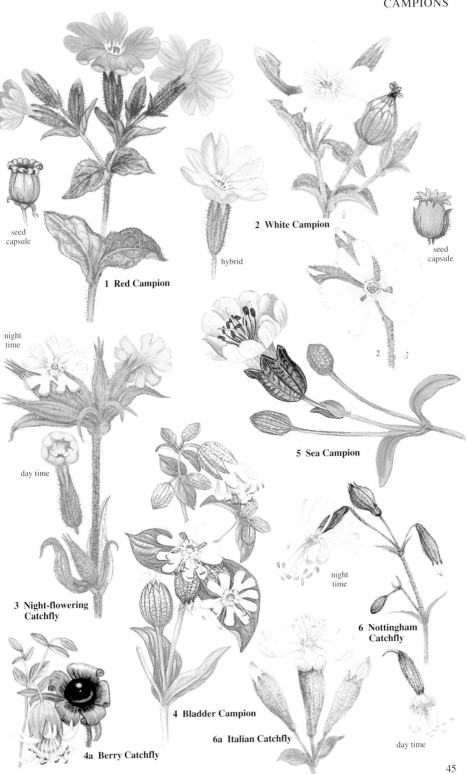

seed
capsule

1 Red Campion

hybrid

2 White Campion ♀

seed
capsule

2 ♂

night
time

day time

**3 Night-flowering
Catchfly**

5 Sea Campion

4 Bladder Campion

night
time

**6 Nottingham
Catchfly**

4a Berry Catchfly

6a Italian Catchfly

day time

1 **Spanish Catchfly *Silene otites*. A most puzzling plant at first sight, appearing quite unlike other Catchflies; an unbranched, medium, stickily hairy perennial, to 80cm. Flowers only 3-4mm, yellowish-green, with unnotched petals, in leafless spikes of *whorl-like clusters*; June-July. Leaves dark green, broadest towards the tip, mainly in basal rosettes. Grass heaths in E Anglian Breckland.

2 *Small-flowered Catchfly *Silene gallica*. A short stickily hairy annual, to 45cm. Flowers yellowish-white or pink (rarely, **2a** var. *quinquevulnera*, red-blotched), 10-12mm, the petals notched and the bladder *inflated* in fruit; June-Oct. Leaves lanceolate, the lower broader at tip, Bare and sparsely grassy sandy places.

3 *Sand Catchfly *Silene conica*. A neat greyish, stickily hairy, erect or sprawling annual, to 35cm. Flowers *tiny, 4-5mm*, variably pink, with notched petals, the bladder inflated to hide the fruit; May-July. Leaves narrow lanceolate. Sandy places, especially dunes.

4 **Sticky Catchfly *Lychnis viscaria*. A short/medium tufted perennial, to 60cm; stems often purplish, *sticky at leaf-nodes*. Flowers bright rosy red, 18-20mm, with petals notched, apparently whorled, in long spikes; May-June. Leaves lanceolate. Cliffs and rocks inland, not on lime.

5 ***Alpine Catchfly *Lychnis alpina*. Shorter than Sticky Catchfly (**4**), to 20cm, with leaf-nodes not sticky and compact clusters of smaller, 6-12mm, pinker flowers; June-July. Two native localities only, high mountains in Cumbria and Angus.

6 Ragged Robin *Lychnis flos-cuculi*. Easily told by its 'ragged' red petals, a medium/tall perennial to 75cm. Flowers 3-4cm, with petals *deeply cleft* into four narrow lobes; May-July; also differs from Red Campion (p. 44) in having its stamens and styles in the same flower and 5-toothed fruits. Leaves lanceolate. Marshes, fens and wet meadows.

7 Moss Campion *Silene acaulis*. The most distinctive of the campions and one of our most attractive high-mountain flowers; a low tufted perennial to 10cm. Flowers 10-12mm, rose-pink, starring the *cushions* of tiny pointed leaves, which end in a more prominent tooth than the yellow-green Cyphel (p. 54); June-July. Mountain tops, ledges and screes, but near sea-level in the far north.

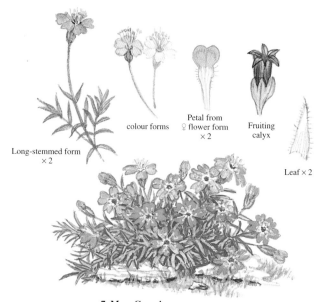

Long-stemmed form
× 2

colour forms

Petal from
♀ flower form
× 2

Fruiting
calyx

Leaf × 2

7 Moss Campion

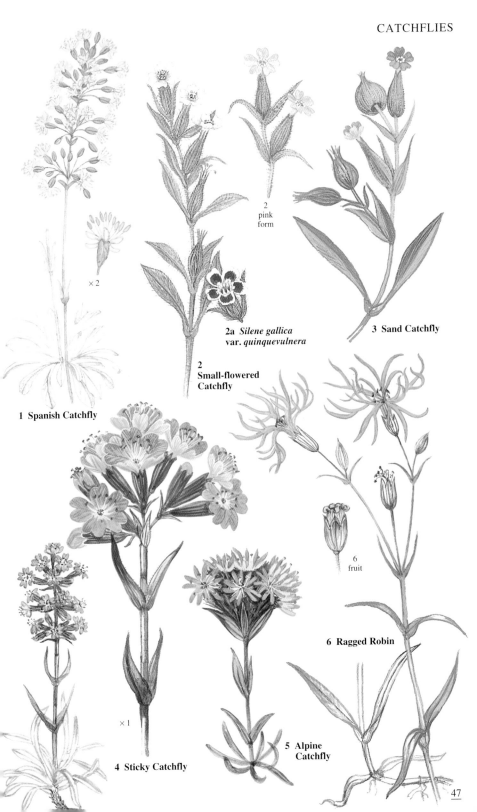

× 2

1 Spanish Catchfly

2a *Silene gallica*
var. *quinquevulnera*

2
Small-flowered
Catchfly

2
pink
form

3 Sand Catchfly

6
fruit

6 Ragged Robin

4 Sticky Catchfly

× 1

5 Alpine
Catchfly

1 Soapwort *Saponaria officinalis*. A medium/tall straggling pale green perennial with runners, formerly used to make soap; stems rather thick and brittle, to 90cm. Flowers soft pink, 2-2.5cm, the *petals unnotched*, and standing clear of the scarcely inflated sepal-tube; double-flowered forms (**1a Bouncing Bett**) are frequent; July-Sept. Leaves lanceolate. Hedge-and stream-banks, grassy places; perhaps native in the SW.

2 Corn-cockle *Agrostemma githago*. A once abundant cornfield weed that is now effectively extinct, except as a casual or when (as it often is) sown in "wildflower mixtures"; a medium/tall softly hairy annual, to 1m. Flowers red-purple, *large, 3-5cm*, the slightly inflated sepal-tube with five long narrow teeth protruding starfish-like well beyond the petals; June-August. Leaves narrow lanceolate.

Pinks *Dianthus*. Distinguished by the epicalyx below the sepal-tube, formed by bracteoles. Petals usually toothed. Leaves linear to narrow lanceolate.

3 *Maiden Pink *Dianthus deltoides*. Loosely tufted, shortly hairy, often greyish perennial, to 45cm. Flowers pink, with darker or paler spots, *12-20mm*, unscented; the epicalyx with two long-pointed scales half as long as the sepal-tube; in dull weather the flowers close and the plant merges into the surrounding grass; June-August. Leaves rough-edged. Decreasing in dry grassland, usually on sand.

4 *Deptford Pink *Dianthus armeria*. Slightly downy, dark green or greyish, short/medium, annual/biennial; stems stiff, to 60cm. Flowers bright pink, with darker or paler spots, *8-13mm*, unscented in *small crowded heads*, the buds hidden among the long narrow sepal-like bracts; epicalyx nearly as long as sepal-tube; June-August. Decreasing in dry grassy places. **4a Sweet William** *D. barbatus*, the well known garden plant, often escaping for short periods, is larger in all its parts and hairless, with flowers more conspicuous and often red, and sterile shoots at flowering time.

5 ***Cheddar Pink *Dianthus gratianopolitanus*. One of our most attractive rarities, native only on limestone cliffs and rocks around Cheddar Gorge, Somerset. A low hairless greyish perennial to 20cm, mat-forming with long creeping sterile shoots. Flowers pink, 14-30mm, solitary and *clove-scented*, petals hairy near the base; epicalyx with 2-4 short pointed teeth; June-July. Leaves rough-edged. Both Cheddar Pink and its hybrid with Pink (**6**) are often grown in gardens and escape.

6 Pink *Dianthus plumarius*. Greyish tufted low/short perennial, to 30cm. Flowers pale mauvish-pink or white, 20-40mm, fragrant, the petals *almost hairless* and cut to half-way with feathery teeth and long sepal-teeth; epicalyx with 2-4 short pointed teeth; June-August. Leaves rough-edged. Old walls, e.g. Beaulieu Abbey, Hants, often long established; also as a more recent escape. Hybridises with both Cheddar (**5**) and Clove Pinks. **6a Clove Pink** *D. caryophyllus*, the origin of the garden Carnation, is taller, to 60cm, with slightly smaller flowers, petals only toothed, a longer sepal-tube and smooth-edged leaves. On fewer old walls, e.g. Rochester Castle, Kent, for more than 300 years.

7 ***Childing Pink *Petrorhagia nanteulii*. Together with Proliferous Pink (**7a**) differs from all other Pinks in the *large brownish chaffy bracts* that enfold the close cluster of small pink flowers, 6-9mm, which only open one at a time; late June-Sept. A short greyish annual; stems hairless or slightly downy, to 50cm. Leaves linear, rough-edged, with sheaths about as long as wide. Now only one site, on sand and shingle near the sea in West Sussex. **7a ***Proliferous Pink** *P. prolifera* differs especially in its more thickly downy stem and leaf-sheaths up to twice as long as wide; flowering June-August. May be native in its two sites on dry banks in Bedfordshire and Norfolk.

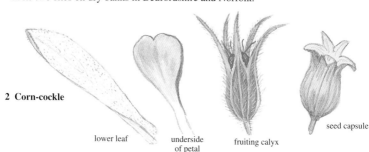

2 Corn-cockle

lower leaf   underside of petal   fruiting calyx   seed capsule

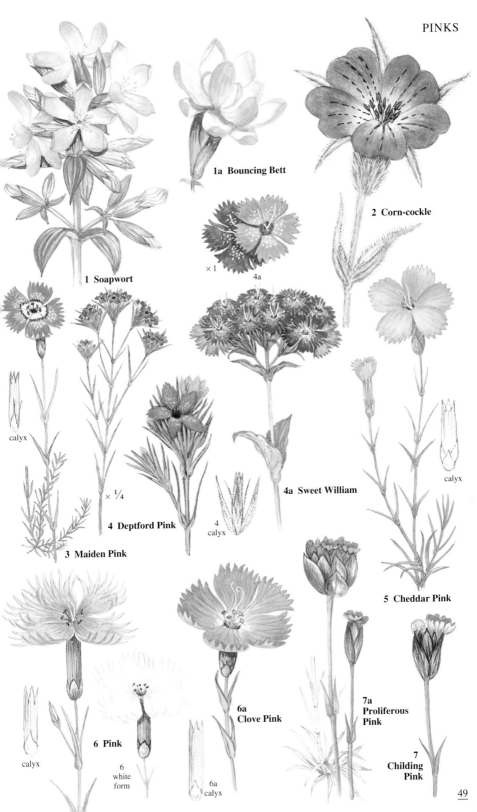

1a Bouncing Bett

1 Soapwort

2 Corn-cockle

×1
4a

calyx

× ¼

4 Deptford Pink

4
calyx

4a Sweet William

3 Maiden Pink

calyx

5 Cheddar Pink

6a
Clove Pink

7a
Proliferous
Pink

6 Pink

6
white
form

calyx

6a
calyx

7
Childing
Pink

Stitchworts and **Chickweeds** *Stellaria*. Flowers white, petals notched; stems rather weak and straggling; stamens usually 10. Stitchworts tend to be perennials with larger flowers and narrower unstalked leaves and chickweeds annuals with smaller flowers and broader stalked leaves.

1 Greater Stitchwort *Stellaria holostea*. The largest-flowered short/medium stitchwort, conspicuous in the spring hedgerows, often in patches; stems rough-edged, 4-angled, to 60cm. Flowers with deeply cleft petals, *15-30mm*; bracts all green; March-June. Leaves narrow lanceolate, minutely rough-edged, slightly greyish. Woods, scrub, hedges, usually in light shade.

2 Marsh Stitchwort *Stellaria palustris*. Intermediate between Greater (**1**) and Lesser (**3**) Stitchworts, differing from Greater in its smooth-angled stems, flowers *12-18mm*, the sepals with broader whitish edges; May-August; also in its narrower greyer smooth-edged leaves, the bracts pale with a green midrib. It has larger flowers than Lesser Stitchwort, as well as partly green bracts. Fens and lowland wet grassland.

3 Lesser Stitchwort *Stellaria graminea*. The smallest-flowered true stitchwort; stems short/medium, smooth-angled, to 80cm. Flowers *5-12mm*, with petals deeply cut; bracts all pale; May-August. Leaves narrow. Grassy, often heathy, places on acid soils.

4 Bog Stitchwort *Stellaria uliginosa*. Intermediate between true stitchworts and chickweeds; stems low/short, smooth-angled, to 40cm. Flowers 5-7mm, shorter than sepals; *bracts pale with a green midrib*; May-Sept. Leaves elliptic to pointed oval, unstalked on flowering stems, but otherwise stalked. Mires, usually unshaded, by or sometimes in streams.

5 Wood Stitchwort *Stellaria nemorum*. A confusingly named stitchwort, much more like Greater Chickweed (**8**) than the true stitchworts (above); stems short/medium, to 60cm, hairy, especially below the swollen leaf-nodes, with runners. Flowers 10-18mm, petals deeply cleft, sepals with narrow pale edges; May-August. Leaves pale green, the lower long-stalked, *heart-shaped*. Damp woods, hedge-banks and streamsides.

6 Common Chickweed *Stellaria media*. Almost our commonest weed – challenged perhaps only by Groundsel (p. 280); annual, prostrate or sprawling, to 50cm; hairs in lines on alternate sides of the rounded stems between the leaf-nodes. Flowers *5-9mm*, petals very deeply notched or sometimes none, not exceeding sepals, which are downy with narrow pale margins; stamens 3-5; mature fruit-stalks drooping; Jan-Dec. Leaves *pale green*, pointed oval, the lower stalked. Cultivated ground and bare places on rich soils; occasionally in upper saltmarshes.

7 Lesser Chickweed *Stellaria pallida*. Differs from the occasional petalless Common Chickweed (**6**) in its slenderer and more brittle stems, flowers *3-6mm*, sepals sometimes hairless, stamens 1-2, fruit-stalks not drooping, and smaller, pale *yellowish-green* leaves; March-May. Shingle and dunes by the sea; bare sandy places inland.

8 Greater Chickweed *Stellaria neglecta*. Like an outsize Common Chickweed (**6**), which can have confusing large shade-forms – but usually more robust and luxuriant, with stems straggling upwards to 80cm, flowers *9-11mm*, stamens 10 and fruit-stalks finally erect; April-July. Differs from Wood Stitchwort (**5**) in its lines of hairs on the stem, smaller flowers and shorter leaf-stalks. In at least light shade in *woods and hedge-banks* and by streams.

~

9 Water Chickweed *Myosoton aquaticum*. An outsize, fleshy chickweed, a straggling medium perennial, to 1m; hairless below but stickily downy above. Flowers white, *12-15mm*, with 5 deeply cleft petals, 10 stamens and 5 styles (*Stellaria* has 3); June-Oct. Leaves pointed oval, often wavy-edged, the lower stalked. *Marshes, by fresh water.*

10 Upright Chickweed *Moenchia erecta*. Another misnamed plant, not being a chickweed, and having the narrow leaves of a stitchwort and the *unnotched petals* of neither; a tiny, usually erect annual, to 12mm. Very hard to detect in the turf, especially when its 7-9mm white flowers are closed (as they usually are, except in sunshine), but the practised eye seeks the *glaucous* hue of the stiff linear unstalked leaves. Petals 4, not notched, shorter than the white-edged sepals; styles 4; April-June. Sandy and gravelly turf.

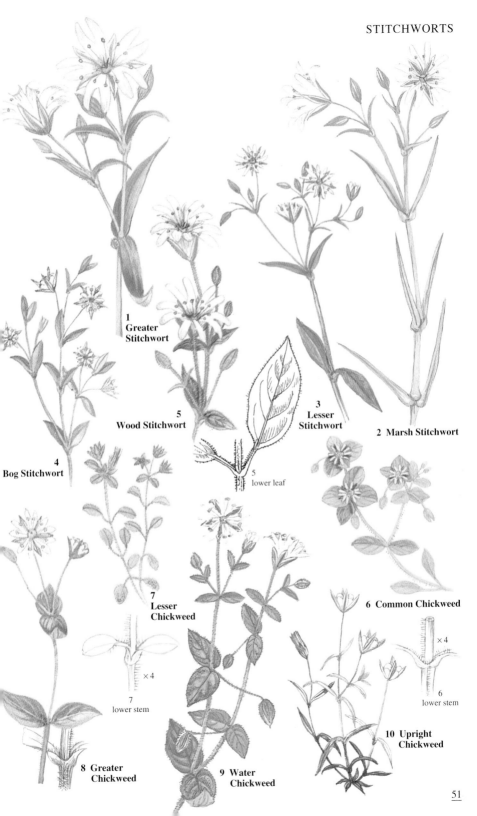

1 Greater Stitchwort

5 Wood Stitchwort

3 Lesser Stitchwort

2 Marsh Stitchwort

4 Bog Stitchwort

5 lower leaf

7 Lesser Chickweed

7 lower stem

×4

6 Common Chickweed

6 lower stem

×4

8 Greater Chickweed

9 Water Chickweed

10 Upright Chickweed

Mouse-ears *Cerastium*. Hairy annuals/perennials. Flowers white, with five petals (except Sea Mouse-ear), deeply notched (except Little Mouse-ear), and (except Starwort Mouse-ear) five styles. Leaves unstalked. Starwort, Alpine and Arctic Mouse-ears grow only on mountains, and Sea Mouse-ear usually by the sea. Aka Mouse-ear Chickweeds.

Flowers usually less than 15mm across. All, except Common and Starwort Mouse-ears, are annuals, with sticky hairs and no non-flowering shoots.

1 Common Mouse-ear *Cerastium fontanum*. Erect to sprawling perennial, almost ubiquitous in grassy places; hairy, but much less so (ssp. *holosteoides*) in wetter places; stems to 50cm with leafy non-flowering shoots. Flowers 6-10mm, from slightly longer than to slightly shorter than sepals, tending to be larger on mountains; sepals and bracts with *narrow pale margins*; April-Nov. Leaves lanceolate to oblong, dark grey-green. Grassland, less frequent on bare ground. The larger-flowered ssp. ***scoticum* occurs on Meikle Kilrannoch in Angus. **1a ***Grey Mouse-ear** *C. brachypetalum* is erect, to 30cm, silvery grey with long, often purple-based hairs, flowers 8-11mm, sepals hairy to the tip and sometimes all green, *bracts all green*; April-June; bare ground on lime in two smallish areas in the S, possibly native.

1   soz   ▫

2 Sea Mouse-ear *Cerastium diffusum*. Shorter, to 30cm, than Common Mouse-ear (**1**), with hairs sticky, flowers *3-6mm*, and petals much shorter than sepals; April-July; bracts *all green*. Bare sandy ground, mostly by the sea.

1a   ▫↓

3 Little Mouse-ear *Cerastium semidecandrum*. Shorter than Common Mouse-ear (**1**), to 20cm, with hairs sticky, flowers *5-7mm* with petals only slightly notched and much shorter than sepals, which have *broad pale edges*; April-May; bracts pale at tip. Leaves pale green. Bare places on sand or lime.

4 *Dwarf Mouse-ear *Cerastium pumilum*. Shorter than Common Mouse-ear (*1*), to 12cm, with stems often reddish at base, sticky hairs, flowers *6-7mm*, petals about as long as *broadly pale-edged sepals*, and bracts with pale tip; April-May. Bare or sparsely grassy places on lime.

2   soz   ▫

5 Sticky Mouse-ear *Cerastium glomeratum*. The most distinctive of the smaller mouse-ears, with its *compact* flower clusters; low, erect, stickily hairy, often *yellowish-green*, to 45cm. Flowers 5-8mm, rarely opening fully, the sepals with narrow pale edges and long whitish hairs; bracts all green; April-Oct. Leaves ovate. Bare and disturbed ground, walls, dunes.

3   ▫

6 *Starwort Mouse-ear *Cerastium cerastoides*. Low, mat-forming, hairless except for two lines of hairs on alternate sides of the stem. Flowers *9-12mm*, sepals with a narrow pale margin, bracts all green; the only mouse-ear with only *three styles*; July-August. Leaves narrow lanceolate, pale green. Very high on mountains, around springs, in sparse grassland and on screes.

Flowers more than 12mm across; petals notched. Perennials.

7 Field Mouse-ear *Cerastium arvense*. Spreading, often forming broad patches, with shoots to 30cm; *grey downy all over*. Flowers 15-20mm, recalling Greater Stitchwort (p. 50); April-August. Leaves narrow. Dry grassland with bare patches on lime and slightly acid sand and gravel. **7a Snow-in-summer** *C. tomentosum* is an increasing escape, almost white with short woolly hairs, with longer and erecter flower stalks and narrower petals; May-August; and longer, broader leaves often on banks and walls away from gardens.

4   ▫↓

8 *Alpine Mouse-ear *Cerastium alpinum*. Low perennial, often tufted, to 20cm; covered with *long white woolly hairs*. Flowers 15-20mm, sepals narrowly pale-edged; bracts white-edged; June-August. Leaves oval to elliptical. Mountain rocks on lime.

9 *Arctic Mouse-ear *Cerastium arcticum*. Tufted, to 15cm, with runners; *hairs short white or yellowish*, flowers 15-30mm, sepals broadly white-edged; June-August; bracts all green. Leaves often narrow. Mountain rocks and ledges. **9a ***Shetland Mouse-ear** *C. nigrescens* is more compactly tufted with many short glandular hairs and leaves usually dark green tinged purple; only on serpentine rocks on two hills in Shetland.

5   soz   ▫↑

6   ▫

7   ▫↓   8   ↓   9   ▫

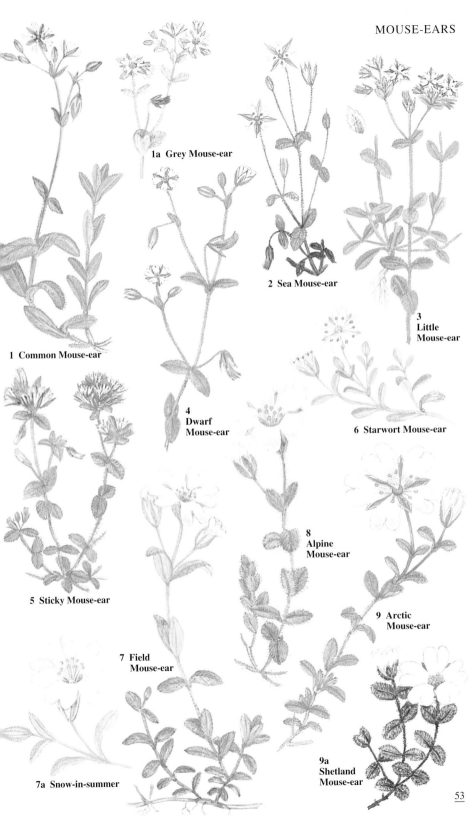

1a Grey Mouse-ear

2 Sea Mouse-ear

3
Little
Mouse-ear

1 Common Mouse-ear

4
Dwarf
Mouse-ear

6 Starwort Mouse-ear

8
Alpine
Mouse-ear

9 Arctic
Mouse-ear

5 Sticky Mouse-ear

7 Field
Mouse-ear

7a Snow-in-summer

9a
Shetland
Mouse-ear

Sandworts. Flowers white (green or greenish in Sea Sandwort and Cyphel), petals not notched.

1 Thyme-leaved Sandwort *Arenaria serpyllifolia*. Prostrate to bushy, greyish hairy annual, to 30cm. Flowers *3-5mm*, petals *shorter* than pointed oval sepals, anthers yellow; April-Sept. Leaves pointed oval. Fruits with curved sides (straight sides in slenderer ssp. *leptoclados*, which may be a full species). Bare and disturbed places, walls; near the sea flower clusters may be denser.

2 **Arctic Sandwort *Arenaria norvegica*. Low, loosely tufted, almost hairless perennial, to 6cm. Flowers 9-10mm, petals longer than sepals; May-Sept. Bare places, screes, usually on lime. **2a ***English Sandwort** ssp. *anglica* is annual/biennial with larger flowers, to 23mm, and narrower leaves. Confined to the Craven Pennines, W Yorkshire. **2b Fringed Sandwort** *Arenaria ciliata* has larger (12-16mm) flowers, with hairier sepals and leaves with a more distinct midrib. Confined to limestone cliffs, Ben Bulben, Co. Sligo.

3 Mossy Sandwort *Arenaria balearica*. Mat-forming perennial, to 5cm; stems thread-like. Flowers solitary, long-stalked, 5-7mm, petals *much longer* than sepals; June-August. Leaves tiny, ovate to rounded. Frequent garden escape to damp rocks, walls and paths.

4 Three-nerved Sandwort *Moehringia trinervia*. A short weak *straggly* downy annual, to 40cm; stem hairy all round. Flowers on long slender stalks, 5-7mm, the petals *half as long* as the narrow pointed petals; April-July. Leaves pointed oval, like Chickweeds (p. 50), with *3-5 conspicuous veins* beneath. Woods, hedge-banks, on richer soils.

5 Sea Sandwort *Honckenya peploides*. A distinctive prostrate hairless perennial, to 40cm. Flowers *greenish-white*, 6-10mm, the narrow petals about equalling the sepals on the male ones, much shorter on the female ones, which may be on different plants. Leaves numerous, *yellowish-green*, broad, pointed, in angular rows up the stems. Fruits *yellow-green*, like small peas. Coastal sand and shingle.

6 *Fine-leaved Sandwort *Minuartia hybrida*. A delicate low annual, erect to 20cm. Flowers 5-6mm, petals *much shorter* than the narrow, pointed, *white-edged*, veined sepals; May-July. Leaves linear, sometimes curved. Dry stony or disturbed ground, walls.

7 *Spring Sandwort *Minuartia verna*. A dainty, often downy, mat-forming perennial, to 15cm. Flowers *8-12mm*, petals usually longer than the veined, white-edged sepals; May-August. Leaves linear, 3-veined. Dry rocky and sparsely grassy places, usually on lime, often on old lead-mine spoil.

8 *Cyphel *Minuartia sedoides*. Rather like a Moss Campion (p. 46) with *yellow-green* flowers, a perennial that forms pale green *cushions*, to 8cm. Flowers often with no petals, sometimes scarcely emerging above the cushion; June-August. Leaves stiff, linear, pointed. Mountains.

9 **Mountain Sandwort *Minuartia rubella*. An insignificant tufted perennial, to 6cm. Flowers 5-8mm, usually solitary, on hairy stalks, the petals *much shorter* than the pointed veined sepals; July-August. Leaves linear. Mountains.

10 ***Teesdale Sandwort *Minuartia stricta*. Not unlike a starved Spring Sandwort (**7**), a perennial, tufted but not mat-forming, to 10cm. Flowers 5-8mm, with *narrow petals* no longer than the unveined sepals; June-July. Leaves linear, unveined. One Durham moor, on sugar limestone.

11 Recurved Sandwort *Minuartia recurva*. Tufted perennial, to 5cm. Flowers 6-12mm, the petals equalling or slightly longer than the *grey-edged* sepals; bracts *white-edged*; June-Oct. Leaves *curved*. Cracks in acid mountain rocks; three localities in SW Ireland.

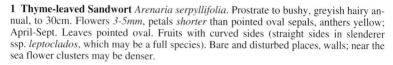

1   SZ   ·

2,2a   Z   ·

2b   ·

4   ·↑

5   SOZ   ■

6   ·↓↓

7   □

8   □

9   ·

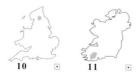

10   ·

11   ·

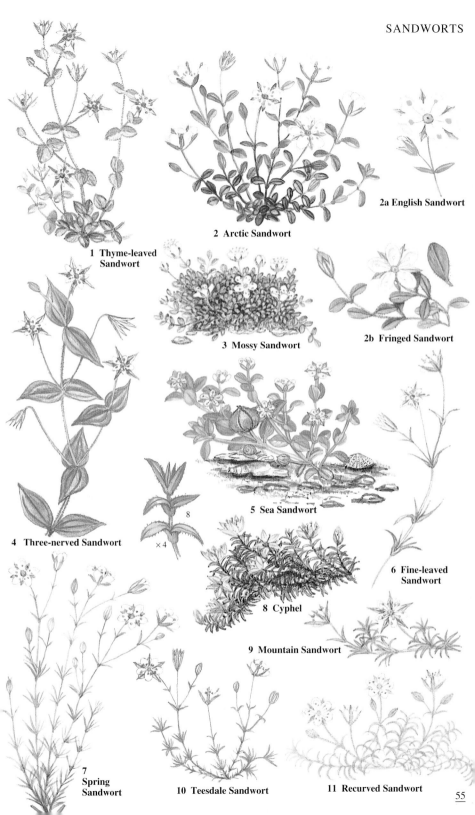

1 Thyme-leaved
Sandwort

2 Arctic Sandwort

2a English Sandwort

2b Fringed Sandwort

3 Mossy Sandwort

4 Three-nerved Sandwort

8

×4

5 Sea Sandwort

6 Fine-leaved
Sandwort

8 Cyphel

9 Mountain Sandwort

7
Spring
Sandwort

10 Teesdale Sandwort

11 Recurved Sandwort

1 Corn Spurrey *Spergula arvensis.* A low, rather straggly, stickily hairy annual, to 40cm. Flowers *white*, petals unnotched, 4-7mm, with *five styles*, in leafless forked clusters; April-Sept. Leaves greyish, linear, apparently whorled, *furrowed beneath*; stipules soon falling. Arable weed, not on lime.

1   soz ☐↓↓

Sea-spurreys *Spergularia.* More or less stickily hairy, with flowers pink, unnotched petals and *three styles*. Leaves opposite or whorled, usually with a tiny bristle, *not furrowed* beneath, and with pale or silvery stipules at stem-nodes. All except Sand Spurrey (**2**) grow by the sea, and sometimes on salted inland road verges.

2 Sand Spurrey *Spergularia rubra.* The only sea-spurrey to grow *inland*, a sprawling annual/biennial, to 25cm. Flowers pale pink, 3-5mm; May-Sept. Leaves greyish, whorled, always ending in a tiny bristle; stipules silvery. Bare, sandy or gravelly places, not on lime.

2   s   ▪

3 Greater Sea-spurrey *Spergularia media.* Sprawling, largely hairless perennial, to 40cm. Flowers pale violet-pink, usually white-centred, 8-12mm, *petals longer than sepals*; late June-Sept. Leaves often yellowish-green with stipules not silvery. Fruiting stalks shorter than or equalling fruit. Drier parts of salt and brackish marshes.

4 Lesser Sea-spurrey *Spergularia marina.* Differs from Greater Sea-Spurrey (**3**) in being often annual, and having smaller, pinker flowers, 6-8mm, with petals usually *shorter than sepals*; April-Sept; and fruiting stalks usually longer than fruit.

3   oz   ☐

5 Rock Sea-spurrey *Spergularia rupicola.* Differs from Greater (**3**) and Lesser (**4**) Sea-spurreys especially in habitat – *cliffs, rocks and walls* by the sea. Perennial with a more or less woody base, sprawling, often purplish stems to 35cm. Flowers without white centres, petals equalling sepals; June-Sept. Stipules somewhat silvery.

6 **Greek Sea-spurrey *Spergularia bocconei.* The smallest-flowered Sea-spurrey, with pale or whitish pink flowers only 2mm across and shorter than sepals; May-Sept. Low annual, densely stickily hairy, to 20cm. Leaves opposite, stipules not silvery. Dry bare ground and rock crevices by the sea. Very rare ancient introduction in the SW, also casual on salted road verges.

4   soz ☐↑↑

~

7 Annual Knawel *Scleranthus annuus.* A small, easily overlooked, annual/biennial; stems erect or sprawling to 20cm. Flowers in heads, tiny, petalless, the five pointed green sepals *narrowly bordered whitish* and usually spreading outwards in fruit; May-Oct. Leaves linear, pointed, in opposite pairs fused at base. Dry bare sandy places.

5   s   ▪

8 **Perennial Knawel *Scleranthus perennis.* Differs from Annual Knawel (**7**) in being biennial/perennial, with stems woody at base (as biennial Annual Knawel may also be) and less branched, some sterile shoots at flowering time (June-August), and *broader whitish edges* to the slightly blunter sepals, which curve in over the ripe fruit. Confined to three sandy heaths in Breckland (ssp. *prostratus*) and one rocky outcrop in Radnorshire (ssp. *perennis*).

6   ▪

9 ***Strapwort *Corrigiola littoralis.* A small prostrate greyish hairless annual; stems may be red, to 25cm. Flowers tiny, in conspicuous leafy clusters, five white, sometimes red-tipped petals somewhat shorter than the *broadly white-edged* sepals, often maroon in the centre; July-Sept. Leaves narrow, alternate. Now only native on shore of Slapton Ley, S Devon; casual on railway ballast elsewhere.

7   ▪↓↓

10 **Smooth Rupturewort *Herniaria glabra.* Variable, prostrate, to 30cm, annual/biennial (rarely perennial with stems slightly woody at base). Flowers green, with five tiny narrow whitish petals, in clusters at base of narrow *hairless* leaves that join round stem; June-Oct. Dry sandy places, Lincolnshire to Suffolk. **10a **Fringed Rupturewort** *H. ciliolata* is always perennial with stems woody below and has evergreen leaves *fringed with hairs*; flowers May-August. Rocks and grassy places by the sea, locally common, Lizard Peninsula, Cornwall.

8   ▪↓

9   ▪↓   10   ▪↓   10a   ▪

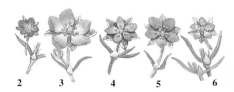

2   3   4   5   6

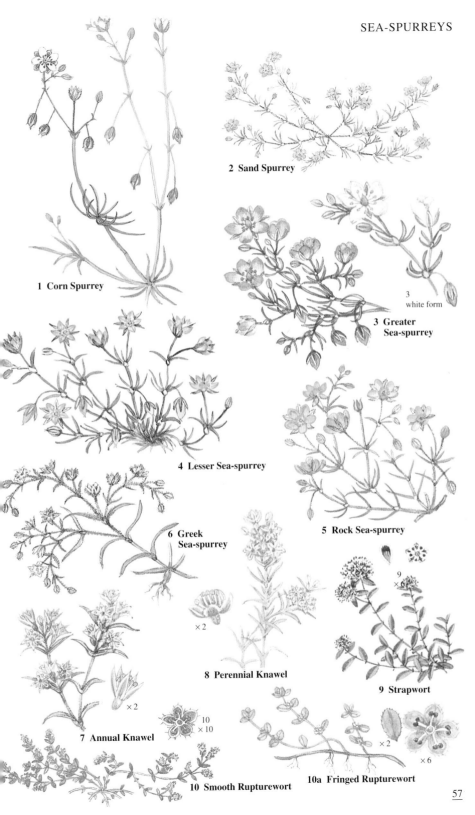

1 Corn Spurrey

2 Sand Spurrey

3
white form

**3 Greater
Sea-spurrey**

4 Lesser Sea-spurrey

5 Rock Sea-spurrey

**6 Greek
Sea-spurrey**

×2

8 Perennial Knawel

9
×6

9 Strapwort

×2

7 Annual Knawel

10
×10

×2

×6

10a Fringed Rupturewort

10 Smooth Rupturewort

Pearlworts *Sagina*. Low-growing perennials (except Annual (**6**) and Sea (**7**) Pearlworts), with small, usually solitary, white (greenish-white in Procumbent (**1**) and Annual (**6**); absent in Sea Pearlwort (**7**)) flowers with 4-5 unnotched petals. Leaves linear, opposite, fused at the base, ending, except in Sea Pearlwort (**7**), with a tiny bristle.

Petals 4:	Procumbent, Annual, Scottish, Snow, Sea (if any)
Petals 5:	Heath, Alpine, Scottish, Snow, Knotted

1 Procumbent Pearlwort *Sagina procumbens*. Much the commonest pearlwort, prostrate and hairless, not unlike a tuft of a rather leafy moss, with rooting stems to 20cm and a central *non-flowering* rosette. Flowers on long slender stalks, with 4 (or 0, rarely 5) minute greenish-white petals, *much shorter* than the four blunt green sepals, which spread crosswise in ripe fruit; April-Sept. All kinds of bare ground from the Duke of York's Steps in London to unkempt lawns in Yorkshire and Ben Lawers in Scotland.

2 Heath Pearlwort *Sagina subulata*. Differs from Procumbent Pearlwort (**1**) in its shorter stems, to 10cm, and larger white flowers, the five petals *equalling* the sepals, which are erect in fruit; June-August. Dry, bare, heathy, sandy or gravelly places, especially near the coast.

3 *Alpine Pearlwort *Sagina saginoides*. A mountain species, with a cushion of matted stems to 10cm and a flowering central rosette. Flowers white, the five petals *almost equalling* the blunt sepals, which are erect in fruit; June-August. Bare ground and ledges on mountains. **3a **Scottish Pearlwort** *S.* × *normaniana*, the hybrid between Alpine and Procumbent (**1**) Pearlworts, is intermediate between its parents (but sometimes grows without them) with runners rooting at the nodes and ripe fruit very rare. Wet mountain rock ledges.

4 **Snow Pearlwort *Sagina nivalis*. Our rarest pearlwort, a mountain species, easily overlooked, its *tiny compact cushion* being often no more than 2-3cm across with the flower-stalks, to 3cm, scarcely emerging from it, and the 4-5 white petals no longer than the often purple-edged sepals; July-Sept. Bare ground high up on mountains, on or near Ben Lawers.

5 Knotted Pearlwort *Sagina nodosa*. Our largest-flowered pearlwort, the sprawling stems to 15cm. Flowers with usually five white petals, 5-10mm, *twice as long as the sepals*; July-Sept. Leaves short, blunt, in *tight knotlike clusters* up the stem nodes, rarely with bulbils. Damp, grassy, rather bare, peaty, sandy or gravelly places.

6 Annual Pearlwort *Sagina apetala*. Well branched erect pale green annual to 15cm. Flowers April-August, similar to Procumbent Pearlwort (**1**), from which *lack of rosette* at once distinguishes; sepals either erect (ssp. *apetala*) or spreading (ssp. *erecta*) in fruit. Var. *filicaulis*, perhaps another species, has glandular hairs on sepals and flower-stalks.

7 Sea Pearlwort *Sagina maritima*. A dark green or purplish, *fleshy* annual, to 15cm. Flowers with petals *minute or absent*, sepals four; April-Sept. Leaves thick, blunt, with no bristle. Bare places near the sea, also on mountains and salted road verges.

~

8 *Coral Necklace *Illecebrum verticillatum*. A slender sprawling hairless annual; stems reddish-pink, to 20cm. Flowers tiny, with five petals and sepals both white, July-Sept, in conspicuous opposite clusters at the base of the bright green, bluntly oval leaves. Damp sandy heathy places.

9 **Four-leaved Allseed *Polycarpon tetraphyllum*. Low, much-branched hairless annual, erect to 25cm. Flowers tiny, in leafless forked heads, with tiny chaffy bracts at their base; the five white petals fall soon after opening and are shorter than the keeled hooded *white-edged sepals*; April-Dec. Leaves oval, *in fours* (rarely pairs), with small chaffy stipules at their base. Bare, often sandy, places near the sea.

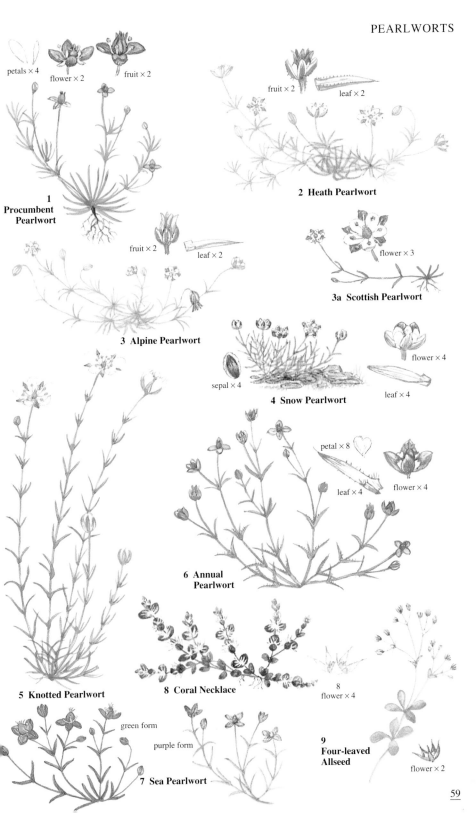

petals × 4

flower × 2

fruit × 2

1 Procumbent Pearlwort

fruit × 2

leaf × 2

2 Heath Pearlwort

fruit × 2

leaf × 2

3 Alpine Pearlwort

flower × 3

3a Scottish Pearlwort

sepal × 4

4 Snow Pearlwort

flower × 4

leaf × 4

petal × 8

leaf × 4

flower × 4

6 Annual Pearlwort

5 Knotted Pearlwort

8 Coral Necklace

8 flower × 4

9 Four-leaved Allseed

flower × 2

green form

purple form

7 Sea Pearlwort

DOCK FAMILY Polygonaceae

Characterised by a sheath at the base of the leaves forming a whitish papery tube (ochrea) around the stem at the more or less swollen leaf-nodes. Leaves alternate, usually undivided and untoothed. Flowers small, pink, white or green, with no petals but petaloid sepals (tepals).

Docks *Rumex*. The great majority of our docks – Dockens in the north – are both hairless and perennial. All have more or less branched terminal, usually leafy, spikes with whorls of small stalked greenish flowers, often tinged reddish, with six tepals. Leaves alternate, untoothed, mostly broad to narrow lanceolate, narrowing up the stem, with thin papery unfringed sheaths at their base. Fruit a 3-sided nut, sometimes with one or three small warts. Ripe fruits are essential for accurate identification of some docks. The brown dead flowering stems of the larger docks persist conspicuously into the winter.

sheath →   flower   toothed   fruit   untoothed   round warts   elongated warts   one wart   no warts

Leaves wavy or crisped:	Patience, Greek, Curled, Northern, Argentine, Shore, Golden, Marsh
waisted:	Clustered (slightly), Fiddle
Fruits toothed:	Broad-leaved, Water, Greek, Argentine, Fiddle, Golden, Marsh
untoothed:	Patience, Curled, Northern, Wood, Clustered, Shore, Monk's Rhubarb, Scottish
with rounded warts:	Broad-leaved, Patience, Greek, Curled, Wood
with elongated warts:	Water, Argentine, Clustered (slightly), Fiddle, Shore, Golden, Marsh
with 3 warts:	Broad-leaved. ssp. *transiens*, Water, Curled, ssp. *littoreus*, Argentine, Clustered, Fiddle, Shore, Golden, Marsh
with 1 wart:	Broad-leaved, Patience, Greek, Curled, Wood
with no warts:	Northern, Monk's Rhubarb, Scottish

Root leaves broad, 8cm or more across

1 Broad-leaved Dock *Rumex obtusifolius*. The sturdier of our two commonest docks, with tall stout stems to 1m or even 2m. Root leaves large, 8-10cm, *heart-shaped* at the base. Flowers with tepals triangular to oblong; May-Oct. Fruits with prominent teeth and *one rounded wart* (three in the alien ssp. *transiens* found along the Thames near London). Hybridises with Curled Dock (p. 62), the hybrid having slightly curly leaves. All kinds of lowland grassland and disturbed ground, including stream banks, farmyards, spoil heaps, road verges and waste ground.

1   SOZ   ☐

2 Water Dock *Rumex hydrolapathum*. Our tallest native dock, a stately plant to 2m. Root leaves *very large*, up to 1m long and 16cm across, not heart-shaped at base. Flowers with triangular tepals; July-Sept. Fruits with a few tiny teeth and three large elongated warts. Fresh-water margins and marshes.

2   ☐

3 Patience Dock *Rumex patientia*. Intermediate between Broad-leaved (**1**) and Water (**2**) Docks, with stems sometimes red-brown and up to 2m tall. Leaves 10-13cm broad, *slightly wavy*, not heart-shaped at base, the lateral veins at less than 60 deg. from the midrib. Flowers (May-June) in dense spikes with ace-of-spades tepals, and untoothed fruits with one small rounded wart. Well naturalised on bare and waste ground around a few large towns, e.g London and Bristol. **3a Greek Dock** *R. cristatus* has leaves *heart-shaped* at base, the lateral veins at more than 60° from the midrib, flowers in June-July and toothed fruits with one large rounded tubercle. Similarly naturalised around London and Cardiff and along the Thames estuary.

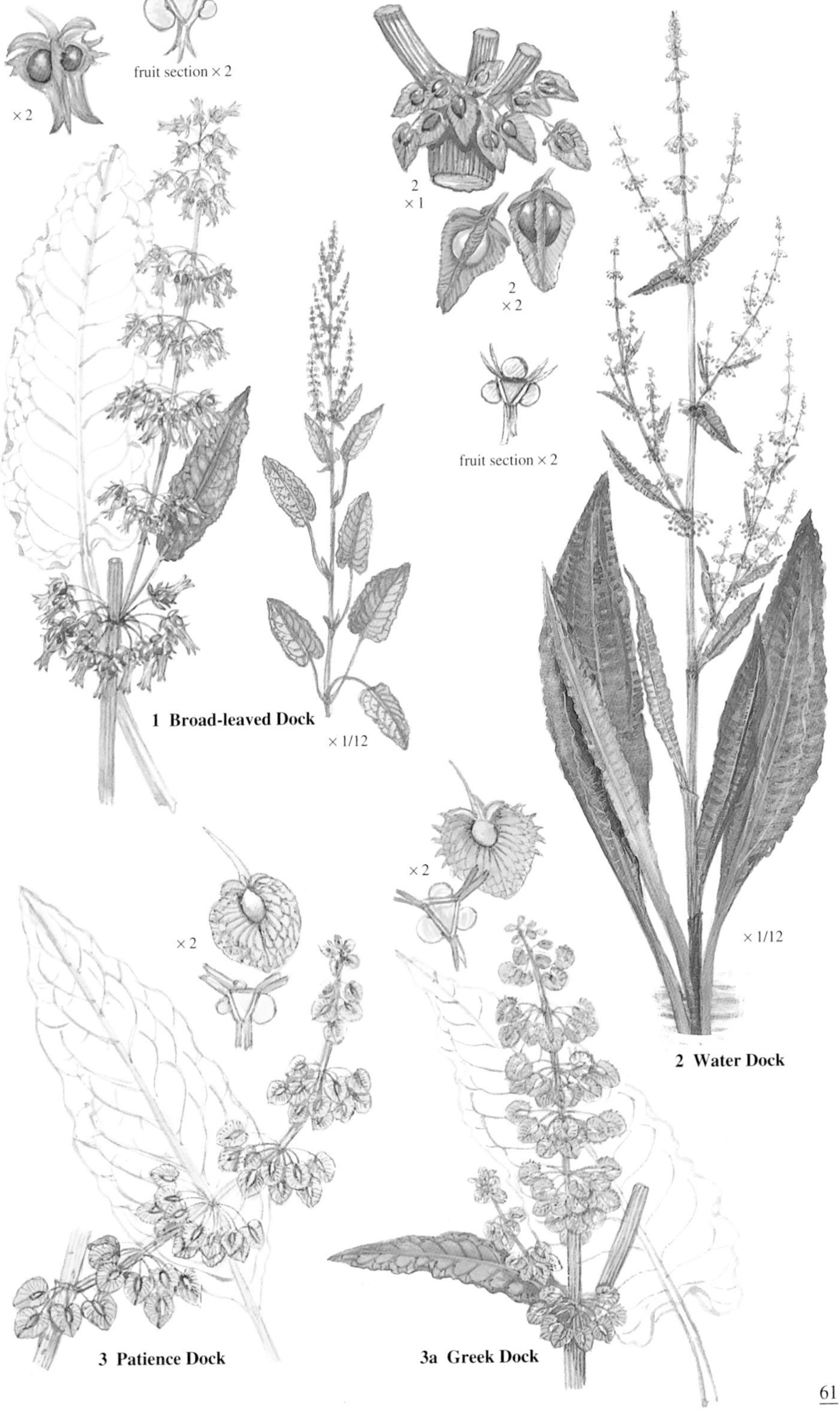

fruit section × 2

× 2

2
× 1

2
× 2

fruit section × 2

1 Broad-leaved Dock

× 1/12

2 Water Dock

× 1/12

× 2

× 2

3 Patience Dock

3a Greek Dock

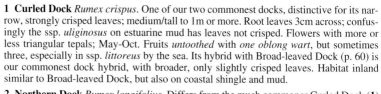

Root leaves with strongly crisped edges

1 Curled Dock *Rumex crispus*. One of our two commonest docks, distinctive for its narrow, strongly crisped leaves; medium/tall to 1m or more. Root leaves 3cm across; confusingly the ssp. *uliginosus* on estuarine mud has leaves not crisped. Flowers with more or less triangular tepals; May-Oct. Fruits *untoothed* with *one oblong wart*, but sometimes three, especially in ssp. *littoreus* by the sea. Its hybrid with Broad-leaved Dock (p. 60) is our commonest dock hybrid, with broader, only slightly crisped leaves. Habitat inland similar to Broad-leaved Dock, but also on coastal shingle and mud.

2 Northern Dock *Rumex longifolius*. Differs from the much commoner Curled Dock (**1**) especially in its larger and broader (5cm) crisped leaves, its almost rounded tepals (June-August) and its fruits *lacking warts*. Disturbed ground, especially near fresh water and around farms.

3 **Shore Dock *Rumex rupestris*. One of the rarest Docks in the world (Wales to N Spain); short/medium to 50cm. Root leaves wavy, greyish, 4-5cm across. Flowers with oblong tepals; June-July. Fruits untoothed, with *three large oblong warts*. Near fresh water on rocky coasts, dune slacks.

4 Argentine Dock *Rumex frutescens*. Stout, rather floppy and creeping, to 25cm. Leaves oval/lanceolate, somewhat leathery, with crisped margins. Flowers with oblong tepals; July-August. Fruits with *small teeth* and three oblong warts. Naturalised among dunes at Braunton Burrows, N Devon, and elsewhere in the SW.

Leaves 4-8cm across

5 Wood Dock *Rumex sanguineus*. Our only shade-loving dock, with *straight* medium stems to 60cm. Flowers in spikes *leafy only near the bottom*, with oblong tepals; June-July. Fruits untoothed, with one rounded wart. Leaves lanceolate, 6-8cm across, red-veined in a rare variety. Woods, especially on clay, and shady road verges, sometimes in the open.

6 Clustered Dock *Rumex conglomeratus*. Often confused with Wood Dock (**5**), but has stems often *slightly zigzag*, branches more spreading, root leaves sometimes slightly waisted, flower spikes *leafy almost to the top* and fruits with three slightly oblong warts. Damp places, especially marshy grassland and freshwater margins.

7 Fiddle Dock *Rumex pulcher*. A rather squat dock, to 40cm. Root leaves especially the early ones, markedly *waisted* or fiddle-shaped, 4-6cm across. Flowers in relatively leafless spikes, on long stiff branches, spreading *at right angles* with a jizz recognisable yards away, and often becoming tangled. Flowers with ovate tepals; June-July. Fruits usually well toothed, with usually three oblong warts. Dry grassy places, often in churchyards and at the base of walls.

Leaves up to 4cm across

8 *Golden Dock *Rumex maritimus*. Short annual/perennial, to 40cm or more, the whole plant turning *golden-yellow* in fruit. Root leaves narrow, 1-3cm across, wavy-edged. Flowers in spikes containing longer leaves than other Docks, the tepals more or less triangular; July-Sept. Fruits well toothed, with three large oblong warts. Damp places, often by ponds and reservoirs which dry out in summer.

9 *Marsh Dock *Rumex palustris*. Short/medium biennial/perennial, to 60cm or more. Like Golden Dock (**8**), but the whole fruiting plant turns *red-brown*, the flower-whorls (June-August) are more widely spaced, the sepals are longer-pointed and the fruits have thicker stalks, shorter teeth and somewhat larger warts. Habitat similar.

1 SOZ

2 Z

3 S

5

6 S

7 S

8

9

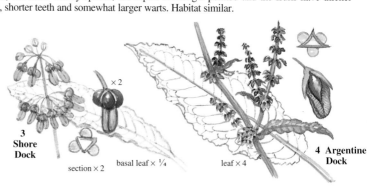

3 Shore Dock

× 2

section × 2

basal leaf × ¼

leaf × 4

4 Argentine Dock

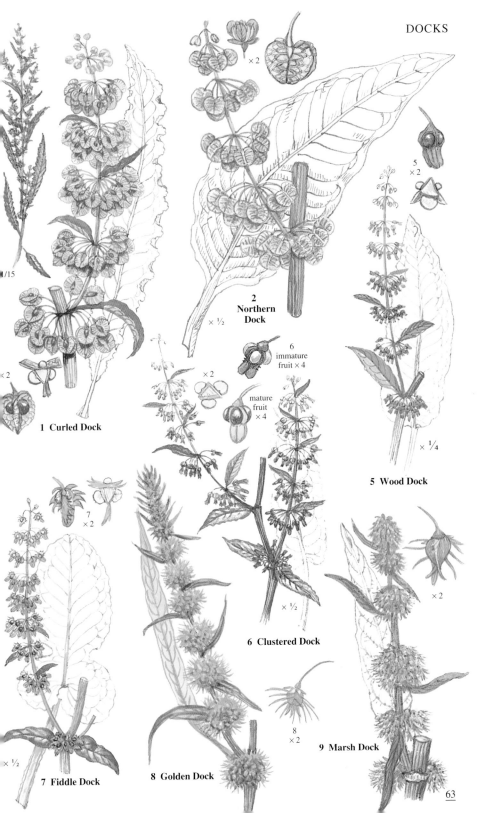

×2

5
×2

1/15

×2

1 **Curled Dock**

2
**Northern
Dock**

× 1/2

6
immature
fruit ×4

×2

mature
fruit
×4

5 **Wood Dock**

× 1/4

7
×2

6 **Clustered Dock**

×2

× 1/2

8
×2

9 **Marsh Dock**

× 1/2

7 **Fiddle Dock**

8 **Golden Dock**

Root leaves as long as broad

1 Monk's Rhubarb *Rumex pseudoalpinus.* Medium, stout and patch-forming, with stems to 70cm. Root leaves broad, *blunt*, heart-shaped. Flowers with rounded tepals; June-August. Fruits untoothed, with no warts. A former potherb surviving by streams and on road verges, usually near houses.

2 ***Scottish Dock *Rumex aquaticus.* Tall, to 2m, differing from other tall Docks especially in its pointed, more or less triangular root leaves. Flowers with oblong tepals; July-August. Fruits oblong, untoothed, with no warts. Readily hybridises with Broad-leaved Dock (p. 60). Native, only by or near the SE shores of Loch Lomond.

Sorrels *Rumex* and *Oxyria.* Sorrels *Rumex* are smaller than docks (p. 60) with arrow-shaped leaves and six tepals. Mountain Sorrel *Oxyria digyna* (**5**) has kidney-shaped leaves and four tepals. Wood Sorrel (p. 172) is quite unrelated.

3 Common Sorrel *Rumex acetosa.* An unbranched tufted acid-tasting perennial, medium/tall, to 80cm, but usually much shorter. Flowers small, red, in fairly compact leafless branched spikes; May-July. Leaves *arrow-shaped*, the basal lobes pointing *backwards*, the topmost unstalked and clasping the stem; fleshy on the coast. Fruit roundish with a tiny wart. Grassland, including mountains; less common on disturbed ground. **3a French Sorrel** *R. scutatus*, is shorter, to 45cm. with shorter broader greyish leaves with *silvery sheaths*; flowering June-July. An ancient salad plant naturalised on a number of old walls, as at Craigmillar Castle, Edinburgh, and Clitheroe Castle, Lancs.

4 Sheep's Sorrel *Rumex acetosella.* Smaller and slenderer than Common Sorrel (**3**), scarcely branched, with low stems to 20cm, the flower spike more open (late April-July), the leaves with the basal lobes pointing *sideways or forwards* and fruits with no wart. Grassy and heathy places, usually with bare soil, but less often in disturbed ground, avoiding limy soils.

5 Mountain Sorrel *Oxyria digyna.* A low/short pale green acid-tasting tufted perennial, to 30cm. Flowers like a slender Common Sorrel (**3**), with only four green but red-edged tepals; June-August. Leaves *kidney-shaped*, wavy-edged. Fruits with no warts. Mountain grassland and ledges.

~

6 Black Bindweed *Fallopia convolvulus.* Climbing or prostrate annual, twining clockwise to 1m or more; stems angled. Flowers small, the tepals greenish, often tinged red and with *narrow* dull white margins, in long loose spikes at the base of the leaves; June-Oct. Leaves heart-shaped, not unlike true Bindweeds (p. 204), but with *silvery sheaths* at base. Fruit a dull black triangular nut on 2mm stalks jointed above the middle. Arable fields, less often in other disturbed ground.

7 *Copse Bindweed *Fallopia dumetorum.* A climbing annual, to 3m or more, nearer the much commoner Black Bindweed (**6**) than Russian Vine (**8**). Flowers like Black Bindweed, the tepals with a *broader* white edge, but never as white as Russian Vine; July-Sept. Leaves more narrowly pointed than Black Bindweed. Fruits shiny black, tepals broadly winged and *running down* on to the stalk, which is up to 8mm long and jointed at or below the middle. Liable to be confused with a not uncommon variety of Black Bindweed, which has the tepals narrowly winged but not running down on to the stalk. Hedges, scrub, woodland edges.

8 Russian Vine *Fallopia baldschuanica.* Rampant deciduous perennial *climber*; lower stems woody, scrambling to 10m or more. Flowers small, bright white, in *showy trusses*; June-August. Leaves below ovate/triangular, wavy-edged, often bronzy when young. Naturalised in hedges and scrub and on cliffs.

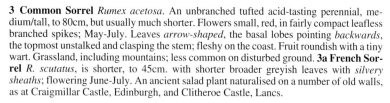

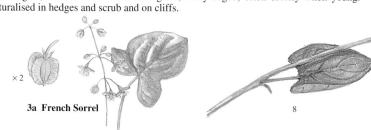

×2

3a French Sorrel   8

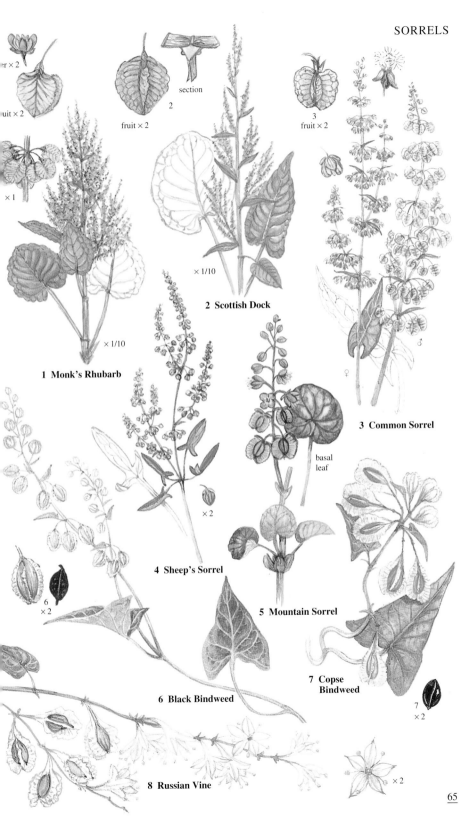

er × 2

uit × 2

2

section

fruit × 2

× 1

3
fruit × 2

× 1/10

2 Scottish Dock

× 1/10

1 Monk's Rhubarb

3 Common Sorrel

basal
leaf

× 2

4 Sheep's Sorrel

5 Mountain Sorrel

6
× 2

6 Black Bindweed

**7 Copse
    Bindweed**

7
× 2

8 Russian Vine

× 2

Bistorts *Persicaria.* Flowers pink or white, mostly in spikes.

1 Common Bistort *Persicaria bistorta.* Medium unbranched perennial, to 1m, often in conspicuous patches. Flowers pink, in compact spikes; May-August. Leaves *narrowly triangular*, on long, winged stalks; stem-leaves may be *arrow-shaped*. Damp grassland, open woods, often near water and in the hills.

2 Amphibious Bistort *Persicaria amphibia.* Creeping perennial with two forms: in water the leaves *floating*, oblong, almost heart-shaped and hairless; on land the stems medium, to 60cm and the leaves smaller, slightly hairy, and with a *rounded base*. Flowers pink, in compact spikes, much less frequent in the land form, where whole colonies are often barren; July-Sept. In and by still and slow fresh water, also on bare ground well away from water.

3 Alpine Bistort *Persicaria vivipara.* Low/short unbranched perennial, to 30cm. Flowers pale pink or white, in slender spikes, the lower ones usually replaced by purplish bulbils; June-August. Leaves dark green, linear to *narrow lanceolate*, tapering at both ends, often with turned-down margins, the root ones broader and withering early. Damp turf and ledges on *mountains*; lower down in the far north.

4 Red Bistort *Persicaria amplexicaulis.* Medium/tall perennial, woody at base, to 1m. Flowers *red*, in compact single or twin spikes; August-Oct. Leaves ovate or lanceolate heart-shaped, with a *long slender tip*, the upper clasping the stem, their stalks unwinged. Naturalised, in damp shady places, such as road and railway banks, thickets, and by streams.

5 Redleg *Persicaria maculosa.* A weedy, almost hairless, sprawling to erect annual; stems often red, to 80cm. Flowers pink, in spikes with the flowers overlapping, both at tip and up the stems, rarely with shiny glands; June-Sept. Leaves lanceolate, often with a *dark blotch* and sometimes silky white beneath; sheaths *all fringed*. Fruit a 3-sided nut. Damp bare ground and mud. (An unfortunate victim of name-changing; formerly Persicaria *Polygonum persicaria*).

6 Pale Persicaria *Persicaria lapathifolia.* Usually larger (to 1m) and bushier than Redleg (**5**), sometimes downy and with stems usually green, flowers very variable, ranging from greenish-white and greenish-pink to pink and reddish-pink, the flower-spike and leaves covered with *shiny glands*, the sheaths *scarcely fringed* and the nuts rounded. Disturbed ground, preferring richer soils.

7 Water-pepper *Persicaria hydropiper.* An erect to sprawling, almost hairless annual, to 75cm, with a distinctive *peppery taste*. Flowers small, *greenish-white*, in a slender, more or less nodding spike, with the flowers not overlapping, covered with *shiny yellow glands*; July-Oct. Leaves narrow lanceolate, the lower gradually tapering to a short stalk; sheaths not or only shortly fringed. Wet places, from pond-sides and damp grassland to woodland rides.

8 *Tasteless Water-pepper *Persicaria mitis.* Low/short annual, to 40cm, not tasting peppery and much more like a small Redleg (**5**) than Water-pepper (**7**). Flowers usually *reddish*, in a slender spike, the flowers hardly overlapping, not usually nodding at the tip and lacking shiny glands; June-Sept. Leaves lanceolate, 10-25mm across, abruptly narrowed at the base; sheaths fringed. Wet nutrient-rich mud by pond-sides as they dry out in summer. **8a *Least Water-pepper** *P. minor* is also not peppery and is shorter, to 30cm, and slenderer, differing especially in its *pinker* flowers, not overlapping, and still narrower leaves, 5-8mm. Habitat similar.

~

9 ***Iceland Purslane *Koenigia islandica.* One of our tiniest land-plants, a prostrate annual; stems to 6cm. Flowers minute, with three white tepals; July-Sept. Leaves *broad oval*, unstalked. Fruit a 3-sided nut. Bare damp ground on Skye and Mull. Cf. Water Purslane (p. 114) with green flowers and often no petals, 4-angled stems and tapering leaves, and Blinks (p. 138) with five petals and paler, narrower leaves.

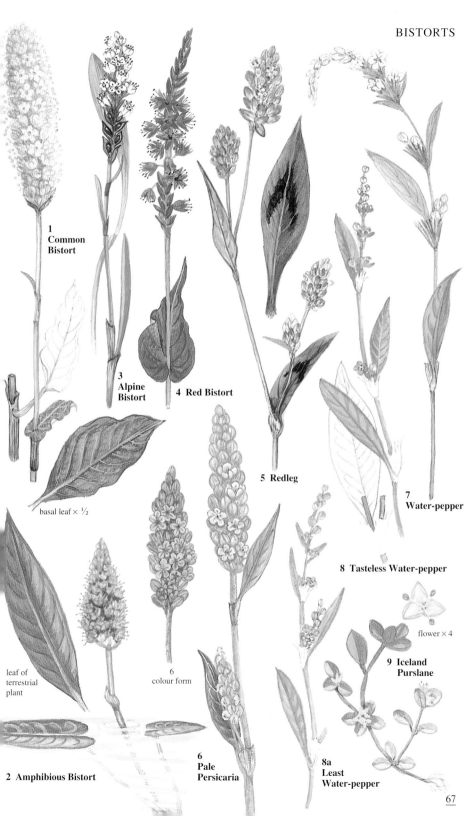

1 Common Bistort

3 Alpine Bistort

4 Red Bistort

basal leaf × 1/2

5 Redleg

7 Water-pepper

8 Tasteless Water-pepper

flower × 4

9 Iceland Purslane

leaf of terrestrial plant

6 colour form

6 Pale Persicaria

8a Least Water-pepper

2 Amphibious Bistort

1 Himalayan Knotweed *Persicaria wallichii.* Very tall patch-forming perennial, to 1.5m, distinguished from Japanese Knotweed (**3**) by its broad, red-veined, *lanceolate* leaves, 20cm long and hairless or downy beneath, not heart-shaped, and from Giant Knotweed (**4**) by the leaves *tapering to the base.* Flowers white, in long branched spikes; July-Oct; a shy flowerer. Naturalised on roadsides, waste ground, railway and river banks.

2 Lesser Knotweed *Persicaria campanulata.* Tall perennial, to 1m. Flowers *bell-shaped,* usually pink, in branched spikes; June-Oct. Leaves lanceolate to ovate, always *downy beneath,* 15cm long. Naturalised by streams and other damp ground.

3 Japanese Knotweed *Fallopia japonica.* Aggressively thicket-forming perennial; stems stout, slightly zigzag, glaucous or reddish, to 2m. Flowers small, white, in loose, often branched spikes at base of upper leaves; August-Oct. Leaves large, *broadly ovate to triangular.* An occasional dwarf variety has thicker wavy-edged leaves, as wide as long, flowers often tinged red. Thoroughly naturalised and spreading on tips, verges and other waste, marginal urban sites, stream banks. Hybridises with Giant Knotweed (**4**).

4 Giant Knotweed *Fallopia sachalinensis.* Taller than Japanese Knotweed (**3**), to 3m or more, less aggressively thicket-forming, with a longer denser spike of greenish-white flowers and *more elongated, long-pointed,* heart-shaped leaves. Cf. Himalayan Knotweed (**1**). Naturalised in similar places, mainly on roadsides. Hybridises with Japanese Knotweed.

5 Buckwheat *Fagopyrum esculentum.* Medium annual, with stems often red, to 60cm. Flowers greenish-white tipped pink, similar to bistorts (p. 66) and knotweeds (**1-4**), with five tepals, in broad branched clusters; July-August. Leaves *broad arrow-shaped,* the sheaths at their base not fringed. Fruit markedly and *sharply 3-angled.* Casual, especially relic of crop sown as food for game-birds.

Knotgrasses *Polygonum.* Prostrate to half-erect annuals (Sea Knotgrass and sometimes Ray's Knotgrass are perennial), the tiny flowers in an often ragged silvery sheath at the base of the small, more or less lanceolate leaves, giving the so-called knotted effect. Tepals five, white or pink, with a green central vein. Fruit a 3-sided nut.

Commonest:	Knotgrass, Equal-lvd	Fruit protruding:	Cornfield (slightly), Ray's, Sea
Lvs of 2 sizes:	Knotgrass, Cornfield, Northern	Inland:	Knotgrass, Equal-lvd, Cornfield, Northern
June-flowering:	Knotgrass, Cornfield	Seashore:	Knotgrass, Equal-lvd, Ray's, Sea

6 Knotgrass *Polygonum aviculare.* Our commonest knotgrass, a hairless annual, to 1m or more, usually very much shorter. Flowers 3-6 together; tepals white, pink or reddish-pink; June-Nov. Leaves 5-15mm wide, those on the main stem *2-3 times as long* as those on the branches, the silvery sheaths later turning brownish. Fruit more or less hidden by dead flower. Cultivated and other bare ground, seashores and coastal gull colonies.

7 Equal-leaved Knotgrass *Polygonum arenastrum.* Almost as common as Knotgrass (**6**), from which it differs especially in having its stems mat-forming and not usually more than 30cm, its stubbier leaves all the same size, its flowers 2-3 together and slightly smaller, the tepals greenish-white or pink, and in flowering a month later, July-Nov. Habitat like Knotgrass, especially bare, trodden places.

8 Cornfield Knotgrass *Polygonum rurivagum.* Easily confused with narrow-leaved forms of Knotgrass (**6**), but is slenderer and often shorter (to 30cm) with *very narrow pointed* leaves, 1-4mm, distinctive longer *red-brown sheaths* and fruits *just protruding* from the dead flower. Flowers 1-2 together, tepals reddish; late July-Nov. Limy arable fields only.

9 *Northern Knotgrass *Polygonum boreale.* The commonest knotgrass in the Northern Isles, differing from Knotgrass (**6**) especially in its larger leaves being usually *stubbier,* from Equal-leaved Knotgrass (**7**) in its two leaf-sizes, and from all other Knotgrasses in the leaf-stalks being *well clear* of the sheaths. Flowers slightly larger than Knotgrass; tepals white, pink-edged; June-Oct. Bare, usually cultivated ground.

10 Ray's Knotgrass *Polygonum oxyspermum.* Compacter and more thick-set than Knotgrass (**6**) and sometimes perennial, but has conspicuous glossy chestnut-brown *fruit projecting* from the dead flower. Flowers 2-6 together, larger than Knotgrass; tepals white, pink-edged; June-Sept. Leaves narrow; sheaths short, brownish with silvery tips, with 3-6 unbranched veins. Coastal sand and shingle.

11 **Sea Knotgrass *Polygonum maritimum.* Our rarest knotgrass and the only one always perennial, sharing the large flowers and prominent fruit of Ray's Knotgrass (**10**), but stouter, with a *woody base,* and flowers (July-Sept) 1-4 together, the tepals pinkish-white, leaves slightly leathery with *down-turned margins* and longer silvery sheaths (to 10mm) with 8-12 branched veins. Sandy seashores.

3 SOZ ■↑↑

4 Z ■↑

6 SOZ ▢

7 SOZ ▣

8 ▫

9 OZ ▫

10 ▫

11 ⌐↑ ▫

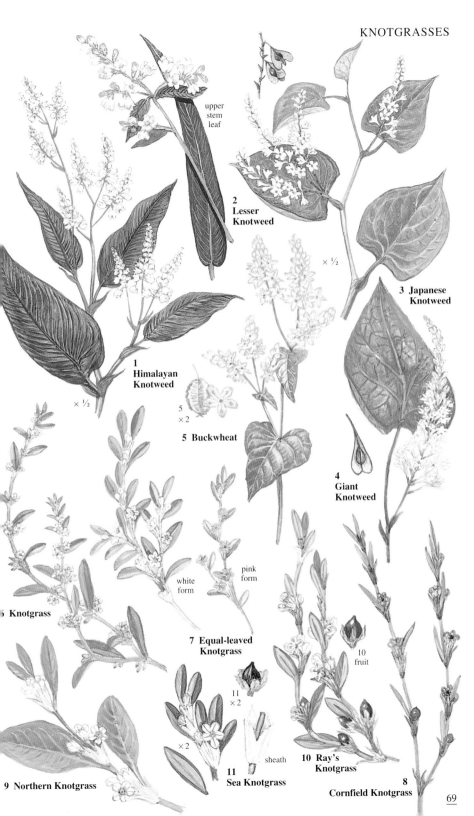

upper stem leaf

2 Lesser Knotweed

× ½

3 Japanese Knotweed

1 Himalayan Knotweed

× ½

5 × 2

5 Buckwheat

4 Giant Knotweed

white form

pink form

6 Knotgrass

7 Equal-leaved Knotgrass

10 fruit

11 × 2

× 2

sheath

9 Northern Knotgrass

11 Sea Knotgrass

10 Ray's Knotgrass

8 Cornfield Knotgrass

THRIFT FAMILY Plumbaginaceae

1 Thrift *Armeria maritima*. A short tufted perennial, to 30cm. Flowers small, pink, in tight roundish heads above small brown *papery bracts*; on downy leafless stalks above cushions of rather fleshy linear leaves; April-Oct. Aka Sea Pink. Cliffs, rocks and salt-marshes by the sea; also on mountains. Ssp. *elongata* with hairless stems to 55cm, formerly more widespread in Lincolnshire, still survives at Ancaster.

Sea-lavenders *Limonium*. Short hairless maritime perennials resembling true Lavender *Lavandula* only in their flower colour. Flowers small, in leafless branched spikes, closely crowded and overlapping, 1-5 together usually in rather flat-topped heads along the upper branches. Leaves untoothed, in basal tufts.

2 Common Sea-lavender *Limonium vulgare*. Stems *rounded*, to 30cm. Flowers on the *upper parts* of branches; July-Sept. Leaves deciduous, elliptic to broad lanceolate, with *pinnate* veins. Hybridises with Lax-flowered Sea-Lavender (**3**) Saltmarshes, usually in masses.

3 *Lax-flowered Sea-lavender *Limonium humile*. Differs from Common Sea-lavender (**2**), with which it hybridises, in its stems often being *angled*, flowers scattered along the *whole length* of the branches and leaves narrower.

4 Rock Sea-lavender *Limonium binervosum*. Very variable, and recently split into 9 spp and 17 subspecies, very hard for non-experts to identify, except by knowing where you are, e.g. 4a***L. paradoxum* at St David's, ***L. parvum* at Saddle Point and ***L. transwallianum* at Giltar Point, all Pembrokeshire. Usually slenderer than Common Sea-lavender (**2**), the stems to 50cm, the lowest branches sometimes flowerless, the flower-heads smaller and the leaves evergreen, smaller and narrower with winged stalks and 1-3 *unbranched* veins. Coastal *cliffs and rocks*, less often shingle, sand and saltmarshes.

5 **Matted Sea-lavender *Limonium bellidifolium*. Smaller than Common Sea-lavender (**2**) and with sprawling stems, to 30cm, divided almost from the base into *zigzag* branches, the lower ones *always flowerless*, and pinker flowers; July-August. Leaves oblong. Drier saltmarshes.

ROCK-ROSE FAMILY Cistaceae

Rock-roses *Helianthemum*. Low-growing woody undershrubs, with five petals and sepals and untoothed opposite 1-veined leaves.

6 Common Rock-rose *Helianthemum nummularium*. Well known in gardens in many colour forms, the *20-25mm* flowers of the wild plant are a pleasant sulphur yellow, sometimes with an orange spot and occasionally smaller or creamy, white or orange; May-Sept. Stems often prostrate, to 50cm. Leaves broad to narrow lanceolate, hairless above and downy white beneath, on stalks shorter than the very narrow *leaf-like stipules* at their base. Hybridises with White (**8**) and Hoary (**7**) Rock-roses. Grassland on chalk and limestone, also on acid soils in Scotland.

7 *Hoary Rock-rose *Helianthemum oelandicum*. Differs from Common Rock-rose (**6**) in its smaller (*10-15mm*) flowers (May-June) and narrower leaves, sometimes downy above, with inrolled margins and *no stipules*. Limestone turf and rocks.

8 **White Rock-rose *Helianthemum apenninum*. Differs from Common Rock-rose (**6**) most obviously in its bright *white* flowers, but also in its narrower leaves, which are downy above, the lower with stalks equalling the stipules. Limestone turf.

9 **Spotted Rock-rose *Tuberaria guttata*. A downy annual, not obviously a Rock-rose, with stems erect to sprawling, to 10cm or more. Flowers 8-15mm, yellow, often with a *red spot* at the base of the five petals, which drop early in the day, so to find it in the afternoon you have to discern the five unequal *black-dotted* sepals or the egg-shaped fruits on down-turned stalks. Leaves narrow lanceolate, 3-veined, downy below. Dry bare or rocky moorland near the sea.

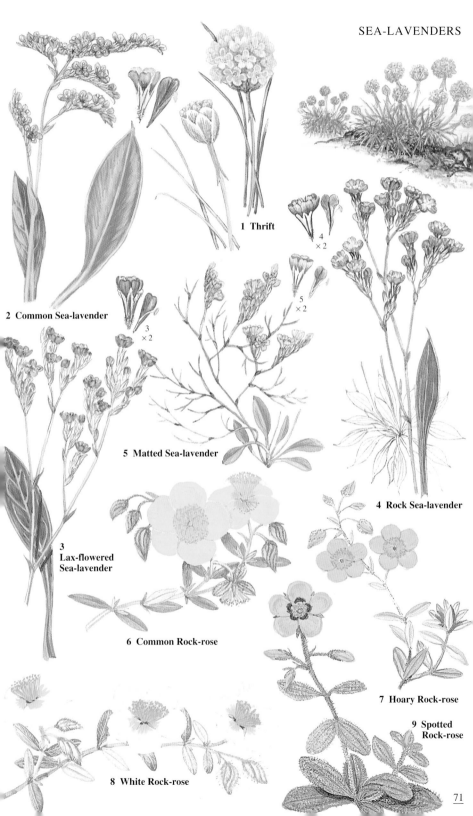

1 Thrift

4
× 2

2 Common Sea-lavender

3
× 2

5
× 2

5 Matted Sea-lavender

4 Rock Sea-lavender

3
Lax-flowered
Sea-lavender

6 Common Rock-rose

7 Hoary Rock-rose

9 Spotted
Rock-rose

8 White Rock-rose

ST. JOHN'S WORT FAMILY Clusiaceae

St. John's Worts *Hypericum.* Mostly medium hairless perennials (Irish St. John's Wort may be annual) or undershrubs (tutsans, Rose of Sharon), with branched, usually leafy clusters (Rose of Sharon is solitary) of open yellow flowers with five, usually black-dotted, petals and sepals, and looking almost furry with their many stamens. Leaves opposite, untoothed, with translucent veins and often black and/or translucent dots. Fruit a dry capsule (except tutsans).

Prostrate:		Trailing, Flax-leaved, Marsh
Downy:		Hairy, Pale, Marsh
Stems	square:	Imperforate, Square-stalked, Wavy, Irish, Stinking Tutsan, Rose of Sharon
	with 2 ridges:	Perforate, Trailing, Tutsan, Tall Tutsan
	with no ridges:	Hairy, Slender, Pale, Flax-leaved, Marsh
Flowers 1cm across or more:		Tutsans, Rose of Sharon
	with some red:	(Hairy), Slender, Flax-leaved, Marsh (sepals), Irish, Rose of Sharon (anthers)
	without black dots:	Square-stalked (usually), Marsh, Irish, Tutsans, Rose of Sharon
Leaves	+/- linear:	Flax-leaved, Irish
	wavy-edged:	Wavy
	without translucent dots:	Imperforate, Pale, Flax-leaved, Tutsans, Rose of Sharon
	with black dots:	Imperforate, Pale, Wavy, Trailing
Habitat	prefers lime:	Perforate, Hairy, Pale
	prefers acid:	Slender, Wavy, Trailing, Flax-leaved, Marsh
	wet:	Square-stalked, Wavy, Marsh

1 Perforate St. John's Wort *Hypericum perforatum.* Generally the commonest St. John's Wort, with *two raised lines* down the stems, to 80cm. Flowers golden-yellow, 15-25mm, with black dots and streaks on the petals and sepals pointed; July-Sept. Leaves small, oval to linear, with *many translucent dots*, almost clasping the stem. Hybrids with Imperforate St. John's Wort (**2**) not infrequent, sometimes without either parent nearby. Dry grassy places, hedge-banks, quarry floors and other bare ground, often on lime.

2 Imperforate St. John's Wort *Hypericum maculatum.* Stems square but not winged, to 60cm. Flowers darker yellow than Common St. John's Wort (**1**), 15-25mm, with black dots and streaks on the petals and broader *blunt* sepals; July-Sept. Leaves usually with black dots but *without translucent dots*, abruptly narrowed at the base and hardly clasping the stem. Hybridises with Common St. John's Wort (**1**). Shadier grassy places, usually dampish and on heavier soils.

3 Hairy St. John's Wort *Hypericum hirsutum.* The only common *downy* St. John's Wort of dry places; stems unridged, medium/tall, to 1m. Flowers *pale yellow*, sometimes red-veined, 15-22mm, with black dots on the edges of the pointed sepals; July-Sept. Leaves yellowish-green, elliptical, with translucent dots but no black dots. Open woods, grassy places, usually on lime or clay.

4 Square-stalked St. John's Wort *Hypericum tetrapterum.* Stems thick-set, *4-winged* to 60cm or more. Flowers pale yellow, 9-13mm, sepals pointed; July-Sept. Black dots rare on both flowers and translucent-dotted leaves. *Damp* grassland, by fresh water.

5 Slender St. John's Wort *Hypericum pulchrum.* The most elegant St. John's Wort, with unridged stems to 60cm or more. Flowers 12-18mm, *rich* yellow, the petals *red beneath* and edged with both red and black dots, the sepals also black-dotted; June-August. Leaves heart-shaped, half-clasping the stem, with translucent dots and often inrolled margins. Heaths, scrub, open woods, *not on lime.*

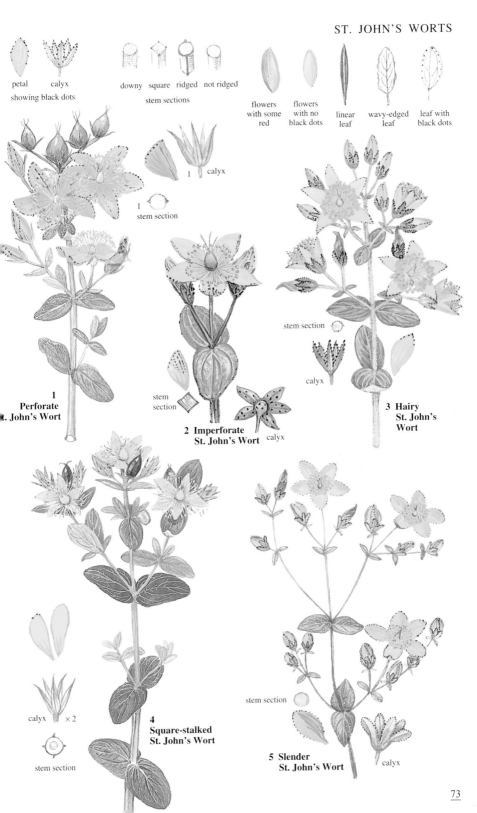

73

1 Pale St. John's Wort *Hypericum montanum*. Stems downy, *rather stiff*, not ridged, medium/tall to 1m, flowers pale yellow, 10-15mm, the sepals black-dotted; July-Sept. Leaves rather broad, with *no translucent dots* but black dots on the edge beneath. Open woods, hedge-banks, rocky places, usually on lime.

2 *Wavy St. John's Wort *Hypericum undulatum*. Stems narrowly 4-winged, to 60cm. Flowers bright yellow, *red-tinged* beneath, 12-25mm, the sepals black-dotted; August-Sept. Leaves *wavy-edged*, with translucent dots. Damp heaths and grassland, bogs.

3 Trailing St. John's Wort *Hypericum humifusum*. Prostrate, with thin wiry *2-ridged* stems to 20cm. Flowers rich yellow, 8-12mm, usually with a few black dots; June-Sept. Leaves pale green, ovate to lanceolate, often with black and translucent dots. Open woods, heaths, preferring *acid soils*.

4 **Flax-leaved St. John's Wort *Hypericum linariifolium*. Stouter, stiffer and often more erect than Trailing St. John's Wort (**3**), with *unridged*, often reddish stems to 40cm. Flowers similar, but 15-20mm and more black-dotted; June-August. Leaves *twice as long*, linear or linear-lanceolate, black-dotted but usually not translucent-dotted. Dry heathy, often rocky slopes on acid soils.

5 Marsh St. John's Wort *Hypericum elodes*. The most un-St. John's-Wort-like St. John's Wort (its flowers being *less widely open*) and the only one that grows right *in the water*, with sprawling and rooting mat-forming stems to 40cm. Flowers yellow, resin-scented, 12-20mm; sepals fringed with red dots; June-Sept. Leaves roundish, greyish with down. Bogs, in and by fresh water, on acid soils.

6 Irish St. John's Wort *Hypericum canadense*. Low red-tinged annual/perennial with slightly winged square stems to 20cm. Flowers star-like, 5-7mm, golden-yellow with *red line* on back of petals; sepals red-streaked with no black dots; July-Sept. Leaves *narrow*, 3-veined, almost clasping stem, with translucent dots. Two wet grasslands near L. Mask, Co Mayo, see p. 460. Probably native.

7 Tutsan *Hypericum androsaemum*. A tall undershrub, with 2-ridged, often reddish stems to 1m. Flowers yellow, 1.5-2.5cm, stamens about *as long as petals*; sepals very unequal, some as long as petals; June-August. Leaves broad oval, 4-15cm long, half-evergreen, *faintly aromatic* if crushed. Fruit a succulent berry, green, then red, finally purplish-black. Damp woods and other shady places, cliff ledges; native, also widely bird-sown from gardens. **7a Stinking Tutsan** *H. hircinum* is deciduous with square stems to 1.5m, flowers 2.5-4cm, stamens slightly *longer* than and sepals all shorter than petals, and leaves 2.5-6cm long, often smelling strongly of *billy-goat* when crushed. Introduced; bird-sown in similar places. **7b Tall Tutsan** *H.* × *inodorum*, the hybrid between **7** and **7a**, is deciduous with 2-ridged stems to 2m, with flowers 1.5-3cm, stamens and sepals like Stinking Tutsan, and (despite its Latin name) crushed leaves with an *aromatic* smell. Introduced, bird-sown in similar places, including walls, especially the red-berried cv. Elstead.

8 Rose of Sharon *Hypericum calycinum*. Much the largest-flowered St. John's Wort, a creeping evergreen undershrub, with square, often reddish stems, short/medium to 60cm. Flowers unmistakable, *solitary, 5-8cm*, with red anthers. Leaves elliptical, 5-8cm long. Introduced, frequently colonising hedge and railway banks and shrubberies.

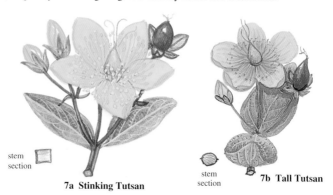

stem section

7a Stinking Tutsan

stem section

7b Tall Tutsan

74

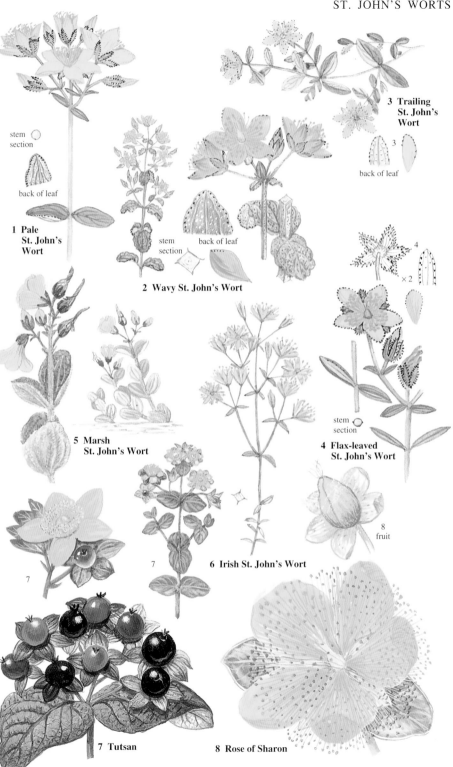

3 Trailing St. John's Wort

3

back of leaf

stem section

back of leaf

1 Pale St. John's Wort

stem section

back of leaf

2 Wavy St. John's Wort

×2

4

5 Marsh St. John's Wort

stem section

4 Flax-leaved St. John's Wort

7

7

6 Irish St. John's Wort

8 fruit

7 Tutsan

8 Rose of Sharon

MALLOW FAMILY Malvaceae

Non-woody plants except Tree Mallow (**4**), usually downy or softly hairy. The often large flowers have five notched petals, a double row of joined sepals, the inner ring often larger, the outer (epicalyx) sometimes forming a cup, and a prominent bunch of stamens. Leaves palmately lobed or cut, stalked and toothed. Fruits disc-shaped nutlets.

1 Musk Mallow *Malva moschata*. A graceful medium/tall perennial, to 80cm, with stem-hairs often purple-based. Flowers a distinctive and handsome *rose-pink*, 3-6cm, in loose spikes; June-August. Leaves *deeply and narrowly cut*. Grassy places, open scrub.

2 Common Mallow *Malva sylvestris*. An erect to sprawling perennial, to 1m. Flowers *pinkish-purple* with darker veins, 2.5-4cm, in conspicuous clusters; the outer sepal-ring may be joined only right at the base; June-Sept. Leaves crinkly, *ivy-like*, often with a small dark spot at the base. Fruits markedly net-veined sharp-edged discs, 'rounde and flat, made lyke little cheeses' whence the names Cheesecakes, Pick-cheese and Bread-and-cheese. Bare ground, waysides, especially near houses and by the sea.

3 Dwarf Mallow *Malva neglecta*. A sprawling or prostrate annual, to 60cm. Flowers *pale lilac* or whitish with lilac veins, 2-2.5cm across, petals bearded at the base; May-Sept. Leaves *rounded, crinkled, lobed*. Fruits smooth, with round edges, distinguishing it from four somewhat similar small-flowered rare casuals, which all have net-veined nutlets. Bare ground, waysides and farmyards.

4 Tree Mallow *Lavatera arborea*. Our only woody mallow, a distinctively tall, softly downy biennial *to 3m*, with lower stems *woody* below. Flowers pinkish-purple, veined purple, 3-4cm, the outer sepal-ring conspicuously *cup-shaped*, with three broad lobes; two or more at each leaf-node; June-Sept. Bare ground and rocks by the sea. Inland could be confused with escaped **Garden Mallow** *L. thuringiaca* agg., which has larger, pinker flowers, only one at each leaf-node.

5 ***Smaller Tree Mallow *Lavatera cretica*. Remarkably like Common Mallow (**1**), but always told by the outer sepal-ring forming a *lobed cup*, also by being a paler green annual/biennial with pinkish-lilac flowers (April-June), much less lobed leaves and smooth, yellowish, blunt-angled nutlets, Bare ground near the sea, waysides and bulbfields. Now regular only in Scilly and Tenby, Pembrokeshire, occasionally naturalised elsewhere.

6 Marsh Mallow *Althaea officinalis*. A tall *velvety grey* perennial, in clumps to 1.5m, whose root yields the sweetmeat. Flowers *pink*, 2.5-4cm, the outer sepal-ring 6-9 lobed; August-Sept. Leaves to 8cm across, 3-5-lobed. Brackish dykes, banks and grassland *near the sea*, and drier saltmarshes. Inland could possibly be taken for a short, very small-flowered **6a Hollyhock** *Alcea rosea*, a frequent garden escape, which is usually much taller, to 3m, and less softly downy, with pink, red, white or yellow flowers 5-7cm across, and 3-9-lobed leaves to 30cm.

7 ***Rough Marsh Mallow *Althaea hirsuta*. Slightly recalling a smaller Musk Mallow (**1**), but annual/biennial, and stems almost bristly and often prostrate, to 50cm or more. Flowers *lilac*, 2.5cm, with petals scarcely notched and the outer sepal-ring forming a *lobed cup*; May-July. Leaves 3-5-lobed or palmate, the upper deeply, the lower shallowly. Bare or disturbed ground, especially at edge of woods and fields. Perhaps native in Kent and Somerset, mainly casual elsewhere.

1 s ☐↓

2 s ☐

3 s ·

4 s ·

5 s ☐

6 ☐↓

7 ·

3 Dwarf Mallow

3
× 1

1 Musk Mallow

1
fruit

2
fruit

2 Common Mallow

4
fruit

4

4 Tree Mallow

5
fruit

**5
Smaller
Tree Mallow**

6
fruit

**6
Marsh
Mallow**

**6a
Hollyhock**

7
fruit

**7
Rough
Marsh
Mallow**

← spur

lower petal

calyx

petalless
flower

VIOLET FAMILY Violaceae

Violets and **Pansies** *Viola*. Low-growing plants with long-stalked solitary flowers, similar to the garden violets, violas and pansies, with five irregular petals, the lowest one spurred, and five unequal sepals with persistent, slightly leafy appendages. Fruits egg-shaped. In summer inconspicuous petalless flowers, which are the main seed-bearers, are produced. Hybrids are frequent. The Water Violet (p. 350) is quite different, belonging to the Primrose Family.

Violets are perennials, mostly with toothed, heart-shaped leaves and inconspicuous stipules. Several species may flower again in late summer. Dog violets were so called because being scentless they were fit only for dogs.

Flowers	blue:	Heath Dog	Flowering times (latitude of Thames Valley)	
	blue-violet:	Sweet, Hairy, Common Dog, Wood Dog	February:	Sweet
	pale blue-violet:	Wood Dog, Teesdale, Marsh	late March:	Wood Dog, Hairy
	bluish-white:	Pale Dog, Fen	early April:	Common Dog
	white:	Sweet, Fen	late April:	Heath Dog, Marsh
	fragrant:	Sweet	May:	Pale Dog, Fen
Sepals	blunt:	Sweet, Hairy, Marsh		
Leaves longer than broad:		Heath Dog, Pale Dog, Fen	Wet habitats:	Fen, Marsh
	roundish:	Marsh, Teesdale		

1 S

2 S

3 SOZ

3a

4 S

5 SZ

6

1 Sweet Violet *Viola odorata*. Our only *fragrant* violet; flowers blue-violet, often white (commoner in some districts), occasionally lilac, pink or yellow, 12-18mm, sepals blunt; Feb-May. Stems with *long rooting runners* and short down-turned or no hairs on 5-10cm leaf-and flower-stalks, which arise in tufts directly from the stem base. Leaves heart-shaped, downy, enlarging in summer. Woods, scrub, hedge-banks.

2 Hairy Violet *Viola hirta*. Differs from Sweet Violet (**1**), in having *no runners*; flowers *not fragrant* and a paler, slightly bluer violet colour, March-May; and leaves longer, narrower and hairier, especially at first, the hairs on their stalks longer and spreading. *Blunt sepals* separate it from all Dog Violets. The late-flowering ssp. *calcarea* has narrower petals and a very short spur. Grassland and open scrub on lime.

3 Common Dog Violet *Viola riviniana*. Generally our commonest wild violet, easily separated from Sweet and Hairy Violets by its *pointed sepals* and hairless or only slightly downy leaves and stalks, not arising from the stem-base. Stems to 4cm in flower, 10cm in fruit. Flowers blue-violet, 12-18mm, the petals usually overlapping, with a *stout curved pale, often creamy spur, notched at the tip*; March-May and sometimes July-Sept. Leaves heart-shaped, as broad as long, mostly in a central non-flowering rosette. In fruit the sepal-appendages enlarge. Woods, hedge-banks, grassland, mountains. **3a ***Teesdale Violet** *V. rupestris* is smaller, to 4cm in flower and 10cm in fruit, and minutely downy all over, with flowers (including spur) pale blue-violet, 10-15mm, May-June; and *rounder* leaves, their stipules broader and with fewer, shorter teeth. It is our only dog violet with *downy fruits*. Beware the hybrid with Common Dog Violet. Limestone turf with bare patches.

4 Wood Dog Violet *Viola reichenbachiana*. Less robust than Common Dog Violet (**3**), with smaller *slenderer* paler flowers, 12-18cm, the narrower petals not overlapping and the *straight spur dark violet and not notched*; earlier-flowering, late March-May. Leaves more pointed, longer than broad. Sepal-appendages less prominent in fruit. Woods and hedge-banks, especially on lime.

5 Heath Dog Violet *Viola canina*. Differs from Common Dog Violet (**3**) especially in its distinctively *bluer* flowers, with a blunt *yellowish* spur, not starting to flower till late April; leaves longer than broad with no central rosette; and sepal appendages not enlarging in fruit. Heaths, dry and wet, fens.

6 *Pale Dog Violet *Viola lactea*. Like a taller, to 20cm, pale-flowered Heath Dog Violet (**5**), which often hybridises with it aggressively at the edge of its range. Flowers *pale milky blue*, sometimes almost white, with a short *greenish* spur; May-June. Leaves broad lanceolate, *wedge-shaped* not heart-shaped below, often tinged purple. Heaths.

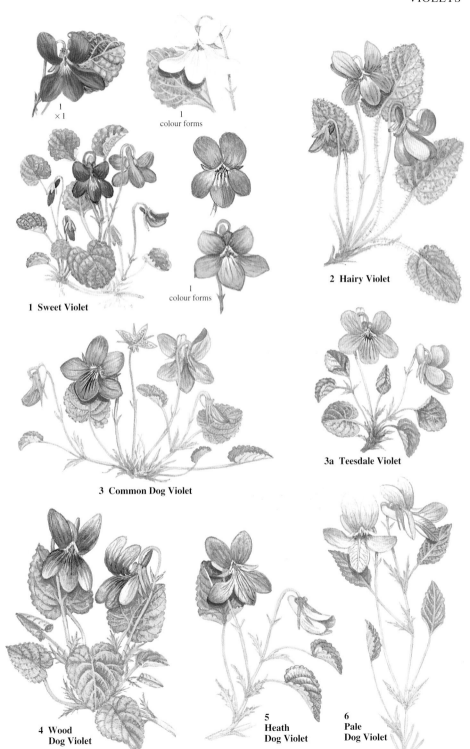

1
×1

1
colour forms

1
colour forms

1 Sweet Violet

2 Hairy Violet

3 Common Dog Violet

3a Teesdale Violet

4 Wood Dog Violet

5 Heath Dog Violet

6 Pale Dog Violet

1 ***Fen Violet *Viola persicifolia*. Differs from Heath Dog Violet (p. 78), with which it may grow and hybridise in its wetter habitats, especially in its *paler*, bluish-white to white flowers, with roundish petals and a *short greenish* spur, hardly longer than the sepal-appendages; May-June. Leaves narrow, scarcely heart-shaped at base. Fens, damp grassland, and in Ireland turloughs (damp hollows on limestone).

2 Marsh Violet *Viola palustris*. Our only violet with *rounded* leaves; stems to 10cm, rootstock creeping. Flowers pale blue-lilac, veined dark purple, 10-15mm, the spur hardly longer than the appendages to the blunt sepals; April-July. Leaves kidney-shaped, either rounded at tip or (ssp. *juressii*) bluntly pointed, with heart-shaped base. Bogs, marshes, wet heaths and woods on *acid soils*.

Pansies. Annuals/perennials with flowers flatter than violets (p. 78) and longer vertically than across, and leaves broad to narrow lanceolate, well toothed and with prominent pinnate leaf-like stipules, the lobes lanceolate. Pansies hybridise with each other even more readily than violets.

3 Field Pansy *Viola arvensis*. Our commonest wild pansy, annual, with stems usually erect, to 40cm. Flowers extremely variable both in size, 8-20mm, and in colour, the basic creamy yellow being varied with patches of orange and streaks of violet, often due to hybridisation with Wild Pansy; spur about *equalling* sepal-appendages and sepals usually *longer* than petals; April onwards and through mild winters. Arable fields. **3a ***Dwarf Pansy** *V. kitaibeliana* is a diminutive version, with stems to 10cm and flowers *4-6mm*, creamy, often flushed pale blue-violet, with spur often violet; March-May-(July). Lower leaves and stipule-lobes more rounded. Dunes; Scilly only.

4 Wild Pansy *Viola tricolor*. A variable annual/perennial, to 45cm. The annual form (perennial in some hill districts) has flowers violet, violet and yellow or rarely yellow, *15-25mm* down and spur *longer* than sepal-appendages; April-Sept. Stipules with end lobe longer. Bare and cultivated ground, preferring slightly acid soils. The maritime perennial ssp. *curtisii* is shorter, to 15cm, and has flowers much more often all yellow. Widespread on dunes, also inland on heaths in E Anglia and by lakes in N Ireland. A largely purple-flowered cultivar often occurs as a garden weed and escape, not to be confused with the **Garden Pansy** *V.* × *wittrockiana*, with flowers broader than long, to 10cm across.

5 Mountain Pansy *Viola lutea*. The most attractive and largest-flowered of our wild pansies, a creeping perennial with erect stems to 20cm. Flowers *20-35mm* down, all yellow or with upper petals often blue-violet or a mixture of the two, the spur usually *2-3 times as long* as the sepal-appendages; May-August. Stipules with end lobe equalling the others. Grassland and rocks, mainly in hill districts and preferring lime. **5a Horned Pansy** or Garden Viola *V. cornuta*, a fragrant, pale blue-violet garden escape, with the lower petal white has a very long spur, 10-15mm. Especially frequent in E Scotland.

SUNDEW FAMILY Droseraceae

Sundews *Drosera*. Insectivorous perennials, with rosettes of untoothed undivided yellowish-green leaves covered with sticky red hairs, curving inwards to trap the insects on which the plants feed. Flowers small, white, 5-petalled, in spikes on leafless stalks. Bogs, wet heaths and moors, often in sphagnum moss.

6 Round-leaved Sundew *Drosera rotundifolia*. Much the commonest sundew, with straight stems to 10cm, arising *near the centre* of the basal rosette of leaves, which are *roundish* and *sharply narrowed* into their downy stalk. Flowers June-August. Hybridises with both other Sundews.

7 Great Sundew *Drosera anglica*. Stouter and taller than Round-leaved Sundew (**6**), to 18cm, with *narrow* leaves *gradually tapering* into a more or less hairless stalk. Flowers July-August. Wetter bogs, also gravelly loch shores.

8 Oblong-leaved Sundew *Drosera intermedia*. Markedly smaller than Great Sundew (**7**), the leaves narrow but half as long, to *c*. 5cm, about equalling the flower-stalks, which arise *from the sides* of the rosette and are curved at the base. Flowers June-August.

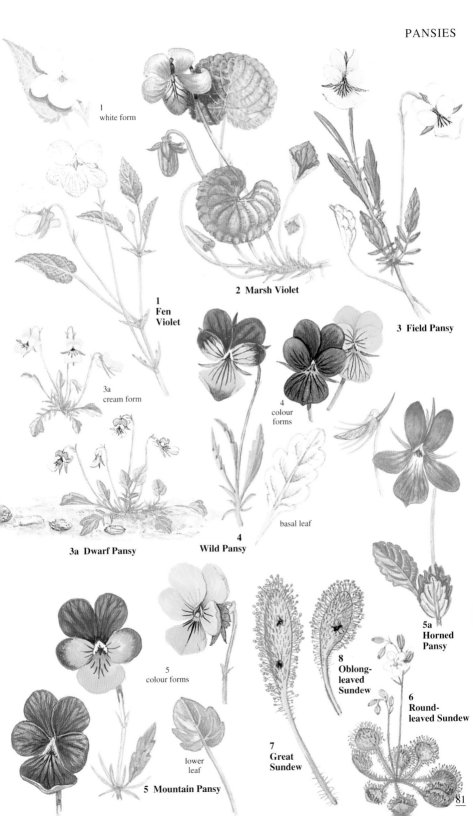

1
white form

1
**Fen
Violet**

2 **Marsh Violet**

3 **Field Pansy**

3a
cream form

4
colour
forms

3a **Dwarf Pansy**

4
Wild Pansy

basal leaf

5a
**Horned
Pansy**

5
colour forms

8
**Oblong-
leaved
Sundew**

6
**Round-
leaved Sundew**

7
**Great
Sundew**

lower
leaf

5 **Mountain Pansy**

CABBAGE FAMILY Brassicaceae (Cruciferae)

Annuals/perennials, almost all non-woody, with flowers, often called crucifers (from the Latin for cross) from the four (usually none in Narrow-leaved Pepperwort, p. 98, rarely none in other species), petals arranged crosswise; stamens usually six; sepals four; mostly in stalked erect spikes or clusters. The seeds are contained in a usually beaked pod, either long and thin (siliqua) or of various shapes less than three times as long as broad (silicula).

Flowers yellow

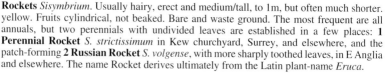

Pods narrow cylindrical (siliquae); all with projecting (sometimes very short) style, except those marked *, which are beaked:	Hedge Mustard, Eastern/Tall/London/False London Rockets, Flixweed, Treacle Mustard, Wallflower, Winter-cresses, Creeping Yellow-cress, Tower Mustard, Bristol Rock-cress, *Wall Rockets, *Brassicas, *Black/Hoary/White Mustards, *Charlock, *Radishes (p. 90), *Hairy Rocket, *Isle of Man/Wallflower/Lundy Cabbages.
broad (siliculae):	Woad (winged), Warty Cabbage (warty), Great/Marsh/Western Yellow-cresses, Yellow Whitlowgrass, Gold of Pleasure (pear-shaped), Bastard/Steppe Cabbages

Rockets *Sisymbrium*. Usually hairy, erect and medium/tall, to 1m, but often much shorter, yellow. Fruits cylindrical, not beaked. Bare and waste ground. The most frequent are all annuals, but two perennials with undivided leaves are established in a few places: **1 Perennial Rocket** *S. strictissimum* in Kew churchyard, Surrey, and elsewhere, and the patch-forming **2 Russian Rocket** *S. volgense*, with more sharply toothed leaves, in E Anglia and elsewhere. The name Rocket derives ultimately from the Latin plant-name *Eruca*.

3 Hedge Mustard *Sisymbrium officinale*. One of the commonest wayside crucifers, sometimes biennial, with *stiff stems*. Flowers pale yellow, c. *3mm*; late April-Oct and sporadically through mild winters. Rosette leaves deeply pinnately lobed, the end lobe the largest. Pods short, 10-15mm, *closely appressed* to stem, downy, but occasionally hairless, when the whole plant may be a paler green.

4 Eastern Rocket *Sisymbrium orientale*. Sometimes sprawling, to 80cm. Flowers *6-8mm*; April-Dec. Lower leaves pinnate with narrow lobes, the end one long, the topmost scarcely lobed. Pods long, 4-10cm, hairy at first, *not* appressed.

5 Tall Rocket *Sisymbrium altissimum*. Flowers pale yellow, *11mm*; late May-Oct. Leaves all pinnate, with *very narrow lobes*, especially the topmost, recalling the very small-flowered Flixweed (**8**). Pods long, *not* appressed, 5-10cm.

6 London Rocket *Sisymbrium irio*. Medium, stems to 60cm, often hairless. Flowers pale yellow, *3-4mm*, scarcely longer than sepals; May-Dec. Leaves *deeply and narrowly pinnately lobed*, the end lobe shorter. Pods 3-5cm, distinctively slender, *almost wire-like*, hairless, the younger ones overtopping the flowers. Named from its abundance after the Great Fire of London in 1666; still at the Tower of London and London Zoo.

7 False London Rocket *Sisymbrium loeselii*. Taller, to 1m or even 1.5m, than London Rocket, and with spreading *bristly hairs* on at least the lower stem, *golden yellow* flowers 4-7mm, about twice as long as sepals; May-Nov. Pods slightly shorter, 2-4cm, never overtopping the flowers. More frequent around London than London Rocket.

8 Flixweed *Descurainia sophia*. An often quite bushy medium/tall annual, to 1m; hairy below. Flowers pale yellow, c. *3mm*, with narrow petals; May-Oct. Leaves 2-3-pinnate, *very finely divided*. Pod cylindrical, slender, long-stalked, 15-40mm. Cf. Tall Rocket (**5**).

9 **Hairy Rocket *Erucastrum gallicum*. The only yellow crucifer with both hairy, *pinnately lobed* leaves and erect sepals. A slender bristly short/medium annual, to 60cm. Flowers 9-11mm; May-Nov. Pods cylindrical, beaked, the lower with distinctive *leafy bracteoles* at their base. Established on the Devil's Dyke, Cambs, and a few other places; an infrequent casual.

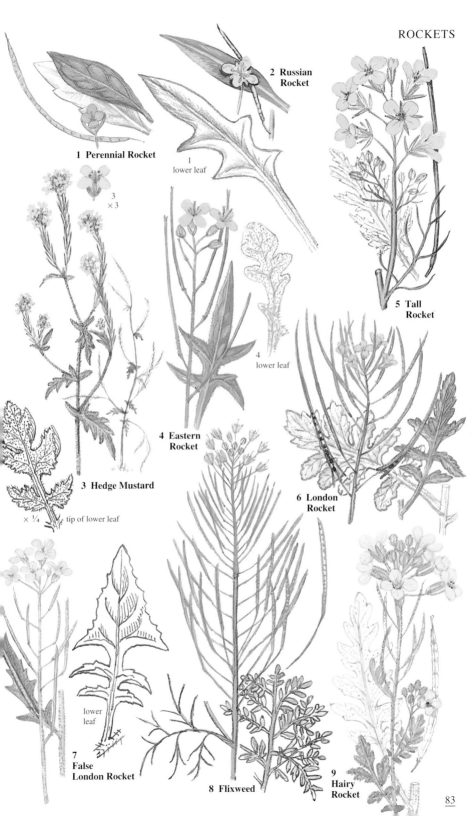

1 Perennial Rocket

2 Russian Rocket

1 lower leaf

3
× 3

5 Tall Rocket

4 Eastern Rocket

4 lower leaf

3 Hedge Mustard

× ¼   tip of lower leaf

6 London Rocket

7 False London Rocket

lower leaf

8 Flixweed

9 Hairy Rocket

1 Woad *Isatis tinctoria*. The only crucifer whose *pods hang like earrings*; a tall, largely hairless biennial, to 1.5m. Flowers bright golden yellow, in trusses, 3-5mm; May-August. Leaves grey, lanceolate, untoothed, the lower downy, the upper hairless, *arrow-shaped* and clasping the stem. Pods long (siliqua) with broad wings that make them look like siliculae, flattened, shiny, purple-brown. Long naturalised on cliffs in Gloucestershire and Surrey; casual elsewhere: most recently and spectacularly appearing at an archaeological dig in Dorset, a startling relic of its prehistoric use as a blue dye.

2 Warty Cabbage *Bunias orientalis*. A tall stout hairy perennial, *stems warty*, to 1m or more. Flowers sulphur-yellow, long-stalked, 7-15mm; May-August. Leaves dark green, lanceolate, pinnately lobed, pointed, the lower long-stalked, toothed and lobed, the topmost lanceolate and unstalked. Fruits distinctively shiny, *warty* and asymmetrically *egg-shaped*. A locally established casual of railway embankments and other waste ground.

3 Treacle Mustard *Erysimum cheiranthoides*. A slender short/medium annual, appressed downy with 3-rayed hairs; stems square, to 60cm. Flowers yellow, 5-7mm; June-Sept. Leaves lanceolate, often slightly toothed; rosette leaves soon dying. Pods cylindrical, markedly *long* (up to 2.5cm) and *4-angled*, held upright. Disturbed ground, often sandy, including stream-banks.

4 Wallflower *Erysimum cheiri*. Well known spring-bedding garden plant; a bushy medium perennial, appressed downy with 3-rayed hairs; stems to 50cm or more. Flowers *large*, 20-30mm, fragrant, very variable in colour, yellow, orange or brick-red; late March-June. Leaves narrow lanceolate, untoothed. Pods long (to 7cm) cylindrical. Long established on *old walls*, cliffs and railway cuttings, also a casual garden escape.

Wintercresses *Barbarea*. Medium/tall, almost hairless biennials/perennials, with bright yellow flowers, pinnate basal leaves upper leaves clasping the stem and pods 4-angled unbeaked siliquae, usually held erect. The most frequent wintercress of commerce is Hybrid Watercress (p. 90) but the hybrid between Wintercress and Small-flowered Wintercress is also sold as Wintercress.

5 Wintercress *Barbarea vulgaris*. Much the commonest species, said to taste bitter; stems to 90cm. Flowers *7-9mm*, the buds hairless; May-July. Basal leaves ending in a *large lobe*, the upper leaves often toothed or lobed to half-way. Pods ending in a *long style* (not a beak). The uncommon var. *arcuata* has yellow-green leaves and curved pods. Road- and streamsides, hedge-banks, waste ground, often dampish.

6 Early Wintercress *Barbarea intermedia*. The next commonest and *earliest-flowering* (often starting in late March) wintercress; stems to 60cm. Also differs from Wintercress in having smaller flowers 5-7mm, stem leaves *all pinnately lobed*, lower leaves with a less prominent end lobe and pods *shorter-styled*. Aka Medium-flowered Wintercress. Habitat similar, sometimes a weed of cultivated ground; not native. **6a American Wintercress** *B. verna* has larger flowers (7-10mm across), pods *curving* upwards, and paler green leaves with more numerous lobes on the basal ones, and stem-leaves narrowly pinnate with only a *small end lobe*. A salad plant, locally established in a few places, otherwise a casual.

7 Small-flowered Wintercress *Barbarea stricta*. Differs from Wintercress (**5**) especially in its basal leaves having the end lobe much the *broadest*, and the upper leaves less deeply toothed, smaller flowers 5-6mm across with *buds hairy at tip* (May-August) and pod slightly longer and *much shorter-styled*. Habitat similar.

4 Wallflower

colour forms

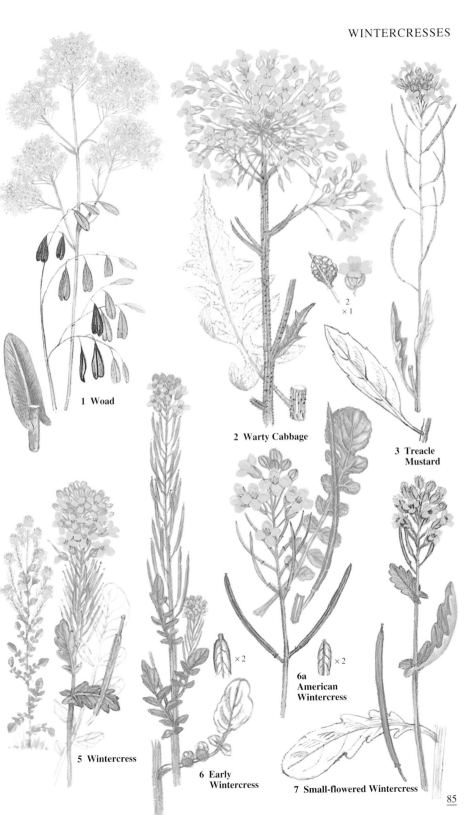

1 Woad

2 Warty Cabbage

2 ×1

3 Treacle Mustard

5 Wintercress

6 Early Wintercress

6a American Wintercress

×2

×2

7 Small-flowered Wintercress

1

1a ⊡

2 ⊡↑

3 ☐

3a ○ ☐

4 ⊡↓↓

5 ☐

7 so ☐↑

8 ☐

1 Great Yellow-cress *Rorippa amphibia*. Hairless creeping semi-aquatic medium/tall perennial; stems hollow, erect to 1m. Flowers bright yellow, *5-7mm*; May-Sept. Leaves lanceolate, variably *toothed or lobed*, the upper often *half-clasping* the stem. Pods *egg-shaped*, short-beaked, long-stalked. Hybridises frequently with Creeping Yellow-cress (**2**) and more locally (Thames near London, Stratford Avon) with Marsh Yellow-cress (**3**). By fresh water. **1a Austrian Yellow-cress** *R. austriaca* has *smaller* flowers, 2-4mm, June-August; leaves only *toothed*, and smaller long-beaked *globular* pods. An increasing casual of waysides, river banks and waste ground, occasionally established.

2 Creeping Yellow-cress *Rorippa sylvestris*. Hairless sprawling short/medium perennial; stems angled, to 60cm. Flowers yellow, *4-6mm*, much longer than the sepals; June-Sept. Leaves pinnate or pinnately lobed, usually looking rather tattered from the well toothed lobes. Pods cylindrical, *long*, long-stalked, usually curved, *pointing upwards*. Damp, bare and disturbed ground, often by rivers, sometimes a garden weed.

3 Marsh Yellow-cress *Rorippa palustris*. A short/medium annual or short-lived perennial, less sprawling than Creeping Yellow-cress, with stems usually shorter, to 30cm. Flowers smaller, *2-4mm*, the petals no longer than the sepals; June-Sept. Leaves darker green, often with *auricles*. Pods *short, dumpy* and less curved, *thick-valved,* from slightly shorter to twice as long as the long, horizontal or deflexed stalks. Mud by fresh water, especially drying-out ponds, also on railway tracks and other dry bare ground. The extremely similar **3a Northern Yellow-cress** *Rorippa islandica* is always annual, more often prostrate, to 15cm, and with no or smaller auricles; the thin-valved pods, *2-3 times as long* as their stalks, are held to one side. Damp places, often near the sea.

4 *Tower Mustard Arabis glabra*. Medium/tall perennial, *hairless above*, to 1m. Flowers *creamy to pale yellow*; May-July. Rosette leaves *greyish*, toothed, often withering before the flowers appear; upper leaves clasping the stem with *arrow-shaped bases*. Pods cylindrical, Dry, open and often sandy places.

5 **Yellow Whitlowgrass *Draba aizoides*. Neat low/short perennial; stems hairless, leafless, to 15cm. Flowers *bright yellow*, 8-9mm; March-April. Leaves in a *cushion*, stiff, lanceolate, fringed with *white bristles*. Pods elliptical. Limestone walls, rocks and cliffs, 10 miles of Gower peninsula, S Wales.

6 Gold of Pleasure *Camelina sativa*. An almost hairless annual, short/medium, to 70cm. Flowers yellow, 3-8mm; June-Sept. Leaves lanceolate, half-clasping the stem with *arrow-shaped* points. Pods elliptical, yellowish. A frequent casual, especially from bird-seed.

7 Annual Wall Rocket *Diplotaxis muralis*. With the next species the only pale yellow crucifer with a an *unpleasant smell* when bruised, hence aka Stinkweed. Short/medium annual, with stems usually *hairy*, to 60cm; rarely a short-lived perennial slightly woody at base. Flowers yellow, *10-15mm*; May-Sept. Leaves pinnately lobed, mostly in a rosette. Pods cylindrical with a short beak, held parallel to the stem but with their stalks *at an angle*; seeds in two rows. Disturbed and waste ground, especially sandy.

8 Perennial Wall Rocket *Diplotaxis tenuifolia*. Differs from more frequent Annual Wall Rocket (**7**) in being always perennial and hairless, and usually taller, to 80cm, greyer and bushier; and having the stem woody at the base; flowers *paler, larger*, 15-30mm, and longer-stalked; leaves not in a rosette but in a bushy bunch on the stem; and the stalks of the pods being held *at a more acute angle* to the stem. Walls, railway cuttings and bare waste ground.

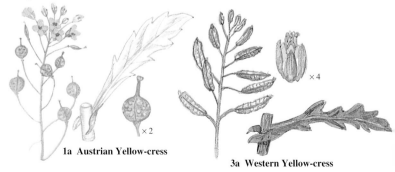

×4

×2

1a Austrian Yellow-cress

3a Western Yellow-cress

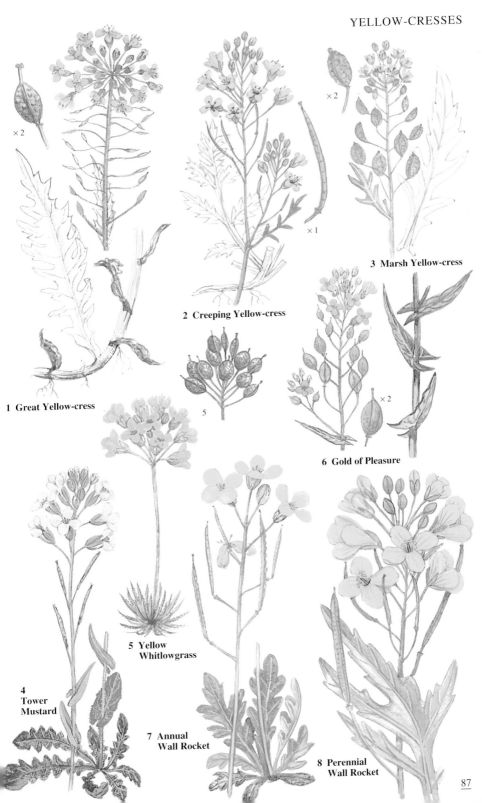

×2

×2

×1

3 Marsh Yellow-cress

2 Creeping Yellow-cress

5

×2

6 Gold of Pleasure

1 Great Yellow-cress

5 Yellow
Whitlowgrass

4
Tower
Mustard

7 Annual
Wall Rocket

8 Perennial
Wall Rocket

Brassicas *Brassica*. Annuals/perennials with yellow flowers, pinnately lobed leaves and long-beaked cylindrical pods with seeds in one row – two rows in wall rockets (p. 86).

1 Oil-seed Rape *Brassica napus* var. *oleifera*. Thanks to the Common Agricultural Policy, now by far the commonest brassica seen wild over most of the South and Midlands; medium/tall annual/biennial, to 1.5m. Flowers bright yellow, 18-30mm across, *slightly overtopped by the buds*; March-Sept. Leaves greyish, the upper clasping the stem. Field borders and waysides in arable country. **1a Swede** var. *rapifera* is a similar but much less common relic of cultivation, often with buffer yellow flowers.

2 Wild Turnip *Brassica rapa* var. *campestris*. A river-bank speciality, differing from Oil-seed Rape (**1**) in its smaller (10-20mm) flowers *overtopping the buds*; April-Sept; and its lower leaves being green. Bare ground, especially by rivers and streams. **2a Turnip** var. *rapa* with a swollen root tuber occurs as a relic of cultivation.

3 Wild Cabbage *Brassica oleracea*. A coastal speciality very like the frequent relics of cultivation; medium perennial, with a stout stem to 60cm and woody at the base. Flowers pale yellow, 30-40mm, in a long spike *well overtopped by the buds*; May-August. Leaves all cabbagey and greyish, the upper clasping the stem. Chalk/limestone sea-cliffs, where various cultivated varieties, such as Curly Greens, may also occur; also a widespread casual.

4 Black Mustard *Brassica nigra*. Tall, rather greyish annual, bristly below, to 2m. Flowers yellow, 14-16mm, with *half-spreading sepals*; May-Sept. Lower leaves pinnately lobed, the upper lanceolate and hairless. Pods with a *short thin seedless beak*, appressed to the stem. Disturbed ground, waste places, and on sea-cliffs and stream-banks.

~

5 Hoary Mustard *Hirschfeldia incana*. An increasing alien, tiresomely similar to Black Mustard (**4**), from which it differs in being paler green with *coarse whitish hairs* all over the lower stems and leaves, and having paler yellow flowers, erecter sepals and a *waisted, 2-segmented pod*. Waste places and road verges, including motorways near London (try the Heston Services on the M4!).

6 Charlock *Sinapis arvensis*. A coarse, usually bristly, short/tall annual, to 1m (usually much shorter). Flowers bright yellow, 15-20mm, with sepals spreading or down-turned; April-Nov. Lower leaves pinnately lobed, the upper *toothed and unstalked*. Pods cylindrical, usually hairless, *longer than their flattened beak*. Waysides, field borders; arable fields coloured yellow by Charlock are coming back thanks to set-aside.

7 White Mustard *Sinapis alba*. The mustard of 'mustard and cress', very like Charlock (**6**), but differing in its paler leaves, the upper also being *stalked and pinnately lobed*, and the flattened beak being *as long as or longer than* the stubbier pod, which is covered with short stiff hairs. Prefers limy soils.

8 Bastard Cabbage *Rapistrum rugosum*. An often bushy medium/tall annual, to 80cm; whitely hairy below. Flowers pale yellow, 6-8mm; June-August. Leaves pinnately lobed. Pods *waisted*, the upper part ovoid, with a *long style*. An increasing casual of bare and sparsely grassy places, established in a few places. **8a Steppe Cabbage** *R. perenne*, a biennial/perennial with a distinctively waisted fruit,the two parts more equal, the upper *narrowing* into a beak, is much less frequent but also established in a few places.

2 SOZ ☐

3 S ⊡

4 SZ ⊡

5 ⊡↑

6 SOZ ☐↓↓

7 O ☐↓

8 ⊡

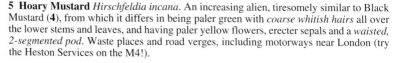

1a Swede   2a Turnip

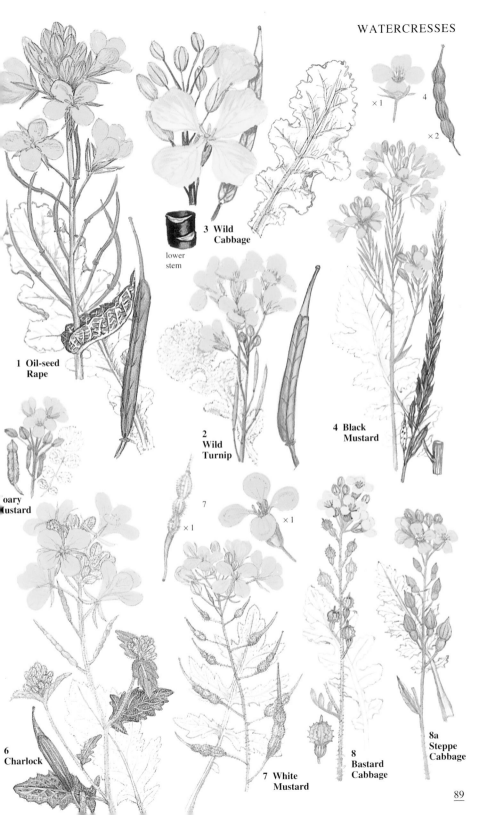

1 Oil-seed Rape

3 Wild Cabbage

lower stem

×1   4

×2

2 Wild Turnip

4 Black Mustard

oary Mustard

7

×1

×1

6 Charlock

7 White Mustard

8 Bastard Cabbage

8a Steppe Cabbage

1 **Isle of Man Cabbage* *Coincya monensis*. A short/medium maritime biennial, to 60cm; sometimes hairy below. Flowers yellow, 20-25mm, sepals erect, *never shorter* than their stalks; June-August. Leaves dark green, shiny, pinnate, the basal in a rosette. Pods cylindrical, *waisted*, beaked, with seeds in one row and *in the beak*. Dunes and other sandy places by the sea. **1a Wallflower Cabbage** ssp. *cheiranthos*, is taller, to 1m, often hairier, more branched and leafier above. Waste places inland, casual but naturalised in Monmouthshire. **1b ***Lundy Cabbage** ssp. *wrightii* is a taller, bushier and downier short-lived perennial to 1m, with stem woody at base, deeper yellow flowers and stalks usually longer than sepals. Only on Lundy I, Bristol Channel.

Flowers white

Petals	notched/cleft:	Hoary/Rock Whitlowgrasses, Common Whitlowgrass (deeply cleft)
	unequal:	Shepherd's Cress, Candytufts
absent (so flowers green):		Narrow-leaved Pepperwort
Anthers	violet:	Large Bittercress, Alpine Pennycress, Smith's Pepperwort, Garden Cress
Pods cylindrical (siliquae):		Garlic Mustard, Thale Cress, (Dame's Violet), Watercresses, Bittercresses, Rock-cresses, (Radishes)
broad (siliculae) flattened:		Whitlowgrasses, Pennycresses, Hoary Cress, Dittander, Pepperworts, Garden Cress, Swinecresses
	twisted:	Hoary Whitlowgrass
	gnarled:	Swinecress
	globular/ovoid:	Scurvygrassses, Horse-radish, Hutchinsia, Shepherd's Cress, Sea Kale
	triangular:	Shepherd's Purse

2 Wild Radish *Raphanus raphanistrum*. Short, medium bristly annual, to 75cm, somewhat recalling a straggly Charlock (p. 88). Flowers either pale yellow, mauve or very often *white with lilac veins*, larger (25-30mm), on longer stalks, with erect sepals; May-Oct. Leaves pinnately lobed with a *large rounded end lobe*. Pods more markedly beaded with a slender beak. Arable weed. **2a Sea Radish** ssp. *maritimus* is a remarkably different biennial/perennial, tall, to 1.5m, with flowers always yellow and pods still more conspicuously beaded. May hybridise with Wild Radish. Bare ground by the sea. **2b Garden Radish** *R. sativus*, much shorter (8-25mm), with flowers usually white or lilac and pods scarcely beaded, is an occasional escape.

3 Garlic Mustard *Alliaria petiolata*. One of the commonest spring hedgerow plants; a medium/tall biennial, *garlic-smelling* when crushed, hairy only below, with stems to 1m or more. Flowers *white*, 5-7mm; April-June. Leaves fresh green, stalked, heart-shaped, well toothed. Pod cylindrical, 4-angled, 3-7cm long. Preferring light shade on hedgebanks and in woods.

4 Watercress *Rorippa nasturtium-aquaticum*. The well known salad plant, a hairless creeping short/tall aquatic perennial, with hollow stems sprawling or erect to 60cm or more. Flowers white, 5-7mm, the petals *gradually narrowed* to their base; May-Oct. Leaves pinnate, *green all year*, those of the extreme form var. *siifolium* being confusable with the umbellifer Fool's Watercress (p. 192). Pods cylindrical, with seeds in *two rows*. In, or on mud by, shallow flowing fresh water, often on lime. **4a Narrow-fruited Watercress** *R. microphylla* has larger petals *abruptly narrowed* to their base, leaves and stems turning purple-brown in autumn and seeds in *a single row* in each pod, which is also usually longer, narrower and longer-stalked. **Hybrid Watercress** *R. × sterilis*, the hybrid between the two, also has leaves purple-brown in autumn and winter, and in summer can be told by its usually short and deformed pods, only rarely containing seeds. Both Watercress, known as green or summer cress, and Hybrid Watercress, known as brown or winter cress (not to be confused with Wintercress, p. 84), are grown as crops.

5 Thale Cress *Arabidopsis thaliana*. A small erect hairy annual, to 30cm, usually much shorter. Flowers white, *2-4mm*; March-Oct. Leaves lanceolate, sometimes slightly toothed, the lowest in a rosette, the upper neither stalked nor clasping the stem. Pods *cylindrical*, distinguishing it at once from Shepherd's Purse (p. 94). Bare and disturbed ground, walls, tending to avoid lime. Has recently become the experimental botanist's equivalent to the fruit-fly *Drosophila*, thanks to its small genome (minimum set of chromosomes).

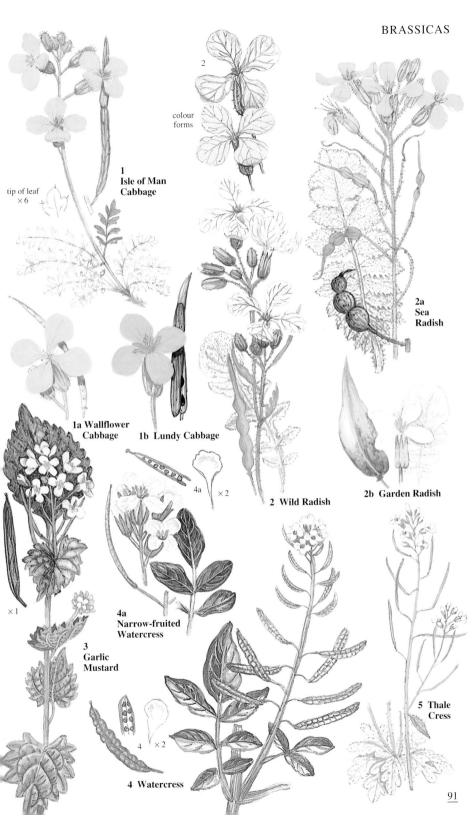

2

colour
forms

**1
Isle of Man
Cabbage**

tip of leaf
×6

**2a
Sea
Radish**

**1a Wallflower
Cabbage**

1b Lundy Cabbage

4a ×2

2 Wild Radish

2b Garden Radish

×1

**4a
Narrow-fruited
Watercress**

**3
Garlic
Mustard**

4 ×2

4 Watercress

**5 Thale
Cress**

Bittercresses *Cardamine*. Flowers white (lilac/purple in Cuckooflower, p. 100, and Coralroot, p. 100) with anthers usually yellow. Leaves pinnate, except Trefoil Cress **4a**). Pods are cylindrical siliquae.

1 Hairy Bittercress *Cardamine hirsuta*. One of our commonest small weedy crucifers, with *straight*, sometimes hairy low/short stems, to 30cm, but usually much shorter. Flowers white, 2-3mm, usually with *four stamens*; Feb-Nov and through mild winters. Leaves, hairy above, the stem leaflets narrower than the rounded basal ones. Pods *overtopping* the flowers. All kinds of bare ground, including rocks, walls, dunes and garden beds.

2 Wavy Bittercress *Cardamine flexuosa*. Easily confused with more luxuriant specimens of Hairy Bittercress (**1**), but is usually biennial, with taller, leafier and often *zigzag* stems to 50cm, and ripe pods normally *not or scarcely* overtopping the *6-stamened* flowers, which appear only April-Sept. Damp shady and often muddy places, such as marshes and streamsides, also on mountains and can be a garden weed.

3 Narrow-leaved Bittercress *Cardamine impatiens*. Short/tall biennial, larger, bushier and more straggling than Wavy Bittercress (**2**), but is hairless and has *straight* stems to 80cm; flowers 5-7mm and often petalless with *greenish-yellow anthers* (stamens 6), May-August; leaves with numerous deeply toothed leaflets, their stalks *clasping the stem*; and pods spreading when ripe. Damp woods (especially ash); rocks and scree on lime.

4 Large Bittercress *Cardamine amara*. Short/medium perennial, broader, more open and leafier than Cuckooflower (p. 100), but with *creeping stems* to 60cm, rooting at the nodes. Flowers usually *white*, rarely lilac, 11-13mm, *anthers violet*; May-June. Leaves pale green, pinnate, all similar, with *no rosette*. Pods cylindrical. Damp shady places (but in the open in the hills), such as freshwater margins and marshy woods. **4a Trefoil Cress** *C. trifolia* with trefoil leaves purplish beneath is established in a few places.

Rock-cresses *Arabis*. More or less hairy, little- or unbranched low-growing perennials. Flowers white, except Tower Mustard (p. 86) and Bristol Rock-cress (**7**). Leaves mostly in a basal rosette, toothed or lobed. Pods cylindrical siliquae with projecting style.

5 Hairy Rock-cress *Arabis hirsuta*. A stiff, usually unbranched, noticeably hairy, short/medium biennial, to 60cm. Flowers white, usually 7-10mm; May-August. Leaves lanceolate, slightly toothed, the lower in a rosette, the upper erect and usually *clasping the stem*. Pods closely appressed to the stem. Grassland and rocks on lime, dunes. Var. *brownii*, p. 460.

6 *Northern Rock-cress *Arabis petraea*. Short, slightly hairy unbranched *mountain* perennial, to 25cm. Flowers white, sometimes lilac, 5-7mm; June-August. Lower leaves pinnately lobed, long-stalked, the upper lanceolate and toothed. Pods *spreading*. Rocks and ledges, usually limy, on mountains; also washed down on river shingle.

7 ***Bristol Rock-cress *Arabis scabra*. A low/short, sometimes branched perennial, hairy below, to 25cm. Flowers *creamy white* or very pale yellow, 5-7mm; March-May. Lower leaves in a rosette, *dark green*, well toothed; stem *almost leafless*. Rocky places on lime in the Avon Gorge, Bristol.

8 ***Alpine Rock-cress *Arabis alpina*, Low/short *mat-forming* hairy perennial, creeping with long runners, to 40mm; not unlike Garden Arabis (**9**). Flowers white, 6-14mm; May-June. Leaves grey-green, short-stalked, *wavy-toothed*. High mountain ledges, Skye.

9 Garden Arabis *Arabis caucasica*. The well known rockery plant; a *hoary grey* mat-forming low/short perennial, to 40cm. Flowers white, *fragrant*, 14-16mm; March-May. Leaves hoary, long-stalked, oblong, slightly toothed, the upper *clasping the stem* with arrow-shaped lobes. Frequent in gardens; well established on rocks at Matlock, Derbyshire, and elsewhere.

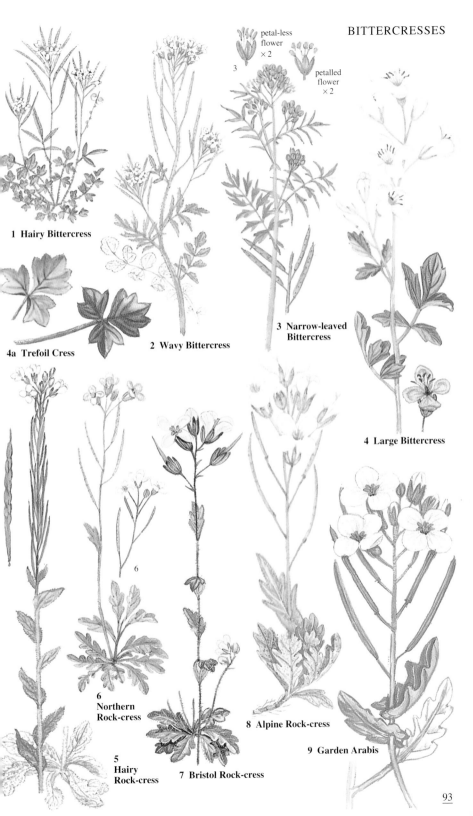

petal-less
flower
× 2

3

petalled
flower
× 2

1 Hairy Bittercress

4a Trefoil Cress

2 Wavy Bittercress

3 Narrow-leaved
Bittercress

4 Large Bittercress

6
Northern
Rock-cress

8 Alpine Rock-cress

9 Garden Arabis

5
Hairy
Rock-cress

7 Bristol Rock-cress

1 Sweet Alison *Lobularia maritima*. A familiar fragrant garden edging plant, now increasingly away from gardens; low/short annual, to 30cm, *greyish* with appressed hairs. Flowers white, occasionally pale purple, 5-7mm; April-Sept. Leaves *linear-lanceolate, untoothed*, unstalked. Pods egg-shaped. Waste ground, at foot of walls, often on sandy ground by the sea.

2 Hoary Whitlowgrass *Draba incana*. Stiff hoary low/medium short biennial/perennial, to 50cm. Flowers white, 3-5mm, the petals *slightly notched*; May-July. Stem and rosette leaves short, lanceolate, toothed. Pods egg-shaped, flattened, *twisted* when ripe. Rock ledges, dunes, mainly on lime.

3 *Wall Whitlowgrass *Draba muralis*. Differs from Hoary Whitlowgrass (**2**) in being a low/short annual, to 40cm, with smaller flowers, 2-3mm, with petals *not notched*; April-June; leaves ovoid, partly clasping the stem and shorter pods *not twisted* when ripe. Limestone rocks and cliffs (on map), occasionally naturalised elsewhere.

4 Rock Whitlowgrass *Draba norvegica*. A tiny low *mountain* perennial, *to 5cm*, differing from small specimens of Hoary Whitlowgrass (**2**) in having stems usually leafless, petals *more deeply notched*, leaves stalked, sometimes untoothed and pods *not twisted* when ripe. Rocks and ledges on limestone, usually high.

5 Common Whitlowgrass *Erophila verna*. A slender, early-flowering, very variable low annual, downy below; to 10cm, or more. Flowers white, 3-5mm, petals *deeply cleft* to more than half-way; late January-April. Leaves lanceolate, sometimes toothed, all in a basal rosette. Pods flattened oval. Dry bare ground, walls, rocks, mountains. **5a Hairy Whitlowgrass** *E. majuscula* is *densely grey-downy*. **5b Glabrous Whitlowgrass** *E. glabrescens* is only *sparsely downy*, and has longer leaf-stalks. Both have petals cleft only to half-way.

6 Shepherd's Purse *Capsella bursa-pastoris*. Generally the commonest small white crucifer, easily told by its flattened *triangular pods*; low/medium, usually downy annual, to 50cm. Flowers white (if tinged pink or red they are an uncommon casual *C. rubella*), 2-3mm; throughout the year, except in hard winters. Leaves very variable, from untoothed to deeply lobed, the upper clasping the stem. Cultivated and other disturbed ground.

7 *Hutchinsia *Hornungia petraea*. A low, often bushy, hairless, early-flowering annual, to 10cm. Flowers *greenish-white*, tiny (1-1.5mm), petals scarcely longer than sepals; March-May. Leaves all pinnate. Pods flattened, rounded, notched. Bare places on limestone, rocks, walls, dunes.

8 Shepherd's Cress *Teesdalia nudicaulis*. Low/short hairless annual, *almost leafless stems* to 25cm. Flowers white, *petals unequal, c.* 2mm; April-Oct. Leaves pinnate, almost all in a rosette. Pods flattened, rounded, notched. Bare or sparsely grassy places on sand, gravel and shingle, avoiding lime.

9 Field Penny-cress *Thlaspi arvense*. A rather stout hairless *foetid* short/medium annual, to 60cm; named from its distinctive flattened and broadly winged pods, notched and *rounded* like pennies. Flowers white, 4-6mm; anthers yellow; April-Sept. Leaves yellowish, shiny, toothed, clasping the stem with arrow-shaped points, the lower *not in a rosette*. Arable and other disturbed ground.

10 *Alpine Penny-cress *Thlaspi caerulescens*. Variable low/short hairless perennial, to 40cm. Flowers white or lilac, 4-8mm; *anthers violet*; April-August. Leaves *untoothed*, clasping the stem with bluntish points. Pods heart-shaped, winged, with a *long style*. Limestone rocks, old lead- and zinc-mining spoil heaps, sometimes in woods away from lime in hill districts.

11 **Perfoliate Penny-cress *Thlaspi perfoliatum*. A Cotswold speciality; a greyish low/short annual, to 25cm, distinguished by its leaf-bases *almost encircling* the stem. Flowers white, 2-3mm, anthers yellow; March-May. Leaves sometimes slightly toothed. Pods flattened, rounded, with a short style. Old quarries and other bare or sparsely grassy places on limestone.

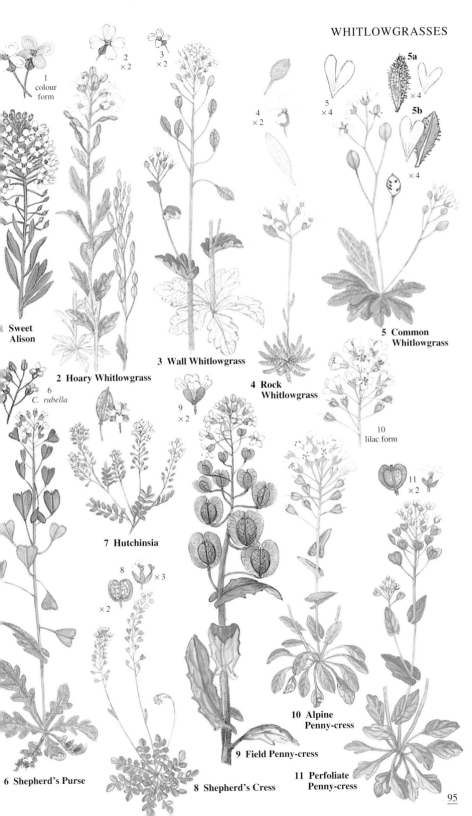

1 colour form

2 ×2

3 ×2

4 ×2

5 ×4

5a ×4

5b ×4

Sweet Alison

2 Hoary Whitlowgrass

3 Wall Whitlowgrass

4 Rock Whitlowgrass

5 Common Whitlowgrass

6 *C. rubella*

9 ×2

10 lilac form

11 ×2

7 Hutchinsia

8 ×2 ×3

10 Alpine Penny-cress

9 Field Penny-cress

6 Shepherd's Purse

8 Shepherd's Cress

11 Perfoliate Penny-cress

Scurvygrasses *Cochlearia*. A variable and perplexing group; mostly biennial/perennials. Flowers white or lilac. Leaves usually fleshy, the lower in a rosette, stalked. Pod a globular to elliptical silicula. Mostly coastal. So named because formerly used to cure scurvy, especially by sailors.

1 Common Scurvygrass *Cochlearia officinalis*. Generally the commonest scurvygrass; stems erect to sprawling, short/medium to 40 or even 60cm. Flowers white, 8-15mm, fragrant; April-August. Lower leaves *rounded*, heart-shaped, upper leaves clasping the stem. Pod globular to egg-shaped. Cliffs, banks and drier saltmarshes by the sea, also, mainly in the W, hedge-banks a few miles inland and salted centre-reservations of roads further inland. A small form with lilac flowers 4-8mm across in N and E Scotland is **1a** ssp. *scotica*; another small form (*atlantica*) has white flowers 9-11mm across, on stony and sandy seashores in W Scotland.

2 Danish Scurvygrass *Cochlearia danica*. The earliest-flowering Scurvygrass; annual/biennial, slender, more or less prostrate and short to 20cm. Flowers white or lilac, 4-5mm; late Jan-Sept. *Stem-leaves stalked*, the topmost ivy-like. Pods egg-shaped, Bare ground near the sea; spreading rapidly along the *centre-reservations* of 2-track inland roads.

3 English Scurvygrass *Cochlearia anglica*. Generally the largest-flowered and most upright scurvygrass; short, stems to 40cm. Flowers white, 10-16mm; April-May. Lower leaves *narrowed gradually* into the stalk, the upper coarsely toothed and often stalked. Pods *flattened*. Muddy shores, estuaries.

4 Pyrenean Scurvygrass *Cochlearia pyrenaica*. The most frequent inland scurvygrass away from roads; stems short, prostrate/sprawling, to 30cm. Flowers white, 5-8mm; April-August. Leaves often darker green and less fleshy than Common Scurvygrass (**1**), the upper *scarcely clasping* the stem, the lower roundish. Pods egg-shaped, *net-veined* when ripe. Bare ground inland, often on lime, especially in the hills and on old metal mine workings and river cliffs; coastal in the far North.

5 Mountain Scurvygrass *Cochlearia micacea*. The only scurvygrass confined to high mountains; slender, slightly woody at base, low/short to 20cm. Flowers white, 5-8mm; June-August. Lower leaves heart-shaped, the upper unstalked but not clasping the stem. Pods *elongated, pointed at both ends, scarcely net-veined* when dry. Bare limy ground on mountains.

~

6 Sea Kale *Crambe maritima*. Our only white crucifer with *large cabbagy leaves*, the origin of the vegetable. A thick-set hairless medium perennial, to 75cm, growing in large clumps with stems woody at base. Flowers in a broad flat-topped cluster, 10-15mm; May-August. Pods small, globular. *Coastal* shingle and sand.

7 *Wild Candytuft *Iberis amara*. A Chiltern speciality; a slightly downy low/short annual, to 35cm; distinctive for the *large outer petals* of its white or deep lilac flowers, 6-8mm, which are in *flat heads*; May-August. Leaves pinnately lobed with no rosette. Pods roundish, notched, broadly winged, in elongated heads. Bare and sparsely grassy places on chalk. Not to be confused with two garden candytufts which may escape: the somewhat similar annual **7a** *I. umbellata*, with flowers of various colours, and the much larger bushy perennial **7b** *I. sempervirens* with white flowers and contrasting dark green leaves, often on walls.

8 Horse-radish *Armoracia rusticana*. The kitchen-garden plant, well known for its roots providing the sauce, but now more frequent on waysides. A medium/tall hairless patch-forming perennial, to 1.5m. Flowers white, 8-9mm, numerous, in trusses; May-August. Leaves *dock-like*, to 50cm or more, shiny, usually wavy and slightly toothed, but sometimes deeply cut and almost pinnate. Pods small, globular, rarely ripening in Britain/Ireland. Widely naturalised on roadsides and waste ground.

1   SOZ   □

1a   Z   □

2   SZ   □↑↑

3   □

4   ⊡

5   □

6   SZ   ⊡

7   □↓↓

8   O   □

1a *Cochlearia officinalis* ssp. *scotica*

5 Mountain Scurvygrass

7a *Iberis umbellata* colour forms

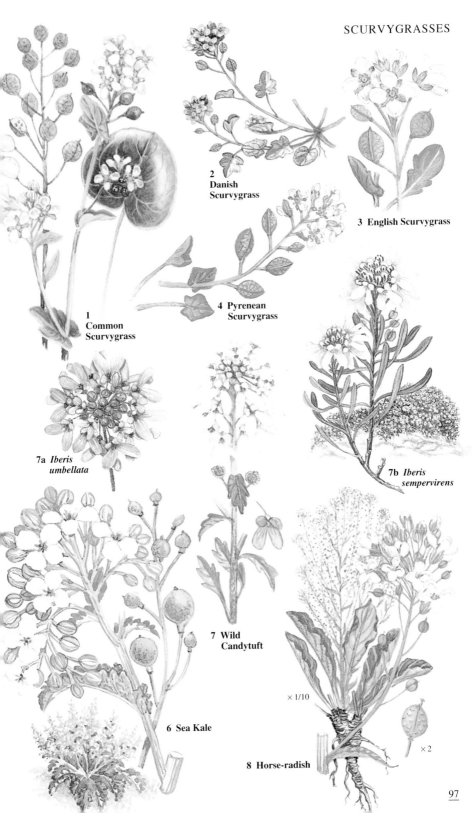

1 Common Scurvygrass

2 Danish Scurvygrass

3 English Scurvygrass

4 Pyrenean Scurvygrass

7a *Iberis umbellata*

7b *Iberis sempervirens*

7 Wild Candytuft

6 Sea Kale

× 1/10

8 Horse-radish

× 2

Pepperworts *Lepidium*. Annuals – Hoary Cress (**1**) and Dittander (**2**) perennial – with white flowers (Narrow-leaved Pepperwort (**5**) usually petalless) usually 2-3mm, and flattened pods (siliculae). Some 30-40 other species have occurred as casuals, including yellow-flowered *L. perfoliatum*.

1 Hoary Cress *Lepidium draba*. Generally the commonest pepperwort in the South; an untidy, often hairless, medium creeping perennial to 60 or even 90cm. Flowers white, in a *loose cluster*, 5-6mm; April-July. Leaves *greyish*, broad lanceolate, toothed or not, the upper clasping the stem. Pods kidney-shaped, flattened, with projecting style, net-veined and as wide as long. The much less frequent ssp. *chalepense* has leaves greener and pod not net-veined and longer than wide. A long-established introduction; disturbed ground, often by roads and railways.

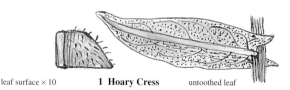

leaf surface × 10   **1 Hoary Cress**   untoothed leaf

2 Dittander *Lepidium latifolium*. Easily the most distinctive pepperwort, with its *broad dock-like leaves*. A tall greyish hairless creeping perennial, to 1.5m. Flowers in a cluster, white, 2-3mm, *sepals white-edged*; July-August. Leaves broad lanceolate like Horse-Radish (p. 96), but smaller, never lobed and more abruptly narrowed into the stalk, the topmost narrow and unstalked. Pods rounded, scarcely notched. Bare ground near the sea, also increasingly naturalised inland, notably in the Colne Valley near Harefield, Middx. Unaccountably named after a mountain in ancient Crete.

3 Field Pepperwort *Lepidium campestre*. A stiff greyish dense, often unbranched, erect to sprawling medium annual, to 60cm. Flowers white, 2-3mm, petals *scarcely longer* than sepals, *anthers yellow*; May-August. Leaves lanceolate, the lower untoothed and soon withering, the upper toothed and clasping the stem. Pods oblong, flattened, winged and notched, held parallel to the stem on spreading stalks. Sparsely grassy places, from dry pastures to arable fields, road verges and coppiced woodlands; also on walls.

4 Smith's Pepperwort *Lepidium heterophyllum*. Like Field Pepperwort (**3**), but flowers with *violet anthers* and petals *longer than* sepals. Also differs in being a usually shorter, more often sprawling, perennial, to 50cm, and having more oval, longer-beaked pods. More often in undisturbed dry grassland.

5 Narrow-leaved Pepperwort *Lepidium ruderale*. A somewhat foetid, often bushy, slender hairless short/medium annual/biennial, to 45cm. Flowers usually petalless and thus *green* from the sepals, 2-3mm; June-August. Lower leaves narrowly pinnate, the upper linear, not clasping the stem. Pods flattened, notched, *shorter* than their stalks. Bare and waste ground, mainly near the sea, where probably native; decreasing.

6 Garden Cress *Lepidium sativum*. The cress of 'mustard and cress', a strong-smelling short/medium annual, to 50cm or more. Flowers white, 2-3mm, petals longer than sepals; May-August. All leaves narrowly pinnate, the upper *stalked*. Pods flattened, longer than their stalks. A frequent casual of waste and disturbed ground.

~

7 Swine-cress *Coronopus squamatus*. A coarse greyish hairless prostrate low annual, to 30cm. Flowers white, 2-3mm, *tightly bunched* at the base of the pinnate leaves; May-Sept. Pods *gnarled*, flattened, broader than long, with a very short beak and *longer* than their very short stalk. Gateways and other well trodden places.

8 Lesser Swine-cress *Coronopus didymus*. A loose, pale green, often prostrate, low/short annual, to 40cm; *smelling like Garden Cress* (**6**) when crushed. Flowers white, or petalless and green, 2-3mm, in spikes *opposite the pinnate leaves*; May-Sept. Pods like Swine-cress (**7**), but *scarcely wrinkled*, notched instead of beaked and *shorter* than their long stalk. Disturbed and waste ground, especially near the sea, but also in the London parks.

1 Hoary Cress

2 Dittander

3 Field Pepperwort

4 Smith's Pepperwort

5 Narrow-leaved Pepperwort

6 Garden Cress

7 Swine-cress

8 Lesser Swine-cress

Pods cylindrical (siliquae):	Dame's Violet, Stocks, Cuckooflower, Coralroot, Northern Rock-cress (p. 92), Aubrietia, (Radishes), p. 90), Sea Rocket (waisted)
broad (siliculae):	Honesty, (Sweet Alison, p. 94), (Common/Danish Scurvygrasses, p. 96), (Alpine Pennycress, p. 94), (Wild Candytuft, p. 96), Sea Rocket

1 z ▫↑

1 Dame's Violet *Hesperis matronalis*. A stout green hairy medium/tall, perennial, to 1m. Flowers *very fragrant*, lilac, purple or white, 15-20mm; May-August. Leaves lanceolate, toothed. Pods cylindrical, long, to 100mm, *curving upwards*. The confusable Honesty (**7**) has both leaves and pods rounded. Well established on hedge-banks, roadsides and grassy places. Dame's refers to Damascus, not dames.

2 s ▫↑

2 **Hoary Stock *Matthiola incana*. Very like the garden Brompton Stock, a hoary grey medium/tall annual/perennial with stems to 80cm and woody at the base. Flowers fragrant, purple, pink or white, 30-40mm; April-July. Leaves narrow lanceolate, *untoothed*. Pods cylindrical, long (to 15cm). Perhaps native on sea cliffs in Sussex and the Isle of Wight; established or casual elsewhere, especially if flowers pink or white.

3 ▫

3 ***Sea Stock *Matthiola sinuata*. Stouter than Hoary Stock (**2**) and much woollier and bushier, with *black dots* mixed with its down. Flowers paler purple and slightly smaller. Basal leaves wavy, *toothed or lobed*. Pods curved, making the fruiting plant a tangled mass. Native on cliffs and dunes in N Devon and S Wales.

4 soz ▫

4 Cuckooflower *Cardamine pratensis*. A graceful early flowerer of spring meadows, in bloom when the Cuckoo arrives. An unbranched hairy short/medium perennial, to 60cm. Flowers 11-20mm, *pale to deep lilac*, rarely white, *anthers yellow*; late March-June. Leaves variably pinnate, the root ones in a rosette, the stem ones with narrower leaflets. Pods held almost erect. Aka Lady's Smock. Damp grassy places, including fens, woods and mountain ledges. **4a Greater Cuckooflower** *C. raphanifolia*, may be taller and stouter and has deeper purple flowers and stem leaves the same size as the rosette ones, all with large end leaflets; established in a few shady places.

5 ▫

5 Coralroot *Cardamine bulbifera*. Rather stiffly erect unbranched short/medium perennial, to 75cm. Flowers lilac-purple, 13-14mm; April-May. Leaves dark green, the lower pinnate, with 1-7 often toothed leaflets and distinctive *dark purple bulbils* at their base up the stem. Pods rarely ripen in Britain. Dampish *woods*. A speciality of the Chilterns and the eastern Weald. **5a Pinnate Coralroot** *C. heptaphylla*, with 5-11 toothed leaflets but *no bulbils*, flowers sometimes white and pods to 80mm long, is established in a few places.

6 Aubretia *Aubrieta deltoidea*. Low/short, prostrate or sprawling downy perennial, to 30cm. Flowers *bright violet*, 20-30mm; March-June. Leaves undivided, with a few teeth. Pods elliptical. Favourite garden plant, on many walls where probably planted, sometimes on rocks and walls away from gardens.

7 s ▫

7 Honesty *Lunaria annua*. Medium/tall biennial, to 1m, best known for its large (to 7cm across) *flattened pods*, used as decorations. Flowers *purple or white*, 28-31mm; April-June. Leaves *heart-shaped*, well toothed. Cf. Dame's Violet (**1**). Increasingly common escape on hedge-banks and waysides.

8 soz ▫

8 Sea Rocket *Cakile maritima*. The only lilac-coloured flower of the seashore that has shiny, pinnately lobed, sometimes linear, fleshy leaves. Floppy, rather bushy, greyish, hairless short/medium annual, to 50cm. Flowers pale to darker lilac; June-August. Pods oval, waisted, the upper part larger. Usually on the drift-line and above on sandy shores; rarely on shingle.

6 Aubretia

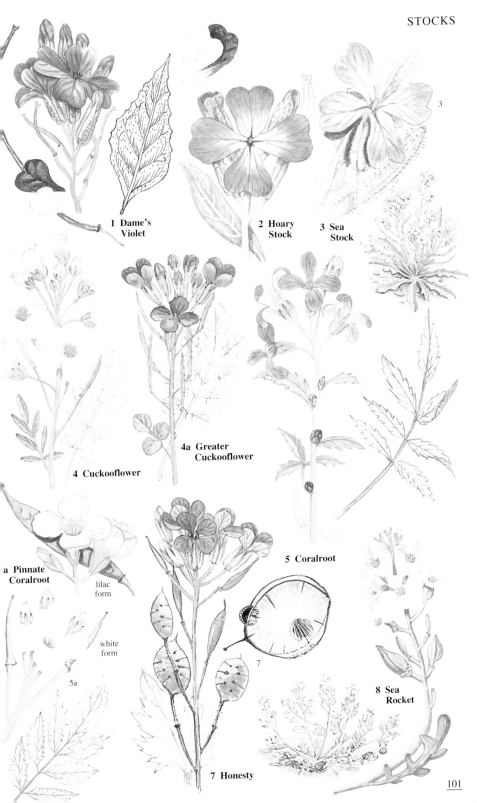

1 Dame's Violet

2 Hoary Stock

3 Sea Stock

3

4 Cuckooflower

4a Greater Cuckooflower

5 Coralroot

a Pinnate Coralroot

lilac form

white form

5a

7

7 Honesty

8 Sea Rocket

MIGNONETTE FAMILY Resedaceae

1 Weld *Reseda luteola*. Tall *erect* hairless biennial, to 1.5m. Flowers yellow-green, *4-petalled*, 4-5mm, in long spikes; June-Sept. Leaves dark green, *narrow lanceolate*, untoothed, wavy-edged. Pods globular, open at the top, with three distinct points. Disturbed ground, especially on lime. Formerly known as Dyer's Rocket and used for a yellow dye.

2 Wild Mignonette *Reseda lutea*. Short/medium, rather *floppy*, biennial, to 75cm. Flowers yellow-green, *6-petalled*, 5-7mm, in short spikes, hardly fragrant; May-Sept. Leaves *pinnate*, wavy-edged, rather pale green. Pods oblong, with three obscure points. Sparsely grassy places, usually on lime. Two white-flowered aliens are established in a few places: **2a White Mignonette** *R. alba* with long flower-spikes, pinnately lobed leaves and 4-pointed pods, and **2b **Corn Mignonette** *R. phyteuma* with most leaves unlobed and 3-pointed pods.

MARROW FAMILY Cucurbitaceae

A family with only one native member, White Bryony (**3**), but numerous casuals deriving from human food wastes and most often encountered at sewage works. All these have yellow flowers, palmately lobed and coarsely hairy leaves, tendrils (except Squirting Cucumber) and distinctive (and mostly well known) yellow or green fruits. The commonest are Marrow *Cucurbita pepo* and Melon *Cucumis melo*, but Pumpkin *Cucurbita maxima* is established at least one place in Hertfordshire, and Cucumber *Cucumis sativus*, Water Melon *Citrullus lanatus* and Squirting Cucumber *Ecballium elaterium* (no tendrils and leaves often not lobed) all occur more rarely. Fruits are rounded in the two melons and Pumpkin and elongated in the rest.

3 White Bryony *Bryonia dioica*. A hairy perennial climber with *long tendrils* opposite the leaf-stalks, to 4m. Flowers in open clusters, greenish-white, dark-veined, 5-petalled, 12-18mm, male and female on separate plants; May-Sept. Leaves pale green, *palmately lobed*. Fruit a red berry. Hedges, scrub, often on lime. Cf. Black Bryony (**4**).

YAM FAMILY Dioscoreaceae

4 Black Bryony *Tamus communis*. A monocotyledon (see p. 9), described here because it is sometimes confused with the totally unrelated White Bryony (**3**). A hairless perennial climber, differing from White Bryony in *twining clockwise*, with smaller yellowish-green 6-petalled, 3-6mm, flowers, (May-Sept) in long loose interrupted, sometimes branched spikes, and dark green shiny *broad heart-shaped* leaves. Fruit a scarlet berry. Hedges and scrub.

CROWBERRY FAMILY Empetraceae

5 Crowberry *Empetrum nigrum*. Prostrate, often mat-forming, evergreen undershrub, trailing to 1m or more. Flowers tiny, pale pink, at the base of the leaves; April-May; male and female on separate plants except in ssp. *hermaphroditum* (5a), growing higher up. Leaves like Heaths (p. 104), but *flatter and shinier*, spirally up the stem. Fruit a berry, green at first, then pink, purple and finally black. Moors, mountains.

SEA-HEATH FAMILY Frankeniaceae

6 Sea-heath *Frankenia laevis*. A prostrate, often matted, heath-like woody perennial, to 35cm. Flowers with five small pinkish petals, *solitary* at the base of the leaves; July-August. Leaves short, fleshy, dark green, opposite, *almost linear*, with inrolled margins. Drier saltmarshes. Introduced on cliffs, West Bay, Dorset.

1 flower and fruit × 2   2 flower and fruit × 2   2a flower and fruit × 2

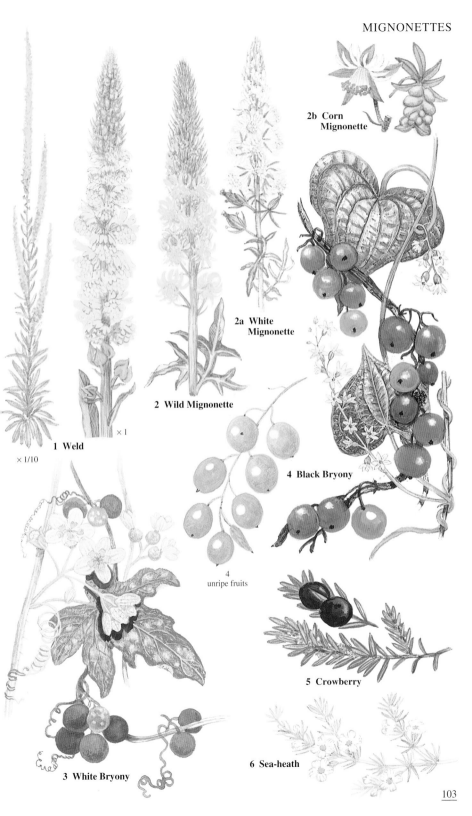

2b Corn Mignonette

2a White Mignonette

2 Wild Mignonette

× 1

1 Weld

× 1/10

4 Black Bryony

4
unripe fruits

3 White Bryony

5 Crowberry

6 Sea-heath

HEATH FAMILY Ericaceae

Mostly low/tall *evergreen* shrubs, but some trees and taller shrubs (p. 384) and some bilberries (p. 106) are deciduous. Flowers often distinctively globular/bell-shaped. Fruit usually a capsule or berry. Avoiding lime, except Strawberry Tree (p. 384).

1 Heather *Calluna vulgaris*. By far our commonest heath, turning huge tracts of moorland purple in late summer; a short/medium *carpeting* undershrub, to 60cm or more. Flowers *pale purple* (rarely the 'lucky' white), 4-petalled, 3-4mm, in spikes; July-Sept. Leaves linear, in opposite rows, sometimes grey with down. Fruit a capsule. Aka Ling. Heaths, moors, bogs, open woods, fixed dunes. The favoured food of the red grouse, on whose behalf many northern moors are managed by muirburn in the spring.

Heaths *Erica*. Flowers globular/bell-shaped, with four teeth. Leaves in whorls, short, linear, the margins inrolled. Fruit a capsule.

2 Bell Heather *Erica cinerea*. Short/medium hairless undershrub, to 60cm. Flowers *red-purple*, much brighter-coloured than Heather (**1**) or other Heaths (below), 4-6mm, in spikes or heads; May-Sept. Leaves dark green, often bronzy, the inrolled margins hiding the underside, in whorls of three with clusters of smaller leaves at their base. *Drier* heaths and moors.

3 Cross-leaved Heath *Erica tetralix*. Short/medium *greyish-downy* undershrub, to 70cm. Flowers *rose-pink*, 5-9mm, in heads; June-Oct. Leaves in whorls of four. Capsules downy. *Wet* heaths and moors, bogs.

4 **Dorset Heath *Erica ciliaris*. Often taller and more straggly than Cross-leaved Heath (**3**), from which it differs especially in being not grey-downy and in its *spikes* of larger (8-12mm), redder-pink flowers, curved and narrowed at the tip with *projecting style*, May-Oct; leaves in whorls of three, broader, greener and hairless above; and hairless capsules. Hybridises with Cross-leaved Heath. Damp heaths.

5 Mackay's Heath *Erica mackaiana*. An Irish speciality, tall/medium, to 60cm. Flowers *purplish*-pink, 5-7mm, in *spikes*, August-Sept. Leaves dark green, hairless above, less inrolled and so broader than most other Heaths. Hybridises with Cross-leaved Heath (**3**). Blanket bog.

6 **Cornish Heath *Erica vagans*. The commonest rare plant in Britain, being abundant on heaths in its restricted range on the *Lizard peninsula*. Hairless medium/*tall* undershrub, to 80cm. Flowers pink or lilac, the chocolate-brown anthers *protruding* prominently from the open mouth, 2-4mm, in dense leafy spikes; July-Sept. Leaves in whorls of four. Dry heaths.

7 Irish Heath *Erica erigena*. Our tallest heath, to *2m*. Flowers pale pink-purple, the red-brown anthers slightly *protruding*, 5-7mm, in a leafy 1-sided spike; March-May, and sporadically in winter. Leaves in whorls of four. Wet moors, heaths.

Four other species are naturalised in a few places: **8 Portuguese Heath** *E. lusitanica* and **8a Tree Heath** *E. arborea*, both with pinkish-white flowers, January-April; **8b Darley Dale Heath** *E.* × *darleyensis* with pink-purple flowers, Nov-June; and **Corsican Heath** *E. terminalis*, June-Sept, p. 460.

~

9 ***Blue Heath *Phyllodoce caerulea*. A low/short heath-like undershrub, to 20cm, hard to detect when not in flower. Flowers mauve-purple, globular/bell-shaped, in small terminal clusters, nodding on slender hairy stalks, 7-12mm, *larger and paler* than Bell Heather (**2**); June-July, a shy flowerer. Leaves short linear, alternate, rough-edged, *green beneath* and rather like Crowberry (p. 102), with which it may grow. Fruit a capsule. Rocky moors.

10 St. Dabeoc's Heath *Daboecia cantabrica*. A hairy, rather straggling, heathlike short/medium undershrub, to 50cm. Flowers pink-purple, globular/bell-shaped, with four teeth, nodding on curving stalks, in short stalked spikes, 8-14mm; May-Sept. Leaves narrow lanceolate, alternate, *whitish beneath* with inrolled margins. Fruit a capsule. Moors and heaths, a Connemara speciality.

Heather moorland with red grouse

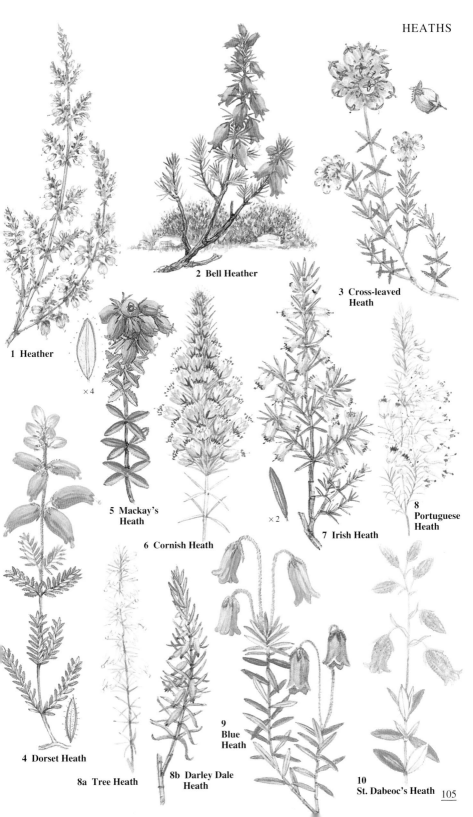

1 Heather

2 Bell Heather

3 Cross-leaved Heath

×4

5 Mackay's Heath

6 Cornish Heath

×2

7 Irish Heath

8 Portuguese Heath

4 Dorset Heath

8a Tree Heath

8b Darley Dale Heath

9 Blue Heath

10 St. Dabeoc's Heath

1 *Bog Rosemary *Andromeda polifolia.* A short hairless undershrub, to 35cm, often straggling in sphagnum moss. Flowers *pale pink* or white, few, 5-8mm, *long-stalked*, globular/bell-shaped, nodding; late April-June; Sept-Oct. Leaves narrowly elliptical, greyish and shiny above, *white* beneath, the margins inrolled. Fruit a capsule. Bogs, wet peaty heaths.

2 Bilberry *Vaccinium myrtillus.* Short *deciduous* undershrub, to 30mm; twigs *green*, angled. Flowers *reddish*-pink tinged green, globular/bell-shaped, 4-6mm, 1-2 at base of leaves; April-June. Leaves *bright* green, pointed oval, slightly toothed, not leathery. Fruit a small *bluish-black* berry with a white bloom, edible and much relished. Heaths, moors, woods on acid soils. Bilberry is the local name in N England; in Scotland it is Blaeberry and in S England Whortleberry, the fruit being whort or hurt (cf. Hurtwood, Surrey) and on the Bedfordshire Greensand Huckleberry, transferred to the N American *V. caesium*, whence Mark Twain's Huckleberry Finn. **2a***Blueberry** *V. corymbosum*, its North American equivalent, taller, with unridged stems and white or pale pink flowers, leaves and bluer fruits all larger, is naturalised in two places in Dorset.

3 Bog Bilberry *Vaccinium uliginosum.* Taller than Bilberry (**2**), to 50cm, and can be a low broad bush, with *brownish* twigs; a shy flowerer with small clusters of up to four *pale pink* flowers, May-June; leaves *bluish* green, rounder and untoothed, netted and paler beneath; and berries bluer. Moorland.

4 Cowberry *Vaccinium vitis-idaea.* A low/short creeping *evergreen* undershrub, to 30cm. Flowers pale pink, more open-mouthed than Bilberry (**2**), 5-8mm, in small drooping terminal clusters; May-June. Leaves glossy *dark* green, somewhat leathery, untoothed, the margins slightly inrolled. Fruit a *red* berry. Hybridises with Bilberry in England. Cf. Bearberry (**6**). Moors, heaths, open woods.

5 Cranberry *Vaccinium oxycoccos.* Short sprawling evergreen undershrub, with threadlike stems to 30cm. Flowers *bright* pink, the four petals *spreading* to reveal eight prominent yellow stamens, 6-10mm, 1-4 together, on long, minutely downy stalks; June-July. Leaves dark green above, whitish beneath, the margins inrolled. Fruit a round to pearshaped red berry, often spotted white or brown, much esteemed and used for sauce. Bogs and wet heaths, often among sphagnum moss. **5a *Small Cranberry** *V. microcarpum*, perhaps just a subspecies, has flowers only 1-2 together, their stalks *hairless*, leaves more triangular, and fruits often lemon-shaped. **5b Large Cranberry** *V. macrocarpon* from N America, stouter, with oblong leaves and larger flowers and all-red berries, is naturalised in the New Forest and two other places.

6 Bearberry *Arctostaphylos uva-ursi.* A prostrate, mat-forming, undershrub, *far-trailing* to 1.5m. Flowers white, tinged pink or green, globular/bell-shaped, 5-8mm; May-June. Leaves *evergreen*, rather leathery, ovate, untoothed, dark green but paler beneath. Fruit a red berry. Differs from Cowberry (**4**) in being never erect, with young stems usually hairless, and leaves *markedly net-veined* with *no glands* beneath. Bare rocky and peaty places on moors and mountains.

7 *Arctic Bearberry *Arctostaphylos alpinus.* Like Bearberry (**6**), but has stems shorter, to 60cm; flowers *white* and smaller (3-5mm), May-August; leaves wrinkled but not leathery, toothed and *deciduous*, turning red in autumn but staying dead on stems till spring; and berry *black*. Moors and lower mountain slopes.

7 Arctic Bearberry

2a Blueberry

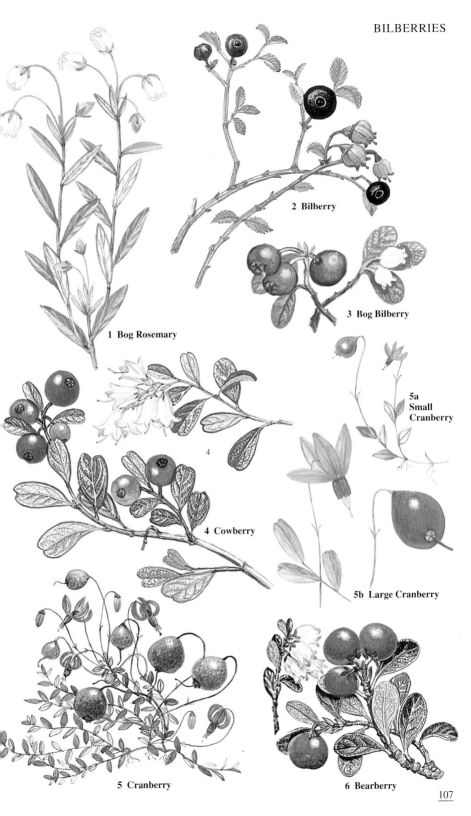

1 Bog Rosemary

2 Bilberry

3 Bog Bilberry

4 Cowberry

5a
Small
Cranberry

4

5b Large Cranberry

5 Cranberry

6 Bearberry

1 Trailing Azalea *Loiseleuria procumbens*. A hairless prostrate mat-forming undershrub, to 25cm; young shoots red. Flowers pink, open bell-shaped with five joined petals, 3-6mm; May-July. Leaves numerous, tiny, *opposite* oblong, thick, the margins inrolled. Fruit a capsule. Bare mountain tops.

2 Labrador Tea *Ledum palustre*. Tall broad thick-set *bush*, to 1m. Flowers creamy white, 5-petalled, 8-16mm, in terminal clusters; May-June. Leaves oblong, untoothed, short-stalked, wrinkled above with their margins inrolled, and (twigs also) covered beneath with *rust-coloured down*. Fruit a capsule. Bogs and mosses. Possibly native on Flanders Moss, Perthshire; bird-sown elsewhere.

American Laurels *Kalmia*. Medium/tall shrubs to 1m, the pink saucer-shaped flowers with five teeth; May-July. Leaves elliptic. Fruit a capsule. Bird-sown and sometimes long established on bogs, heaths and moors.

3 Bog-laurel *Kalmia polifolia*, the least rare, and long established on Chobham Common, Surrey, has flowers *10-16mm*, twigs 2-edged, leaves mostly opposite, un- or very short-stalked, with inrolled margins and *whitish* beneath. **3a Mountain-laurel** *K. latifolia* is stouter and can be much taller than 1m, with twigs rounded, flowers *20-25mm*, and leaves mostly alternate with flat margins and *pale yellow-green* beneath. **3b Sheep-laurel** *K. angustifolia* has twigs rounded, flowers *6-12mm* and leaves stalked, opposite or whorled, with flat or slightly inrolled margins and *pale green* beneath.

~

4 Shallon *Gaultheria shallon*. Medium/tall creeping patch-forming shrub, to 1m or more. Flowers pink or white, globular/bell-shaped, 8-10mm; May-June. Leaves *ace-of-spades*, rather leathery. Fruit a purplish-black berry. Naturalised; woods, heaths, on acid soils; often planted for game.

5 Prickly Heath *Gaultheria mucronata*. Medium/tall suckering and thicket-forming shrub, to 1m or more. Flowers white, globular/bell-shaped, 5-6mm; May-June. Leaves elliptical, toothed and *spine-tipped*. Fruit a berry, purple, pink-purple or white. Naturalised in woods and scrub, often on sand.

WINTERGREEN FAMILY Pyrolaceae

Hairless perennials with flowers generally white, 5-petalled and bell-shaped – except One-flowered Wintergreen (**10**) – in leafless spikes (or solitary, **10**) on long leafless stalks. Leaves variable, ovate to rounded, toothed. Fruit a capsule. Some species are superficially like large-flowered Lily of the Valley (p. 312), but the leaves are quite different. A group badly in need of more imaginative official English names. Chickweed Wintergreen (p. 112) belongs to the Primrose Family.

6 Common Wintergreen *Pyrola minor*. Low/short, to 20cm. Flowers white or *pale pink*, 4-7mm; style *straight*, 1-2mm, not protruding, often shorter than stamens; June-August. Leaves in a rosette. Woods, moors, mountain-ledges, rarely on dunes.

7 *Intermediate Wintergreen *Pyrola media*. Low/short, to 20cm. Flowers white, 7-11mm, style *straight*, 4-6mm, just protruding; June-August. Leaves sometimes rounded. Moors, woods.

8 *Round-leaved Wintergreen *Pyrola rotundifolia*. Low/short, to 20cm. Flowers white, 8-12mm, more open than other Wintergreens, style *curved*, 4-10mm; June-Sept. Leaves more often rounded than other Wintergreens, especially on dunes. Woods, limestone rock-ledges, bogs, fens, chalk turf, dune slacks.

9 Serrated Wintergreen *Orthilia secunda*. Low, to 10cm. Flowers *greenish*-white, 4-6mm, in a *one-sided* spike, the long straight style protruding. Leaves pale green. Aka Yavering Bells. Pinewoods, mountain ledges.

10 **One-flowered Wintergreen *Moneses uniflora*. Low, to 10cm; much the most distinctive Wintergreen, with its *solitary large*, 12-20mm, fragrant white flowers and prominent straight style, 5-7mm; May-July. Leaves pale green, roundish, opposite. Aka St. Olaf's Candlestick. Pinewoods.

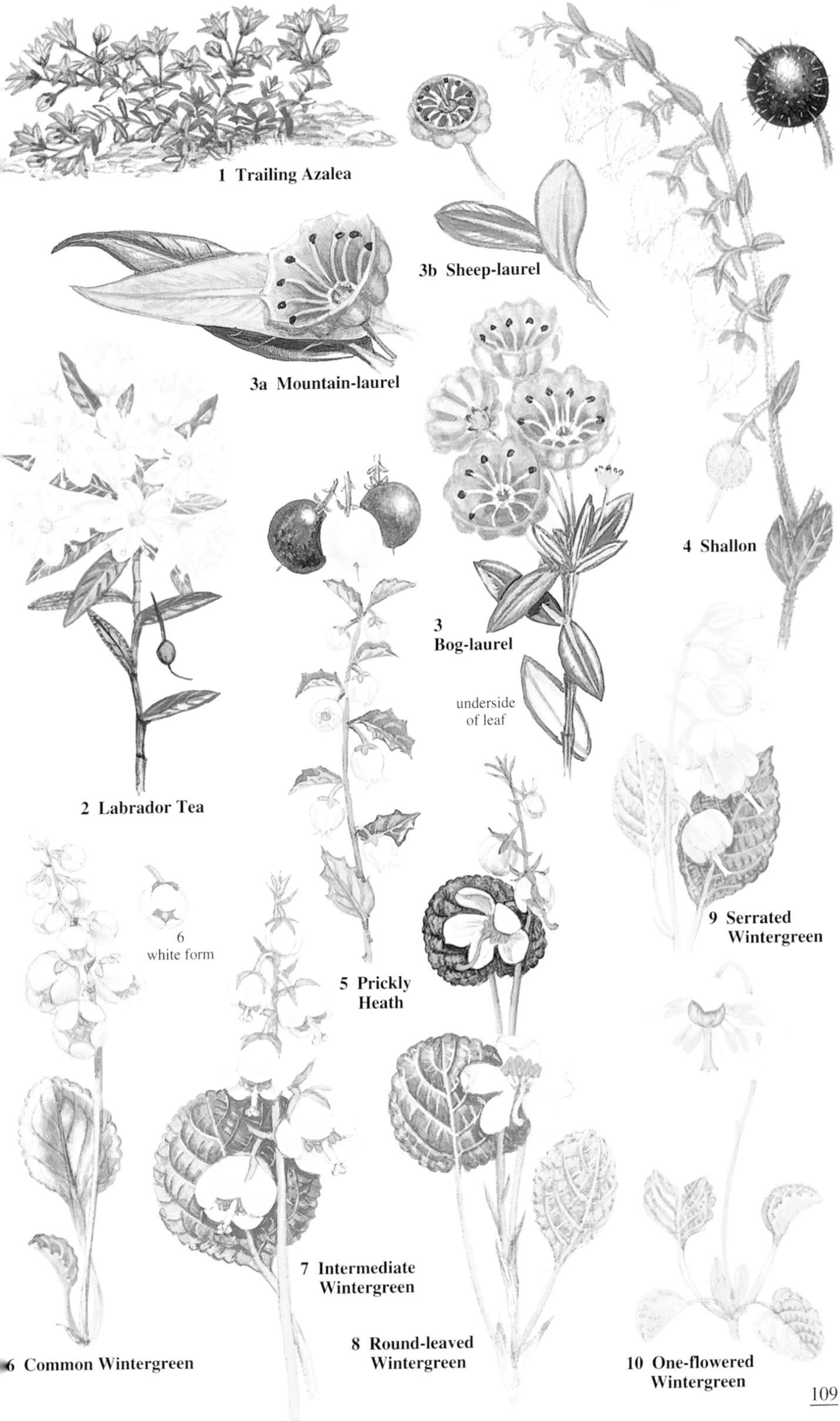

1 Trailing Azalea

3b Sheep-laurel

3a Mountain-laurel

4 Shallon

3 Bog-laurel

underside
of leaf

2 Labrador Tea

6
white form

**9 Serrated
Wintergreen**

**5 Prickly
Heath**

**7 Intermediate
Wintergreen**

6 Common Wintergreen

**8 Round-leaved
Wintergreen**

**10 One-flowered
Wintergreen**

PRIMROSE FAMILY Primulaceae

Mostly perennials. Flowers usually with five joined petals. Fruit a capsule.

Primroses *Primula*. Leaves undivided and all at the base. Several garden species are very locally naturalised, the most frequent being **7 Tibetan Cowslip** *P. florindae* with an umbel of yellow flowers and **7a Japanese Cowslip** *P. japonica* with a whorled spike of red-purple or white flowers.

1 soz □

1 Primrose *Primula vulgaris*. A universal favourite; a low carpeter, to 12cm. Flowers *solitary*, pale yellow with a deep yellow eye and honey-guides, 20-40mm, on long *shaggy* stalks; March-May, often much earlier in milder areas; pink-purple forms, usually pale, occur, especially in hedge-banks near gardens. Leaves lanceolate, crinkly, *tapering* to the base. In two marked variations: (a) the flower-stalks can form a spreading umbel on a single extended stouter common stalk, which is normally underground; and (b) the stigmas may be either above (pin-eyed) or below (thrum-eyed) the anthers; thrum is a weaving term for a fringe of threads. Woods, scrub, hedge-banks, sea cliffs, also on mountains; rare near large towns, due to overpicking and (now illegal) digging up for gardens.

2 o □

2 Cowslip *Primula veris*. Much loved for its graceful fragrant flowers; low/medium, to 30cm. Flowers *deep* yellow, orange at the base, 8-15mm, in *umbels* usually drooping to one side, on *downy* stalks; April-May. Leaves smaller than Primrose (**1**) and *abruptly* narrowed at the base. Confusable with both Oxlip (**4**) and False Oxlip (**3**) and the occasional escaped garden Polyanthus, whose much larger flowers are more often pink-purple. Grassland, mostly on chalk, limestone or limy clay.

3 o □

3 False Oxlip *Primula × polyantha*. The hybrid between Primrose (**1**) and Cowslip (**2**), intermediate between the two and liable to occur wherever they grow close together, usually in scrub. Often taken for the very local true Oxlip (**4**), but it is *not a carpeter*, and also differs in its shorter stem, *deeper yellow* flowers, especially in the centre, the umbels not one-sided and leaves more gradually tapered to the base, From the Cowslip it can be told by its larger, flatter, paler yellow flowers and leaves tapered to the base; and from the occasional umbelled Primrose by its smaller, deeper yellow flowers on shorter stalks, and longer-stalked leaves. Rarer hybrids include those between Oxlip and both Primrose and Cowslip, which will only be found in, and especially on the edges of, the limited Oxlip territory.

4 □

4 *Oxlip *Primula elatior*. The true Oxlip has a highly restricted range in eastern England. Low/short *carpeter*, to 30cm. Resembling Cowslip (**2**) in its flowers being in a one-sided drooping *umbel* and its abruptly narrowed (but larger) leaves, and Primrose (**1**) in its larger (15-20mm) pale yellow flowers. Confusable with both False Oxlip (**3**) and the occasional umbelled Primrose. Hybridises with both Primrose and Cowslip, the latter being the rarest of the three hybrids. Dampish woods on clay, where it largely replaces Primrose.

5 □↓

5 *Birdseye Primrose *Primula farinosa*. A gay (in the old sense) little plant, the Bonny Birdseye of Scotland; recalling the much larger garden Drumstick Primrose *P. denticulata*, but low, to 15cm. Flowers lilac-pink with a yellow eye, 7-15mm, in an umbel; May-June. Stem and narrow lanceolate rosette-leaves *mealy white*, but hairless. Damp bare or sparsely grassy places on limestone.

6 o □↓

6 *Scots Primrose *Primula scotica*. An even bonnier gem than Birdseye Primrose, as a Scottish endemic the emblem of the Scottish Wildlife Trust. Low biennial, to 8cm. Flowers like Birdseye Primrose (**5**), but *deeper purple* with a richer yellow eye and broader petals, 7-15mm; two flowering periods, May-June; July-August – don't hope to see it in late June or early July. Short coastal turf and dunes; very rare inland.

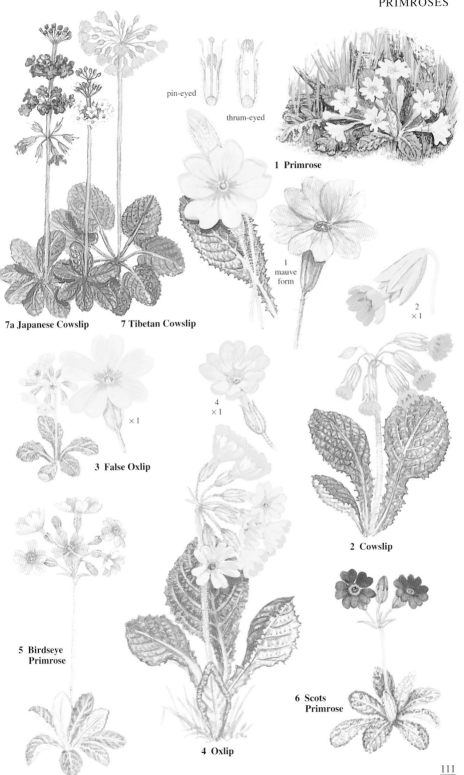

pin-eyed

thrum-eyed

1 Primrose

1
mauve
form

2
×1

7a Japanese Cowslip   **7 Tibetan Cowslip**

3 False Oxlip

×1

4
×1

2 Cowslip

5 Birdseye Primrose

6 Scots Primrose

4 Oxlip

1 Water Violet *Hottonia palustris*. A graceful, pale green aquatic, with short aerial stems to *c.* 30cm. Misnamed, since its flowers are not violet but lilac-pink with a yellow throat, 15-25mm, in a whorled spike; May-June. Leaves pinnate, whorled, submerged. Ponds and ditches.

2 Sowbread *Cyclamen hederifolium*. Low and tufted, to *c.* 10cm. Flowers pink, with large down-turned petals in the well known cyclamen shape, 12-25mm; appearing before the leaves, August-Sept. Leaves heart-shaped, toothed, dark green and often purple beneath. Naturalised in woods and scrub. Two spring-flowering Cyclamens are much less often naturalised: **2a Eastern Sowbread** *C. coum*, with a dark basal blotch on the bright pink petals and kidney-shaped leaves; and **2b Spring Sowbread** *C. repandum*, with purpler flowers and angled leaves.

3 Chaffweed *Anagallis minima*. One of our tiniest plants, a very low erect annual, to 5cm, but often only 1-2cm. Flowers pink or white, 1-2mm, petals *shorter* than sepals; short-stalked and hidden at base of leaves; June-August. Leaves oval, scarcely stalked, the *upper alternate*. Cf. Allseed (p. 170), which has more conspicuous white flowers and all leaves opposite. Damp bare sandy ground, on heaths and in woodland rides.

4 Chickweed Wintergreen *Trientalis europaea*. A delicate short perennial, to 20cm. Flowers white or pale pink, *star-like*, 5-9-petalled, 15-18mm, more like a small Wood Anemone (p. 30) than a large Chickweed (p. 50); long-stalked in a loose umbel above the leaves; May-August. Leaves pale green, broad lanceolate, all in a single whorl. Heather moors and heaths, coniferous woods.

5 Sea Milkwort *Glaux maritima*. A low, usually prostrate, pale green perennial, to 30cm; quite unlike and unrelated to the true Milkworts (p. 170). Flowers petalless, with five *pale pink* sepal-lobes, 3-5mm, solitary at the base of the leaves; May-Sept. Leaves elliptic or oval fleshy, opposite. *By the sea*, usually in barish places.

6 Brookweed *Samolus valerandi*. Short hairless perennial, often unbranched, to 45cm. Flowers white, 2-4mm, in leafless stalked spikes with a *tiny bract* about the middle of each stalk; June-August. Leaves oval, some in a basal rosette. Fruits globular. Can be quite puzzling and crucifer-like when first encountered, but has five petals – Crucifers (p. 82) have four. Marshy meadows and other damp places, especially near the sea.

7 Scarlet Pimpernel *Anagallis arvensis*. Prostrate annual; stems square, to 40cm. Flowers usually *vermilion red* with a purple eye, but can be pink, flesh, maroon, lilac or (most often) blue; petals fringed with hairs; 4-7mm; May-Oct; aka Poor Man's Weatherglass because they close when the sun goes in. Leaves pointed oval, unstalked, in pairs or whorls. Bare and disturbed ground, including dunes.

8 Bog Pimpernel *Anagallis tenella*. A charming delicate prostrate, often mat-forming perennial, to 20cm. Flowers *pink, bell-shaped*, 6-10mm, solitary on long stalks, opening in the sun; May-Sept. Leaves oval to rounded, short-stalked, opposite. *Bogs* and other peaty places.

1 ■↓

2 ☐↑↑

3 S ☐↓↓

4 OZ ☐

5 SOZ ☐

6 O ☐

7 SOZ ☐

8 SOZ ☐

2a Eastern Sowbread

2b Spring Sowbread

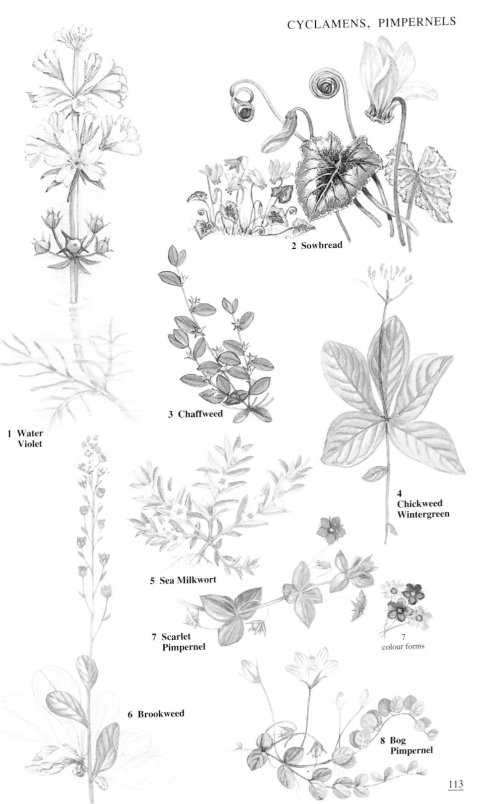

1 Water Violet

2 Sowbread

3 Chaffweed

4 Chickweed Wintergreen

5 Sea Milkwort

7 Scarlet Pimpernel

7 colour forms

6 Brookweed

8 Bog Pimpernel

Loosestrifes *Lysimachia*. Perennials with yellow flowers and undivided leaves. Lysimachus was a Greek King of Sicily; loosestrife is just a translation.

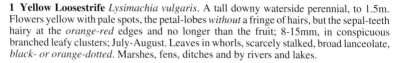

1 Yellow Loosestrife *Lysimachia vulgaris*. A tall downy waterside perennial, to 1.5m. Flowers yellow with pale spots, the petal-lobes *without* a fringe of hairs, but the sepal-teeth hairy at the *orange-red* edges and no longer than the fruit; 8-15mm, in conspicuous branched leafy clusters; July-August. Leaves in whorls, scarcely stalked, broad lanceolate, *black- or orange-dotted*. Marshes, fens, ditches and by rivers and lakes.

2 Dotted Loosestrife *Lysimachia punctata*. Shorter, downier and not, or less, branched than Yellow Loosestrife (**1**), with flowers paler, the petals *fringed with hairs*, the very narrow *all-green* hairy sepal-teeth, longer than the fruit; June-August. Leaves short-stalked, with downy margins, *dotted beneath*. An increasing escape on road- and riversides and among rough herbage. A similar escape, **2a Fringed Loosestrife** *L. ciliata*, with red and black markings on the petals is more frequent in the North. Another, recently discovered but probably widespread, escape is **2b Whorled Loosestrife** *L. verticillaris*, with petals tinged pale orange at the base and the leaf-junctions pale purple.

3 *Tufted Loosestrife *Lysimachia thyrsiflora*. An almost hairless medium perennial, to 70cm. Flowers yellow, bell-shaped, with five black-dotted petal-lobes, feathery with *prominent yellow stamens*, 4-6mm, in pairs of short dense leafy stalked spikes, in the *middle* of the stem, with more leaves at the top; June-July, but a shy flowerer. Leaves narrow lanceolate, black-dotted, unstalked. Marshes, fens and by ditches and canals; well known but non-flowering at Gormire, N Yorkshire. **3a Lake Loosestrife** *L. terrestris* has black-streaked flowers with five petal-lobes at the top of the stem; introduced by Lake Windermere and in Sussex

4 Creeping Jenny *Lysimachia nummularia*. A prostrate low perennial, creeping to 60cm. Flowers yellow, black-dotted, *bell-shaped*, 8-18mm; sepal-teeth broader and stalks shorter and thicker than Yellow Pimpernel (**5**); June-August. Leaves blunter than Yellow Pimpernel, *black-dotted*. Native in damp woods and grassy places; also a favourite cottage garden plant, frequently escaping.

5 Yellow Pimpernel *Lysimachia nemorum*. A prostrate perennial, creeping to 40cm. Flowers yellow, star-like, 5-8mm, sepal-teeth very narrow, on long thin stalks, open in fine weather; May-August. Leaves pointed oval, opposite. Damp woods.

LOOSESTRIFE FAMILY Lythraceae

6 Purple Loosestrife *Lythrum salicaria*. A conspicuous waterside perennial, stems 4-sided, to 1.5m. Flowers *bright red-purple*, with six narrow petals, in whorls up the stem; June-August. Leaves lanceolate, unstalked, untoothed, opposite or whorled. Fruit a capsule. By fresh water, fens, marshes.

7 Water Purslane *Lythrum portula*. A prostrate hairless annual, creeping and rooting, with stems often reddish, to 25cm. Flowers tiny, *c.* 1mm, pinkish, with six or no petals, *solitary* at the base of the leaves; June-Oct. Leaves *broadest at the tip*, often reddish. Damp bare ground, especially by (sometimes in) muddy pools, avoiding lime.

8 **Grass Poly *Lythrum hyssopifolium*. Erect to sprawling hairless annual, to 25cm. Flowers with six *pink* petals, 4-6mm, solitary or paired at the base of the leaves; June-Sept. Leaves narrow, alternate above, opposite below. Bare *wet or moist* ground, often in slight hollows. Not to be confused with the more frequent birdseed alien **False Grass Poly** *L. junceum*, which has longer stems, to 70cm and *purple* flowers, on drier ground.

petal × 4   × 2   sepal × 2

3 Tufted Loosestrife details

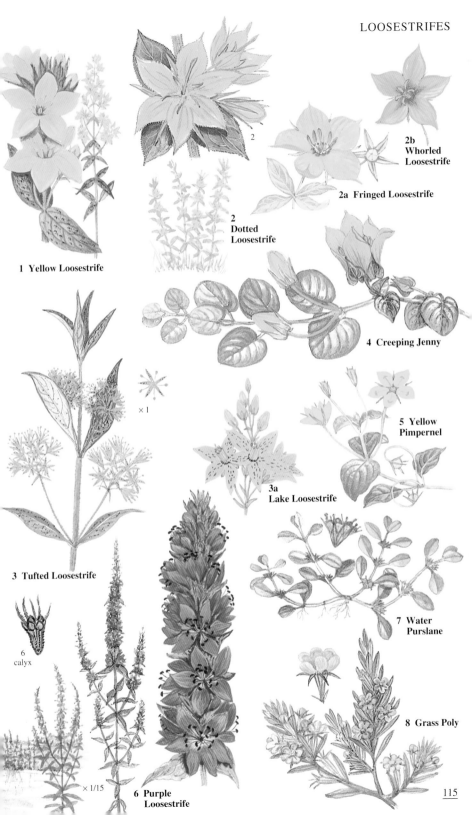

1 Yellow Loosestrife

2 Dotted Loosestrife

2a Fringed Loosestrife

2b Whorled Loosestrife

×1

4 Creeping Jenny

3a Lake Loosestrife

5 Yellow Pimpernel

3 Tufted Loosestrife

6 calyx

7 Water Purslane

×1/15

6 Purple Loosestrife

8 Grass Poly

SAXIFRAGE FAMILY Saxifragaceae

Annuals/perennials, with flowers 4-5-petalled and 3-styled, leaves usually alternate or basal and fruit a capsule. Among many locally established, distinctly unsaxifragelike escapes familiar in larger gardens are three species of **False Bucksbeard** *Astilbe* with spiraea-like panicles of pink or red flowers, and pinnate leaves, in a few woodlands; several species of **Bergenia** *Bergenia* with pink flowers and large rounded leaves; and two usually by fresh water, **Rodgersia** *Rodgersia podophylla* with yellowish-white flowers and large long-stalked palmate red-green leaves; and **Indian Rhubarb** *Darmera peltata* with pink flowers and large long-stalked palmately lobed leaves. Cf. giant rhubarbs *Gunnera*, p. 306.

Saxifrages *Saxifraga*. Mostly hairy or downy perennials, with loose clusters of 5-petalled flowers. Leaves undivided but sometimes deeply lobed, at base and usually up stems. Fruit a capsule. Three flower-colour groups below: White, Purple and Yellow.

Flowers white

Species 3-5 are Irish specialities. Species 4-5, but not 5a, are sometimes known as as Robertsonian Saxifrages (after a disused classification). Species 2-8 on p. 118 are largely confined to mountains.

1 Meadow Saxifrage *Saxifraga granulata*. Our largest-flowered saxifrage and the only one in lowland grassland; short/medium, to 50cm. Flowers white, *18-30mm*, the five petals spaced out; April-June. Leaves kidney-shaped, with rounded lobes, the rosette ones with *bulbils* at their base. A confusing double-flowered form may escape from gardens. Grassland, preferring limy soils.

2 Mossy Saxifrage *Saxifraga hypnoides*. Variable, *mat-forming* and low/short, to 20cm. Flowers white, 14-20mm, with *nodding*, often pink-tipped buds; May-July. Leaves *linear* or 3-lobed, sharply pointed, many on barren stems. Aka Dovedale Moss. Cultivars are familiar in gardens, but rarely escape. Cliffs, rocks, e.g. at Cheddar Gorge, Somerset, dunes, ledges and streams on mountain-sides.

3 Irish Saxifrage *Saxifraga rosacea*. One of several Irish saxifrages, like Mossy Saxifrage (**2**), but with flowers erect in bud, leaves *3-5-lobed*, broader and less sharply pointed. Damp cliffs and rocks, especially in the Burren, mountain stream-sides.

4 St Patrick's Cabbage *Saxifraga spathularis*. The most frequent of a rather difficult group, Irish as natives but widely scattered as introductions elsewhere. A graceful, *almost hairless* short perennial, to 40cm, very like London Pride (**4a**). Flowers white, with many red and *two yellow* spots on each petal, 7-9mm, on reddish stems; June-August. Leaves all in a rosette, long-stalked, spoon-shaped, tapering to the base, well toothed, often reddish beneath. Hybridises with Kidney Saxifrage (**5**). Damp rocks from sea-level to mountain tops. **4a London Pride** *S. × urbium*, its hybrid with Pyrenean Saxifrage (**4b**), and intermediate between the two, is well known in gardens and a frequent escape, especially in the Isle of Man. **4b Pyrenean Saxifrage** *S. umbrosa*, the second parent, hairier and with shorter-stalked leaves and down-turned sepals, has been known for 200 years in one ghyll in the Yorkshire Dales.

5 Kidney Saxifrage *Saxifraga hirsuta*. Differs from the more frequent St Patrick's Cabbage (**4**), with which it often hybridises, in being hairier, with a yellow *patch* and usually some *pink* spots on the petals, the sepals down-turned and the leaves *kidney-shaped*. Also hybridises with Pyrenean Saxifrage (**4b**), as a rare established escape. Shadier places, such as woods, stream-sides and shady rocks and ghylls. **5a Round-leaved Saxifrage** *S. rotundifolia* is less hairy with larger flowers, 12-20mm, petals spotted both red-purple and yellow, spreading sepals (June-Sept) and leaves often more rounded. Well naturalised in several shady places, especially in Stirlingshire.

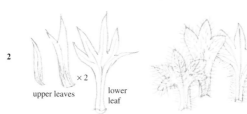

2

× 2

upper leaves   lower leaf

3
leaves from
different plants

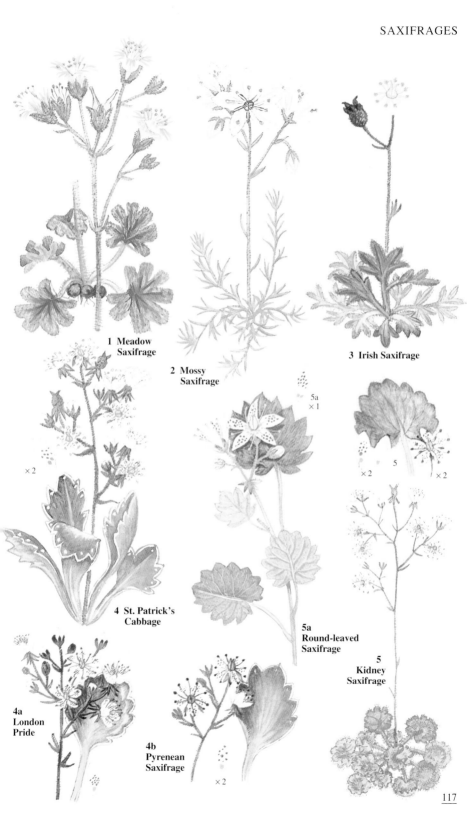

1 Meadow
Saxifrage

2 Mossy
Saxifrage

3 Irish Saxifrage

× 2

4 St. Patrick's
Cabbage

5a
× 1

5

× 2

× 2

5a
Round-leaved
Saxifrage

5
Kidney
Saxifrage

4a
London
Pride

4b
Pyrenean
Saxifrage

× 2

1 Rue-leaved Saxifrage *Saxifraga tridactylites.* One of our commonest and most distinctive saxifrages, and our only white annual: a dainty, often *reddish*, stickily hairy, low winter annual, with somewhat zigzag stems to 10cm. Flowers white, 4-6mm, bell-shaped; April-May. Leaves *3-5-lobed*, narrowed at the base. Fruits egg-shaped. Walls, rocks, dunes and other dry, bare, often sandy places, usually on lime.

2 Starry Saxifrage *Saxifraga stellaris.* The commonest of the white mountain saxifrages; low/short, graceful and slightly hairy, to 20cm. Flowers white, with two yellow spots, 10-15mm, with *down-turned* sepals, in a *loose cluster* on leafless stems; June-August. Leaves ovate, toothed, unstalked, in a rosette. Wet places on mountains.

3 *Alpine Saxifrage *Saxifraga nivalis.* Differs from Starry Saxifrage (**2**) especially in its *tightly packed* flowerhead on a black-hairy stem, smaller (5-6mm) flowers with *unspotted* petals usually tipped pink and erect sepals (July-August), and leaves more stalked and usually *purple* beneath. High mountain ledges.

4 **Highland Saxifrage *Saxifraga rivularis.* Low, hairless, to 12cm. Flowers white *or pink*, 8-10mm, petals scarcely longer than sepals, 1-3 on a stem; July-August. Leaves shallowly *palmately lobed*, with hard-to-see bulbils and runners at their base. Wet rocky places on the Cairngorms and other Highland mountains. A circumpolar species first discovered by Linnaeus on his 1732 Lapland journey.

5 **Tufted Saxifrage *Saxifraga cespitosa.* Our second rarest mountain saxifrage; low and cushion-forming, to 10cm. Flowers whitish, usually tinged *greenish or creamy*, 7-9mm, 1-5 to a stem; May-July. Leaves almost all basal, *glandular-hairy*, with usually three blunt lobes. High, sheltered mountain ledges.

6 **Drooping Saxifrage *Saxifraga cernua.* Our rarest saxifrage, with only five localities; low, slender, almost unbranched, to 15cm. Flowers white, *solitary*, large (12-18mm) for the size of the plant. Leaves 3-5-lobed, with tiny *red bulbils* at their base up the stems, which do not always end in flowers. High mountain corries and rock crevices.

Flowers purple

7 Purple Saxifrage *Saxifraga oppositifolia.* Our only purple saxifrage and one of the first and most unmistakable mountain plants to flower. Prostrate and mat-forming, with often long trailing stems. Flowers *purple* or pink, solitary, short-stalked, 10-20mm, usually in sheets visible from a distance; *March-May.* Leaves oval, opposite, unstalked. Rocks, screes, ledges, usually on lime, as far S as Ingleborough and Pen-y-ghent in the Craven Pennines.

Flowers yellow

8 Yellow Saxifrage *Saxifraga aizoides.* Much the commoner of our two native yellow saxifrages; low/short mat-forming, sparsely hairy perennial, to 25cm. Flowers yellow, rarely orange, often red-spotted, the petals well spaced, *5-10mm*, in loose clusters; June-August. Leaves narrow lanceolate, *toothed*, scarcely stalked. Wet lime-rich places on mountains, also on dunes in the far North.

9 **Marsh Saxifrage *Saxifraga hirculus.* Differs from Yellow Saxifrage (**8**) in being *reddish-hairy*, with much *larger* (20-30mm), often solitary, almost buttercup-like, yellow flowers (late July-early Sept, a shy flowerer), the hairy sepals *turned down* after flowering, and narrower, longer-stalked leaves. Marshy grassland on moors.

10 Caucasian Saxifrage *Saxifraga cymbalaria.* One of our two annual saxifrages, low/short, with sprawling stems to 20cm. Flowers *yellow*, 5-9mm, in loose clusters; April-Sept. Leaves *kidney-shaped, lobed* often heart-shaped at base, long-stalked. An introduced nursery and garden weed.

1
×2

3
calyx

5
×2

6
bulbils ×4

×2
9
fruit ×1

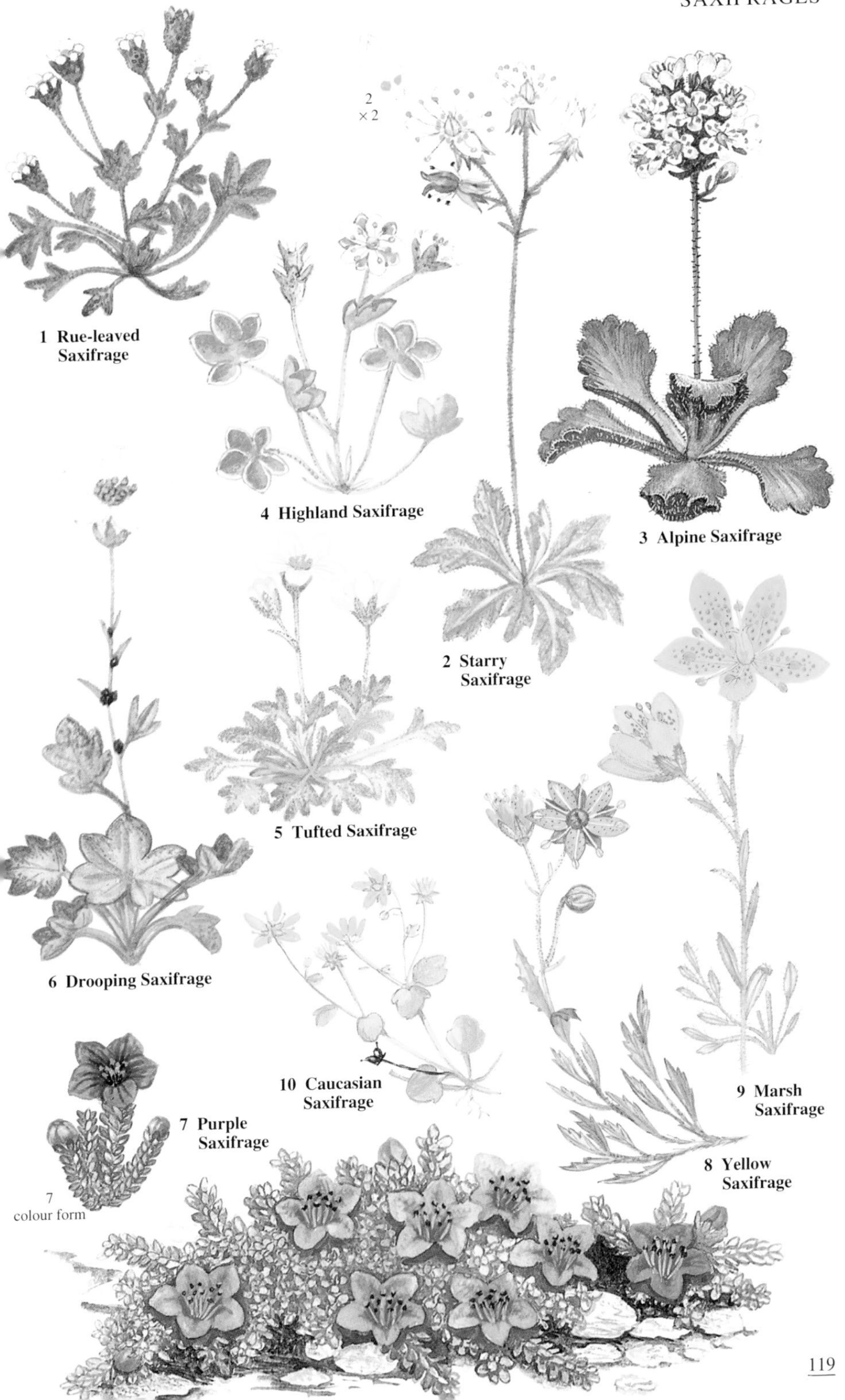

1 Rue-leaved Saxifrage

2
× 2

4 Highland Saxifrage

3 Alpine Saxifrage

2 Starry Saxifrage

5 Tufted Saxifrage

6 Drooping Saxifrage

10 Caucasian Saxifrage

7 Purple Saxifrage

7
colour form

9 Marsh Saxifrage

8 Yellow Saxifrage

1 Golden Saxifrage *Chrysosplenium oppositifolium.* Low creeping perennial; stems *square*, to 15cm. Flowers petalless, 3-4mm, coloured by yellow-green sepals and bracts and bright yellow anthers; February-July. Leaves in mossy mats, roundish, *bluntly* toothed, *opposite*; root leaves as long as stalks. Springs, flushes, stream-sides, wet mountain ledges. **1a Alternate-leaved Golden Saxifrage** *C. alternifolium* is less mat-forming, with a taller, *triangular* stem, larger flowers with glossier bracts, broader, more heart-shaped and clearly toothed alternate leaves and longer-stalked root leaves. May grow with (**1**), but more often on limy soils; under overhanging rocks grows further in.

2 Grass of Parnassus *Parnassia palustris.* A short pale green tufted perennial, to 30cm. Flowers *white*, 5-petalled, 15-30mm; buttercup-like but the five stamens alternate with *scales*; July-Sept. Leaves pointed oval, heart-shaped, long-stalked, basal, but one unstalked leaf usually clasps the stem. Marshes, fens, damp grassland, dune slacks.

3 Pick-a-back Plant *Tolmiea menziesii.* Creeping short/medium downy perennial, to 70cm. Flowers *red-brown* with purple-veined sepals, *4-petalled*, 6-15mm, in stalked spikes; April-August. Leaves heart-shaped, lobed, *yellow-green*, with buds at their base in autumn. Naturalised in damp shady places. There are also several similar but much less frequent escapes from the genera *Heuchera*, × *Heucherella* and *Tiarella*.

4 Fringe Cups *Tellima grandiflora.* Similar to Pick-a-back Plant (**3**), but has *greenish* flowers, later reddening, with five *jaggedly-toothed petals*, in nodding spikes, and *dark green* leaves without autumnal buds. Habitat similar.

STONECROP FAMILY Crassulaceae

Mostly hairless perennials, with star-like, 5-petalled flowers; untoothed, *fleshy*, un- or short-stalked leaves and dry, many-seeded fruits. Most stonecrops (*Sedum*) prefer walls and dry rocky places, and many are grown in gardens; nearly a dozen species, besides those described here, are liable to escape. Three colour groups below, yellow, white and pink.

Flowers yellow

5 Biting Stonecrop *Sedum acre.* Our commonest yellow stonecrop, *peppery-tasting*, low, often mat-forming, to 10cm. Flowers bright yellow, 10-14mm; May-July. Leaves small, ovoid, broadest near base, yellow-green. Aka Wall-pepper. Walls, rocks and other dry bare places, including coastal sand and shingle, often on lime. **5a Tasteless Stonecrop** *S. sexangulare* with taller stems, to 25cm, and longer, *tasteless* cylindrical leaves, is an occasional escape, notably at Wick Rocks, NE of Bristol.

6 *Rock Stonecrop *Sedum forsterianum.* Mat-forming, short, to 30cm. Flowers yellow, usually 7-petalled, 10-12mm, in slightly domed heads; June-August. Leaves grey-green, *flattened above*, sharply pointed; sterile shoots have a tassel of living leaves above *persistent dead* ones below, *Native* on rocks and screes, occasionally on banks and shingle; also as a garden escape.

7 Large Rock Stonecrop *Sedum rupestre.* Generally larger and stouter than Rock Stonecrop (**6**), to 35cm, with flowers 14-15mm and often 6-petalled. Leaves somewhat longer and more spreading, *not flattened above* or sharply pointed, and with *no* persistent dead leaves. A confusingly frequent *garden escape*, especially on walls.

8 Roseroot *Sedum rosea.* Tufted, short, to 35cm. Flowers *yellow-green*, 4-petalled, 5-7mm, in slightly domed heads; sometimes purple-tinged with purple anthers; male and female on different plants; May-June. Leaves broad, slightly *toothed*, up the stems, *greyish*, often tinged purple-red. Fruits *orange*, mistakable for flowers. Sea cliffs, mountain ledges. Named from the rose-like scent of its roots when cut.

♀ × 4

♂ × 4

fruit
× 2

8
Roseroot details

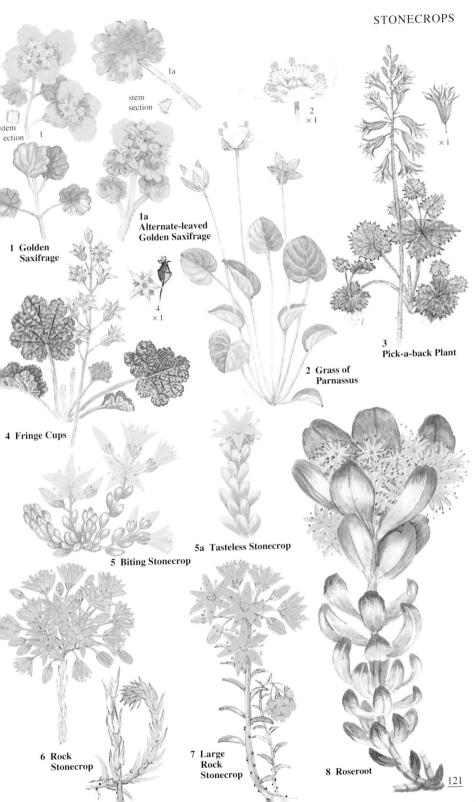

1a

stem
section

stem
section

1 Golden
Saxifrage

1a
Alternate-leaved
Golden Saxifrage

2
× 1

× 1

3
Pick-a-back Plant

4
× 1

2 Grass of
Parnassus

4 Fringe Cups

5a Tasteless Stonecrop

5 Biting Stonecrop

6 Rock
Stonecrop

7 Large
Rock
Stonecrop

8 Roseroot

121

Flowers white

1 English Stonecrop *Sedum anglicum.* Our commonest white stonecrop, low and mat-forming, to 5cm. Flowers white *tinged pink*, 11-12mm; June-Sept. Leaves stubby, *alternate*, grey-green, often *reddening*. Fruits red. Rocks, cliff-tops, dunes and shingle on acid soils, often by the sea.

2 Thick-leaved Stonecrop *Sedum dasyphyllum.* Low and *grey-downy*, to 10cm. Flowers white, *pink beneath*, 5-6-petalled, 5-7mm; May-July. Leaves stubby, usually *opposite*, with minute green or red spots. Long established, locally frequent garden escape, usually on walls.

3 White Stonecrop *Sedum album.* Short, to 20cm. Flowers white with *no* pink tinge, 6-9mm, in broad, slightly domed *heads*; June-August. Leaves stubby, alternate, *green* but sometimes reddish. Rocks, walls, bare ground; a scarce native, much more frequent as an escape.

Flowers pink

4 Orpine *Sedum telephium.* Our tallest native stonecrop, to 60cm, the most frequent native pink one, and the only pink succulent found in woods; short/medium, to 60cm. Flowers *purplish-pink* to lilac, 9-12mm, in loose clusters; July-Sept. Leaves broad, toothed, *alternate*. Woods, rocks, hedge-banks. **4a Ice Plant** *S. spectabile*, with broader, flatter heads of pale pink to red-purple flowers and leaves *opposite* or whorled is a frequent escape on waysides and elsewhere. Its hybrid with Orpine, cv. Herbstfreude, may also occur. **4b Caucasian Stonecrop** *S. spurium*, much lower, creeping and mat-forming, with slightly larger flowers but much smaller, more toothed, leaves, and often covering the ground without flowering, is the most frequent of several similar escaped stonecrops.

5 *Pink Stonecrop *Sedum villosum.* The smaller of our two native pink stonecrops, a low *downy* biennial/perennial, to 10cm. Flowers *pink*, 5-8mm, in clusters; June-August. Leaves short, alternate. In the hills: by streams, in flushes and abundant on an old Wensleydale quarry floor.

~

6 *Mossy Stonecrop *Crassula tillaea.* A tiny prostrate annual, usually to no more than 5cm. Starts greyish and inconspicuous, soon turns *brilliant red*. Flowers white, 1-2mm, usually *3-petalled*, solitary at the base of the tiny (1-2mm) crowded leaves; May-Sept. Bare patches on sand and gravel.

7 ***Pigmyweed *Crassula aquatica.* A tiny prostrate annual, to 5cm. Flowers greenish-white, 4-petalled, 1-2mm, solitary at the base of the small (3-5mm) *linear* leaves up the stem; June-August. Remarkably abundant in and on the muddy shores of L. Shiel, N Argyll.

8 Navelwort *Umbilicus rupestris.* A distinctive low/medium fleshy perennial, anything from 2 to 50cm. Flowers greenish- or pinkish-white, bell-shaped, 7-10mm, in a long stalked spike; May-August. Named from its *rounded* leaves with a navel-like *dimple* in the centre, varying from 1 to 7cm across. Aka Wall Pennywort. Rocks, walls, hedge-banks, especially near the sea.

9 House-Leek *Sempervivum tectorum.* Short/medium perennial, to 50cm, with conspicuous rosettes of thick fleshy. often reddish leaves, and leafless flowering stems. Flowers pink-purple, *c.* 12-petalled, 15-30mm; June-July. Roofs, walls and quarry cliffs, almost always planted.

DIAPENSIA FAMILY Diapensiaceae

10 ***Diapensia *Diapensia lapponica.* A low evergreen cushion-forming undershrub, to 6cm. Flowers white, 5-petalled, solitary, short-stalked, 10-20mm, not unlike a Saxifrage (p. 116), but with only one style, a 3-lobed stigma and *three sepal-like bracts* close under the five leathery sepals, which redden in fruit. Leaves narrow, shiny, leathery, untoothed. Fruit a capsule. Discovered in 1951 on a single hilltop near the head of L. Shiel, Inverness-shire.

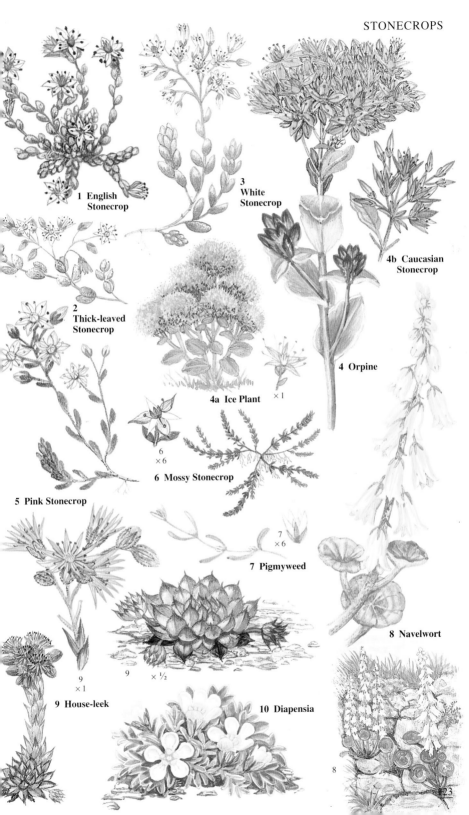

1 English Stonecrop

2 Thick-leaved Stonecrop

3 White Stonecrop

4a Ice Plant × 1

4b Caucasian Stonecrop

4 Orpine

5 Pink Stonecrop

6 × 6

6 Mossy Stonecrop

7 × 6

7 Pigmyweed

8 Navelwort

9 × 1

9 × ½

9 House-leek

10 Diapensia

8

ROSE FAMILY Rosaceae

A large family, including many trees and tall shrubs (p. 364). Flowers very variable in size, with five petals and sepals, numerous yellow stamens, leaves usually alternate and with stipules, and fruit usually compound, of several to many achenes (dry) or drupes (fleshy).

Roses *Rosa*. Scrambling deciduous shrubs, with thin spiny or thorny stems. Flowers large, with usually five floppy pink, white or red petals; sepals usually pinnate. Leaves pinnate with toothed leaflets and stipules at the base. Fruit (hip), red (except Burnet Rose, p. 126) egg-shaped, shiny and berry-like, enclosing the seeds. Very variable, with many hybrids. Some 26 alien species, hybrids and cultivars are established in various parts of Britain and Ireland, but only two are frequent enough to be included below.

1 Dog Rose *Rosa canina*. The 'English unofficial Rose', generally our commonest and most variable wild rose, but most frequent in the South; tall, to 3 or even 4m, with arching stems and stout hooked or curved prickles. Flowers pale pink or white, fragrant, 30-60mm, on *hairless stalks*; June-July. Leaves rather dark green, sometimes downy beneath. Hip egg-shaped, bright red, almost always hairless, *losing the sepals* before they redden. Hedges, scrub, woods. **1a Northern Dog Rose** *R. caesia* has its young stems distinctively wine-red on the sunlit side (a feature often found in its hybrids), flowers usually pink, leaves usually glaucous beneath, hips larger with *spreading/erect* sepals on short stalks often hidden by the bracts. **1b Round-leaved Dog Rose** *R. obtusifolia* has flowers usually white, sepals 2-pinnate, down-turned and soon falling, leaves rounder and downy, often on both sides, with small dark red-brown glands on the teeth, and hips often more rounded.

2 Field Rose *Rosa arvensis*. One of our most distinctive wild roses, with the styles making a *stout column* longer than the stamens in the middle of the cup-shaped flowers, which are always *creamy-white*, slightly smaller (30-50mm) and flowering about a fortnight later (June-August) than Dog Rose (**1**) and with sepals often *purplish*, without lobes and with glands on their stalks. Almost hairless, with hooked prickles on the long glaucous green and dull purple trailing stems, to 2m, which often form matted brakes and may hang down like lianas. Hips smaller and often rounder than Dog Rose. Woods, scrub, hedges. Our only other wild rose with styles in a column is **2a Short-styled Field Rose** *R. stylosa*, otherwise more like a Dog Rose, with pale pink or white flowers, a narrower style-column arising from a conical base and distinctively sharply pointed dark green leaflets, the lower ones often bent backwards, and stem-thorns almost an equilateral triangle.

Downy Roses. A group of three roses with deeper pink flowers on glandular stalks, the *unstalked* glands faintly resin-scented (Cf. sweetbriars, p. 126) leaves downy beneath and also often above, prickles nearly straight and hips globular and bristly. Wood margins, scrub, chalk downs, moors.

The most frequent in the South is **3 Southern Downy Rose** *Rosa tomentosa*, a climber, with flowers occasionally white, long-stalked, leaves pale or greyish green and hips with down-turned sepals falling early. The most frequent in the North is the early-flowering **3a Northern Downy Rose** *R. mollis* with erect suckering stems, purplish when young, completely straight prickles, very deep pink flowers, large, softly hairy leaflets, grey beneath, and large, short-stalked hips with persistent erect sepals. Intermediate in both appearance and distribution and generally the most widespread is the non-climbing **3b Sherard's Downy Rose** *R. sherardii*, with flowers sometimes white (in Scotland), leaves bluish-green and hips with more spreading sepals.

1 s

1a oz

1b

2

2a

3

3a o

hedgerow with wild roses

3b o

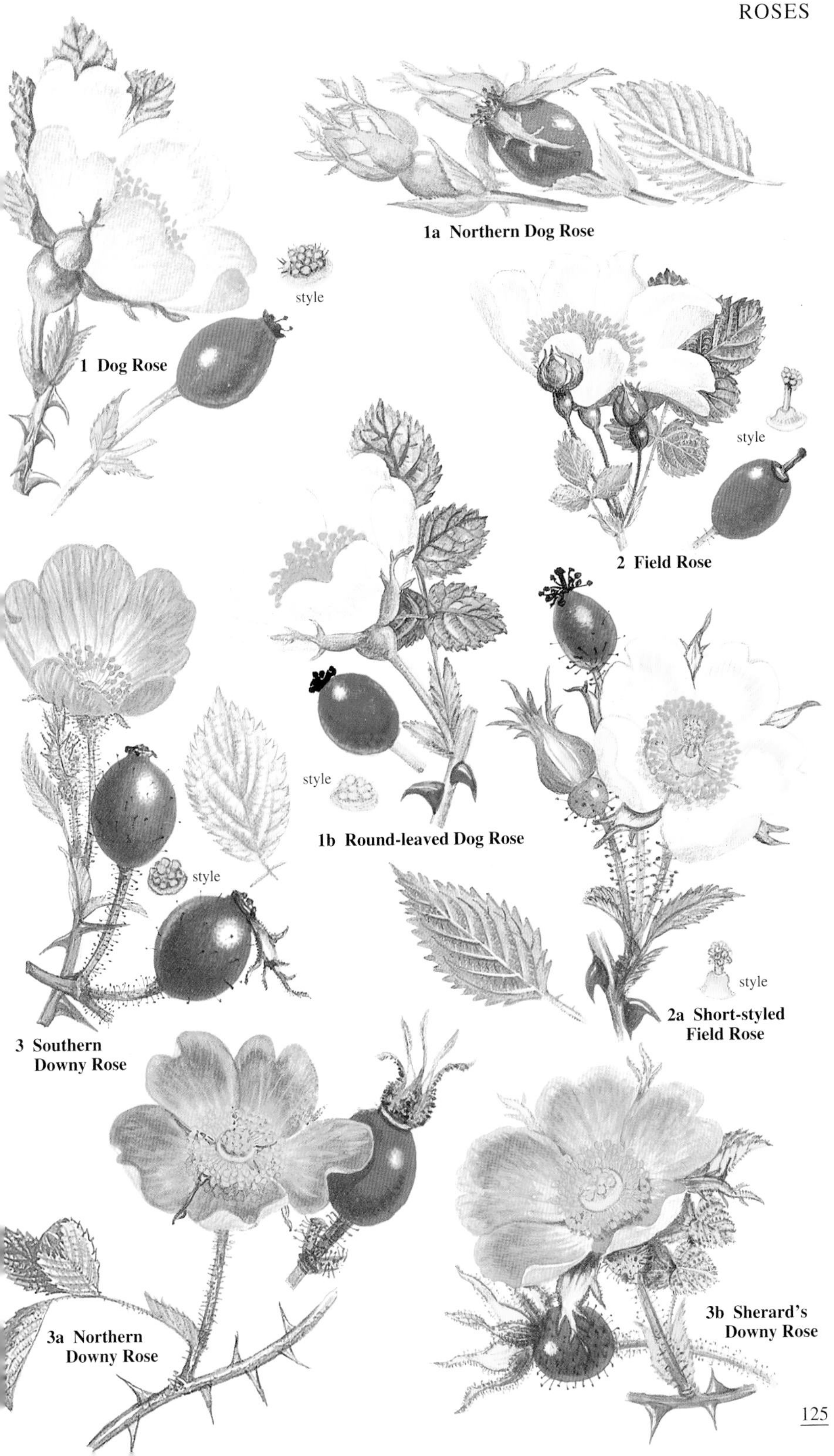
1a Northern Dog Rose
style
1 Dog Rose
style
2 Field Rose
style
1b Round-leaved Dog Rose
style
3 Southern
Downy Rose
style
2a Short-styled
Field Rose
3a Northern
Downy Rose
3b Sherard's
Downy Rose

Sweetbriars. A group of three roses noted for the strong sweet *apple scent* of the numerous stalked glands on their leaves and flower-stalks. Stems to 2 or 3m with curved or hooked prickles. Flowers usually pink, 25-40cm; June-July. Leaves stickily hairy beneath. Hips red, the sepals falling early. Scrub, hedges, usually on lime, especially chalk downs.

The erect **1 Sweetbriar** *Rosa rubiginosa* has unequal prickles mixed with *hair-like acicles*, bright pink flowers, 30-40cm, and hips with erect sepals. The erect or climbing **1a Small-flowered Sweetbriar** *R. micrantha* has more equal prickles with *no acicles*, slightly smaller, paler pink flowers, longer leaflets and hips with turned-down sepals; the most likely to be seen away from limy soils. The rare erect **1b **Small-leaved Sweetbriar** *R. agrestis* has no acicles, smaller (20-40mm) *white* or pale pink flowers, narrower leaflets, and smaller hips with turned-down sepals.

2 Burnet Rose *Rosa pimpinellifolia*. Low-growing, to 30cm, suckering to form *extensive bushy patches*. Flowers creamy white, rarely pale pink, fragrant, solitary, 20-40cm; May-July. Leaves with 7-9 small roundish leaflets. Hips *purple-black*, with undivided sepals persisting. Hybrids can be confusing, as they may have red hips. Dunes, coastal heaths, chalk downs and mountain ledges inland.

3 Japanese Rose *Rosa rugosa*. The most frequent and the largest-flowered of the introduced Roses; erect, stems downy with many straight prickles and hair-like acicles, to 2m, suckering to form extensive thickets. Flowers bright pink-purple, occasionally white, 60-80mm; June-July. Leaves dark green and ridged above, greyish and downy beneath. Hips large, 20-25mm, with both glands and acicles. Dunes and shingle by the sea, e.g. at Skinburness, Cumbria, and rough or waste ground inland.

Many-flowered Rose *Rosa multiflora* is a scrambler, to 5m. Flowers 10 or more in a cluster, usually white, and quite small (20-30mm). Leaves with much divided, almost hairlike stipules. Hips small, bristly. Hedges, woods; an escape.

Brambles *Rubus*. Mostly spiny deciduous shrubs. Flowers white or pink, 5-petalled. Leaves mostly variously divided. Fruit fleshy, often edible. Besides those described below, two white-flowered and red-fruited species with undivided but lobed leaves are sometimes naturalised: The erect **4 Thimbleberry**, aka Salmonberry, *Rubus parviflorus* with rounded leaves and the **4a Creeping Chinese Bramble** *R. tricolor* with brownish bristles and ovate leaves.

5 Bramble *Rubus fruticosus* agg. One of the most familiar and most variable plants in our flora; a very prickly, prostrate to clambering, half-evergreen perennial, to 4m tall or long. Flowers white or pink, 20-32mm, sepals down-turned in fruit; May-Nov. Leaves with 3-5 broad, toothed leaflets. Fruit the familiar edible Blackberry, green, then red, finally purple-black, not coming easily off its base till quite ripe. Ubiquitous: woods, scrub, hedges, heaths, dunes, cliffs, waste ground. More than 400 microspecies are known, almost all requiring some expertise to identify. The easier ones include: **5a Cut-leaved Blackberry** *R. laciniatus*, discovered in the Berlin Botanic Garden in 1909, and easily told by its very deeply cut leaves; the aggressive escape **5b Himalayan Giant** (not from the Himalayas!) *R. armeniacus* with its large pale pink flowers and large leaves, increasingly common in and around towns and villages; the comparatively recent arrival from Germany, **Slender-spined Bramble** *R. elegantispinosus*, with unusually thin 8mm purple spines and pink flowers, increasing, especially on suburban railway banks and in E Scotland; and the common and widespread **5c Elm-leaved Bramble** *Rubus ulmifolius*, which appears easy to identify from its pink flowers and elm-like leaves, dark green above and downy-white beneath, until you realise that it often hybridises with those other so confusingly similar brambles.

6 Dewberry *Rubus caesius*. Less robust and prickly, and more often prostrate than Bramble (**5**); stems *greyish* when young, to 1m or more. Flowers white, 20-25mm, the earliest often strikingly larger than the later ones; May-Sept. Leaves trefoil. Fruit blue-black with a *waxy bloom*, with fewer and larger segments, edible but rather insipid. Hybridises readily with Bramble. Woodland edges, scrub, grassy places, fens, dunes.

5
pink form

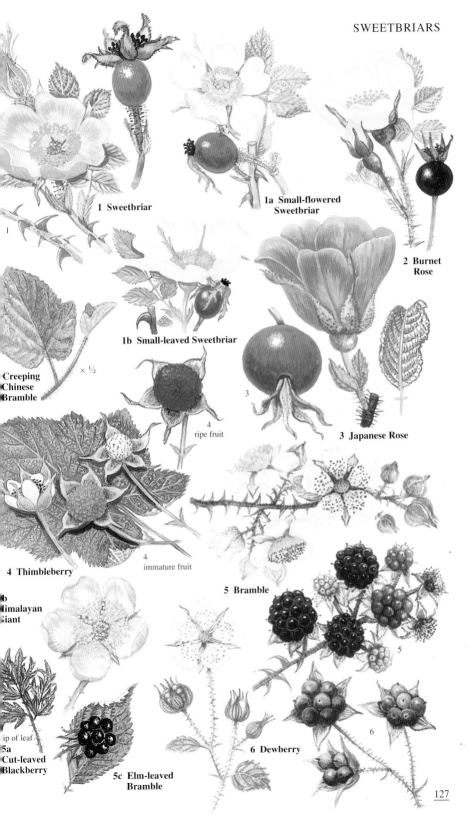

1 Sweetbriar

1a Small-flowered Sweetbriar

2 Burnet Rose

1b Small-leaved Sweetbriar

Creeping Chinese Bramble

× ½

4 ripe fruit

3 Japanese Rose

3

4 Thimbleberry

4 immature fruit

5 Bramble

5

b Himalayan Giant

tip of leaf

5a Cut-leaved Blackberry

5c Elm-leaved Bramble

6 Dewberry

6

127

1 Raspberry *Rubus idaeus*. The familiar garden fruit, but quite native; tall perennial, with little-branched, usually weakly prickly, *biennial* stems to 2m. Flowers *dull* white, 9-11mm, often drooping; May-August. Leaves trefoil, downy-white below. Fruits red, edible, easily coming off their base when ripe. Woods, scrub, heaths; also as an escape near gardens and allotments. **1a Loganberry** *R. loganobaccus* is an artificial hybrid (by Judge J.H. Logan in California in 1881) between Raspberry and the N American *R. vitifolius* that often escapes or is bird-sown. Its stems are pricklier and root at the tips; the fruit is longer and slightly purplish and comes away with part of its base when ripe.

1 S ■

2 Cloudberry *Rubus chamaemorus*. Our only native bramble with undivided leaves and orange fruits; short annual stems from creeping perennial rootstock, to 20cm. Flowers white, *solitary*, 20-30mm, male and female on different plants; June-July, a shy flowerer. Leaves rounded, *palmately lobed*, often solitary. Fruit edible, like a large raspberry, red, then *orange*. Damp heather moors and bogs on mountainsides.

2 O □

3 Stone Bramble *Rubus saxatilis*. Medium annual stems from creeping perennial rootstock, *weakly* or not prickled, to 40cm. Flowers *dull* white, 8-15mm, the narrow petals making green sepals conspicuous, in small clusters; June-August. Leaves *trefoil*, downy beneath, long-stalked. Fruits red. Woods, rocks, screes in hill districts, often on lime.

3 OZ □

4 False Salmonberry *Rubus spectabilis* is the most frequent, especially in N Ireland, of four naturalised *Rubus* with deep pink to red-purple flowers. Stems erect, biennial, weakly prickly to 2m. Flowers bright pink, 20-30mm; March-May, before the leaves. Leaves trefoil, hairless. Fruit orange. Wood edges, scrub, hedges; planted as game covert. The others are: **5 Purple-flowered Raspberry** *R. odoratus*, with hairs not prickles; flowers bright purple, June-August; leaves rounded, lobed; and fruit red; **6 Wineberry** *R. phoenicolasius*, with both reddish bristles and weak spines; flowers pink, May-July; leaves downy-white beneath and with reddish veins; and fruit red; and **7 White-stemmed Bramble** *R. cockburnianus*, with conspicuously white, erect and arching stems, to 5m; purple flowers, June; pinnate leaves; and blue-black fruit.

~

8 Meadowsweet *Filipendula ulmaria*. A tall hairless perennial, forming extensive stands, to 1m or more. Flowers *creamy*-white, fragrant, 4-8mm, with numerous stamens, in *foamy clusters*; June-Sept. Leaves pinnate, usually *silvery* beneath, the larger toothed leaflets interspersed with *small ones*. Fruits fused in a spiral. By fresh water, marshes, fens, damp woods. **8a Goatsbeard Spiraea** *Aruncus dioicus* is like an outsize Meadowsweet, to 2m, but with usually *white* flowers in spikes in larger, more open clusters and 2-3-pinnate leaves. Well established in two places in Scotland; usually planted elsewhere. Not to be confused with the much less frequent **Giant Meadowsweet** *F. kamtschatica*, with red, pink or white flowers and no smaller leaflets

8 SOZ □

9 Dropwort *Filipendula vulgaris*. The downland Meadowsweet (**8**), medium, to 50cm, differing from its larger waterside relative in its more open clusters of fewer. *larger* (8-16mm), unscented flowers (May-August), the usually six petals tinged pink on the back, and its darker green leaves, largely in a basal *rosette*, and with many small, crowded, finely cut leaflets. Fruit a group of downy nutlets. Chalk and limestone turf.

9 ·

tip of young stem

7 White-stemmed Bramble

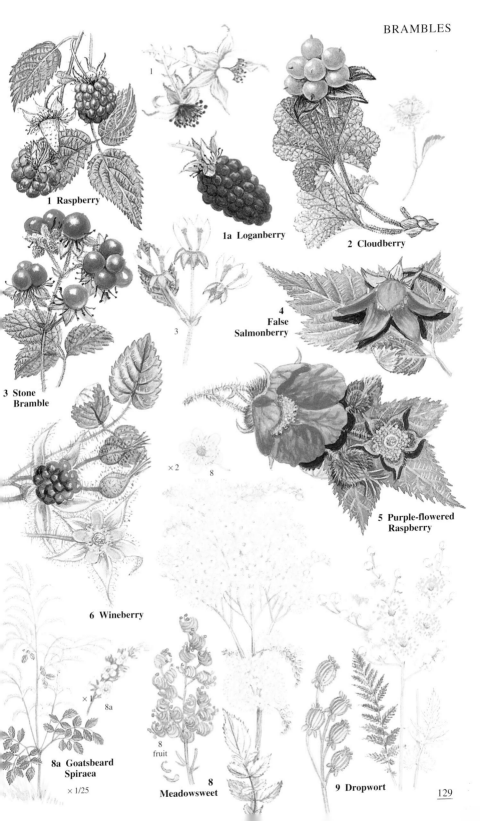

1 Raspberry

1a Loganberry

2 Cloudberry

3 Stone Bramble

3

4 False Salmonberry

5 Purple-flowered Raspberry

× 2

8

6 Wineberry

8a Goatsbeard Spiraea

× 1/25

× 1

8a

8 fruit

8 Meadowsweet

9 Dropwort

Cinquefoils *Potentilla*. Low/medium, usually downy, mostly herbaceous, with flowers open, yellow or white (purple in Marsh Cinquefoil, p. 132), 5-petalled, except in the Tormentil complex (below), leaves variously divided and fruit a head of dry nutlets (achenes). **Strawberries** *Fragaria* have 5-petalled white flowers, trefoil leaves and fleshy fruits, but *Duchesnea* has yellow flowers and dry fruits.

Flowers yellow, low/short

1 Silverweed *Potentilla anserina*. Our only common yellow flower with silvery pinnate leaves; a low/short silky prostrate perennial with long runners, to 80cm. Flowers yellow, 15-20mm, *solitary*, long-stalked, to 25cm; May-August. Leaves pinnate, with alternate large and small well-toothed leaflets, *silvery* on both sides, the underside only, or on neither side, apparently never on the upper side only. Damp bare and sparsely grassy places, waysides, dunes.

1   SOZ ■

The Tormentil Complex *Potentilla erecta/reptans/ × mixta/anglica*. All are prostrate perennials, with creeping stems, *rooting* at the stems in all but Tormentil and early-flowering Trailing Tormentil. Flowers *4-petalled*, almost always in Tormentil (smallest), usually in Trailing Tormentil, often in Hybrid Cinquefoil, never in Creeping Cinquefoil (largest). Leaves with three leaflets, usually in Tormentil, sometimes in the others; with four leaflets, sometimes in all; with five leaflets, usually in Creeping Cinquefoil, much less often in the others. Leaves almost *unstalked* in Tormentil, very short-stalked on upper stem in Trailing Tormentil, mediumly stalked on lower stem in Trailing Tormentil and in Hybrid Cinquefoil, and long-stalked in Creeping Cinquefoil.

2 Tormentil *Potentilla erecta*. A slender, prostrate to sprawling perennial, with threadlike stems that *do not root*, to 45cm. Flowers yellow, almost always *4-petalled*, 7-11mm; May-Sept. Leaves *usually with 3*, sometimes with 4-5 toothed leaflets, but often appearing 5-foliate due to the two large toothed leaflike stipules at their base; *almost unstalked*. Cf. Hybrid Cinquefoil (**4a**). Heaths, moors, grassland, scrub, bogs, mountainsides, usually on

2   SOZ ▢   acid, much less often on limy soils.

3 Trailing Tormentil *Potentilla anglica*. Intermediate between Tormentil (**2**) and Creeping Cinquefoil (**4**), but most likely to be confused with the more frequent triple hybrid *P. × mixta* (**4a**). Prostrate perennial, with runners rooting only in *late summer*, to 80cm. Flowers 14-18mm, 4-5-petalled; June-Sept. Leaves with 3-5 leaflets, distinguished from Tormentil by being *shortly* stalked on the upper stem and longer-stalked below. Heaths, woodland edges, banks.

4 Creeping Cinquefoil *Potentilla reptans*. A rather coarse, low perennial, with far-creeping, rooting runners to 1m. Flowers 17-25mm, solitary, on long slender stalks; June-Sept. Leaves *palmate*, with 3-5 toothed lanceolate leaflets; *long-stalked*. Bare and sparsely grassy places, waysides. **4a Hybrid Cinquefoil** *P. × mixta* is a triple hybrid between Creeping Cinquefoil and the two Tormentils (**2** and **3**). Flowers with 4-5 petals, leaves with 3-5 leaflets and leaf-stalks *medium throughout*. Fairly common and probably much overlooked

4   s   ▢   because so confusing. Rarely fruiting. More likely to be found in man-made bare and sparsely grassy places than Trailing Tormentil.

~

5 *Spring Cinquefoil *Potentilla neumanniana*. The earliest-flowering of our small yellow cinquefoils; a low creeping *undershrub*, to 10cm. Flowers yellow, *5-petalled*, 10-18mm, in small clusters; *March*-June. Leaves *dark* green, palmate, with *5-7 leaflets*, the

5   ▢↓   upper ones *trefoil and unstalked*. Dry, sometimes rocky grassland on limy soils in *lowlands*.

6 *Alpine Cinquefoil *Potentilla crantzii*. The mountain counterpart of Spring Cinquefoil (**5**), but can be taller, to 20cm, slenderer and more tufted, with larger (10-25mm), often orange-spotted flowers; June-July. Leaves usually with five, occasionally three leaflets. Rocky grassland and ledges on limy soils on *mountains*.

6   ▢   **7 Hoary Cinquefoil** *Potentilla argentea*. A short sprawling perennial, to 30cm. Flowers yellow, 10-12mm, in clusters; June-Sept. Leaves palmate, with 3-5 toothed leaflets, dark green above, *silvery-white* beneath. Sandy and heathy grassland.

~

8 Yellow-flowered Strawberry *Duchesnea indica*. Low creeping perennial, to 10cm. Flowers yellow, 5-petalled, solitary, 8-16mm; May-July. Leaves trefoil. Fruits reddish,

7   ▢↓   strawberry-like but dry and tasteless. Mainly near gardens.

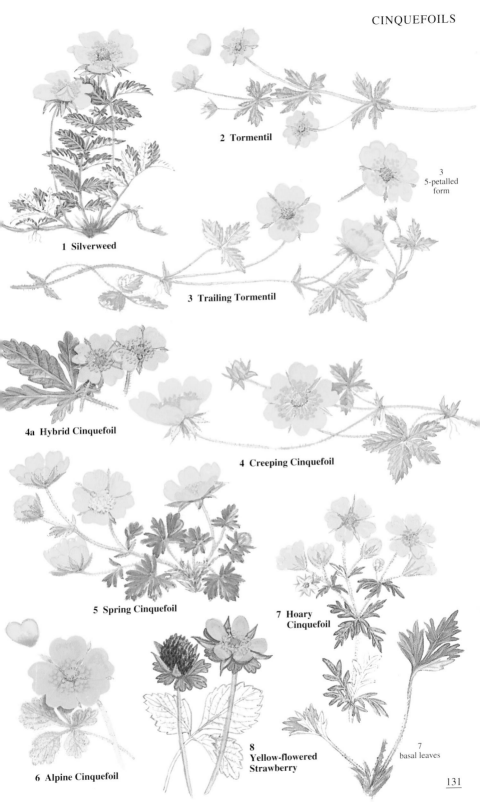

1 Silverweed

2 Tormentil

3
5-petalled
form

3 Trailing Tormentil

4a Hybrid Cinquefoil

4 Creeping Cinquefoil

5 Spring Cinquefoil

7 Hoary
Cinquefoil

6 Alpine Cinquefoil

8
Yellow-flowered
Strawberry

7
basal leaves

Flowers yellow, medium/tall

1 Sulphur Cinquefoil *Potentilla recta*. Medium hairy perennial, erect to 70cm. Flowers yellow, usually *pale*, petals *longer* than sepals, 15-25mm, in loose clusters; June-August. Leaves palmate, with 5-7 sharply toothed leaflets. Increasingly established in sparsely grassy places. Two similar locally established or casual cinquefoils, mainly of waste places: **1a Trefoil Cinquefoil**, *P. norvegica* is often annual and shorter, to 50cm, with much brighter yellow, smaller (10-15mm) flowers, petals equalling or shorter than sepals, and leaves always with three leaflets. **1b Russian Cinquefoil**, *P. intermedia* is like Trefoil Cinquefoil, but with slightly larger flowers, petals equalling or slightly longer than sepals and lower leaves with five leaflets.

2 **Shrubby Cinquefoil *Potentilla fruticosa*. A deciduous *bush*, to 1m. Flowers yellow, male and female usually on separate plants; May-Oct. Leaves grey-hairy, palmate, with 3-5 leaflets, paler beneath. Many garden varieties, some with orange flowers, but these rarely escape. Limestone rocks, usually by water, as at High Force in the Durham Pennines.

Flowers white

3 Barren Strawberry *Potentilla sterilis*. A low hairy perennial, to 15cm. Confusable with Wild Strawberry (**4**), but is smaller, with shorter and less erect stems, *gaps* between the slightly notched white petals; earlier-flowering (February-May); *spreading hairs* beneath the rather bluish-green, *matt*, less sharply veined trefoil leaves, which have the end tooth of the terminal leaflet shorter than its neighbours; and dry, quite *unstrawberry-like* fruits. Wood margins, scrub, dry hedge-and other banks.

4 Wild Strawberry *Fragaria vesca*. Easily recognisable in fruit as a diminutive Garden Strawberry (**5**); a low hairy perennial, with rooting runners; low/short, to 30cm. Flowers white, 12-18mm, with no gaps between the five *unnotched* petals; April-July. Leaves trefoil, *shiny green* above when fresh, paler beneath and silky with appressed hairs. The reddish strawberries have *pips protruding* and the sepals turned down. Cf. Barren Strawberry (**3**). Open woods and scrub, banks and other grassy places. The garden **4a Alpine Strawberry**, with no runners and fruiting until autumn, is a cultivar that may escape. **4b Hautbois Strawberry** *F. moschata* is larger, to 40cm, with flowers 20-25mm and leaves matt above when fresh; formerly cultivated, and surviving on a few banks and elsewhere.

5 Garden Strawberry *Fragaria* × *ananassa*. Larger in all its parts than Wild Strawberry (**4**), with numerous runners, flowers 20-35mm, flower-and fruit-stalks less erect, sepals erect in fruit and *pips sunk* into the surface of the strawberry. Waste ground, especially railway banks.

6 **Rock Cinquefoil *Potentilla rupestris*. Short/medium downy perennial, to 60cm. Flowers white, 16-28mm, often solitary; May-July. Leaves pinnate below, trefoil up stems, toothed. Limestone rocks, 4 sites only.

Flowers purple

7 Marsh Cinquefoil *Potentilla palustris*. A hairless short/medium perennial, to 50cm. Flowers strikingly unlike any other native flower, dull *dark purple*, 20-30mm, star-shaped, with *narrow pointed* petals, backed by much broader and paler purple pointed sepals, 20-30mm; May-July. Leaves grey-green, pinnate, with 3-7 toothed leaflets. *Very wet places*: marshes, fens, bogs and swamps.

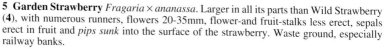

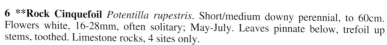

4a Alpine Strawberry

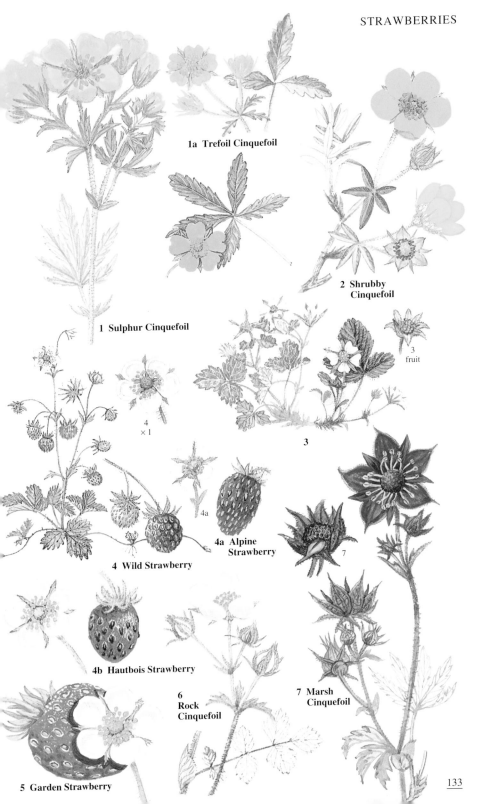

1a Trefoil Cinquefoil

2 Shrubby Cinquefoil

1 Sulphur Cinquefoil

3
fruit

4
× 1

3

4a

4a Alpine Strawberry

4 Wild Strawberry

7

4b Hautbois Strawberry

6
Rock
Cinquefoil

7 Marsh Cinquefoil

5 Garden Strawberry

1 Water Avens *Geum rivale*. A medium downy perennial, to 50cm. Flowers with five pale *pinkish-purple* notched rounded petals contrasting with the darker purple sepals *bell-shaped*, nodding, 10-18mm, the stalks purple; April-Sept. Lower leaves pinnate, stems leaves trefoil with small stipules at their base. Fruits hooked, in a bur-like head. Damp or wet, often shady places, in woods and marshes, by streams and on mountain ledges. The name avens appears to be of Anglo-Saxon origin. **1a Hybrid Geum** *G.* × *intermedium*, its hybrid with Herb Bennet (**2**), often found where the parents grow together, is generally intermediate between them, with the flowers pale yellow, the rounded petals scarcely notched, and their stalks purple and green.

2 Herb Bennet *Geum urbanum*. One of our commonest hedge-bank flowers, a hairy medium perennial, to 70cm. Flowers *yellow*, their stalks green, star-shaped, 8-15mm, with gaps between the five unnotched pointed petals, sepals soon down-turned, a bunch of kinked red styles and many stamens; May-Nov and through mild winters. Lower leaves pinnate, the end lobe *much the largest*, stem leaves 3-lobed. Fruits bronze-tipped, hooked, in a bur-like head. Bennet means blessed (*benedictus*) Woods, hedge-banks and other places in light shade.

3 Mountain Avens *Dryas octopetala*. One of the most beautiful 'alpines' of the rock garden, as well as a long-standing native since the end of the Ice Age. A low creeping undershrub, to 50cm. Flowers solitary, somewhat anemone-like, with 7-10, usually 8, *brilliant white* petals and a mass of golden-yellow stamens. Leaves oak-like, evergreen, dark green above, *downy white* beneath. Fruit a nutlet with a long feathery plume. A lime-lover, in short turf or on rock-ledges on mountains, but down to sea-level in the far North and the Burren, Co Clare.

4 Agrimony *Agrimonia eupatoria*. A softly hairy, sometimes slightly aromatic, medium/tall perennial, to 1m; the hairs on the stems and beneath the leaves *sparsely* interspersed with glands. Flowers yellow, in a spike, 5-petalled, star-shaped, 5-8mm; June-Sept. Leaves pinnate, the larger leaflets toothed and alternating with smaller ones. Fruit a small *obconical* (i.e. the cone pointing downwards) bur, deeply furrowed, hooked, the outer spines *spreading or erect* when ripe. Grassy places.

5 Fragrant Agrimony *Agrimonia procera*. Confusingly like Agrimony (**4**), but usually more robust, *more fragrant* because the glands are *more numerous* than the hairs, the stems leafier, leaves more deeply toothed and burs *bell-shaped* with the outer spines *down-turned*. Grassy places, often on wood margins on acid soils.

6 Bastard Agrimony *Aremonia agrimonioides*. A short sprawling perennial, to 30cm. Flowers yellow, 5-petalled, in *clusters*, 7-10mm or sometimes not opening; May-July. Leaves mostly *trefoil*. Fruit rounded, with no bristles. Locally naturalised, woods and shady road verges; a Scottish speciality.

7 Salad Burnet *Sanguisorba minor*. A short/medium perennial, smelling of cucumber when crushed; to 50cm or more. Flowers in *rounded* 10-20mm heads, tiny and green and easily overlooked except when displaying red styles in the upper half of the head and yellow anthers in the lower; May-August. Leaves greyish, pinnate, with up to 12 pairs of toothed leaflets. Fruits *ridged*. Dry grassland on limy soils. **7a Fodder Burnet** ssp. *muricata*, larger, with more deeply toothed leaves and fruits winged; sometimes sown for fodder or on road banks, and may persist.

8 Great Burnet *Sanguisorba officinalis*. Much taller than Salad Burnet (**7**), to 1.2m or more, not cucumber-scented, and has *dark red-purple* flowers, in *elongated* heads 10-30m deep, and with both stamens and styles in each flower; June-Sept; and up to seven pairs of larger, less deeply toothed leaflets. *Damp* grassland. **8a White Burnet** *S. canadensis* is still taller, to 2m, with elongated heads of white flowers; sometimes naturalised in marshes. A Scottish speciality, especially by the Lower Tay.

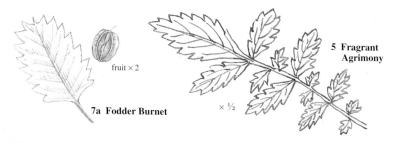

fruit × 2

5 Fragrant Agrimony

7a Fodder Burnet

× ½

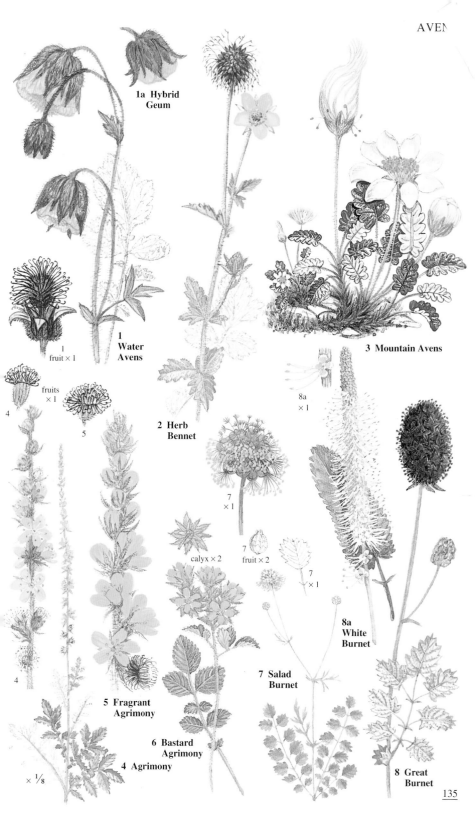

1a Hybrid
Geum

1
fruit × 1

1
Water
Avens

fruits
× 1

4

5

2 Herb
Bennet

3 Mountain Avens

8a
× 1

7
× 1

calyx × 2

7
fruit × 2

7
× 1

4

8a
White
Burnet

5 Fragrant
Agrimony

7 Salad
Burnet

6 Bastard
Agrimony

4 Agrimony

× ¹/₈

8 Great
Burnet

Lady's Mantles *Alchemilla*. Without *leaves* you will not be able to identify the 15 species in this notoriously difficult group. Fortunately, only five species are at all common. Mostly low/short pale green perennials, very variable in size, hairiness and leaf-shape. Flowers tiny, 2-3mm, petalless, with two rings of four green or yellow-green sepals, but coloured by the yellow anthers, in loose clusters; May-Sept. Leaves usually palmately lobed, toothed; the shape of the sinus between the two basal lobes is important. Fruit a dry nut. Grassy places. The five most frequent species, all with a broad sinus, are:

1 Southern Lady's Mantle *Alchemilla filicaulis* is densely hairy, but an uncommon species on hills in the North, where it can be very small, has the upper stem and flower clusters hairless; leaf-lobes usually nine, sinuses toothed to base and leaf-teeth pointed, incurved; often tinged *purple* at base of stems.

2 Hairless Lady's Mantle *Alchemilla glabra*. One of the larger species with down largely confined to the stems and the only lowland species to have *appressed hairs*; the gaps between the 7-9 leaf-lobes toothed to the base, and leaf-teeth pointed, incurved. Also on mountains.

3 Pale Lady's Mantle *Alchemilla xanthochlora*. The only common species with upper leaf surface hairless, except sometimes for a few hairs in the folds, and many *spreading* hairs elsewhere, the leaf-teeth sharply pointed and straight.

4 Alpine Lady's Mantle *Alchemilla alpina*. Leaves darker and greyer than other species, divided *to the base* into 5-9 narrow toothed lobes and covered beneath with silkily *silvery* appressed hairs. Mountains. **4a Silver Lady's Mantle** *A. conjuncta* with the leaf-lobes joined at the base is long naturalised in Glen Clova, Angus, and elsewhere; otherwise a garden escape.

5 Garden Lady's Mantle *Alchemilla mollis*. Much the largest of our species and an aggressively spreading garden escape. Medium, to 50cm or more, densely hairy and with leaves up to 14cm across; leaf-teeth pointed, slightly incurved. Two much smaller introduced species are: **5a Crimean Lady's Mantle** *A. tyttantha*, the stems and leaf-stalks with spreading and down-turned hairs, leaves with nine lobes, narrow sinus and dense spreading hairs. Scotland only, especially the Bowhill estate, Selkirk; and **5b Caucasian Lady's Mantle** *A. venosa* with appressed hairs on lower parts, upper parts almost hairless and more deeply lobed leaves with broad sinus; two localities in England.

The rest of our lady's mantles are localised, in two groups: Highlands/N Pennines; and Upper Teesdale/Yorkshire Pennines.

The Highlands/N Pennines Group includes **6** *Alchemilla wichurae*, rather small and hairless except for appressed hairs on the leaf-stalks and short spreading hairs on the veins beneath the leaves, 7-11 lobes, sinus narrow and leaf-teeth incurved; **6a** *A. glomerulans* with semi-appressed hairs on stems, leaf-stalks and leaves, lobes 7-11, sinus broad, and leaf-teeth slightly incurved; **6b** *A. glaucescens*, small and densely hairy, with 7-9 lobes, sinus almost closed, blunt leaf-teeth and stem bases *brownish*; and **6c** *A. micans*, medium, with hairs both spreading and semi-appressed, leaf-lobes 9, sinus narrow and leaf-teeth sharply pointed and unequal; S Northumberland only.

The Upper Teesdale/Yorkshire Pennines Group includes **7** *Alchemilla acutiloba*, a large plant with leaf-stalks and lower stems densely hairy and leaves downy beneath and sparsely so or hairless above, 9-11 lobes, sinus broad and leaf-teeth sharp, straight; **7a** *A. monticola*, medium, hairy except on parts of the flower cluster, with 9-11 leaf-lobes, sinus closed and leaf-teeth sharply pointed and slightly incurved; **7b** *A. subcrenata*, hairy, often with down-turned hairs on lower stems and leaf-stalks, leaves downy, especially beneath, lobes 9-11, sinus narrow and leaf-teeth blunt; and **7c** *A. minima*, our smallest species, perhaps only a variety of Southern Lady's Mantle (**1**), with almost whole plant downy, but leaf-lobes only five and sinus not toothed to base; an early-flowerer. **7**, the most frequent, **7a** and **7b** in Upper Teesdale, **7c** in two localities in Yorkshire.

1 oz ·

2 oz □

3 □

4 z ·

5 z □↑

6 ·

6a ·

6b ·

7 ·   7a ·↓   7b ·   7c ·

×2

×2

×2

4
×4

2 Hairless Lady's Mantle

1 Southern Lady's Mantle

3 Pale Lady's Mantle

4 Alpine Lady's Mantle

5 Garden Lady's Mantle

5a Crimean Lady's Mantle

5b Caucasian Lady's Mantle

4a Silver Lady's Mantle

6 *Alchemilla wichurae*

6a *Alchemilla glomerulans*

6b *Alchemilla glaucescens*

6c *Alchemilla micans*

7 *Alchemilla acutiloba*

7a *Alchemilla monticola*

7b *Alchemilla subcrenata*

7c *Alchemilla minima*

1 Parsley Piert *Aphanes arvensis*. An inconspicuous, usually prostrate, greyish downy little annual, to 10cm. Flowers minute, 1-2mm, petalless, with two rings of four joined green sepals, in tight clusters up the stem; April-Sept. Leaves 3-lobed, short-stalked, with three deeply toothed lobes, above prominent toothed leaflike stipules. Fruit with a distinct constriction where it joins the *erect* sepals, which *equal* the tip of the stipules. Arable and other dry bare ground, *usually* on lime. **1a Slender Parsley Piert** *A. australis* is slenderer, but otherwise extremely similar, except for the fruits, which lack the constriction and are shorter than the stipule-tips. Habitat similar, but *avoiding* lime.

2 Mountain Sibbaldia *Sibbaldia procumbens*. A low prostrate tufted perennial, to 10cm. Flowers pale yellow, with five or no petals, 4-5mm, in *tight leafy heads*; July-August. Leaves trefoil, each leaflet 3-toothed. High bare *mountains*, often where snow lies in winter, scarcely below 600m.

Pirri-pirri-burs *Acaena*. Creeping, mat-forming perennials, woody at the base, with flowers in distinctive *globular* heads, recalling Salad Burnet (p. 134), petalless but with four greenish-white sepals; June-July. Leaves pinnate with toothed leaflets. In fruit the heads develop long *red spines*, soft at first but later barbed at base. Four species are naturalised on bare or sparsely vegetated ground.

The two most frequent have bright green glossy leaves, the end leaflet oval: **3 Pirri-pirri-bur** *Acaena novae-zelandiae* with smooth leaves and four spines per flower, well known on Kelling Heath, N Norfolk; and **3a Two-spined Acaena** *A. ovalifolia* with finely wrinkled leaves and two spines per flower. The two less frequent have matt leaves tinged brown, the end leaflet rounded: **3b Bronze Pirri-pirri-bur** *A. anserinifolia* with markedly bronzed leaves, well established at St Fillans on L. Earn and elsewhere, and **3c Spineless Acaena** *A. inermis* with glaucous, slightly bronzed, sometimes orange-tinged leaves and often no barbs or even spines.

PURSLANE FAMILY Portulacaceae

4 Spring Beauty *Claytonia perfoliata*. Low/short pale green introduced annual, to 30cm. Flowers white, 4-6mm, the five petals sometimes slightly notched; April-July; unmistakable in their stalked cluster immediately above a pair of fused leaves. Root leaves pointed oval, long-stalked. Disturbed ground on sandy soils.

5 Pink Purslane *Claytonia sibirica*. Low/short, rather fleshy introduced annual, to 40cm. Flowers pink or white, 16-20mm, the five petals well notched; April-July; in a stalked cluster above an opposite, but not joined, pair of leaves. Root leaves pointed oval, long-stalked. Damp shady places.

6 Purslane *Portulaca oleracea*. Erect or sprawling, slightly succulent introduced annual, to 50cm. Flowers yellow, 5-petalled, 1-3 at base of opposite spoon-shaped leaves. Disturbed ground. Established in Scilly, otherwise casual.

7 Blinks *Montia fontana*. A low, very variable, 1-20cm, gregarious annual/ perennial, usually prostrate on mud, but may be erect or floating, or even form a cushion; stems sometimes reddish. Flowers tiny, white, 5-petalled, in clusters of 1-3 on short stalks towards tip of stem; April-Oct. Leaves small, narrow oval, opposite. Bare places, usually wet, sometimes only seasonally damp; avoiding lime.

3c Spineless Acaena

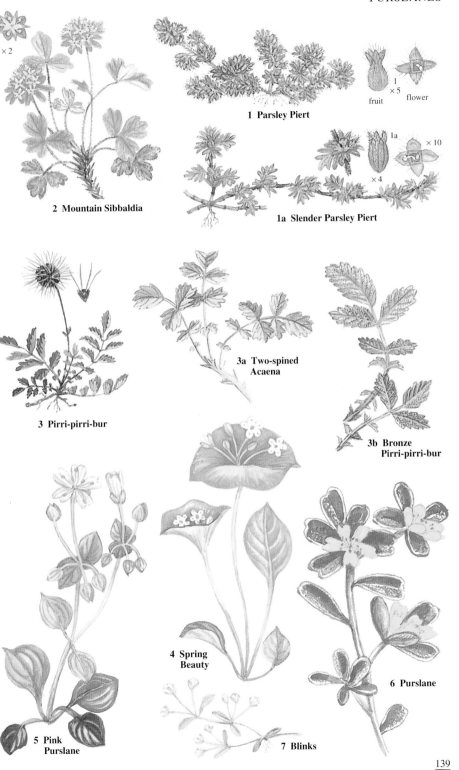

× 2

1 Parsley Piert

1
× 5
fruit   flower

2 Mountain Sibbaldia

1a
× 10

× 4

1a Slender Parsley Piert

3a Two-spined
Acaena

3 Pirri-pirri-bur

3b Bronze
Pirri-pirri-bur

4 Spring
Beauty

6 Purslane

5 Pink
Purslane

7 Blinks

Pea Family Fabaceae

Distinctive for its 5-petalled flower-shape: the broad and often erect *standard* at the top, the two narrower *wings* at the sides, and the two lowest joined as the *keel*, which hides the stamens and styles. Flowers usually in heads, the unique shape not being immediately apparent when the flowers are small and in a tight head, as with some of the clovers (p. 150). Leaves alternate and usually either pinnate (with or without a terminal leaflet) or trefoil. Fruit a pod (legume), usually long and resembling a cultivated pea or bean – **1 Garden Pea** *Pisum sativum* with white to purple flowers is a frequent relic of cultivation.

1. Flowers in loose heads or short spikes: (below)
   - 1a. Leaves with many leaflet pairs, ending with a leaflet (below)
   - 1b. Leaves with many leaflet pairs, ending with a tendril (p. 142)
   - 1c. Leaves with many leaflet pairs, ending with neither leaflet nor tendril (p. 144)
   - 1d. Leaves with 3-5 leaflets (p. 146)
   - 1e. Leaves with 1-2 leaflet pairs (p. 148)
   - 1f. Leaves undivided (p. 148)

2. Flowers in tight heads: (p. 148)
   - 2a. Yellow (p. 150)
   - 2b. Pink or pink-purple (p. 150)
   - 2c. White (p. 152)

3. Flowers in long spikes: (p. 154)

4. Flowers solitary or paired: (p. 158)

~

1a. Flowers in loose heads or short spikes: Leaves with many leaflet pairs ending with a leaflet

Flowers	white:	Crown Vetch
	pink:	Birdsfoot, Crown Vetch
	yellow:	Yellow Oxytropis, Kidney Vetch, Birdsfoot (yellowish-white), Orange Birdsfoot (orange-yellow), Horseshoe Vetch
	greenish-cream:	Wild Liquorice
	lilac:	Alpine Milk-vetch, Crown Vetch
	purple:	Purple Milk-vetch, Purple Oxytropis, Crown Vetch, Common Vetch, Spring Vetch

2 Purple Milk-vetch *Astragalus danicus*. Low/short downy perennial, to 30cm. Flowers bright *violet*, 15-18mm, more or less erect, with a blunt keel and joined sepals; May-July. Leaves pinnate with a terminal leaflet. Pods with spreading *white hairs*, short, 7-9mm. Short limy turf, including dunes and mountains.

3 **Alpine Milk-vetch *Astragalus alpinus*. Differs from Purple Milk-vetch (**2**) in having *pale lilac*, purple-tipped flowers, often turned down, with free sepals, June-July; and pods with appressed *brownish* hairs. Mountains, four localities only.

4 Wild Liquorice *Astragalus glycyphyllos*. Tall straggling perennial, to 1m or more; stems *zigzag*. Flowers *greenish-cream*, 11-15mm, in open heads or short stalked spikes; June-August. Pods stout, curved, to 40cm. Grassland, scrub, open woods, often on lime. The plant from which liquorice used to be made at Pontefract, W. Yorks, was *Glycyrrhiza glabra* from SE Europe.

5 **Purple Oxytropis *Oxytropis halleri*. Not unlike the much commoner Purple Milk-Vetch (**2**), but has a *sharply pointed* tip to the keel of the soon-fading rosy-purple flowers, 15-20mm, May-June, and very *silky* leaves. Pods 15-20mm. Rocky coastal and mountain grassland, dunes.

6 **Yellow Oxytropis *Oxytropis campestris*. Almost identical with Purple Oxytropis (**5**), except for its *yellow*, often purple-tinged flowers, and pods being only partially instead of fully divided into two cavities. Coastal and mountain rock ledges in six places.

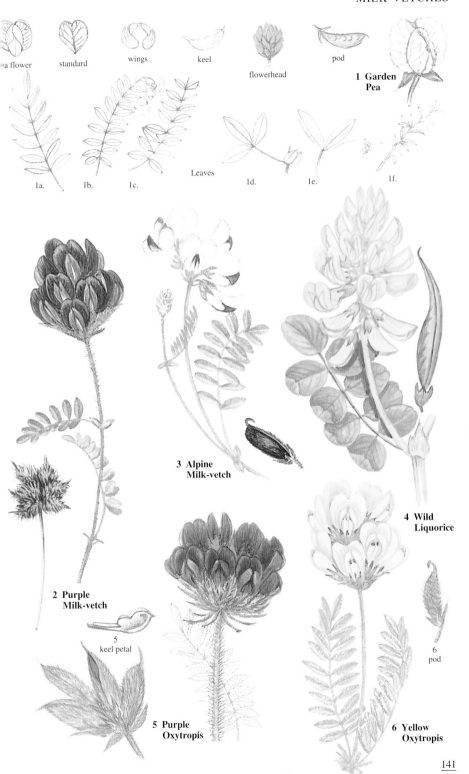

a flower standard wings keel

flowerhead pod

1 Garden Pea

1a. 1b. 1c. Leaves 1d. 1e. 1f.

3 Alpine Milk-vetch

4 Wild Liquorice

2 Purple Milk-vetch

5 keel petal

5 Purple Oxytropis

6 Yellow Oxytropis

6 pod

1 Kidney Vetch *Anthyllis vulnereria*. A very variable (four or five subspecies), silky, often greyish perennial, sprawling/medium, to 60cm. Flowers pale to deep yellow, orange or a fiery red, 12-15mm, with *downy-white* joined sepals and conspicuously *leafy palmate bracts*; May-Sept. Leaves undivided at the base, pinnate above, often rather fleshy. Pods roundish, 2-4mm, hairless. Dry, rather open, often limy grassland, often on sea cliffs, also mountain ledges.

2 Birdsfoot *Ornithopus perpusillus*. Slender downy prostrate/sprawling annual, to 30cm. Flowers with standard pale *pink* with darker streaks, and *whitish* wings and *yellow* keel, 3-5mm, in heads of 3-8, with a pinnate bract at their base; May-August. Leaves with many leaflets. Pods *beaded*, curved, so that 2-3 together look like a bird's foot. Dry, sandy or gravelly places, avoiding lime.

3 ***Orange Birdsfoot *Ornithopus pinnatus*. Differs from Birdsfoot (**2**) especially in its flowers being *orange-yellow* veined with red, usually only 1-2 in a head, with no or only a tiny bract, many fewer leaflets and much less beaded pods. Short turf in Scilly.

4 Horseshoe Vetch *Hippocrepis comosa*. Superficially like Birdsfoot Trefoil (p. 146), but apart from its mats of quite different *multi-pinnate* leaves, is usually shorter, with smaller (5-10mm), harder yellow flowers (May-July), often veined but never suffused red, the joined sepals blackish-green, and slender wavy pods with *curved joints*, supposedly like horseshoes joined together. *Confined* to short chalk and limestone turf, including cliff-tops.

5 Crown Vetch *Securigera varia*. A hairless perennial, straggling to 1m. Flowers *parti-coloured*, purple, lilac, pink and white, 8-15mm, on stalks longer than the leaves; June-August. Leaves with 11-25 leaflets, differing from all true vetches (below) in having no tendril. Pods slender, beaded, *4-angled*, ending in a whisker. Naturalised in grassy and waste places.

1b. Flowers in loose heads or short spikes: Leaves with many leaflet pairs ending with a tendril

Vetches *Vicia*. The true vetches use their usually branched tendrils (except Upright Vetch. p. 144) to climb or scramble over other plants. Flowers in heads or (Tufted/Fine-leaved/Fodder/Wood Vetches, p. 154) spikes, usually on stalks at the base of the leaves. Pods long, more or less flattened. They differ from peas and vetchlings *Lathyrus* (pp. 144, 148) in not having winged or angled stems and (except Bithynian Vetch, p. 148) having more leaflets.

6 Common Vetch *Vicia sativa*. A very variable sprawling or scrambling annual. Flowers *purple*, with standard *much paler* than wings, solitary or paired, 10-25mm; May-Sept. Leaves with 3-8 pairs of leaflets, the upper slightly narrower, and tendrils *branched*. Pods smooth, hairless, usually black or brown, 28-70mm. Grassy and waste places. Three marked subspecies: *segetalis*, the commonest, to 1m, as above; **6a** ssp. *nigra*, to 75cm, with flowers *uniformly coloured*, 14-19mm, upper leaflets *much narrower* and pods smaller (23-38mm); and the now quite rare cultivation relic ssp. *sativa*, as above, but stouter, to 1.5m, with beaded, often downy, brown to yellowish-brown pods.

7 Spring Vetch *Vicia lathyroides*. Can be confused with the much commoner ssp. *nigra* of Common Vetch (**6a**), with which it often grows, but is shorter, to 20cm, with flowers dull purple, turning *bluish* as they fade, solitary and smaller (5-9mm), leaves with only 2-4 pairs of leaflets, tendrils *unbranched* or none, and pods smaller (15-30mm). Sandy turf on heaths and by the sea.

8 Bush Vetch *Vicia sepium*. A medium scrambling perennial, to 60cm. Flowers *dull purple*, fading bluish and bluer in the N, 12-15mm, 2-6 in the head, on short stalks; April-Nov. Leaves with 5-8 pairs of leaflets and tendrils branched or not. Pods 20-35mm, hairless. *black* when ripe. Hedges, scrub, woodland edges, grassy places, rarely on dunes.

6a ssp. *nigra*

1
colour forms

1 Kidney Vetch

2 Birdsfoot

3 Orange Birdsfoot ×3

5 Crown Vetch

4 Horseshoe Vetch

6 Common Vetch

7 Spring Vetch

8 Bush Vetch

1 Hairy Tare *Vicia hirsuta*. A medium scrambling annual, to 80cm. Flowers pale to bluish lilac, *small* (3-5mm), sepal-teeth all more or less *equal*, 2-7 in a long-stalked *spike-like* head; May-August. Leaves with 6-8 pairs of usually alternate narrow leaflets and branched tendrils. Pods black, *downy*, 6-11mm. Rough grassy places.

2 Smooth Tare *Vicia tetrasperma*. A medium clambering annual, to 60cm. Flowers *larger* (4-8mm) and clearer lilac than Hairy Tare (**1**), *1-2* in the head, with the 2 upper sepal-teeth *shorter* than the rest. Leaves with fewer (3-6) pairs of longer leaflets, with unbranched tendrils. Pods brown, *hairless*, 12-16mm. Rough grassy places.

3 Slender Tare *Vicia parviflora*. Differs from more frequent Smooth Tare (**2**) especially in its flowers being bluer, *larger still* (6-9mm) and 1-4 in the head; June-August. Leaves with 2-4 pairs of *markedly longer* leaflets. Pods and habitat similar.

4 *Yellow Vetch *Vicia lutea*. The only native peaflower with both solitary yellow flowers and tendrils, a *sprawling* grey-green annual, to 60m. Flowers pinkish-white turning *dirty yellow*, 15-25mm, 1-3 at base of leaves; June-Sept. Leaves with 3-8 leaflet pairs. Pods black or yellowish-brown, usually hairy, 20-40mm. Coastal shingle and cliff-tops, waste ground inland. **4a Hungarian Vetch** *V. pannonica* is a *climber* with 2-4, often browner flowers, leaflets up to 19 pairs and pods never black. A frequent casual, naturalised in W Kent.

5 *Sea Pea *Lathyrus japonicus*. Prostrate mat-forming fleshy *bluish-green* perennial, with unwinged stems to 90cm. Flowers purple turning blue, 15-25mm, 2-10 in a short-stalked short spike; June-August. Leaves with 2-5 oval leaflet pairs, tendrils branched or not. Pods brown, 30-50mm, said to have once saved Suffolk villagers from famine. *Coastal* shingle and, less often, sand.

6 *Marsh Pea *Lathyrus palustris*. Slender medium/tall climbing perennial, with *winged* stems to 1. 2m. Flowers blue-purple, 12-20mm, 2-6 in a long-stalked short spike; June-July. Leaves with 2-3 narrow leaflet pairs, the tendrils branched. Pods brown, 25-60mm. *Fens* and other tall damp grassland.

1c. Flowers in loose heads or short spikes: Leaves with many leaflet pairs with neither end leaflet nor tendril

Spring Vetch *Vicia lathyroides*, p. 142.

7 Upright Vetch *Vicia orobus*. The only true vetch with its leaves ending in a *tiny point* instead of tendrils; a medium erect perennial, to 60cm. Flowers *white*, but with *purple veins* making them look lilac, 12-15mm, 6-20 to the head; May-Sept. Leaves with 6-15 leaflet pairs and half-arrowlike stipules. Pods yellow-brown, 20-30mm. Rocky woods and scrub, heathy grassland. (We use the old name Upright Vetch instead of the modern Wood Bitter-vetch, to avoid confusion with Bitter Vetchling (**8**), which is actually a pea with winged stems and may grow in woods, and equally confusingly was formerly called Tuberous Pea.)

8 Bitter Vetchling *Lathyrus linifolius*. Medium erect perennial, to 40cm. Flowers red-purple, fading bluish, joined sepals dark blue-green, 10-16mm, 2-6 in the long-stalked head; April-July, the earliest pea/vetch to flower. Leaves with 2-4 pairs of narrow leaflets, the tendril replaced by a point. Pods red-brown, 25-45mm. Heaths, scrub, wood-margins, on acid soils. The current official name, Bitter Vetch, is confusing, since, having winged stems, it is not a Vetch, and its old name Tuberous Pea has been assigned to the Fyfield Pea (p. 148). Cf. Upright Vetch, (**7**).

The familiar white-flowered **Broad Bean** *Vicia faba* is a frequent relic of cultivation.

5

5
back of
leaf

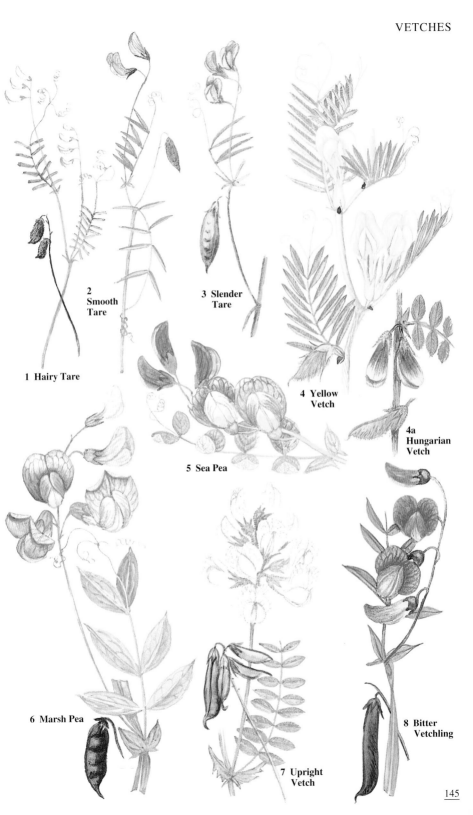

2 Smooth Tare

3 Slender Tare

1 Hairy Tare

4 Yellow Vetch

4a Hungarian Vetch

5 Sea Pea

6 Marsh Pea

7 Upright Vetch

8 Bitter Vetchling

Birdsfoot Trefoils *Lotus*. Flowers yellow. Leaves with five leaflets, but the lower pair either bent back or looking like stipules on the stem, so making the leaf appear *trefoil*. Pods in a head supposedly like a bird's foot.

1 Birdsfoot Trefoil *Lotus corniculatus*. One of our commonest and most attractive yellow peaflowers, prostrate or short/medium, to 50mm. Flowers deep yellow or *orange*, often partly red, 2-7 in the head, 10-16mm; May-Sept. Pods to 30mm. *Dry* grassland (on motorway verges a large alien form is often sown). Aka Common Birdsfoot Trefoil; (folk names, Eggs and Bacon, Tom Thumb).

2 Greater Birdsfoot Trefoil *Lotus pedunculatus*. Larger, more luxuriant and darker green than Birdsfoot Trefoil (**1**); stems medium, stouter and hollow, to 1m. Flowers a distinctive rich dull yellow, *5-12 in the head*, with the sepal-teeth spreading in bud and the two upper at an acute angle; June-August. Leaves bluish-green. Pods 15-35mm. *Damp* grassy places, marshes, woodland rides.

3 Narrow-leaved Birdsfoot Trefoil *Lotus glaber*. Taller, to 90cm, slenderer, wirier, erecter, more branched and forming larger tufts than Birdsfoot Trefoil (**1**). Flowers of a more *lemony* yellow, *fewer* (2-4) to the head and smaller (6-12mm), with the rear sepal-teeth converging; June-August. Winter leaves similar but summer ones *much narrower*. Much less common; dry grassy places, often on heavier soils and near the sea.

4 *Hairy Birdsfoot Trefoil *Lotus subbiflorus*. A small, *shaggy* prostrate or sprawling annual, to 30cm Flowers *orange-yellow*, 5-10mm, 2-4 in the head; June-Sept; on stalks much *longer* than the leaves. Pods 6-12mm. Dry grassland near the coast, but sometimes a bulbfield weed, when can be much lusher and grow to 80cm.

5 **Slender Birdsfoot Trefoil *Lotus angustissimus*. Like Hairy Birdsfoot Trefoil (**4**), with which it may grow, but downy rather than hairy, and with yellower flowers, only *1-2 in a head*, on stalks usually *shorter* than the leaves and *much longer* (12-30mm), slenderer pods. Dry grassland near the coast.

~

6 Lucerne *Medicago sativa* ssp. *sativa*. Medium perennial, to 90cm. Flowers various shades of *violet or red-purple*, 5-12mm, in short spikes; June-Oct. Leaves trefoil. Pods coiled, 8-11mm. Its hybrid, **6a**, with Sickle Medick (**7**) produces a remarkable range of colours, including purples, yellows, greens, livid grey, and the only black flower in our flora; pods curved to coiled. Grassy and waste places; formerly cultivated for fodder.

7 Sickle Medick *Medicago sativa* ssp. *falcata*. Very like Lucerne (**6**), except that its flowers are *yellow* and its pods slightly to markedly curved. Habitat similar; especially in the E Anglian Breckland.

8 Spotted Medick *Medicago arabica*. Prostrate to sprawling annual, downy only when young, to 60cm. Flowers, bright yellow, 4-6mm, 1-5 together; April-Sept. Leaves larger than other Medicks, each usually with a *dark blotch*; stipules toothed. Pods coiled, hairless, spiny, *faintly* netted. Grassy and waste places, especially on sand and near the sea.

9 *Toothed Medick *Medicago polymorpha*. Like a Spotted Medick (**8**) with *unspotted*, leaves, but has smaller flowers (3-5mm), 1-8 in a head, May-Sept, more *deeply toothed* stipules, and pods more strongly netted. Native in bare sandy and gravelly places near the sea, but often inland as a casual on rubbish tips and waste ground.

10 *Bur Medick *Medicago minima*. Smaller than **8** and **9**, *thickly downy* usually more or less prostrate, to 20cm. Flowers yellow, 2-5mm, 1-6 to the head, May-July. Leaves with stipules usually *untoothed*. Pods often slightly downy, coiled, usually with thin spines. Native on sandy heaths, dunes and shingle near the sea, also in the E Anglian Breckland; elsewhere usually a casual.

Slender Trefoil *Trifolium micranthum*, p. 150.

Birdsfoot Clover *Trifolium ornithopodioides*, p. 158.

Burrowing Clover *Trifolium subterraneum*, p. 154.

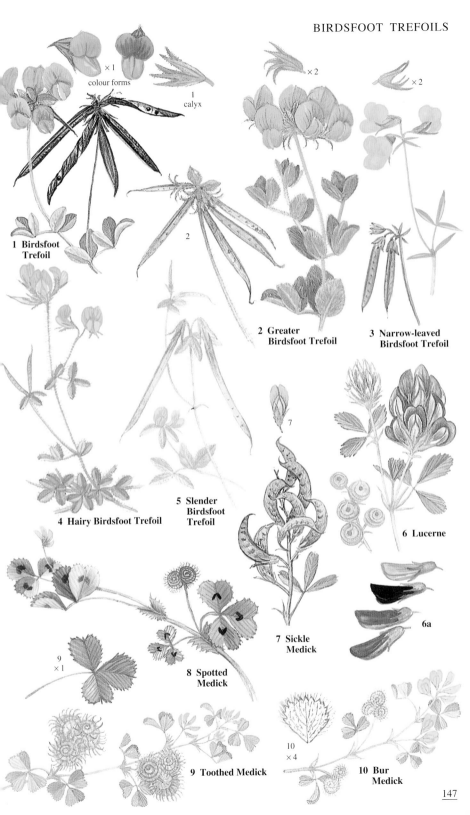

×1

colour forms

×2

×2

1
calyx

1 Birdsfoot Trefoil

2

2 Greater Birdsfoot Trefoil

3 Narrow-leaved Birdsfoot Trefoil

7

4 Hairy Birdsfoot Trefoil

5 Slender Birdsfoot Trefoil

6 Lucerne

6a

7 Sickle Medick

9
×1

8 Spotted Medick

10
×4

9 Toothed Medick

10 Bur Medick

1 Meadow Vetchling *Lathyrus pratensis*. Far the commonest tendrilled yellow peaflower, a short/tall scrambling perennial, stems angled, to 1. 5m, but often quite short. Flowers *yellow*, 10-18mm, 5-12 to the short spike-like head, long-stalked; May-August. Leaves with 1 pair of narrow lanceolate leaflets, with arrow-shaped stipules and tendrils branched or not. Pods black, 25-35mm. Grassy places.

2 *Bithynian Vetch *Vicia bithynica*. A medium scrambling annual, to 60cm, pea-like, but with unwinged stalks. Flowers *particoloured*, the purple standard often hiding the mostly creamy wings and keel, 16-20mm, *solitary or paired*, long-stalked; May-June. Leaves with 1-2 pairs of *broad lanceolate* leaflets. Pods brown or yellowish, hairy, abruptly beaked, 25-50mm. Scrub, hedges, grassy places, mostly near the coast. Bithynia is in NW Turkey.

Smooth Tare *Vicia tetrasperma*, and **Slender Tare** *Vicia parviflora*, p. 144.

Yellow Vetch *Vicia lutea,* and **Hungarian Vetch** *Vicia pannonica*, p. 144.

3 Broad-leaved Everlasting Pea *Lathyrus latifolius*. A tall or sprawling, aggressively far-scrambling perennial, stems broadly winged, to 3m. Flowers *bright magenta-pink*, 15-30mm, 3-12 in a well stalked short spike; June-August. Leaves with one pair of broadly elliptical leaflets, with branched tendrils. Pods brown, 50-100mm. Frequently established on railway banks and other waste ground, especially around London. **Two-flowered Everlasting Pea** *L. grandiflorus*, with unwinged stems and 1-4, often larger (25-35mm) flowers, is a less frequent escape. *L. heterophyllus* is established on dunes in N Norfolk.

4 Narrow-leaved Everlasting Pea *Lathyrus sylvestris*. Differs from its Broad-leaved relative (**3**) in being less tall, to 2m, with slightly smaller (12-20mm), *yellowish-or greenish-pink* flowers, the wings *tipped violet*, narrower leaflets and shorter (40-70mm) pods. Native in wood-margins, scrub and hedges.

5 Fyfield Pea *Lathyrus tuberosus*. Medium/tall scrambling perennial, stems angled, to 1-2m. Flowers *bright red-purple*, surprisingly large (12-20mm), 2-7 in the short spikelike head, slightly fragrant; June-August. Leaves with one pair of *oval* leaflets and a tendril. Pods brown, 20-40mm. Aka Tuberous Pea. Formerly grown for its edible tubers, now naturalised in grassy places, perhaps still at Fyfield, Essex, where first found wild in 1859.

Sea Pea *Lathyrus japonicus,* and **Marsh Pea** *Lathyrus palustris,* p. 144.

Petty Whin *Genista anglica*, and **Hairy Greenweed** *Genista pilosa*, p. 158.

6 Black Medick *Medicago lupulina*. The commonest of the small yellow medicks (p. 146). Sprawling to erect low/short annual or short-lived perennial, to 60cm. Flowers *bright* yellow, 10-50 to a 3-6mm head, the joined sepals *downy*; April-Oct. Leaves *downy*, the leaflets minutely toothed. Pods coiled, netted and *black* when ripe. Differs from Lesser and Hop Trefoils (p. 150) especially in the leaves ending in a *minute point* and the coiled black ripe fruits not being covered by the dead flowers. Barish grassy and waste places.

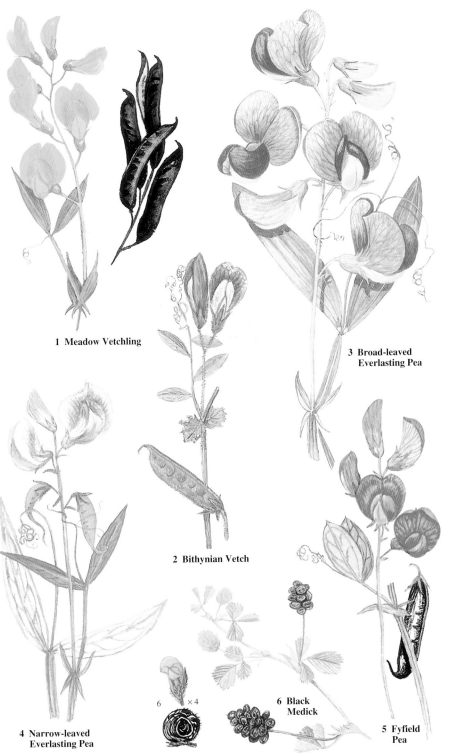

1 Meadow Vetchling

3 Broad-leaved
Everlasting Pea

2 Bithynian Vetch

6 Black
Medick

6 ×4

4 Narrow-leaved
Everlasting Pea

5 Fyfield
Pea

Clovers and **Trefoils** *Trifolium*. A large group, whose small, often tiny, flowers are in usually tight heads, the wings always longer than the keel, with trefoil leaves and straight pods, often covered by the dead flowers. Several of the smaller, more or less prostrate species grow in short sandy turf near the sea in the SE. They include, with pink flowers: Knotted and Clustered Clovers; with white flowers: Rough, Suffocated and Burrowing Clovers; and with both, Birdsfoot Clover.

2a. Flowers small, in tight heads: Flowers yellow

1 Lesser Trefoil *Trifolium dubium*. Low, almost hairless, erect to sprawling annual, sometimes turning purplish, to 25cm. Flowers dull yellow, 3-4mm, short-stalked, 10-20 in the head, the joined sepals hairless; May-Sept. Leaves with the leaflets *notched*, the middle leaflet with the longest stalk. Pods egg-shaped with a short hooked beak, drooping when ripe, covered by the dead flowers. Cf. Black Medick (p. 148). Dry grassland, rock outcrops and other bare ground.

2 Hop Trefoil *Trifolium campestre*. Short, slightly downy annual, to 30cm. Flowers *pale* yellow, 4-7mm, 20-30 in a *globular* 10-15mm head; May-Sept. Leaves like Lesser Trefoil (**1**), but larger. Pods similarly covered by pale brown dead flowers. Dry grassland, especially on lime. **2a Large Trefoil** *T. aureum* has slightly larger *golden* yellow flowers, *July-August*, and all leaflets with equal stalks. Naturalised in grassy and bare places, decreasing.

3 Slender Trefoil *Trifolium micranthum*. Low sprawling to erect annual, to 15cm. Flowers darker yellow than Lesser Trefoil (**1**), also smaller (2-3mm) and longer-stalked, with *fewer* (2-6) in the smaller, *more open*, (3-5mm), longer-stalked head, May-August. Leaves smaller, with all leaflet-stalks *equal*. Pods smaller. Dry turf on light soils.

4 Sulphur Clover *Trifolium ochroleucon*. The only larger clover with yellow flowers, except for the Lizard speciality Long-headed Clover (p. 156). Downy short/medium patch-forming perennial, to 50cm. Flowers like a lemony-yellow Red Clover (**5**), 15-20mm in a narrower ovoid head; June-July. Distinguished from occasional white Red Clovers by narrower leaflets without pale markings. Pods egg-shaped. Grassland, road verges, especially on clay.

Long-headed Clover *Trifolium incarnatum* ssp. *molinerii*, p. 152.

2b. Flowers small, in tight heads: Flowers pink or pink-purple

5 Red Clover *Trifolium pratense*. Much the commonest pink or pink-purple clover, a usually erect short/medium perennial, stems solid, to 60cm. Flowers pink-purple, never red, 12-15mm, in egg-shaped, very *short-or unstalked* 20-40mm heads; May-Nov. Leaves stalked below, unstalked above; leaflets toothed, often with a whitish crescent; stipules narrow, *bristle-pointed*. Pods egg-shaped. The cultivated form is usually taller and more luxuriant, with paler flowers, hollow stems and less toothed leaflets. Native form in not too limy natural grassland, cultivated form in sown grassland and other disturbed ground.

6 Zigzag Clover *Trifolium medium*. Rather like Red Clover (**5**), but its flowers are a harder, darker pink-purple and its flowerheads are more spreading, *flatter* and much longer-stalked. Growing in larger patches, the stems often in a gentle zigzag. Leaves darker green, the upper usually well stalked, the leaflets narrower with less conspicuous pale marks and the stipules *not* bristle-pointed. Natural grassland, especially on clay.

Alsike Clover *Trifolium hybridum*, p. 152.

7 Haresfoot Clover *Trifolium arvense*. Short erect softly hairy annual, to 20cm. Flowers pale pink to white, 3-6mm, in somewhat *elongated*, to 25mm, heads, often obscured (the pods also) by the long fine *pale brown teeth* of the joined sepals; June-August. Leaflets narrow, hardly toothed. Dry grassy, often bare or sandy places, dunes, usually avoiding lime.

1   SOZ ☐

2   SO ☐↓

3   S ☐↑

4   ☐↓

5   SOZ ☐

6   ☐↓

7   S ☐↓

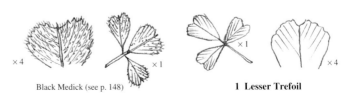

Black Medick (see p. 148)   ×4   ×1   ×1   ×4   **1 Lesser Trefoil**

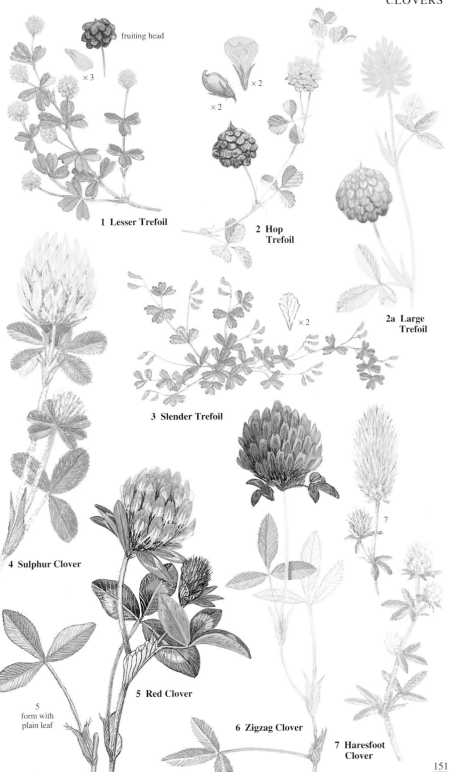

fruiting head

× 3

1 Lesser Trefoil

× 2

× 2

2 Hop Trefoil

2a Large Trefoil

× 2

3 Slender Trefoil

4 Sulphur Clover

7

5 Sulphur Clover

5 form with plain leaf

5 Red Clover

6 Zigzag Clover

7 Haresfoot Clover

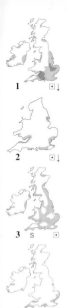

1 Strawberry Clover *Trifolium fragiferum*. Sprawling perennial, to 30cm; only this and White (**8**) and Western Clovers (**9**) have rooting stems. Flowers pink, 5-7mm, in tight rounded long-stalked 10-22mm heads, like miniature White Clovers; June-Sept. Leaves like White Clover, but smaller and with thicker, *recurved* veins. Most easily identified in fruit, when the pods enclosed in the inflated joined sepals make the whole head look like a small dull pink *strawberry*. Natural grassland, especially on clay and near the sea. **1a Reversed Clover** *T. resupinatum* is annual with stems not rooting, and has the flowers *upside down*, with the keel at the top and the standard below. Fruits covered by downy sepals. A casual, established in a few places.

2 *Sea Clover *Trifolium squamosum*. Short erect annual, to 40cm. Flowers pale pink, 7-9mm, like a miniature Red Clover (p. 150), in short-stalked egg-shaped 10-20mm heads, with a pair of leaves at the base; June-August. Leaflets and stipules narrow. In fruit the teeth of the joined sepals spread outwards, star-like. Short turf by the sea.

3 Knotted Clover *Trifolium striatum*. Short, erect to sprawling annual, to 30cm. Flowers pale pink, 4-7mm, in *unstalked* egg-shaped, 10-15mm heads; June-July. The only small pink annual clover with leaves downy *on both sides*. The base of the joined sepals *swollen* in fruit, and the teeth erect. Short turf and bare places, often on sand and near the sea.

4 *Clustered Clover *Trifolium glomeratum*. Prostrate to sprawling annual, to 25cm. Flowers pink-purple, 4-5mm, embedded in the green sepals of *unstalked* 8-12mm heads; June-July. Leaflets oval, toothed, often with a pale patch at the base. Pods covered by the dead sepals with tips spreading *star-like*. Short turf, usually on sandy soils and near the sea.

The Lizard Clovers. The next three species are confined (but see p. 457) to grassy places in the Lizard Peninsula in Cornwall.

5 ***Upright Clover *Trifolium strictum*. A slender low/short hairless annual, to 15cm. Flowers *pink-purple*, 5-7mm, with base of joined sepals *markedly angled*, in globular 7-10mm heads; May-July. Leaflets narrow, well veined, with small sharp *glandular* teeth and broad *white-centred* toothed stipules.

6 **Twin-headed Clover *Trifolium bocconei*. A low/short erect downy annual, to 20cm. Flowers usually *pale pink*, sometimes white, 4-6mm, in small unstalked egg-shaped 9-15mm heads, almost always in *unequal pairs*; June-July. Leaflets downy beneath.

7 **Long-headed Clover *Trifolium incarnatum* ssp. *molinerii*. Short erect to sprawling annual, to 20cm. Flowers pale pink to (more often) *yellowish white*, 9-15mm, in *elongated heads*, to 60mm; June-July. The bright red **7a** ssp. *incarnatum* used to be cultivated, but is now rarely seen.

Birdsfoot Clover *Trifolium ornithopodioides*, p. 158.

White (8) and **Alsike (10) Clovers**, below.

2c. Flowers small, in tight heads: Flowers white

8 White Clover *Trifolium repens*. One of our two commonest clovers, a low sprawling perennial with solid rooting stems (cf. Strawberry Clover, **1**), to 50cm. Flowers dull white, sometimes pinkish, rarely purple, scented, 7-12mm, with joined sepals white but with teeth and sometimes veins green; in roundish 15-20mm *long-stalked* heads, May-Nov. Leaflets toothed, usually with a *white mark* at the base and veins translucent when fresh. Grassy places, often sown. Aka Dutch Clover and known to farmers as "wild white" or Kentish clover.

9 Western Clover *Trifolium occidentale*. Smaller and slenderer than White Clover (**8**), and with smaller heads of always white unscented flowers, appearing earlier, *April-July*; leaflets thicker, more *rounded*, unmarked and bluish-green, the veins never translucent and the stipules often *tinged red*. Coastal turf.

10 Alsike Clover *Trifolium hybridum*. Not unlike a more erect White Clover (**8**), but with stems *taller*, to 40cm, *not* creeping and often hollow. Flowers usually white, but often pink or even purple, especially as they fade, 7-10mm, in much *shorter-stalked* 24-26mm heads; June-Sept. Leaflets narrower and *without* pale marks. Naturalised in grassy and waste places.

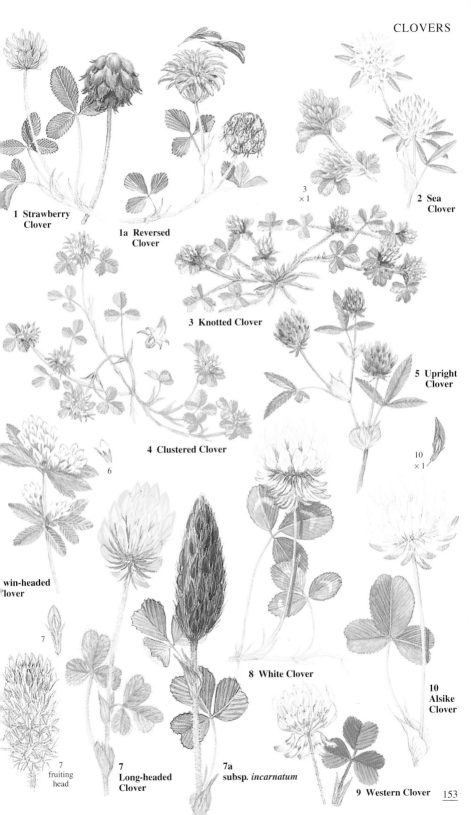

1 Strawberry Clover

1a Reversed Clover

2 Sea Clover

3
× 1

3 Knotted Clover

4 Clustered Clover

5 Upright Clover

6

10
× 1

win-headed
lover

7

7
fruiting
head

7 Long-headed Clover

7a subsp. *incarnatum*

8 White Clover

9 Western Clover

10 Alsike Clover

1 Rough Clover *Trifolium scabrum*. The white-flowered counterpart of Knotted Clover (p. 152), with which it often grows, a low, often prostrate annual, to 20cm. Flowers *white*, 4-7mm, in unstalked 5-12mm heads along the stems; May-June. Leaflets downy on both sides, the side veins curving backwards. Sepal-teeth *curving backwards* in fruit, unlike Knotted Clover. Dry grassy places, usually near the sea.

1   S   ·

2 Burrowing Clover *Trifolium subterraneum* A usually prostrate hairy annual, to 20cm or more. Flowers *creamy white*, 8-14mm, in a rather open head of 2-5, together with numerous *sterile* ones with only the green joined sepals; May-June. Leaflets broad. The fruiting heads have the unique habit of *burrowing* into the ground. Aka Subterranean Clover. Bare dry grassy places.

2   S   ·

3 Suffocated Clover *Trifolium suffocatum*. A most distinctive small prostrate, to 8cm, hairless annual, often detectable by the way its *sharply toothed* leaves are held aloft above the *close clusters* of unstalked heads of tiny (3-4mm) white flowers; April-August. The flowers are largely hidden by the green sepal-teeth, which *turn back* in fruit. Short turf or bare sandy or gravelly ground, mainly near the sea.

3   S   ·

Haresfoot and **Birdsfoot Clovers** *Trifolium arvense*, p. 150 and *Trifolium ornithopodioides*, p. 158.

Twin-headed and **Long-headed Clovers** *Trifolium bocconei* and *Trifolium incarnatum* ssp. *molinerii*, p. 152.

3. Flowers in spikes, leaves pinnate with terminal leaflet

4 Goat's Rue *Galega officinalis*. Medium/tall *erect*, often hairless perennial, to 1.5m. Flowers pinkish-lilac or white, 12-15mm, with five *bristle-like* sepal-teeth, in stalked spikes; June-Sept. Pods rounded, short, to 3cm. Increasingly naturalised in waste, usually grassy places.

4   ·

Wild Liquorice *Astragalus glycyphyllos*, p. 140.

5 Sainfoin *Onobrychis viciifolia*. Our only peaflower with conspicuous stalked *spikes* of bright *pink* flowers, in two forms. A large, more or less upright medium perennial, to 60cm, with flowers 10-14mm, June-August, leaves with narrow leaflets, and pods 5-8mm, derives from former fodder crops and is frequent in dry grassy places, especially on lime. A much less frequent and probably native form is more or less *prostrate*, with duller pink flowers and is confined to undisturbed chalk turf (see map).

5   ·

Hairy Tare *Vicia hirsuta*, p. 144.

6 Tufted Vetch *Vicia cracca*. The most conspicuous of the commoner vetches, often festooning the hedges with its showy flowers; a tall scrambling perennial, to 2m. Flowers violet-purple, 8-12mm, the standard about equalling the claw, 10-30 in a *1-sided spike*; June-August. Leaves with 8-12 pairs of leaflets. Pods brown, hairless, 10-25mm. Hedges, scrub, wood margins, rough grassland. **6a Fine-leaved Vetch** *V. tenuifolia* has larger (12-18mm) flowers, with the standard *longer* than the claw. A not infrequent casual, established in the Cotswolds and Surrey. **6b Fodder Vetch** *V. villosa* is annual, differing especially in its larger (10-20mm) flowers being *variably* purple/violet/bluish, sometimes with the wings white or yellow, and pods longer (20-40mm). Mainly casual, sometimes established locally for a few years.

6   SOZ   ■

7 Wood Vetch *Vicia sylvatica*. Far-scrambling tall/medium perennial, to 2m. Flowers looking *white* at a distance, but actually particoloured, with the wings and keel creamy white, contrasting with the *purple veins* on the pale lilac standard, 12-20mm, 4-15 in 1-sided spikes; June-August. Leaves with 4-12 pairs of leaflets and branched tendrils. Pods black, 25-30mm. Woodland edges, scrub, also on mountains, screes and coastal cliffs and shingle.

7   ■↓

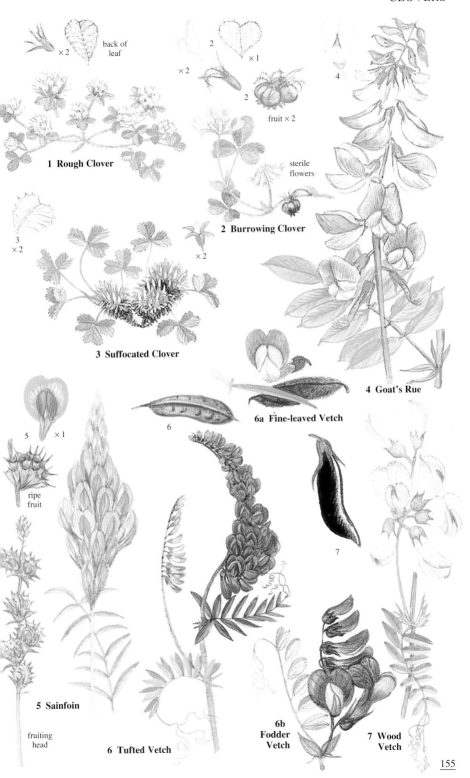

×2   back of leaf

1 Rough Clover

2

×2   ×1

2

fruit ×2

2

sterile flowers

2 Burrowing Clover

4

3
×2

×2

3 Suffocated Clover

4 Goat's Rue

6a **Fine-leaved Vetch**

5   ×1

6

7

ripe fruit

5 Sainfoin

fruiting head

6 Tufted Vetch

6b
Fodder Vetch

7 **Wood Vetch**

155

1 Rest-harrow *Ononis repens*. Short/medium, erect or sprawling undershrub, with stems tough – 'arresting the harrow', hairy all round, usually *spineless*, but sometimes with soft spines, often creeping and rooting, to 60cm. Flowers pink, 12-20mm, the wings equalling the hooked keel, in leafy stalked spikes; June-Sept. Leaves small, well toothed, *blunt or notched*, solitary or trefoil, with prominent toothed leaf-like stipules clasping the stem at their base. Pods 5-7mm, shorter than joined sepals. Dry grassland, especially on lime, dunes.

2 Spiny Rest-harrow *Ononis spinosa*. Like Rest-harrow (**1**), with which it hybridises, but always more or less erect, usually taller, stems usually with *two lines of hairs*, never creeping or rooting and almost always *sharply spiny*, to 70cm. Flowers *red*-pink, 12-20mm, wings distinctly shorter than keel; July-Sept. Leaflets narrower, *pointed*. Pods longer than joined sepals. Similar, but less often limy, grassy places.

3 ***Small Rest-harrow *Ononis reclinata*. Like a miniature Rest-harrow (**1**), a stickily hairy, grey-green, always erect annual, with slender stems, hairy all round, to 15cm. Flowers pink, 5-10mm, the petals scarcely longer than the joined sepals; May-June. Leaves trefoil. Pods 8-14mm, hanging down as they ripen, like a miniature Christmas tree. Bare patches on limestone cliffs and sandy turf by the sea.

Melilots *Melilotus*. Medium/tall annuals, with long spikes of yellow or white flowers, trefoil leaves and straight pods.

4 Golden Melilot *Melilotus altissima*. Badly named in Latin because though it can be as tall as Ribbed Melilot (**5**), to 1.5m, it is usually shorter, also compacter with darker stems. Flowers *golden* yellow, 5-7mm, with standard, wings and keel *equal*; June onwards. Pods *black*, ridged. Aka Tall Melilot. Rough grassland, waysides, woods, waste places; probably native.

5 Ribbed Melilot *Melilotus officinalis*. Very like but often taller than Golden Melilot (**4**), to 1.5m, flowers a more *lemony* yellow, with *keel shorter* than standard and wings and pods *brown*. Well established on waste ground. **5a Small Melilot** *M. indica* is much shorter, to 40cm, much smaller (2-3mm) flowers, the *standard longer* than the wings and keel and drooping, net-veined *olive-green* pods. A locally frequent casual.

6 White Melilot *Melilotus albus*. Much the easiest Melilot to identify because of its *white* flowers; July-August. Tall annual/biennial, to 1.5m. Pods brown. Frequent by railways and other waste ground. Formerly grown for fodder as Bokhara Clover.

~

Long-headed Clover *Trifolium incarnatum* ssp. *molinerii*, p. 150.

7 Nootka Lupin *Lupinus nootkatensis*. Tall hairy perennial, to 1m. Flowers blue-purple, sometimes almost white or particoloured, 12-16mm; May-July. Leaves palmate, with 6-9 leaflets almost as long as the stalks. Pods brown, silky. Aka Scottish Lupin. Long established on river shingle in Scotland and on moorland in Orkney. Nootka is an island near Vancouver, BC. **7a Russell Lupin** *L. × regalis*, the well known garden plant, is taller, with flowers often also pink and leaflets 9-15, half as long as the stalks. A frequent escape on railway banks and other waste land. **7b White Lupin** *L. albus*, increasingly sown and escaping, is annual with white to blue-violet flowers.

Tree Lupin *Lupinus arboreus*, p. 394.

7a Russell Lupin

colour forms

7a
leaflet × 1

1 **Rest-harrow**

2 **Spiny Rest-harrow**

3

5a ×3

5a

×2

6 ×2

6

4 ×2

4 ×2

4 ×2

5 ×2

5 ×2

5 ×2

6 **White Melilot**

5a **Small Melilot**

5 **Ribbed Melilot**

4 **Golden Melilot**

4

7b colour form

7 **Nootka Lupin**

×1

7a **Russell Lupin**

7b **White Lupin**

Greenweeds *Genista*. Undershrubs with yellow flowers and *undivided* leaves.

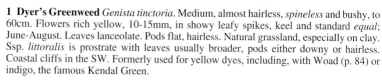

1 Dyer's Greenweed *Genista tinctoria*. Medium, almost hairless, *spineless* and bushy, to 60cm. Flowers rich yellow, 10-15mm, in showy leafy spikes, keel and standard *equal*; June-August. Leaves lanceolate. Pods flat, hairless. Natural grassland, especially on clay. Ssp. *littoralis* is prostrate with leaves usually broader, pods either downy or hairless. Coastal cliffs in the SW. Formerly used for yellow dyes, including, with Woad (p. 84) or indigo, the famous Kendal Green.

2 Petty Whin *Genista anglica*. Short/medium, hairless, usually *spiny*, with wiry stems to 1m. Flowers yellow, 7-10mm, keel *longer* than standard, in rather short spikes; April-July. Leaves pointed oval. Pods short, inflated. Heaths and moors, especially with Heather (p. 104).

3 **Hairy Greenweed *Genista pilosa*. Prostrate to sprawling *spineless* downy, *half-evergreen*, to 50cm. Flowers yellow, 7-11mm, in short spikes; May-June. Leaves dark green, oval, hairy below. Pods downy. Dry heaths and cliff-tops.

Broom *Cytisus scoparius* ssp. *maritimus*, p. 394, and **Gorse, Western Gorse, Dwarf Gorse** *Ulex europaeus, gallii, minor*, p. 398.

4. Flowers solitary or paired

4 Dragon's Teeth *Tetragonolobus maritimus*. A hairy grey-green perennial, prostrate/sprawling to 30cm. Flowers pale yellow, the standard veined brown, the sepal-cup sometimes streaked red, *solitary*, 25-30mm, with trefoil bract at base; May-Sept. Leaves trefoil. Pods dark brown, 4-winged, 30-60mm. Well naturalised in scattered grassy places.

Slender Birdsfoot Trefoil *Lotus angustissimus*, p. 146 and **Smooth** and **Slender Tares** *Vicia tetrasperma* and *V. parviflora*, p. 144.

Bithynian Vetch *Vicia bithynica*, p. 148 and **Yellow** and **Hungarian Vetches** *Vicia lutea* and *V. pannonica*, p. 144.

5 Yellow Vetchling *Lathyrus aphaca*. A medium grey-green annual, with winged stems to 40cm. Most distinctive for its true leaves becoming *tendrils* on the stems and its stipules becoming broad *triangular* pseudo-leaves. Flowers *yellow*, 10-13mm, *solitary*, long-stalked; June-August. Pods brown, 20-35mm. Dry grassy places.

6 Grass Vetchling *Lathyrus nissolia*. Erect medium/tall annual, stems angled, to 90cm. The only peaflower with long narrow pseudo-leaves, so *grass-like* as to be invisible in long grass when the long-stalked solitary or paired *crimson-red* flowers are not out; May-July. No leaves/tendrils. Pods pale brown, 30-60mm. Grassy places.

7 Hairy Vetchling *Lathyrus hirsutus*. Medium/tall scrambling grey-green annual, stems angled, to 1m. Flowers *particoloured*, with a purple standard, paler wings fading blue, and a creamy keel, 8-15mm, 1-2 together, long-stalked; June-August. Leaves with one pair of narrow leaflets and narrow, half-arrowshaped stipules. Pods brown, 20-50mm, *silkily hairy*. Grassy places, possibly native (known in S Essex for over 300 years, but now extinct), otherwise established or casual, in grassy places.

Spotted, Toothed and **Bur Medicks** *Medicago arabica, M. polymorpha* and *M. minima*, p. 146, and **Slender Trefoil** *Trifolium micranthum*, p. 150.

8 Birdsfoot Clover *Trifolium ornithopodioides*. Prostrate annual, to 20cm. Flowers pale pink or white, 6-8mm, *1-4 together*, on stalks *shorter* than the leaves, sometimes looking like rows of teeth upright in the turf; June-July. Leaves trefoil. Pods longer than dead sepals. Differs from Burrowing Clover (p. 154) in being not hairy. Aka Fenugreek. Dry bare sandy and gravelly places, usually near the sea.

Burrowing Clover *Trifolium subterraneum*, p. 154.

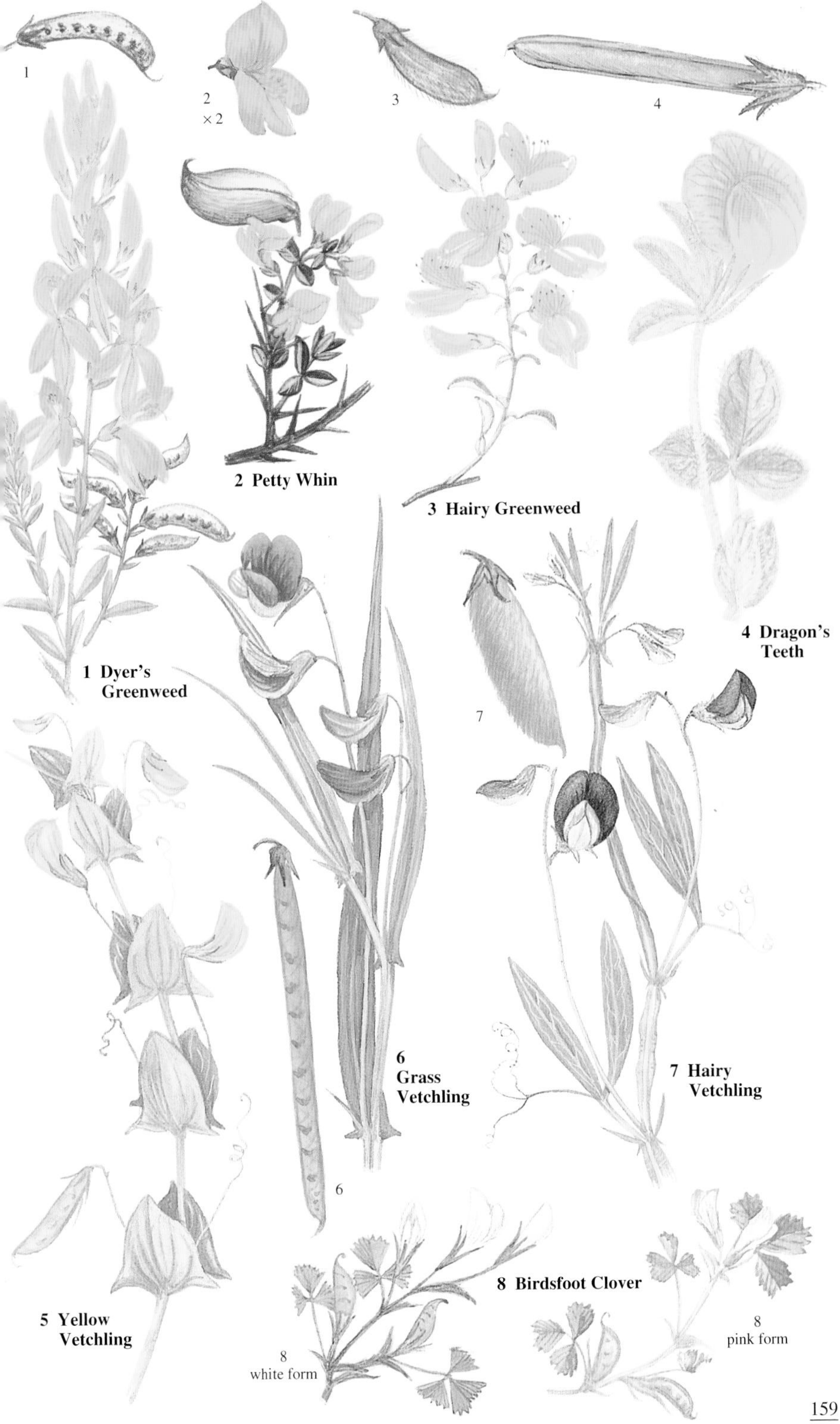

1

2
× 2

3

4

2 Petty Whin

3 Hairy Greenweed

4 Dragon's Teeth

1 Dyer's Greenweed

7

6 Grass Vetchling

6

7 Hairy Vetchling

5 Yellow Vetchling

8 Birdsfoot Clover

8
white form

8
pink form

WILLOWHERB FAMILY Onagraceae

Willowherbs *Epilobium.* Perennials, usually with runners, easily recognisable as a group, by their pink flowers with four notched petals and undivided leaves, but much less so as species, due to their *frequent hybridisation.* The shape of both leaves and stigmas is important, especially the stigmas, either club-shaped or divided into four lobes like a short-armed (Maltese) cross. Seeds with plumes of long silky hairs in long narrow 4-sided pods that split when ripe. Three groups: tall, medium/tall (below) and short (p. 162).

Tall, more than 1m

1 Great Willowherb *Epilobium hirsutum.* Our tallest, to 1.8m, *largest-flowered* and most easily recognised willowherb, profusely covered with *soft spreading hairs,* Flowers purple-pink, stigma 4-lobed; 15-23mm; July-Sept. Leaves lanceolate to oblong, unstalked. Aka Codlins-and-Cream. By fresh water and in other damp, wet, or even dry places.

1   soz ■↑

Medium/tall, usually to 75cm

Except where stated, stems have four (sometimes two) ridges, hairs are both appressed downy and erect glandular, flowers have club-shaped stigma, and leaves are un- or quite short-stalked; habitat bare ground in woods, spoilheaps and other waste places, gardens.

Stems rounded:	Hoary, Broad-leaved, Marsh
No glandular hairs:	Hoary, Square-stemmed, Short-fruited (except on sepals)
Stigma 4-lobed:	Hoary, Broad-leaved, Spear-leaved
Leaves long-stalked:	Pale, Spear-leaved

2 Hoary Willowherb *Epilobium parviflorum.* Like a miniature Great Willowherb (**1**), but with *much smaller* (7-12mm) flowers; stems and leaves covered with *soft whitish hairs,* to 75cm. Flowers pale pink-purple, with deeply notched petals and stigma *4-lobed*; July-Sept. Leaves more sharply pointed. Preferring damp places on limy soils.

2   o   ▢

3 Broad-leaved Willowherb *Epilobium montanum.* Generally our commonest medium-sized willowherb, the stems *rounded.* Flowers purple-pink, petals deeply notched, 12-15mm, stigma *4-lobed*; June-August. Leaves usually broad lanceolate. Prefers shady places.

4 Square-stemmed Willowherb *Epilobium tetragonum.* Another common medium-sized Willowherb, the conspicuously *4-sided stems* with all hairs appressed downy. Flowers pale purple-pink, 6-8mm; June-August. Leaves narrow, *strap-shaped,* shiny, unstalked and running down on to ridges on stem. Prefers damper places.

3   soz   ▢

5 American Willowherb *Epilobium ciliatum.* A fast-spreading invader, with stems often reddish. Flowers pale pink-purple, 8-10mm, with *gaps* between the petals, stigma club-shaped; June-August. Leaves narrow lanceolate. Fruits short. Especially in towns.

6 Short-fruited Willowherb *Epilobium obscurum.* Most easily recognised by its long, broad lanceolate, pale green, scarcely stalked leaves, rose pink 7-9mm flowers and short (4-6cm) fruits. Glandular hairs only on sepals. Flowers late, *July*-August. Prefers damper places.

4   s   ▢↑↑

7 Pale Willowherb *Epilobium roseum.* Look for the long-stalked leaves and white flowers turning pale pink. Stems with glandular hairs often sparse. Flowers 8-10mm, *late,* July-August. Leaves broad lanceolate, like stalked Broad-leaved Willowherb (**3**). Fruits short. Prefers shadier and damper places.

8 Spear-leaved Willowherb *Epilobium lanceolatum.* The least frequent of the group, but instantly recognisable by its long-stalked, narrowly elliptical, blunt-tipped leaves. Stems only faintly ridged. Flowers pale pink to pink, 12-13mm; late flowering, July-Sept. Waste places, walls; has a curious liking for Midland churchyards.

5   sz   ▢↑↑

9 Marsh Willowherb *Epilobium palustre.* Slender, with a rounded stem, to 60cm. Flowers pale pink, sometimes lilac or white, *small,* 8-12mm; June-August. Leaves *narrow* lanceolate, tapering at both ends. *Wet places* on acid soils.

6   z   ▢

7   z   ▣

8   ▣↑

9   oz   ▢

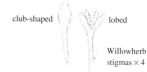

club-shaped   lobed

Willowherb
stigmas × 4

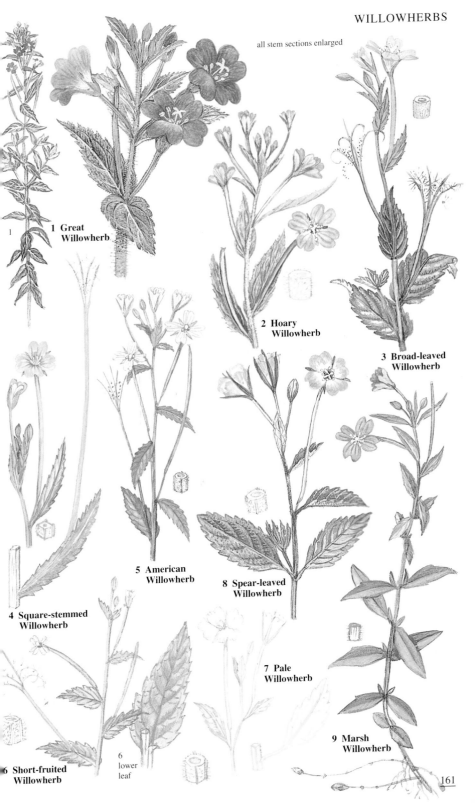

all stem sections enlarged

1 Great Willowherb

2 Hoary Willowherb

3 Broad-leaved Willowherb

4 Square-stemmed Willowherb

5 American Willowherb

6 Short-fruited Willowherb

6 lower leaf

7 Pale Willowherb

8 Spear-leaved Willowherb

9 Marsh Willowherb

Short, to 25cm, or creeping

1 Alpine Willowherb *Epilobium anagallidifolium*. The smaller and more frequent of our two native mountain willowherbs, with slender reddish, usually unbranched stems, to 20cm. Flowers with rose-pink petals and reddish sepals, 7-10mm; June-August. Leaves narrowly elliptical, *scarcely toothed*, often *yellowish-green*. Pods dark red. Wet places in mountains.

2 Chickweed Willowherb *Epilobium alsinifolium*. Lusher and slightly taller than Alpine Willowherb (**1**), with stems thicker and more often branched, to 25cm. Flowers of a bluer pink, larger, *14-16mm*; June-August. Leaves larger, longer-stalked, broader, more pointed, *more toothed*, shiny and of a *bluer green*. More often on limy soils.

3 New Zealand Willowherb *Epilobium brunnescens*. A rapidly spreading invader, now much the most frequent small willowherb in hill districts; prostrate and *mat-forming* with rooting stems, to 20cm. Flowers pale pink to white, with deeply notched petals and sepals often reddish, 6-7mm, solitary on *long* (to 4cm) stalks; May-Oct. Leaves *rounded*, toothed, bronzy green above, often purplish beneath. Damp bare ground, from peat to railway sidings. Two similar New Zealand rock-garden escapes with leaves *green beneath* are also established locally: **3a Rockery Willowherb** *E. pedunculare* with larger, rounder, more *sharply toothed* leaves, especially in W Ireland; and **3b Bronzy Willowherb** *E. komarovianum*, with *untoothed, elliptical* leaves.

~

4 Rosebay *Chamerion angustifolium*. The most conspicuous red-purple flower after the Foxgloves (p. 232) have gone over; a tall, aggressively spreading perennial, to 1.5m. Flowers a garish red-purple, with four *unequal petals* but looking multipetalled because of the long narrow reddish sepals, in showy spikes, 20-30mm; June-Sept. Leaves narrow lanceolate. Pods like Willowherbs (p. 160). Now commoner on railway banks and other waste places in towns than in its original rural habitat of woodland clearings, heaths and mountains.

Enchanter's Nightshades *Circaea*. Short/medium perennials. Flowers white, with *two notched petals*, in leafless stalked spikes. Leaves heart-shaped, sharply pointed, toothed, stalked, opposite. Fruits club-shaped. Woods and shady places. Not related to the true nightshades (p. 202); named for the ancient Greek enchantress Circe.

5 Enchanter's Nightshade *Circaea lutetiana*. Stems to 60cm. Flowers often faintly tinged pink, with *no bracts*; petals well notched, sepals glandular-hairy, stigma deeply lobed, 4-7mm; June-August. Leaves shallowly toothed, scarcely heart-shaped, on stalks *downy on both sides*. Fruits clinging bur-like to clothes with their many tiny white hooked bristles. A carpeter, sometimes unwelcome in gardens.

6 Intermediate Enchanter's Nightshade *Circaea × intermedia*. The stable hybrid between the two other Enchanter's Nightshades (**5** & **7**); stems to 45cm. Flowers with *tiny hairlike bracts* at their base, deeply notched petals, sepals glandular-hairy and stigma only notched, 3-7mm; July-August. Leaves crinkly, shiny, more deeply toothed and more heart-shaped than **5**, on stalks downy above, *almost hairless beneath*. Fruits rarely produced. In hill districts, often without one or both parents.

7 *Alpine Enchanter's Nightshade *Circaea alpina*. The smallest and slenderest of the three Enchanter's Nightshades, to 30cm. Flowers *tiny*, 1-3mm, in a closer spike, elongating in fruit, with *hairlike bracts*, the sepals *hairless*; July-August. Leaves sharply toothed, markedly heart-shaped, on *hairless* winged stalks. Fruits with soft bristles, not clinging. Rocky woods, damp shady rocks on acid soils; rare away from the Lake District and Arran.

4
lower leaf

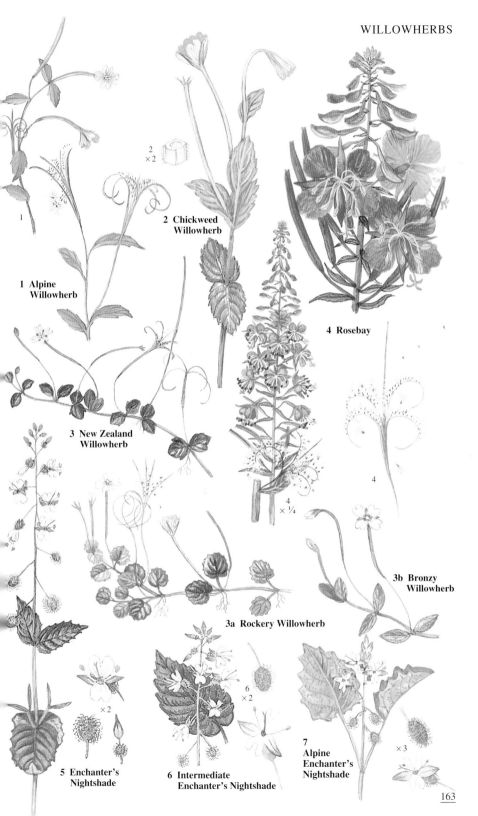

1 Alpine
Willowherb

2 Chickweed
Willowherb

2
×2

3 New Zealand
Willowherb

4 Rosebay

4
× 1/4

4

3b Bronzy
Willowherb

3a Rockery Willowherb

×2

6
×2

7
Alpine
Enchanter's
Nightshade

×3

5 Enchanter's
Nightshade

6 Intermediate
Enchanter's Nightshade

Evening Primroses *Oenothera*. Invaders from N America, quite unrelated to our Primrose; medium/tall with large yellow 4-petalled flowers that become fragrant at dusk (all, not just Fragrant Evening Primrose), alternate lanceolate leaves, and fruit an elongated capsule. Bare and waste places, dunes. When many plants are present, as on the Lancashire coastal dunes, they are likely to be a *hybrid swarm*, making it very hard to identify individual plants. Indeed some experts believe 'pure' plants are scarce throughout Britain.

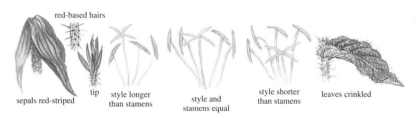

red-based hairs

sepals red-striped | tip | style longer than stamens | style and stamens equal | style shorter than stamens | leaves crinkled

Stems with red-based hairs:	Large-flowered, Intermediate, Small-flowered
Tip of flower-spike red:	Large-flowered, Intermediate, Fragrant
Sepals red-striped:	Large-flowered, Intermediate, Fragrant
Styles *longer than* stamens:	Large-flowered
equalling stamens:	Fragrant
shorter than stamens:	Common, Intermediate, Small-flowered
Leaves crinkled:	Large-flowered, Intermediate

1 Large-flowered Evening Primrose *Oenothera glazioviana*. Generally the commonest and largest-flowered evening primrose; stems to 1.8m and with many *red-based* hairs and the tip of the flower-spike red. Flowers 50-80mm, petals wider than long, sepals red-striped, and styles *longer* than stamens; June-Sept. Leaves *crinkled*, midrib usually white. Capsules with red-based hairs.

2 Common Evening Primrose *Oenothera biennis*. No longer our commonest evening primrose; differs from Large-flowered (**1**) in having *no red-based hairs* on stems or capsules, tip of flower-spike green, *smaller* flowers (40-50mm), green sepals, shorter styles and *flat* leaves with *red* midrib. **2a Intermediate Evening Primrose** *Oe.* × *fallax*, the rather uncommon true-breeding hybrid between **1** and **2**, has red-based hairs, tip of flower-spike red, flowers 40-50mm, sepals red-striped and crinkled leaves with red midrib. In hybrid swarms, however, and indeed elsewhere, there will be many plants with a different mix of these characters.

3 Small-flowered Evening Primrose *Oenothera cambrica*. Differs from Large-flowered (**1**) in having tip of flower-spike green, flowers 40-50mm, petals about as wide as long, sepals *green*, short styles and flat leaves with a red midrib; and from Common (**2**) in usually having red-based hairs and in having petals about as wide as long.

4 Fragrant Evening Primrose *Oenothera stricta*. Usually shorter (to 1m) than other Evening Primroses, and rarely hybridising with them. Has no red-based hairs, tip of flower-spike usually red, buds sometimes red, sepals red-striped, flowers 35-60mm, reddening when dried, styles about *equalling* stamens, and *narrower* flat leaves. Sandy ground, usually by the sea.

~

5 **Hampshire Purslane *Ludwigia palustris*. A short sprawling aquatic perennial, stems red-purple below, to 30cm. Flowers petalless, the four green sepals often *red-edged*, 2-5mm, solitary at base of leaves; June-July. Leaves opposite, elliptical, *pointed* (unlike the much smaller Water Purslane, p. 114). Wet places on acid soils. Now only in the New Forest, Hants; elsewhere likely to be a hybrid thrown out by aquarists.

1 S ◼↑

2 S ◼↑

2a ▫

3 ▫↑

4 ◻

5 ▫

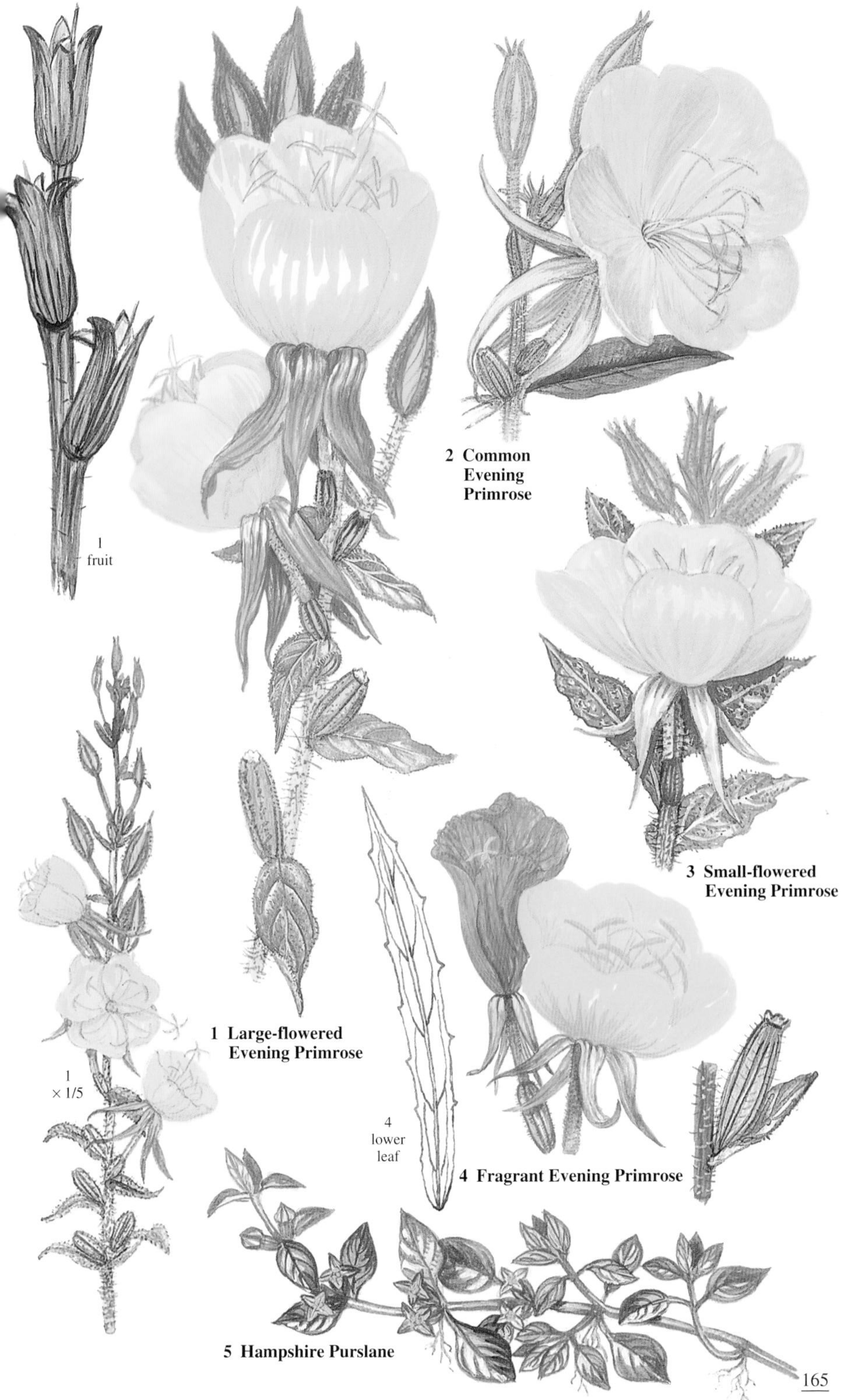

1
fruit

2 Common
Evening
Primrose

3 Small-flowered
Evening Primrose

1 Large-flowered
Evening Primrose

1
× 1/5

4
lower
leaf

4 Fragrant Evening Primrose

5 Hampshire Purslane

SPURGE FAMILY Euphorbiaceae

P **Spurges** *Euphorbia*. Stems with acrid *milky juice*, formerly used by poachers to kill fish. Individual flowers tiny, with no petals or sepals, within usually broadening umbel-like clusters. What appear to be large yellow, yellowish-green or green petals are actually outer bracts. Within them is a fleshy cup with four conspicuous oval or crescent-shaped lobes containing one stalked female with three often forked styles among many minute 1-stamened male flowers. ('the woodspurge has a cup of three' – D. G. Rossetti); Leaves undivided, usually alternate and untoothed. Fruit a stalked capsule. Best divided as follows, below: weeds of bare and disturbed ground; woods and shady places; and on p. 168, coastal; very tall; aliens.

Weeds of bare and disturbed ground

1 Petty Spurge *Euphorbia peplus*. Our commonest weedy spurge, a short hairless unbranched annual to 30cm. Flowerheads *green*, in less conspicuously flattened clusters than Sun Spurge (**2**), with slender crescent-shaped lobes; April-Nov and through mild winters. Leaves oval, mid-green and *untoothed*. Fruits with wavy ridges. Gardens, allotments and other cultivated and waste ground.

1   SOZ☐↓↓

2 Sun Spurge *Euphorbia helioscopia*. Our only common spurge with *toothed* leaves, a short/medium hairless, sometimes branched annual to 50cm, but usually much shorter. Flowerheads *bright yellowish-green* at first, distinctly flattened, with roundish green lobes; April-Nov and through mild winters. Leaves oval. Fruits smooth. Habitat as Petty Spurge (**1**).

3 Dwarf Spurge *Euphorbia exigua*. Slender *greyish* low/short annual, to 20cm. Flowerheads yellow, the lobes with very slender crescentic horns; June-Sept. Leaves short, *linear*. Fruits smooth. Arable fields, especially on lime.

2   SOZ ☐

4 *Broad-leaved Spurge *Euphorbia platyphyllos*. Medium, sometimes downy, usually branched, annual, often tinged red, to 80cm. Flowerheads open, with rounded lobes; June-Sept. Leaves egg-shaped, *finely toothed* in the outer half and half-clasping the stem. Fruits with rounded warts. Arable fields.

3   ☐↓↓

Woods and shady places

5 Wood Spurge *Euphorbia amygdaloides*. The common spring spurge of *southern woodlands*, a medium/tall downy unbranched perennial, to 90cm. Flowerheads with converging crescentic horns on the lobes; March-May. Leaves narrow lanceolate, untoothed, often reddish. Fruits almost smooth. Woods, hedges, occasionally naturalised elsewhere. Ssp. *robbiae* with shiny dark green hairless leaves is an increasing garden escape.

4   ☐

6 **Upright Spurge *Euphorbia serrulata*. Hairless medium/tall annual to 80cm, often tinged red. Flowerheads a graceful open cluster; June-Sept. Upper leaves pointed oval, the lower narrower fruits covered with *tall cylindrical warts*. Woods on *limestone* and as a casual, occasionally naturalised elsewhere.

5   S ☐

7 **Irish Spurge *Euphorbia hyberna*. A little-branched, clump-forming, medium perennial, to 60cm. Flowerheads bright yellow, with rounded lobes later turning brown; April-July. Leaves lanceolate, untoothed, downy beneath. Fruits with prominent cylindrical warts. Woods, hedges, also in *rough grassland*. See p. 461.

6   ☐↓

7   ☐

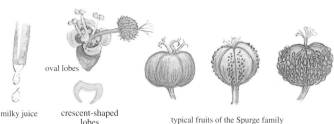

milky juice oval lobes crescent-shaped lobes typical fruits of the Spurge family

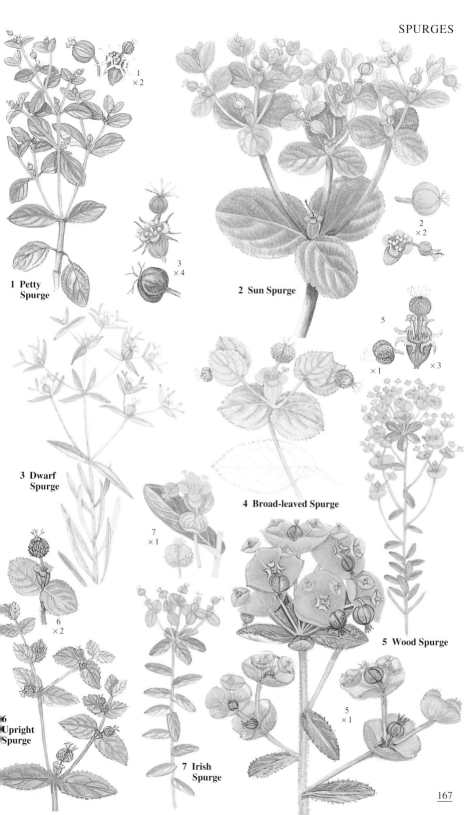

1 Petty
Spurge

1
×2

3
×4

2 Sun Spurge

2
×2

5

×1
×3

3 Dwarf
Spurge

4 Broad-leaved Spurge

7
×1

6
×2

5 Wood Spurge

6
Upright
Spurge

5
×1

7 Irish
Spurge

Coastal

1 Sea Spurge *Euphorbia paralias*. The more widespread of our two coastal spurges; medium perennial, to 60cm. Flowerheads with lobes short-horned; June-Sept. Leaves grey, fleshy, oval, the midrib *obscure below*, closely packed up the stem. Fruits wrinkled. Sandy places by the sea.

2 *Portland Spurge *Euphorbia portlandica*. Differs from Sea Spurge (**1**) in being often tinged red, with long crescentic horns in the flowerheads, earlier-flowering (April-Sept), narrower, *minutely pointed* leaves, the midrib *prominent below*, and fruits only slightly rough. Also on cliffs.

Very tall

3 Caper Spurge *Euphorbia lathyris*. Strikingly tall biennial, to 2m. Flowerheads with bluntly horned lobes; June-Aug. Leaves *greyish*, lanceolate, the upper broader-based; our only inland spurge with *opposite* leaves, strikingly arranged up the stem, so that shorter young plants are easily recognised. Fruits large, 3-sided, resembling capers (but poisonous to eat). Very local as a native in woods; widespread as a garden escape, especially young plants.

Aliens

We have 10 locally established medium/tall perennial alien spurge species or hybrids, best distinguished by leaf-shape. Most flowering May-July, on hedge or railway banks and other waste places, mostly with a few scattered sites.

Much the most frequent is **4 Twiggy Spurge** *Euphorbia × pseudovirgata*, with pointed, often narrow, lanceolate leaves, broadest at or below the middle. One of its parents, **5 Leafy Spurge** *E. esula*, is shorter and slenderer, with blunt-tipped leaves broadest above the middle.

6 Cypress Spurge *Euphorbia cyparissias*, familiar in gardens, but possibly native in limy grassland in the S (abundant at one site in Wiltshire), has almost linear leaves crowded up the stems, reddening as they go over.

~

7 Dog's Mercury *Mercurialis perennis*. A hairy foetid low/short unbranched creeping and *carpeting* perennial, to 40cm. Flowers greenish, petalless, 4-5mm, February-May; the male in catkins, yellow from their anthers, the female, on separate plants, 1-3 together on stalks that lengthen as their hairy fruits ripen. Leaves *dark green*, broad lanceolate, opposite, mainly at the top of the stem. Woods, shady banks, mountains, often the only plant over many square metres.

8 Annual Mercury *Mercurialis annua*. An almost hairless, often branched short/medium annual, to 50cm. Flowers like Dog's Mercury (**7**), but the female *scarcely stalked* and occasionally on the same plant; April-August. Leaves similar, but *pale green* and also down the stem. Fruits bristly. A weed of bare ground.

DOGWOOD FAMILY Cornaceae

9 Dwarf Cornel *Cornus suecica*. Short, little-branched perennial, to 25cm, often hidden under Bracken, Heather or Bilberry. Flowers dark purple, tiny, 2-3mm, in a tight head, offset by four conspicuous petal-like creamy white bracts, 10-15mm across; June-Sept, a shy flowerer. Leaves pointed oval, unstalked, opposite, with conspicuous veins. like Dogwood (p. 370). Fruit a red berry. Heaths, moors, mountains, not on lime.

SANDALWOOD FAMILY Santalaceae

10 Bastard Toadflax *Thesium humifusum*. A slender prostrate, semi-parasitic perennial, to 20cm; often mat-forming and hard to see among the grass. Flowers yellowish-green outside, whitish inside, *star-like* with five joined petals, 2-3mm, in loose spikes with long narrow leaf-like bracts at their base; June-August. Leaves linear, alternate. Fruit a nut. Short turf on lime.

4 Twiggy Spurge   **5 Leafy Spurge**

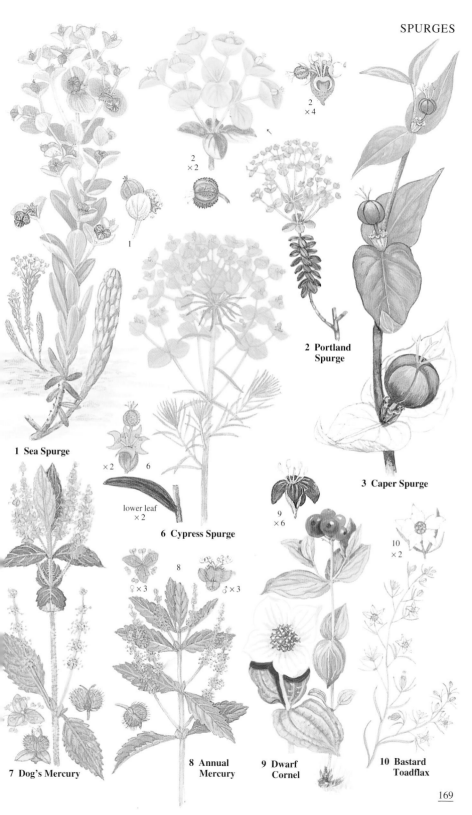

2
×4

2
×2

1

**2 Portland
Spurge**

3 Caper Spurge

1 Sea Spurge

×2 **6**

lower leaf
×2

6 Cypress Spurge

9
×6

10
×2

♀×3 **8** ♂×3

**8 Annual
Mercury**

**9 Dwarf
Cornel**

**10 Bastard
Toadflax**

7 Dog's Mercury

FLAX FAMILY Linaceae

Flowers 5-petalled. Leaves opposite, undivided. Fruit a globular capsule.

1 Cultivated Flax *Linum usitatissimum*. Now that it is a subsidised crop, much the most familiar flax in the countryside; a slender hairless grey-green medium/tall annual, to 80cm. Flowers *soft blue*, 16-24mm, sepals *shorter* than the fruit; June-Aug. Leaves narrow lanceolate, 3-veined. A relic of cultivation.

2 Pale Flax *Linum bienne*. Like Cultivated Flax (**1**), but with a wirier stem, to 60cm, biennial/perennial, with flowers *pale bluish-lilac* (May-Sept), sepals more sharply pointed and *almost equalling* the fruit, and leaves almost linear. Dry grassy places, especially near the sea.

3 Perennial Flax *Linum perenne*. Greyer than Cultivated Flax (**1**), and perennial, with a wirier stem to 60cm, *darker blue* flowers (May-July), narrower leaves and blunt sepals *much shorter* than the fruit. Limy grassland.

4 Fairy Flax *Linum catharticum*. A slender hairless low/short annual, to 25cm, recalling the Sandworts (p. 54), but with five petals. Flowers white with a yellowish centre, 4-6mm, on thread-like stalks in loose branched clusters; May-Sept. Leaves oblong. Short, especially limy, turf, fens.

5 Allseed *Radiola linoides*. A tiny delicate, often well branched low annual, with stiff thread-like forked stems, to 6cm, often less. Flowers white, 1-2mm, in branched clusters, the petals no longer than the toothed sepals; July-August. Leaves tiny, pointed oval. Heaths, woodland rides, with bare moist patches on sand or peat.

MILKWORT FAMILY Polygalaceae

Milkworts *Polygala*. Low, often more or less prostrate, slender, hairless perennials. Flowers in spikes, of a unique shape, appearing 5-petalled, but with the two inner of the five sepals large and petal-like on either side of the three small true petals, which are joined at the base, uniquely together with the two Y-shaped bundles of four stamens. Leaves lanceolate, unstalked, usually alternate up the stems. Fruit a capsule. All on limy soils except Heath Milkwort and sometimes Common Milkwort.

6 Common Milkwort *Polygala vulgaris*. Our commonest milkwort, with stems to 30cm. Flowers *very variable* in colour, usually blue, but also often mauve, pink, white or white tipped mauve or blue, 4-7mm; May-Sept. Leaves *not* forming a basal rosette. Fruit shorter than inner sepals. Dry, limy or acid grassland.

7 Heath Milkwort *Polygala serpyllifolia*. Smaller than Common Milkwort (**6**), to 25cm, and flowers smaller, 5-6mm, in shorter spikes, dark blue, dark pink or white, the inner sepals more pointed, and at least the lower leaves *opposite* and more crowded. *Heaths*, dry acid grassland. Northern plants often look different from southern ones.

8 Chalk Milkwort *Polygala calcarea*. Often instantly recognised by its distinctive *bright gentian-blue* flowers, 6-7mm, but these can also be paler blue, pink or white; *April*-June. An equally good distinction from Common Milkwort (**6**) is the irregular false *rosette* of the blunter leaves at the base of the stem (to 20cm), Fruits broader than inner sepals. Chalk and limestone turf, differing slightly at its N and S extremes.

9 **Dwarf Milkwort *Polygala amarella*. Our smallest milkwort, to 10cm. Flowers *small*, 3-5mm and blue or pink in the N, and 2-4mm and a rather dingy greyish blue or mauve in the S; May-July. Leaves rather broad, the lower ones in a *rosette*. Limestone turf in the N, chalk turf in Kent.

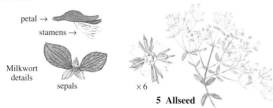

petal →
stamens →

Milkwort
details

sepals

×6

5 Allseed

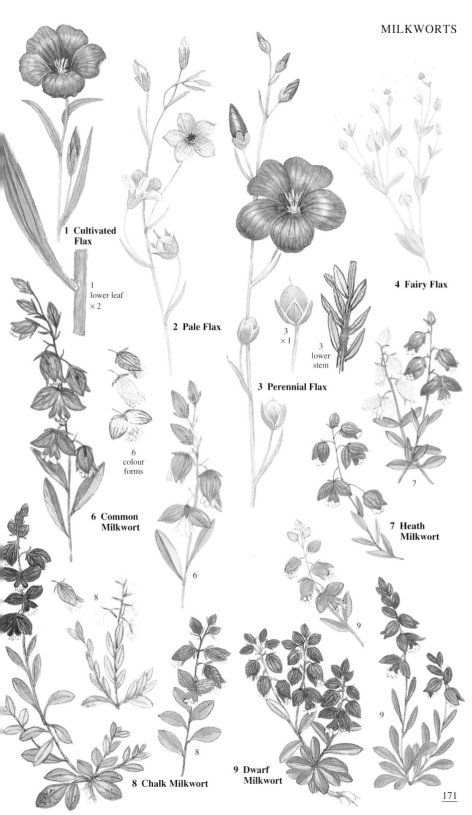

1 Cultivated Flax

1 lower leaf × 2

2 Pale Flax

4 Fairy Flax

3 × 1

3 lower stem

3 Perennial Flax

6 colour forms

6 Common Milkwort

6

7 Heath Milkwort

8

8 Chalk Milkwort

9

9 Dwarf Milkwort

9

WOOD-SORREL FAMILY Oxalidaceae

Perennials, often with bulbils. Flowers 5-petalled. Leaves trefoil. Fruit a capsule. Besides the native Wood-sorrel, there are 17 introduced species, only the more frequent being described below. For two Scilly species, see p. 457. Divided into white, yellow and pink flowers.

Flowers white

1 Wood-sorrel *Oxalis acetosella*. Much the commonest and the only native wood-sorrel; delicate, pale green, creeping and patch-forming. Flowers white, usually veined mauve, rarely pink or mauve, 12-18mm, cup-shaped, solitary, on leafless stalks to 10cm; April-May. Leaves in tufts, sometimes purple beneath. *Woods*, hedge-banks, also in shade on mountains.

Pink Sorrel *O. articulata* (**5**) and **Pale Pink Sorrel** *O. latifolia* (**6a**), see below.

Flowers yellow

2 Spreading Yellow Sorrel *Oxalis corniculata*. The most frequent of the yellow sorrels, *sprawling* to 50cm. Flowers 6-10mm, long-stalked, in small clusters, rarely solitary, up the stems; May-Sept. Leaves *often* dark purple. Fruits on *spreading or down-turned* stalks. A weed in many gardens and nurseries. **2a Least Yellow Sorrel** *O. exilis* is smaller in all its parts with thread-like stems, flowers always solitary and leaves always green. Much less frequent.

3 Upright Yellow Sorrel *Oxalis stricta*. Like Spreading Yellow Sorrel (**2**), but has *erect* stems to 40cm, leaves less often purple and fruits on *erect* stalks. Less frequent.

4 Bermuda Buttercup *Oxalis pes-caprae*. Much the largest-flowered yellow sorrel, a perennial reproducing by numerous bulblets, to 20cm. Flowers bright sulphur-yellow, much larger than buttercups at *20-25mm*, in umbel-like clusters; almost all the year, but especially February-June. Leaves sometimes with a pale brown blotch. A vigorous weed of bulb-fields and elsewhere, especially in the Scillies.

Flowers pink

Bulbils	around bulb:	Pink-Purple
	on creeping stems:	Pale Pink, 4-leaved (p. 457)
	at base of leaves:	Lilac
	none:	Wood-sorrel
Leaves	spotted beneath:	Pink, Pink-purple

Wood-sorrel *Oxalis acetosella* (**1**), see above.

5 Pink Sorrel *Oxalis articulata*. The most frequent pink-flowered wood-sorrel, tufted, to 35cm. Flowers deep pink, sometimes pale pink or white, 10-15mm, in an umbel; May-Sept. Leaves with numerous *pale orange spots* beneath. A favourite garden plant, often escaping.

6 Pink-purple Sorrel *Oxalis debilis*. Tufted, with many bulbils *around bulb*; stems to 20cm. Flowers *purplish*-pink, larger than Pink Sorrel (**5**), 15-20mm, in clusters; July-Sept. Leaves with *dark or orange spots* beneath, especially on margins. Fruits rare. A garden weed, readily spread by its bulbils to nearby bare ground, the leaves often present without the flowers. **6a Pale Pink Sorrel** *O. latifolia* has the bulbils *long-stalked*, flowers smaller (8-13mm), pinker, sometimes white, and leaves *not spotted beneath.*

7 Lilac Sorrel *Oxalis incarnata*. Perennial, with bulbils at the *base of leaves*; stems to 20cm. Flowers pale lilac, with darker veins, *solitary*; May-July. Leaves without spots. A weed of cultivation and nearby banks and walls.

1 Wood-sorrel
colour forms

2 Spreading Yellow Sorrel

2 purple leaved form

1 Wood-sorrel

2a Least Yellow Sorrel

3 Upright Yellow Sorrel

4 Bermuda Buttercup

6 back of leaf

6 Pink-purple Sorrel

5 Pink Sorrel

colour forms

6a white form

6a Pale Pink Sorrel

7 Lilac Sorrel

CRANESBILL FAMILY Geraniaceae

Cranesbills *Geranium.* All except Shining Cranesbill (p. 176), conspicuously hairy or downy. Flowers 5-petalled, divided below by size. Distinguished from storksbills (p. 178) by their toothed and *palmately lobed* leaves, usually deeply cut to more than half-way. Fruit with five segments curling upwards from the base when ripe and ending in a long pointed beak, the 'crane's bill'. Only the most frequent of the 15 or more naturalised species and hybrids are described below, divided into large, medium, and small flowers (p. 176).

Petals	deeply notched:	Hedgerow, Dovesfoot, Small-flowered, Cut-leaved
	shallowly notched:	Purple, Wood, Bloody, French, Pencilled, Round-leaved, Long-stalked
	not notched:	Meadow, Wood, Herb Robert, Little Robin, Shining, Round-leaved, Long-stalked

Flowers large, 20mm or more across

1 Meadow Cranesbill. *Geranium pratense.* A most handsome medium/tall perennial, stems long-hairy, often reddish, to 1m. Flowers a soft *violet blue*, petals *not notched*, 25-30mm; June-Sept. Leaves 7-9-lobed, cut almost to base. Fruit stalks *bent down* when ripe. Grassland on lime, mainly in the lowlands, especially the Cotswold road verges. Numerous cultivars, hybrids and similar species are liable to escape, the most frequent being **1a Purple Cranesbill** G. × *magnificum*, whose slightly larger, more purplish flowers have notched petals; leaves less deeply cut.

2 Wood Cranesbill *Geranium sylvaticum.* Much like Meadow Cranesbill (**1**), near which it may grow in N England, but has rather smaller, *mauver* and less blue flowers, the petals sometimes slightly notched; June-August; stems to 75cm, leaves less deeply cut and fruit stalks *erect* when ripe. Open woods, hedge-banks, upland meadows, moors, mountain ledges.

3 Bloody Cranesbill *Geranium sanguineum.* A showy, clump-forming short perennial, to 40cm. Flowers bright *red-purple* (sometimes pink on Walney I, Cumbria), 25-30mm; May-August. Leaves small, 5-7-lobed, narrowly and sharply cut. Dry grassland, dunes, rocks, mainly on limy soils; widely naturalised.

4 French Cranesbill *Geranium endressii.* Short/medium perennial, to 60cm. Flowers deep *salmon-pink*, the veins darkening as they fade, 24-28mm; May-August. Leaves broadly 5-lobed. A frequent garden escape. Its hybrid with Pencilled Cranesbill (**5**). G. × *oxonianum*, is very similar, with flowers deep to pale pink, the veins often conspicuous, and no ripe fruits; may be commoner than French Cranesbill.

5 Pencilled Cranesbill *Geranium versicolor* is quite distinct from both French Cranesbill (**4**) and the hybrid (as well as all other native or escaped cranesbills), having flowers *white* or very pale lilac, with *purple veins*; leaves less deeply cut. A less frequent garden escape.

Flowers medium, 10-20mm across

6 Herb Robert *Geranium robertianum.* A strong-smelling short/medium hairy annual, with stems often reddish, to 50cm. Flowers clear deep pink, occasionally white, petals not notched, pollen *orange*; 14-18mm; Apr-Nov. Leaves 3/5-lobed. Fruits slightly ridged. Woods, hedge- and other banks, shingle (when may be prostrate and hairless), mountain screes.

7 Little Robin *Geranium purpureum.* Often taller and greener than Herb Robert (**6**), of which it may be a subspecies, with smaller (7-14mm) flowers, *yellow* pollen, more narrowly cut leaves and more *conspicuously ridged* fruits. Dry, often limy banks, shingle (when often prostrate) and cliffs by the sea.

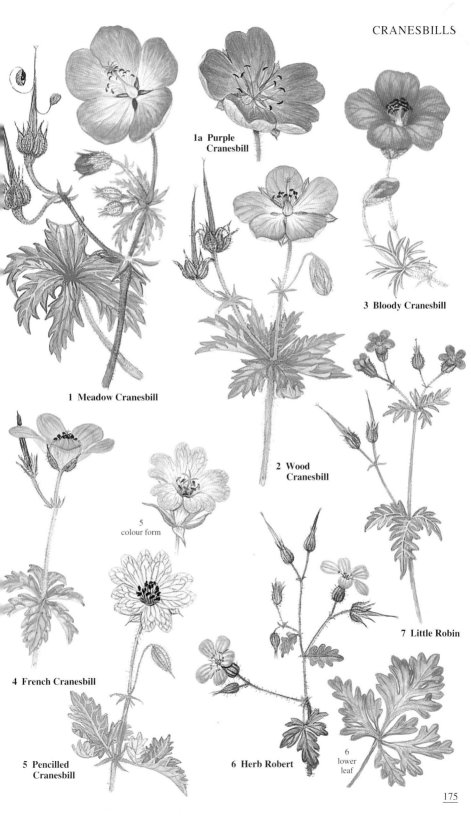

1a Purple Cranesbill

3 Bloody Cranesbill

1 Meadow Cranesbill

2 Wood Cranesbill

5 colour form

7 Little Robin

4 French Cranesbill

5 Pencilled Cranesbill

6 Herb Robert

6 lower leaf

1 Hedgerow Cranesbill *Geranium pyrenaicum*. Medium downy perennial, to 60cm. Flowers pink-purple, petals *deeply notched*, 14-18mm; May-Sept. Leaves 7-lobed. Fruits downy, *smooth*. Grassy places, hedge- and other banks.

2 Shining Cranesbill *Geranium lucidum*. Our only cranesbill with *glossy* roundish leaves; scarcely downy, often *reddish*, erect to sprawling medium perennial, to 40cm. Flowers deep pink, petals not notched, sepals ending with a bristle, 10-14mm; May-Sept. Leaves roundish, 5-lobed. Walls, rocks, hedge-banks, bare places, often on lime.

3 Round-leaved Cranesbill *Geranium rotundifolium*. Medium hairy, usually erect annual, to 40cm. Flowers pink, petals sometimes slightly notched, 10-12mm; April-August. Leaves *roundish*, 5/9-lobed, cut to half-way. Fruits hairy. smooth. Hedge- and other banks, walls, bare ground.

4 Long-stalked Cranesbill *Geranium columbinum*. More or less erect, often reddish, downy, short/medium annual, to 60cm. Flowers rosy pink, 12-18mm, solitary on *slender stalks*, the petals not or shallowly notched, the sepals ending in a bristle; May-August. Leaves with almost linear lobes, cut almost to the base. Grassy places, chiefly on lime.

5 Dusky Cranesbill *Geranium phaeum*. By far our darkest-flowered cranesbill; medium/tall perennial, to 80cm. Flowers often almost *blackish purple*, 15-20mm; May-Sept. Leaves broadly 7-lobed, often with a darker blotch. Frequent escape in shady places.

Flowers small

6 Dovesfoot Cranesbill *Geranium molle*. Low/short, erect to sprawling, hairy annual, to 40cm. Flowers variably *pink-purple*, 6-10mm, petals notched, all stamens with anthers; April-Sept. Leaves roundish, 7-9-lobed, cut to at least half-way. Fruits hairless, usually ridged. Grassy and waste places, often with bare patches, usually on lime.

7 Small-flowered Cranesbill *Geranium pusillum*. Differs from Dovesfoot Cranesbill (**6**) in its *smaller* (4-6mm), usually *pale dingy lilac* flowers, the outer five stamens without anthers, leaves more narrowly cut to over half-way and fruits downy and not ridged. Habitat similar.

8 Cut-leaved Cranesbill *Geranium dissectum*. Short/medium, erect to sprawling annual, to 60cm. Flowers pink-purple, 8-10mm, well notched, sepals ending in a bristle. Leaves cut *nearly to base* with seven very narrow lobes. Fruits downy. Cultivated, waste and grassy places with bare patches.

Little Robin *Geranium purpureum*, p. 174.

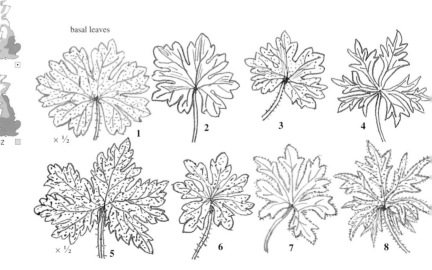

basal leaves

× ½   1   2   3   4

× ½   5   6   7   8

176

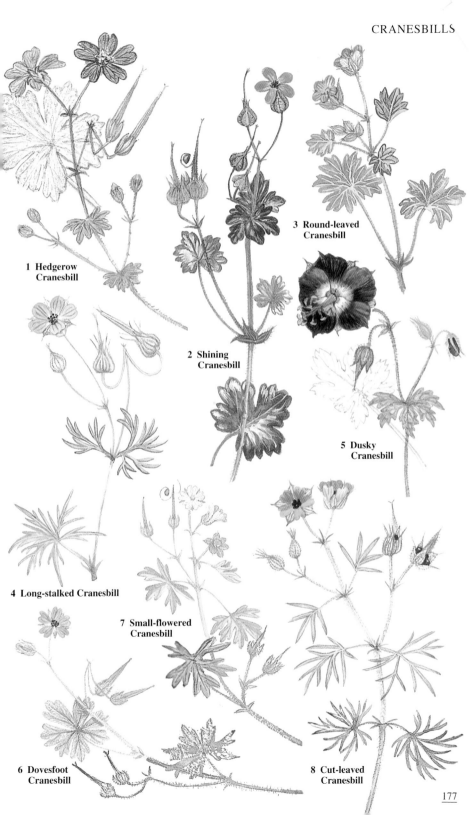

1 Hedgerow
  Cranesbill

2 Shining
  Cranesbill

3 Round-leaved
  Cranesbill

4 Long-stalked Cranesbill

5 Dusky
  Cranesbill

6 Dovesfoot
  Cranesbill

7 Small-flowered
  Cranesbill

8 Cut-leaved
  Cranesbill

Storksbills *Erodium*. Hairy annuals, like small cranesbills (p. 176), but with leaves pinnate or pinnately lobed, never palmately lobed. Flowers usually pink or pink-purple. Fruits with a spirally twisted beak. None of the 20 alien species are described, as they are rarely seen away from fields manured with shoddy.

1 Common Storksbill *Erodium cicutarium*. Variable short annual, prostrate, sprawling or erect, to 60cm; sometimes slightly foetid, but not musky. Flowers pink-purple, sometimes white, often with a *blackish spot* at the base of the two upper petals, usually 10-18mm, in clusters of 3-7; April-Sept. Leaves 2-pinnate with *narrow stipules* at their base. Fruits with beak 2-4cm. Dunes and other dry grassy and sandy places, especially on lime and near the sea.

2 Sticky Storksbill *Erodium lebelii*. Shorter than Common Storksbill (**1**), with sand adhering to many *sticky hairs*. Flowers pale lilac-pink or white, with no black spots, smaller (usually 7-10mm), 2-4 in the cluster; leaves similar but sticky; and fruits with shorter beak, to 2.2cm. Coastal dunes.

3 *Musk Storksbill *Erodium moschatum*. Generally larger and coarser than Common Storksbill (**1**), more profusely white-hairy and often with a faint sweetish musky smell; with or without a central stem, to 60cm. Flowers of a more purplish pink, with no blackish spots, larger (16-24mm), in heads of 5-12, the stalks *sticky-haired*; February-Oct. Leaves *1-pinnate*. Fruits with beak 2-4.5cm. As a native, bare or sparsely grassy places, mainly near the sea (inland in the Mendips); as an alien, mainly a weed of cultivation, notably with several other species in fields manured by shoddy.

4 Sea Storksbill *Erodium maritimum*. A prostrate downy annual, usually compact or just a tiny rosette, to 10cm. Flowers pale pink, but rarely seen as the *petals drop* so early, 4-6mm, solitary or paired; April-Sept. Leaves *pinnately lobed*. Fruits with beak *c.* 1cm. Bare ground near the sea.

BALSAM FAMILY Balsaminaceae

Hairless annuals with fleshy stems. Flowers with a unique shape, 5-petalled with a broad lower lip, a small upper hood and a usually curved spur behind; in loose clusters. Leaves oval, stalked, slightly toothed. The seeds explode from the ripe cylindrical fruits. Only one native species, Touch-me-not Balsam (**7**).

5 Himalayan Balsam *Impatiens glandulifera*. Our tallest and commonest balsam, with thick-ribbed, often reddish stems to 2m or more. Flowers variably *pink-purple*, sometimes almost white, with a short thin bent spur, fragrant, 25-40mm; June-Oct. Leaves in whorls of 2-5. Aka Indian Balsam or Policeman's Helmet. An aggressive coloniser of river, canal and stream banks, also on waste ground.

6 Orange Balsam *Impatiens capensis*. Tall and bushy, to 1.5m. One of our very few *orange*-flowered plants, with numerous blood-red spots, 20-30mm, the long slender spur *bent into a crook*; July-August. Leaves alternate. River and canal banks.

7 Touch-me-not Balsam *Impatiens noli-tangere*. Differs from Orange Balsam (**6**) in having stems to 1m and larger flowers, *yellow* speckled red, with the spur only *curved*. Named for its explosive fruits. Damp or wet woods.

8 Small Balsam *Impatiens parviflora*. Medium, to 60cm. Flowers *yellow*, and unspotted, with a short straight spur, 6-18mm, much smaller than our other balsams; May-Sept. Leaves alternate. Bare and shady places.

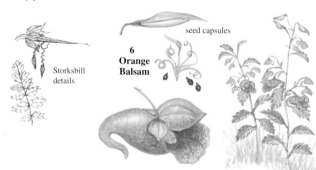

Storksbill details

6 Orange Balsam

seed capsules

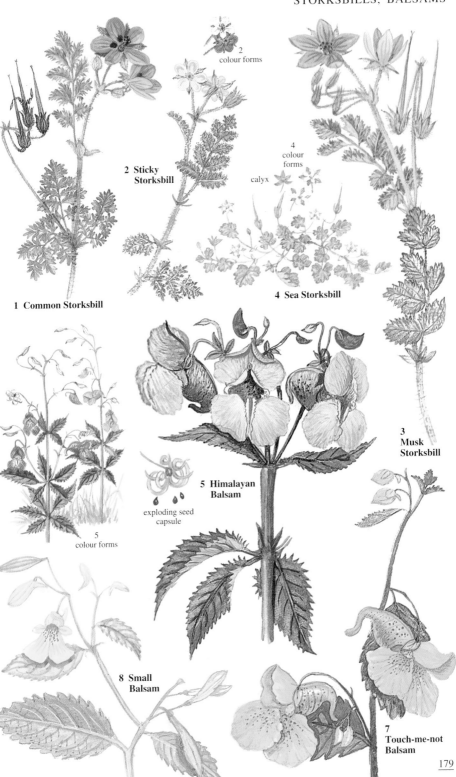

2
colour forms

2 **Sticky Storksbill**

4
colour
forms

calyx

4 **Sea Storksbill**

1 **Common Storksbill**

3 **Musk Storksbill**

exploding seed capsule

5 **Himalayan Balsam**

5
colour forms

8 **Small Balsam**

7 **Touch-me-not Balsam**

179

CARROT FAMILY Apiaceae (Umbelliferae)

Typical umbellifers are easily identified: their flowers are arranged in a flat umbrella-like head or umbel. (The few atypical umbellifers are described on p. 196. Yarrow (p. 268) is an umbellifer-like composite). The spokes (rays) of the umbel end in secondary umbels, with a number of small 5-petalled flowers arranged in a smaller umbel, usually with a flattish top, but becoming domed as they go over. The tops of these smaller umbels make up the top of the whole umbrella. In some country districts the larger umbellifers are still called Keck or Kecks. The hollow stems of, for instance, Hogweed and Wild Angelica, used to be, and perhaps still are, cut by country boys to make whistles. Umbellifers look disconcertingly alike at first; the most important clues to their identity are:

* flower colour, white (sometimes pink) or yellow.

* the presence or absence of small green bracts at the base of both the main umbel (lower bracts) and the smaller umbels (upper bracts).

* whether the leaves are 1-2- or 3-pinnate, some being finely divided and fern-like.

* the shape and presence or absence of wings, ridges, spines or hooks on the fruits.

Only a few of the *c*. 90 established aliens and casuals can be described here, divided thus:

1. Flowers white/pink: drier places (below)
   1a. Over 1m. 1b. 60-100cm (p. 182). 1c. 30-60cm (p. 184). 1d. Less than 30cm (p. 188).

2. Flowers white/pink: damper/wetter places (p. 188)
   2a. Over 1m (p. 188). 2b. 60-100cm (p. 190). 2c. 30-60cm (p. 192). 2d. Less than 30cm (p. 192).

3. Flowers yellow (p. 194)

4. Atypical umbellifers (p. 196)

Flowers sometimes pink:	Hogweed, Hedge Parsley, Greater Burnet-saxifrage, Coriander, Cumin, Corky-fruited/Tubular Water Dropworts, Sulphurwort
No upper or lower bracts:	Greater Burnet-saxifrage, Ground Elder, Burnet-saxifrage, Caraway (usually), Wild Celery, Wild Parsnip, Fennel, Giant Fennel, Alexanders
No lower bracts: S = sometimes U = usually	Hogweeds, Cow Parsley, Rough Chervil, Pignut (S), Bur Chervil, Knotted Bur Parsley, Caraway, Spignel (S), Coriander, Fool's Parsley (U), Spreading Hedge Parsley (S), Honewort (S), Angelicas, Hemlock/Fine-leaved (U)/River Water Dropworts, Cowbane, Masterwort, Sulphurwort, Cambridge Milk Parsley, Fool's Watercress (U), Tubular Water Dropwort (U), Lesser Marshwort, Pepper-saxifrage, Hog's Fennel (S)
Rootstock covered with fibrous dead leaf-stalks:	Burnet-saxifrage (usually), Spignel, Moon Carrot, Honewort, Whorled Caraway, Hog's Fennel

1a. Flowers white/pink: drier places: Very tall, often over 1m.

1 Hogweed *Heracleum sphondylium*. The commonest tall wayside white umbellifer of the summer and autumn; a stout coarse, roughly hairy biennial, with hollow stems to 2 or even 3m. Flowers usually white, but sometimes pink or even purple, and rarely greenish-white in E Anglia, (**1a** ssp. *sibiricum*), the umbels 50-200mm across, the petals of the outer flowers very unequal, usually no lower bracts; May-Nov, and throughout mild winters. Leaves 1/3-pinnate, with usually very broad, toothed leaflets. Fruits flattened, oval, winged, with dark streaks. Aka Cow Parsnip. Grassland, road verges, waste and cultivated ground.

2 P Giant Hogweed *Heracleum mantegazzianum*. An outsize Hogweed (**1**), with often reddish stems 5-10cm wide and *attaining 5m*. Flowers white, in umbels *up to 1m across*; June-August. Leaves 1m long, equalling their stout stalks, Fruits narrower. An aggressive alien invader of road and stream banks and other waste places. Causes skin damage.

3 P Hemlock *Conium maculatum*. The only white umbellifer with both hollow *purple-spotted* stems and an unpleasant smell when bruised; hairless biennial, to 2.5m or more. Flowers white, umbels 20-60mm, upper bracts only round the edge of the small umbels; June-August. Leaves 2/5-pinnate, finely cut. Fruits globular with *wavy ridges*. Road- and stream-banks and other waste ground. *Very poisonous*; many other umbellifers are loosely referred to as hemlock, but this is the plant that killed Socrates.

1 SOZ ▪

2 Z ▪↑↑

3 SO ▪

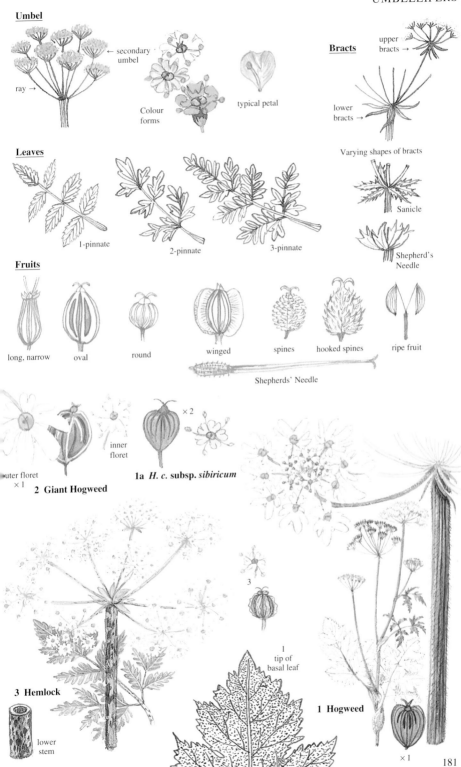

Umbel

← secondary umbel

ray →

Colour forms

typical petal

Bracts

upper bracts →

lower bracts →

Varying shapes of bracts

Sanicle

Shepherd's Needle

Leaves

1-pinnate

2-pinnate

3-pinnate

Fruits

long, narrow

oval

round

winged

spines

hooked spines

ripe fruit

Shepherds' Needle

inner floret

outer floret
× 1

× 2

1a *H. c.* subsp. *sibiricum*

2 Giant Hogweed

3

1
tip of basal leaf

3 Hemlock

lower stem

1 Hogweed

× 1

1b. Flowers white/pink: drier places: Tall, usually 60-100cm.

1 Cow Parsley *Anthriscus sylvestris*. Much the commonest umbellifer of the spring hedge-rows, often whitening roadsides, a downy perennial to 1m or more; stems hollow, often be-coming purple. Flowers white, umbels 20-60mm, no lower bracts, the upper pointed oval; April-June, sporadically later and through mild winters. Leaves fresh green, 3-pinnate, sharply cut, appearing in January, or even earlier. Fruits smooth, long, broad-based. Wood borders, hedge-banks and other shady places.

2 Rough Chervil *Chaerophyllum temulum*. Starts to flower between Cow Parsley (**1**), though never so dominant, and Hedge Parsley (**3**) in the hedge-banks; differing from both in its usually *purple-spotted* stems (shared only by Hemlock, p. 180), markedly swollen at the leaf-junctions. A coarsely hairy biennial, stems *solid*, to 1m, the whole plant later turn-ing purple. Flowers white, umbels 30-60mm, usually no lower bracts, the upper lanceo-late; May-July. Leaves 2-3-pinnate, *bluntly lobed*. Fruits long, narrow, broader above, ridged. Hedge-banks, wood borders and other places in light shade.

3 Hedge Parsley *Torilis japonica*. The latest to flower of the three common white hedgerow umbellifers; a medium/tall grey-green annual, with stiffer stems than Cow Parsley (**1**) and Rough Chervil (**2**), to 2m. Flowers white or pink, umbels 20-40mm, with both upper and lower bracts; July-Sept. Leaves 1-3-pinnate, narrowly triangular oblong, sharply cut. Fruits egg-shaped with purple *hooked bristles*. Hedge-banks, scrub, woodland edges.

4 Sweet Cicely *Myrrhis odorata*. Aromatic downy perennial, to 1m or more. Flowers white, in foamy umbels 10-60mm, no lower bracts; April-June. Leaves 2-4-pinnate, with small *pale flecks*, smelling of *aniseed* when crushed. Fruits upright, ribbed, dark shiny brown, *c.* 2cm long. Established in grassy places, often near houses, and replacing Cow Parsley (**1**) on many road verges in dales in N England.

5 Stone Parsley *Sison amomum*. A bushy hairless biennial, with solid wiry stems, to 1m; when crushed has a *pungent smell* of a mixture of nutmeg and petrol. Flowers white, with deeply notched petals, few to the very *long* but unequally stalked smaller umbels, main um-bels 10-40mm, the whole cluster more like a garden Gypsophila than an umbellifer; July-August. Leaves 1-pinnate, often turning wine-purple as they go over, the upper with very narrow leaflets, the lower larger and coarsely toothed, soon withering. Fruits ridged, almost globular. Hedge-banks, grassy places, especially on clay.

6 Corn Parsley *Petroselinum segetum*. Very like Stone Parsley (**5**), but smells of *parsley*, and has petals less deeply notched and some small umbels very short-stalked; longer, greyer-green leaves, with leaflets more deeply toothed and often lobed at the base; and more markedly ridged fruits. Hedge-banks and other grassy places, often near the sea.

7 Greater Burnet-saxifrage *Pimpinella major*. Tall hairless perennial, with stems hol-low, well grooved, to 1m; unrelated to either burnets or saxifrages. Flowers white or pink, umbels 30-60mm, with *no bracts*; July-Sept. Leaves 1-pinnate, dark green, shiny, coarsely toothed, the end leaflet 3-lobed. Fruits almost globular, hairless, slightly ridged. Grassy, often shady places, including woodland margins and stream banks.

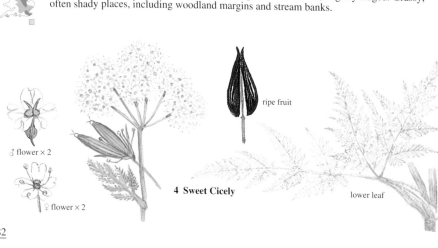

♂ flower × 2

♀ flower × 2

4 Sweet Cicely

ripe fruit

lower leaf

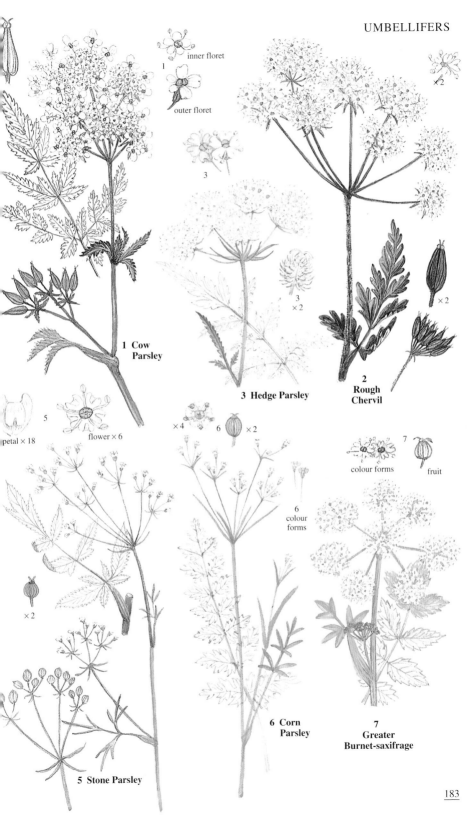

inner floret

1

outer floret

×2

3

1 Cow
Parsley

3
× 2

3 Hedge Parsley

×2

2
Rough
Chervil

5

petal × 18

flower × 6

× 4   6 × 2

colour forms   fruit   7

6
colour
forms

× 2

6 Corn
Parsley

7
Greater
Burnet-saxifrage

5 Stone Parsley

183

1 **Bladder-seed *Physospermum cornubiense*. Almost hairless perennial, with solid stems to 1m. Flowers white, umbels 20-50mm; July-August. Leaves dark green, *2-trefoil* at base, 1-trefoil or undivided up stems, the leaflets well toothed. Fruits distinctively *swollen*, like small bladders. West country woods, with an outlying site near Burnham Beeches, Bucks.

2 ***Hartwort *Tordylium maximum*. A roughly hairy annual, to 1m. Flowers white, the *outermost petals* the largest, umbels 20-25mm; June-July. Leaves *1-pinnate*, the leaflets toothed, narrowing up the stem; the undivided lowest leaves have withered by June. Fruits flattened oval, bristly, with a thickened border and prominent sepal-teeth. Two grassy sites in S Essex.

1c. Flowers white/pink: drier places: Medium, usually 30-60mm.

3 Ground Elder *Aegopodium podagraria*. A hairless perennial and pestilential weed, creeping to form *extensive patches*; stems hollow, grooved, to 1m. Flowers white, umbels dense, 20-60mm, usually with *no bracts*; June-August. Leaves 1/2-trefoil, with irregularly toothed, broad lanceolate leaflets. Fruits egg-shaped, ribbed. Shady places, waysides, all too often in gardens.

4 Wild Carrot *Daucus carota*. The only common white umbellifer with *conspicuous 3-forked or pinnate bracts* fringing the umbels; a roughly hairy biennial with a pungent smell when crushed; stems stiff, solid to 1.5m. Flowers dull white, often with a red flower in the centre, petals often unequal, umbels 30-70mm, folding inwards in fruit; June-Sept. Leaves 3-pinnate, feathery, often grey-green. Fruits with often hooked spines. Grassy places, especially on lime. **4a Sea Carrot** ssp. *gummifer* has stouter, almost succulent stems, darker green leaves and saucer-shaped fruiting umbels; coastal. **Edible Carrot** ssp. *sativus*, an occasional escape or relic, has the familiar stout orange-red edible root.

5 Bur Chervil *Anthriscus caucalis*. Upright to sprawling annual with *hairless* hollow stems to 70cm. Flowers white, umbels 10-40mm, on stalks *opposite* the very finely cut, almost feathery, *2/3-pinnate* leaves; no lower bracts; May-June. Fruits egg-shaped, beaked, covered with *short hooked* bristles. Bare and waste, often sandy or shingly, ground, most often near the sea.

6 Knotted Hedge-parsley *Torilis nodosa*. Upright to sprawling, roughly hairy annual, to 50cm. Flowers white, umbels 5-12mm, on *very short* stalks *opposite* the finely cut *1/3-pinnate* leaves; no lower bracts; May-July. Fruits egg-shaped, warty on the inside, covered with *long, scarcely hooked*, bristles on the outside. Arable fields inland, dry sunny banks near the sea.

7 Burnet-saxifrage *Pimpinella saxifraga*. Neither a burnet nor a saxifrage; a usually downy perennial, with tough, almost solid, slightly ridged stems, to 70cm. Flowers white, umbels 20-50mm, no bracts; May-Sept. Root leaves 1-pinnate with broad, toothed leaflets *quite distinct* from the almost linear leaflets of the 2-pinnate stem leaves; leaf-stalks sheath-like. Fruits globular, shiny. Grassland, usually on lime.

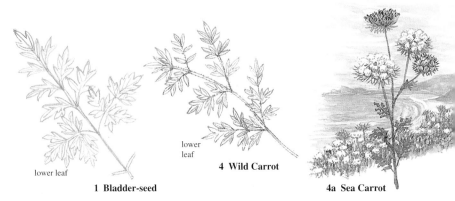

lower leaf
1 Bladder-seed

lower leaf
4 Wild Carrot

4a Sea Carrot

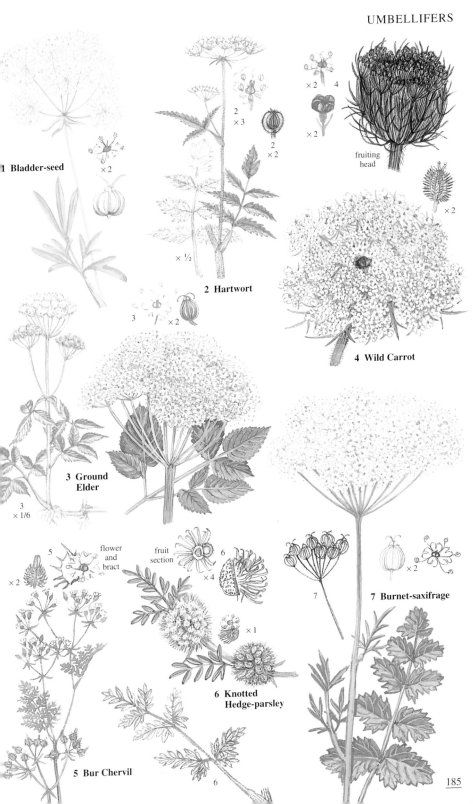

1 Bladder-seed

×2

a

2
×3

2
×2

×½

2 Hartwort

3
×2

×2 4

×2

fruiting
head

×2

4 Wild Carrot

3
×1/6

**3 Ground
Elder**

5

flower
and
bract

fruit
section

6

×4

×2

×1

**6 Knotted
Hedge-parsley**

7

×2

7 Burnet-saxifrage

5 Bur Chervil

6

1 Pignut *Conopodium majus*. A slender hairless perennial, stems to 40cm, arising from a rounded brown tuber, edible for humans as well as pigs. Flowers white, umbels 30-70mm, sometimes no lower bracts; May-July. Leaves 2-3-pinnate, the leaflets *narrowly linear* up the stems, less so at the base, *hairy* along the edges and pointed at the tip. Fruits oblong, styles erect. Woods, open scrub, grassland.

2 **Great Pignut *Bunium bulbocastanum*. Stouter and usually somewhat taller than Pignut (**1**) with lower bracts always present, leaflet margins *hairless*, their tips more narrowly pointed, and longer, more ribbed fruits with the styles *down-turned*. Chalk turf and arable reverting to grass.

3 Caraway *Carum carvi*. Hairless biennial with hollow stems to 60cm. Flowers white, umbels 20-40mm, *folding inwards* in fruit, usually no bracts; June-July. Leaves 2/3-pinnate. Fruits aromatic (used to flavour cakes), egg-shaped, ridged. Native in grassland, introduced on roadsides and waste ground.

4 *Spignel *Meum athamanticum*. A tufted aromatic hairless perennial, with hollow stems to 60cm. Flowers white, sometimes tinged pink, umbels 30-60mm, sometimes no bracts; May-June. Leaves 2-pinnate, with many *thread-like* leaflets in bushy whorls. Fruits egg-shaped, ridged. Hill pastures.

5 Coriander *Coriandrum sativum*. A hairless annual with a nauseous smell; stems solid to 50cm. Flowers pink or white, the outer petals longer, umbels 10-30mm, no lower bracts; June-August. Lower leaves 1/2-pinnate with broad leaflets, the upper 2-pinnate with narrow leaflets. Fruits globular, ridged, red-brown and pleasantly aromatic when ripe and used for flavouring. An increasing casual near where it is cooked or eaten. **5a Cumin** *Cuminum cyminum*, similarly used in cooking, has often 3-lobed lower bracts, 2-trefoil leaves with thread-like leaflets and fruits often bristly.

6 Scots Lovage *Ligusticum scoticum*. A stocky hairless tufted perennial, with stiff, ribbed, usually purple stems, hollow below, to 60cm. Flowers greenish-white, umbels 40-60mm; June-July. Leaves bright green, leathery, glossy, 2-trefoil with broad, toothed leaflets and inflated sheathing stalks. Fruits oval, flattened, ridged. Cliffs and rocks by the sea.

7 **Moon Carrot *Seseli libanotis*. Scarcely downy perennial, with solid grooved stems to 60cm. Flowers pure white, umbels 30-60mm, 15-30-rayed, with long lower bracts, carrot-like but *undivided*; July-Sept. Leaves 2/3-pinnate, deeply cut and somewhat crisped. Fruits egg-shaped, downy, with prominent sepal-teeth. Chalk turf.

8 Longleaf *Falcaria vulgaris*. Easily identified by its *long strap-like leaflets*; a hairless greyish patch-forming perennial, with solid stems to 60cm. Flowers white, in open umbels, the small umbels long-stalked; July-August. Leaves 1-2-trefoil with leaflets toothed and 10-30cm long. Fruits oblong, rarely ripening. Often established in grassy places, road verges and scrub.

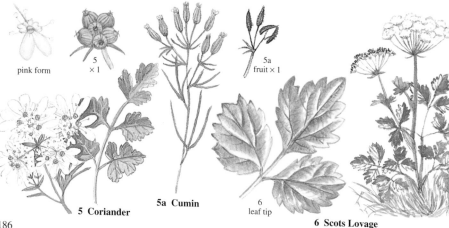

pink form

5 × 1

5a fruit × 1

5 Coriander

5a Cumin

6 leaf tip

6 Scots Lovage

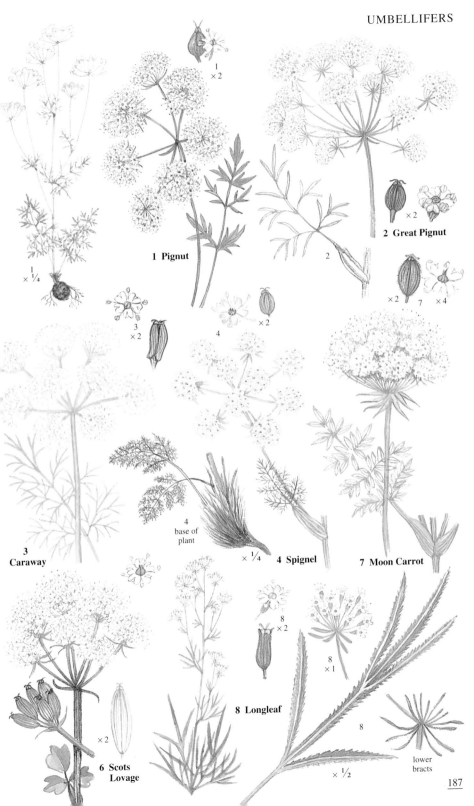

1
×2

2 Great Pignut

×2

1
Pignut

2

7   ×4
×2

1
× ¼

3
×2

4

×2

3
Caraway

4
base of
plant
× ¼   **4 Spignel**

7 Moon Carrot

8
×2

8
×1

×2

8 Longleaf

8

6 Scots
Lovage

× ½

lower
bracts

1d. Flowers white/pink: drier places: Short: usually less than 30cm.

1 Fool's Parsley *Aethusa cynapium.* Easily recognised by the bearded effect of the 3-4 *long upper bracts* on the outer side of each small umbel; a hairless annual with ribbed stems to 1m. Flowers white, umbels 20-60mm, usually no lower bracts; June-Oct. Leaves dark green, 2-3-pinnate. Fruit globular, smooth. A weed of cultivated ground.

2 *Shepherd's Needle *Scandix pecten-veneris.* A somewhat atypical umbellifer because of its only 1-3 small umbels, but its long *needle-like* 3-7cm fruits make it one of the easiest to identify; an almost hairless annual, to 50cm. Flowers white, umbels 70-90mm, upper bracts deeply toothed, no lower bracts; May-August. Leaves fresh green, 2/3-pinnate, finely cut. Arable fields, apparently increasing again.

3 *Spreading Hedge-parsley *Torilis arvensis.* A low/short annual, with spreading wiry stems, to 50cm. Flowers white, umbels 10-25mm, one or no lower bracts; July-Sept. Leaves 1/2-pinnate, the leaflets sharply pointed. Fruits egg-shaped, with long straight spines. Arable fields and other bare ground, especially on lime; much decreased.

4 **Honewort *Trinia glauca.* A low, much branched greyish perennial, with solid stems to 20cm. Flowers white, male and female on different plants, umbels 10-30mm; bracts sometimes 3-lobed, the lower often absent; May-June. Leaves 2/3-pinnate, the leaflets narrow. Fruits egg-shaped, ridged. Dry limestone turf, very local.

2a. Flowers white/pink: damper/wetter places: Very tall or long, often over 1m.

5 Wild Angelica *Angelica sylvestris.* A stout perennial, often suffused *purple,* with *downy to hairless* stems to 2.5m. Flowers white, often tinged pink, umbels 30-150mm, usually with no lower bracts; June-Sept. Leaves 2/3-pinnate with broad toothed leaflets and inflated sheathing stalks. Fruits oval, flattened, with four broad wings and no sepal-teeth. Woods, hedge- and stream-banks, fens and other shady places. **5a Garden Angelica** *A. archangelica* has stems usually green, flowers *yellowish-green,* umbels 5-7cm, May-August; leaf-stalks (the source of the sweetmeat) aromatic and fruits with corky wings. Naturalised on river banks, especially by the Thames at Kew, and waste ground.

6 P Hemlock Water Dropwort *Oenanthe crocata.* Stout, hairless, clump-forming, parsley-scented, *very poisonous* perennial; stems hollow, to 1.5m. Flowers white, umbels 50-100mm, sometimes no lower bracts; May-August. Leaves *glossy,* 3-pinnate, the broad leaflets wedge-shaped at the base and 2-3-toothed. Fruits *cylindrical,* with long styles. By ponds, ditches and other fresh water.

7 Fine-leaved Water Dropwort *Oenanthe aquatica.* A hairless perennial, with stout shiny hollow stems, to 1.5m, but can be much shorter. Flowers white, umbels 20-40mm, on short stalks *opposite* the leaf-stalks, usually no lower bracts; June-Sept. Leaves 2/4-pinnate, with sharply pointed leaflets; also submerged leaves with *threadlike* leaflets. Fruits narrowly oval, the styles and sepal-teeth very short. Cf. River Water Dropwort (**8**). In and by still and slow-moving fresh water.

8 River Water Dropwort *Oenanthe fluviatilis.* Differs from Fine-leaved Water Dropwort (**7**) in being fully submerged, the leaves with narrowly *wedge-shaped* leaflets, until flowering time, July-Sept, when the very similar flowers with no lower bracts, and aerial leaves with *blunter* leaflets emerge; fruits larger. In fast rivers and streams.

5a Garden Angelica

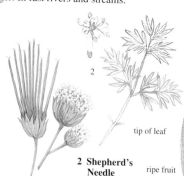

2

2 Shepherd's Needle ripe fruit

tip of leaf

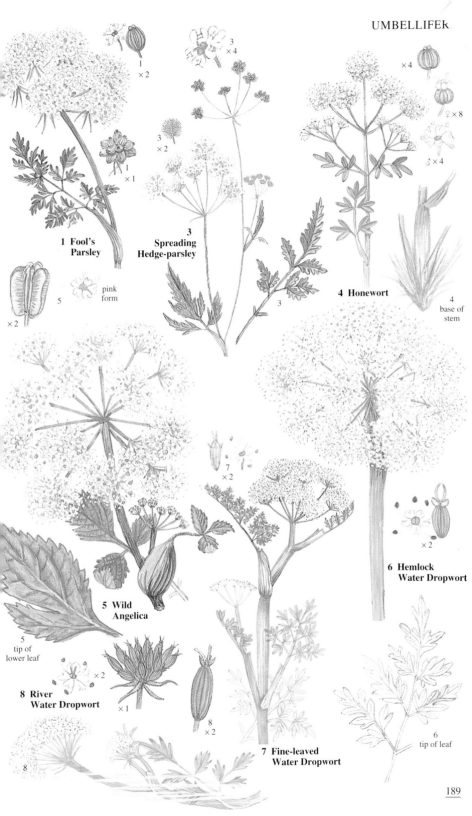

1
× 2

3
× 4

× 4

3
× 2

♀ × 8

♂ × 4

**1 Fool's
Parsley**

1
× 1

**3
Spreading
Hedge-parsley**

3

3

4 Honewort

4
base of
stem

5

pink
form

× 2

5
tip of
lower leaf

**5 Wild
Angelica**

7
× 2

7
× 2

**6 Hemlock
Water Dropwort**

× 2

**8 River
Water Dropwort**

× 1

8
× 2

**7 Fine-leaved
Water Dropwort**

6
tip of leaf

8

1 *Great Water Parsnip *Sium latifolium*. Hairless perennial, with ridged hollow stems to 2m. Flowers white, umbels 50-100mm, with large bracts; June-Sept. Leaves *1-pinnate* (unlike Cowbane, **2**), with *c.* 5 pairs of toothed leaflets; also many finely cut submerged leaves. Fruits egg-shaped, with *prominent* ridges and inconspicuous styles. By fresh water, especially fen dykes.

2 *Cowbane *Cicuta virosa*. Hairless perennial, with hollow stems to 1.5m, but sometimes half-floating. Flowers white, umbels 70-130mm, *no lower bracts*; July-August. Leaves 2/3-pinnate (unlike Great Water Parsnip, **1**). Fruits globular, ridged, with *long styles* and prominent sepal-teeth. In and by fresh water, marshy fields.

3 *Milk Parsley *Peucedanum palustre*. A hairless biennial with milky juice in the stems, to 1.5m. Flowers white, umbels 30-80mm, all bracts reflexed; July-Sept. Leaves 2-4-pinnate, the deeply cut leaflets *blunt-tipped*. Fruits flattened oval, with short styles and two pairs of wings. Fens, fen scrub. The favoured food-plant of the swallowtail butterfly.

4 Masterwort *Peucedanum ostruthium*. A stocky, usually slightly downy perennial, stems hollow, to 1m. Flowers white, umbels 50-100mm, no lower bracts; June-July. Leaves mostly at base, 2-trefoil, with broad toothed leaflets and *inflated* sheathing stalks. Fruits globular, winged, with down-turned styles. A former potherb, still naturalised in damp grassland and on stream banks.

2b. Flowers white/pink: damper/wetter places: Tall, usually 60-100cm

5 Corky-fruited Water Dropwort *Oenanthe pimpinelloides*. Stout perennial with solid ridged stems to 1m. Flowers white or pink, umbels 20-50mm, flat in fruit, lower bracts unequal; June-August. Leaves 1/3-pinnate, the leaflets narrower up the stem, but quite *broad.* wedge-shaped and toothed below, which have usually withered by June. Fruits cylindrical, with a *corky base* and long styles and sepal-teeth, on thickened stalks. Damp, often on acid meadows, sometimes in drier grassy or bare places.

6 *Sulphurwort *Oenanthe silaifolia*. Very like Corky-fruited Water Dropwort (**5**), but has often taller, more ridged *hollow* stems, umbels with usually *no lower bracts* and not flat in fruit, all leaves with narrow leaflets, recalling Pepper-saxifrage (p. 194) and fruits more conical and with shorter styles. Aka Narrow-fruited Water Dropwort. Damp meadows, usually on neutral or limy soils.

7 ***Cambridge Milk Parsley *Selinum carvifolia*. Parsley-scented perennial, stems solid, ridged, to 1m. Flowers white, umbels 30-70mm, upper bracts thread-like, no lower bracts; August-Sept. Leaves 2/3-pinnate, the leaflets with *very pointed tips*. Fruits with *winged ridges*. Cf. Milk Parsley (**3**). Confined to three Cambridgeshire fens.

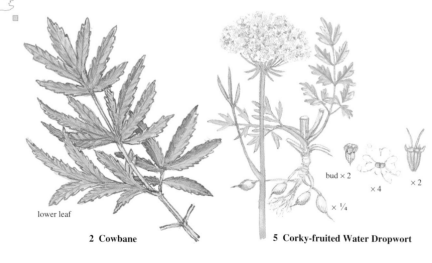

bud × 2

× 4

× 2

× ¼

lower leaf

2 Cowbane   **5 Corky-fruited Water Dropwort**

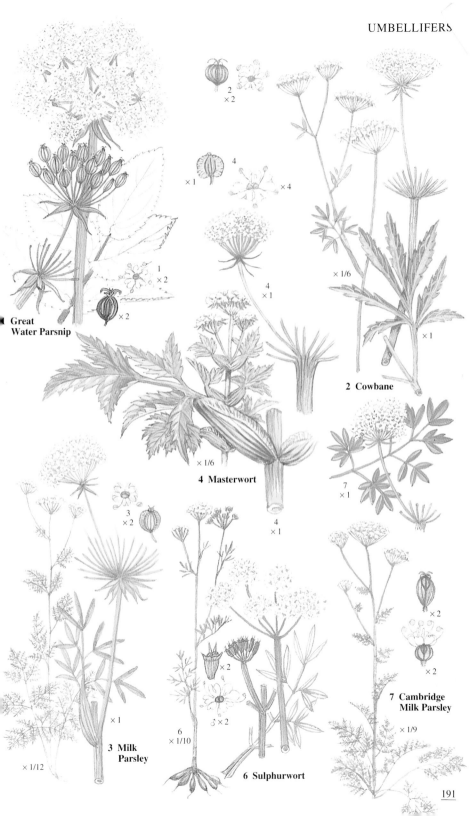

Great Water Parsnip

1
× 2

× 2

2
× 2

4
× 1

× 1

4

4
× 1

2 Cowbane

× 1/6

× 1

4 Masterwort
× 1/6

4
× 1

7
× 1

3
× 2

× 1

3 Milk Parsley

× 1/12

6
× 2

♂ × 2

6
× 1/10

6 Sulphurwort

× 2

× 2

7 Cambridge Milk Parsley

× 1/9

1 Fool's Watercress *Apium nodiflorum*. Sprawling hairless perennial, to 1m. Flowers white, umbels 20-30mm, on stalks *opposite* the leaves, usually no lower bracts; June-Sept. Leaves *bright green*, shiny, 1-pinnate, the leaflets shallowly toothed, sometimes mistaken and eaten (apparently without harm) for Watercress (p. 90), with which it may grow, but Watercress leaves are untoothed and usually have a relatively much larger end lobe. Fruits egg-shaped, ridged. Wet streams, ditches and pond-edges.

2 Lesser Water Parsnip *Berula erecta*. Hairless, often sprawling perennial, with hollow stems to 1m. Flowers white, umbels 30-60mm, on stalks *opposite* the leaves; July-Sept. Leaves 1-pinnate, bluer-green, longer, and with more (5-9) pairs of more *coarsely and sharply toothed* leaflets than Fool's Watercress (1). Fruits globular, almost divided in two, with long styles. In and by still fresh water, fens, marshes.

3 Tubular Water Dropwort *Oenanthe fistulosa*. A greyish hairless perennial, with hollow, slightly ridged stems to 80cm. Flowers white or pale pink, umbels with 2-4 small umbels, 8-12mm, becoming domed in fruit, usually no lower bracts; June-Sept. Leaves with soft *hollow* stalks, the lower 2-pinnate with lanceolate leaflets, the upper 1-pinnate with linear leaflets. Fruits angled, with long styles. Fens, marshes, ditches and other wet places.

4 Parsley Water Dropwort *Oenanthe lachenalii*. A greyish hairless perennial with solid stems to 1m. Flowers white, umbels 50-60mm, with *narrow lower bracts*; July-Sept. Leaves 2-pinnate, the lower with short bluntly elliptical leaflets, the upper with narrower, pointed ones. Fruits egg-shaped, ribbed, with short styles. Fens, salt- and brackish marshes.

5 Wild Celery *Apium graveolens*. Hairless biennial, with a pungent smell of celery when crushed; stems solid to 1m. Flowers white, umbels 35-45mm, no upper or lower bracts; June-August. Leaves yellowish-green, shiny, 1-pinnate, with large toothed leaflets like Garden Celery, the upper trefoil and unstalked. Fruits globular, slightly ridged. Bare damp brackish places, usually coastal.

6 Whorled Caraway *Carum verticillatum*. Hairless biennial with hollow stems to 60cm; best distinguished by its long narrow, somewhat Yarrow-like leaves with *palmate whorls* of *thread-like* leaflets. Flowers white, umbels 20-50mm; June-July. Fruits egg-shaped, ridged, not aromatic. Damp meadows, marshes, streamsides.

7 Lesser Marshwort *Apium inundatum*. Sprawling, creeping and rooting or largely submerged hairless perennial, easily overlooked; stems hollow, to 50cm. Flowers white, umbels few, very small (8-12mm), no lower bracts; June-August. Leaves 2-pinnate, the aerial ones with narrow leaflets, the submerged ones with thread-like leaflets recalling Water Crowfoots (p. 26). Fruits well ridged. In and by shallow water, marshes.

8 ***Creeping Marshwort *Apium repens*. Differs from often very similar prostrate forms of Fool's Watercress (1), with which it hybridises, especially in its broader, more *deeply toothed* leaves; an always prostrate creeping perennial, *rooting at most leaf-nodes*. Flowers white, umbels long-stalked, with *numerous lower bracts*; July-August. Fruits broader. Marshy grassland, now only on or near Port Meadow, Oxford.

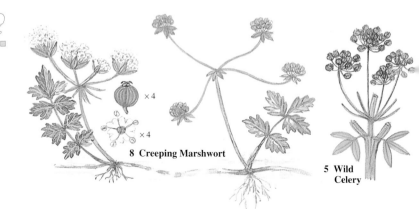

× 4

× 4

8 Creeping Marshwort

5 Wild Celery

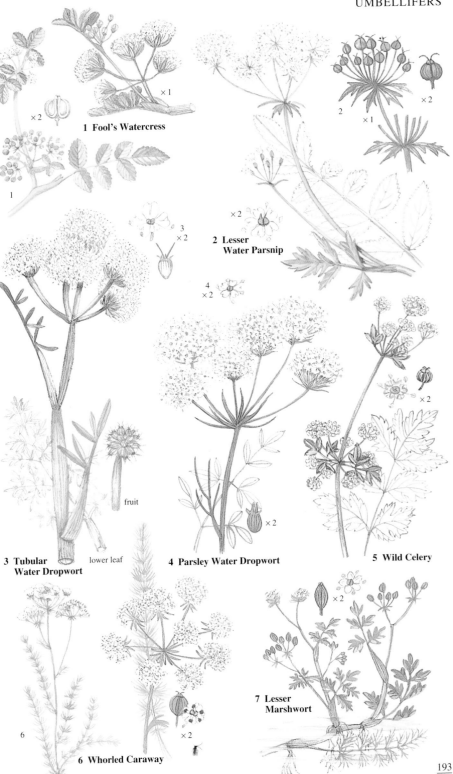

×1
×2
1 Fool's Watercress
1

2
×1
×2
×2
**2 Lesser
Water Parsnip**

3
×2
4
×2

fruit
**3 Tubular
Water Dropwort**
lower leaf

×2
4 Parsley Water Dropwort

×2
×2
5 Wild Celery

×2
**7 Lesser
Marshwort**

6
×2
6 Whorled Caraway

3. Flowers yellow

1 Wild Parsnip *Pastinaca sativa*. Roughly hairy tall biennial, pungent when crushed, to nearly 2m. Flowers yellow, umbels 30-100mm, no upper or lower bracts; June-Sept. Our only yellow umbellifer with *1-pinnate* leaves, the leaflets broad, toothed and sometimes lobed. Fruits oval, flat, narrowly winged. The occasional escaped **Garden Parsnip** ssp. *hortensis* has rather few *short straight* hairs, compared with the many *long wavy* ones of the wild ssp. *sativa*. Grassy and bare places, roadsides, mainly on lime.

2 Fennel *Foeniculum vulgare*. Hairless tall aniseed-scented perennial, with shiny glaucous stems, solid at first, to 2.5m. Flowers yellow, umbels 40-80mm across, no upper or lower bracts; July-Sept. Our only native yellow umbellifer with *thread-like* leaflets to the 3/4-pinnate leaves. Fruits narrowly egg-shaped, ridged, not always ripening. Roadsides and other bare and waste places, often near the sea. **Giant Fennel** *Ferula communis* may be even taller, to 3m, with broad sheathing stalks to the 4/6-pinnate leaves. Rarely established.

3 Pepper-saxifrage *Silaum silaus*. Like so many "saxifrages" it is not a true one; a medium/tall hairless perennial, with solid stems to 1m. Flowers yellow, umbels 20-60mm, sometimes no lower bracts; June-Sept. Leaves 2/3-pinnate, with *narrow, pointed* leaflets. Fruits egg-shaped, ridged. *Damper grassland*, where it is the only yellow umbellifer likely to be found.

4 Alexanders *Smyrnium olusatrum*. Stout clump-forming medium/tall hairless biennial/perennial, with solid stems to 1.5m. Flowers yellow, umbels 10cm, no bracts; March-June. Our only yellow umbellifer with large glossy *dark green* 3-trefoil leaves, with broad, toothed leaflets. Fruits *black*, globular, sharply ridged. Hedge-banks, roadsides, cliffs, waste places, uncommon away from the sea.

5 Rock Samphire *Crithmum maritimum*. Our most distinctive yellow umbellifer, the only one with fleshy leaves and growing only by the sea; bushy short/medium greyish perennial to 45cm. Flowers yellowish-green, umbels 30-60mm; July-Sept. Leaves strong-smelling when crushed, 2/3-pinnate, fleshy, with succulent linear lobes. Cliffs and rocks by the sea. Like Marsh Samphire (p. 42), used for pickling in Shakespeare's day: "halfway down hangs one that gathers samphire – dreadful trade".

6 Garden Parsley *Petroselinum crispum*. Hairless upright biennial, with solid stems to 75cm. Flowers *greenish*-yellow, umbels 20-50mm, lower bracts often lobed; June-August. Leaves bright green, fading yellow, *shiny*, 3-pinnate, with a pleasant fresh green scent, much crisped in the cultivated forms used in cooking. Fruits globular. An escape to rocks, especially by the sea, and waste places.

7 **Hog's Fennel *Peucedanum officinale*. Hairless perennial, stems solid, to 2m. Flowers darker yellow than Fennel (**2**) umbels 50-150mm, often no lower bracts; July-Sept. Leaves very large, 3-6-trefoil, repeatedly cleft into linear segments (not thread-like as in Fennel). Fruits oval, shiny. Rough grassy places by the sea. still almost confined to the two areas in Kent and Essex where Gerard knew it in 1597 "in a meadow neere to the seaside".

5 Rock Samphire

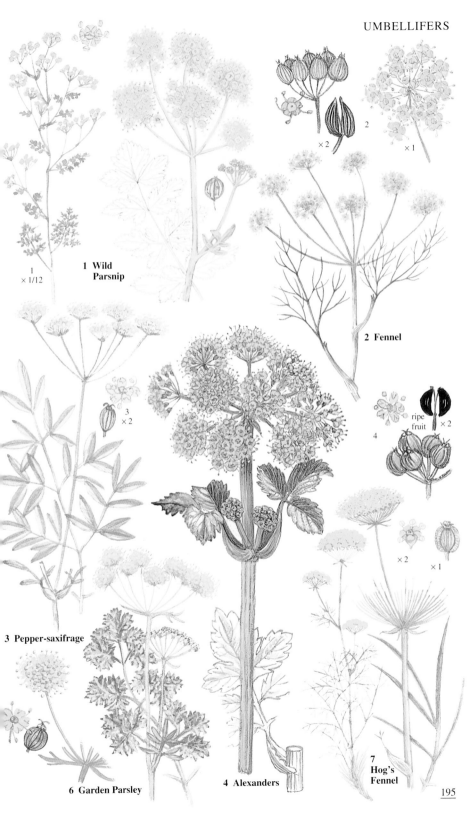

1 Wild
Parsnip

1
× 1/12

2

× 2

× 1

2 Fennel

3
× 2

4

ripe
fruit   × 2

3 Pepper-saxifrage

× 2   × 1

6 Garden Parsley

4 Alexanders

7
Hog's
Fennel

1 Sanicle *Sanicula europaea*. A short hairless perennial, to 40cm. Flowers greenish-white or pale pink, small, in clusters of *tight* head-like umbels; May-Sept. Leaves deeply *palmately* 3/5-lobed, toothed, long-stalked. Fruits with hooked spines. Woods, especially beechwoods on chalk, where it may carpet the ground.

2 Sea Holly *Eryngium maritimum*. Unmistakable with its *spiny* blue-green leaves, a stiff hairless medium clump-forming perennial, to 60cm. Flowers powder blue, small, in striking *rounded* head-like umbels with broad spiny bracts; June-Sept. Leaves with white veins and edges. Fruits egg-shaped with hooked bristles. Sand and shingle by the sea.

3 **Field Eryngo *Eryngium campestre*. Taller than Sea Holly (**2**) and less thick-set with thinner stems and longer branches, to 75cm. Flowers white, in much smaller umbels, with longer, narrower bracts; July-August. Leaves pale green, the basal ones pinnate. Fruits scaly. Aka Watling Street Thistle. Dry bare and grassy places, especially in Devon; still by Watling Street at Dartford, Kent. Three other Eryngos are naturalised in a very few places.

4 Pink Masterwort *Astrantia major*. A medium hairless perennial, to 80cm. Flowers pale pink or greenish-white, with a sickly smell, in close head-like umbels, with *large pale pink sepal-like bracts*, making it look like a scabious; June-August. Leaves deeply palmately lobed, toothed. Fruits scaly. Naturalised in woods and on banks – road, railway and stream; since *c.* 1840 near Stokesay, Shropshire.

5 *Slender Hare's-ear *Bupleurum tenuissimum*. An upright or sprawling short/medium hairless perennial, with wiry stems to 50cm; extremely hard to detect even in short grass. Flowers *yellow*, in tiny umbels, with narrow green upper bracts; July-Sept. Leaves grey-green, linear up the stems. Fruits globular. Sea-walls, upper saltmarshes and other grassy, usually brackish places by the sea.

6 ***Small Hare's-ear *Bupleurum baldense*. Low upright annual, to 25cm, but often only 3-7cm and hard to see in short turf. Flowers yellow, in tiny umbels, largely concealed by the *sharply pointed* leaf-like *brownish* upper bracts; late May-July. Leaves linear, soon withering. Fruits egg-shaped. Two localities only, in short coastal cliff-top turf on lime.

7 False Thorow-wax *Bupleurum subovatum*. Short greyish upright annual, to 30cm. Flowers tiny, yellow, in 2-3 small umbels. cupped by conspicuous *greenish-yellow petal-like* upper bracts; June-August. Leaves mostly narrowly oval, the upper going "thorow" the stem, to quote Gerard. Fruits warty. A birdseed alien, often mistaken for the now extinct arable weed **Thorow-wax** *B. rotundifolium* (p. 463), which has 4-8 small umbels, lower leaves more rounded and fruits ridged.

8 Marsh Pennywort *Hydrocotyle vulgaris*. A prostrate creeping and rooting perennial, to 30cm. Flowers tiny, greenish-pink, with reddish buds and yellow anthers, in tight heads or whorls at the base of the leaves; June-August. Leaves disc-like, 8-35mm, very shallowly lobed, usually held aloft, with the stalk *in the middle*, umbrella-like. Fruits roundish, flattened. Bogs, fens, marshes and other wet places, mainly on acid soils. Two alien species may be planted on lawns.

9 Floating Pennywort *Hydrocotyle ranunculoides*. Like an outsize Marsh Pennywort (**8**), with much *larger*, often *floating* leaves, to 70mm, 3/7-cleft, with the stalk *at the edge*; the younger ones resembling Water Crowfoot leaves (p. 26). Flowers whitish. Fruits stalked. An aggressive mat-forming waterweed spreading from the R Chelmer, Essex, often several metres away from water.

basal leaf × ½

9 Floating Pennywort

7 False Thorow-wax

× 2

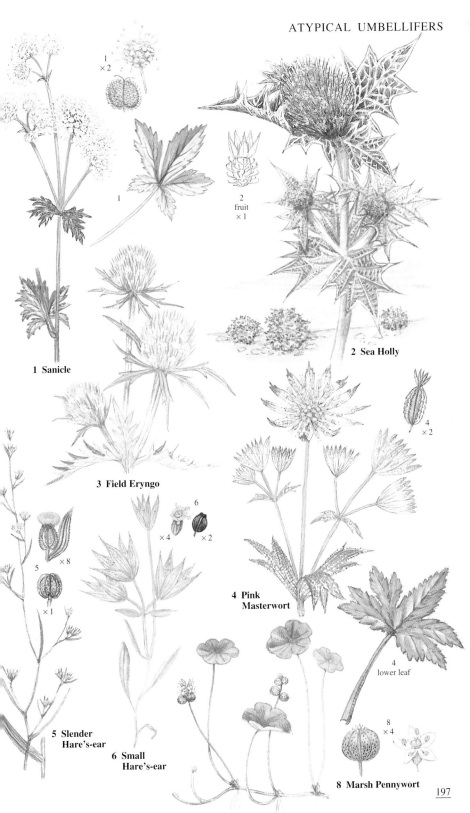

1
× 2

1

2
fruit
× 1

1 Sanicle

2 Sea Holly

4
× 2

3 Field Eryngo

6
× 4   × 2

5
× 8

5
× 1

**4 Pink
Masterwort**

4
lower leaf

**5 Slender
Hare's-ear**

**6 Small
Hare's-ear**

8
× 4

8 Marsh Pennywort

GENTIAN FAMILY Gentianaceae

Hairless annuals/perennials. Flowers in a branched cluster, with 4-5 joined petals and sepals, often opening only in sunshine. Leaves undivided, opposite, usually unstalked. Fruit a capsule.

Gentians: *Gentianella* are annuals/biennials, with flowers purplish (except Fringed Gentian, **6**) and *long fringes* in the petal-tube. *Gentiana* are perennials with flowers blue and small *inner lobes* in the petal tube.

1 Autumn Gentian *Gentianella amarella*. The most frequent gentian, low/short to 30cm, sometimes only 2-3cm. Flowers dull purple (often creamy white inside and red-purple outside in the N; ssp. *septentrionale*); with usually five narrow petals, 12-22mm, the sepals narrow and shorter than their cylindrical tube; late July-early Oct. Leaves ovate-lanceolate, often purplish. Hybridises freely with Chiltern Gentian (**2**). Aka Felwort. Grassland on lime, dunes.

2 *Chiltern Gentian *Gentianella germanica*. Low/short, to 40cm, sometimes only 2-3cm. Flowers of a somewhat brighter purple than Autumn Gentian (**1**), larger (25-35mm) with markedly *larger and broader* petals, the sepal-tube being *broader at the tip*, making the flowers look almost bell-shaped; August-early Oct. Leaves broader. Hybridises freely with Autumn Gentian. Chalk turf. ***Hybrid Gentian** *Gentianella × pamplinii*. No two gentians are easier to distinguish from each other than pure-bred Autumn and Chiltern Gentians. The problem arises in their almost invariable tendency to produce, wherever they meet, hybrid swarms with a complete series of intermediates; because of this it is pointless to describe the often sterile hybrid, which may occur in the absence of either parent, e.g. in Kent. Especially in the Chilterns, pure Autumn Gentian is more distinctive than pure Chiltern Gentian, i.e. most intergrades look more like Chiltern Gentian.

3 Field Gentian *Gentianella campestris*. Has flowers of a paler and bluer purple than Autumn Gentian (**1**), often almost white, 15-25mm, always with *four petals*, the two outer sepals much *larger and broader* and overlapping the two inner ones; July-early Oct. Leaves narrowly ovate-lanceolate. Grassland and dunes, usually avoiding lime.

4 **Early Gentian *Gentianella anglica*. Often a tiny plant, to 2-3cm, but can reach 20cm. Differs from Autumn Gentian (**1**) especially in its main flowering time, *May-June*; but also has usually *four petals*, often paler purple or whitish flowers, 13-20mm, and four narrower sepals. In N Cornwall and N Devon, a probable hybrid with Autumn Gentian starts to flower in April. Chalk turf, grassy cliff-tops, dunes.

5 **Dune Gentian *Gentianella uliginosa*. Usually tiny, rarely more than 7cm, but can reach 15cm. Flowers dull purple, 10-20mm, the end flower-stalk *long*, the sepals *unequal* and spreading; May-early-Nov. Leaves few. Hybridises with Autumn Gentian (**1**). Dunes, dune slacks.

6 ***Fringed Gentian *Gentianella ciliata*. Slender low/short perennial, to 30cm, but usually much shorter. Flowers clear blue, with four large *fringed* petals, 25-40mm across but most often seen more or less folded; Sept-Oct. Chalk turf, one locality only.

7 *Marsh Gentian *Gentiana pneumonanthe*. Low/short perennial, to 40cm. Flowers *trumpet-shaped*, strikingly deep blue with green streaks outside, solitary, 15-40mm; July-Sept. Leaves linear. Wet heaths (not marshes). Two similar garden plants with all-blue flowers are locally naturalised in drier places: **7a Willow Gentian** *G. asclepiadea* with broader leaves and **7b Clusius's Gentian** *G. clusii* with most leaves in a basal rosette.

8 ***Spring Gentian *Gentiana verna*. Low perennial, to 7cm. Flowers the most *brilliant blue* in our flora, 17-30mm; April-June. Leaves pointed oval, in a tuft. Limestone turf in Upper Teesdale and the Burren. Co Clare.

9 ***Alpine Gentian *Gentiana nivalis*. Diminutive low annual, to 15cm. Flowers almost as blue as Spring Gentian (**8**), but only 7-10mm; July-August. Leaves pointed oval. High mountain ledges.

pale
form

2

3

1
× 1

1 **Autumn
Gentian**

2 **Chiltern Gentian**

5

3 **Field
Gentian**

4
× ½

4 **Early
Gentian**

× 1

6
**Fringed
Gentian**

5 **Dune
Gentian**

7a **Willow
Gentian**

7b
**Clusius's
Gentian**

7 **Marsh
Gentian**

8 **Spring Gentian**

9
**Alpine
Gentian**

Centauries *Centaurium.* Annuals/biennials, except Perennial Centaury (**5**) with flowers usually *pink* and 5-petalled, the sepals linear and keeled, longer than their tube. Sometimes reduced to a tiny 1- or 2-flowered stem.

1 Common Centaury *Centaurium erythraea.* Much the commonest centaury, a low/short biennial to 50cm, but can be only 2cm. Flowers *clear* pink, occasionally white, *not* or very short-stalked, 9-15mm, in rather tight clusters; June-Oct. Leaves *pointed oval*, mostly in a *basal rosette*. Grassy places, dunes.

2 *Seaside Centaury *Centaurium littorale.* Very like a dwarf Common Centaury (**1**), but shorter, to 25cm, with flowers of a more bluish pink, 11-14mm, in tighter clusters; June-Sept. Leaves, the safest diagnostic character, mostly in a basal rosette, *strap-shaped*, somewhat leathery. Hybridises with Common Centaury. Dunes and other sandy turf by the sea.

3 Lesser Centaury *Centaurium pulchellum.* Slenderer and more open than Common Centaury (**1**), to 20cm, branching from *below the middle* of the stem. Flowers *redder* pink, sometimes white, with narrower petals, smaller (5-9mm), *longer-stalked*, in looser clusters; June-Sept. Leaves pointed oval, with a *basal rosette* at flowering time. Grassy places, often damp, in woods or near the sea.

4 ***Slender Centaury *Centaurium tenuiflorum.* So like Lesser Centaury (**3**) that it may be only a subspecies., but has a denser, flatter-topped cluster of usually *white* flowers. May be taller, to 35cm, branching above the middle of the stem. One locality only, a damp grassy undercliff in Dorset.

5 **Perennial Centaury *Centaurium scilloides.* Our only perennial centaury, with *sprawling stems*, some non-flowering, to 30cm. Flowers pink, rather *large* (15-20mm), often solitary; June-Nov. Leaves roundish, stalked on the non-flowering stems. Cliff-tops and dunes by the sea, now Pembrokeshire only.

6 Yellow-wort *Blackstonia perfoliata.* Erect greyish annual, to 50cm, easily identified by its combination of yellow flowers (closed when the sun is in) and pairs of greyish leaves *joined at the base*. Flowers 6-8-petalled, 8-15mm; June-Oct. Short turf on lime, dunes.

7 Yellow Centaury *Cicendia filiformis.* A tiny, very slender, upright, scarcely branched annual, to 10cm, often only 2cm. Flowers yellow, *4-petalled*, 3-7mm, *open only in sunshine*, solitary, long-stalked; June-Oct. Leaves linear. Bare patches on sand or peat, most often on heaths near the coast.

DODDER FAMILY Cuscutaceae

Rootless parasites devoid of green colour, with a combination unique in the plant kingdom of red or yellow stems, leaves reduced to tiny scales and tight unstalked heads of flowers with 4-5 petals and joined sepals.

8 Dodder *Cuscuta epithymum.* Annual with a dense network of threadlike reddish stems, twining anticlockwise, usually on *Gorse* (p. 398) or *Heather* (p. 104). Flowers translucent waxy white, tinged pink, bell-shaped, scented, the stamens *as long as the five petals*, in 5-10mm heads; July-Sept. Heaths, chalk downs.

9 Greater Dodder *Cuscuta europaea.* Differs from Dodder (**8**) especially in its favourite hosts, Nettle (p. 36) and other tall herbaceous plants, and having its flowers in larger (10-15mm) heads with the stamens *much shorter than the 4-5 petals*; July-Sept. Often by rivers, canals and other fresh water.

The yellow-stemmed **10 Yellow Dodder** *Cuscuta campestris* is increasing in carrot, tomato and other crops. **Flax Dodder** *C. epilinum* is extinct (p. 464).

10 Yellow Dodder

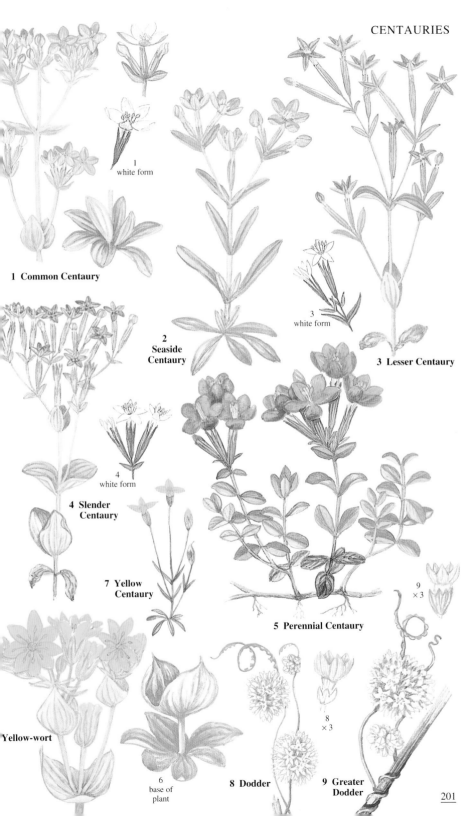

1 white form

1 Common Centaury

2 Seaside Centaury

3 white form

3 Lesser Centaury

4 white form

4 Slender Centaury

7 Yellow Centaury

5 Perennial Centaury

9 ×3

Yellow-wort

6 base of plant

8 ×3

8 Dodder

9 Greater Dodder

P NIGHTSHADE FAMILY Solanaceae

Mostly poisonous; even Potato and Tomato if you eat the wrong parts of the plant. Flowers with five joined petals and sepals. Leaves usually alternate and stalked. 22 other species, including 14 *Solanum*, are either very locally established or casuals, including the white-flowered **Sweet Tobacco** *Nicotiana alata*, the most frequent of five tobaccos to escape from cultivation.

Nightshades *Solanum*. Flowers like those of Potato or Tomato (**3**, **4**), with the petals down-turned and a central column of yellow anthers.

1 Bittersweet *Solanum dulcamara*. A clambering or sprawling, hairless to velvety downy (var. *villosissimum*) perennial, with woody lower stems, to 2m or more; in Darwin's words "one of the feeblest and poorest of twiners", twining "indifferently to the right or left". Flowers *bright purple* with yellow anthers, sepals and stalks often purplish, 10-15mm; June-Sept. Leaves pointed oval, often with one or more pairs of narrow lobes at the base. Fruit an egg-shaped berry, green, yellow, and finally red. Aka Woody Nightshade. Both dry (hedges, woods, walls, waste ground), and damp (fens, by ponds and ditches) places; also the prostrate and fleshy ssp. *marinum* on coastal shingle. Sometimes semantically confused with the quite different Deadly Nightshade (**5**).

1 SO

2 Black Nightshade *Solanum nigrum*. A variably downy, erect to sprawling annual, stems often blackish, to 70cm. Flowers *white* with yellow anthers, 10-14mm; July-Sept. Berry *black*, sometimes purplish or remaining green. A weed of cultivated and waste ground. **2a Green Nightshade** *S. physalifolium* has stems always green and berries green or purplish and *enfolded* in the sepals; leaves larger and paler. Not native and much less common. **Tall Nightshade** *S. chenopodioides* is taller, to 1m, with appressed hairs and purplish-black fruits; recently naturalised in Inner South London. **2b Cock's Eggs** *Salpichroa origanifolia* is perennial, with white bell-shaped flowers, untoothed roundish leaves and white berries. Established at Abbotsbury, Dorset, Lowestoft, Suffolk, and a few other places.

2 S

3 Potato *Solanum tuberosum*. A frequent relic of cultivation near arable fields, its *white or pale purple* nightshade-like flowers (late June-Sept) adorn many a field border or roadside in the arable countryside, where it may even be allowed to produce the green or purplish berries that are rarely seen in gardens.

4 Tomato *Lycopersicon esculentum*. A familiar salad plant, whose *yellow* nightshade-like flowers (July-Sept) and pinnate leaves (but much less often its red fruits) are to be seen wherever sandwiches have been thrown away, and especially at sewage works.

5 P Deadly Nightshade *Atropa belladonna*. A tall stout bushy, often downy perennial, to 2m. Flowers dull purple, sometimes greenish, *bell-shaped*, solitary, 24-30mm; June-August. Leaves broad, pointed oval. Fruit a large *glossy black* berry, 15-20mm, producing a valuable drug but can be *fatally tempting* to young children. Aka Belladonna. Cf. Woody Nightshade (**1**). Scrub, quarries, waste ground, almost always on lime.

5

6 P Henbane *Hyoscyamus niger*. A stout, evil-looking, *evil-smelling* biennial, clammy with *sticky white* hairs, to 80cm. Flowers a lurid pale yellow, purple in the throat, netted with purple veins, 20-30mm, anthers purple, sepals green, with four broad stiff teeth; in a leafy spike; June-August. Lower leaves broad, usually with a few large teeth, the upper narrower, more toothed and unstalked. Fruit a capsule within the swollen sepals. Bare or disturbed ground inland, sand or shingle by the sea.

6

7 Thorn-apple *Datura stramonium*. A distinctive stout hairless annual, with an unpleasant smell, to 1m. Flowers white or purple, solitary, *trumpet-shaped*, 5-10cm; July-Oct. Leaves pointed oval, *jaggedly toothed*. Fruits large (3-7cm), green, usually *spiny* like a Horse-chestnut (p. 394). Not infrequent casual of cultivated and waste ground.

7 S

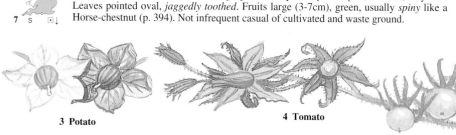

3 Potato   **4 Tomato**

202

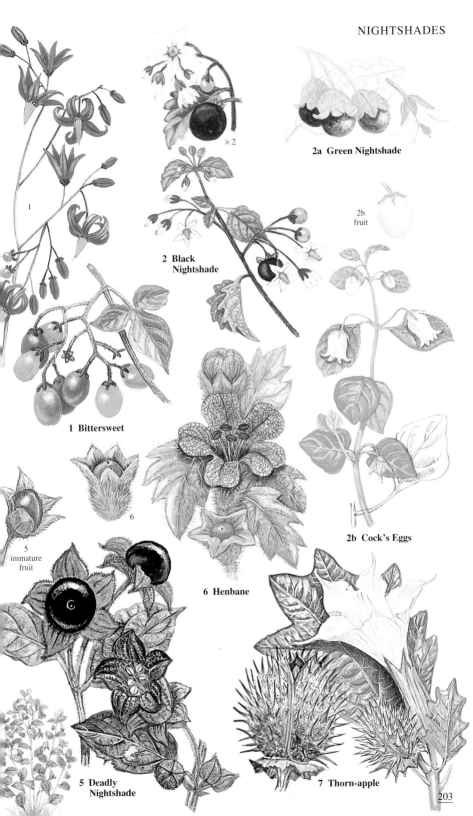

×2

2a Green Nightshade

2b
fruit

**2 Black
Nightshade**

1 Bittersweet

5
immature
fruit

6

2b Cock's Eggs

6 Henbane

**5 Deadly
Nightshade**

7 Thorn-apple

1 P Apple-of-Peru *Nicandra physalodes*. Foetid hairless annual, to 80cm. Flowers pale blue or violet with white throat, *bell-shaped*, with large ace-of-spades sepals, solitary, 30-40mm, opening only for a few hours; June-Oct. Leaves pointed oval, toothed to lobed. Fruit a dry brown berry, *encased* in the net-veined bladder-like sepals. Frequent casual in bare or sparsely grassy places. **1a Japanese Lantern** *Physalis alkekengi* is perennial with smaller white flowers, leaves sometimes untoothed and berry and fruiting sepals red to orange. A less frequent casual. **1b Cape Gooseberry** *P. peruviana* differs from **1a** in being very downy, with yellow flowers and fruits and green fruiting sepals. Another casual, naturalised in Hertfordshire.

BINDWEED FAMILY Convolvulaceae

Perennials with stems usually twining anticlockwise. Flowers large and *trumpet-shaped*, sometimes quite deeply lobed. Leaves usually undivided, untoothed, alternate. Fruit a capsule. Four species of annual **Morning Glory** *Ipomoea*, with blue or white flowers and leaves often lobed, occur as casuals.

2 Field Bindweed *Convolvulus arvensis*. Stems prostrate or twining, to 1m or more. A pernicious weed despite its attractive scented pink, white or pink-and-white flowers, *10-25mm*, with a pair of tiny bracts *on the stalk below*; June-Sept. Leaves arrow-shaped. Cultivated and bare or waste places, often climbing wire fences.

Calystegia **Bindweeds** differ from Field Bindweed (**2**) most obviously in their larger flowers with large bracts immediately beneath them. If they have *white-striped pink* or pink-striped white flowers, they can be differentiated by these bracts. If the flower stalks are hairless, they are either Hedge or Large Bindweed and need to be separated as such. If the stalks are downy, they are either Hedge Bindweed ssp. *roseata* or Hairy Bindweed, and need to be similarly separated, as Hairy Bindweed has the large bracts of Large Bindweed.

3 Hedge Bindweed *Calystegia sepium*. Usually hairless; stems climbing to 2m or more. Flowers white, occasionally, especially in Ireland, pink with five white stripes (stalks hairless in f. *colorata*, downy in ssp. *roseata*), 30-60mm, the five sepals being *half-covered* by two large bracts, often purple-tinged, immediately beneath them; June-Sept. Leaves arrow-shaped. Hedges, fences, fens, marshes, waste places.

4 Large Bindweed *Calystegia silvatica*. Somewhat larger and stouter than Hedge Bindweed (**3**), with which it hybridises. Stems to 3m or more. Flowers white, sometimes with faint pink stripes, *60-90mm* with more inflated bracts *completely enfolding* the sepals Thoroughly naturalised; commoner in towns and suburbs; not in fens or marshes.

5 Hairy Bindweed *Calystegia pulchra*. Differs from Large (**3**) and most Hedge (**4**) Bindweeds in its *downy* upper stems and flower stalks and in its flowers being always *pink with white stripes*, but has the large bracts of Large Bindweed. See also note above. Much less often naturalised.

6 Sea Bindweed *Calystegia soldanella*. Hairless *prostrate* creeping perennial, to 1m. Flowers pink with five white stripes with a yellowish centre, 35-50cm; June-August. Leaves *kidney-shaped*, fleshy. Dunes, less often shingle, *by the sea*. **Kidneyweed** *Dichondra repens*, with *yellowish- or greenish-white* flowers lobed to half-way and kidney-shaped leaves, is naturalised on dunes at Hayle, Cornwall.

2   soz

3   soz

4   s

5

6   so

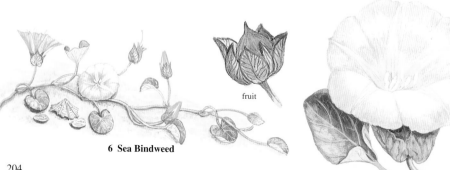

fruit

6 Sea Bindweed

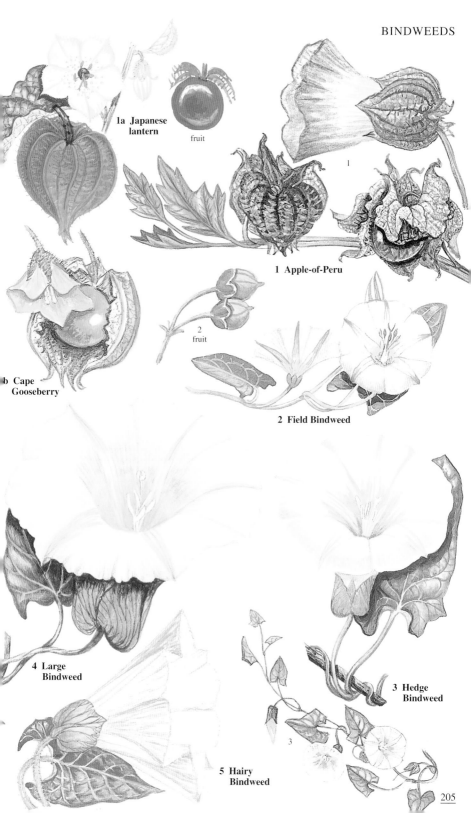

1a Japanese lantern

fruit

1

1 Apple-of-Peru

b Cape Gooseberry

2
fruit

2 Field Bindweed

4 Large Bindweed

3 Hedge Bindweed

3

5 Hairy Bindweed

BORAGE FAMILY Boraginaceae

All except Oysterplant (p. 212) are hairy, often *roughly hairy*. Flowers usually blue, often *pink in bud* with five joined petals and sepals, usually in 1-sided spikes, tightly coiled at first. Leaves undivided, alternate. Fruits four nutlets.

Comfreys *Symphytum*. Roughly hairy perennials, with bell-shaped flowers in spikes, coiled at first, and broad lanceolate leaves, the lower long-stalked. Fruit a nutlet.

Flowers		
	blue:	Russian, Rough, Hidcote Blue, Caucasian
	purple:	Common, Russian
	pink:	Rough, Creeping, Hidcote Blue
	pale yellow/yellowish-cream:	Common, Tuberous, Creeping, Bulbous, Crimean
	white:	White
Leaves	running down on to stem:	Common, Russian, Tuberous, Caucasian, Bulbous
	not running down on to stem:	Russian, Rough, White, Creeping, Crimean

1 Common Comfrey *Symphytum officinale*. Our commonest comfrey of wetter habitats, tall, well branched, erect to 1.5m. Flowers either yellowish cream or dull purple, the long sepal-teeth pointed, at least equalling their tube, 12-18mm; May-July. Upper stem-leaves *run down to the next leaf-junction* on the winged stem. Nutlets shiny. Moist places, especially by still and slow fresh water, and in fens and marshes.

2 Russian Comfrey *Symphytum × uplandicum*. Our commonest comfrey of drier habitats, a hybrid between Common (**1**) and Rough (**2a**) Comfreys, differs from Common Comfrey especially in its flowers being bright *blue* or some shade of purple, upper stem-leaves either *not or only slightly* running down on to the stem, and the nutlets matt. Back-crosses with Common Comfrey produce plants that are especially confusing. A former fodder plant, now well established on both damp and dry waysides and waste or rough ground; a form with clear blue flowers is especially frequent on drier roadsides. **2a Rough Comfrey** *S. asperum* differs especially in its upper stem-leaves being *shortly stalked* and never running down; flowers *pink at first*, then blue; June-July. A much less frequent alien. **2b Hidcote Blue**, a hybrid *Symphytum* with creeping stems to 50cm, pink then blue (often red on the outside) flowers and stalked stem-leaves; well established in Shropshire and widely scattered elsewhere. Its parents may be Russian and Creeping (**5**) Comfreys. **2c Caucasian Comfrey** *S. caucasicum* with clear blue flowers, sepals *divided to halfway* or less (June-August) and stem-leaves unstalked, running shortly on to stem, is a widely scattered garden escape.

3 Tuberous Comfrey *Symphytum tuberosum*. Our only other native comfrey, is medium, often unbranched, to 60cm. Flowers pale yellowish-cream, the sepal-teeth very long and pointed; June-July. Upper stem-leaves *running a short way* down the stem, the middle leaves the longest. Damp woods, hedge-banks and road verges, also stream and river banks. **3a Crimean Comfrey** *S. tauricum* has pale yellow flowers and stem-leaves sometimes stalked but *not* running down on to stem. Naturalised in Cambridgeshire.

4 White Comfrey *Symphytum orientale*. Erect, little-branched, medium to 70cm. Our only comfrey with *pure white* flowers, the sepal-teeth short and blunt; *early*-flowering; April-May. Stem-leaves more rounded than other comfreys, stalked or not, never running down the stem. Well established, hedge-banks, waysides.

5 Creeping Comfrey *Symphytum grandiflorum*. Our most frequent *creeping* and patch-forming comfrey, stems low/short, to 20cm. Flowers *red-pink* at first, later yellowish-cream; sepal-teeth very deeply cut; the first comfrey to flower, *March*-Sept. Leaves not running down on to stem. Established on roadsides and river banks, often in churchyards. **5a Bulbous Comfrey** *S. bulbosum* with pale yellow flowers (June-August) and leaves running shortly on to stem, has long been naturalised in Dorset, and is widely scattered elsewhere.

1

2 soz

3 oz

4 ↑↑

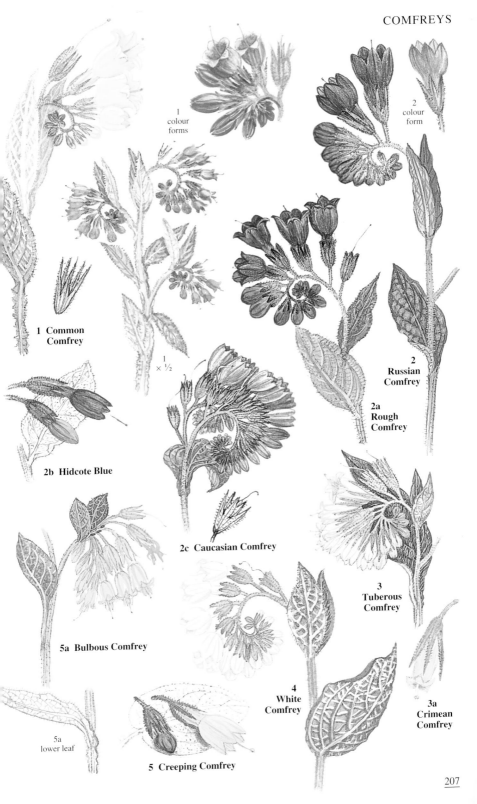

1
colour
forms

2
colour
form

1 Common
Comfrey

1
× ½

2
Russian
Comfrey

2a
Rough
Comfrey

2b Hidcote Blue

2c Caucasian Comfrey

3
Tuberous
Comfrey

5a Bulbous Comfrey

4
White
Comfrey

3a
Crimean
Comfrey

5a
lower leaf

5 Creeping Comfrey

Forgetmenots *Myosotis*. Stems and leaves downy. Flowers usually blue, pink in bud, in forked stalked spikes, elongating in fruit. Leaves oblong, usually unstalked.

Flowers	grey-blue:	Field
	mid-blue:	Field (shade form), Early, Changing
	pale blue:	Pale
	sky-blue:	Wood, Alpine, Water, Tufted, Creeping
	yellow:	Changing

Dry habitats

1 Field Forgetmenot *Myosotis arvensis*. Much the commonest wild forgetmenot, usually annual, low/short, erect to 40cm. Flowers *grey-blue*, sometimes remaining pink, 2-5mm, slightly concave, the petals and style shorter than their tube; April-Oct. Fruiting stalks longer than sepal-tube. Nutlets blackish. A shade form (ssp. *umbrata*) can be much taller, even to 100mm and has larger, somewhat bluer flowers. A weed of cultivation, also in other bare or disturbed places, e.g. woods, plantations, dunes.

2 Early Forgetmenot *Myosotis ramosissima*. Low, sometimes sprawling annual, to 25cm, but often only 2-3cm. Flowers *mid-blue*, 1-3mm, concave with petal-tube shorter than erect sepals; April-June. Lower leaves forming a rosette. Fruiting part of stem much longer than leafy part; sepals spreading in fruit, their tube longer-stalked. Nutlets pale brown. Bare or rocky places on dry, often limy soils, also dunes.

3 Changing Forgetmenot *Myosotis discolor*. Low annual, to 25cm, usually much shorter. Flowers opening *yellow*, bright, pale or creamy, later turning mid-blue, 1-2mm, concave, petal-tube becoming longer than sepal-tube; May-Sept. Fruiting parts of stems not much longer than leafy parts, the stalks shorter than *incurved* sepals. Nutlets dark brown to black. Bare places on dry, often slightly acid soils, also in the N in dune slacks and other damp places.

4 Wood Forgetmenot *Myosotis sylvatica*. Short, softly hairy erect perennial, to 50cm. Flowers *sky-blue*, 6-10mm, flat, petals much longer than their tube; April-July; larger than the shade form of Field Forgetmenot (**1**) and with style longer than sepal-tube. Fruiting stalks longer than sepals, their tube blunt at the base; nutlets *dark brown*, pointed. Woods, shady roadsides, also on upland rocks and screes. Much less widespread than its garden form, which often escapes.

5 **Alpine Forgetmenot *Myosotis alpestris*. Low/short perennial, to 25cm, rather like upland forms of Wood Forgetmenot (**4**), but with slightly larger (4-10mm) richer blue flowers, fruiting sepal-tube *pointed* at the base and nutlets *black* and blunt-tipped. Rock-ledges and limestone grassland in the mountains, especially Ben Lawers, Perthshire, and Upper Teesdale, N Pennines.

Wet habitats

6 Water Forgetmenot *Myosotis scorpioides*. The commonest of the four water forgetmenots, a pale green short creeping perennial, stems with appressed hairs, to 70cm. Flowers sky-blue, sometimes remaining pink, with white honey-guides and a yellow eye, petals flat, style *long*, often longer than the broadly triangular sepals, 8-13mm; June-Oct, but some of the later-flowerers may be hybrids with Tufted Forgetmenot (**7**). Fruiting stalks longer than the short sepals. Nutlets shiny black, blunt. Wet places, especially in mires and by rivers and ponds.

7 Tufted Forgetmenot *Myosotis laxa*. Very like and often growing with Water Forgetmenot (**6**), but has *no creeping runners*, distinctly smaller (3-5mm) flowers, style *shorter* than the narrower sepals, and nutlets dark brown. Habitat similar. Hybrids with Water Forgetmenot have creeping stems, flowers 5-8mm and fruiting stalks often longer than both parents with the sepals brown and shrivelled. not green.

8 Creeping Forgetmenot *Myosotis secunda*. Differs from Water Forgetmenot (**6**) in having stem hairs appressed above but *spreading below*, smaller (4-8mm) flowers, narrower sepals, *style very short* and nutlets pointed. Wet, usually acid, places.

9 *Pale Forgetmenot *Myosotis stolonifera*. Has shorter stems, to 20/30cm, than Water Forgetmenot (**6**), together with smaller (4-6mm) *pale* blue flowers, a *very short style*, and much *shorter*, blunter and more bluish-green leaves. By upland streams, springs and flushes.

flowers × 1
calices × 2
nutlets × 4

1

2

3

4

5

6

7

8

9

2 Early Forgetmenot

3 Changing Forgetmenot

4 Wood Forgetmenot

Field Forgetmenot

5 Alpine Forgetmenot

7 Tufted Forgetmenot

8 Creeping Forgetmenot

9 Pale Forgetmenot

6 Water Forgetmenot

Two casuals with forgetmenot-like flowers: **1 Bur Forgetmenot** *Lappula squarrosa*, covered with appressed and spreading white hairs, has spiralled spikes of tiny (2-4)mm blue flowers; **White Forgetmenot** *Plagiobothrys scouleri*, with white flowers, is locally established in the New Forest and elsewhere.

2 Siberian Bugloss *Brunnera macrophylla*. Short/medium tufted perennial, with appressed downy hairs, to 50cm. Flowers blue, *small* (3-4mm), in clusters, not unlike a small Forgetmenot (p. 208) and has been confused with the much larger-flowered Blue-eyed Mary (**3**); May-June. Leaves *ace-of-spades*, long-stalked. Nutlets ridged. Aka Great Forgetmenot. An increasing escape near gardens (where confusingly called *Anchusa myosotidiflora*), sometimes in woods.

3 Blue-eyed Mary *Omphalodes verna*. Low/short creeping and patch-forming perennial, to 25cm. Flowers bright blue, *10-15mm*; March-May. Leaves fresh green, *pointed oval*. Nutlets smooth, downy. Uncommon escape, but established in woods near Aberystwyth and in Anglesey.

4 Green Alkanet *Pentaglottis sempervirens*. A tufted, roughly hairy, *medium/tall* perennial, to 1m. Flowers *bright blue*, with white honeyguides, flat, 8-10mm, sepals cut ¾-way to base; March-July. Leaves pointed oval, abruptly contracted at the base, the lower stalked. Nutlets ridged. Hedges, wood borders, waysides, a rapidly spreading native, often also a garden escape. **4a Alkanet** *Anchusa officinalis*, with flowers more purplish, sepals cut to half-way and narrower leaves, is an occasional escape; as are **4b Garden Anchusa** *A. azurea* with larger (15 25mm), brighter blue flowers with a tuft of white hairs in the middle, and sepals cut nearly to base; the yellow-flowered **4c Yellow Alkanet** *A. ochroleuca* (p. 210), and **False Alkanet** *Cynoglottis barrelieri* with blue flowers and sepals cut to half-way, established in four places.

4 s □↑↑

5 Houndstongue *Cynoglossum officinale*. Softly *downy, greyish* erect medium biennial, to 60cm; with a strong mousy smell. Flowers *maroon red*, 6-10mm, with velvety scales closing the mouth; May-August. Leaves broad lanceolate. Nutlets rather flattened with a *thickened flange* and covered with short hooked spines that readily adhere to fur and clothing. Dry, rather bare grassy places, dunes, shingle, often on lime.

5 □↓

6 **Green Houndstongue *Cynoglossum montanum* Erect medium biennial, to 60cm, remarkably different from Houndstongue (**5**) due to its *fresh green* leaves, not unlike Wood Dock *Rumex sanguineus* (p. 62); also not mouse-scented. Flowers maroon red, 6-10mm, much *shorter-stalked*; May-July. Nutlets with *no flange*. Woods, spinneys, hedge-banks.

6 □

Among the rarer alien Boraginaceae is **7 Madwort** *Asperugo procumbens*, with tiny (1-3mm) purple flowers, formerly more frequent, but still well established on the shore in Angus. Easily taken for a member of the Borage Family is **8 Tansy-leaved Phacelia** *Phacelia tanacetifolia* (Hydrophyllaceae), with coiled spikes of blue or mauve 6-10mm flowers and *pinnate* leaves, increasingly sown with grass mixtures.

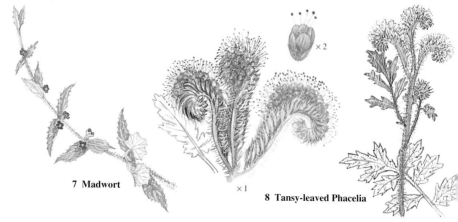

× 2

7 Madwort   × 1   **8 Tansy-leaved Phacelia**

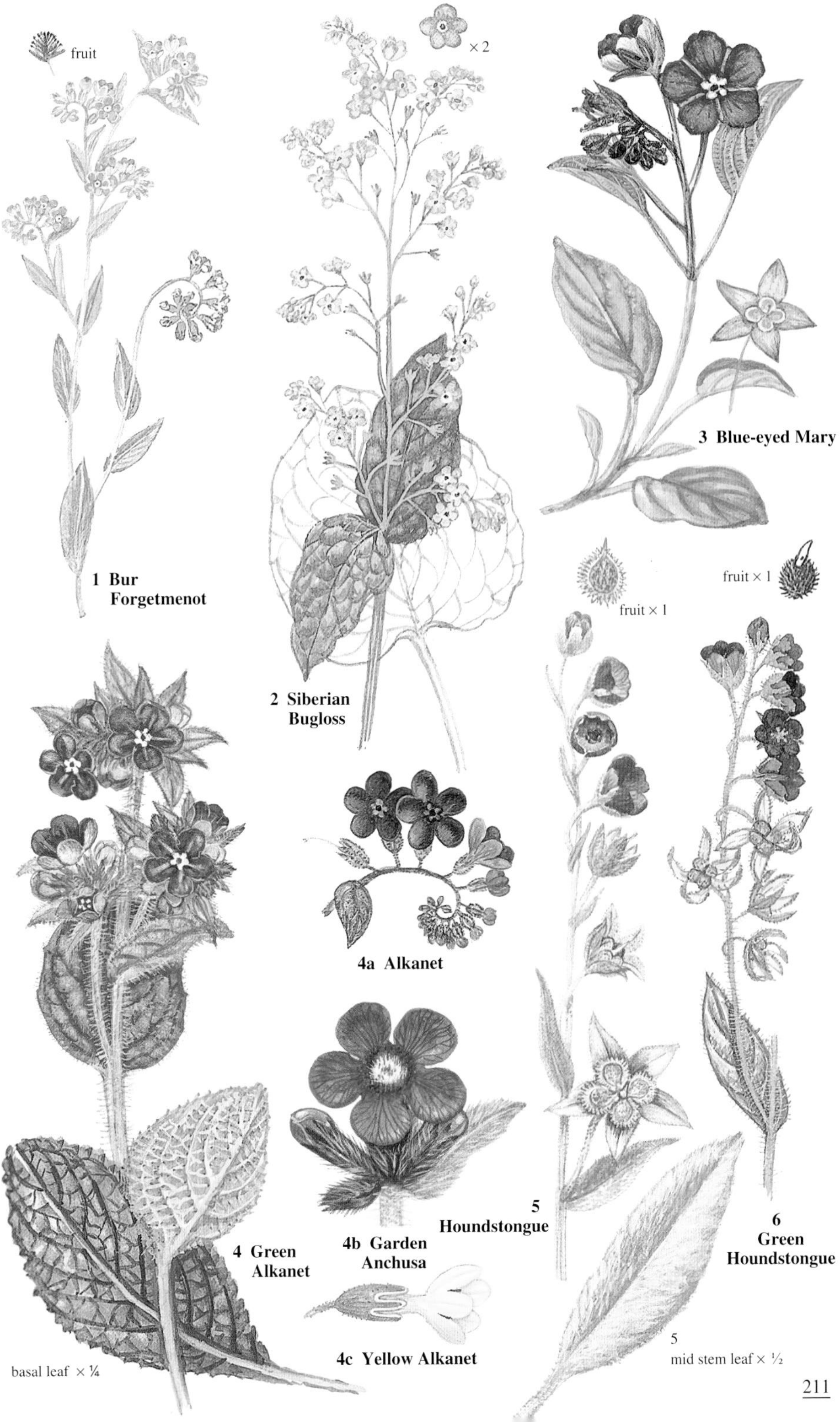

fruit

×2

3 Blue-eyed Mary

1 Bur Forgetmenot

fruit × 1

fruit × 1

2 Siberian Bugloss

4a Alkanet

5 Houndstongue

4 Green Alkanet

4b Garden Anchusa

6 Green Houndstongue

4c Yellow Alkanet

basal leaf × ¼

5
mid stem leaf × ½

1 Bugloss *Anchusa arvensis*. A short erect bristly annual, to 50cm. Flowers blue, with white honeyguides, *4-6mm*, the petal-tube curved; April-Sept. Leaves lanceolate, *wavy*. Nutlets netted. *Arable weed*.

1 SOZ ▫ ↓

2 Common Gromwell *Lithospermum officinale*. A roughly hairy, well branched, medium/tall perennial, to 1m. Flowers cream-coloured to greenish-white, 3-6mm, in leafy spikes; June-July. Leaves lanceolate with *prominent veins*. Nutlets hard, *white*, shiny. *Woods*, scrub, usually on lime.

2 ▫ ↓

3 Corn Gromwell *Lithospermum arvense*. A short/medium annual, to 50cm. Flowers creamy white, 5-9mm; April-Sept. Leaves strap-shaped to lanceolate, with *no* prominent veins. Nutlets *grey-brown*, warty. *Arable weed*.

3 ▫ ↓↓

4 **Purple Gromwell *Lithospermum purpurocaeruleum*. A short/medium unbranched perennial, to 60cm. Flowers red-purple, becoming a startlingly attractive *blue*, 11-16mm; April-June. Leaves *dark green*, narrow lanceolate. Nutlets *white*, shiny. Woods, scrub, on lime.

4 ▫

5 *Oysterplant *Mertensia maritima*. A prostrate mat-forming hairless *greyish* perennial, to 60cm. Flowers pink, turning blue-purple, 5-7mm, petals concave, in clusters; June-August. Leaves oval, *fleshy*, tasting of oysters. Nutlets flattened, fleshy. Coastal shingle, decreasing; especially in N Scotland.

5 OZ ▫

6 Borage *Borago officinalis*. A stout, roughly hairy medium annual, to 60cm. Flowers bright blue, 7-15mm, the narrow petals and sepals bent back to reveal the conspicuous *column of stamens*, in clusters; May-Sept. Leaves pointed oval with wavy margins. Nutlets ridged. Juice smells and tastes of cucumber, whence its herbal use. Established on waysides, rough and waste ground. **6a Slender Borage** *B. pygmaea* with erect petals hiding the stamens is a much rarer escape.

7 Abraham, Isaac and Jacob *Trachystemon orientalis*. Roughly hairy creeping perennial, with erect stems to 40cm. Flowers blue-violet, shaped like `e` (**6**) with a *prominent column* of mauve stamens, 9-12mm, in broad leafy clusters; March-May, before the *large* (15-50cm) broad heart-shaped long-stalked leaves. Nutlets ridged. Naturalised in damp woods, waysides.

8 Lungwort *Pulmonaria officinalis*. A roughly downy perennial, with unbranched stems to 30cm. Flowers *reddish-pink*, often turning bluer, bell-shaped, 9-11mm, sepals broad, in clusters with many *glandular hairs*; March-May. Leaves large, pointed oval, often abruptly narrowed at the base, long-stalked, *pale-spotted*. Nutlets flattened, shiny. Established in woods and on hedge-banks and road verges. **8a Red Lungwort** *P. rubra*, with flowers redder and never blue and leaves usually unspotted, is occasionally established, but usually soon hybridised away if near other Lungworts.

8 Z ▫ ↑↑

9 ***Suffolk Lungwort *Pulmonaria obscura*. The rarer of our two native lungworts, very like Lungwort (**8**), but has fewer glandular hairs and leaves darker green, *unspotted* or with very faint spots. Three woods in Suffolk.

9 ▫

10 *Narrow-leaved Lungwort *Pulmonaria longifolia*. The more frequent of our two native lungworts, differing from Lungwort (**8**) in its smaller (5-6mm), more vividly *blue* flowers with longer, narrower and more pointed sepals, few or no glandular hairs and narrower, *elliptical* leaves. Damp woods and banks in the catchment area of the ancient Solent River. **10a Mawson's Lungwort** *P. 'Mawson's Blue'*. A cultivar of unknown parentage with blunter sepals, numerous glandular hairs and *unspotted* leaves. An increasing escape on shady banks.

10 ▫ ↓

10a Mawson's Lungwort

8a Red Lungwort

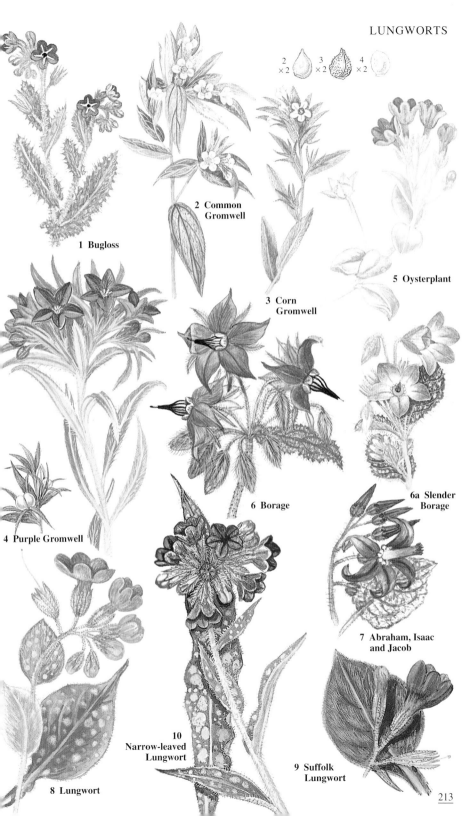

2
×2

3
×2

4
×2

1 Bugloss

2 Common
Gromwell

5 Oysterplant

3 Corn
Gromwell

4 Purple Gromwell

6 Borage

6a Slender
Borage

7 Abraham, Isaac
and Jacob

8 Lungwort

10
Narrow-leaved
Lungwort

9 Suffolk
Lungwort

1 Viper's Bugloss *Echium vulgare*. A roughly hairy medium/tall biennial, to 1m, often forming brilliant blue patches. Flowers in a drooping cluster of pink buds before becoming erect and *blue*, trumpet-shaped, open-mouthed, with 4-5 pink-purple stamens protruding, 10-19mm, the sepals *downy all over*; June-Sept. Leaves, the lower lanceolate, with *only* the midrib prominent. Nutlets wrinkled, the persistent hairy sepals making the fruiting spike look mossy. Dry bare or sparsely grassy places, often on lime.

2 ***Purple Viper's Bugloss *Echium plantagineum*. More spreading and not so tall as Viper's Bugloss (**1**), to 75cm. Flowers *purple*, with only two stamens protruding, larger (18-30mm); sepals downy *only on veins and margins*; June-August. Leaves with *side veins* also prominent. Nutlets warty. Bare places near the sea, now only near Land's End.

3 Common Fiddleneck *Amsinckia intermedia*. Low/short white-bristly annual, to 20cm. Flowers yellow, on upper side of coiled spikes; April-August. Leaves bluntly lanceolate. Fruits wrinkled. Now well established on bare or disturbed, often sandy, ground, often an arable weed. **Scarce Fiddleneck** *A. lycopsoides*, taller, to *c.* 60cm, whose orange-yellow flowers have a hairy throat, is long established on Inner Farne I, Northumberland.

PERIWINKLE FAMILY Apocynaceae

4 Greater Periwinkle *Vinca major*. Evergreen undershrub, with long stems trailing and rooting at the tips, to 1.5m. Flowers blue-violet, 5-petalled, *30-50mm*, solitary; January-June. Leaves *broad* lanceolate, stalked, rather leathery, sometimes variegated. Well established on hedge-banks and road verges, especially near gardens, occasionally in woods. **4a Intermediate Periwinkle** *V. difformis*, with pale blue or whitish flowers and narrower leaves, is much less frequent.

5 Lesser Periwinkle *Vinca minor*. Evergreen undershrub, with a mat of prostrate stems to 1m. Flowers blue-violet, occasionally purple, 5-petalled, *25-30mm*, solitary; January-July. Leaves *narrow* lanceolate. Woods, shrubberies, hedge-banks, may be native, but usually an escape.

BOGBEAN FAMILY Menyanthaceae

6 Bogbean *Menyanthes trifoliata*. A distinctive, far-creeping aquatic perennial, stems sprawling or floating, to 1.5m, but flowers and *trefoil* leaves projecting up to 30cm above the water. Flowers white inside, pink outside, with five petals *fringed with white hairs*, in conspicuous stalked spikes; May-June. Fruit a capsule. Shallow water in marshes, swamps, fens and bogs.

7 Fringed Water-lily *Nymphoides peltatus*. An aquatic plant differing from the true Water-lilies (p. 306) especially in its smaller (30-40mm) projecting yellow flowers with five *fringed petals* and its small (3-10cm) rounded, shallowly toothed floating leaves, *purple below* and sometimes purple-spotted above. Fruit a capsule. Ponds and slow streams, increasing, due perhaps to aquarists' throw-outs.

JACOB'S LADDER FAMILY Polemoniaceae

8 Jacob's Ladder *Polemonium caeruleum*. A handsome medium-tall perennial, to 1m. Flowers purplish-blue, white at the base, five-petalled, 20-30mm, in spike-like clusters; June-August. Leaves *pinnate*, alternate. Fruit a capsule. Grassy and stony places, cliff-ledges, usually on *limestone*, notably at Malham Cove in the Craven Pennines, Yorkshire; occasionally naturalised elsewhere.

VERBENA FAMILY Verbenaceae

9 Vervain *Verbena officinalis*. A roughly hairy medium perennial, with *stiff square* stems to 75cm. Flowers pale lilac, 5-petalled, more or less *2-lipped*, 3-5mm, in spikes; June-Sept. Leaves pinnately lobed, opposite. Fruit a cluster of nutlets. Dry bare or grassy places, especially on lime.

7

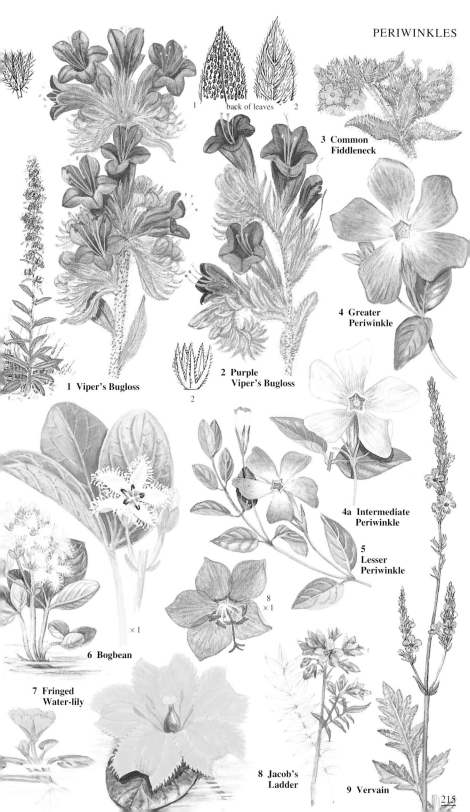

1

back of leaves

2

3 Common Fiddleneck

4 Greater Periwinkle

1 Viper's Bugloss

2

2 Purple Viper's Bugloss

4a Intermediate Periwinkle

5 Lesser Periwinkle

8
× 1

× 1

6 Bogbean

7 Fringed Water-lily

8 Jacob's Ladder

9 Vervain

DEAD-NETTLE FAMILY Lamiaceae

Formerly known as Labiatae, hence still referred to as Labiates. Hairy/downy annuals/perennials, often aromatic or pungent, with *square stems*. Flowers with joined petals and five sepal-teeth, *2-lipped* and open-mouthed (except mints and Gipsywort p. 226); upper lip missing in bugles and germanders (p. 224); usually in whorls up leafy stems. Leaves opposite, toothed, usually stalked and undivided. Fruit a cluster of nutlets. See p. 228 for two-lipped members of Figwort Family. Described below as:

1. Two-lipped, strong-smelling. 2. Two-lipped, pleasantly aromatic p. 220). 3. Two-lipped, faintly or not aromatic (p. 222). 4. One-lipped (p. 224). 5. Scarcely or not lipped, pleasantly aromatic (p. 226).

~

1. Two-lipped, strong-smelling

Flowers	white:	White Dead-Nettle, Common/Bifid Hemp-Nettles (occasional), Bastard Balm
	yellow:	Yellow Archangel, Bifid Hemp-Nettle (pale; rare), Large-flowered Hemp-Nettle (pale), Downy Hemp-Nettle (very rare, p. 464)
	pink:	Red Hemp-Nettle (deep), Bastard Balm
	pink-purple:	Dead-Nettles (except White), Common/Bifid Hemp-Nettles, Marsh/Field/Downy Woundworts, Black Horehound, Lesser Skullcap
	red-purple:	Betony
	purple:	Hedge/Limestone Woundworts
	blue-violet:	Ground Ivy
	blue:	Skullcaps

Dead-nettles *Lamium*. Flowers with lower lip 2-lobed, four stamens within hooded upper lip and sepal-teeth narrow, in whorls at base of leaves.

1 White Dead-nettle *Lamium album*. Short creeping perennial, to 60cm. Flowers *white* with greenish streaks on lower lip, 18-25mm, with a wide open mouth; March-Nov and through mild winters. Leaves heart-shaped, somewhat like Common Nettle (p. 36), but with *no stinging hairs*. Aka White Archangel. Hedge-banks, waysides, bare and waste ground.

2 Red Dead-nettle *Lamium purpureum*. Low erect/sprawling annual, stems to 40cm. Flowers dark/pale pink-purple, 10-18mm; Jan-Dec. Leaves heart-shaped, shortly toothed, *all stalked*. A familiar weed of cultivation. **2a Cut-leaved Dead-nettle** *L. hybridum* may grow with Red Dead-Nettle, but differs especially in its petal-tube being *much shorter*, the flowers (March-Oct) sometimes not opening, and its more *deeply toothed* upper leaves. Mainly cultivated ground.

3 Henbit Dead-nettle *Lamium amplexicaule*. Low erect annual, to 25cm. Flowers pink-purple, more deeply coloured in bud, 14-20mm, but often much shorter, confined within the whitely downy 5-7mm sepals and *not opening*; April-August. Leaves well toothed, those under the flowers *unstalked*. Sepal-teeth more or less erect in fruit. Cultivated and bare ground. **3a Northern Dead-nettle** *L. confertum* is very similar but has sepals *nearly twice as large*, 8-12mm, and the fruiting sepal-teeth *divergent*. Cultivated and bare ground. Differs from Cut-leaved Dead-Nettle (**2a**) in its unstalked upper leaves.

4 Spotted Dead-nettle *Lamium maculatum*. Like a pink-purple-flowered White Dead-Nettle (**1**), a strong-smelling short creeping perennial, to *c.* 30cm. Flowers *pink-purple*, 20-35mm; March-Oct and through mild winters. Leaves heart-shaped, usually with a *large whitish patch*. A frequent garden escape.

~

5 Yellow Archangel *Lamiastrum galeobdolon*. Short hairy patch-forming perennial, with erect flowering stems to 30cm and *long rooting runners* to 1m. Flowers like Dead-Nettles (above), *butter yellow*, with red-brown honeyguides, 17-21mm; April-June. Leaves *dark green*, heart-shaped, long-stalked; with conspicuous whitish blotches in the increasing garden escape, **5a** ssp. ***argentatum***. Woods, scrub, hedge-banks.

6 Ground Ivy *Glechoma hederacea*. A low, often purplish, pungent perennial, to 30cm; *long creeping runners* to 1m. Flowers *blue-violet*, 15-20mm, rarely larger and pink; March-June. Leaves kidney-shaped, blunt-toothed, long-stalked. Woods, hedge-banks, bare ground.

Labiate details

stem

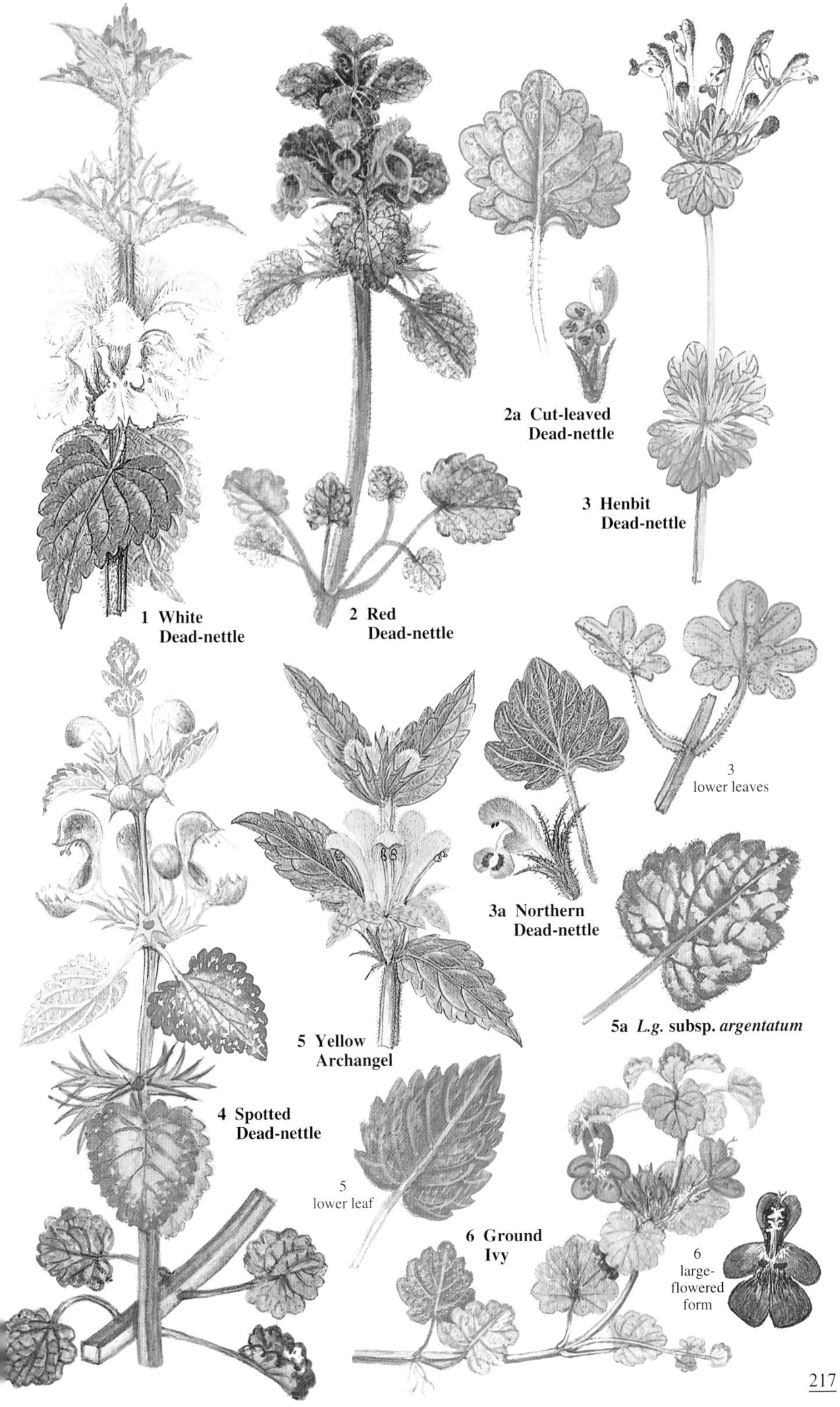

2a Cut-leaved Dead-nettle

3 Henbit Dead-nettle

1 White Dead-nettle

2 Red Dead-nettle

3 lower leaves

3a Northern Dead-nettle

5a *L.g.* subsp. *argentatum*

5 Yellow Archangel

4 Spotted Dead-nettle

5 lower leaf

6 Ground Ivy

6 large-flowered form

Hemp-nettles *Galeopsis*. Coarsely hairy annuals, with stems usually *swollen at nodes*. Flowers like dead-nettles (p. 216), but with with two small humps at the angle between the two outer and the centre lobes of the 3-lobed lower lip; in whorls up leafy stems. Leaves broad lanceolate, well toothed, nettle-like.

1 Common Hemp-nettle *Galeopsis tetrahit*. Stems low/medium, to 1m. Flowers pink-purple, sometimes white, with darker markings on the middle lobe of the lower lip (if very slightly notched may be a hybrid) *not approaching the tip*; sepals tinged purple-brown; 10-20mm; July-Sept. Damp woodland, stream-banks, fens and heaths; also often in arable and other disturbed ground.

2 Bifid Hemp-nettle *Galeopsis bifida*. Extremely like Common Hemp-Nettle (**1**), with which it hybridises. Best distinguished by the darker markings on the lower lip *reaching the usually well notched tip*. Flowers rarely pale yellow.

3 Large-flowered Hemp-nettle *Galeopsis speciosa*. Our largest and bushiest hemp-nettle, medium/tall, to 1m. Flowers pale yellow, the lower lip darker, usually with a *purple* central lobe, sepals green, *20-45mm*; July-Sept. Leaves ovate. An arable weed, often on peat.

4 Red Hemp-nettle *Galeopsis angustifolia*. Stems downy rather than hairy, erect, *scarcely swollen* at the nodes, low/short, to 60cm. Flowers *deep pink*, sepals green, 14-25mm; July-Sept. Leaves *narrow* lanceolate. A decreasing arable weed, usually on lime, also on coastal sand or shingle.

Woundworts *Stachys*. Perennials, except Field Woundwort (**8**). Flowers with upper lip hooded and containing four stamens, lower lip 3-lobed and five spiny-tipped sepal-teeth, in leafy whorls up the stem. Leaves with teeth sometimes rounded.

5 Hedge Woundwort *Stachys sylvatica*. Roughly hairy, rather unpleasantly pungent, medium, with both creeping and erect stems, to 1m. Flowers dark *beetroot-purple* with whitish blotches, 13-18mm with tiny bristle-like bracts; June-Oct. Leaves dark green, heart-shaped, all stalked. Hybridises with Marsh Woundwort (**6**). Hedge-banks and other shady places.

6 Marsh Woundwort *Stachys palustris*. Downy, with some glandular hairs, faintly pungent, medium/tall, with both creeping and erect stems, to 1m. Flowers *pink-purple*, sepals often maroon, 12-15mm; late June-Sept. Leaves narrowly heart-shaped or ovate, the upper unstalked. Hybridises with Hedge Woundwort (**5**). Damp places, often by ditches and other fresh water.

7 Betony *Stachys officinalis*. Slightly hairy, medium, to 75cm. Flowers bright *red-purple*, 12-18mm, in oblong heads; June-Oct. Leaves mostly in a basal rosette, *bluntly* toothed. Heaths, grassy places, usually avoiding clay.

8 Field Woundwort *Stachys arvensis*. Our only annual woundwort, hairy, erect to sprawling, *low*, to 25cm. Flowers *dull* pink-purple, 6-8mm, sepal-teeth long; April-Oct. Leaves oval, bluntly toothed, the upper unstalked. A weed of cultivation, avoiding lime.

9 **Downy Woundwort *Stachys germanica*. Tall biennial, to 1m; thickly covered with a felt of *greyish-white* hairs. Flowers *pale* pink-purple, 12-20mm; July-August. Leaves pointed oval, the lower long-stalked. Hedge-banks and sparsely grassy places N and W of Oxford. **9a Lamb's-ear** *S. byzantina* is even more thickly *whitely* woolly, with creeping stems and shorter erect ones, flowers 15-25mm and many non-flowering rosettes. A garden escape, much more widespread.

10 ***Limestone Woundwort *Stachys alpina*. Not unlike Hedge Woundwort (**5**), but aromatic or creeping, softly downy with glandular hairs, flowers *dull purple* blotched creamy and *broader bracts* nearly as long as the sepals. Woods on lime.

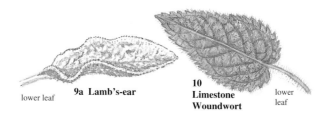

9a Lamb's-ear
lower leaf

10 Limestone Woundwort
lower leaf

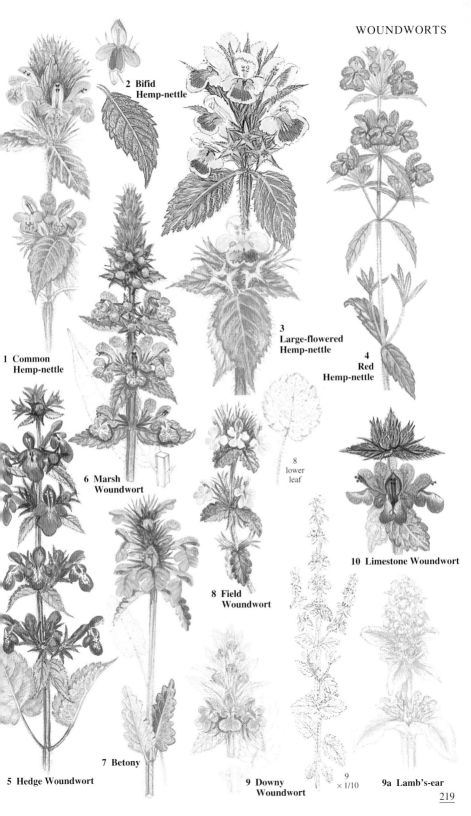

2 Bifid Hemp-nettle

3 Large-flowered Hemp-nettle

4 Red Hemp-nettle

1 Common Hemp-nettle

6 Marsh Woundwort

8 lower leaf

10 Limestone Woundwort

8 Field Woundwort

5 Hedge Woundwort

7 Betony

9 Downy Woundwort

9 × 1/10

9a Lamb's-ear

1 Black Horehound *Ballota nigra*. Coarse, *disagreeably pungent*, erect to straggly medium perennial, to 1m. Flowers *pink-purple*, 9-15mm, sepal-tube *funnel-shaped* with long teeth, often barren with no flowers, in whorls; June-Sept. Leaves pointed oval, well stalked, mid-green. Hedge-banks, waysides rough or waste ground. **1a Motherwort** *Leonurus cardiaca*, 'of a verie ranke smell', has somewhat similar but paler pink and *downy* flowers, but strikingly different *3-5-lobed* leaves. A herbal relic, decreasing.

2 Bastard Balm *Melittis melissophyllum*. Our largest-flowered labiate, a hairy, strong-smelling medium perennial, to 70cm. Flowers white with lower lip mainly pink, *25-40mm*, in whorls; May-July. Leaves pointed oval. Woods, hedge-banks, shady rocks.

2. Two-lipped, pleasantly aromatic

Flowers	white:	White Horehound, Catmint, Balm
	pink-purple:	Wild Basil, Calamints, Thymes
	purple:	Marjoram
	violet:	Garden Catmint

Calamints *Clinopodium*. Pleasantly aromatic perennials (both except Basil Thyme, p. 224), the flowers with upper lip 2-lobed and lower 3-lobed, the sepals 2-lipped, the upper lip with three teeth, shorter and broader than the two teeth of the lower; in whorls at base of leaves; July-Sept. Dry grassy and bushy places, especially on lime.

3 Wild Basil *Clinopodium vulgare*. Downy and faintly aromatic; often only short/medium, to 75cm. Flowers pink-purple 12-22mm, sepals purplish and whitely hairy, in whorls with *no common stalk*. Leaves pointed oval, slightly toothed.

4 Common Calamint *Clinopodium ascendens*. Mint-scented, hairy, short/medium, to 60cm. Flowers pale violet-pink, spotted darker, 10-16mm; sepals often purple, hairs on lower teeth *long*, those in their throat *not* protruding in fruit; whorls with a common stalk, scarcely branched. Leaves up to 40mm, with 3-8 teeth on each side.

5 Lesser Calamint *Clinopodium calamintha*. Greyer than Common Calamint (**4**) and has paler lilac, less spotted flowers, sepals with shorter lower teeth, which have *short or no* hairs, and hairs in the throat *protruding* in fruit, and flower stalks well branched. Leaves smaller, up to 20mm, scarcely toothed.

6 ***Wood Calamint *Clinopodium menthifolium*, an extreme rarity on one chalky bank in the Isle of Wight, has larger flowers, (15-22mm) than Common Calamint (**4**), with longer lower sepal-teeth and larger leaves with 6-10 teeth on each side

~

7 Wild Thyme *Thymus polytrichus*. A prostrate, faintly aromatic evergreen undershrub, with a mat of non-flowering rooting stems, and flowering stems erect, to 10cm, square, bluntly angled, with *dense downy hairs on two faces* and few or none on the others. Flowers pink-purple, obscurely 2-lipped, 6mm, in whorls and terminal heads; May-Sept. Leaves oval, opposite, very small, the veins beneath *curving round at the margin* and joining at the tip. Dry grassy and heathy places, dunes, mainly on chalk in the S. The very similar but usually smaller **7a **Breckland Thyme** *T. serpyllum* flowers later (July-August) and has stem hairs on all four sides, and veins beneath the leaves not reaching the margin. Confined to the E Anglian Breckland.

8 Large Thyme *Thymus pulegioides*. Generally taller, to 25cm, and more strongly and *distinctively* aromatic than Wild Thyme (**7**), with no creeping runners. Stems with *hairs on the sharper angles*, two narrow sides shortly downy and two broader sides hairless. Flowers in often longer heads; *July*-August. Leaves with veins beneath obscure when dry. Short turf on chalk or sand.

9 Marjoram *Origanum vulgare*. A short/medium downy, *strongly aromatic* perennial, to 50cm. Flowers with *dark purple buds* opening pale purple, with usually purple bracts at their base, in loose clusters; July-Sept. Leaves oval, often slightly toothed. Dry grassland, usually on lime.

back of leaf ×2 **7** ×4 ×2 **7a** **8** **7**

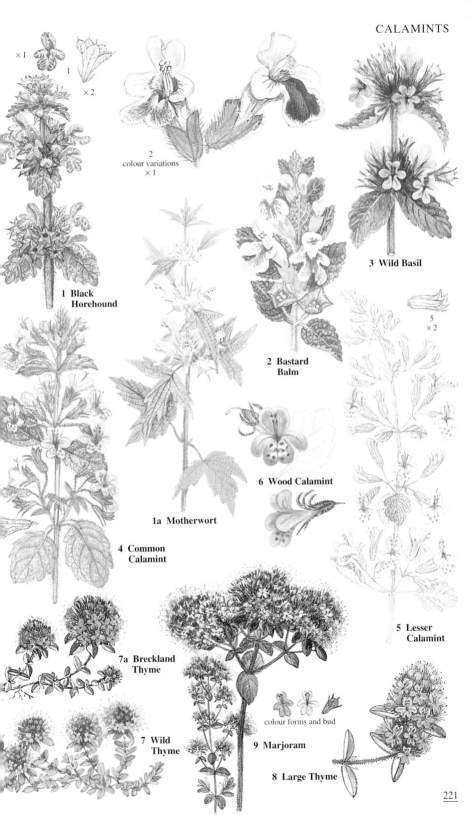

× 1

1

× 2

2
colour variations
× 1

3 Wild Basil

1 Black
Horehound

5
× 2

2 Bastard
Balm

6 Wood Calamint

1a Motherwort

4 Common
Calamint

5 Lesser
Calamint

7a Breckland
Thyme

colour forms and bud

7 Wild
Thyme

9 Marjoram

8 Large Thyme

1 White Horehound *Marrubium vulgare*. Whitely downy. *thyme-scented* medium perennial, to 60cm. Flowers *white*, with hooked sepal-teeth, 12-15mm, in whorls; June-Sept. Leaves roundish, bluntly toothed, wrinkled, grey-green. Bare dry places on lime, e.g. Tennyson Down, Isle of Wight, Great Orme's Head, N Wales.

2 Catmint *Nepeta cataria*. A decreasing short/medium *mint-scented* perennial, thickly *covered with grey down*, to 1m. Flowers *white* with purplish spots, 7-12mm; June-Sept. Leaves heart-shaped, toothed. Quite distinct from the most frequent and sometimes escaping **Garden Catmint** *N. × faassenii*, which is much less thickly downy and has bright violet flowers. Dry and often bare grassy places, roadsides, on limy soils.

3 Balm *Melissa officinalis*. A medium/tall hairy *lemon-scented* perennial, to 1m. Flowers white, relatively *inconspicuous*, 8-15mm; July-Oct. Leaves yellowish-green at first, pointed oval, toothed, wrinkled. A culinary and medicinal herb and bee-plant, frequently escaping and locally established.

3. Two-lipped, faintly or not aromatic

Flowers		
	blue:	Meadow Clary, Whorled Clary, Skullcap
	violet:	Self-heal, Basil Thyme
	purple:	Balkan Clary
	pink-purple:	Garden Clary, Lesser Skullcap
	yellow:	Sticky Clary

4 Self-heal *Prunella vulgaris*. Creeping downy perennial, not aromatic or pungent, prostrate or short, to 30cm. Flowers *violet*, rarely pink or white, sepals purple, 10-15mm, in *oblong* or squarish heads; June-Oct. Leaves pointed oval, *not or slightly toothed*. Hybridises with the very local Cut-leaved Self-heal (**2**), which brings creamy-white to the flowers and toothing to the leaves. Grassy, often rather bare, places, including lawns and woods.

5 Cut-leaved Self-heal *Prunella laciniata*. Has *creamy white* flowers, (June-August), somewhat larger (15-17mm) than Self-heal (**1**), with which it hybridises freely; also hairier leaves, the upper more or less *pinnate*. Dry grassy places, usually on lime.

Claries *Salvia*. Slightly aromatic perennials; flowers open-mouthed, with hooded upper lip and 3-lobed lower lip, the upper lip of their sepals either un- or 3-toothed, the lower 2-toothed. 15 alien species have been recorded:

Fairly widely naturalised are **6 Whorled Clary** *Salvia verticillata*, with pale blue flowers, and **6a Garden Clary** *S. sclarea* with multi-coloured flowers, especially on old walls. Locally established are **6b Sticky Clary** *S. glutinosa*, with red-marked yellow flowers and many sticky hairs, especially in woods by the R Tay at Caputh; and **6c Balkan Clary** *S. nemorosa*, with purple flowers, on dunes in N Cornwall.

7 Wild Clary *Salvia verbenaca*. Our most frequent native clary, medium, to 80cm. Flowers pale purple, often tinged blue, much smaller (10-15mm) and much less showy than Meadow Clary (**8**), for which it can be wishfully mistaken; sepals *white-haired*, 10-15mm; often self-pollinating and so not opening and appearing barren; June-Sept. Leaves broad lanceolate, bluntly toothed, wrinkled, *greyish*. Decreasing in dry grassy, often rather bare, places.

8 **Meadow Clary *Salvia pratensis*. One of our most gorgeous wild flowers, medium/tall, to 1m. Flowers a rich *violet-blue*, 15-30mm, sepals with *brownish* hairs, never self-pollinating; June-July. Leaves like Wild Clary (**7**), but larger and not greyish. Grassland on lime, also as a garden escape.

7 Wild Clary

6b Sticky Clary

6b lower leaf

calyx
× 2

3
Balm

5
Cut-leaved
Self-heal

2
Catmint

4 Self-heal

1
White Horehound

6a Garden
Clary

6c
Balkan
Clary

8 Meadow
Clary

7 Wild
Clary

8

6 Whorled
Clary

1 Basil Thyme *Clinopodium acinos*. Low, often prostrate annual, to 25cm; our only non-aromatic calamint. Flowers *violet*, with a white patch on the lower lip; May-Sept. Leaves oval, slightly toothed, with prominent veins. Habitat as other calamints (p. 220), but more often on barer ground.

2 Skullcap *Scutellaria galericulata*. Short, faintly aromatic perennial, erect to sprawling, to 50cm. Flowers *bright blue*, in pairs, 10-18mm; June-Sept. Leaves lanceolate, short- or unstalked. Hybridises with Lesser Skullcap (**3**). Wet grassy places and by fresh water. **2a Somerset Skullcap** *S. altissima*, with a white lower lip and heart-shaped leaves, has grown since 1929 on a shady wall near Mells and in two other places.

3 Lesser Skullcap *Scutellaria minor*. Low, faintly aromatic perennial, to 25cm. Flowers pale *pink-purple* spotted darker, 6-10mm; July-Oct. Leaves broad lanceolate, scarcely toothed. Hybridises with Skullcap (**2**). Damp heaths, woods, not on lime.

4. One-lipped

Flowers	blue:	Bugle, Pyramidal Bugle
	pink-purple:	Cut-leaved/Water/Wall Germanders
	yellow:	Ground-pine, Wood Sage

4 Bugle *Ajuga reptans*. Low/short perennial, with stems hairy on two opposite sides, to 30cm, with *long rooting runners*. Flowers rich powder-blue, rarely pink, creamy or white, the upper lip *tiny*, five sepal-teeth, 14-17mm; in a leafy spike with leaf-like bracts often purplish, especially beneath, the topmost shorter than the flowers; April-July. Leaves oval, often *bronzy*, the lowest long-stalked and in a rosette. Woods, shady grassy places.

5 Pyramidal Bugle *Ajuga pyramidalis*. Differs from Bugle (**4**) in having stems hairy all round, but with *no runners*. Flowers a deeper blue, shorter than *all* the leafy bracts, 10-18mm; April-May, but a shy flowerer. Rosette leaves short-stalked. Limestone rocks.

6 Ground-pine *Ajuga chamaepitys*. Low grey-green annual, often prostrate, to 20cm. Its faint smell of pine-resin, together with the 3 needle-like linear lobes of the leaves up the stem makes it fancifully like a bushy Pine seedling. Flowers *yellow* with tiny red spots in the throat and a very short upper lip, 1-2 together up the stem, 7-15mm; May-Sept. Arable weed, also in sparsely grassy places on chalk.

Germanders *Teucrium*. Flowers with *no upper lip*, 5-lobed lower lip and 5 sepal-teeth not lipped.

7 Wood Sage *Teucrium scorodonia*. Short/medium downy perennial, to 50cm. Flowers *pale greenish-yellow*, with prominent stamens and purplish anthers, 7-9mm, in pairs; July-Sept. Leaves pointed oval, bluntly toothed, wrinkled. Dry heathy places, often in light shade, usually on acid soils, also on dunes and screes.

8 **Cut-leaved Germander *Teucrium botrys*. A low downy annual, erect to 30cm. Flowers pink-purple, 15-20mm, in small whorls; July-Sept. Leaves triangular, *deeply cut*, the lower almost pinnate. Bare ground on lime, decreasing.

9 ***Water Germander *Teucrium scordium*. Sprawling short grey-downy perennial, to 50cm. Flowers pink-purple, 7-10mm, July-Oct. Leaves oblong, toothed, *unstalked*. Dune slacks, Braunton Burrows, N Devon, also by fresh water S of Ely; Ireland, see p. 461.

10 ***Wall Germander *Teucrium chamaedrys*. Short undershrub, to 40cm. Flowers pink- to red-purple, 9-16mm, the whorls *clustered* at the top of the stem; July-Sept. Leaves pointed oval, toothed, *dark green*, shiny. Native only on chalk downs above Cuckmere Haven, Sussex; otherwise widely scattered on old walls, since 1714 on Camber Castle, E Sussex.

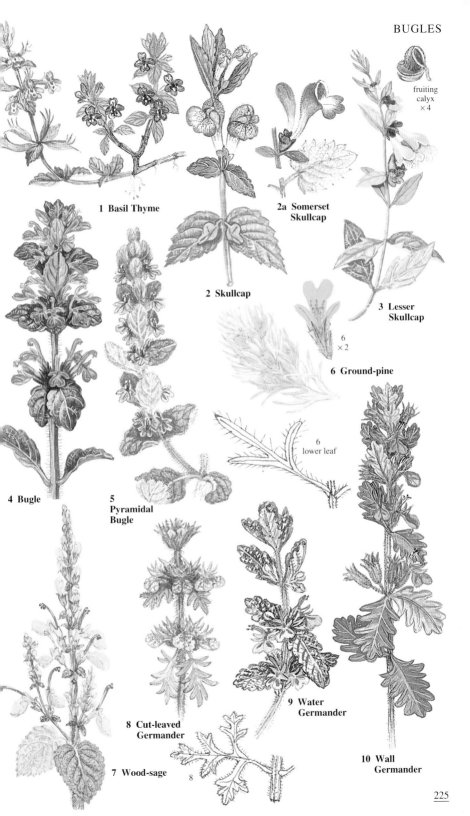

fruiting
calyx
×4

1 Basil Thyme

2a Somerset
Skullcap

2 Skullcap

3 Lesser
Skullcap

6
×2

6 Ground-pine

6
lower leaf

4 Bugle

5
Pyramidal
Bugle

8 Cut-leaved
Germander

9 Water
Germander

7 Wood-sage

8

10 Wall
Germander

Flowers lilac:	Mints, (Round-leaved Mint pinkish)	**Flowers white**:	Gipsywort

Mints *Mentha*. Highly *aromatic* perennials, each with a distinctive scent. Flowers lilac, small, bell-shaped, with four more or less equal petals, in tight whorls up the leafy stem; sepal-teeth 5; stamens 4, protruding except in Pennyroyal (**3**) and hybrids. Leaves toothed, usually stalked. The many hybrids are very difficult and some cannot be certainly identified.

1 Water Mint *Mentha aquatica*. Much the commonest waterside mint, short/medium, usually downy, often purplish, to 90cm; scent very pleasant. Flowers lilac, with hairy sepals, 3-4mm, in a large (20-30cm) round *terminal head*, often with a few whorls at the base of the upper leaves; sepal-tube and teeth narrow and hairy; flower-stalks hairy; July-Sept. Leaves pointed oval. Hybridises with Corn (**2**) and Spear (**4**) Mints. Wet grassy places and by fresh water.

2 Corn Mint *Mentha arvensis*. Our most frequent mint away from water and the least pleasantly aromatic, sickly to some people, acrid to others, downy, low/short, often sprawling, to 60cm. Flowers lilac, 3-4mm, *all in whorls up the stem*, sepal-tube and teeth broad and hairy, flower-stalks hairy or not; July-Sept. Leaves pointed oval. Damp, often grassy places, woodland clearings, by fresh water; often an arable weed. **2a Whorled Mint** *M.* × *verticillata,* the hybrid between our two commonest mints, resembles Corn Mint in its flowers being all in whorls up the stem, but Water Mint (**1**) in its nearly always hairy flower-stalks and narrow sepal-tube and teeth; stamens normally *not protruding*.

3 *Pennyroyal *Mentha pulegium*. Downy, low/short, usually prostrate, sometimes erect to 30cm. Flowers not unlike Corn Mint (**2**), but sepal-tube markedly ribbed with hairs in the throat and the two lower sepal-teeth are longer and narrower than the three upper; August-Oct. Leaves small, pointed oval, bluntly toothed, often drooping. Damp heaths and grassland, decreasing; occasionally naturalised elsewhere.

4 Spear Mint *Mentha spicata*. The most frequent garden mint, strongly and sweetly aromatic; usually hairless, short/medium, to 90cm. Flowers lilac, in *terminal spikes*, 2-4mm, stamens *protruding*; July-Oct. Leaves lanceolate, usually shiny, almost unstalked. A frequent escape on waysides and waste ground. Hairy forms used to be mistaken for the non-British Horse Mint *M. longifolia*, one of the parents from which Spear Mint itself originated – the other was Round-leaved Mint (**5**). The often purple-tinged **4a Peppermint** *M.* × *piperita*, its hybrid with Water Mint (**1**), has the well known peppermint smell (also Eau-de-Cologne), with a terminal head and darker, well stalked leaves and stamens not protruding. Much less frequent. Three locally established spearmint-scented hybrids are: **4b Bushy Mint** *M.* × *gracilis* (× **2**), with stems often purplish and sepals hairy only on teeth; **4c Tall Mint** *M.* × *smithiana*, a triple hybrid with **1** and **2**, often taller, to 1.5m, with stems often purplish and leaf-teeth sharp and forwardly directed; and **4d Sharp-leaved Mint** *M.* × *villosonervata,* Spear Mint's hybrid with Horse Mint, frequent in gardens, always downy, with very sharply pointed leaf-teeth and pinkish flowers.

5 Round-leaved Mint *Mentha suaveolens*. Well covered with whitish down, apple-scented, short/medium, to 90mm. Flowers *pink*-lilac to whitish, 2-3mm, in a branched spike; August-Sept. Leaves broadly oval to roundish, *wrinkled*, the teeth bent back to appear blunt. Ditches, rivulets, damp waysides. **5a Apple Mint** *M.* × *villosa*. Very variable and not infrequent cultivated hybrid of Round-leaved and Spear (**4**) Mints. Intermediate between parents, mixing the spearmint and apple scents, the flower colour and leaf shape (usually roundish) and either downy or hairless. Waste and rough ground, often near gardens. The Apple Mint of gardens is its var. *alopecuroides*, which is closer to **5** but with the sharp teeth not bent back. **5b False Apple Mint** *M.* × *rotundifolia*, the hybrid between Round-leaved and Horse Mints, is always downy, with less rounded leaves.

6 Corsican Mint *Mentha requienii*. Prostrate, rooting and *mat-forming*, to 12cm; distinctively and pleasantly aromatic. Flowers lilac, *1-2mm*, rather few to the cluster; June-Sept. Leaves tiny, *roundish*, untoothed, well stalked. Naturalised in a few damp woodland rides, and see p. 461.

7 Gipsywort *Lycopus europaeus*. Short/medium perennial, to 1m; not aromatic. Flowers *white, dotted purple*, 4-petalled, 3-5mm, in whorls at base of upper leaves; June-Sept. Leaves lanceolate, *deeply toothed*. By fresh water.

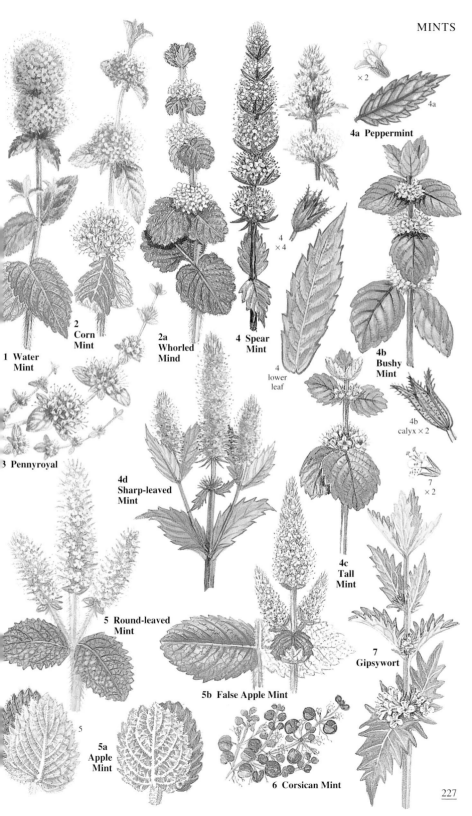

×2

4a

4a Peppermint

2 Corn Mint

2a Whorled Mind

4 Spear Mint

4 ×4

4 lower leaf

4b Bushy Mint

4b calyx × 2

1 Water Mint

3 Pennyroyal

4d Sharp-leaved Mint

7 ×2

4c Tall Mint

5 Round-leaved Mint

7 Gipsywort

5

5a Apple Mint

5b False Apple Mint

6 Corsican Mint

227

FIGWORT FAMILY Scrophulariaceae

Annuals/perennials, with two quite distinct flower-types, some 2-lipped, the lips not always well developed and sometimes closed, the rest with 4-5 petals, joined at the base (see p. 238). Stems usually rounded, sometimes square. Leaves very variable. Fruit a capsule. The 2-lipped flowers are described first, to be near the also 2-lipped labiates (p. 216), most of which are aromatic.

Flowers 2-lipped

Flowers white:	Foxglove 232
pink-purple:	Weasel's Snout 232, Foxglove 232, Lousewort 234. Red Bartsia 234, Crested/Field Cow-wheats 234
red:	Snapdragon 232
red-purple:	Marsh Lousewort 234
red-brown:	Water Figwort 228, Coppery Monkeyflower 232
yellow:	Yellow Figwort 228, Common/Sand/Prostrate Toadflaxes 230, Fluellens 230, Straw Foxglove 232, Monkeyflowers 232, Musk 232, Yellow Rattles 234, Yellow Bartsia 234, Cow-wheats 234
yellow-brown:	Common Cow-wheat 234
lilac:	Pale/Ivy-leaved Toadflaxes 230
purple:	Italian/Malling Toadflaxes 230, Alpine Bartsia 234
violet:	Purple Toadflax 230
purple-brown:	Common/Green/Balm-leaved Figworts 228
Flowers with spur:	Yellow Toadflax (long) 230, Other Toadflaxes (short) 230, Fluellens 230
pouch:	Trailing Snapdragon 230, Snapdragon 230, Weasel's Snout 232
mouths closed:	Toadflaxes 230, Snapdragons 230, Fluellens 230

Figworts *Scrophularia*. Perennials with 4-angled stems and opposite leaves. Flowers, rather small, almost globular, open-mouthed, with 2-lobed upper and 3-lobed greenish lower lips; stamens four with anthers and (except Yellow Figwort, **5**) one without (staminode) located between the two lobes of the upper lip, sepal-lobes pale-edged, toothed, in an open leafy cluster.

1 Common Figwort *Scrophularia nodosa*. Much the commonest figwort of drier places, rather foetid, almost hairless, tall, with stems square but *not winged*, to 1m. Flowers purple-brown, the staminode blunt, lobed and *broader than long*, the sepal-lobes with a very narrow pale border, 7-10mm; late May-August. Leaves pointed oval, well toothed, on unwinged stalks. Woods, hedge-banks and other places in half-shade.

2 Water Figwort *Scrophularia auriculata*. Much the commonest figwort of wetter places, only slightly foetid, usually hairless, tall, with stems conspicuously *winged*, to 1.2m. Flowers red-brown, brighter than other Figworts, the staminode *rounded* and not lobed and the sepal-lobes broadly edged whitish, 5-9mm; June-Sept. Leaves blunter than Common Figwort (**1**), usually with a pair of leaflets at the base, on *winged* stalks. By fresh water and in marshy places, occasionally unexpectedly in drier spots.

3 Green Figwort *Scrophularia umbrosa*. Tall, with stems even more conspicuously winged than Water Figwort (**2**), to 1m. Flowers purple-brown like Common Figwort (**1**), but staminode more 2-lobed and sepal-lobes more toothed and with a broader pale edge, 7-10mm; July-Sept. Leaves like Common Figwort but more sharply toothed. Damp shady places.

4 Balm-leaved Figwort *Scrophularia scorodonia*. Whole plant *downy*, tall, with stems not winged, sometimes rounded, to 1m. Flowers purple-brown, like Common Figwort (**1**), but staminode rounded and sepal-lobes with a broader pale edge, 8-11mm; June-Sept. Leaves bluntly pointed oval, *wrinkled*. Dry places in half-shade near the sea.

5 Yellow Figwort *Scrophularia vernalis*. Medium/tall, softly hairy, slightly foetid, with stems to 80cm. Flowers *pale yellow*, in small leafy clusters, with no staminode, 6-8mm; April-June. stems to 80cm. Leaves pointed oval. well toothed, nettle-like. Shady places, as in pinewoods on N Norfolk coast, an often established garden escape.

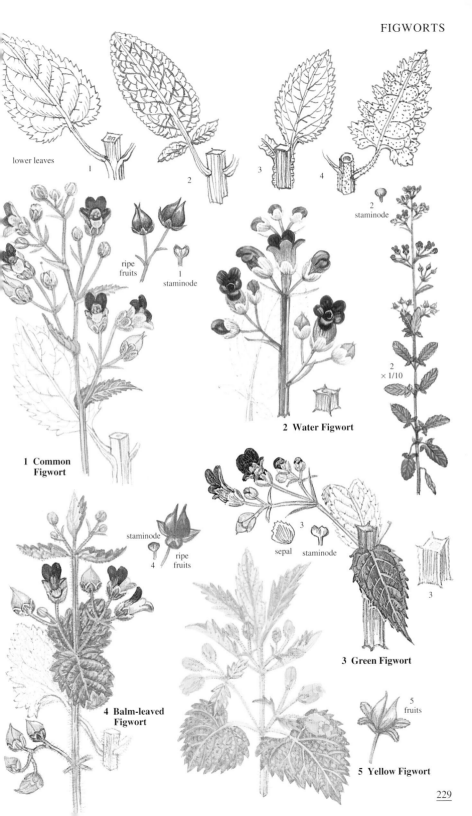

lower leaves

1

2

3

4

ripe fruits

1 staminode

2 staminode

2 × 1/10

2 Water Figwort

1 Common Figwort

staminode

4 ripe fruits

sepal

3

staminode

3

3

3 Green Figwort

4 Balm-leaved Figwort

5 fruits

5 Yellow Figwort

Toadflaxes *Linaria*. Mostly perennials, with flowers snapdragon-like (**9**), but spurred not pouched. the mouth more or less closed by a bulge on the lower lip. Leaves broad linear, untoothed, up the stems.

Two very localised long-established annual aliens are **1 Sand Toadflax** *Linaria arenaria*, erect, to 15cm, downy all over, the yellow flowers often with a pale violet spur, on Braunton Burrows, N Devon; and **1a Prostrate Toadflax** *L. supina*, sprawling, to 20cm, downy only above, with flowers pale yellow with a pale orange bulge, at Par Harbour, S Cornwall.

2 Common Toadflax *Linaria vulgaris*. By far our commonest toadflax, a short/medium erect greyish perennial, hairless or downy above, to 80cm. Flowers *yellow* with an *orange* bulge and a long straight spur, 18-35mm, in spikes; June-Oct. if pale yellow with violet veins is a hybrid with Pale Toadflax (**3**). Grassy banks, road verges, waste places.

3 Pale Toadflax *Linaria repens*. Greyish, hairless, often sprawling perennial, to 80cm. Flowers pale *lilac with violet veins* with an orange spot on the bulge and a short straight spur, 8-15mm, in spikes; June-Sept. Hybridises with Common (**2**) and Purple (**4**) Toadflaxes. Dry, rather bare, grassy and waste places.

4 Purple Toadflax *Linaria purpurea*. Greyish hairless medium/tall perennial, to 1m. Flowers *bright violet* or pale violet with darker veins (pink in the much less frequent cultivar Canon Went), sometimes with a whitish bulge, with a long curved spur, 7-15mm; June-August. Hybridises with Pale Toadflax (**3**). An increasing semi-naturalised garden escape; walls and other dry bare places.

~

5 Ivy-leaved Toadflax *Cymbalaria muralis*. A trailing hairless perennial, often tinged purple, to 60cm. Flowers like typical Toadflaxes, *lilac* with a yellow bulge on the lower lip, short-spurred, long-stalked at the base of the leaves, 9-15mm; April-Dec. and through mild winters in the S. Leaves palmately lobed, often not very ivy-like. *Walls*, less often on other rocky places, one of our most widely and longest established aliens, since 1617 in Essex. **5a Italian Toadflax** *C. pallida*, downy and not trailing, has flowers darker purple with a white bulge and larger (15-25mm); much less frequent and mainly in the N. **5b Trailing Snapdragon** *Asarina procumbens* has much larger (30-35mm) flowers pale yellow with pink-purple veins, a pouch instead of a spur, and shallowly palmately lobed leaves; an alien with a well known site on a cliff in Nottingham, elsewhere scattered on walls.

6 Small Toadflax *Chaenorhinum minus*. A slender, greyish, usually downy, low annual, to 25cm. Flowers like miniature typical Toadflaxes, pale purple with a pale yellow bulge, mouth slightly open, spur short and blunt, 6-9mm, solitary on long stalks at the base of the leaves; June-Oct. Leaves broad linear. Bare places, often on railway tracks and arable fields, especially on lime. **Malling Toadflax** *C. origanifolium*, with larger (8-15mm), darker purple flowers, was naturalised on walls in W Malling, Kent, for many years.

7 Sharp-leaved Fluellen *Kickxia elatine*. Rather sprawling, softly hairy annual, to 50cm. Flowers like typical Toadflaxes, yellow with violet upper lip, long-spurred, 7-12mm, solitary on slender stalks, downy at the top, at base of leaves; July-Oct. Leaves *arrow-shaped*. An arable weed, usually on lime.

8 Round-leaved Fluellen *Kickxia spuria*. Very like Sharp-leaved Fluellen (**7**), with which it often grows, but has *rounded* leaves and slightly larger (8-15mm) flowers with spur more curved and stalks all downy.

9 Snapdragon *Antirrhinum majus*. A stocky, bushy, medium perennial, to 80cm. Flowers of the well known snapdragon shape, familiar in several colours in gardens but usually some shade of red in the wild, with a *pouch* instead of a toadflax-like spur, 30-45mm; May-Oct. Leaves narrow lanceolate. Well established on walls, railway cuttings and other waste places.

6a Malling Toadflax   **7 Sharp-leaved Fluellen**

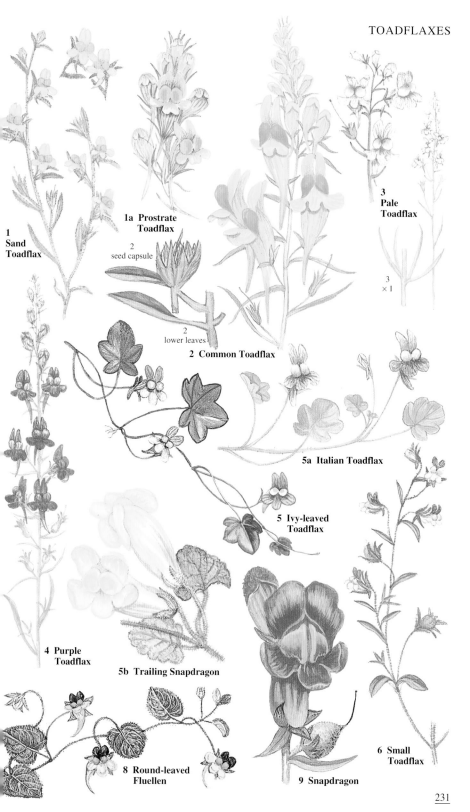

1 Sand Toadflax

1a Prostrate Toadflax

2 seed capsule

2 lower leaves

2 Common Toadflax

3 Pale Toadflax

3 × 1

5a Italian Toadflax

5 Ivy-leaved Toadflax

4 Purple Toadflax

5b Trailing Snapdragon

6 Small Toadflax

8 Round-leaved Fluellen

9 Snapdragon

1 Weasel's Snout *Misopates orontium*. Short, usually downy annual, to 50cm. Flowers bright pink-purple, *snapdragon-like* (p. 230) with a pouch, sepal-teeth unequal, 10-17mm; July-Oct. Leaves linear. Aka Lesser Snapdragon. A weed of cultivation.

2 Foxglove *Digitalis purpurea*. A tall stately biennial, to 2m, familiar in gardens but native. Flowers bright pink-purple, sometimes white, like a *weakly 2-lipped* glove-finger, 40-55mm, up to 80 in long unbranched stalked spikes; June-Sept. Leaves large, softly downy, broad lanceolate, wrinkled, the lowest in a basal rosette. Woods, heaths, banks, preferring acid soils. **2a Straw Foxglove** *D. lutea*, with flowers 9-25mm, is the only one of several yellow-flowered garden Foxgloves, to be fully established, in five quarries or roadside banks in S England, including the verge of the Leatherhead By-pass, Surrey.

Monkeyflowers *Mimulus*. A difficult group of three naturalised species and five hybrids, of which only the most frequent are described here. Perennials with leafy runners; large and showy 2-lipped flowers, bright yellow usually marked with red, 25-45mm (except Musk, **7**) June-Sept; and broad toothed opposite leaves, the lower often stalked. Wet places, especially by shallow streams.

3 Monkeyflower *Mimulus guttatus*. The most frequent monkeyflower in the lowlands; hairless below, densely sticky-downy above, to 75cm. Flowers all yellow except for *red spots in throat*, which is almost closed by two large bulges on the lower lip, anthers with pollen (if not the plant is a hybrid).

4 Hybrid Monkeyflower *Mimulus × robertsii*. The hybrid between Monkeyflower (**3**) and Blood-drop Emlets (**5**), the second most frequent monkeyflower, but mainly in the uplands; hairless below, sparsely sticky-downy above, to 50cm. Flowers bright yellow, spotted or *blotched* variably orange, red or purplish all over, the throat more or less open, anthers without pollen.

5 Blood-drop Emlets *Mimulus luteus*. Less frequent than Hybrid Monkeyflower (**4**), and differing from it in being scarcely sticky-downy above, the flowers with pollen-bearing anthers and having many fewer reddish blotches, and leaves with irregular, often twisted teeth.

6 Coppery Monkeyflower *Mimulus × burnetii*. A hybrid between Monkeyflower (**3**) and *M. cupreus* from western N America, with distinctive *copper-coloured* flowers, also found in some of the rarer hybrids; no pollen on anthers.

7 Musk *Mimulus moschatus*. Much the smallest-flowered of our monkeyflowers, sticky-downy *both above and below*, to 40cm. Flowers paler yellow with no red spots, *10-20mm*; June-Sept. Leaves paler green, very shortly stalked. Has long lost the scent that gave it its name.

~

8 *Cornish Moneywort *Sibthorpia europaea*. A delicate hairy mat-forming prostrate perennial, to 40cm. Flowers 4-5-petalled, not 2-lipped, whitish, usually tinged pink or yellow, tiny (1-3mm), long-stalked at base of leaves; June-Oct. Leaves rounded, palmately lobed. Damp shade: woods, hedge-banks, marshes, streamsides.

9 Fairy Foxglove *Erinus alpinus*. An erect unbranched low, often tufted perennial, to 20cm. Flowers purple, with a long petal-tube and five spreading notched petals, not 2-lipped, 6-9mm, in a leafy spike; May-August. Leaves small, toothed, broadest at the tip, many in basal rosettes. Widely naturalised on walls.

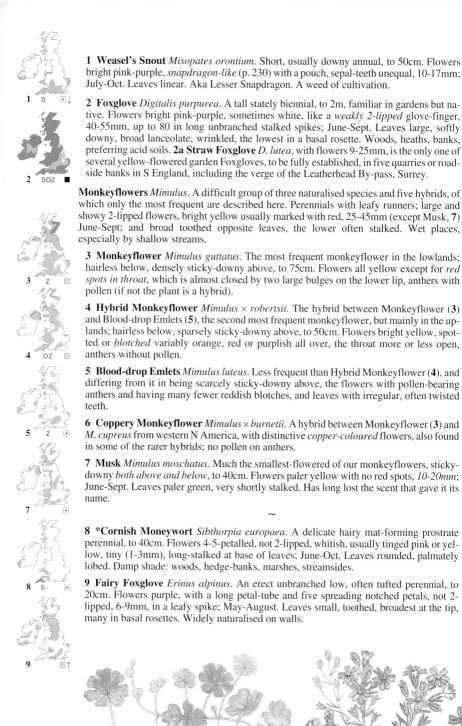

8 Cornish Moneywort

9 Fairy Foxglove

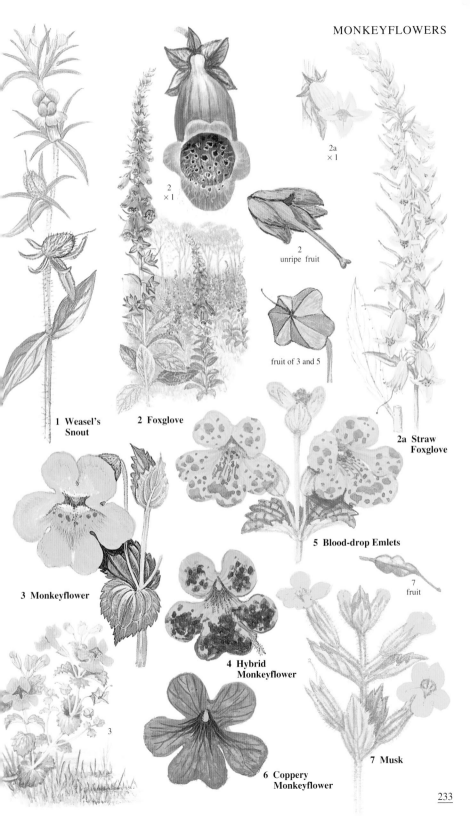

2
× 1

2a
× 1

2
unripe fruit

fruit of 3 and 5

1 Weasel's
Snout

2 Foxglove

2a Straw
Foxglove

3 Monkeyflower

5 Blood-drop Emlets

7
fruit

4 Hybrid
Monkeyflower

3

6 Coppery
Monkeyflower

7 Musk

233

The next 11 species, to Eyebright (p. 236) are *hemi-parasites*, depending partly on the roots of other plants for their nutriment. All have 2-lipped, more or less open-mouthed flowers.

1 Lousewort *Pedicularis sylvatica*. A low/short spreading perennial, to 25cm. Flowers pink-purple, the upper lip *longer* and 3-toothed, 20-25mm, in leafy spikes, the joined sepals inflating in fruit; April-July. Leaves pinnate, toothed. Damp heaths and moors, bogs.

2 Marsh Lousewort *Pedicularis palustris*. A short/medium, erect, often purple-stalked, annual/biennial, to 60cm. Flowers like Lousewort (**1**), but *redder pink* with the two lips *equal*, the upper 5-toothed; May-Sept. Aka Red Rattle. Marshes and wet, often less acid, grassy places.

3 Yellow Rattle *Rhinanthus minor*. Very variable low/medium annual, to 50cm. Flowers yellow, sometimes tinged brownish, mouth variably open, the upper lip with two white or purple teeth, the lower lip *down-turned*, stigma *scarcely protruding*, 12-15mm; joined sepals inflated, sometimes tinged reddish; May-Sept. Leaves oblong/linear, toothed, unstalked, opposite. Named from its ripe fruit *rattling* in the still more inflated joined sepals. Aka Hay-rattle. Grassland, lowland and upland, fens. **3a** *****Greater Yellow Rattle** *R. angustifolius* differs especially in having its lower lip horizontal and stigma protruding; June-July. Lowland grassland, heaths, cornfields.

4 Red Bartsia *Odontites vernus*. A downy, rather bushy, often purple-stemmed, short annual, to 50cm. Flowers *pink-purple*, the lower lip 3-lobed, 8-10mm, in leafy 1-sided spikes; June-Sept (despite its vernal name). Leaves narrow lanceolate, toothed, opposite. Grassy and bare places.

5 Yellow Bartsia *Parentucellia viscosa*. A stickily hairy, usually unbranched, short/medium annual, to 50cm. Flowers *yellow*, with a *long* 3-lobed lower lip, 16-24mm, in leafy spikes; June-Sept. Leaves broad to narrow lanceolate, toothed, unstalked, opposite. Increasing in damp grassy places, usually near the sea, occasionally naturalised elsewhere.

6 **Alpine Bartsia *Bartsia alpina*. Low downy unbranched perennial, to 25cm. Flowers a distinctive rich *dark purple*, among large leaf-like dull purple bracts, 15-20mm; July-August. Leaves oval, untoothed, unstalked, often purplish. Uplands: damp grassland in N England, rock ledges in Scotland.

Cow-wheats *Melampyrum*. Annuals, flowers with the upper lip hooded, the 3-lobed lower lip with bulges usually largely closing the mouth; joined sepals not inflated. Leaves lanceolate, usually narrow, scarcely toothed or stalked, opposite. Seeds wheat-like.

7 Common Cow-wheat *Melampyrum pratense*. Much the commonest of our four species; short/medium, to 60cm. Flowers pale to deep yellow, often marked pink-purple and on moors sometimes all pink-purple, 10-18mm; sepal-teeth *appressed*; in pairs facing much the same way, with toothed green leaflike bracts at their base; May-Sept. Leaves untoothed, broader on limy than on acid soils. Woods, scrub, heaths, moors.

8 *Small Cow-wheat *Melampyrum sylvaticum*. Like Common Cow-wheat (**7**), but smaller and slenderer, to 35cm. Flowers always deep yellow, speckled purple, the lower lip *down-turned*, so opening the mouth, 8-12mm; sepal-teeth *spreading*; in pairs further apart, their bracts scarcely toothed; June-Aug. Mountain woods.

9 *Crested Cow-wheat *Melampyrum cristatum*. Widely branched, short/medium, to 50cm. Flowers in a short spike, the upper lip pink-purple, the lower yellow, almost hidden in the *bright pink-purple* long-toothed strongly *recurved* bracts, 12-16mm; June-Sept. Woodland edges, scrub.

10 **Field Cow-wheat *Melampyrum arvense*. Short, to 35cm. Flowers in a short spike, *pink-purple* with the throat and often the lower lip yellow, 20-25mm, visually merging into the brightly coloured bracts, pink-purple and toothed at the base, green at the long narrow *spreading* or drooping tip; June-Sept. Leaves narrow. Cornfields, grassy field margins, hedge-banks.

1 soz ▫↓↓

2 oz ▫↓

3 oz ▫

3a ▫↓

4 oz ▫

5 s ▫↑

6 ▫

7 oz ▫↓   8 ▫↓   9 ▫↓   10 ▫↓

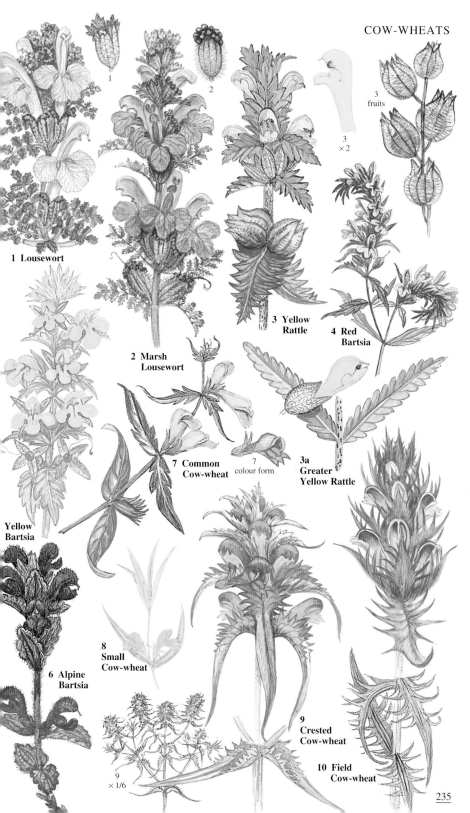

1 Lousewort

2 Marsh Lousewort

3 Yellow Rattle

3 fruits

3 ×2

4 Red Bartsia

Yellow Bartsia

6 Alpine Bartsia

7 Common Cow-wheat

7 colour form

3a Greater Yellow Rattle

8 Small Cow-wheat

9 Crested Cow-wheat

9 ×1/6

10 Field Cow-wheat

Eyebright *Euphrasia*. One of the half-dozen most difficult groups in our flora, with at least 20 microspecies, only Irish Eyebright (**20**) having an English name. They all overlap so much with at least one or two others that experts demand six specimens before they will positively identify them. Moreover, they all hybridise with each other and in some districts these intermediates are commoner than their parents. So, since the non-expert can basically only make intelligent guesses, only the briefest descriptions are given here.

Eyebrights are extremely variable, often well branched, low/short hairy annuals, to 50cm, but usually much shorter. Flowers white, often tinged purple or purple-veined, open-mouthed, the lower lip with three spreading lobes and often a yellow spot, 3-12mm, in leafy spikes; June-Oct. Leaves small, deeply toothed, more or less oval, pale, dark or bronzy green. Fruits hairy, except Irish Eyebright (**20**). Grassy and heathery places, high and low.

<u>Throughout</u>: **1** *E. nemorosa*. Generally the commonest eyebright in England and Wales. Low/short, to 35cm. Flowers usually white, sometimes wholly or partly lilac, 5-8mm; late May-Sept. Leaves dark green. Grassy places. **2** *E. confusa* is well named, being so like *nemorosa*, but is often shorter, to 20cm, and slenderer and flowers can be red-purple or, on Exmoor, yellow, 5-9mm; leaves paler green. Short turf. Uncommon in the SE. **3** *E. tetraquetra*. Low, to 15cm. Flowers white/lilac, 5-7mm. Leaves fleshy. Coastal turf only, except in Cheddar Gorge, Somerset, but beware *nemorosa* on cliffs.

<u>Southern</u>: **4** *E. anglica*. Low, to 20cm. Densely hairy, flowers 6-8mm, lilac, lower lip sometimes white. Leaves dark green, often roundish. Short turf, heaths. **5** * *E. pseudokerneri*. Low, to 20cm. Flowers white, pale lilac, large (7-10mm); July-Sept. Limy grassland, especially chalk. **6** ** *E. vigursii*. Low, to 20cm. Densely hairy. Flowers lilac/purple, 7-8mm. Leaves often purplish. Heaths, grassy cliffs.

<u>Northern/Western</u>: **7** *E. arctica*, the commonest eyebright in Scotland and parts of Ireland. Low/short, to 30cm, often our most robust species. Flowers white/lilac, 6-9mm. **8** ***E. cambrica*. Low, to 8cm. Flowers with upper lip white/lilac, lower lip white/yellow, 4-5mm. **9** *E. micrantha*. Low/short, slender, to 25cm. Flowers lilac/purple, or lower lip white, 4-7mm. Stems/leaves sometimes purplish. Among heather. **10** ***E. rivularis*. Low, to 15cm. Densely hairy. Flowers lilac, lower lip sometimes white, 7-9mm. Mountain flushes. **11** *E. rostkoviana*. Low/short, to 35cm. Densely hairy. Flowers large (8-12mm), upper lip lilac to violet, lower lip white. Leaves pale green. **12** *E. scottica*. Low/short, slender, to 25cm, Flowers white, or upper lip lilac, 4-7mm. Leaves purple beneath. Wet flushes in the hills.

<u>Mainly Northern</u>: **13** ***E. campbelliae*. Low, to 10cm. Flowers with upper lip pink-lilac, lower lip white, 5-7mm. Damp heaths near sea. Lewis only. **14** *E. foulaensis*. Low, to 6cm. Flowers deep violet or white, 4-6mm. Leaves deep green, almost round, fleshy. Damp turf, saltmarsh edges, near the sea. **15** *E. frigida*. Low, to 20cm. Flowers white/lilac, 4-7mm. Mountain ledges. **16** ***E. heslop-harrisonii*. Low, to 15cm. Flowers usually white, 4-6mm. Leaves fleshy, basal teeth curving upwards and outwards. Edge of saltmarshes. **17** *E. marshallii*. Low, to 12mm. Densely hairy. Flowers white, or upper lip lilac, 5-6mm. Short rocky turf. **18** *E. ostenfeldii*. Low, to 12cm. Densely hairy. Flowers white or upper lip lilac, 3-6mm. Mainly grassy/bare places near the sea. **19** ***E. rotundifolia*. Low, to 10cm. Densely hairy. Flowers white/lilac, or lower lip purplish/yellow, 5-6mm. Short turf by sea.

<u>Ireland only</u>: **20 Irish Eyebright** *E. salisburgensis*. Low, to 12cm. Flowers white, upper lip sometimes lilac, 4-7mm. Fruits almost hairless.

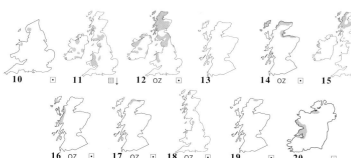

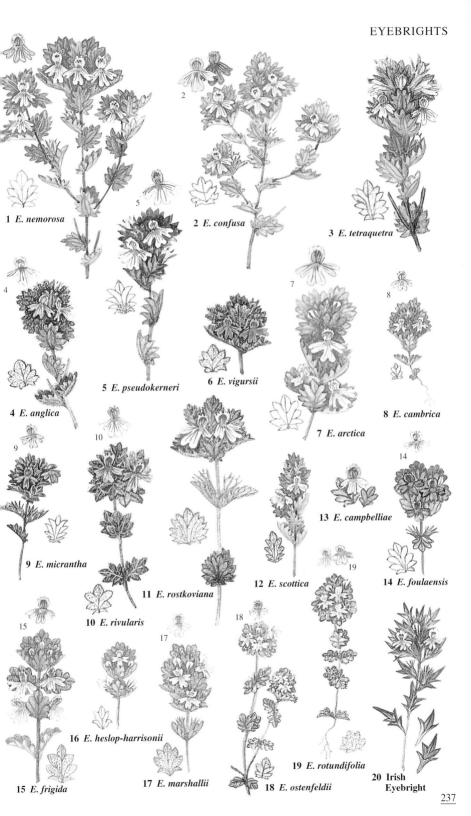

1 *E. nemorosa*

2 *E. confusa*

3 *E. tetraquetra*

4 *E. anglica*

5 *E. pseudokerneri*

6 *E. vigursii*

7 *E. arctica*

8 *E. cambrica*

9 *E. micrantha*

10 *E. rivularis*

11 *E. rostkoviana*

12 *E. scottica*

13 *E. campbelliae*

14 *E. foulaensis*

15 *E. frigida*

16 *E. heslop-harrisonii*

17 *E. marshallii*

18 *E. ostenfeldii*

19 *E. rotundifolia*

20 Irish Eyebright

Flowers 5-petalled (see also numbers **8** and **9**, p. 232)

Mulleins *Verbascum*. Tall erect biennials, scarcely branched or with stems arranged like a candelabra. Flowers yellow, except Purple Mullein, flat, rather large, with five petals, joined sepals and stamens with orange anthers, the three upper usually kidney-shaped. Leaves usually broad lanceolate; leaves (and anthers) sometimes *decurrent* (i.e. running down on to the stem or stamen). Fruits more or less egg-shaped. Dry grassy and bare places, the natives mainly on lime. Eight garden species escape and both these and the natives readily interbreed; the most distinctive is the purple-flowered **6 Purple Mullein** *Verbascum phoeniceum*. Two established candelabra-branched species, especially on active or disused railway banks, are **Caucasian Mullein** *V. pyramidatum*, with purple-haired stamens, at Swaffham Prior NE of Cambridge and Melton Mowbray NE of Leicester; and **Hungarian Mullein** *V. speciosum*, with white stamen-hairs, at Great Blakenham, Suffolk.

Stamens	with white hairs:	Great, Orange, White, Hoary, Hungarian
	purple hairs:	Dark, Twiggy, Moth, Purple, Caucasian

1 Great Mullein *Verbascum thapsus*. Much the commonest of our mulleins; stout, woolly with white or greyish down, usually unbranched, to 2m. Flowers yellow, 15-30mm; stamens three white-woolly, two hairless, stigma *club-shaped*; June-August. Leaves thickly woolly, strongly *decurrent*. **1a Orange Mullein** *V. phlomoides*, the most frequent of the garden escapes, has deeper yellow (not orange!) flowers with longer stalks, stamens *all* woolly and *spoon-shaped* stigma decurrent on to the style; the upper leaves *scarcely decurrent* and the down sometimes yellowish.

2 Dark Mullein *Verbascum nigrum*. Our second most frequent native mullein, hairy but not woolly, stems ridged, comparatively slender, little branched, to 1.2m. Flowers rich yellow, speckled purple at the base, with *purple hairs* on all stamens, 12-22mm; June-Sept. Leaves dark green, stalked, the lower heart-shaped.

3 *White Mullein *Verbascum lychnitis*. Candelabra-branched, thinly woolly with grey down, to 1.5mm. Flowers *white* (yellow in N Somerset), with linear woolly sepal-teeth and whitish hairs on all stamens, 15-20mm; June-Sept. Leaves dark grey-green, almost *hairless* above.

4 *Hoary Mullein *Verbascum pulverulentum*. Candelabra-branched, densely covered at first with loose *white mealy down*, becoming hairless later, to 1.5m. Flowers yellow, stamens all white-hairy, 18-25mm, in large pyramidal clusters; June-August. Leaves *mealy on both sides*, the upper heart-shaped. An East Anglian speciality, often by the A 14 near Bury St Edmunds.

5 *Twiggy Mullein *Verbascum virgatum*. Scarcely branched, stickily hairy *throughout*, to 1m. Flowers yellow, occasionally white or pale pink, often pale reddish beneath, stamens with violet hairs, the three upper anthers kidney-shaped, the lower two decurrent on to stamens, 20-30cm, *1-5* at the base of a leaf-like bract, on stalks shorter than the sepals; June-Sept. Leaves hairless, shallowly lobed. Native only in Devon and Cornwall, sometimes in hedge-banks; more widespread as a casual. **5a Moth Mullein** *V. blattaria* is stickily hairy only above, with only one flower per bract on stalks longer than sepals. A widespread and perhaps more frequent casual.

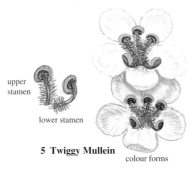

upper
stamen

lower stamen

5 Twiggy Mullein

colour forms

6 Purple Mullein

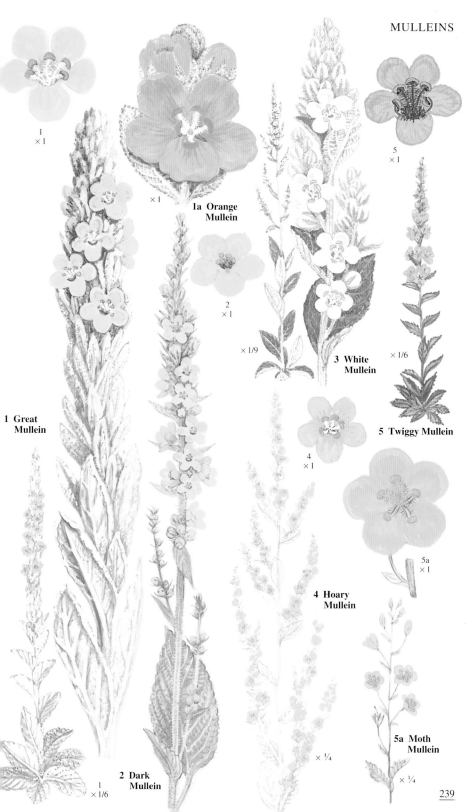

1
× 1

1a Orange
Mullein

× 1

2
× 1

× 1/9

3 White
Mullein

5
× 1

× 1/6

5 Twiggy Mullein

1 Great
Mullein

4
× 1

4 Hoary
Mullein

5a
× 1

2 Dark
Mullein

1
× 1/6

× ¼

5a Moth
Mullein

× ¼

Speedwells *Veronica*. Low/medium annuals/perennials. Flowers typically *blue*, sometimes lilac, small, and in stalked spikes, either terminal or at the base of the leaves up the stem. Leaves opposite, undivided, mostly toothed. Fruits flattened, notched.

1   soz

Lowland habitats, dry: flowers in spikes up the stem

1 Germander Speedwell *Veronica chamaedrys*. A rather sprawling hairy low/short perennial, with two opposite lines of whitish down on the stems, to 50cm. Flowers brilliant *azure blue* with a white eye, on stalks no shorter than the tiny leaf-like bracts at their base, 8-12mm; April-July. Leaves pointed oval, well toothed, short- or unstalked. Fruits broadly heart-shaped, hairy, shorter than the pointed sepal-lobes. Grassy places.

2   soz

2 Heath Speedwell *Veronica officinalis*. A low/short mat-forming hairy perennial, with stems creeping, rooting and hairy all round, to 40cm. Flowers *lilac*, sometimes purple in bud, 6-9mm, the stalks no longer than the leaf-like bracts at their base; May-August. Leaves oval, toothed, narrowed to their short stalks. Fruits longer than broad, exceeding the sepal-teeth. Dry grassy and heathy places, open woods.

3   s

3 Wood Speedwell *Veronica montana*. Low/short, sprawling perennial, with stems hairy all round, to 40cm. Flowers *pale lilac-blue*, smaller and much paler blue than Germander Speedwell (**1**) but larger and bluer than Heath Speedwell (**2**), 8-10mm, their stalks twice as long as the bracts; April-July. Leaves oval, toothed. Fruits disc-like, larger than the small, rather blunt sepal-teeth. Woods, often on clay and so damp.

4   soz

Lowland habitats, dry: flowers in terminal spikes

4 Thyme-leaved Speedwell *Veronica serpyllifolia*. A neat low creeping and rooting perennial, to 30cm. Flowers *very pale blue* or white with violet veins, 5-10mm, on stalks as long as the sepal-teeth but shorter than the small leaf-like bracts at their base; April-Oct. Leaves oval, shiny, *untoothed*. Fruits slightly broader than long, with a long style and about equalling the oblong sepal-teeth. Bare and sparsely grassy places; for ssp. *humifusa* on mountains, see p. 242.

5   soz

5 Wall Speedwell *Veronica arvensis*. A low, often very low, hairy, sometimes stickily hairy, annual, 2-30cm. Flowers *blue*, tiny (2-3mm), often almost hidden by the untoothed, upper leaves; late March-Oct. Leaves oval, *toothed*. Fruit heart-shaped, about as long as broad, notched, shorter than the often spreading sepal-teeth. Dry, usually more or less bare places, including walls. **5a American Speedwell** *V. peregrina* is usually hairless, with pale lilac flowers and narrowly elliptical, often untoothed leaves. An increasing alien, especially

5a

in Ireland. **5b French Speedwell** *V. acinifolia* has dark blue flowers and rounded, un- or scarcely toothed leaves. Established for 40 years at Beaminster, Dorset.

The Rare Breckland Speedwells. Three low annuals largely confined to the heaths and arable fields of the E Anglian Breckland.

6

6 **Spring Speedwell *Veronica verna*, with stems to 15cm, differs from the smallest Wall Speedwells (**5**), in both upper and lower leaves being *always* stickily hairy, and the upper leaves *pinnately lobed*. Flowers blue, April-May. Fruits broader than long, on stalks shorter than the sepal-teeth. **6a **Fingered Speedwell** *V. triphyllos* is stickily hairy, to

6a

20cm, with *dark blue* flowers, 3-4mm (April-June), leaves *palmately lobed*, and fruits like Wall Speedwell (**5**). **6b Breckland Speedwell** *V. praecox*, has stems to 20cm, flowers *dark blue*, 2-4mm on stalks longer than both upper leaves and sepal-teeth; March-June; leaves *rounder* and more shallowly toothed than the other two and often purple beneath; and fruits like Wall Speedwell (**5**) but narrower. First discovered, 1933; also in Oxfordshire.

6b

~

7 *Spiked Speedwell *Veronica spicata*. The handsomest of our native speedwells, a short/medium downy perennial, to 60cm. Flowers *intensely blue*, with prominent stamens, 4-8mm, in a long showy spike; July-Oct. Leaves toothed, the lower oval and often in a rosette, the upper narrower, unstalked. Fruits hairy, no shorter than the short sepal-teeth. Ssp. **hybrida* on limestone rocks in the W; ssp. ***spicata* in grassland in the E (Breckland). **7a Garden Speedwell** *Veronica longifolia* is a taller, to 1.2m, and longer-spiked plant of waste ground. Often a cultivar hybrid with **7**.

7

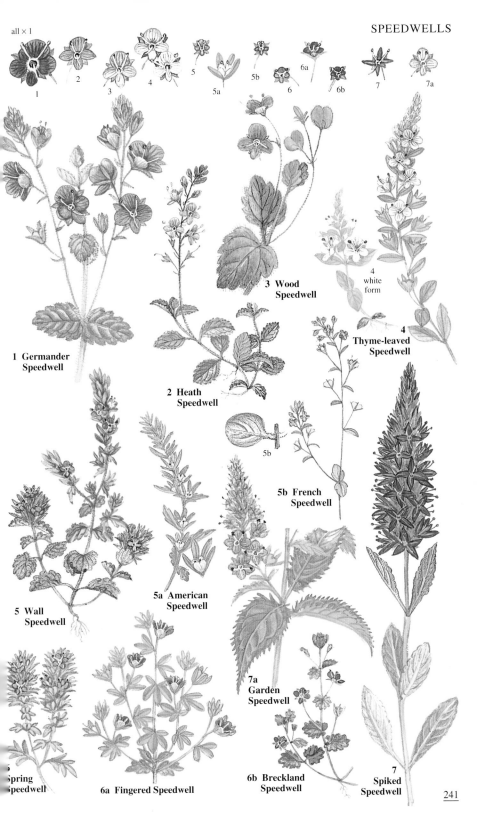

all × 1

1

2

3

4

5

5a

5b

6

6a

6b

7

7a

3 Wood Speedwell

4 white form

4 Thyme-leaved Speedwell

1 Germander Speedwell

2 Heath Speedwell

5b

5b French Speedwell

5a American Speedwell

5 Wall Speedwell

7a Garden Speedwell

Spring Speedwell

6a Fingered Speedwell

6b Breckland Speedwell

7 Spiked Speedwell

241

Lowland habitats, dry: flowers solitary at base of leaves

1 Common Field Speedwell *Veronica persica*. A low sprawling hairy annual, to 60cm. Flowers a clear *sky blue* with darker veins, the lower petal usually white, 8-12mm; Jan-Dec. Leaves *pale green*, more or less oval, toothed. Fruits with two *widely diverging* lobes. An alien weed of cultivation, first recorded 1825.

2 Grey Field Speedwell *Veronica polita*. A more or less prostrate annual, to 30cm. Flowers *dark blue*, 3-8mm; March-Nov. Leaves *greyish-green*, oval, toothed. Fruits oblong with a slight notch, the sepal-teeth pointed. Bare, often cultivated ground.

3 Green Field Speedwell *Veronica agrestis*. Similar to Grey Field Speedwell (**2**), but with flowers *pale blue*. at least the lowest petal usually white, leaves *pale green*, and fruits with a shorter style, the sepal-teeth blunter. A decreasing weed of cultivation.

4 Slender Speedwell *Veronica filiformis*. A prostrate mat-forming perennial, to 50cm. Flowers *mauvish-blue*, 8-15mm; March-June. Leaves kidney-shaped, bluntly toothed. Fruit rare. An alien that has spread fast since 1927 in grassy places, especially lawns, but may now have stabilised.

5 Ivy-leaved Speedwell *Veronica hederifolia*. A more or less prostrate hairy annual, to 50cm. Flowers *blue* and 6-9mm in ssp. *hederifolia*, *lilac* and 4-6mm in the more frequent **5a** ssp. *lucorum*; March-August. Leaves palmately lobed, more sharply toothed in ssp. *hederifolia*. Fruits globular, hairless. A weed of disturbed ground. **5b Crested Field Speedwell** *V. crista-galli*, with pale blue flowers 5-7mm, leaves oval and toothed and notched fruits almost hidden by the large pointed sepal-teeth, is well naturalised in N Somerset.

Lowland habitats, wet: flowers in stalked spikes up the stem

6 Brooklime *Veronica beccabunga*. A hairless fleshy sprawling, creeping and rooting perennial, to 60cm. Flowers *deep blue*, 5-7mm; May-Sept. Leaves oval, bluntly toothed, stalked. Fruits roundish. Small streams and other wet places.

7 Water Speedwell *Veronica anagallis-aquatica*. More erect than Brooklime (**6**), to 50cm. Flowers *paler blue*, 5-10mm, in longer denser spikes, with tiny narrow pointed bracts at their base; June-August. Upper leaves lanceolate, longer and unstalked, the lower sometimes broader and shortly stalked. Fruits very slightly notched. Similar wet places.

8 Pink Water Speedwell *Veronica catenata*. Differs from Water Speedwell (**7**) in its often purple-tinged stem, shorter spikes of *pale pink* flowers, with broader bracts, all leaves narrow, the fruits wider than long, on more erect stalks. Frequently grows and hybridises with Water Speedwell, the hybrid often being taller and stouter than either.

9 Marsh Speedwell *Veronica scutellata*. A slender downy perennial, to 15cm. Flowers *whitish*, often tinged pale blue, 5-6mm, rather few in the spike; June-August. Leaves short, narrow, minutely toothed, often olive-brown. Fruits deeply notched. Marshes, wet meadows, by fresh water, on acid soils.

Upland habitats: mountains

10 Mountain Speedwell *Veronica serpyllifolia* ssp. *humifusa*. The commonest speedwell high on mountains, where the smaller-flowered Thyme-leaved Speedwell (p. 240) itself may also grow. More prostrate than Thyme-leaved Speedwell, with stems rooting along their length. Flowers *bright* blue with *no red eye*, 7-10mm, fewer in the spike; July-August. Leaves roundish. Fruits with a long style, downy. Rock ledges, gravelly patches.

11 *Alpine Speedwell *Veronica alpina*. Low, scarcely downy perennial, mainly erect, to 15cm. Flowers dark blue with *no red eye*, small (5-10mm), the sepals often bluish-green; July-August. Leaves bluish-green, oval, scarcely toothed, unstalked. Fruits hairless, shortly styled, slightly notched. Rocks above 500m.

12 **Rock Speedwell *Veronica fruticans*. The rarest and largest-flowered of our three mountain speedwells, a low perennial, to 20cm. Flowers bright blue with a *red eye*, at 10-15mm looking rather large for the plant; July-August. Leaves pointed oval, toothed, unstalked. Fruits elliptical, long-styled. High mountain ledges.

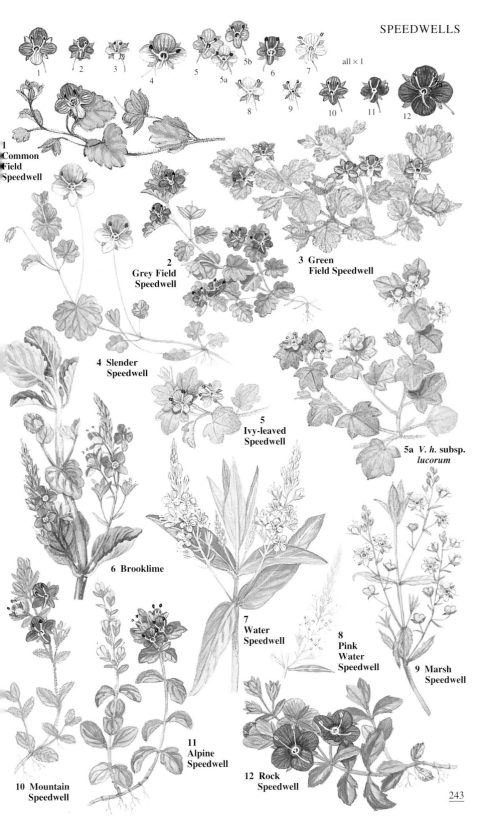

all × 1

1 Common Field Speedwell

2 Grey Field Speedwell

3 Green Field Speedwell

4 Slender Speedwell

5 Ivy-leaved Speedwell

5a *V. h.* subsp. *lucorum*

6 Brooklime

7 Water Speedwell

8 Pink Water Speedwell

9 Marsh Speedwell

10 Mountain Speedwell

11 Alpine Speedwell

12 Rock Speedwell

BROOMRAPE FAMILY Orobanchaceae

Broomrapes *Orobanche*. Perennial parasites on the roots of other plants and so with *no green pigment*. A difficult group: the host plant is an important clue to identity, though it can be several metres away, and it may not be easy to decide which of several nearby plants is the host. Stems stiff, erect, unbranched, often persisting, brown with the dead flowers, into the winter. Flowers 2-lipped, in spikes, usually coloured like the rest of the plant and with only one bract, which may be hard to distinguish from the deeply divided sepals. No leaves, but large fleshy pointed scales up the stem. Fruit a capsule, mostly egg-shaped. Grassy places.

BROOMRAPE HOSTS	
Peaflowers:	Clovers (p. 150) – Common Broomrape; Broom (p. 394) and Gorse (p. 398) – Greater Broomrape; coastal, Rest-harrow (p. 156) – Common Broomrape var. *maritima*; Cultivated Beans – *O. crenata*, rare in S Essex.
Ivy (p. 396):	Ivy Broomrape
Umbellifers:	coastal, Wild Carrot (p. 184) – Common Broomrape var. *maritima*
Labiates:	Wild Thyme (p. 220) – Thyme Broomrape
Plantains:	coastal, Buckshorn Plantain (p. 248) – Common Broomrape var. *maritima*
Bedstraws:	Hedge Bedstraw (p. 254) – Bedstraw Broomrape
Composites:	especially long-rooted Catsear (p. 296) & Smooth Hawksbeard (p. 298) – Common Broomrape, especially var. *compositarum*; Greater Knapweed (p. 286) – Knapweed Broomrape; Yarrow (p. 268) – Yarrow Broomrape; Thistles *Cirsium/Carduus* (p. 290) – Thistle Broomrape; Oxtongues (p. 298) – Oxtongue Broomrape.

1 Common Broomrape *Orobanche minor*. Much the most frequent species, stems short/medium, usually reddish or purple, rarely yellow, to 60cm. Flowers veined dark violet, stamens hairless, stigma usually purple; equalling or shorter than their bracts, which are longer than the flowers, unscented, 10-18mm; June-Sept. Numerous hosts, especially Clovers (p. 150), Wild Carrot (p. 184), var. *maritima*, and Composites (p. 264), var. *compositarum*.

2 Knapweed Broomrape *Orobanche elatior*. The next most frequent species, but confined to *Greater Knapweed* (p. 286) on limy soils; medium, stoutish, to 75cm. Flowers *honey-yellow*, usually tinged purple, upper lip 2-lobed, stamens hairless below, stigma yellow, 18-25mm; bracts equalling flowers; June-July.

3 *Greater Broomrape *Orobanche rapum-genistae*, Our tallest and stoutest broomrape, preying on woody peaflowers, especially Broom and Gorse (p. 394, 398) on acid soils; medium/tall. to 90cm. Flowers honey-yellow, usually tinged purple, 20-25mm; upper lip hooded, not lobed, lower 3-lobed; stamens hairless below, stigma pale yellow, sepals 4-lobed; May-July.

4 *Ivy Broomrape *Orobanche hederae*. Differs from Common Broomrape (**1**) especially by growing among *Ivy* (p. 396), but also has more creamy flowers with stamens sometimes downy, stigma yellow, 12-20mm; June-July. Notably in Cheddar Gorge, Somerset.

5 Thyme Broomrape *Orobanche alba*. One of the smaller species, short, to 25cm. Stems often deep red-purple, with the flowers partly yellowish or sometimes white (whence the misleading name), scented, 15-20mm, with stamens hairy below, stigma reddish and bracts shorter than flowers; June-August. Mainly on Wild Thyme (p. 220) near the coast.

6 **Yarrow Broomrape *Orobanche purpurea*. The only species with *three bracts*, short/medium, rarely branched, to 45cm. Stems and flowers bluish-purple, flowers large (18-30mm), with petals pointed, stamens hairless and stigma white; June-July. Increasing, mainly on Yarrow (p. 268).

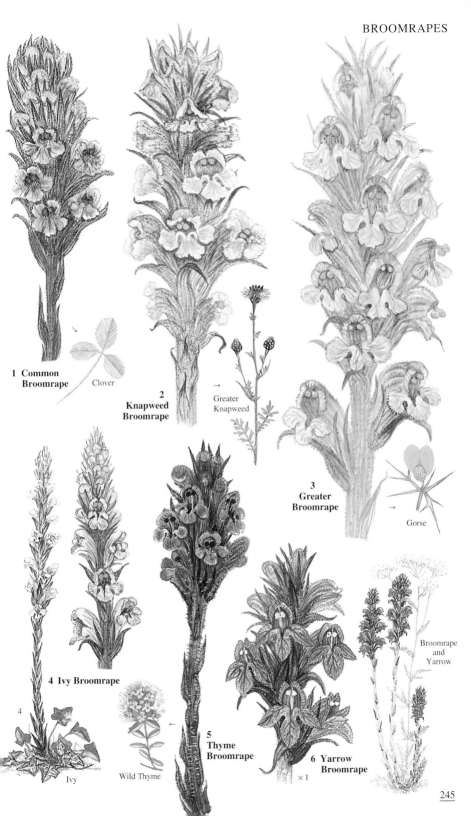

1 Common Broomrape

Clover

2 Knapweed Broomrape

→ Greater Knapweed

3 Greater Broomrape

→ Gorse

4 Ivy Broomrape

4

Ivy

Wild Thyme

→ **5 Thyme Broomrape**

× 1

6 Yarrow Broomrape

Broomrape and Yarrow

1 **Thistle Broomrape *Orobanche reticulata*. One of the taller species, to 70cm, yellowish/purplish, the flowers yellow tinged purple, unscented, 12-22mm, with stamens downy and stigma red/purple; June-August. On Thistles (p. 290) in Yorkshire.

2 ***Bedstraw Broomrape *Orobanche caryophyllacea*. Shortish, to 40cm, stems and flowers yellow tinged purplish, large (20-32mm), stamens downy, stigma purple, reputedly clove-scented; June-July. On Hedge Bedstraw (p. 254) in two sites in Kent.

3 ***Oxtongue Broomrape *Orobanche artemisiae-campestris*. Now almost our rarest species, with only two sites left, on Oxtongues (p. 298) on chalk cliffs in Kent. Stems (to 60cm) and flowers yellowish-white tinged purple, the flowers purple-veined, 14-22mm, stamens downy below, stigma purple; June-August. Despite its (new) name does not grow on Field Wormwood (p. 284) in Britain.

Two species are accidentally established in Oxford Botanic Garden: *Orobanche flava* on *Petasites* (p. 288) and relatives, and *Orobanche lucorum* on Barberries (p. 370).

4 Toothwort *Lathraea squamaria*. A low creamy-pink leafless perennial, to 30cm; parasitic like the Broomrapes (p. 244) and so with *no green pigment* and scales instead of leaves. Flowers 2-lipped, open-mouthed, *pink*, 14-20mm, drooping in a 1-sided spike; April-May. Scales broad, up the stem. Fruit egg-shaped. In clumps on the roots of Hazel (p. 358) and other shrubs and trees. **4a Purple Toothwort** *L. clandestina* has larger (40-50mm) stemless *violet-purple* flowers arising straight off the rootstock; March-May. Occasionally naturalised, e.g. on willows at Coe Fen, Cambridge.

BIRDSNEST FAMILY Monotropaceae

5 Yellow Birdsnest *Monotropa hypopitys*. A short perennial, to 30cm. As a saprophyte that lives off decaying vegetable matter, it needs no chlorophyll and so is not green, the whole plant being waxy pale brownish-yellow. Flowers tubular, 4/5-petalled. on a drooping stem that becomes erect in fruit. Leaves scale-like, up the stems. Fruit a capsule. Leaf-litter in beech, pine and other woods; also on dunes. Not to be confused with Birdsnest Orchid (p. 336).

BEARSBREECH FAMILY Acanthaceae

6 Bearsbreech *Acanthus mollis*. A tall erect, almost *hairless* perennial, to 1m. Flowers white, purple-veined, with a lower lip only, often with purplish bracts, 25-50cm, in stout spikes; June-August. Leaves to 60cm long, deeply pinnately lobed, the lobes *sharply pointed* but not spiny. Fruit a capsule. Widely naturalised, especially in SW England. The much less frequent **6a Spiny Bearsbreech** *A. spinosus* is downy and has leaves with *spiny* teeth on the lobes.

MOSCHATEL FAMILY Adoxaceae

7 Moschatel *Adoxa moschatellina*. A low hairless perennial, to 15cm. Flowers greenish, 4/5-petalled, tiny, in fives at right angles to each other to make a 5-7mm head; March-May. Leaves trefoil, one pair on each flower-stalk. Woods, hedge-banks, also on mountains. The only species in its family.

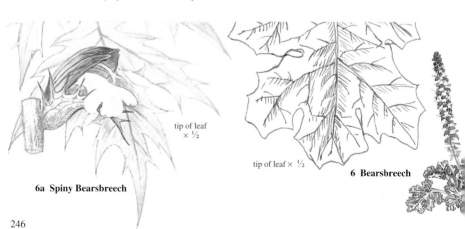

tip of leaf
× ½

tip of leaf × ½

6 Bearsbreech

6a Spiny Bearsbreech

246

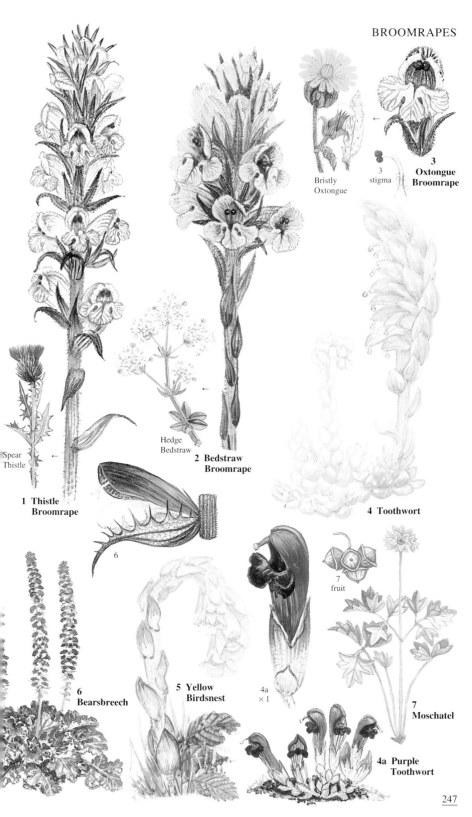

3 Oxtongue Broomrape

Bristly Oxtongue

3 stigma

Spear Thistle

1 Thistle Broomrape

Hedge Bedstraw

2 Bedstraw Broomrape

4 Toothwort

6

6 Bearsbreech

5 Yellow Birdsnest

4a × 1

7 fruit

7 Moschatel

4a Purple Toothwort

Adderstongue
Fern

PLANTAIN FAMILY Plantaginaceae

Plantains *Plantago*. Rather dull perennials (Buckshorn Plantain (**4**) may be annual), whose tiny flowers, with their parts in fours and prominent stamens, are in dense spikes on unbranched leafless stems. Leaves ribbed or veined, in basal rosettes. Fruit a capsule. Other plants that might be mistaken for plantains are Mousetail (p. 306), arrow-grasses (below), and the three adderstongue ferns (p. 440), of which the commonest is *Ophioglossum vulgatum* with a spore-bearing spike rising out of a single pointed oval leaf.

1 Ribwort Plantain *Plantago lanceolata*. A familiar short plant, often downy, stems to 50cm. Flowers in dense stubby spikes, 2-4cm, *blackish-brown* at first but pale brown later, with anthers usually pale yellow and furrowed stalks; April-Oct. Leaves *lanceolate*, slightly toothed, with 3-5 prominent ribs beneath. Grassy and waste places.

2 Greater Plantain *Plantago major*. Rather stout and coarse, usually hairless, low, stems to 40cm. Flowers in elongated *greenish* spikes, to 20cm, pale yellow with purple anthers fading warm brown and unfurrowed stalks; June-Oct. Leaves *broad oval*, often wavy, with prominent veins beneath. Waysides, farmyards, lawns and other bare or well-trodden places; in damp fresh or brackish places leaves may be toothed (ssp. *intermedia*).

3 Hoary Plantain *Plantago media*. Downy and rather grey, short, stems to 40cm. Flowers in 4-6cm spikes, grey-green but looking *pale pink-purple* from the fuzz of stamens, on unfurrowed stalks; May-August. Leaves broad to narrow elliptical, *gradually narrowing* to the very short winged stalk, in a flat rosette. Grassland, usually limy.

4 Buckshorn Plantain *Plantago coronopus*. Low downy annual/perennial, to 20cm, but often quite small and prostrate; our only plantain with (usually) pinnate leaves. Flowers in 2-4cm spikes, *brownish* with yellow anthers; May-Oct. Leaves varying from *pinnate* to linear, with only one vein beneath. Bare ground *near the sea*, sandy places inland.

5 Sea Plantain *Plantago maritima*. Short, hairless, to 30cm. Flowers in greenish 6-8cm spikes, *brownish* with pale yellow anthers, on unfurrowed stems; June-Sept. Leaves thick, *fleshy, linear*, sometimes slightly toothed, with 3-5 obscure veins beneath, flatter and broader than Sea Arrow-grass (**7**). Saltmarshes, bare ground by the sea.

Shore-weed *Littorella uniflora*, p. 344.

ARROW-GRASS FAMILY Juncaginaceae

A monocotyledon family (see p. 9) described here to compare with the plantains (above). Hairless perennials with spikes of *stalked* green flowers with six sepals/petals and styles forming a short whitish tuft. Leaves linear, in basal rosettes.

6 Marsh Arrow-grass *Triglochin palustris*. Slender, short/medium, to 60cm. Flowers green, edged purple, 2-3mm, *irregularly* up a spike that elongates in fruit; May-August. Leaves long, grass-like, *deeply furrowed*. Fruit erect, narrowly arrow-shaped. Marshes, marshy meadows.

7 Sea Arrow-grass *Triglochin maritima*. Stout, short/medium, to 60cm. Flowers green, 3-4mm, longer-stalked and in a longer spike than Marsh Arrow-grass (**6**); May-August. Leaves fleshy, *unfurrowed*, broader than Marsh Arrow-grass, but narrower than Sea Plantain (**5**). Fruit oblong. Saltmarshes.

RANNOCH-RUSH FAMILY Scheuchzeriaceae

8 Rannoch-rush *Scheuchzeria palustris*. Another monocotyledon, a short/medium hairless perennial. Flowers yellows, 6-petalled; June-August. Leaves linear, flat, with inflated sheathing bases, longer than the flower cluster. Bog pools on Rannoch Moor.

1 SOZ □

2 SOZ □

3 □↓

4 SOZ □

5 SOZ □

6 OZ □   7 OZ □   8   ·

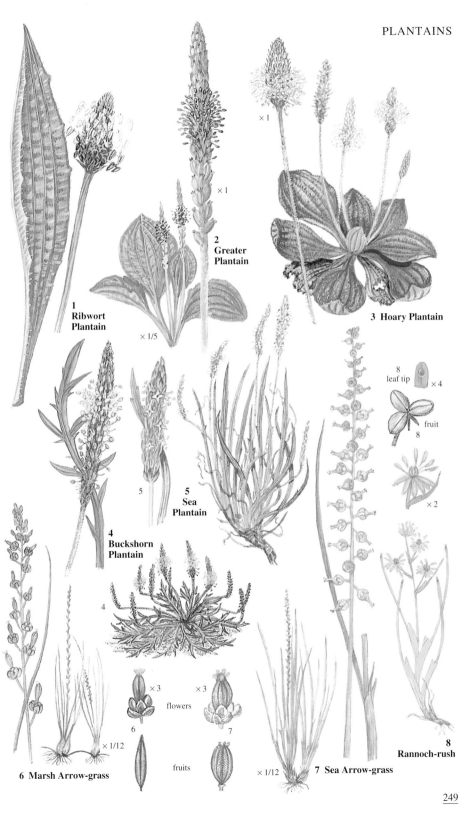

PLANTAINS

1 Ribwort Plantain

2 Greater Plantain

× 1

× 1/5

3 Hoary Plantain

× 1

8 leaf tip × 4

fruit 8

× 2

4 Buckshorn Plantain

5

5 Sea Plantain

× 3 flowers × 3

6 7

fruits

× 1/12

6 Marsh Arrow-grass

× 1/12 7 Sea Arrow-grass

8 Rannoch-rush

BLADDERWORT FAMILY Lentibulariaceae

Bladderworts *Utricularia*, see p. 352.

Butterworts *Pinguicula*. Low/short perennials with leaves slimy (to catch insects on which they feed), oblong, untoothed, all in a basal starfish-like rosette. Flowers solitary, rather the size and shape of a Violet (p. 78), with five petal-lobes, spurred, long-stalked. Fruit a capsule.

1 Common Butterwort *Pinguicula vulgaris*. Flowers *violet* with a broad pale patch in the throat, the lobes of the lower lip diverging and a pointed spur, 14-22mm; stems to 18cm; May-July. Leaves *yellow-green*, 2-8cm, not overwintering. Bogs, wet heaths and moors, fens, limestone flushes.

2 Pale Butterwort *Pinguicula lusitanica*. Flowers much smaller (7-11mm) than Common Butterwort (**1**), *pale lilac*, with the throat patch pale yellow and the spur blunt and down-turned; stems to 15cm; June-Oct. Leaves *olive-green*, smaller (1-3)cm, overwintering. Bogs, wet heaths, only on acid soils.

3 Great Butterwort *Pinguicula grandiflora*. Flowers much larger (25-35mm) and spur stouter than Common Butterwort (**1**) but colour similar; stems to 18cm; May-June. Leaves similar, sometimes present in winter. Bogs, damp moors, always on acid soils. Native only in Ireland, rarely naturalised elsewhere. Aka Large-flowered Butterwort.

BELLFLOWER FAMILY Campanulaceae

Mostly perennials. Flowers usually stalked, bell-shaped, usually blue, with five usually short lobes. Leaves undivided, alternate. Fruit usually a capsule.

4 Harebell *Campanula rotundifolia*. Slender, hairless, short/medium, erect to 50cm, with creeping underground stems. Flowers pale to mid blue, nodding on long thin stalks, in a loose truss, 12-20mm; July-Nov. Leaves *linear* on the stems, those at the base roundish, usually withering before the flowers appear. Dry grassland and other grassy places, acid and limy. Formerly aka Bluebell, in the N.

5 Clustered Bellflower *Campanula glomerata*. Stiff, hairy, low/short, to 80cm, but often quite dwarfed and when 1-flowered has been mistaken for a Gentian (p. 198, with opposite leaves). Flowers among the most vivid in our flora, a handsome *violet*, unstalked, 12-25mm, mostly in heads; June-Oct. Leaves narrow and half-clasping, the lower more triangular and stalked. Grassland on lime.

6 Nettle-leaved Bellflower *Campanula trachelium*. Medium/tall, roughly hairy perennial, with stems rather *sharply* angled, to 80cm. Flowers usually *mid blue*, 25-35mm, 1-3 together in a stalked spike, the top ones opening first, sepal-teeth *broad, hairy*; June-Sept. Leaves triangular, the upper narrower and shorter-stalked. Cf. Giant Bellflower (**7**). Woods, hedge-banks, especially on lime.

7 Giant Bellflower *Campanula latifolia*. A handsome tall perennial, a striking sight on northern hedge-banks; stems softly hairy, *bluntly* angled, unbranched, to 1.2m. Flowers usually *pale blue*, 35-55mm, singly in a long leafy stalked spike, the lower ones opening first, sepal-teeth *narrow, hairless*; July-Sept. Leaves lanceolate to narrowly triangular, the lower with a winged stalk. Woods, hedge-banks. **7a Milky Bellflower** *C. lactiflora* is even taller, to 2m, with flowers pale to bright blue, 15-25mm; well naturalised, especially by streams in Scotland.

8 *Spreading Bellflower *Campanula patula*. A graceful, almost hairless short/medium perennial, with angled stems to 60cm. Flowers pale to purplish-blue, *lobed to halfway*, 15-25mm, on many *spreading* few-flowered branches; June-July. Leaves bluntly lanceolate. Woods, hedge-banks, grassy places. **8a Creeping Bellflower** *C. rapunculoides* is a slightly hairy garden escape, with creeping underground runners, with stems hardly angled, narrower leaves and stalked spikes of *drooping* flowers, lobed to less than halfway. Apparently decreasing.

Clustered Bellflower

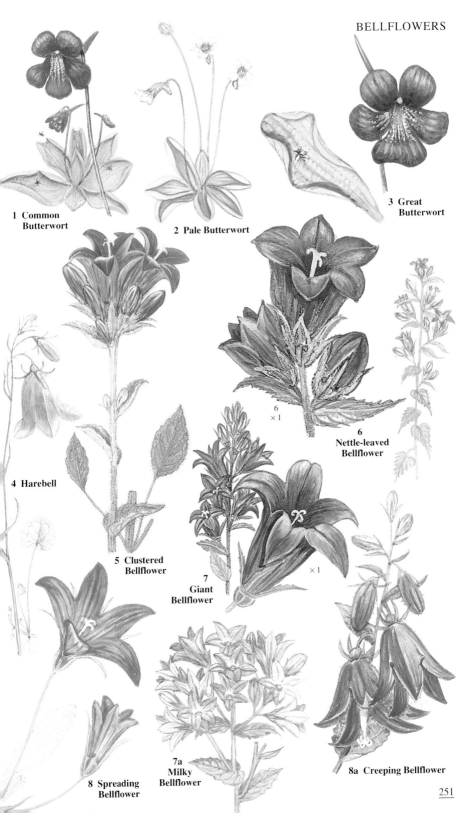

1 Common Butterwort

2 Pale Butterwort

3 Great Butterwort

4 Harebell

5 Clustered Bellflower

6
×1

6 Nettle-leaved Bellflower

7
Giant Bellflower

×1

8 Spreading Bellflower

7a
Milky Bellflower

8a Creeping Bellflower

Other naturalised Bellflowers. Gardeners being especially attracted to bellflowers/campanulas, 10 species, including Milky and Creeping Bellflowers above, have escaped and become established in various places.

Two Balkan species with regrettably forbidding names are widely established on walls: **1 Adria Bellflower** *Campanula portenschlagiana* with violet-blue flowers lobed less than halfway; and **2 Trailing Bellflower** *C. poscharskyana* with paler, greyer blue flowers lobed more than halfway. **3 Peach-leaved Bellflower** *C. persicifolia*, with large, broadly bell-shaped blue flowers and narrow leaves, frequent in gardens, is widely established in woods and scrub. Three species are found especially on railway banks: **4 Canterbury Bells** *C. medium*, once more familiar in gardens, with very large flowers, usually violet-blue, but sometimes pink or white, especially on chalk in NW Kent; **5 Cornish Bellflower** *C. alliariifolia*, with white flowers, increasing in Cornwall, Somerset and elsewhere. **6 Rampion Bellflower** *C. rapunculus*, with pale blue flowers, once grown for its edible root, decreasing, but still at Kelvedon, Essex, and Worms Heath, Surrey, as well as in rough fields at Pulborough, Sussex, since 1805.

7 Ivy-leaved Bellflower *Wahlenbergia hederacea*, A hairless creeping pale green perennial, with delicate stems, to 30cm. Flowers pale blue, bell-shaped, 6-10mm, on long *thread-like* stalks; July-August. Leaves roundish, lobed but scarcely ivy-like. *Damp places on acid soils*, in woodland rides, on heaths and moors and by streams.

8 Venus's Looking-glass *Legousia hybrida*. A low hairy annual, to 30cm. Flowers dark or pale purple, the petal-lobes flat and only half as long as the sepal-teeth, 4-10mm, *visible only in sunshine*, otherwise showing only their pale undersides; May-August. Leaves oblong, *wavy*, unstalked. Fruits triangular, very long and narrow. Arable weed, mainly on limy soils. **8a Large Venus's Looking-glass** *L. speculum-veneris* is strikingly different, its *much larger* (15-20mm) *bright purple* flowers being the origin of the strange name. Established since *c.* 1942 in arable fields in N Hampshire.

9 Sheepsbit *Jasione montana*. A low/short, slightly hairy, somewhat scabious-like, variable biennial, to 50cm. Flowers soft blue, with *prominent* petal-lobes and orange-yellow *anthers*, in a rounded 5-35mm head; May-Sept. Leaves narrow oblong, sometimes wavy, untoothed, the upper unstalked. Grassland on *acid* soils, heaths, sea cliffs, shingle, varying according to habitat: in sparsely grassy or heathy places is low and rather bushy, with thread-like stems and small flowerheads, but on cliffs can be taller, stout, erect, less branched and with larger heads.

10 Round-headed Rampion *Phyteuma orbiculare*. A short/medium unbranched perennial, usually hairless, to 50cm. Flowers dark blue, narrow, long and curved in bud, in rounded 10-20cm heads; June-August. Differs from Sheepsbit (**9**) in its petal-lobes being at first joined at the top around the long slender style, enclosing the five stamens. Leaves oval, narrower up the stem, long-stalked at the base. *Chalk* turf. A very similar plant naturalised on limestone in Sutherland is **10a Inchnadamph Rampion** *P. scheuchzeri* from the Alps.

11 **Spiked Rampion *Phyteuma spicatum*. A hairless medium/tall perennial, to 80cm. Flowers like Round-headed Rampion (**10**), but pale greenish-white, in a 30-80mm *spike*; May-July. Leaves heart-shaped, toothed and long-stalked at the base, narrower and shorter-stalked up the stem. Woods, copses and road verges in E Sussex.

1 Adria Bellflower

2 Trailing Bellflower

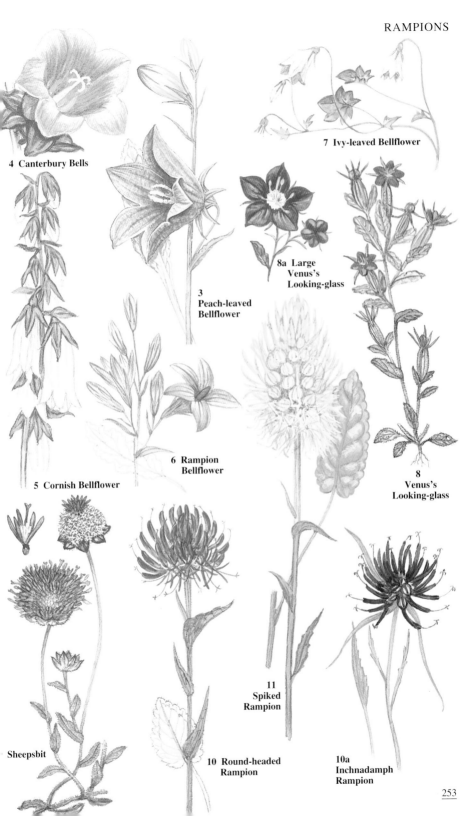

4 Canterbury Bells

7 Ivy-leaved Bellflower

8a Large
Venus's
Looking-glass

3
Peach-leaved
Bellflower

6 Rampion
Bellflower

8
Venus's
Looking-glass

5 Cornish Bellflower

Sheepsbit

11
Spiked
Rampion

10 Round-headed
Rampion

10a
Inchnadamph
Rampion

1 **Heath Lobelia *Lobelia urens*. A slightly downy short/medium perennial, stems with acrid milky juice, to 80cm. Flowers purple-blue, *2-lipped*, the upper lip 2-lobed, the lower lip 3-lobed, 10-15mm, in a long stalked spike; August-Sept. Leaves oblong, toothed, alternate. Damp woods and heaths, on *acid* soils.

Water Lobelia *Lobelia dortmanna*, see p. 344.

Three escaped Lobelias. Much the most frequent is **2 Garden Lobelia** *Lobelia erinus*, with blue or white 2-lipped flowers, increasing in bare places near gardens, especially the bright blue cultivar Sapphire, popular at garden centres. **2a Lawn Lobelia** *Pratia angulata*, increasing in lawns, has star-like white flowers and (unlike other Lobelias) purple berries. **Californian Lobelia** *Downingia elegans*, sometimes found where grass seed has been sown, has white-centred blue flowers with only a lower lip.

BEDSTRAW FAMILY Rubiaceae

Annuals/perennials, often climbers, with clusters of small flowers, with four petals (except Wild Madder and Madder, p. 258) and minute or no sepals, and whorls of undivided leaves and leaflike stipules. Fruit usually a nutlet.

Climbers/Clamberers:		Cleavers, False/Corn Cleavers, Hedge B, Marsh/Fen B, Wild Madder, Madder
Flowers	white:	Cleavers, Hedge B, Heath B, Woodruff, Northern B, Marsh B, Fen B
	creamy-white:	Corn Cleavers, Limestone/Slender B, Slender Marsh B (inside)
	greenish-white:	False Cleavers, Wall B (inside)
	yellow:	Lady's B, Crosswort, Madder
	yellow-green:	Wild Madder
	pinkish:	Slender Marsh B (outside), Squinancywort, Pink Woodruff, Field Madder
	reddish:	Wall B (outside)
Habitat	damp:	Marsh B, Fen B, Slender Marsh B
	acid:	Heath B, Slender Marsh B
	limy:	Hedge B ssp. *erectum*, Lady's B, Limestone B, Slender B, Woodruff, Fen B, Field Madder, Crosswort

Bedstraws *Galium*. Flowers 4-petalled. Leaves in whorls of 4-12, unstalked, 1-veined, except Northern Bedstraw (p. 256). Nutlets often with bristles, sometimes hooked. Named from their medieval use for human bedding.

3 **Cleavers** *Galium aparine*. By far the commonest member of the family in farming country, a straggling annual, clambering over other vegetation, to 3m, and *clinging* to animal fur and human clothing with its numerous curved prickles with *bulbous* bases on stems, leaves and fruits. Flowers *white*, inconspicuous (1-2mm), in small stalked clusters at base of and on common stalks *longer* than the leaves; May-Sept. Leaves in whorls of 6-8, narrow but broader at the tip, and ending in a minute bristle. An increasingly tiresome weed of hedges and disturbed ground, due to its resistance to many herbicides, also in fens and on coastal shingle. Aka Goosegrass. **3a False Cleavers** *G. spurium* is shorter, to 1m, with *greenish*-white flowers, July-Sept, narrower leaves, prickles *not bulbous* at base and fruits blackish, sometimes with no bristles, flowering/fruiting stalks straight. Established in cultivated ground near Saffron Walden, Essex, since 1844.

4 **Corn Cleavers** *Galium tricornutum* is shorter than Cleavers (**3**), to 60cm, and has backward-directed prickles, *creamy*-white flowers, June-Sept, on common stalks *shorter* than the leaves and fruits rough but with *no prickles* and on recurved stalks. A much decreased arable weed.

5 **Hedge Bedstraw** *Galium mollugo*. A sprawling/scrambling medium/tall perennial, with smooth square stems, to 1.5m. Flowers white, 2-5mm, the petals ending in a fine point, in large spreading clusters; June-Sept. Leaves elliptical, ending in a point, 6-8 in a whorl. Fruits wrinkled but with no prickles. Hedge-banks, dry bushy grassland. On limier soils **5a** ssp. *erectum* has larger flowers with much less finely pointed petals and narrower leaves.

6 **Lady's Bedstraw** *Galium verum*. Our only bedstraw with yellow flowers (but see Crosswort, p. 258), an often sprawling short/medium perennial, to 1m. Flowers bright *golden yellow*, 2-4mm; June-Sept. Leaves linear, smelling of new-mown hay (whence their allocation to ladies). Dry grassland, especially on lime.

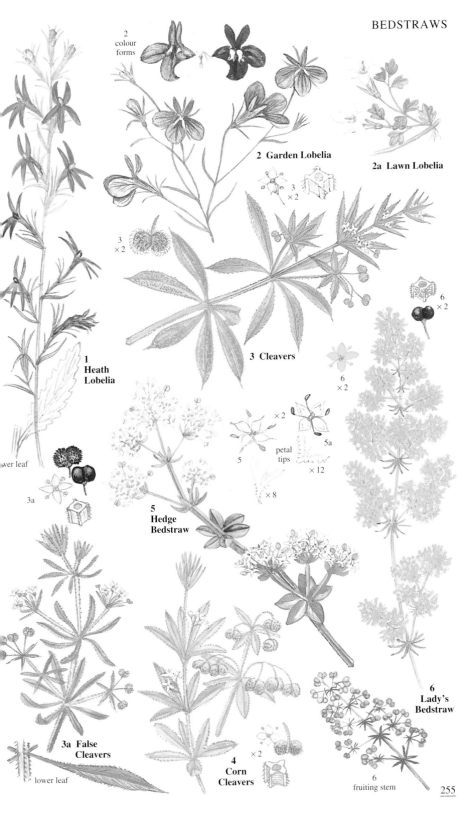

2
colour
forms

2 Garden Lobelia

2a Lawn Lobelia

3
× 2

3
× 2

3
× 2

3 Cleavers

6
× 2

6
× 2

**1
Heath
Lobelia**

lower leaf

3a

× 2

5

5a

petal
tips

× 12

× 8

**5
Hedge
Bedstraw**

**3a False
Cleavers**

**6
Lady's
Bedstraw**

lower leaf

**4
Corn
Cleavers**

× 2

6
fruiting stem

1 Woodruff *Galium odoratum.* Our only woodland bedstraw, a short *carpeting* perennial, to 45cm. Flowers white, 4-6mm, the petals lobed to halfway; *April*-June. Leaves *dark green*, slightly shiny, 6-8 per whorl. Fruit with hooked bristles. Woods, hedge-banks, mainly on lime.

2 Heath Bedstraw *Galium saxatile.* Much the commonest bedstraw of acid soils, a somewhat sprawling mat-forming hairless short perennial, to 30cm. Flowers white, with a sickly fragrance, *c.* 3mm, in opposite clusters; May-August. Leaves 5-8 per whorl, abruptly and sharply pointed, edged with minute forwardly pointing prickles; *blackening* when dried. Fruits with high-domed warts. Acid grassland, heaths, moors.

3 Limestone Bedstraw *Galium sterneri* and **3a *Slender Bedstraw** *G. pumilum* are the much scarcer and slenderer northern and southern limestone counterparts of acid-loving Heath Bedstraw (**2**). Flowers a creamier white, 2-3mm; June-July. Leaves longer and narrower with a short bristle at the tip and *backward*-pointing marginal prickles; *not* blackening when dried. Limestone Bedstraw tends to be more mat-forming, but the only real non-geographical difference between them is that Limestone Bedstraw has high-domed warts on its fruits like Heath Bedstraw, but Slender Bedstraw has them low-domed. Limestone rocks and grassland, including Cheddar Gorge, Somerset, home to some slightly aberrant, more tufted Slender Bedstraw, with stems reddish at base.

4 Northern Bedstraw *Galium boreale.* Our only white bedstraw with *3-veined* leaves, a short erect perennial, to 45cm. Flowers white, *c.* 3mm, in leafy clusters; June-Sept. Leaves dark green, rough-edged. Fruits with hooked bristles. Dampish bare and rocky places, usually in the hills, often by streams, also on dunes.

5 *Wall Bedstraw *Galium parisiense.* A slender, often sprawling, low/short annual, stems with tiny curved prickles, to 30cm. Flowers *greenish*-white inside, reddish, outside, *minute* (less than 1mm); June-July. Leaves becoming down-turned, edged with *forwardly directed* prickles, 5-7 per whorl. Fruit blackish, almost smooth. Old walls, bare sandy ground.

6 Marsh Bedstraw *Galium palustre.* A variable hairless, often clambering medium perennial, stems usually roughish but *without prickles*, to 1m. Flowers white, 2-4mm, in loose cylindrical clusters; June-August. Leaves blunt, edged with minute prickles, 4-5 in the whorl. Fruit slightly wrinkled. **6a** ssp. *elongatum,* with flowers larger in conical clusters, is perhaps commoner. Wet grassy places, by ditches and ponds, fens, marshes.

7 Fen Bedstraw *Galium uliginosum.* Shorter than Marsh Bedstraw (**6**), to 60cm, its stems edged with *down-turned prickles*. Flowers white, 2-3mm, in loose clusters; June-August. Leaves narrow, with a *minute bristle* at the tip, in whorls of 5-8. Fruits with *low-domed* warts. Fens and other damp limy places.

8 **Slender Marsh Bedstraw *Galium constrictum.* Much smaller, slenderer and weaker than either Marsh (**6**) or Fen Bedstraw (**7**), to 40cm. Flowers creamy-white inside, *pale pink* outside, 2-3mm; May-July. Leaves linear, blunt to pointed, 4-6 per whorl. Fruit with *high-domed* warts. Marshes and by ditches and ponds, on *acid* soils, most frequent in the New Forest, Hants.

Fruits and leaves of Bedstraws

256

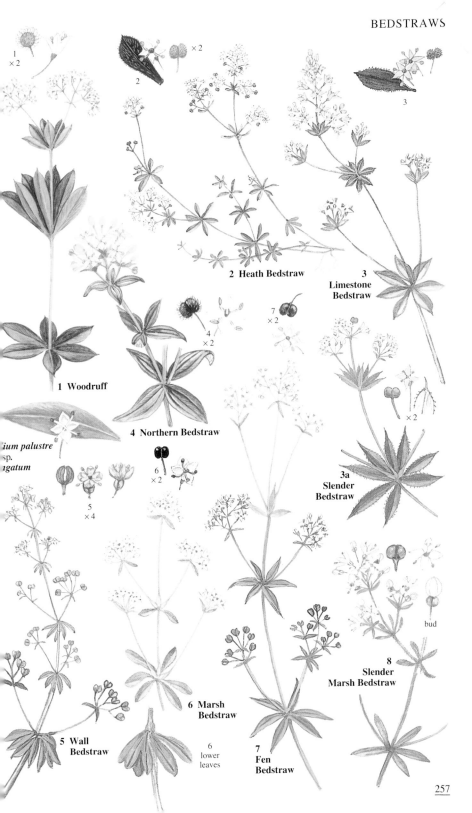

1
× 2

2

3

2 Heath Bedstraw

**3
Limestone
Bedstraw**

7
× 2

4
× 2

1 Woodruff

4 Northern Bedstraw

ium palustre
sp.
ıgatum

6
× 2

5
× 4

**3a
Slender
Bedstraw**

bud

**8
Slender
Marsh Bedstraw**

**6 Marsh
Bedstraw**

**5 Wall
Bedstraw**

6
lower
leaves

**7
Fen
Bedstraw**

1 Squinancywort *Asperula cynanchica*. A low, usually prostrate slender hairless perennial, to 50cm. Flowers pale. sometimes very pale, pink, petals pointed, 3-4mm, in terminal clusters; June-Sept. Leaves linear, in whorls of four, sometimes unequal. Limy grassland, dunes. Named as a medieval cure for quinsy. **1a Pink Woodruff** *A. taurina* is downy, with much larger (10-14mm) yellowish-pink to white flowers and a whorl of leaf-like bracts at their base. Naturalised in damp woods in C Scotland.

2 Crosswort *Cruciata laevipes*. A short tufted perennial, *softly hairy*, branched only at the base, to 60cm. Flowers *pale yellow*, fragrant, 2-3mm, in small clusters at the base of the leaves; April-June. Leaves pale green, elliptical, 3-veined. Grassy places, mostly on lime.

3 Field Madder *Sherardia arvensis*. A prostrate hairy annual, with square stems to 40cm. Flowers *pale pink-purple*, 4-5mm, in small heads surrounded by leaf-like bracts; May-Sept. Leaves in whorls of 4-6, elliptical, narrowing up the stem. Bare and thinly grassy places, especially arable fields and on lime.

4 Wild Madder *Rubia peregrina*. A vigorous clambering evergreen perennial, with stout, sharply 4-angled, *prickly* stems, to 1.5m. Leaves *dark green*, shiny, leathery, prickly, lanceolate, in whorls of 4-6. Flowers rather inconspicuous, yellowish-green, 4-6mm, 5-petalled, in small clusters at the base of the leaves; June-August, Fruit a pea-sized *black berry*. Hedges and scrub, often on sea cliffs. **4a Madder** *R. tinctorum*, with softer narrower pale green leaves, brighter yellow flowers and a reddish berry, still grows on a village wall S of Lincoln, where it used to be cultivated for its red dye.

HONEYSUCKLE FAMILY Caprifoliaceae

5 Honeysuckle *Lonicera periclymenum*. A deciduous woody climber, twining clockwise to 7m or more. Flowers yellowish-cream, deepening to orange-buff when pollinated, tinged crimson outside, very sweet-scented; 2-lipped with a long slender tube, 40-50mm, in close heads with small bracts at their base; June-Sept. Leaves oval, untoothed, opposite, short- or unstalked, appearing in December and January. Fruit a red berry. Woods, scrub, hedges.

For introduced shrubby species, including the perhaps native Fly Honeysuckle *Lonicera xylosteum*, see p. 376.

Introduced Climbing Honeysuckles: four locally established species: **6 Perfoliate Honeysuckle** *Lonicera caprifolium*, like Honeysuckle but with upper leaves fused at base and berries orange; the most frequent, since 1700 at Bagley Wood, N Berks, and 1763 at Cherry Hinton, Cambridge; **Garden Honeysuckle** *L. × italica*, like Perfoliate Honeysuckle (one of its parents), but with larger flowerheads and a tiny bract at the base of each flower; **7 Japanese Honeysuckle** *L. japonica*, with pairs of purple-tinged pale yellow flowers, pointed oval leaves and black berries; since 1930s at Bere Ferrers, Devon, also at Beaconsfield Station, Bucks, and elsewhere; and **8 Henry's Honeysuckle** *L. henryi*, with dark red flowers, paired but in terminal clusters, lanceolate leaves and black berries; especially on Holmwood Common, Surrey.

7 Japanese Honeysuckle

8 Henry's Honeysuckle

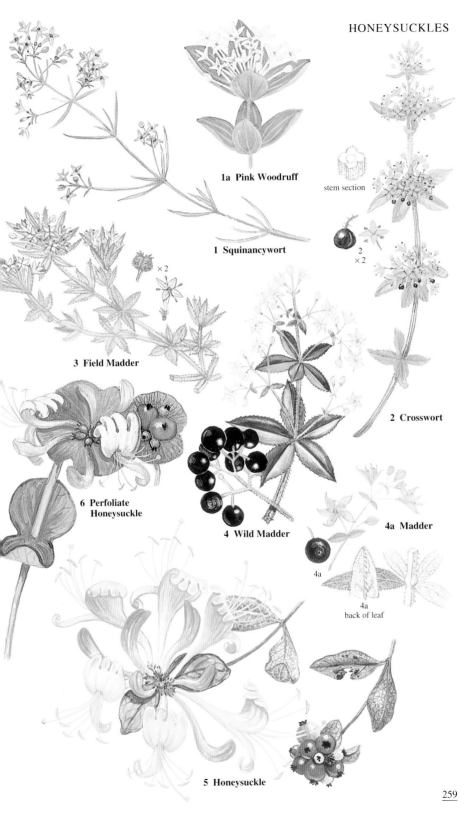

1a Pink Woodruff

stem section

1 Squinancywort

× 2

2
× 2

× 2

3 Field Madder

2 Crosswort

**6 Perfoliate
Honeysuckle**

4 Wild Madder

4a Madder

4a

4a
back of leaf

5 Honeysuckle

1 Dwarf Elder *Sambucus ebulus*. A tall, somewhat foetid, clump-forming, unbranched perennial, to 1.5m. Confusable with small or cut-back Elder bushes (p. 388), but dies back in winter. Flowers white, in large (7-10cm) umbel-like heads like Elder, but often pink-tipped, with anthers violet, not pale yellow; July-Oct. Leaves pinnate, with more numerous and narrower leaflets. Not native, usually by roadsides.

2 Twinflower *Linnaea borealis*. A delicate short creeping undershrub, to 40cm. Flowers pink, bell-shaped, 5-10mm, in drooping pairs on leafless stalks, to 8cm; June-August. Leaves small, oval, toothed, stalked. Woods, usually of Pine. The favourite flower of the great Swedish botanist, Linnaeus.

VALERIAN FAMILY Valerianaceae

3 Common Valerian *Valeriana officinalis*. A tall, variable, usually unbranched, perennial, to 2m. Flowers very pale pink (but darker in bud), 5-petalled, pouched at the base, 4-5mm, in *loose* roundish clusters; June-August. Leaves *pinnate*, with broad to narrow leaflets, toothed (especially on lime in the S) or not, the lower stalked. Woods, damp and dry grassland. **3a Pyrenean Valerian** *V. pyrenaica* has pinker flowers and basal and sometimes stem leaves *undivided* and heart-shaped, Naturalised, scattered woods and hedgebanks, mainly in the N & W.

4 Marsh Valerian *Valeriana dioica*. An unbranched perennial with rooting runners, short, to 40cm. Flowers pale to dark pink, 5-petalled, large (4-6mm) male and small (2-4mm) female flowers on different plants, in *tight* clusters; *April*-June. Basal leaves oval, untoothed, often long-stalked, the upper often pinnate. *Marshes*, marshy grassland, fens, bogs.

5 Red Valerian *Centranthus ruber*. A greyish *bushy* medium perennial, to 80cm. Flowers usually dark pink, often white, fragrant, 5-petalled, spurred, 4-6mm, in loose clusters; *April*-Oct (March in the far S). Leaves usually pale green, pointed oval, the lowest stalked. Fully naturalised on *rocks*, cliffs, walls, quarries and chalky banks, especially near the sea.

Cornsalads *Valerianella*. Low annuals with forked stems, to 20cm. Flowers tiny (c 2mm), pale lilac, 5-petalled, in umbel-like heads. Leaves oblong, unstalked, opposite. Very similar and best identified by their tiny nut-like fruits.

Fruits	hairy:	Narrow-fruited (sometimes), Hairy-fruited
	hairless:	Common, Narrow-fruited, Keeled-fruited, Broad-fruited
	grooved:	Common (scarcely), Keeled-fruited (deep), Broad-fruited
	keeled:	Keeled-fruited
	flattened:	Smooth-fruited (on one face, rounded on the other)
Sepal-teeth	conspicuous:	Broad-fruited (short), Hairy-fruited (long)
	obscure:	Common

6 Common Cornsalad *Valerianella locusta*, is much the most frequent. Flowers can be single, often in the fork of the branches; April-June. Leaves narrow oval, sometimes slightly toothed, eatable as salad, hence old name Lamb's Lettuce. Bare and sparsely grassy ground, walls, rocks, dunes. **7 Narrow-fruited Cornsalad** *V. dentata*, the next most frequent, has paler flowers, late June-August, and narrower untoothed leaves often with a tooth at the base. Arable fields, especially on lime. **8 Keeled-fruited Cornsalad** *V. carinata* differs from Common Cornsalad (**6**) as in fruit key above. **9 **Broad-fruited Cornsalad** *V. rimosa* is like Narrow-fruited Cornsalad (**7**), but has *white* flowers, still narrower and more toothed leaves, and see fruit key above. **10 **Hairy-fruited Cornsalad** *V. eriocarpa*, flowering May-July, has narrow oval leaves. Banks, old walls.

×6 ×6 ×4 ×4 ×4

6 7 8 9 10

9 10

3
fruit × 2

3
× 2

3
Common
Valerian

4
fruit × 2

2 Twinflower

1
Dwarf
Elder

3a
× 2

renean
lerian

♀ × 2

4

♂ × 2

4
lower
leaves

4 Marsh
Valerian

5
white
form

5
pink
form

5 Red
Valerian

ower
stem
× 2

× 2

9
lower
stem
× 1

× 4

9
Broad-fruited
Cornsalad

7
× 4

8
Keeled-fruited
Cornsalad

lower
stem
× 2

× 6

× 4

6 Common
Cornsalad

7 Narrow-fruited
Cornsalad

10
Hairy-fruited
Cornsalad

lower
stem
× 4

TEASEL FAMILY Dipsacaceae

Perennials/biennials, like the Daisy Family (p. 264), with their dense compound flower-heads, somewhat mimicking a single large stalked flower. But the small individual flowers have 4-5 joined petals, with four *separate* stamens, and very narrow, sometimes bristle-like joined sepals sitting in a small green cup of bracts. What look like green sepals around the whole flowerhead are also actually bracts. Leaves opposite. Fruit a small seed.

1 Wild Teasel *Dipsacus fullonum*. Tall biennial with prickly stems to 3m, easily recognised by its bluntly *conical* 4-8cm flowerheads, which persist on the gaunt dead stems through the winter. Flowers *pale purple*, a band of those in the middle of the head opening first; July-Sept. Individual flowers are surrounded by small spines and the whole flower-head by larger *straight* ones. Leaves prickly, the basal ones oblong and goose-fleshy, over-wintering but withering before flowering, the stem ones narrower, often cupped at the base and holding rain water. Rough grassy, bushy and waste places. **1a Fuller's Teasel** *D. sativus* is still cultivated in Somerset for its dead flowerheads, whose *recurved* outer spines are used to card wool. Also an occasional escape. Two other scattered aliens are: **1b Cut-leaved Teasel** *D. laciniatus* with pale pink flowers and leaves *pinnately lobed*, mainly W of Oxford, and **1c Yellow Teasel** *D. strigosus* with larger flowerheads and yellow flowers, mainly around Cambridge.

2 Small Teasel *Dipsacus pilosus*. A tall biennial, with short prickles on its stems to 1.5m. Flowers *white* with violet anthers, in small *globular* 15-25cm heads, with woolly purple-tipped spines; July-Sept. Leaves oblong, the upper narrower, all often with a pair of leaf-lets at their base. Damper woods and hedge-banks, stream-sides.

3 Field Scabious *Knautia arvensis*. A medium/tall hairy, fairly stout perennial, to 1m. Flowers in flattish 15-30mm heads, *bluish-lilac* with pink anthers, the four petal-lobes *unequal*, especially on the larger outer flowers; sepal-like bracts lanceolate in two *unequal rows*, June-Oct. Leaves lanceolate, varying from untoothed to pinnately lobed, the basal ones overwintering. Dry grassy and cultivated places, avoiding heavy soils. **3a Giant Scabious** *Cephalaria gigantea* is much taller, to 2m, with much larger, 40-100mm, *yellow* flowerheads and all leaves pinnately lobed. An increasing and conspicuous escape in rough grassy and waste places.

4 Small Scabious *Scabiosa columbaria*. Slenderer, less hairy and shorter, to 70cm, than Field Scabious (**3**). Flowers paler blue, with five petal-lobes, the petal-like bracts in *one row* and ending in a dark purple *bristle*, in smaller flattish 15-35mm heads (which elongate in fruit); June-Oct. Grassland on lime, dunes. **4a Sweet Scabious** *S. atropurpurea*, with flowers usually *dark purple*, is established in Kent (Folkestone since 1862) and Cornwall, elsewhere a garden escape.

5 Devilsbit Scabious *Succisa pratensis*. A short/tall downy perennial, to 1m; rootstock very short, alleged to have been bitten off in a devilish plot. Flowers usually *dark blue-purple*, sometimes pink, with pink or purple anthers, in roundish 15-25mm heads, both flowers and heads with green bracts; June-Oct. Leaves elliptical, often blotched purplish, the few stem ones narrower and sometimes toothed. Damp grassy places on acid soils, less often in grassland on lime.

seeding head

4a Sweet Scabious

3a Giant Scabious

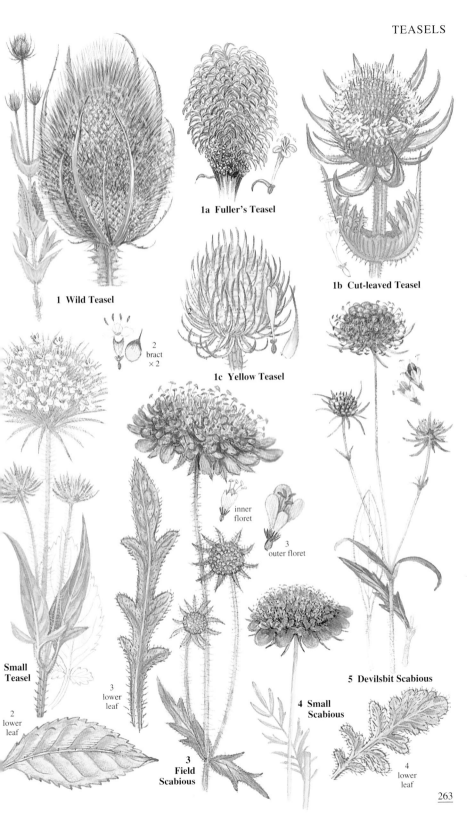

1 Wild Teasel

1a Fuller's Teasel

1b Cut-leaved Teasel

2

1c Yellow Teasel

2
bract
×2

inner
floret

3
outer floret

**Small
Teasel**

2
lower
leaf

3
lower
leaf

5 Devilsbit Scabious

**4 Small
Scabious**

4
lower
leaf

**3
Field
Scabious**

DAISY FAMILY Asteraceae (Compositae)

The largest family of flowering plants, often called composites; their tiny flowers are closely packed into a compound head, which resembles a single flower, surrounded by sepal-like bracts. (These flowerheads are referred to below as flowers, and the individual flowers as florets). Petals are joined in a tube so that the florets are of two kinds: *disc florets* with the tube ending in five short teeth and *ray florets*, ending in a conspicuous flat petal-like flap. Composite flowers are thus of three kinds: *daisy-type* with a flat or conical base of yellow disc florets usually surrounded by ray florets; *brush-like* or *thistle-type* (p. 280), usually with disc florets only; *dandelion-type* (p. 294) with (almost always yellow) ray florets only. In some daisy-type flowers the florets' true sepals become chaffy scales. In the two other groups they become hairs, simple in thistle-type, and feathery in dandelion-type flowers. These become the thistle-down and dandelion-clocks, on which the tiny nut-like seeds float away in the wind.

Some 600-700 casual and established alien composites occur in Britain and Ireland – only a few of those well naturalised can be included here.

disc floret

ray floret

1. Daisy-type flowers, disc florets yellow, except where stated (below)

    1a. Flowers white, rays long, below
    1b. Flowers white, rays very short, p. 268
    1c. Flowers purple, p. 268
    1d. Flowers yellow, p. 270
    1e. Flowers not, or obscurely, rayed, p. 278

~   simple   feathery

1a. Daisy-type, disc florets yellow: Flowers white, rays long

1 Daisy *Bellis perennis.* Everybody knows the 'wee, modest, crimson-tipped' Daisy in a lawn (especially if they think it ought not to be there). A low perennial, to 12cm. Flowers white, the rays sometimes tipped red, 12-25mm, solitary on *leafless* stalks; Jan-Dec. Leaves spoon-shaped, in a basal rosette. Lawns and other short grassland.

2 Ox-eye Daisy *Leucanthemum vulgare.* Our largest native daisy, a medium unbranched perennial, to 75cm. Flowers white, *25-60mm*, solitary, on sparsely leafy stalks; May-Sept, earlier from various seed mixtures on roadsides. Leaves long-stalked, spoon-shaped, toothed, the upper slightly clasping the stem; can be deeply lobed on mountains. Grassy places. Aka Moon Daisy, Marguerite. **2a Shasta Daisy** *L.* × *superbum* is taller, to 1.2m, with flowers *60-100mm* across, sometimes double, and flowering much later, July-Sept, and leaves dark green. Waysides and waste places, especially on railway banks around Birmingham. **2b Autumn Oxeye** *Leucanthemella serotina* is later-flowering still, *Sept-Oct*, with flowers between Ox-eye and Shasta Daisies in size and paler green, more sharply toothed leaves. A much less frequent escape, in damper areas.

3 Feverfew *Tanacetum parthenium.* Medium downy perennial, *pungently aromatic* to 70cm. Flowers white, with short broad rays, often double, 15-23mm, in clusters on leafy stems; June-Sept. Leaves 1-2 pinnate, often yellowish. Widely established, most often near gardens and at the base of walls. **3a Rayed Tansy** *T. macrophyllum*, with still shorter rays and leaf-tips more pointed, has been naturalised on a road verge outside Jervaulx Abbey, North Yorkshire since 1912.

4 Tall Fleabane *Erigeron annuus* is sometimes much taller, to 1m or more, than Feverfew (**3**). Flowers 10-20cm; July-Sept, Leaves always green, *lanceolate*, sometimes toothed, and not clasping the stem. Established in a quarry near Portland, Dorset, and on waste ground elsewhere. **Robin's Plantain** *E. philadelphicus* has leaves clasping the stem and larger (15-25mm), sometimes pink flowers and leaves *clasping the stem*. Established on two walls in S Wales and a few banks elsewhere.

5 Mexican Fleabane *Erigeron karvinskianus.* Low sprawling perennial, to 50cm. Flowers usually white, sometimes pale pink-purple, the rays often deeper pink-purple beneath, 12-18cm, in loose clusters; April-Oct. Leaves lanceolate. Well established on many walls in the S.

1   soz   □

2   soz   □

3   soz   □

5   s   □↑↑

5

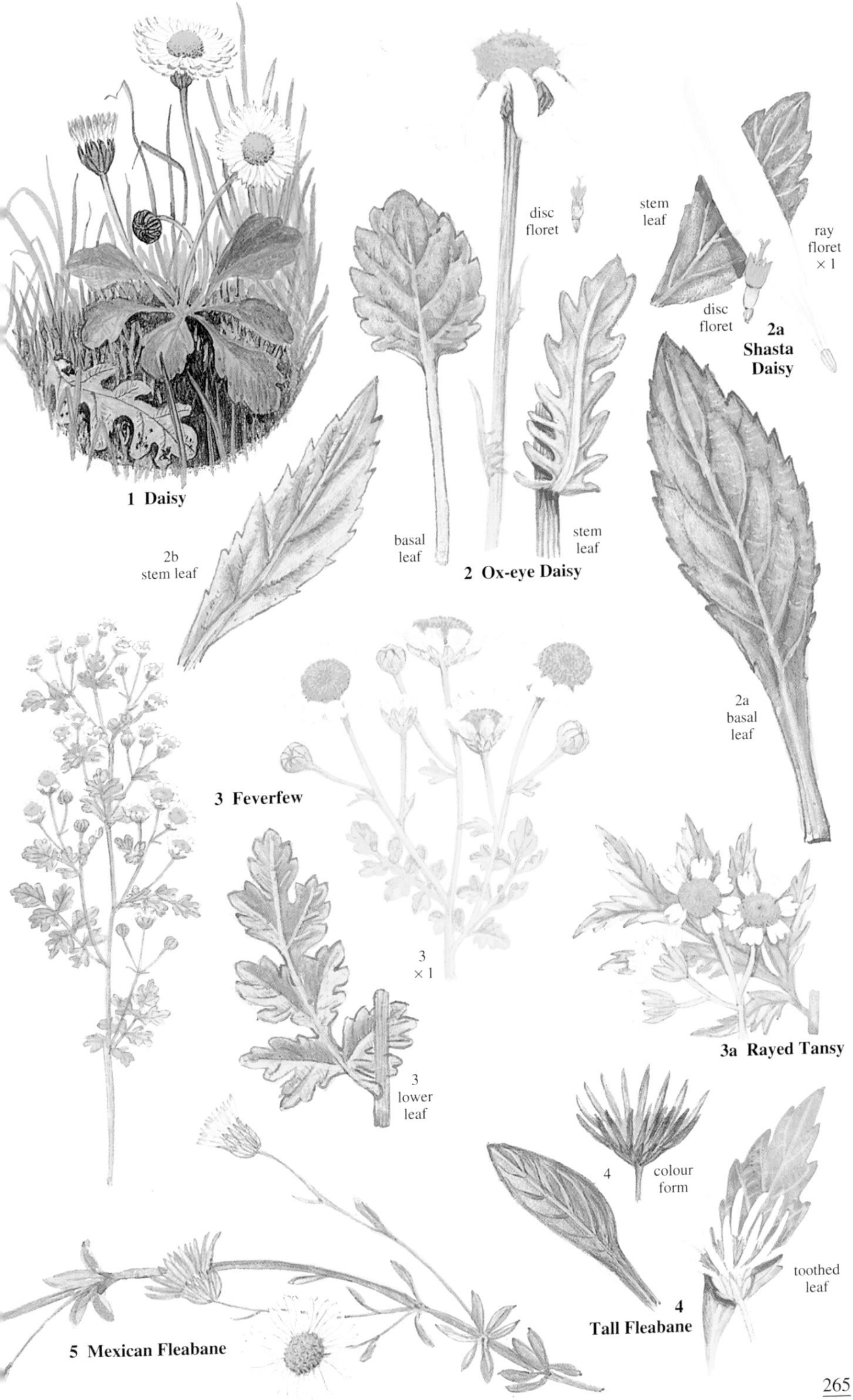

1 Daisy

disc floret

stem leaf

2a Shasta Daisy

ray floret × 1

disc floret

2b stem leaf

basal leaf

stem leaf

2 Ox-eye Daisy

2a basal leaf

3 Feverfew

3 × 1

3 lower leaf

3a Rayed Tansy

4 colour form

4 Tall Fleabane

toothed leaf

5 Mexican Fleabane

Mayweeds and **Chamomiles**. *Tripleurospermum, Matricaria, Anthemis* and *Chamaemelum*. A group of superficially similar white daisy-like flowers in open clusters that can in fact be fairly easily identified, especially by their leaflets and sepal-like bracts. *Tripleurospermum* and *Matricaria* have flowerheads flat, becoming conical and solid in fruit. *Anthemis* and *Chamaemelum* have solid domed flowerheads throughout and also have transparent scales among their disc florets.

	AROMATIC	SEPAL-LIKE BRACTS	LEAFLETS
Scentless Mayweed	No	Brown-edged	Thread-like
Sea Mayweed	No	Brown-edged	Fleshy
Scented Mayweed	Yes	Edged greenish-white	Thread-like
Stinking Mayweed	Foetid	Whitish, midrib green	Broader
Corn Chamomile	Scarcely	All green	Broader still
Chamomile	Yes	White-edged	Thread-like
Sicilian Chamomile	Yes	Brown-edged	Linear/broader

flower bracts

1 SOZ

2 SOZ

3 SZ

4

5 OZ

6 S

8 OZ

1 Scentless Mayweed *Tripleurospermum inodorum*. The commonest of the group; short hairless non-aromatic annual/biennial, to 60cm. Flowers large, 30-45mm, with *brown-edged* sepal-like bracts; April-Nov. Leaves 2-3-pinnate, with thread-like, often bristle-tipped leaflets. Bare and disturbed ground.

2 Sea Mayweed *Tripleurospermum maritimum*. Like Scentless Mayweed (**1**), but stouter, more spreading, slightly fleshy, often purplish and sometimes perennial. Shingle and other bare places *by the sea*. In N Scotland has still darker-edged bracts.

3 Scented Mayweed *Matricaria recutita*. Short/medium hairless, usually *aromatic* annual, to 60cm. Flowers *smaller* than Scentless Mayweed (**1**), 10-25mm, with *greenish-white* bracts; May-July. Bare and disturbed ground.

4 Stinking Chamomile *Anthemis cotula*. Short, slightly hairy annual, with a *sickly smell*, to 50cm. Flowers *smaller* than Scentless Mayweed (**1**), 12-25mm, the bracts *whitish with a green midrib*; June-Sept, with Scentless Mayweed, which has narrower leaflets, the most likely to be seen in early autumn. Bare and disturbed ground, an arable weed.

5 Corn Chamomile *Anthemis arvensis*. Short *grey-downy*, scarcely aromatic annual, to 50cm. Flowers as large as Scentless Mayweed (**1**), 20-40mm, the bracts *all green*; June-Sept. Leaves with distinctly broader leaflets, often markedly downy beneath. A decreasing arable weed, usually on limy soils.

6 *Chamomile *Chamaemelum nobile*. Low/short spreading, *strongly aromatic*, hairy perennial, to 30cm. Flowers like Scentless Mayweed (**1**), but smaller, 18-25mm, bracts *white-edged*; June-Sept. Leaflets threadlike, not downy beneath. Decreasing in well grazed turf on acid soils, especially in the New Forest; now less often planted in lawns.

7 Sicilian Chamomile *Anthemis punctata*. Medium *bushy* aromatic perennial, to 60cm. Flowers white, large (40-60mm); June-Dec. Leaves *greyish*. Established on cliffs and banks in Cornwall, the Isle of Wight, Fishguard, W Wales (since 1823) and elsewhere.

~

Michaelmas Daisies *Aster* spp, p. 270.

8 Magellan Ragwort *Senecio smithii*. A tall, unbranched, whitely downy perennial, to 1m. Flowers white, sometimes tinged yellowish, large (30-40mm); June-July. Leaves dark glossy green, downy beneath, oblong, heart-shaped at base, narrower up the stem. Well established in far N Scotland, especially by streams and near the sea.

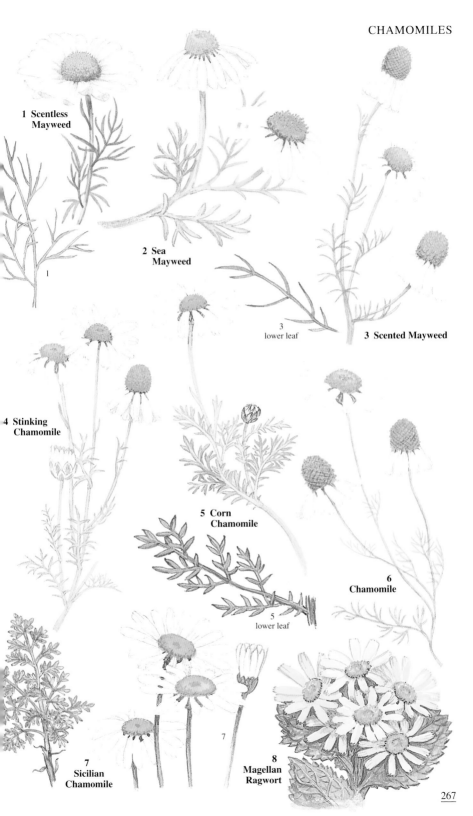

1 Scentless
Mayweed

1

2 Sea
Mayweed

3
lower leaf

3 Scented Mayweed

4 Stinking
Chamomile

5 Corn
Chamomile

5
lower leaf

6
Chamomile

7
Sicilian
Chamomile

7

8
Magellan
Ragwort

1 Yarrow *Achillea millefolium*. A downy, dark green, *strongly aromatic*, short/medium perennial, with creeping runners, but erect and little-branched, to 80cm. Flowers white, sometimes tinged pale or deep pink by cross-pollination from the many deep pink cultivars in gardens, 4-6mm, the disc florets creamy, many in a flat *umbel-like* head; June-Dec. Leaves long, narrow, 2-3-pinnate, rather feathery. Grassy places.

2 Sneezewort *Achillea ptarmica*. A greyish medium perennial, with slightly hairy erect stems to 60cm. Flowers white, 12-18mm, the disc florets *greenish-white*, sometimes double-flowered in garden escapes, in loose clusters; July-Sept. Leaves linear, pointed, finely saw-toothed. *Damp* grassy or heathy places, mainly on acid soils.

3 Mountain Everlasting *Antennaria dioica*. A short neat *white-woolly* perennial, with rooting runners and erect unbranched stems to 20cm. Flowers white, 6-12mm, with pink disc florets, male with *white or pale pink* bracts and female with *deeper pink* bracts, on separate plants; June-July. Leaves narrow, spoon-shaped in the basal rosette, narrow lanceolate and appressed to the stem. Dry grassland, heaths, moors, mainly in hill districts, often on mountains.

4 Shaggy Soldier *Galinsoga quadriradiata*. Short/medium annual with many *long white* and short sticky hairs, to 80cm. Flowers white, 5-7mm, the scales among the yellow disc florets *not or scarcely* lobed, in branched clusters; June-Oct. Leaves opposite, pointed oval, toothed, narrowing up the stem. Established on bare and waste ground since 1909.
4a Gallant Soldier *G. parviflora* is either hairless or with *much shorter* hairs, and has slightly smaller flowers with the scales in the disc *3-lobed*. Similarly established since escaped from Kew Gardens, Surrey, in 1860, but less frequent. Both species are most frequent in London.

Rayed Tansy *Tanacetum macrophyllum*, p. 268.

5 Blue Fleabane *Erigeron acer*. Short/medium, roughly hairy annual/biennial, stems often purple, to 60cm. Flowers with *erect dingy purple* rays not much longer than the yellow disc florets, in loose clusters of small cylindrical 12-18mm heads; July-Sept. Leaves lanceolate, untoothed, narrower and half-clasping on the stems. Pappus reddish-white. Hybridises with Canadian Fleabane (p. 280). Dry grassy places, dunes.

Robin's Plantain *Erigeron philadelphicus*, p. 264.

6 **Alpine Fleabane *Erigeron borealis*. A low/short hairy perennial, to 20cm. Flowers solitary, pink-purple, 16-20mm, with ray florets spreading, much longer than the disc florets; July-August. Leaves narrowly spoon-shaped in a basal rosette, narrower up the stems. *Mountain rock ledges*, especially around Ben Lawers, Perthshire.

7 Seaside Daisy *Erigeron glaucus*. Short/medium perennial, to 50cm. Flowers pale purple, *30-40mm*, solitary; May-August. Leaves slightly fleshy, spoon-shaped, narrower up the stems. Increasing garden escape *by the sea* in the Isle of Wight and elsewhere in the S.

7 Seaside Daisy

1 Yarrow
pink form

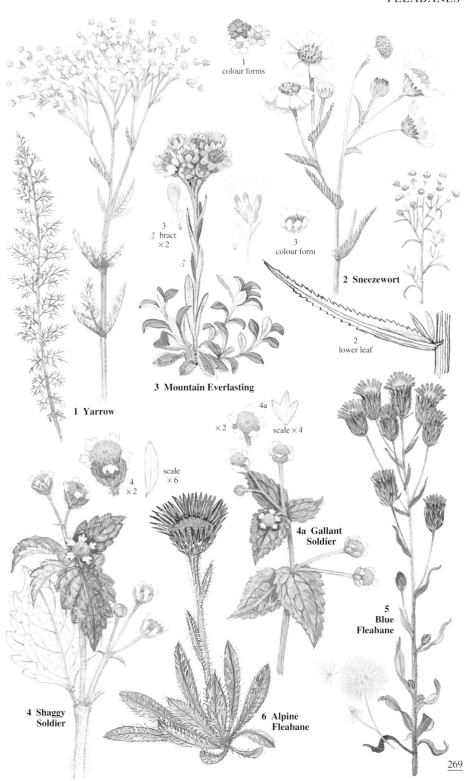

1
colour forms

3
♂ bract
× 2

♂

♀

3
colour form

2 Sneezewort

2
lower leaf

3 Mountain Everlasting

1 Yarrow

4a

× 2

4a
scale × 4

scale
× 6

4
× 2

**4a Gallant
Soldier**

**5
Blue
Fleabane**

**4 Shaggy
Soldier**

**6 Alpine
Fleabane**

269

1 Sea Aster *Aster tripolium*. A stout hairless fleshy biennial, short/medium, to 1m. Flowers in open clusters, of two kinds: most often looking like michaelmas daisies (below) with pale blue-purple, occasionally whitish, rays (12-20mm), and without them (8-10mm) and so all-yellow and more like an erect outsize yellow groundsel (p. 280); July-Oct. Leaves dark green, lanceolate with a prominent midrib. *By the sea* or tidal rivers, usually in saltmarshes.

1 Z ▢

Michaelmas Daisies *Aster.* Our most difficult group of naturalised aliens, with perhaps hardly any pure-bred strains in this huge well-established hybrid swarm of North American perennials. The six 'species' are often best distinguished by their sepal-like bracts. Medium/tall, mostly to 1.5m. Flowers pale (except Hairy Michaelmas Daisy, **7**) blue-purple to whitish, 25-40mm; August-Nov. Leaves lanceolate. Damp and waste places, waysides, streamsides. Common (**2**), Changing (**6**) and Narrow-leaved (**4**) appear to be our three most frequent species; Common is a hybrid between the other two. Three species each have a distinctive character: Narrow-leaved (**4**) its small whitish flowers, Glaucous (**5**) its glaucous leaves, and Hairy (**7**) its both long and sticky hairs

2 Common Michaelmas Daisy *Aster* × *salignus*, the hybrid between Confused and Narrow-leaved, has all-green bracts appressed and widest below the middle, and leaves narrow lanceolate and scarcely clasping the stem. **3 Confused Michaelmas Daisy** *A. novibelgii* has the bracts widest near the middle, loosely appressed, and leaves slightly broader and clasping the stem. **4 Narrow-leaved Michaelmas Daisy** *A. lanceolatus* has smaller (14-20mm), whitish or pale purple flowers, the bracts pale-edged, the lower spreading, and the leaves narrow lanceolate. **5 Glaucous Michaelmas Daisy** *A. laevis* has stems to 1m, flowers blue-purple with bracts green only at the tip, the outer less than half as long as the inner, and leaves lanceolate and *glaucous* above. **6 Changing Michaelmas Daisy**, *A* × *versicolor*, the hybrid between Confused (**3**) and Glaucous (**5**), is taller than Glaucous, to 2m, with stems often red, flowers whitish *at first*, turning purple and appearing Sept-Oct, with outer bracts at least half as long as the inner, and all-green leaves. **7 Hairy Michaelmas Daisy** *A. novae-angliae* is taller, to 2m, with many *long hairs* and shorter *sticky* ones; flowers usually bright purple, larger, to 50mm, and bracts either purple or green.

1d. Daisy-type, disc florets yellow: Flowers yellow

Ragworts *Senecio*. The largest group of yellow daisy-like flowers. Flowers in clusters. Leaves mostly pinnate or pinnately lobed. Fruit a pappus with simple hairs, not forming a clock. Several species hybridise. For the rayless groundsels, see p. 280. Several species are favourite food plants of the striking black and yellow caterpillars of the Cinnabar Moth (*Tyria jacobaeae*).

The four commonest ragworts can be distinguished as follows: *Inner bracts dark-tipped*: Common Ragwort (**8**), Oxford Ragwort (p. 272). *Inner bracts edged whitish*: Marsh Ragwort (**10**). *End leaf-lobe pointed*: Hoary Ragwort (**9**).

8 Common Ragwort *Senecio jacobaea*. An often hairless medium/tall perennial, branched only at the top, to 1.5m. Flowers yellow, 15-25mm, the outer bracts few, *much shorter* than the dark-tipped inner; in large *flat-topped* clusters; June-Nov. Leaves dark green, deeply pinnately lobed, the lobes toothed and the end one short and *blunt*. *Dry*, sandy or limy grassy places and dunes, often with bare patches due to overgrazing.

8 SOZ ▢

9 Hoary Ragwort *Senecio erucifolius*. Branched lower down and *greyer* with down than Common Ragwort (**8**) and with very short creeping runners; to 1.2m. Flowers paler yellow, 12-20mm, the outer bracts about *half as long* as the usually *green-tipped* inner; in a more *rounded* and open cluster; July-Sept, at its best when Common Ragwort is past its best. Leaves paler green, more deeply and narrowly lobed, the end lobe narrow and *pointed*. Grassy places, mainly on lime or clay.

9 ▣

10 Marsh Ragwort *Senecio aquaticus*. Shorter, to 80cm, and more widely branched than Common Ragwort (**8**). Flowers markedly *larger*, 25-40mm, the inner bracts sharply pointed, *green with whitish edges*, the outer much shorter; in broader, looser clusters; June-Oct. Leaves glossier, with a *large end lobe* and much smaller, forward-pointing side lobes; root-leaves oval, often *undivided*. Beware autumnal shoots from mutilated Common Ragwort plants. *Wet grassland*.

10 OZ ▢↓

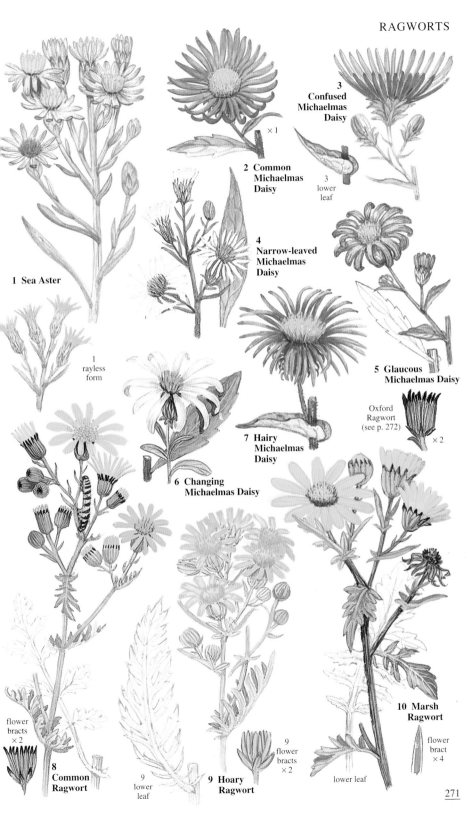

3 Confused Michaelmas Daisy

3 lower leaf

2 Common Michaelmas Daisy

× 1

4 Narrow-leaved Michaelmas Daisy

1 Sea Aster

1 rayless form

5 Glaucous Michaelmas Daisy

7 Hairy Michaelmas Daisy

Oxford Ragwort (see p. 272)

× 2

6 Changing Michaelmas Daisy

flower bracts × 2

8 Common Ragwort

9 flower bracts × 2

9 lower leaf

9 Hoary Ragwort

10 Marsh Ragwort

flower bract × 4

lower leaf

271

1 Oxford Ragwort *Senecio squalidus*. A well branched, straggling, short/medium annual/perennial, to 50cm. Flowers yellow, 16-20mm, with inner bracts *black-tipped*, the outer much shorter; *April*-Nov and through mild winters. Leaves glossy, hairless, pinnately lobed or deeply toothed, sometimes undivided. Well established on bare and waste ground, especially in London and other *towns*, since escaping from Oxford Botanic Garden in 1794. **1a Welsh Groundsel** *S. cambrensis* and **York Groundsel** *S. eboracensis* (see p. 280) are true-breeding hybrids with Groundsel, (see also p. 280). **1c Eastern Groundsel** *S. vernalis*, an increasing weed from grass mixtures, is markedly downy with somewhat smaller flowers and more shallowly lobed leaves, but closely resembles the ordinary Oxford Ragwort/Groundsel hybrid (p. 280).

1   sz   ☐↑

2 Silver Ragwort *Senecio cineraria*. A medium/tall bushy *silvery* perennial, woody at the base, to 60cm. Flowers yellow, with the centre often darker, 8-20mm, stalks and bracts whitely woolly; June-August. Leaves oval to oblong, *toothed to pinnately lobed*, green above but covered beneath and on the stalks with a dense white felt. Well established on cliffs, shingle and rough ground, especially near the sea. **2a Shrub Ragwort** *Senecio* cv. Sunshine is the common garden plant, often escaping, and differing especially in its undivided oblong leaves.

1a   ☐

3 ***Fen Ragwort *Senecio paludosus*. By far our rarest native ragwort, extinct between 1857 and 1972, when it was refound in a Cambridgeshire dyke. A tall perennial, to 1.5m. Flowers with 12-20 yellow rays, 18-22mm; May-July. Leaves lanceolate to narrow lanceolate, saw-toothed, downy white beneath, clasping the stem. Not to be confused with two species naturalised in scattered damp or wet places: **3a Broad-leaved Ragwort** *S. fluviatilis* with 6-8 rays, downy bracts and flower-stalks and broader, often blunt-toothed leaves; or **Golden Ragwort** *S. doria*, which has golden-yellow flowers with bracts and flower-stalks hairless, and leaf-teeth pointed and incurved.

2   s   ☐↑↑

Other naturalised perennial Ragworts include: **4 Narrow-leaved Ragwort** *Senecio inaequidens* from S Africa, almost hairless, bushy, medium, to 80cm, and with flowers 10-20mm and narrow, well toothed *unstalked* leaves; well established in France and now spreading from E Kent and S Essex; otherwise a casual. **5 Wood Ragwort** *S. ovatus*, to 1.5m, with 6-8 yellow rays and narrowly elliptical *stalked* leaves, is in a few damp woods in N England. **6 Chamois Ragwort** *S. doronicum*, to 1m, with 15-22 golden-yellow rays and leaves linear-lanceolate, short-toothed and unstalked, is on river banks in Perthshire. **Chinese Ragwort** *Sinacalia tangutica*, to 2m, with large clusters of tiny (2-4mm) flowers and large oval, deeply pinnately lobed leaves, to 20cm long, is in many damp shady places in the N.

3   ☐

3a   ☐

Groundsels *Senecio*, with rayed flowers are described, for convenience, with the unrayed ones on p. 280.

7 Field Fleawort *Tephroseris integrifolia*. Short/medium unbranched downy perennial, to 60cm. Flowers yellow, 15-25mm, the disc florets often darker; in a loose, umbel-like cluster; May-June. Leaves oval, in a basal rosette, wrinkled and hairless above, cottony beneath; narrower up the stem. Short, with leaves usually untoothed, in limy turf in the S; medium, with leaves usually toothed, on sea cliffs in Anglesey; now extinct in Westmorland.

7   ☐↓

2a Shrub Ragwort

leaf × 1

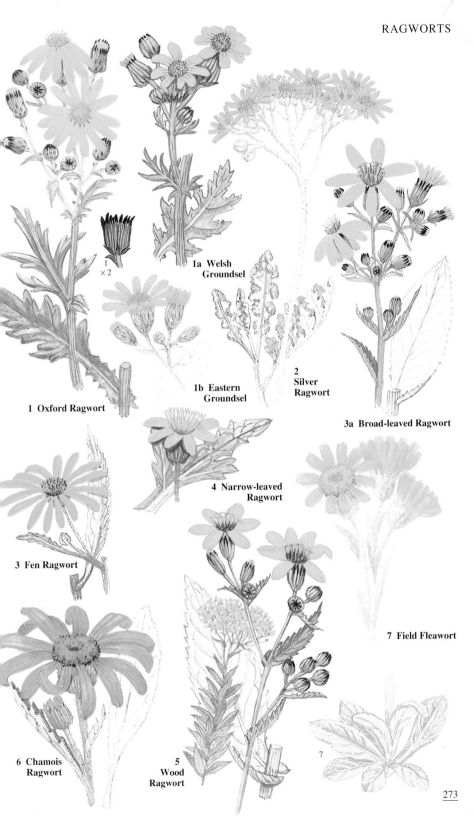

1 **Oxford Ragwort**

1 ×2

1a **Welsh Groundsel**

1b **Eastern Groundsel**

2 **Silver Ragwort**

3a **Broad-leaved Ragwort**

3 **Fen Ragwort**

4 **Narrow-leaved Ragwort**

7 **Field Fleawort**

6 **Chamois Ragwort**

5 **Wood Ragwort**

7

1 OZ ■↓

2 SOZ■↓↓

4 S ▢

5 ·▢↓

6 ▢

7 ▢↓

1 Coltsfoot *Tussilago farfara.* Low erect perennial, with whitely woolly, purplish stems, leafless but with many overlapping fleshy scales, to 15cm. Flowers yellow, with *both disc and ray* florets, 15-35mm, solitary; late Jan-April, *long before the leaves.* Leaves broadly heart-shaped, polygonal, whitely downy at first. Fruit with a conspicuous white pappus. Beware early Dandelions (p. 294), which have no disc florets, much broader rays and pinnately lobed leaves that appear before the flowers.

2 Corn Marigold *Chrysanthemum segetum.* A short/medium greyish hairless annual, to 60cm. Flowers bright yellow, 30-70mm; June-Oct. Leaves fleshy, jaggedly toothed. Often yellowing *arable fields,* also waysides, preferring acid soils; decreasing. **2a Yellow Chamomile** *Anthemis tinctoria* has smaller (25-40mm) flowers and pinnate leaves. Mainly a garden escape.

3 Pot Marigold *Calendula officinalis.* Short/medium, roughly hairy, slightly aromatic annual/perennial, to 80cm. Flowers *orange,* 40-70mm; May-Oct, sometimes through mild winters in the S and W. Leaves oblong, often broadest at the tip. Waste ground, a familiar garden escape.

4 Common Fleabane *Pulicaria dysenterica.* A short/medium, shaggily downy perennial, to 1m. Flowers golden-yellow, 15-30mm, in *flat-topped* clusters; July-Sept. Leaves lanceolate, the upper wrinkled. *Damp* grassy places, by ditches.

5 **Small Fleabane *Pulicaria vulgaris.* Well branched short downy annual, to 45cm. Flowers dull yellow, with the rays erect, *small* (6-12mm); August-Sept. Leaves narrow oblong, wavy-edge, toothed or not. Bare ground flooded in winter, often pond-edges, a New Forest speciality.

6 Golden Samphire *Inula crithmoides.* Medium perennial, to 1m. Flowers golden-yellow, 15-25mm, in loose umbel-like clusters; July-August. Leaves *linear* up the stem, *fleshy* – unlike all our other daisy-type flowers. Bare ground *by the sea,* especially cliffs and drier saltmarshes. **6a Woody Fleabane** *Dittrichia viscosa.* Stickily hairy and resinous-smelling, with smaller (10-15mm) flowers and often broader but not fleshy leaves, is established on Landguard Common, Suffolk.

7 Irish Fleabane *Inula salicina.* Short/medium perennial, to 70cm. Flowers yellow, 20-30mm, solitary or in small clusters; July-Sept. Leaves oblong, arched back. Shores of L. Derg. Now very rare.

8 Elecampane *Inula helenium.* Very tall stout hairy perennial, to *2.5m.* Flowers *yellow, unusually large* (60-90mm), with many *narrow* rays; July-August. Leaves elliptical, *bluntly* toothed, stalked, not heart-shaped, the basal to 60cm long, shorter and broader up the stems. A former medicinal/veterinary herb for men and horses; long established on waysides and near cottages. **8a Yellow Oxeye** *Telekia speciosa* has flowers with leaves somewhat smaller, heart-shaped at the base and sharply toothed. A favourite border plant, often established near fresh water.

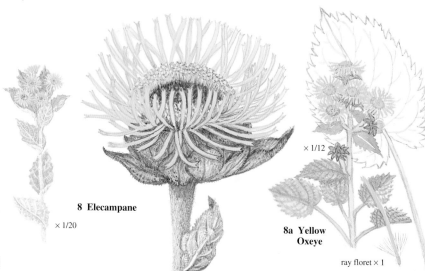

8 Elecampane

× 1/20

× 1/12

8a Yellow Oxeye

ray floret × 1

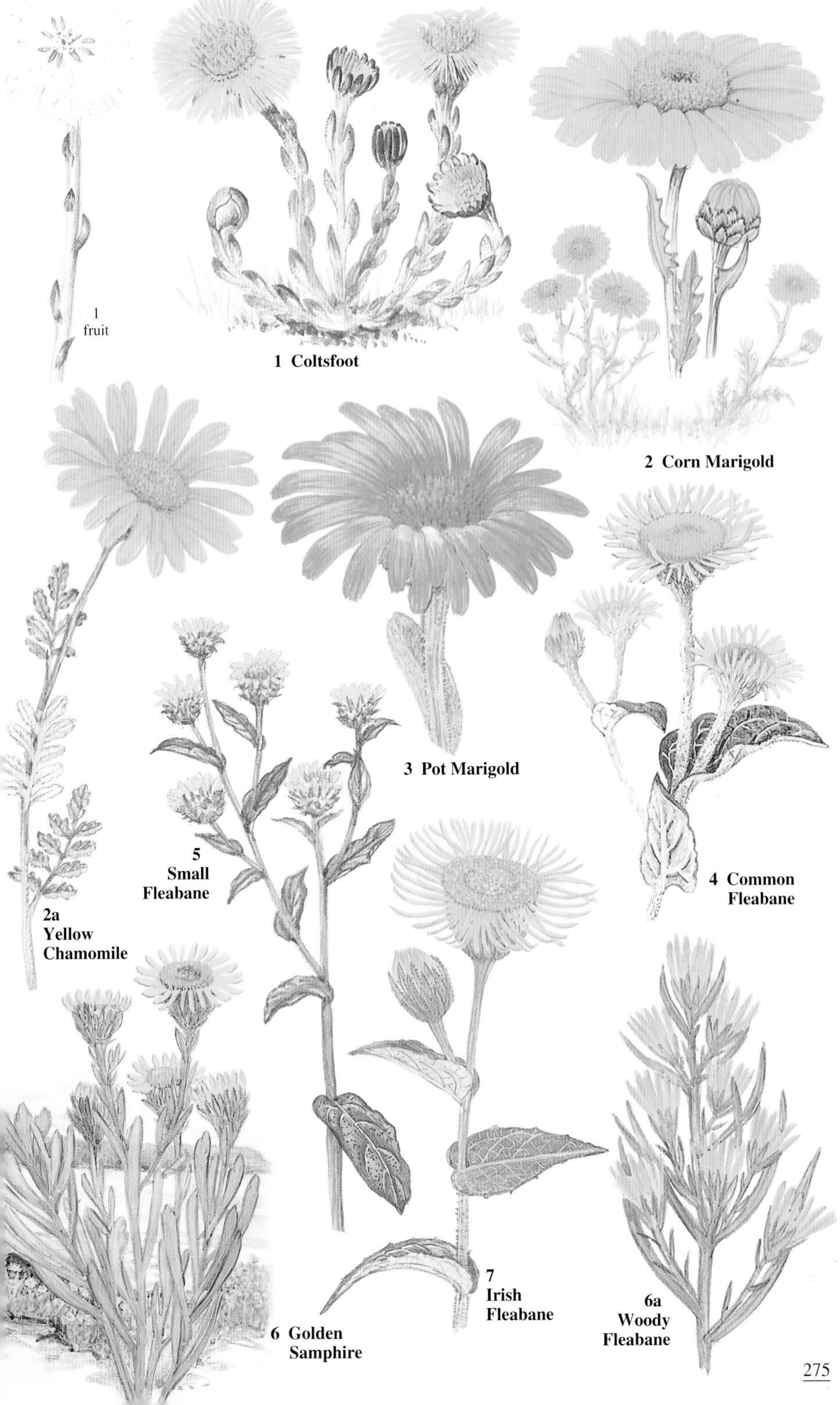

1
fruit

1 Coltsfoot

2 Corn Marigold

3 Pot Marigold

4 Common Fleabane

5 Small Fleabane

2a Yellow Chamomile

6 Golden Samphire

7 Irish Fleabane

6a Woody Fleabane

275

Leopardsbanes *Doronicum*. Medium/tall, to 1m, yellow-flowered perennial garden escapes, best distinguished by their leaves. The two main species are quite distinctive; their hybrids are the problem. Long established in woods, shrubberies and hedge-banks.

The most frequent is **1 Leopardsbane** *Doronicum pardalianches*, with flowers usually 30-45mm; May-July; and leaves *heart-shaped*, often overlapping at the base, and almost *rounded* at the tip. **1a Plantain-leaved Leopardsbane** *D. plantagineum* and its hybrids all have leaves more or less *pointed* at the tip and larger (50-80mm) flowers, some flowering in April. Plantain-leaved itself has leaves *sharply pointed* at the tip and *gradually narrowed* to the base. The hybrid between the two, *D. × willldenowii* has leaves rounded to sharply cut off at the base, and a triple hybrid also involving both, *D. × excelsum*, has leaves shallowly heart-shaped. The third parent **1b Eastern Leopardsbane** *D. columnae* (one site in Surrey) has leaves deeply heart-shaped, the bases not overlapping.

1 ■↑

1a ▢

Sunflowers *Helianthus*. Tall annuals/perennials with large yellow daisy-type flowers, sometimes doubled, the disc florets flattish, and undivided leaves, opposite below and alternate above. Widely established in waste places.

2 Annual Sunflower *Helianthus annuus*. The common garden Sunflower, a *very tall*, roughly hairy annual, to 3m. Flowers golden-yellow, with disc florets brownish and bracts abruptly contracted to a point, very large (10-30cm); August-Oct. Leaves broad, often heart-shaped, to 40cm long. Grown as a crop for the oil from its seeds. A frequent casual, especially along the S shore of the Thames from Erith to Sheppey. **Lesser Sunflower** *H. petiolaris* is smaller, to 1m, with flowers 30-80mm, the disc florets red-purple, bracts gradually tapering to the tip, and leaves paler green, to 15cm. Much less frequent, but also often by the Thames at Erith.

3 Perennial Sunflower *Helianthus × laetiflorus*. Our most frequent perennial sunflower, patch-forming, with stems all *roughly hairy*, to 1.5m. Flowers 60-100mm, the disc florets turning dark purple, the sepal-like bracts *tightly appressed*, August-Oct. Leaves broad lanceolate, scarcely toothed, clearly 3-veined beneath, and rough to the touch. The often taller (to 3m) and shy-flowering **3a Jerusalem Artichoke** *H. tuberosus* with edible tubers on its roots is a frequent allotment throw-out, further differing from Perennial Sunflower in its more toothed leaves with *winged stalks* and flowers with *loosely* appressed bracts. The much less frequent **Thin-leaved Sunflower** *H. × decapetalus (multiflorus)* has stems *hairless* below, to 1.5m.

~

4 Coneflower *Rudbeckia laciniata*. Very tall, almost hairless perennial, to 3m. Flowers daisy-like, the golden-yellow rays broad and *down-turned*, the greenish-brown disc florets making a flattened *cone*, 70-140mm across; June-Oct. Leaves lanceolate, lobed or toothed, alternate. A frequent escape, established by two rivers in Scotland. The smaller **4a Black-eyed Susan** *R. hirta*, to 80cm, is roughly hairy, smaller (50-100mm) flowers with a *purplish* cone and its leaves not lobed. Much less frequent. **4b Sneezeweed** *Helenium autumnale*, to 1m, has still smaller (40-65mm) flowers yellow to purplish-brown, the rays soon turned down and leaves scarcely toothed. Established in a chalk pit and by a plantation in Surrey. All three are familiar in gardens.

5 Blanketflower *Gaillardia × grandiflora*. Medium annual/perennial, to 70cm. Flowers yellow/purple, large (40-100mm); June-Nov. Leaves lanceolate, toothed. Garden escape, making a great show on shingle at Greatstone-on-Sea, Kent, and on Witley Heath, Surrey.

6 Tyneside Leopardplant *Ligularia przewalskii*. Tall perennial, to 1.2m, Flowers yellow, in a strikingly long spike; June-August. Leaves large, jaggedly palmately lobed. Well established by the R Tyne, Northumberland. **Leopardplant** *L. dentata* has flowers tinged orange and leaves kidney-shaped and toothed. Established in scattered woods and damp places.

Bur-Marigolds *Bidens*, p. 278, may also have rayed flowers.

1
× 1/8

1 Leopardsbane

1a Plantain-leaved Leopardsbane

1a
× 1/6

1b Eastern Leopardsbane

2 Annual Sunflower

× 1/20

× ¼

× 1

3 Perennial Sunflower

4 Coneflower

4a Black-eyed Susan

× ¼

× 1

20

× 1/20

× ½

6 Tyneside Leopardplant

5 Blanketflower

4b Sneezeweed

3a Jerusalem Artichoke

1 Goldenrod *Solidago virgaurea*. Variable short/medium little-branched perennial, downy or not, to 70cm. Flowers yellow, 6-10mm, with very short rays, in *straight* branched spikes; July-Sept (June in the hills). Leaves narrow lanceolate, sometimes slightly toothed. Wooded, grassy and rocky places.

1 soz ▣↓

2 Canadian Goldenrod *Solidago canadensis*. Tall perennial, with stems *downy below*, to 2.5m. Flowers yellow, 4-6mm, with very short rays, in *curved* branched spikes; July-Sept. Leaves lanceolate, toothed, *downy on both sides*. Well established on waysides and waste ground. The less frequent **2a Early Goldenrod** *S. gigantea* has stems more or less *hairless* and leaves *hairless* except sometimes on underside veins. **2b Grass-leaved Goldenrod** *S. graminifolia*, with a flat-topped flower spike and *much narrower* leaves, is established in a wood in N Devon and a few other places. Eight more alien Goldenrods have been recorded.

2 s ■↑

1e. Daisy-type, disc florets yellow: Flowers not, or obscurely, rayed

3 Pineappleweed *Matricaria discoidea*. A dark green, hairless, rather bushy, strongly *pineapple-scented* low annual, to 35cm. Flowers yellowish-green, in a *conical head*, 5-10mm; May-Nov. Leaves 2-3-pinnate, with thread-like segments. Well established (since 1871) in bare, disturbed and often well trodden places.

2a ■↑

4 Tansy *Tanacetum vulgare*. A tall stout, dark green, *strongly aromatic* perennial, to 1.2m. Flowers golden-yellow, button-like, 6-10mm, in *flat-topped* clusters; July-Oct. Leaves pinnate, the leaflets toothed. Bare and grassy waste places, waysides.

3 soz ▢

5 **Norwegian Mugwort *Artemisia norvegica*. An aromatic low grey-downy, perennial, to 8cm. Flowers yellow, nodding, button-like, 8-13mm, usually solitary or paired; June-Sept. Leaves deeply pinnately cut, in a basal rosette. Bare mountain tops; a native not found till 1951.

4 oz ▢

6 Trifid Bur-marigold *Bidens tripartita*. Low/short annual, to 60mm. Flowers yellow, normally unrayed, 15-25mm, but sometimes with short broad rays, bracts blackish; July-Oct. Leaves opposite, with short, winged stalks, lanceolate, toothed with *a pair of lobes* at the base. Fruits flattened, oblong, with two barbed bristles at the top, so that it adheres to fur and clothing. By fresh water, especially on the dry margins of ponds and reservoirs. **6a Beggarticks** *B. frondosa* has leaves with unwinged stalks and often two pairs of lobes. Waste ground, mainly by canals and rivers, especially around London and Birmingham and in S Wales. **6b London Bur-marigold** *B. connata* has leaves not lobed and fruits warty but not flattened. By canals around London, especially the Grand Union.

5 ▣

7 Nodding Bur-marigold *Bidens cernua*. Differs from Trifid Bur-marigold (**6**) in having larger broader *nodding* flowers, very rarely rayed, except in NW England, thicker hairy stems, unstalked undivided leaves and narrower fruits with *3-4* barbed bristles. Habitat similar.

6 s ▢↓

8 Cottonweed *Otanthus maritimus*. A short creeping perennial, covered all over in a *thick white down*, to 30cm. Flowers yellow, button-like, 6-9mm, in small clusters; August-Nov. Leaves oblong, toothed. *One site* by the sea in Co Wexford. **8a Lavender-cotton** *Santolina chamaecyparissus*, a low shrub with pinnately lobed leaves, is established on two sandy shores in W Cornwall.

6a ▣

7 ▢

6a Beggarticks

6b London Bur-marigold

7 Nodding Bur-marigold

rayed form

8 ▣↓↓

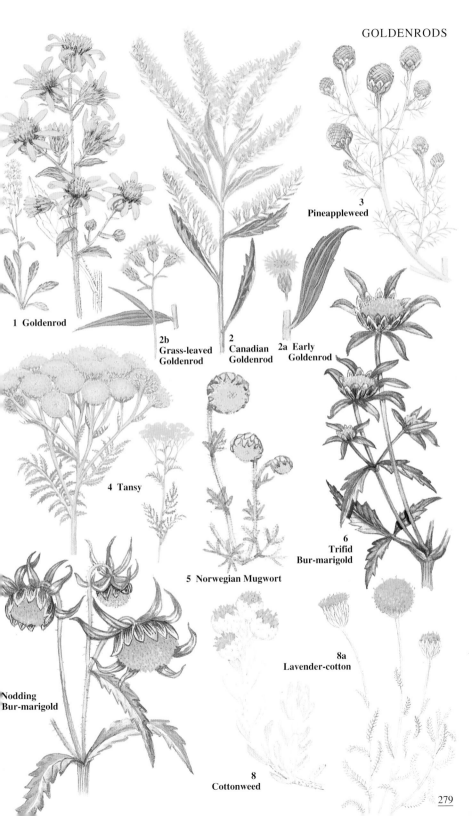

1 Goldenrod

2b
Grass-leaved
Goldenrod

2
Canadian
Goldenrod

2a Early
Goldenrod

3
Pineappleweed

4 Tansy

5 Norwegian Mugwort

6
Trifid
Bur-marigold

Nodding
Bur-marigold

8a
Lavender-cotton

8
Cottonweed

1 Buttonweed *Cotula coronopifolia*. A short hairless aromatic fleshy annual, to 30cm. Flowers yellow, button-like, 8-12mm, solitary, always facing the sun; July-Oct. Leaves yellowish-green, *varying*, even on the same stem, from broad linear and undivided to deeply pinnate. Marshy, usually *brackish* places, naturalised in the Wirral, Cheshire, since the 1880s, more recently in Yorks and Hants. Two other species occur as lawn weeds, not always flowering: **1a Leptinella** *C. squalida*, with leaves deeply lobed and abruptly pointed, and **Hairless Leptinella** *C. dioica*, with leaves shallowly lobed and gradually pointed. 10 other species have been recorded.

2. Brush-like/Thistle-type:
    2a. Flowers yellow, not spiny (below).
    2b. Flowers yellow, spiny (p. 284).
    2c. Flowers purple, not spiny (p. 286).
    2d. Flowers purple, spiny (p. 288).
    2e. Flowers blue (p. 292).
    2f. Flowers white or green (p. 292).

**5b
Argentine
Fleabane**

2a. Brush-like/Thistle-type: Flowers yellow, not spiny

2 Groundsel *Senecio vulgaris*. Variable, often downy, low/short annual, to 30cm. Flowers yellow, 4-5mm, usually unrayed but sometimes with narrow yellow rays, bracts narrow, *black-tipped*, in loose clusters of cylindrical heads; *Jan-Dec*. Leaves pinnately lobed, hairless above. Hybridises with other groundsels and ragworts (p. 270). The familiar weed of gardens and other disturbed ground. **2a Welsh Groundsel** *S. cambrensis* is a very similar but larger true-breeding hybrid of Groundsel with Oxford Ragwort (see also p. 272), usually with ray florets broader than rayed Groundsel but soon rolling back. Spreading from N Wales, where first found 1948; similar plants elsewhere are more likely to be the ordinary hybrid between the two. **York Groundsel** *S. eboracensis* is another hybrid species, but has fewer, shorter bracts, and more lobes on the leaves. Waste places, as yet only in York.

3 Heath Groundsel *Senecio sylvaticus*. Medium annual, slightly foetid, often somewhat stickily downy, to 70cm, but on fen tracks can grow to well over 1m, when it can be very puzzling. Flowers like Groundsel (**2**), the more conical heads with very short *rolled-back* rays and the bracts *purple-tipped*; June-Sept. Leaves more deeply and irregularly lobed. Heaths and other sandy or gravelly places.

4 Sticky Groundsel *Senecio viscosus*. Stickier, more *foetid* and later-flowering than Heath Groundsel (**3**), to 60cm. Flowers similar, the rays quickly rolling back, but the bracts *green-tipped*; July-Sept. Leaves darker grey-green, clammily *sticky-hairy*. Hybridises with Oxford Ragwort (p. 272). Bare and waste ground, often by the sea.

5 Canadian Fleabane *Conyza canadensis*. A medium/tall annual, to 1m. Flowers appearing rayless but with very short whitish rays bordering the *4-lobed* yellow disc florets, 3-5mm, the bracts *yellowish-green*, hairless to slightly downy; in loose, somewhat *cylindrical* clusters; late June-Sept. Leaves *mid green*, narrow lanceolate, often obscurely toothed, usually edged with *straight* hairs. Disturbed and waste ground. Three similar plants are spreading in the S. The most frequent is **5a Guernsey Fleabane** *C. sumatrensis*, with disc florets *5-lobed*, bracts grey-green and much downier, more pyramidal clusters and leaves *greyer*-green often more strongly toothed, edged with *hooked hairs*; especially around London and Yeovil, Somerset. The much rarer **5b Argentine Fleabane** *C. bonariensis* has distinctive *red-tipped* bracts and long-branched clusters. A roughly hairy plant with a flatter cluster of slightly larger flowers and greyish leaves edged with hooked hairs is **Bilbao Fleabane** *C. bilbaoana*, a recent arrival.

6 Ploughman's Spikenard *Inula conyzae*. Tall downy perennial, stems purplish, to 1.2m. Flowers dull yellow, with no or obscure ray florets, bracts *purple-brown* (prominent in bud), 9-11mm, in loose umbel-like clusters; July-Sept. Leaves lanceolate, the lower large, *foxglove-like* and in an overwintering basal rosette. Open woods, grassy places, especially on lime. Spikenard was an expensive medieval perfume; ploughmen were reduced to hanging this up in their hovels to sweeten the air.

7 **Goldilocks Aster *Aster linosyris*. Medium perennial, to 50cm. Flowers with bright golden-yellow disc florets only and prominent yellow stigmas, 12-18mm, in a loose erect cluster; Sept.-Nov. Leaves numerous, *very narrow*, not fleshy (cf. Golden Samphire, p. 274). Limestone cliffs in the W.

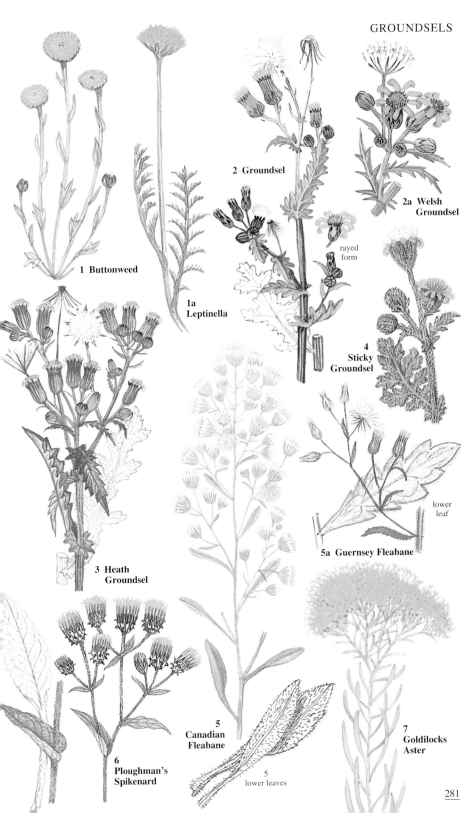

1 Buttonweed

1a Leptinella

2 Groundsel

rayed form

2a Welsh Groundsel

4 Sticky Groundsel

3 Heath Groundsel

lower leaf

5a Guernsey Fleabane

5 Canadian Fleabane

5 lower leaves

6 Ploughman's Spikenard

7 Goldilocks Aster

Cudweeds. *Gnaphalium* and *Filago*. Annuals/perennials, all more or less covered with grey, white or yellowish wool or down. Flowers small, unrayed, mostly 3-5mm, in clusters or loose spikes, the tiny florets often almost hidden by the bracts, whose tips usually give the flower its most conspicuous colour, usually brownish in *Gnaphalium* and yellowish, or red, in *Filago*. Female *Filago* flowers contain chaffy scales. Mostly preferring acid soils.

1 Marsh Cudweed *Gnaphalium uliginosum*. The most frequent of the group, a low bushy annual, to 25cm. Flowers yellowish-brown, unstalked, with bracts browner in the upper half, yellower brown in the lower, in crowded clusters; July-Sept. Leaves narrow, cottony on both sides but the upper sides greener, the topmost overtopping the flowers. Pappus white. Not a marsh plant, preferring all kinds of damp bare ground.

2 Heath Cudweed *Gnaphalium sylvaticum*. A greyish woolly short/medium perennial, with leafy shoots at the base and an erect unbranched stem to 60cm. Flowers pink to pale yellow, narrow oblong, the outer bracts warm brown and the inner pinkish with a pale green midrib; July-Sept. Leaves linear, dark green and hairless above, white-felted beneath. Pappus red-brown. Dry open heathy woods, banks and fields.

3 Dwarf Cudweed *Gnaphalium supinum*. Low tufted silvery grey perennial, to 12cm. Flowers bright pink, with warm brown bracts, edged and tipped dark brown, greenish on the back, in compact terminal heads or spikes; June-July. Leaves narrow, thickly downy on both sides. Bare *mountain tops*.

4 **Highland Cudweed *Gnaphalium norvegicum*. Low/short perennial, to 30cm. Flowers pinkish, in leafy spikes, the bracts warm brown, the inner pinkish with a green midrib and a dark brown tip; August. Leaves narrow, 3-veined. *Mountain tops*, usually on granite.

5 **Jersey Cudweed *Gnaphalium luteo-album*. Short/medium grey-woolly annual, with unbranched stems to 50cm. Flowers yellow with bright red stigmas, oval with shiny chaffy straw-coloured bracts, in dense terminal umbel-like clusters; July-Sept. Leaves grey on both sides, the margins inrolled, the root ones broader and blunt. Dunes, N Norfolk.

6 Small Cudweed *Filago minima*. Inconspicuous slender low erect annual, greyish with silky down, to 25cm. Flowers yellow from the tips of the bracts, the outer ones sharply angled and spreading *star-like* in fruit; in narrowly conical clusters; June-Sept. Leaves linear, *4-10mm*, the topmost *below* the flower clusters. Bare dry sandy and gravelly places.

7 Narrow-leaved Cudweed *Filago gallica* is often more widely branched than Small Cudweed (**6**) and also has longer (*12-20mm*) and narrower green-edged leaves *above* the flower clusters, with the outer fruits enclosed by swollen-based inner bracts. Long-established (Essex since 1696) but became extinct in the 1950s, and has recently been reintroduced.

8 Common Cudweed *Filago vulgaris*. A low/short annual, silvery-grey with woolly down, with spreading wiry branches, sometimes overtopping the main stem, to 40cm. Flowers *deep yellow* from the tips of the bracts, the almost hidden florets being white, tipped red, 4-6mm, 20-40 in globular 10-12mm clusters; July-August. Leaves narrow oblong, *widest at the base*, wavy-edged, the upper not overtopping the flowers. Heaths, dry bare sandy and gravelly places.

9 **Broad-leaved Cudweed *Filago pyramidata*. Differs from Common Cudweed (**8**) especially in the flowers, 10-20 in the cluster, having bracts tipped *buff* or reddish-buff and often curved, and the leaves more sharply pointed, *widest at the tip*, not wavy-edged and with the 2-4 larger top ones usually overtopping the flowers. Also on lime.

10 **Red-tipped Cudweed *Filago lutescens*. Easily told from Common and Broad-leaved Cudweeds (**8, 9**) both by its distinctively *bright red-tipped* bracts and by its *yellowish wool*. Further differs from Common in its leaves being more sharply pointed, not wavy-edged and overtopping the flowers, which are fewer (10-25) in the cluster; and from Broad-leaved in its bracts being not curved and in having only 1-2 overtopping leaves.

1   SOZ ⊡↑

2   OZ ⊡↓↓

3   ⊡

4   ⊡

5   ⊡↓

6   s   ⊡↓

8   s   ▢↓↓

9   ⊡↓↓

10   ⊡↓

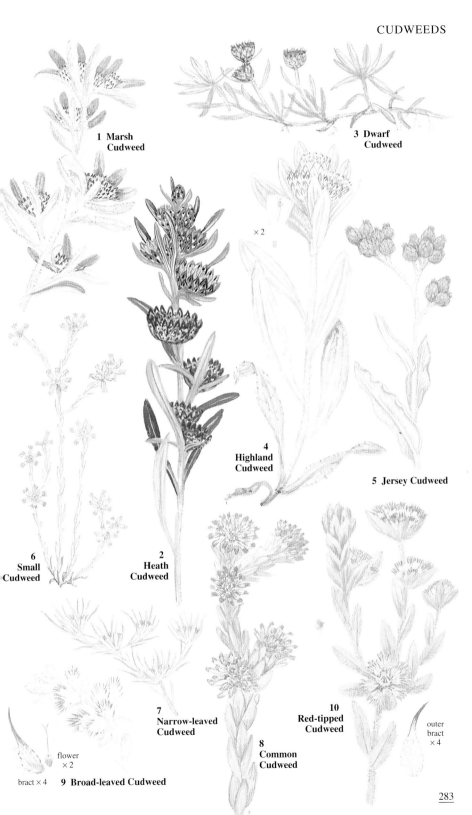

1 Marsh Cudweed

3 Dwarf Cudweed

× 2

4 Highland Cudweed

5 Jersey Cudweed

6 Small Cudweed

2 Heath Cudweed

7 Narrow-leaved Cudweed

10 Red-tipped Cudweed

8 Common Cudweed

flower × 2

bract × 4 **9 Broad-leaved Cudweed**

outer bract × 4

Mugworts and **Wormwoods**. *Artemisia*. Mostly perennials, often aromatic, usually more or less white-downy, with dense branched stalked spikes of small, usually yellow, more or less groundsel-like, rayless flowers. Leaves usually multi-pinnate. Mostly on various kinds of bare ground. Norwegian Mugwort *A. norvegica*, see p. 278.

1 Mugwort *Artemisia vulgaris*. Tall, slightly aromatic perennial, to 1.5m. Flowers brown, tinged yellow or purple, 2-4mm; *July-Sept*. Leaves 1-2-pinnate, *dark green* and almost hairless above, silvery downy beneath. Waysides, rough and waste ground. Named from its supposed ability to repel midges. The patch-forming **1a Chinese Mugwort** *A. verlotiorum* is more aromatic, with flowers, appearing *Oct-Dec*, when the whole plant still looks fresh, its leaves darker green and less downy beneath. Well established, especially around London.

2 Wormwood *Artemisia absinthium*. Strongly aromatic, distinctively *grey-downy*, tall perennial, to 1m. Flowers yellow, 3-5mm, flatter than Mugwort (**1**); July-Sept. Leaves whitely downy on *both sides*. Makes absinthe bitter. Waysides, hedge-banks, rough ground. **2a Hoary Mugwort** *A. stelleriana* is not aromatic and has flowers 5-9mm with white-felted bracts and leaves pinnately lobed. Established mainly on coastal dunes. **2b Perennial Ragweed** *Ambrosia psilostachya* has a simpler spike of somewhat similar flowers, but is not aromatic and has pinnately lobed leaves. Established on dunes in Lancashire and elsewhere.

3 **Field Wormwood *Artemisia campestris*. Medium perennial, *not* aromatic, stems almost hairless, to 75cm. Flowers yellow, 3-4mm; May-Sept. Leaves silky on both sides at first, becoming *hairless*. Grassy and heathy places in Breckland. **3a Slender Mugwort** *A. biennis* is a strongly aromatic annual/biennial with smaller flowers and hairless leaves, established in two places in Somerset (near Bath since 1925) and one in Sussex.

4 Sea Wormwood *Seriphidium maritimum*. Strikingly *silvery-downy* short perennial, to 50cm. Flowers yellow/orange, 2-4mm; July-Sept. Leaves 1-2-pinnate. Drier *saltmarshes*, sea-walls.

2b. Brush-like/Thistle-type: Flowers yellow, spiny

5 Carline Thistle *Carlina vulgaris*. Stiff short biennial, to 60cm. Flowers brownish-yellow, often solitary, 15-30mm, with conspicuous narrow *purple-based straw-yellow* ray-like inner bracts, which fold over in wet weather; the outer bracts spiny, cottony and leaf-like; July-Sept. Leaves prickly, the lower cottony. Dead plants, looking much as they do in flower, often survive the winter. Grassland on lime.

Four yellow-flowered spiny aliens are mainly casuals: two softly spiny thistles, **5a Cabbage Thistle** *Cirsium oleraceum*, long known on the Tay marshes below Perth and elsewhere, and **5b Yellow Thistle** *C. erisithales* in an old quarry near Bristol; also **5c Yellow Star-thistle** *Centaurea solstitialis*, with strong spines around the flower, and **5d Safflower** *Carthamus tinctorius* with bright orange-yellow 20-30mm flowers.

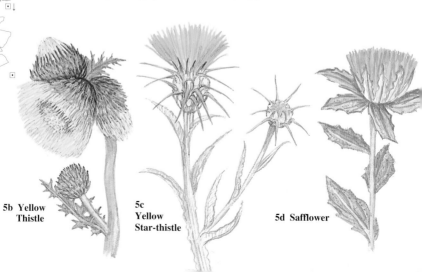

5b Yellow Thistle

5c Yellow Star-thistle

5d Safflower

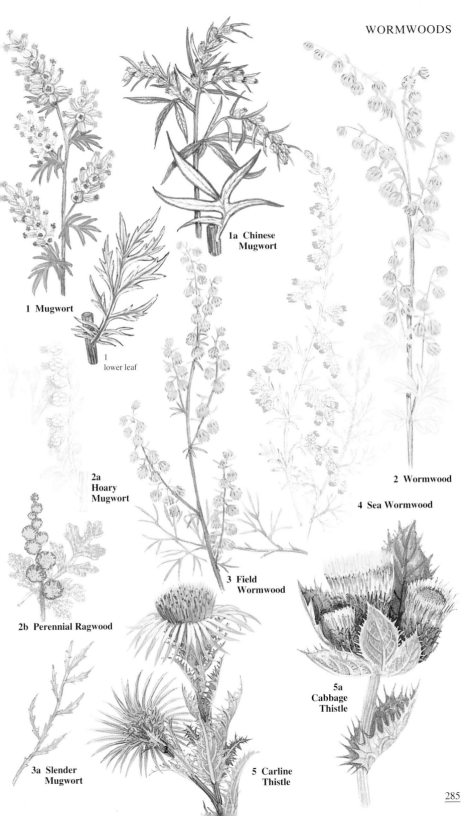

1 Mugwort

1 lower leaf

1a Chinese Mugwort

2a Hoary Mugwort

2b Perennial Ragwood

3 Field Wormwood

3a Slender Mugwort

5 Carline Thistle

5a Cabbage Thistle

2 Wormwood

4 Sea Wormwood

ray
floret

bract

Knapweeds *Centaurea*. Perennials with stiff downy stems. Flowers with disc florets only, but often with sterile outer ones enlarged and mimicking rays, the bracts with toothed or cut appendages. Leaves alternate.

Common Knapweed *Centaurea nigra* agg. Medium perennial, with very stiff ribbed stems, to 1m. Flowers brush-like, purple, rayed or not, 20-40mm, the bracts *pale brown* with blackish-brown appendages; June-Sept. Leaves *lanceolate*, the lower toothed. Grassy places. Aka Black Knapweed, Hardhead (from the hard globular buds). The aggregate has four forms, often locally quite distinct but linked by many intermediates. The rather stout **1 Common Knapweed** '*Centaurea nigra*' has two forms, the commoner unrayed and the less frequent rayed, both with the stem *markedly swollen* under the flower. The distinctly slenderer and more branched **1a Lesser Knapweed** '*C. nemoralis*', its stem scarcely swollen at the top, also has both a rayed and an unrayed form. The rayed form is locally frequent and later-flowering, and looks quite different from Common Knapweed. On rough or waste ground beware also surviving hybrids sharing the pale brown appendages of the almost extinct alien Brown Knapweed *C. jacea*. The grey-downy **Russian Knapweed** *Acroptilon repens* has pink flowers and has been established on waste ground at Hereford since 1959.

2 Greater Knapweed *Centaurea scabiosa*. Erect medium/tall perennial, to 1.2m. Flowers purple, *always rayed*, 30-50mm, with grey-green bracts and blackish-brown appendages; July-Sept. Leaves *pinnately lobed*, sometimes undivided on coastal cliffs. Grassy places, especially on lime.

~

3 Saw-wort *Serratula tinctoria*. Slender hairless short/medium perennial, with stiff stems to 70cm. Flowers purple with greenish-purple bracts, *smallish* (15-20mm), in loose clusters; July-Sept. Leaves lanceolate, very variably pinnately lobed, finely and sharply *saw-toothed*. Grassland, heaths, open woods, cliff-tops.

4 Alpine Saw-wort *Saussurea alpina*. A stout unbranched white-hairy short/medium perennial, to 45cm. Flowers purple, 15-20mm, solitary or in a compact terminal cluster; August-Sept. Leaves broad lanceolate, not or sharply toothed, *cottony white beneath*. Ledges on *mountain* and sea cliffs.

1 SOZ

2

3

4 OZ

Burdocks *Arctium*. Well branched medium/tall biennials, to 2m in shade. Flowers purple, in brush-like heads whose bracts end in hooked bristles, which remain in fruit to attach themselves to fur and clothing. Leaves large and broad, all except Greater Burdock (**5**) with *hollow stalks*. Many intermediates, including occasional Lesser/Greater hybrids, occur. Waysides, woods, waste and rough ground.

Florets longer than bracts:	Lesser		Bracts green:	Lesser, Wood
equalling bracts:	Lesser, Greater, Wood, Intermediate		purplish:	Lesser, Wood
shorter than bracts:	Lesser, Greater		yellowish:	Greater, Intermediate

The most distinctive is **5 Greater Burdock** *Arctium lappa*, differing from all the others in its *solid* leaf-stalks and flowers in a *flat-topped* cluster, with their stalks up to 10cm. The commonest is **5a Lesser Burdock** *A. minus* with flower-stalks very short, to 1cm, and florets sometimes sticky-downy. **5b Wood Burdock** *A. nemorosum* has flower-stalks very short, less than 1cm, and florets never sticky-downy. **5c Intermediate Burdock** *A. pubens* has flower-stalks 1-4cm.

5

5a SOZ

5b Wood Burdock

5c Intermediate Burdock

286

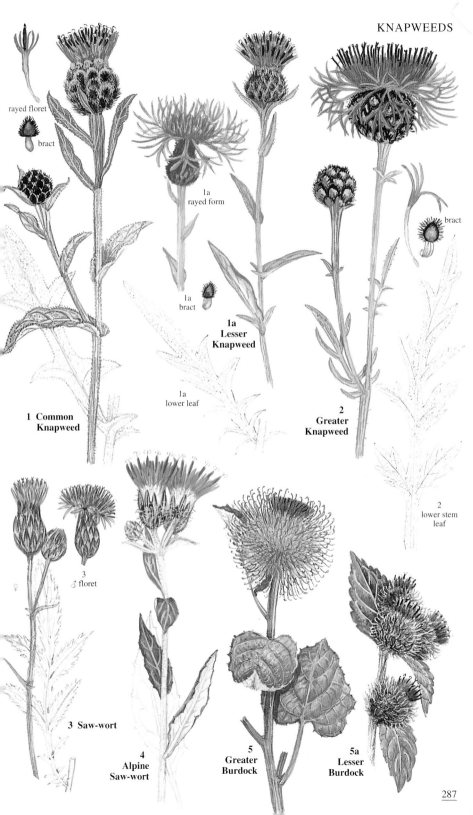

rayed floret

bract

1a
rayed form

1a
bract

1a
Lesser
Knapweed

1a
lower leaf

1 Common
Knapweed

bract

2
Greater
Knapweed

2
lower stem
leaf

♀

3
♂ floret

3 Saw-wort

4
Alpine
Saw-wort

5
Greater
Burdock

5a
Lesser
Burdock

1 Butterbur *Petasites hybridus*. A patch-forming perennial. Flowers *lilac-pink*, male (7-12mm) and female (3-6mm) on separate plants, *not fragrant*, in spikes on stems with many strap-shaped bracts, to 40cm, elongating in fruit to 80cm; March-May, *before* the leaves. Leaves huge, up to 1m across and 1.5m tall, *rhubarb-like*, heart-shaped, toothed, green above and grey-downy beneath. Wet ground, by streams and ditches, road verges, damp copses. Female plants very localised, in N Central England, from Lancashire to Lincolnshire. **1a Giant Butterbur** *P. japonicus* has fragrant *creamy-white* flowers, whose dense branched cluster when young is framed by broad green bracts up the stem, looking like a small cauliflower; later it elongates to 1m; Feb-April, before the leaves, which are green on both sides. Well established. **1b White Butterbur** *P. albus* has fragrant *pure white* flowers and leaves on shaggy stalks, downy-white beneath. Increasing alien, especially in E Scotland.

2 Winter Heliotrope *Petasites fragrans*. A patch-forming perennial, with leaves and flower-spikes both much shorter than Butterbur (**1**), to 30cm. Flowers lilac, like male Butterbur but housing both sexes, *fragrant* with a vanilla or heliotrope scent; *Nov-March*. Leaves much *smaller and rounder*, to 20cm, present throughout the year in the S and W, sometimes without flowers even in winter. Well established on waysides and hedge-banks.

3 ***Purple Coltsfoot *Homogyne alpina*. Short perennial, to 35cm. Flowers purple, rayless, solitary, 10-15mm; May-July. Leaves kidney-shaped, leathery, to 40mm across. One site in the high Clova mountains of Angus, first found *c.* 1800, but may have been planted; refound 1951.

4 Hemp Agrimony *Eupatorium cannabinum*. Tall perennial, to 1.5m; stems often reddish. Flowers small, in dense trusses, more like Common Valerian (p. 260) than a Composite, rayless, with 5-6 loose pale to darker pink-purple florets, with long white styles and long purple-tipped sepal-like bracts; July-Sept. Leaves palmate with lanceolate segments, the upper undivided. Damp woods, fens, by fresh water; sometimes in drier places.

2d. Brush-like/Thistle-type: Flowers purple, spiny

Thistles *Cirsium* and *Carduus*. Little-branched biennials/perennials, notoriously spiny, often sharply so, but also with many softer spines. Flowers brush-like, usually purple. Leaves usually pinnate or pinnately lobed and spiny. Pappus (thistledown) of feathery hairs in *Cirsium* and simple hairs in *Carduus*. Hybrids are not infrequent.

Stems	spiny:	Spear, Marsh, Welted (below), Musk, Slender, Plymouth, Cotton
	spineless:	Creeping, Welted (above), Dwarf, Woolly, Melancholy, Meadow, Tuberous, Milk
	none:	Dwarf
Leaves	white/grey beneath:	Creeping, Welted, Slender, Plymouth, Woolly, Melancholy, Meadow, Cotton
	green beneath:	Creeping, Spear, Marsh, Dwarf, Musk, Tuberous, Milk

5 Creeping Thistle *Cirsium arvense*. One of our two commonest thistles, and the only one with fragrant *lilac* or pale purple flowers; medium/tall erect perennial, to 2m or more, with a *creeping* rootstock. Flowers 10-20mm, sometimes all female, bracts purplish-green and scarcely spiny; in terminal clusters; June-Oct. Leaves variably lobed, sometimes cottony beneath, only shortly running down on to the *spineless* stems. Grassy and waste places, waysides.

6 Spear Thistle *Cirsium vulgare*. Our commonest large-flowered thistle, a tall stout biennial, with *spiny-winged stems*, to 1.5m. Flowers purple, *20-40mm*, often solitary, the bracts with *yellow-tipped* spines; July-Sept. Leaves pinnately lobed and spiny. Grassy and waste places, waysides.

1a
× 1

1a
Giant
Butterbur

1

1 ♂ ♀
× 2

1 Butterbur

× 2
♂ ♀

1b White
Butterbur

× ¼

3 Purple
Coltsfoot

4
p of leaf

× 1

2 Winter
Heliotrope

2

Hemp
Agrimony

4
× 1/12

5
Creeping
Thistle

6
Spear
Thistle

× ½

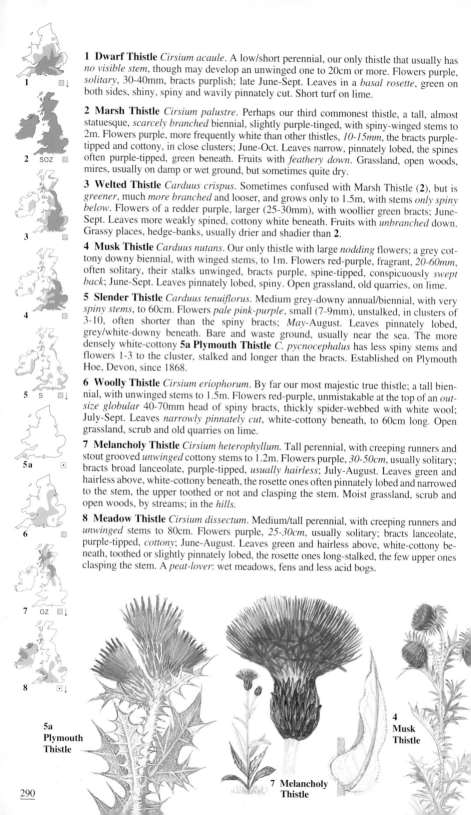

1 Dwarf Thistle *Cirsium acaule*. A low/short perennial, our only thistle that usually has *no visible stem*, though may develop an unwinged one to 20cm or more. Flowers purple, *solitary*, 30-40mm, bracts purplish; late June-Sept. Leaves in a *basal rosette*, green on both sides, shiny, spiny and wavily pinnately cut. Short turf on lime.

2 Marsh Thistle *Cirsium palustre*. Perhaps our third commonest thistle, a tall, almost statuesque, *scarcely branched* biennial, slightly purple-tinged, with spiny-winged stems to 2m. Flowers purple, more frequently white than other thistles, *10-15mm*, the bracts purple-tipped and cottony, in close clusters; June-Oct. Leaves narrow, pinnately lobed, the spines often purple-tipped, green beneath. Fruits with *feathery down*. Grassland, open woods, mires, usually on damp or wet ground, but sometimes quite dry.

3 Welted Thistle *Carduus crispus*. Sometimes confused with Marsh Thistle (**2**), but is *greener*, much *more branched* and looser, and grows only to 1.5m, with stems *only spiny below*. Flowers of a redder purple, larger (25-30mm), with woollier green bracts; June-Sept. Leaves more weakly spined, cottony white beneath. Fruits with *unbranched* down. Grassy places, hedge-banks, usually drier and shadier than **2**.

4 Musk Thistle *Carduus nutans*. Our only thistle with large *nodding* flowers; a grey cottony downy biennial, with winged stems, to 1m. Flowers red-purple, fragrant, *20-60mm*, often solitary, their stalks unwinged, bracts purple, spine-tipped, conspicuously *swept back*; June-Sept. Leaves pinnately lobed, spiny. Open grassland, old quarries, on lime.

5 Slender Thistle *Carduus tenuiflorus*. Medium grey-downy annual/biennial, with very *spiny stems*, to 60cm. Flowers *pale pink-purple*, small (7-9mm), unstalked, in clusters of 3-10, often shorter than the spiny bracts; *May*-August. Leaves pinnately lobed, grey/white-downy beneath. Bare and waste ground, usually near the sea. The more densely white-cottony **5a Plymouth Thistle** *C. pycnocephalus* has less spiny stems and flowers 1-3 to the cluster, stalked and longer than the bracts. Established on Plymouth Hoe, Devon, since 1868.

6 Woolly Thistle *Cirsium eriophorum*. By far our most majestic true thistle; a tall biennial, with unwinged stems to 1.5m. Flowers red-purple, unmistakable at the top of an *out-size globular* 40-70mm head of spiny bracts, thickly spider-webbed with white wool; July-Sept. Leaves *narrowly pinnately cut*, white-cottony beneath, to 60cm long. Open grassland, scrub and old quarries on lime.

7 Melancholy Thistle *Cirsium heterophyllum*. Tall perennial, with creeping runners and stout grooved *unwinged* cottony stems to 1.2m. Flowers purple, *30-50cm*, usually solitary; bracts broad lanceolate, purple-tipped, *usually hairless*; July-August. Leaves green and hairless above, white-cottony beneath, the rosette ones often pinnately lobed and narrowed to the stem, the upper toothed or not and clasping the stem. Moist grassland, scrub and open woods, by streams; in the *hills*.

8 Meadow Thistle *Cirsium dissectum*. Medium/tall perennial, with creeping runners and unwinged stems to 80cm. Flowers purple, *25-30cm*, usually solitary; bracts lanceolate, purple-tipped, *cottony*; June-August. Leaves green and hairless above, white-cottony beneath, toothed or slightly pinnately lobed, the rosette ones long-stalked, the few upper ones clasping the stem. A *peat-lover*: wet meadows, fens and less acid bogs.

5a
Plymouth
Thistle

7 Melancholy
Thistle

4
Musk
Thistle

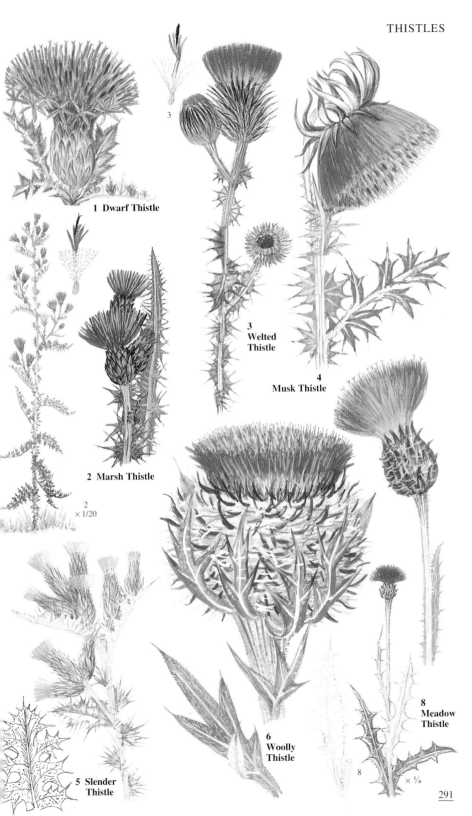

1 Dwarf Thistle

3

2 Marsh Thistle

2
× 1/20

3 Welted Thistle

4 Musk Thistle

5 Slender Thistle

6 Woolly Thistle

8 Meadow Thistle

8
× ¼

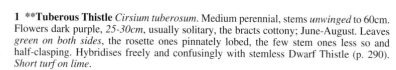

1 **Tuberous Thistle *Cirsium tuberosum.* Medium perennial, stems *unwinged* to 60cm. Flowers dark purple, *25-30cm*, usually solitary, the bracts cottony; June-August. Leaves *green on both sides*, the rosette ones pinnately lobed, the few stem ones less so and half-clasping. Hybridises freely and confusingly with stemless Dwarf Thistle (p. 290). *Short turf on lime.*

2 Milk Thistle *Silybum marianum.* Our only thistle whose leaves usually have conspicuous *white veins* above; a stout medium/tall annual/biennial, with unwinged stems to 1m. Flowers purple, solitary, 40-50mm, the lower bracts with long *sharp yellow spines*; June-August. Long naturalised in bare and sparsely grassy places, often on the coast.

3 Cotton Thistle *Onopordum acanthium.* Our tallest and most striking thistle, with all its stems *stoutly winged* and triangular-spined; a huge branched biennial *covered all over* with cottony white down, to 2.5m. Flowers pale purple, 20-60mm, solitary, guarded by ferociously spiny bracts; July-Sept. Leaves oblong, very spiny. Bare and sparsely grassy ground, waysides, probably native in the E Anglian Breckland, but a widespread garden escape elsewhere.

4 Red Star-thistle *Centaurea calcitrapa.* A medium, well branched biennial, to 60cm. Flowers pale purple, 8-10mm, with stout *yellow spiny* bracts; July-Sept. Leaves *greyish*, pinnately lobed, spine-tipped. Bare places, established on the Sussex coast since 1765 and at Chatham, Kent, since 1839.

2e. Brush-like/Thistle-type: Flowers blue

Globe-thistles *Echinops.* Tall perennials, 2m. Flowers bluish, in 30-60mm globular heads; July-August. Leaves pinnately lobed, weakly spined, grey/white-downy beneath. Frequent garden escapes on roadsides, railway banks and other waste places.

5 Blue Globe-thistle *Echinops bannaticus*, the most frequent, has pale blue flowers and sticky glands only on upper leaf-surfaces. **5a Globe-thistle** *E. exaltatus* has white or greyish flowers, strongly recurved bracts, and no glandular hairs. **5b Glandular Globe-thistle** *E. sphaerocephalon*, perhaps the least frequent, has greyish flowers and bracts with many stalked glands.

~

6 Cornflower *Centaurea cyanus.* A grey downy medium/tall annual, to 80cm. Flowers *blue*, with ray-like enlarged outer florets, 15-30mm; June-August. Leaves pinnately lobed, the upper narrow lanceolate. Formerly a colourful cornfield weed, but now much more often originating from 'wildflower' seed mixtures or gardens.

7 Perennial Cornflower *Centaurea montana.* Medium clump-forming perennial, to 80cm. Flowers blue, rayed, *much larger* (60-80mm) than Cornflower (**6**); May-July. Leaves lanceolate. A frequent garden escape.

2f. Brush-like/Thistle-type: Flowers white or green

8 Rough Cocklebur *Xanthium strumarium.* Medium, often pungent spineless annual, to 1m. Flowers green, the 5-8mm *globular* male, with reddish anthers, and the larger *egg-shaped* female on the same plant; July-Oct. Leaves shallowly palmately lobed. Mainly a casual, but frequent on the S Thames shore below London. Two other, spiny, species are casuals.

Giant and **White Butterburs**, p. 288.

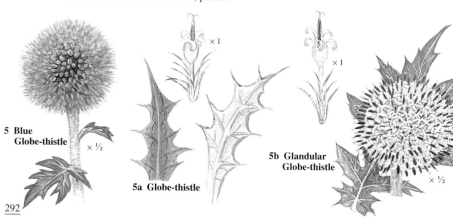

5 Blue Globe-thistle × ½

× 1

× 1

5a Globe-thistle

5b Glandular Globe-thistle

× ½

292

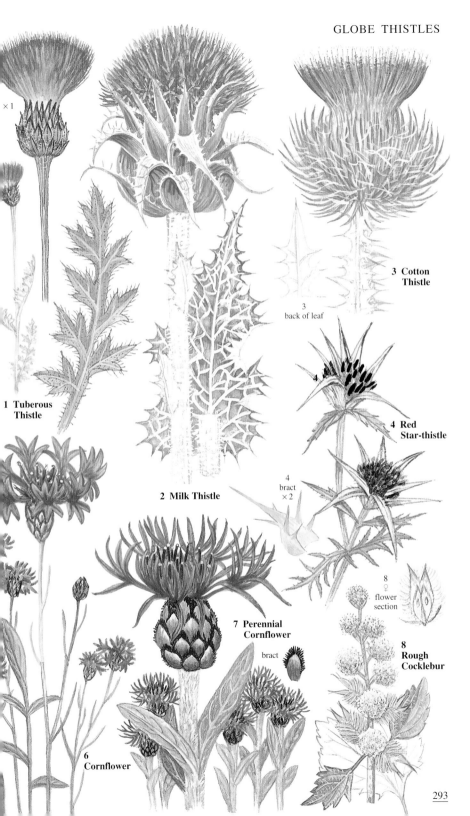

× 1

1 **Tuberous Thistle**

2 **Milk Thistle**

3 **Cotton Thistle**

3
back of leaf

4

4 **Red Star-thistle**

4
bract
× 2

6 **Cornflower**

7 **Perennial Cornflower**

bract

8
♀
flower section

8 **Rough Cocklebur**

3. Dandelion-type flowers:
   3a. Flowers yellow (below).
   3b. Flowers blue/purple/lilac (p. 304)

~

3a. Dandelion-type: Flowers yellow

Stems with milky juice:		Dandelion, Goatsbeard, Viper's Grass, Sow-thistles, Lettuces
Flowering stems leafless:		Dandelion, Catsears, Hawkbits, some Hawkweeds, Mouse-ear Hawkweeds
Runners:		Mouse-ear Hawkweeds, Fox-and-Cubs
Leaves	grass-like:	Goatsbeard
	pimply:	Bristly Ox-tongue
	prickly:	Prickly/Great Lettuces
Flowers	orange:	Fox-and-Cubs

Dandelion. *Taraxacum officinale*. A group of some 240-250 diverse short perennials to 20cm, some very common, some quite rare, the great majority difficult for the non-expert to distinguish. All have *milky juice* in their *hollow leafless* flower-stalks and a rosette of basal leaves, sometimes with dark blotches and usually lobed, those with large lobes like a lion's tooth having given rise to the name. Flowers yellow, the outer rays often reddish on the back, 15-75mm. Fruits with a beak, topped by a non-feathery spreading pappus, and making the well known 'dandelion clock'. They can be divided into nine sections. The two most frequent and distinctive are:

1 Section *Ruderalia*. The very variable, often large and coarse common Dandelions of grassy fields, waysides and waste places. Flowers large (25-75mm), making a golden blaze in spring meadows; bracts usually down-turned; *Jan-Dec*. Fruits usually grey-brown. 121 species, some introduced.

2 Section *Erythrosperma*. Generally our smallest and slenderest dandelions, with flowers often pale yellow, small (15-35mm), April-June, and fruits often reddish; preferring warm dry sunny habitats, such as chalk grassland, heaths and dunes. 30 species.

The other sections are: ***Celtica***, 35 species of damp meadows and other semi-natural habitats, with flowers 15-50mm, their stalks and leaf-midribs red or purple; ***Hamata***, 18 'weedy' species with flowers 30-55mm and leaves hooked at the tip; ***Naevosa***, 12 northern/western species with flowers 25-60mm and leaves with many large dark spots; ***Taraxacum***, six high mountain species with flowers 30-45mm and bright green leaves; **3** ***Palustria***, four fen species with flowers 25-40mm, June-(July), the bracts appressed and pale-bordered; **4 *Spectabilia***, three species of damp, usually acid places, mainly in the hills, with flowers 35-55mm, June-July; and leaves often unlobed; and ***Obliqua***, two coastal species, like *Erythrosperma* (**2**) but flowers deep or orange-yellow, 10-25mm, with grey-brown fruits.

~

5 Goatsbeard *Tragopogon pratensis*. Our only dandelion-type flower with *grass-like* leaves; a greyish, little branched, medium perennial, to 75cm, with milky juice. Flowers yellow, 18-30mm (if larger, probably an alien subspecies), the florets usually markedly *shorter* than the long pointed bracts; often only opening in the mornings (whence the folk-name Jack-go-to-bed-at-noon); May-August. Fruits beaked, pappuses forming a conspicuous clock. Grassy places.

6 ***Viper's Grass *Scorzonera humilis*. An almost hairless, pale green, short/medium perennial, to 50cm, with milky juice. Flowers lemon-yellow, 20-30cm, distinguished from Goatsbeard (**5**) by their *short*, pale green bracts; May-July. Leaves lanceolate, untoothed, *narrowing* up the stem to become like the bracts of Catsears (p. 296). Fruits not beaked, pappus whitish. Two meadows, in Dorset and S Wales.

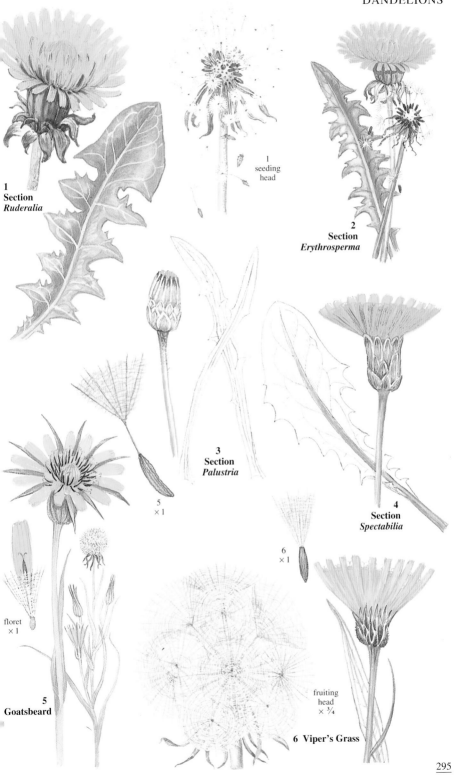

1
Section
Ruderalia

1
seeding
head

2
Section
Erythrosperma

3
Section
Palustria

5
× 1

4
Section
Spectabilia

6
× 1

floret
× 1

5
Goatsbeard

fruiting
head
× ¾

6 Viper's Grass

The Hawkish Complex. Hawkbits, hawksbeards and hawkweeds, together with the closely allied catsears and ox-tongues, form the core of the problems many people have with dandelion-type flowers. Part of the trouble is the confusing similarity of their seemingly irrelevant English names. The hawk connection dates back to Ancient Greek folklore. None of them have milky juice like dandelions (p. 294), but two catsears, all hawkbits and the very rare Leafless Hawksbeard share their leafless stems. The rest, including sometimes the uncommon Spotted Catsear, have leafy stems. *Hawksbeards* (p. 298) can always be told by their sepal-like bracts, and *catsears* (p. 296) by the chaffy scales among their florets. The commonest species are Catsear, Autumn and Rough Hawkbits, Smooth and Beaked Hawksbeards and Mouse-ear Hawkweed.

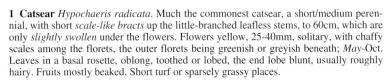

1 Catsear *Hypochaeris radicata*. Much the commonest catsear, a short/medium perennial, with short *scale-like bracts* up the little-branched leafless stems, to 60cm, which are only *slightly swollen* under the flowers. Flowers yellow, 25-40mm, solitary, with chaffy scales among the florets, the outer florets being greenish or greyish beneath; *May*-Oct. Leaves in a basal rosette, oblong, toothed or lobed, the end lobe blunt, usually roughly hairy. Fruits mostly beaked. Short turf or sparsely grassy places.

1   soz   □

2 Autumn Hawkbit *Leontodon autumnalis*. The commonest hawkbit, a variable short, often sprawling perennial, to 60cm, not unlike Catsear (**1**), but usually shorter, and with most of the scale-like bracts at the much *more swollen* top of the stem. Flowers usually smaller (12-35mm), with no chaffy scales, the outer florets usually reddish beneath; in loose clusters; *July*-Oct. Leaves distinctly more *sharply* tipped and with much *sharper* lobes. Fruits not beaked. Habitat similar, but sometimes damper.

2   soz   □↑

3 Rough Hawkbit *Leontodon hispidus*. Short perennial, with stems *very hairy*, without leaves but sometimes with 1-2 tiny bracts, slightly swollen at the top, to 60cm. Flowers golden-yellow, 25-40mm, solitary, the outer florets often reddish/orange, the bracts *very shaggy*; late May-Oct. Leaves in a basal rosette, bluntly lobed. Pappuses making a dandelion-like clock. Grassland, especially on lime.

3   □

4 Lesser Hawkbit *Leontodon saxatilis*. Low/short perennial, with leafless, bractless and only sparsely hairy stems, scarcely swollen at the top, to 40cm. Flowers yellow, *12-20mm*, solitary, the outer florets *greyish-purple* beneath; June-Oct. Leaves in a basal rosette, rather bluntly lobed. Dry grassy turf, dunes.

4   s   □

5 Smooth Catsear *Hypochaeris glabra*. A low, somewhat sprawling annual, stems with a few bracts, to 40cm. Flowers yellow, 5-15mm, solitary, inconspicuous because opening widely only in *full sun*, the florets about equalling the bracts; June-Oct. Leaves shiny, almost *hairless*. Grassy places, mainly on *sand*.

6 Spotted Catsear *Hypochaeris maculata*. Stout, short/medium, roughly hairy, usually unbranched perennial, to 60cm. Flowers pale yellow, 30-45mm, solitary, with shaggy, sometimes black-tipped bracts; June-August. Leaves in a basal rosette, well toothed, with a reddish midrib and usually heavily *blotched* with purplish-black; the only catsear or hawkbit to have sometimes a few *leaves on the stem*. Limy turf inland, also on sea cliffs.

5   □↓

7 Nipplewort *Lapsana communis*. A rather shaggy, medium/tall annual, to 1m. Flowers yellow, *small*, usually 15-20mm, sometimes to 30mm, with very short outer bracts, on long slender stalks in open clusters; June-Oct. Leaves pointed oval, toothed, usually lobed at the base. Disturbed ground, also often in half-shade in open woods and on hedge-banks.

6   □↓

Fruits of Hawkbits and Catsears

all × 1

7   soz   □

1   2   3   4   5 outer fruit / inner fruit   6   7

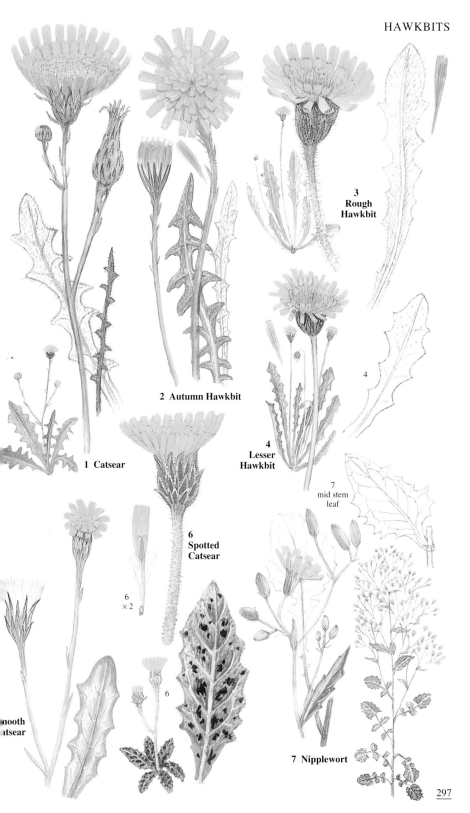

**3
Rough
Hawkbit**

4

2 Autumn Hawkbit

**4
Lesser
Hawkbit**

1 Catsear

7
mid stem
leaf

**6
Spotted
Catsear**

6
× 2

6

mooth
atsear

7 Nipplewort

Hawksbeards *Crepis* are readily distinguished, especially from hawkweeds (p. 300), by their sepal-like bracts, with one conspicuously erect row above another much smaller and half-spreading. Flowers in clusters. Fruits not beaked, except Beaked and Stinking Hawksbeards (**2, 7**). Three more species occur as casuals. Cf. Hawkweed Oxtongue (p. 300).

1 Smooth Hawksbeard *Crepis capillaris*. Generally the commonest hawksbeard, a rather variable, branched, erect or sprawling, sometimes stickily hairy, *short*/medium annual/biennial, to 75cm. Flowers yellow, the outer florets often reddish on the back, small, 10-15mm, on rather slender stalks; June-Dec, the *latest* of the group to last into the winter. Leaves usually shiny, lobed or toothed, mostly basal, but a few clasping the stem. Grassy and waste places, path-sides.

2 Beaked Hawksbeard *Crepis vesicaria*. A stout erect downy medium/tall perennial, to 80cm. Flowers yellow, the outer florets usually orange beneath, *15-25mm*; May-July. Leaves sharply pinnately lobed, half-clasping the often reddish stem. Fruits *long-beaked*. Established since 1713 and still spreading N, in waste places and on waysides and walls.

3 Rough Hawksbeard *Crepis biennis*. Downier, more robust and branched above and usually *taller*, to 1.2m, with a less reddish stem, than the much commoner Beaked Hawksbeard (**2**). Flowers usually *larger*, 20-35mm, and fewer in the cluster; June-July. Leaves similar. Fruits *not beaked*. Road verges and other rough grassy places, often on lime.

4 Marsh Hawksbeard *Crepis paludosa*. Medium/tall, almost hairless perennial, to 80cm, very like one of the leafier Hawkweeds (p. 300). Flowers of a distinctive hard dull *orange-yellow*, the styles greenish-black, 15-25mm; June-Sept. Leaves yellow-green, usually shiny, sharply toothed, clasping the stem with downward-pointing bases. Pappus *yellowish- or brownish-white*. Damp and wet, usually grassy, places, mainly in the hills.

5 *Northern Hawksbeard *Crepis mollis*. Another Hawkweed-like perennial, usually shorter than the much more frequent Marsh Hawksbeard (**4**), to 60cm, and having *larger* (20-30mm) flowers, leaves *not or scarcely toothed*, and pappus *pure white*. Similar but somewhat drier places.

6 ***Leafless Hawksbeard *Crepis praemorsa*. One of our two rarest hawksbeards, a slightly downy medium perennial, to 60cm. Flowers yellow, 15-18mm, with *hairless* bracts, a few in a closer cluster than other Hawksbeards; May-July. Leaves *scarcely* toothed, *none* on the stems. A group of limestone banks in Westmorland.

7 Stinking Hawksbeard *Crepis foetida*. Medium annual/biennial, smelling strongly of *bitter almonds*, to 60cm. Flowers golden-yellow, 15-20mm, *drooping in bud*; June-August. Leaves very hairy, the basal with a large diamond-shaped end-lobe, the upper sharply toothed and clasping the stem. Fruits *beaked*, the inner long, the outer short, the pappuses strikingly white. Extinct since 1980 but reintroduced on the Dungeness shingle, Kent.

~

8 Bristly Oxtongue *Picris echioides*. One of our most distinctive dandelion-type flowers, its leaves *pimply* with the large pale swollen bases of the bristles. Medium annual/biennial, bristly, almost prickly, all over, to 80cm. Flowers pale yellow, 20-25mm, in rather tight clusters, with broad triangular half-spreading outer bracts; June-Nov. Fruit long-beaked. Rough grassy places, especially on clay and near the sea.

1 soz ▢↑

2 s ▢↑

3 ▢

4 ▫

5 ▫↓↓

6 ▢

7 ▫

8 s ▢

Fruits of Hawksbeards

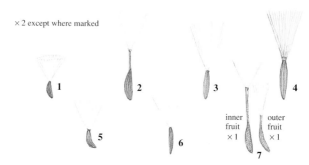

× 2 except where marked

1   2   3   4

5   6

inner fruit × 1   outer fruit × 1

7

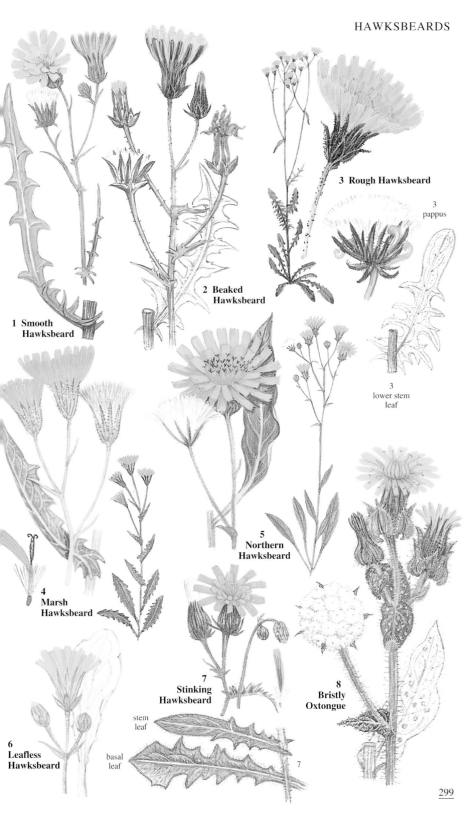

3 Rough Hawksbeard

3
pappus

**2 Beaked
Hawksbeard**

**1 Smooth
Hawksbeard**

3
lower stem
leaf

**5
Northern
Hawksbeard**

**4
Marsh
Hawksbeard**

**7
Stinking
Hawksbeard**

**8
Bristly
Oxtongue**

stem
leaf

**6
Leafless
Hawksbeard**

basal
leaf

7

Hawkweeds *Hieracium*. Short/tall hairy/downy perennials, to 1m. Flowers yellow with several rows of sepal-like bracts (unlike hawksbeards, p. 298). Leaves alternate, broad to narrow lanceolate, usually toothed and never lobed, up the stems and/or in a basal rosette; with dark purplish blotches in a few species. Fruits not beaked, with a non-feathery pale brown pappus. Dry grassy and heathy places, often on walls and mountain rocks. With the brambles (p. 126) and dandelions (p. 294) they are our three most difficult plant groups to identify. Experts recognise some 260 microspecies in 15 sections, some of them introduced, with stickily hairy leaves clasping the stem, often on old garden walls. Here we reduce them to three groups, based on the number of stem leaves: leafy, few-leaved and basal-leaved, and even then the boundaries between the three overlap. Cf. Hawkweed Oxtongue (**4**).

1 s

Leafy Hawkweeds are medium/tall, to 1.2m. Leaves 6-50, any basal ones withering early. Flowers 20-30mm, in more or less flat-topped clusters; July-Sept. Our most distinctive hawkweed is the tall, softly hairy **1 Narrow-leaved Hawkweed** *Hieracium umbellatum*, to *c.* 80cm, with many very narrow strap-like leaves and hairless recurved blackish-green sepal-like bracts; dry heathy places. Two other frequent softly hairy species with more open clusters and somewhat fewer and much broader leaves, rounded at the base, are the southern **1a** *H. sabaudum* with stiff white hairs at the base of the stem and **1b** *H. vagum*, the urban hawkweed of N England.

1a

Few-leaved Hawkweeds, the most numerous group, have up to 10 more or less lanceolate leaves, the basal ones sometimes surviving. Flowers 20-30mm, fewer in the cluster, the bracts often stickily hairy; May-July. **2 Spotted Hawkweed** *Hieracium maculatum*, with short dark gland-tipped bracts and 2-3 stem-leaves, is the most frequent dark-blotched species.

Basal-leaved Hawkweeds can be quite short, to 20-30cm, and have fewer and larger (25-35mm) flowers, some with incurving blackish bracts, May-Sept; and at most one leaf on the stem, the basal leaves always surviving. Cliffs and rocks on hills and mountains, especially in Scotland, where curiously the most frequent hawkweed, with unusually one, slightly clasping, stem-leaf, and pale yellow flowers is named **3** *Hieracium anglicum*.

~

4

4 Hawkweed Oxtongue *Picris hieracioides*. One of our most hawkweedlike non-hawkweeds, a roughly hairy, medium/tall biennial/perennial, with lower stem often reddish, to 1m; Differing from all hawkweeds (above) and most hawksbeards (p. 298) in being *branched*, often at right angles, and having *wavy-edged* lanceolate leaves. Flowers yellow, 20-35mm, with narrow bracts, the outer row short and *recurved*; July-Oct. Fruits short-beaked, pappus creamy. Grassland, usually on lime.

5 oz

5 Fox-and-cubs *Pilosella aurantiaca*. A short/medium perennial, densely covered with blackish hairs, to 40cm; with long leafy runners. Flowers *orange* or brownish, paler in the centre, in close clusters, 13-15mm; June-Sept. Leaves lanceolate, in a rosette and a few up the stems. Two other established escapes, especially on railway banks, are: **5a Yellow Fox-and-cubs** *P. caespitosa*, taller, to 50cm, with pale hairs, *yellow* flowers and *glaucous* leaves; and the very similar **5b Tall Mouse-ear Hawkweed** *P. praealta*, which is taller, to 65cm, and has green leaves.

6 soz

6 Mouse-ear Hawkweed *Pilosella officinarum*. Low/short perennial, shaggy with *white* hairs, to 30cm; producing runners with *small distant* leaves. Flowers lemon-yellow, the outer florets reddish beneath, *solitary*, 20-30mm, in turf with blackish hairs; May-Oct. Leaves elliptical, white-felted beneath. Short turf, dunes and sparsely grassy places, often on lime. **6a Shaggy Mouse-ear Hawkweed** *P. peleteriana* has its runners, if any, ending in a *rosette*, its flowers sometimes larger and its leaves more pointed.

6a

7 ***Shetland Mouse-ear Hawkweed *Pilosella flagellaris*. Unlike Mouse-ear Hawkweed (**6**), has *leafy* runners and *two flowers* together at the top of the stalk. Rocky places in Shetland. Cultivated forms with 2-4 flowers together often escape and are sometimes established, as on railway banks near Edinburgh.

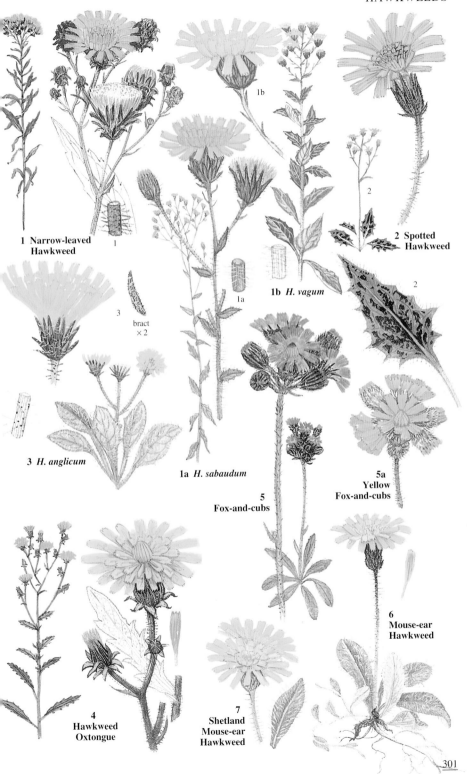

1 Narrow-leaved Hawkweed

1

1b *H. vagum*

1a

1a *H. sabaudum*

2 Spotted Hawkweed

2

2

3

bract ×2

3 *H. anglicum*

5 Fox-and-cubs

5a Yellow Fox-and-cubs

6 Mouse-ear Hawkweed

4 Hawkweed Oxtongue

7 Shetland Mouse-ear Hawkweed

1 Smooth Sow-thistle *Sonchus oleraceus.* Somewhat the commoner of our two smaller and variable sow-thistles, a greyish hairless short/medium annual/biennial, to 2m or more, with milky juice. Flowers usually a rather pale yellow, 20-25mm, in clusters; April-Nov, and through mild winters. Leaves weakly spiny, more or less pinnately lobed, clasping the stem with *pointed* auricles. Disturbed ground.

2 Rough Sow-thistle *Sonchus asper.* So like Smooth Sow-thistle (**1**), that almost its only reliable distinction is the *rounded* auricles of its leaves. However, also tends to have deeper yellow flowers, perhaps less often seen in winter, and leaves more often unlobed and more sharply pointed. In some districts may prefer limy soils.

3 Corn Sow-thistle *Sonchus arvensis.* Tall creeping perennial, to 1.5m, with milky juice. Flowers *deep* yellow, *large* and showy, 40-50mm, the olive-green bracts covered in sticky *yellow* hairs, in open clusters; July-Sept. Leaves greyish beneath, lanceolate, pinnately lobed, with softly spiny teeth, clasping the stem with rounded auricles. Disturbed and other bare ground, once a frequent arable weed.

4 *Marsh Sow-thistle *Sonchus palustris.* Not unlike a giant Smooth Sow-thistle (**1**), a *very tall*, greyish, stickily hairy perennial, to 2.5m, with milky juice. Flowers pale yellow, 30-40mm, with sticky *olive-green* hairs on the bracts, in rather dense clusters; July-Sept. Leaves narrow, untoothed, with sharply pointed lobes, clasping the stem with *pointed* auricles. *Fens, reed-beds.*

5 Prickly Lettuce *Lactuca serriola.* A tall hairless, slightly foetid, biennial, with stems *whitish* (often reddish below) and prickly, to 2m, and milky juice – seeming very unlettucelike, because so few Garden Lettuces (below) are allowed to 'bolt'. Flowers pale yellow, often tinged purple, rather small (11-13mm), with bracts often purple-tinged, in loose clusters; July-Sept. Leaves greyish, un- or pinnately lobed, weakly spiny, with sharper *prickles on the midrib* beneath, the upper clasping the stem. In the sun the upper leaves twist round to hold their margins upright, whence the name of Compass Plant. Fruits *pale brown* with a pale beak. Increasing in disturbed and waste ground. **Garden Lettuce** *L. sativa,* on abandoned allotments and elsewhere, is shorter, to 75cm, and not foetid or prickly, with leaves often unlobed and untoothed and fruits grey-brown with a white beak.

6 Great Lettuce *Lactuca virosa.* Darker green, more widely branched and distinctly *stouter* than Prickly Lettuce (**5**), with stems *tinged purple.* Flowers *greenish*-yellow and slightly smaller (9-11mm), the bracts *white-edged* and red-tipped. Leaves larger, *wavy-edged*, often purple-tinged, less lobed and prickly and more horizontal. Fruits *dark purple* with a white beak. Increasing in similar places, especially near the sea.

7 ***Least Lettuce *Lactuca saligna.* Smaller (to 75mm) and slenderer than Prickly Lettuce (**5**) – though beware of small starved specimens of this – *not prickly* and often prostrate at the base. Flowers yellow, 9-11mm, the bracts tipped green, in *slender stalked spikes*; July-August. Lower leaves pinnately lobed, the upper narrow, untoothed, usually held with margins upright, clasping the stem with arrow-shaped auricles. Fruits *grey-green* with a white beak. Two seawalls in Essex and on shingle in Sussex.

8 Wall Lettuce *Mycelis muralis.* A slender hairless, often *purplish* perennial, short/medium, to at least 1.5m, with milky juice. Flowers yellow, 7-8mm, each with *c.* 5 rather *broad* florets, in a loose cluster; June-Sept. Leaves pinnately lobed, the end lobe large and *triangular*, the upper clasping the stem with blunt lobes. Fruits shortly beaked. Walls, rocks, shady banks and woodland edges, often on lime.

1 SOZ

2 SOZ

3 SOZ

4

5

6

7

8

× 1/25

fruiting head

mid-stem leaf

4 Marsh Sow-thistle

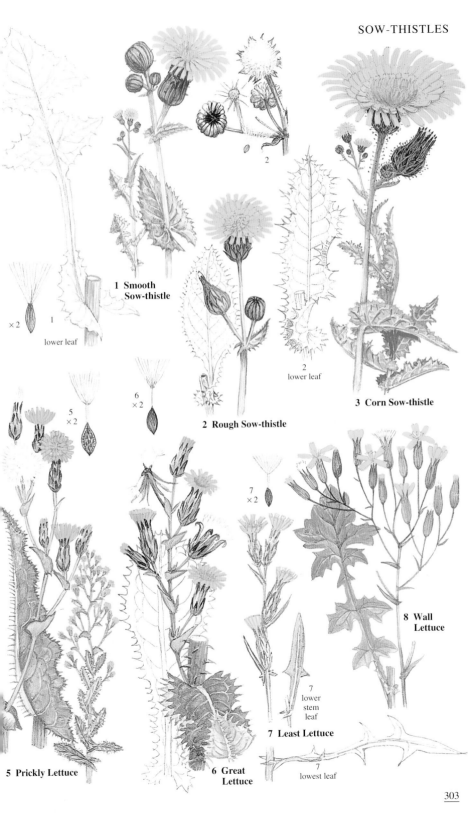

×2

1
lower leaf

1 Smooth Sow-thistle

2

2
lower leaf

3 Corn Sow-thistle

5
×2

6
×2

2 Rough Sow-thistle

7
×2

7
lower
stem
leaf

8 Wall Lettuce

7 Least Lettuce

7
lowest leaf

5 Prickly Lettuce

6 Great Lettuce

1 Chicory *Cichorium intybus*. Our only common native blue dandelion-type flower, a stiff perennial, to 1m. Flowers *clear blue*, 25-40mm, unstalked, scattered up the stem; June-Sept. Leaves unstalked, lanceolate, only the lower pinnately lobed. Aka Succory. Young shoots can be used as salad. Roadsides, rough grassy or waste places, especially on lime.

2 Salsify *Tragopogon porrifolius*. A tall biennial, to 1.2m, with milky juice. Flowers and leaves like those of Goatsbeard (p. 294), but flowers larger and *dull purple*, 30-50mm; June-August. Garden outcast or relic, grassy and waste places, often by the sea; increasing as people start eating its root again.

Blue Sow-thistles *Cicerbita*. Medium/tall perennials, to 1-2m, with milky juice. Flowers blue to lilac; June-Sept. Leaves pinnately lobed with a much larger end lobe. Pappus whitish or yellowish.

3 **Alpine Blue Sow-thistle *Cicerbita alpina*, our only native, has flowers *pale blue*, 18-22mm, and the end leaf-lobe sharply triangular. A very few *high mountain ledges* in E Scotland. Much the most frequent of the three established aliens is **3a Common Blue Sow-thistle** *C. macrophylla*, the only one with creeping roots, and with sticky hairs on its upper stems, *lilac* flowers and blunter end leaf-lobes, the lower leaves with downy veins beneath. An aggressive coloniser of hedge-banks and waste places. **Pontic Blue Sow-thistle** *C. bourgaei*, has no sticky hairs or hairs on leaf-veins, pale purple flowers and more oval end-lobes. **3b Hairless Blue Sow-thistle** *C. plumieri* has no hairs at all, blue flowers and triangular end-lobes. A not dissimilar alien is **3c Russian Lettuce** *Lactuca tatarica*, to 80cm, with creeping roots, lilac-blue flowers, 18-26mm, and dandelion-like pinnately lobed lower leaves with a small pointed end-lobe.

MESEMBRYANTHEMUM FAMILY Aizoaceae

4 Hottentot-fig *Carpobrotus edulis*. A creeping perennial, to 3m, whose densely matted woody stems may drape whole cliffs. Flowers daisy-like, many-petalled, yellow, often fading deep pink, or pink-purple with or without a yellow centre, 5-10cm across; March-August. Leaves dark green, succulent, 3-angled, 5-12cm long, reddening at the tip in autumn. Cliffs and banks by the sea.

5 Sally-my-handsome *Carpobrotus acinaciformis* has flowers always pink-purple and narrower leaves curved and thickest towards the tip. Habitat as Hottentot-fig, mainly in the far SW.

6 Purple Dewplant *Disphyma crassifolium* has red-purple flowers and thick blunt dark green leaves. Especially on the Lizard.

Nine other introduced 'mesems' or dewplants are scattered round the coast from Suffolk to Galloway, but mainly in Scilly; for those most often seen in Scilly, see p. 456.

6 Purple Dewplant

5 Sally-my-handsome

4 yellow form on sea cliff

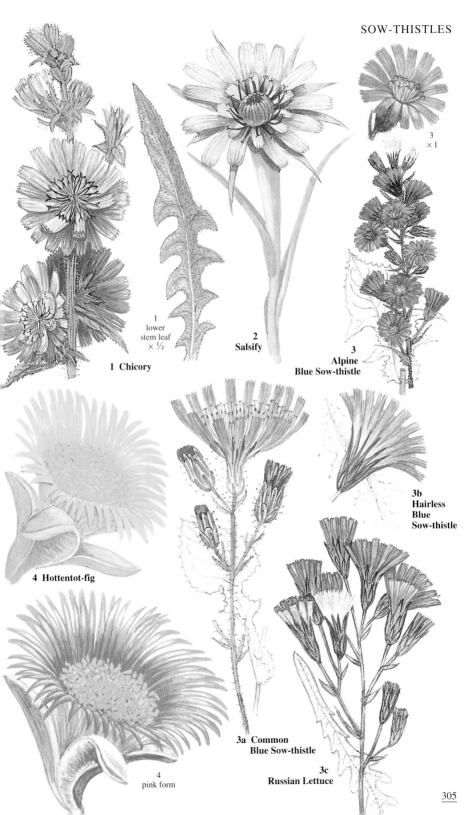

1
lower
stem leaf
× ½

1 Chicory

**2
Salsify**

3
× 1

**3
Alpine
Blue Sow-thistle**

**3b
Hairless
Blue
Sow-thistle**

4 Hottentot-fig

4
pink form

**3a Common
Blue Sow-thistle**

**3c
Russian Lettuce**

WATER-LILY FAMILY Nymphaeaceae

Hairless perennials, with large flowers and large long-stalked leaves. Still and slow-moving fresh water, rooting in the bottom mud.

1 White Water-lily *Nymphaea alba* Our largest floating white flower, 9-20cm, with conspicuous yellow stamens; flowers fragrant, fully open only in sunshine; June-Sept. Leaves broadly oval, 12-35cm, all floating, rather smaller and rounder than Yellow Water-lily (**2**). Fruits green, roundish, warty. Widespread and frequent. Ssp. *occidentalis* in N & W Scotland and W Ireland, has smaller flowers, 5-12cm, not opening so wide. Several related alien species or cultivars, some with pink or yellow flowers, may be planted in lakes and ponds.

2 Yellow Water-lily *Nuphar lutea*. Our largest and commonest floating yellow flower, usually projecting a few cm out of the water; flowers 5-8cm, petals usually shorter than sepals; June-Sept. Smells faintly of brandy, which with the smooth green, carafe-shaped fruits gave rise to the folk-name Brandybottle. Leaves oval, up to 40 × 30cm, leathery when floating, cabbagy when submerged. Widespread and frequent.

3 *Least Water-lily *Nuphar pumila*. Smaller than Yellow Water-lily (**2**), with flowers to 3cm, petals further apart and flowering July-August, and leaves to 17 × 12cm with the lobes further apart. Still water only, mainly in the uplands. Hybrids with **2** are intermediate and may occur away from both parents.

PEONY FAMILY Paeoniaceae

4 Wild Peony *Paeonia mascula*. Medium perennial, to 60cm. Flowers red, solitary, large, to 14cm across; April-May. Leaves large, dark shiny green, 2-trefoil. Fruits downy, curved. Not native; confined to two islands in the Bristol Channel: Steep Holm, where first found in 1803, and Flat Holm, where introduced in 1980s. Similar Peonies seen elsewhere, often with double flowers, are likely to be the Garden Peony *P. officinalis*.

PITCHERPLANT FAMILY Sarraceniaceae

5 Pitcherplant *Sarracenia purpurea*. A singular North American insectivorous perennial, totally unlike any other plant found wild in Britain or Ireland – except the yellow-flowered *S. flava*, which has been planted in a Surrey bog. The pitchers are its curved tube-shaped root-leaves, red-purple mottled green, 10-20cm high, with a flap at the top and usually half-full of water – the plant feeds on the insects which drown in them. Flowers with five red-purple petals and sepals, solitary, nodding, 4-5cm across, with contrasting large yellow-green umbrella-like style *c.* 3cm across, on stems to 60cm; June-July. Well naturalised in Irish bogs, less so in English ones.

GIANT RHUBARB FAMILY Gunneraceae

6 Chilean Giant Rhubarb *Gunnera tinctoria*. Outsize perennial, quite unrelated to Rhubarb (p. 64), but with strikingly *broad rhubarb-like leaves* to 2m across, on 1.5m stalks with *pale bristles*. Flowers rather small, reddish-green, in oblong clusters with stout branches to 1m high; June-August. Widely planted and sometimes self-sown by lakes, ponds and streams in parks and gardens, also wet grassland and woods and (in Ireland) sea cliffs. **Brazilian Giant Rhubarb** *G. manicata* may have broader leaves on taller stalks, which have *reddish* bristles and flower clusters with slenderer branches. Not recorded as self-sown.

BIRTHWORT FAMILY Aristolochiaceae

Two long-established but widely scattered aliens are **7 Birthwort** *Aristolochia clematitis*, source of a drug used to save peccant medieval nuns from their misbehaviour with peccant monks, and **8 Asarabacca** *Asarum europaeum*, a plant so dull that one wonders why it was ever planted, its dull purple bell-shaped flowers being usually hidden under kidney-shaped leaves on a few shady banks. Birthwort is foetid with pale yellow tubular flowers and large heart-shaped leaves; found, in Oxfordshire for instance, at Godstow Nunnery ruins and by a roadside at Kencott.

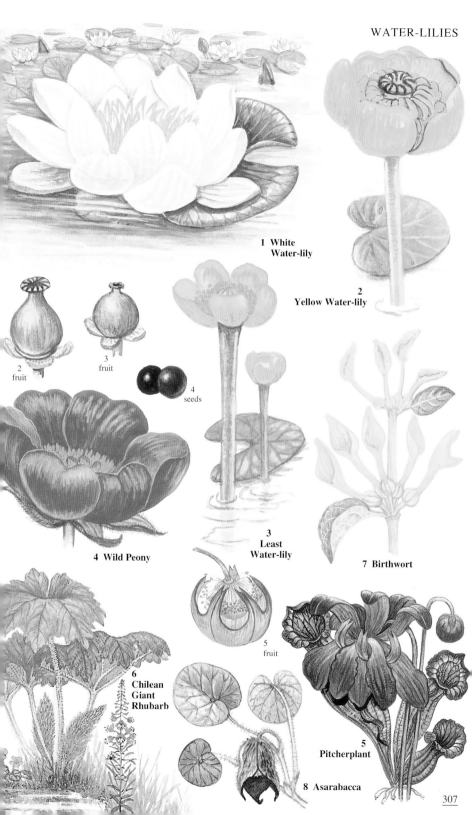

1 White Water-lily

2 Yellow Water-lily

2 fruit

3 fruit

4 seeds

4 Wild Peony

3 Least Water-lily

7 Birthwort

5 fruit

6 Chilean Giant Rhubarb

5 Pitcherplant

8 Asarabacca

MONOCOTYLEDONS (see p. 9)

seed leaf

Plants with only one seed-leaf, with leaves usually narrow and unstalked, often parallel-sided and nearly always parallel-veined. Petals or tepals usually in threes or sixes.

parallel veins

LILY FAMILY Liliaceae

A very diverse group of mostly bulbous hairless plants, though Butcher's Broom (p. 316) is a low shrub. Flowers with three petals and three sepals, sometimes joined at the base and often all the same colour and appearing 6-petalled. Leaves usually *long, fairly narrow, all basal*, iris-like in the two asphodels (p. 312). Fruit usually a capsule. No fewer than 124 species have been recorded as more or less established in our area, so very few can be mentioned here; see also those on Scilly, p. 458.

1 S

1 Bluebell *Hyacinthoides non-scriptus*. The glory of our woods in spring, short/medium, to 50cm. Flowers azure blue with *creamy* anthers, bell-shaped with six *turned-down* lobes, fragrant, 14-20mm, in a *one-sided* spike drooping at the tip; most large populations have a few scattered white spikes; April-June. Leaves keeled, narrow, 7-15mm wide. Fruit a capsule. Hybridises readily with Spanish Bluebell (**1a**), the hybrids often commoner near gardens. Carpeting woods and hedge-banks, also on sea cliffs and mountains. **1a Spanish Bluebell** *H. hispanica*, the common Bluebell of gardens, has *erecter*, not one-sided spikes of larger, flatter flowers, paler blue and often pale pink-purple or white, with anthers *blue* and the petal-lobes *erecter*, leaves broader, to 35mm. Now much less frequent outside gardens than the hybrid.

1a S

2 Spring Squill *Scilla verna*. Much smaller than Bluebell (**1**), with which it shares some sea-cliffs in spring, though never in such dense masses; stems to 15cm. Flowers bright blue, with petals not joined and so *star-like*, 10-16mm, each with a bluish bract at the base, in stalked spikes; *April-June*. Leaves very narrow, with the flowers. Grassy places, usually near the sea.

2 SOZ

3 *Autumn Squill *Scilla autumnalis*. Differs from Spring Squill (**2**) especially in flowering *July-Sept* without the leaves, but also has a longer spike of more purplish flowers with *no bracts*. Dry grassy places, including a large colony in Hampton Court Park, Middlesex.

Seven other squills have become naturalised from gardens. Two of the most frequent, both flowering in spring with the leaves, are: **3a Siberian Squill** *Scilla siberica* with deeper blue, drooping cup-shaped flowers and tiny bracts; and **3b Alpine Squill** *S. bifolia* with no or minute bracts and only two leaves, well established in Abbey Wood, SE London. Very like squills are the three species of more or less naturalised **Glory of the Snow** *Chionodoxa*, with petals joined at the base, no tiny bracts and leaves with the flowers. Much the most frequent is **3c** *C. forbesii* with 4-12 flowers, white in the centre, with white stamens.

3

4 **Grape-hyacinth *Muscari neglectum*. Short, to 30cm, and unmistakable (apart from its garden relatives) for its dense 15-50mm head of small, supposedly grape-like, flowers, the upper pale blue, the lower *dark purplish-blue* and white-toothed; April-May. Leaves narrow, 2-8mm, grooved, rather limp. Dry grassland, field borders; abundant on allotments in one Cotswold village. Occasionally naturalised elsewhere. Very much more frequent is **4a Garden Grape-hyacinth** *M. armeniacum* with lower flowers bright blue and white-toothed. Two much less frequent escapes, with broader leaves, to 20mm, are **4b Compact Grape-hyacinth** *M. botryoides*, with flowers like Garden Grape-hyacinth and leaves hooded at the tip; and the taller, to 60cm, **4c Tassel Hyacinth** *M. comosum* with a much longer spike, the upper flowers bright violet-blue and the lower *dark buff* and pale-toothed, especially on dunes.

4

5 Fritillary *Fritillaria meleagris*. One of our most attractive and distinctive wild flowers; short to 30cm. Flowers varying from dull purple to creamy white, chequered with darker and paler blotches, solitary, *bell-like and nodding*, 30-50mm; April-May. Leaves grass-like, greyish, up the stem. Gregarious in damp meadows, especially near rivers, e.g. Iffley and Magdalen Meadows, Oxford; occasionally naturalised elsewhere.

5

Meadow Saffron *Colchicum autumnale*. Described with the very similar Crocuses on p. 324.

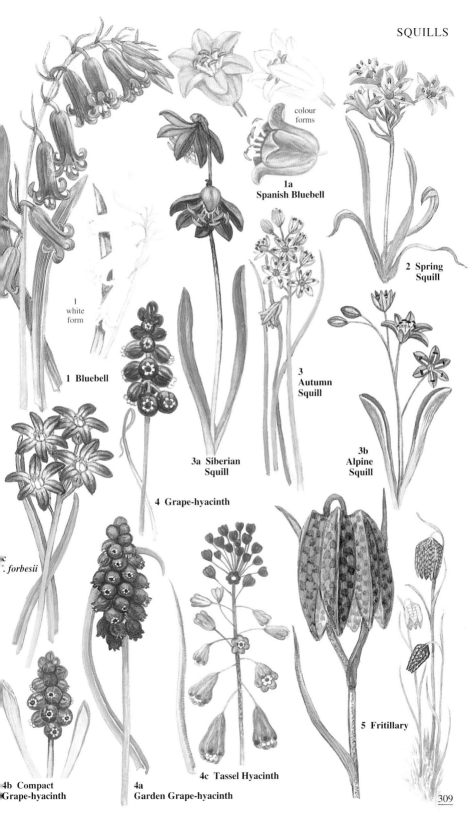

colour
forms

1a
Spanish Bluebell

2 Spring
Squill

1
white
form

1 Bluebell

3
Autumn
Squill

3a Siberian
Squill

3b
Alpine
Squill

4 Grape-hyacinth

c
. forbesii

4c Tassel Hyacinth

5 Fritillary

4b Compact
Grape-hyacinth

4a
Garden Grape-hyacinth

Daffodils *Narcissus.* A diverse group, with two main flower-types, the classical daffodil with a long central trumpet-like corona and the pheasant's-eye-type with a very short corona, both with six yellow or white outer petals. The short-corona type may be either large and solitary or small with several flowers together. Leaves long, narrow, usually greyish, all basal. Specialists have divided daffodils into 11 different groups, but only about half of these include the 16 species or cultivars that have established themselves away from gardens, especially in Cornwall and Scilly (p. 458). The old-fashioned Double Daffodil is now rarely seen.

1 Wild Daffodil *Narcissus pseudonarcissus.* Our only native narcissus is a dainty miniature of the often rather gross Daffodils seen in gardens and shops; short, to 35cm. Flowers yellow, with a somewhat darker trumpet-like central corona, 18-40mm; March-April. Woods, damp grassland, with famous sites in Farndale, N Yorkshire, and at Dunsford Wood, S Devon. The corona of the **1a Tenby Daffodil** ssp. *obvallaris*, naturalised in W Wales, is the same colour as the petals.

1 S ☐

Two miniature daffodils are especially well naturalised on grassy slopes at two much-visited Surrey gardens, the R. H. S. at Wisley and the Savill, Windsor Great Park, and elsewhere: **2 Hoop-Petticoat Daffodil** *Narcissus bulbocodium* with the corona greatly inflated and the petals very narrow, and **2a Cyclamen Daffodil** *N. cyclamineus* with the petals swept right back.

1a ▫

3 Pheasant's Eye *Narcissus poeticus.* Short/medium, to 50cm. Flowers with petals usually *white* and corona very short, *yellow edged with red*, 55-70mm; April-May. Perhaps the most widely naturalised of the narcissi with short coronas.

~

4 Turkscap Lily *Lilium martagon.* Medium/tall, to 1.5m. Flowers very distinctive, *dull purple* with darker spots, nodding with the petals turned back to make the Turk's cap and reveal the very prominent stamens and red-brown anthers, 30-40mm; June-July. Leaves narrow, in whorls up the stem. Familiar in gardens and long naturalised in woods in the lower Wye valley and elsewhere. **4a Pyrenean Lily** *L. pyrenaicum* is somewhat shorter, to 1m, the flowers *yellow* with small dark spots (May-July) and leaves grass-like, spirally up the stem. Well established on hedge-banks, mainly S of Exmoor.

4 ▫

5 Wild Tulip *Tulipa sylvestris.* Slender, short/medium, to 50cm. Distinguished from the variously coloured garden Tulips by the 20-60cm flowers being always *yellow* and *drooping* in bud (April-May, but very shy-flowering) and the leaves much narrower. Long naturalised in woods and copses, e.g. Bayhurst Wood, Middlesex, since 1839; never in the typical wayside and waste-ground habitats of garden Tulips.

5 ▫

6 Yellow Star of Bethlehem *Gagea lutea.* Low, to 25cm. Flowers yellow, usually tinged green, with a *green stripe* on the back of the star-like six petals, 15-25mm; in small umbel-like *clusters* with 2-3 short leaf-like bracts; 15-25mm; Feb-May, often only a few flowers in a large colony. Leaves, none on stem but *one* at base, like Bluebell (p. 308), but smaller, narrower and with *three* instead of one prominent veins on the back, more hooded at the tip and sometimes wavy. Damp woods.

6 ▫

7 ***Early Star of Bethlehem *Gagea bohemica.* Flowers brighter yellow than Yellow Star of Bethlehem (**6**) and usually smaller (10-20mm) and solitary, with 1-2 bracts; January-March. Leaves: up to four on stem; the two at base *thread-like* and wavy. Rocks on the Welsh/English border.

7 ▫

3
Pheasant's Eye

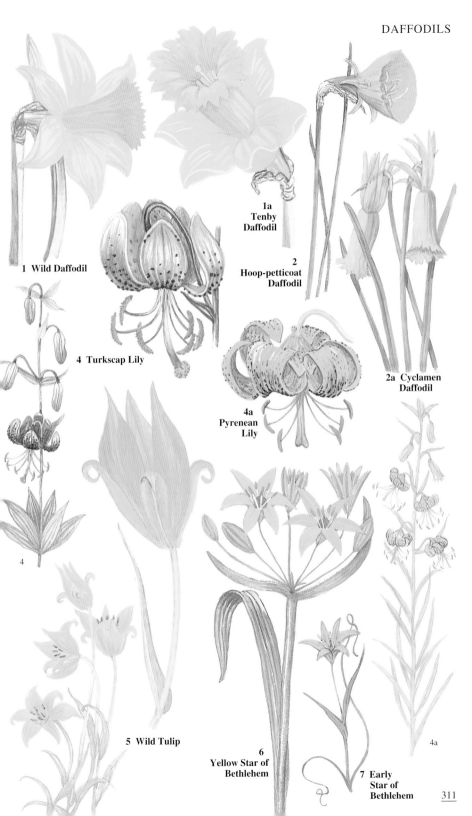

1 Wild Daffodil

1a
Tenby
Daffodil

2
Hoop-petticoat
Daffodil

2a Cyclamen
Daffodil

4 Turkscap Lily

4a
Pyrenean
Lily

4

5 Wild Tulip

6
Yellow Star of
Bethlehem

7 Early
Star of
Bethlehem

4a

311

1 Yellow Day-lily *Hemerocallis lilioasphodelus*. Medium/tall, clump-forming, to 80cm. Flowers *yellow*, trumpet-shaped, 70-80cm, fragrant, in clusters, each lasting only a day; May-June. Leaves to 65cm and 15mm broad, all basal. Widely naturalised, especially in Scotland, on waysides and waste ground, including the old Mendip lead-mine spoilheaps at Charterhouse, Somerset. **1a Orange Day-lily** *H. fulva* is generally larger, with dull *orange* unscented flowers, June-August, in similar places but mainly in England/Wales.

2 Peruvian Lily *Alstroemeria aurea*, a not dissimilar escape, well naturalised in the Isle of Man and elsewhere, has its longer-lasting orange flowers spotted with red and all its much shorter lanceolate leaves on the stems.

3 Bog Asphodel *Narthecium ossifragum*. Short, to 45cm. Flowers deep *yellow*, often tinged orange, anthers orange, star-like, 10-16mm; in a short spike; July-August. Leaves *flattened*, iris-like, in basal tufts. Fruiting spikes deep orange, often colouring the ground. Bogs, peaty heaths and moors.

4 Scottish Asphodel *Tofieldia pusilla*. Low, to 20cm. Flowers *greenish-white*, with 3-lobed bracts, 3-5mm, in a short stalked spike on a flat stem; June-August. Leaves *flattened*, iris-like, in a basal tuft. Wet places in the hills.

Red-hot Pokers *Kniphofia*. Tall, clump-forming, to 2m. Flowers familiar in gardens, reddish-orange at first, becoming yellow, 30-40mm, in a large dense terminal head; August-Sept, Leaves long, narrow, V-shaped. Widely naturalised, especially on coastal dunes, e.g. in Flintshire. Many cultivars are involved; among the more frequent are **5 Common Red-hot Poker** *Kniphofia uvaria* with stamens scarcely protruding and bluntish leaf-tips, and **Greater Red-hot Poker** *K. × praecox* with stamens protruding up to 15mm and leaf-tips sharply pointed.

6 Lily of the Valley *Convallaria majalis*. A favourite, sweetly fragrant garden flower, but fully native; low, carpeting, to 25cm. Flowers creamy-white, *bell-shaped*, nodding, 5-9mm, in one-sided stalked spikes; May-June. Leaves two, basal, broadly elliptical, not unlike Ramsons (p. 318), but a much duller, greyer green and not garlic-scented. Fruit a red berry. Dry woods on limestone or sand; also an escape, when often stouter.

7 **May Lily *Maianthemum bifolium*. Low, carpeting, to 20cm. Flowers white, *4-petalled*, fragrant, 4-6mm, in an erect stalked spike; May-June. Leaves two, *heart-shaped*, on the stem. Fruit a red berry. A few woods on acid soils, native in N England, introduced elsewhere, e.g. Swanton Novers, Norfolk.

8 **Snowdon Lily *Lloydia serotina*. Low, to 15cm. Flowers white with purple veins, bell-shaped, solitary, 18-22mm; May-June. Leaves very narrow, two at base, a few more up stem. Confined to mountain rocks in five sites around *Snowdon*, N Wales.

9 Kerry Lily *Simethis planifolia*. Short, to 40cm. Flowers white, the six petals tinged purplish on the back, anthers yellow, 18-22mm; in a loose cluster; June-July. Leaves linear, greyish, often curled. Dry heathland; see p. 462.

1
Yellow
Day-lily

× ½

× ¼

1a Orange
Day-lily

2 Peruvian Lily

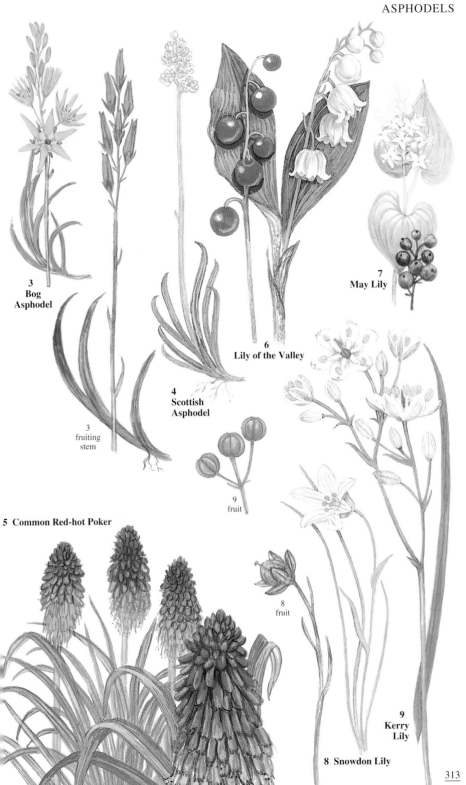

3
Bog
Asphodel

3
fruiting
stem

4
Scottish
Asphodel

6
Lily of the Valley

7
May Lily

9
fruit

5 Common Red-hot Poker

8
fruit

9
Kerry
Lily

8 Snowdon Lily

1 Snowdrop *Galanthus nivalis.* The welcome first-flowerer in the garden, but well established and perhaps in places even native outside it; low, to 20cm. Flowers with three snow-white outer petals and three rather bell-like *inner* ones green outside, white with a green tip inside, sometimes 'double', solitary, drooping, and with a greenish leaflike hood, 12-25mm; January-March, with the leaves. Leaves *greyish,* usually two. Woods, copses, stream-sides, waysides. Five more species and two hybrids are more or less established in scattered places. The most frequent are **1a Pleated Snowdrop** *G. plicatus,* whose leaves have a pale stripe above and their edges distinctively folded under, and the inner petals sometimes with a green patch at the base; The taller **1b Greater Snowdrop** *G. elwesii* with noticeably larger flowers, the inner petals with a green patch at the base; **1c Green Snowdrop** *G. ikariae,* easily told by its bright green leaves; and **1d Queen Olga's Snowdrop** *G. olgae-reginae,* which flowers Nov-January, before the leaves.

2 Summer Snowflake *Leucojum aestivum.* Medium, tufted, to 60cm. Flowers white, green at the tip, bell-shaped with no inner ring, anthers orange, 13-22mm, in small drooping *umbels* on minutely toothed stalks; misnamed as it flowers *April-May.* Leaves green. Aka Loddon Lily. Wet meadows and copses, especially in Thames and Loddon valleys; a garden form with untoothed stalks is an increasing escape.

3 ***Spring Snowflake *Leucojum vernum.* Intermediate between Snowdrop (**1**) and Summer Snowflake (**2**), short, to 40cm. Flowers white, like Summer Snowflake, but larger (15-25mm), sometimes green or yellow near the tip, and *solitary* or paired; *February-March,* with the green leaves. Perhaps native in two damp copses, also an occasional escape.

4 Star-of-Bethlehem *Ornithogalum angustifolium.* Short, to 30cm, often with a few *elongated* bulblets at the base. Flowers *bright white,* anthers yellow, the six petals each with a green stripe on the back, opening star-like in the sun, *28-38mm;* in an open *umbel-like head;* May-June. Leaves linear with a central white stripe. Grassy, scrubby and wooded places. Native but also a widespread garden escape, when it could be confused with the potential escape **4a Garden Star-of-Bethlehem** *O. umbellatum,* which has larger flowers, to 55mm, and many *globular* bulblets.

5 *Spiked Star-of-Bethlehem *Ornithogalum pyrenaicum.* Medium/tall, to 60cm. Flowers greenish/yellowish-white, 6-petalled, star-like, in a stalked spike; June-July. Leaves greyish, linear, all basal, soon withering. Aka Bath Asparagus, its young shoots being formerly marketed in Bath, Somerset, as asparagus. Woods, hedge-banks.

6 Drooping Star-of-Bethlehem *Ornithogalum nutans.* Short/medium, to 60cm. Flowers *dull* white tinged *greenish,* spreading and finally *nodding,* the six petals curved back and with a green stripe on the back 26-40mm; in a stalked spike; April-May. Leaves linear with a broad whitish stripe. A widely scattered garden escape, often on grassy banks.

1 S

2 S

3

4

5

6

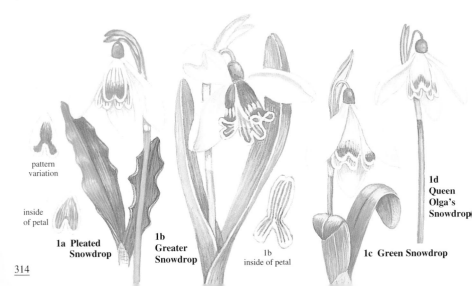

pattern variation

inside of petal

1a Pleated Snowdrop

1b Greater Snowdrop

1b inside of petal

1c Green Snowdrop

1d Queen Olga's Snowdrop

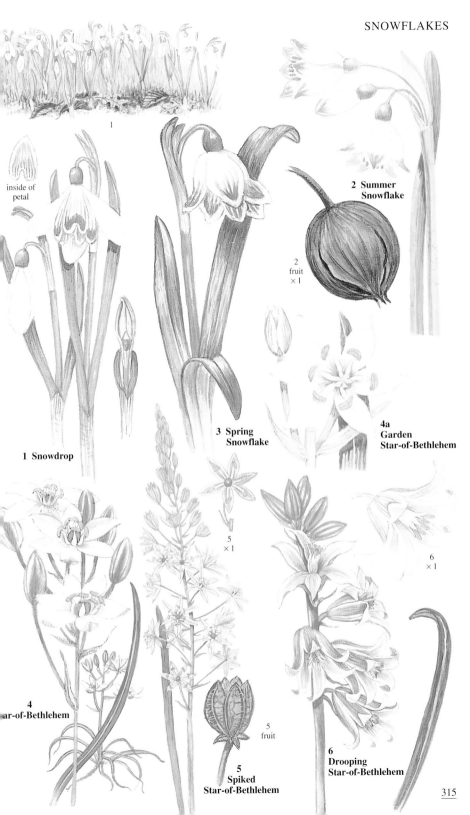

1

inside of
petal

2 Summer
Snowflake

2
fruit
× 1

3 Spring
Snowflake

4a
Garden
Star-of-Bethlehem

1 Snowdrop

5
× 1

6
× 1

4
ar-of-Bethlehem

5
fruit

5
Spiked
Star-of-Bethlehem

6
Drooping
Star-of-Bethlehem

1 Solomon's-seal *Polygonatum multiflorum*. Medium, patch-forming, stems *smooth*, unbranched, arching, to 80cm. Flowers dull white tipped green, anthers yellow, bell-like, *waisted* in the middle, unscented, 9-20mm; 1-3 at the base of the upper leaves; May-June. Leaves broad elliptical, alternate, all on the stems. Fruit a blue-black berry. Ancient woods. **Garden Solomon's-seal** *P.* × *hybridum*, the hybrid between **1** and **2**, has ridged stems and flowers scarcely waisted and 1-6 together; berries uncommon. A frequent escape on waysides and railway banks.

2 Angular Solomon's-seal *Polygonatum odoratum*. Shorter than Solomon's Seal (**1**), to 40cm, the stems more erect and distinctly *angled*. Flowers *fragrant* and not waisted, 1-2 together; June-July. Woods on limestone.

3 **Whorled Solomon's-seal *Polygonatum verticillatum*. Looks very different from the two other Solomon's Seals (**1**, **2**), with *angled* stems to 80cm, hard to see among the herbage. Flowers greenish-white tipped green, unscented, smaller (5-10mm), in *whorls* of small clusters at the base of the leaves; June-July. Leaves much narrower, also in *whorls*. Berry red. A few wooded sites in Perthshire.

4 Herb Paris *Paris quadrifolia*. Short, to 40cm. The star-like flowers resemble small garden Trilliums, the 4(6) very narrow yellow-green petals slightly shorter than the much broader 4(6) lanceolate green sepals, and the eight erect green stamens with yellow anthers, solitary, 40-50mm; May-June. Leaves pointed oval, unstalked, 3-8 but usually four, in a *whorl* a little below the flower. Fruit a purplish-black berry, with four purplish styles. Woods, usually on lime, where colonial but often hard to detect among the Dog's Mercury (p. 168).

5 **Wild Asparagus *Asparagus prostratus*. Prostrate, to 30cm. Flowers greenish-white, bell-shaped, 1-2 together along the stems, 4-6mm; male and female on different plants; June-August. No true leaves, but small needle-like fleshy bluish-green 'leaves' up the stems. Fruit a small red berry. Native, sea cliffs. Much more often seen is **Asparagus** *A. officinalis*, the escaped vegetable, with tall *erect* stems to 1.5m, and much less bluish and fleshy 'leaves'. Frequent on dunes and waste ground.

6 Butcher's Broom *Ruscus aculeatus*. By far the most anomalous member of the Lily Family, a medium stiff *evergreen bush*, to 75cm. Flowers pale yellowish-green, sometimes with purplish spots, tiny (4-5mm), 4-petalled, on what look like oval leaves ending in a sharp spine, but are actually flattened stems; male and female on different plants; February-May and sporadically through the year. True leaves minute at the base of the false leaves. Fruit a rather infrequent red berry. Dry woods, hedges; native, but sometimes an escape.

5 Wild Asparagus

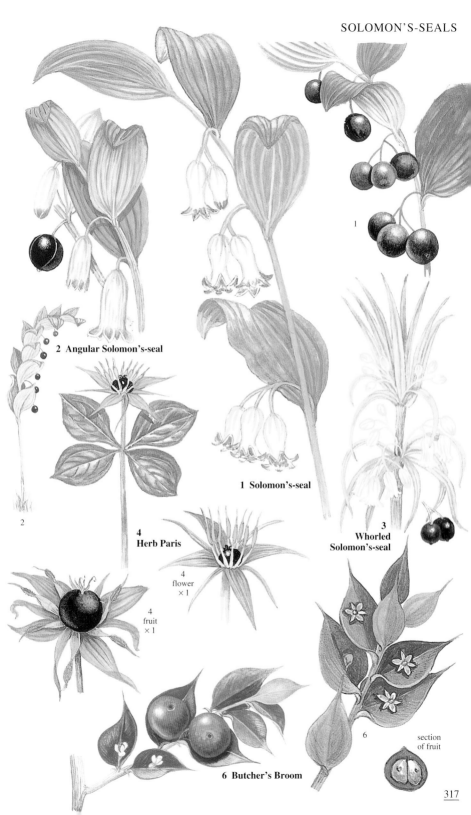

1

2 **Angular Solomon's-seal**

2

4
Herb Paris

4
flower
× 1

4
fruit
× 1

1 **Solomon's-seal**

3
**Whorled
Solomon's-seal**

6

section
of fruit

6 **Butcher's Broom**

Garlics, Leeks and **Onions** *Allium*. Bulbous perennials with a *pungent smell* of garlic or onion. Flowers usually more or less bell-shaped, well stalked, in some species partly or wholly replaced by *bulbils*, in a tight or more open umbel-like heads; enclosed by one or more papery bracts. Leaves, sometimes sheathing up the stem, either cylindrical or linear and keeled, but much broader in Ramsons (**1**) and the rarely established pink-flowered **1a Broad-leaved Leek** *Allium nigrum*.

1a
Broad-leaved
Leek

flower shapes

leaf sections

bulbil

stem sections

Flowers only:	Ramsons, 3-cornered Garlic, Neapolitan Garlic, Hairy Garlic, Crow Garlic (rare), Field Garlic, Chives, Round-headed Leek, Rosy Garlic, Keeled Garlic, Honey Garlic, Onion, Garden Leek, Garlic
Flowers/Bulbils:	Few-flowered Garlic, Crow Garlic, Field Garlic, Field Garlic, Wild Leek, Sand Leek (rare), Rosy Garlic, Keeled Garlic, Onion, Garden Leek, Garlic
Bulbils only:	Crow Garlic, Field Garlic, Chives, Sand Leek, Keeled Garlic, Onion, Garlic

1 Ramsons *Allium ursinum*. Our commonest and only native broad-leaved garlic, a vigorous carpeter, short, to 45cm. Flowers white, star-like, 12-20mm, in a broad umbel on leafless stems with 2-3 ridges; April-June. Leaves broad lanceolate, not unlike Lily of the Valley (p. 312), but much brighter green and easily told by their smell. Damp woods, shady banks, occasionally in the open.

2 Three-cornered Garlic *Allium triquetrum*. Often called White Bluebell, and quite like one until you smell it. Also differs from Bluebell (p. 308) in its short 3-angled stems, to 45cm, more deeply lobed white flowers with a narrow *green stripe* down the centre of each petal, February-June, and sharply keeled leaves, curly at the top. Damper banks and way-sides where the winter climate is warmest.

3 Few-flowered Garlic *Allium paradoxum*. Short, to 40cm. Flowers white or creamy, 10-12mm, 1-5 in a head *mainly of bulbils*; March-June. One very narrow, well keeled root-leaf. Naturalised in plantations and elsewhere, often carpeting the ground, as on a disused canal-bank at Drayton Beauchamp, Bucks.

4 Neapolitan Garlic *Allium neapolitanum*. Stems *triangular, hairless*, short/medium, to 50cm. Flowers white, star-like, 12-14mm, in an open head; March-May. Leaves linear, keeled. Widely naturalised in grassy places, especially S coast of England. **4a Hairy Garlic** *A. subhirsutum* differs in its *rounded hairy* stem and less keeled leaves. Probably less frequent, but perhaps overlooked.

5 Crow Garlic *Allium vineale*. Much the commonest garlic with bulbils; usually medium, sometimes tall, to 1.2m. Flowerhead usually *purplish bulbils only*, 12-20mm, but sometimes also with 2-4mm flowers varying from red to pink to greenish-pink (blue in Co Kerry) and rarely with flowers only; stamens *protruding*, papery bracts short, long-pointed; June-July. Leaves cylindrical, hollow, up the stems. Bare and grassy places, sometimes an arable pest.

6 Field Garlic *Allium oleraceum*. Medium, stems slightly ridged, usually hollow, to 80cm. Flowerheads differ from Crow Garlic in having flowers whitish, tinged pink, green or brown, 6-7mm, stamens *not* protruding, and a *very long* papery bract, and never having flowers only and rarely bulbils only; July-August. Leaves usually semi-cylindrical. Road verges and other dry grassy places.

7 Wild Leek *Allium ampeloprasum*. Very tall, stout, to 2m. Flowers dark or pale lilac-purple to whitish, and anthers yellow, 7-9mm, in *large rounded heads*, 70-100mm, with or without bulbils; July-August. Leaves greyish, broad to narrow, to 40mm, keeled, finely toothed. Cf. Garden Leek (p. 320). **7a Babington's Leek** var. *babingtonii* has flowers in a looser head with both flowers and bulbils and sometimes *secondary heads*. Rocky and sandy places near the sea.

1 ■

2 s ■↑↑

3 □↑↑

5 s □

6 □↓

7 s ▫

7a s □↓

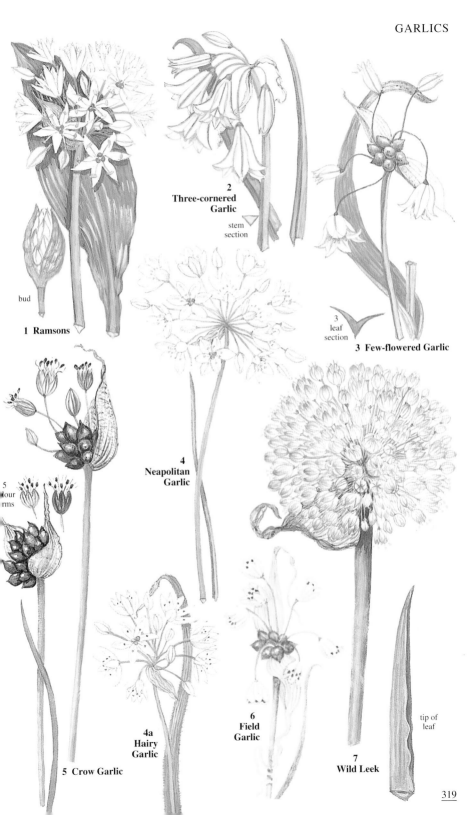

1 Ramsons

bud

2 Three-cornered Garlic

stem section

3 leaf section

3 Few-flowered Garlic

4 Neapolitan Garlic

5 flour rms

4a Hairy Garlic

6 Field Garlic

5 Crow Garlic

7 Wild Leek

tip of leaf

1 Chives *Allium schoenoprasum*. The same plant as the garden herb, tufted, short, to 30cm. Flowers pale pink-purple with a *darker vein* down each petal, the stamens slightly *protruding*, 7-15mm, in a small dense head with two short narrow pointed papery bracts and *no bulbils*; June-Sept. Leaves greyish, cylindrical, hollow, sometimes wavy. Rocky ground, usually on lime; occasionally naturalised elsewhere.

2 Sand Leek *Allium scorodoprasum*. Medium, to 80cm. Flowers pale to dark red-purple, with stamens *not* protruding, stalks of varying lengths, and *purple bulbils* (rarely bulbils only), 5-8mm; in a smallish head with two short broad pointed papery bracts; May-August. Leaves flat, finely toothed and grass-like, making it hard to find when not in flower. Dry grassy and bare places.

3 ***Round-headed Leek *Allium sphaerocephalon*. Medium/tall, with stiff stems, to 80cm. Flowers pink-purple, with *protruding* stamens, 3-5mm; in a dense rounded head, 20-30mm, with short broad papery bracts and *no bulbils*; June-August. Leaves cylindrical, hollow, up the stems. Only on Avon Gorge cliffs, Bristol.

4 Rosy Garlic *Allium roseum*. Medium, to 75cm. Flowers dark to pale pink, petals pointed, stamens *not* protruding, long-stalked, 10-12mm; many in a loose head with *short* papery bracts, with or without bulbils; *May-June*. Leaves *flat*. Established in scattered places, e.g the Avon Gorge, Bristol.

5 Keeled Garlic *Allium carinatum*. Medium, to 60cm. Flowers purplish-pink, petals blunt, stamens *protruding*; 4-6mm; few to the head, with *very long* papery bracts, with or without bulbils, or bulbils only; *July-August*. Leaves *keeled*. Established in scattered places.

6 Honey Garlic *Nectaroscordum siculum*. Tall, garlic-smelling, to 1.2m. Flowers *greenish-red*, bell-shaped, fragrant, 18-22mm; many drooping in a large loose head, no bulbils; May-June. Leaves narrow, 3-angled. Aggressive in gardens, sometimes spreading elsewhere, e.g Abbotsbury, Dorset, and the Avon Gorge, Bristol.

Escaped Leek-like Vegetables. These can look quite different in flower from their vegetable-plot selves, and are likely to be seen on waysides or near gardens and allotments.

7 Onion *Allium cepa* is tall, to 1m, and stout with a rounded head of greenish-white flowers. **7a Garden Leek** *A. porrum* differs from Wild Leek (p. 318) in having stems to 1m, flowers more often whitish with anthers reddish, and leaves much broader, to 1m. **7b Garlic** *A. sativum*, not unlike Sand Leek, with greenish-or pinkish-white flowers, is established by the Lune estuary at Lancaster and by the sea at Port Dinllaen, N Wales.

IRIS FAMILY Iridaceae

Perennials with showy flowers of various shapes. Leaves often iris-like (p. 322) (cf. also Bog and Scottish Asphodels, p. 312).

8 **Wild Gladiolus *Gladiolus illyricus*. Smaller than garden Gladioli in all its parts, medium, stems unbranched, to 50cm. Flowers always bright red-purple, with six pointed petals, and bracts often purple-tipped, 35-50mm; 3-6 in a spike; June-August. Leaves iris-like, narrower. Heathy places, often under Bracken, now apparently only in the New Forest, Hants. **Eastern Gladiolus** *G. communis*, with stems often branched and 10-20 flowers in the spike, is a not infrequent escape in the SW.

9 Montbretia *Crocosmia × crocosmiiflora*. A man-made hybrid from France, familiar in gardens and one of our most widely established escapes; clump-forming, medium, to 60cm. Flowers bright reddish-orange, the six petal-lobes *about as long* as the *gradually* widening tube, 25-40mm; in an unbranched one-sided spike; July-Oct. Leaves iris-like, with a prominent midrib but *not pleated*. Sea cliffs, grassy banks, less frequent inland. Three others are much more local, mainly in Scotland: **Potts's Montbretia** *C. pottsii*, one of Montbretia's parents, with lobes *half as long* as the *abruptly* widening tube; **Aunt Eliza** *C. paniculata*, taller, to 1.2m, with petal-lobes no more than *half as long* as the *abruptly* widening tube, and leaves *pleated;* and **9a Giant Montbretia** *C. masoniorum*, like Aunt Eliza but with lobes about as long as the *gradually* widening tube and stamens *protruding*.

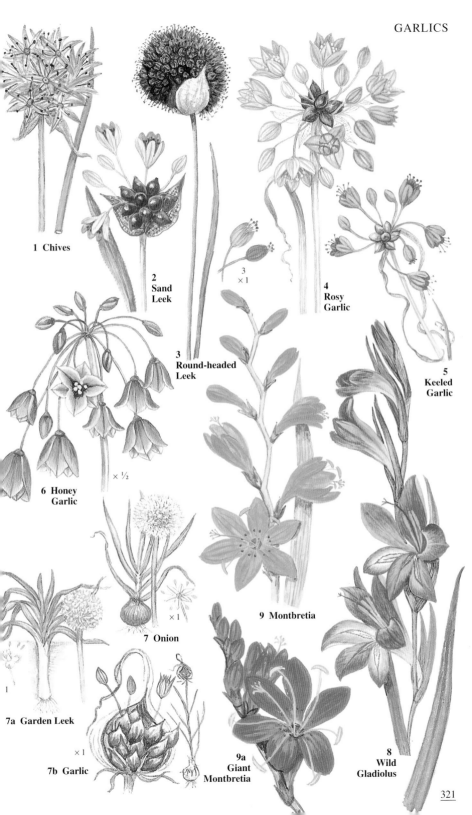

1 Chives

2 Sand Leek

3 Round-headed Leek

3 ×1

4 Rosy Garlic

5 Keeled Garlic

6 Honey Garlic

×½

7 Onion

×1

7a Garden Leek

7b Garlic

×1

8 Wild Gladiolus

9 Montbretia

9a Giant Montbretia

Irises or **Flags**. *Iris*. Rootstock often swollen and above ground. Flowers with three spreading outer petals (falls), three more or less erect and twisted inner ones (standards), all narrow at the base, and three large, almost petal-like stigmas with branched tips (crests). Buds enclosed in a sheath (spathe), which splits at flowering time. Leaves distinctively flat and sword-shaped, usually with a raised midrib, evergreen. Fruit a capsule. Two native species and 10 more or less established aliens.

1 Yellow Iris *Iris pseudacorus*. By far our commonest iris, a tall stout carpeter, to 1.5m. Flowers rich *yellow*, 80-100mm; June-August. Leaves typically iris-like, 10-30mm broad. Seeds pale brown, flattened. Aka Yellow Flag. Marshes, by fresh water, and other wet places.

1   SOZ   ▫

2 Stinking Iris *Iris foetidissima*. Medium, tufted, to 80cm, sometimes called Roast-beef Plant for its sweetly acrid smell reputedly like 'high' medieval meat. Flowers pale *grey-purple*, occasionally yellow, 50-70mm; not appearing in every tuft; June-July. Leaves *dark green*, 10-25mm broad. Seeds bright *orange*, conspicuous in autumn and early winter. Aka Gladdon. Woods, scrub, hedge-banks, sea cliffs, often on lime. The introduced **2a Purple Iris** *Iris versicolor* has purpler flowers, the falls with a broader yellow midrib. Leaves with *no raised midrib*, often tinged red at the base. Established by fresh water in a few places.

2   S   ▫

3 Bearded Iris *Iris germanica*. By far the most frequent naturalised iris, especially on railway banks and near towns. Medium/tall, to 90cm, with conspicuous above-ground rootstock. Flowers usually some shade of purple or blue-violet, with a yellow 'beard' on the falls, 8-15cm; May-June. Leaves 30-60mm broad. **3a Turkish Iris** *I. orientalis*, with white flowers and a yellow patch on the falls, is much less frequent, but common around Northfleet and Swanscombe, N Kent, and increasing in the New Forest.

3   ▫

~

4 Snakeshead Iris *Hermodactylus tuberosus*. Short/medium perennial, to 40cm, with no above-ground rootstock. Flowers fragrant, *iris-like*, yellowish-green, the outer petals (falls) with broad, strikingly *dark purplish-brown* tips, 50-65mm; March-May. Leaves quite *un-irislike*, narrow and 4-angled. Established on grassy banks in SW England.

5 Blue-eyed Grass *Sisyrinchium bermudiana*. Short, tufted, *branched*, to 60cm. Flowers *pale* blue, 6-petalled, starlike, 15-20mm; opening one at a time at the tip of a branch; June-July. Leaves iris-like. Fruiting stems curved or drooping. Grassy places, stony loughshores. Native, *W Ireland* only. **5a American Blue-eyed Grass** *S. montanum* is unbranched with *larger* (25-35mm), more purplish-blue flowers and fruiting stems erect. A scattered escape in Great Britain.

5   ▫

6 Yellow-eyed Grass *Sisyrinchium californicum*. Like American Blue-eyed Grass (**5a**), but with bright *yellow* 12-18mm flowers. A rarer escape, Ireland and Wales. **6a Pale Yellow-eyed Grass** *S. striatum* is much taller, to 75mm, with paler yellow flowers all up the stem and broader leaves. Frequent in gardens, established in a few places.

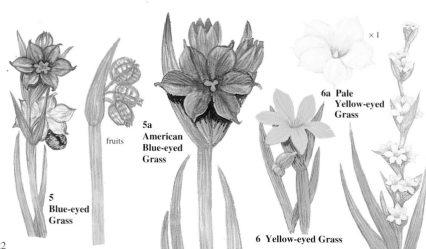

× 1

6a Pale Yellow-eyed Grass

5a American Blue-eyed Grass

fruits

5 Blue-eyed Grass

6 Yellow-eyed Grass

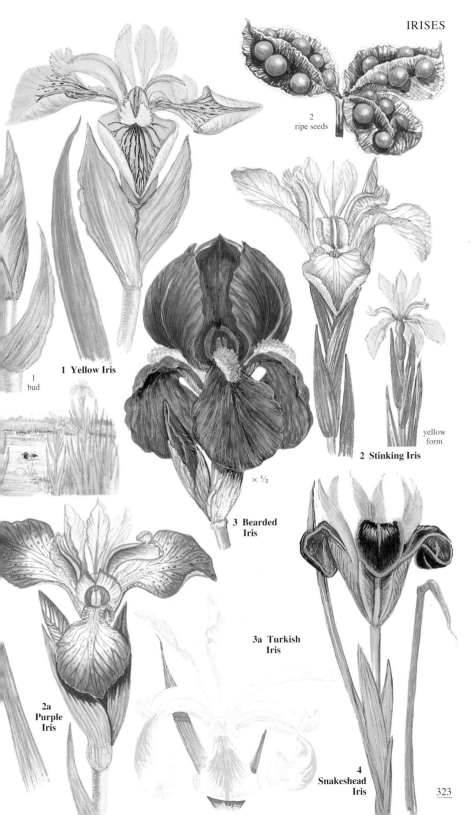

2
ripe seeds

1 **Yellow Iris**

1
bud

× ½

3 **Bearded
Iris**

2 **Stinking Iris**

yellow
form

3a **Turkish
Iris**

2a
**Purple
Iris**

4
**Snakeshead
Iris**

Crocuses *Crocus*. No native species but 13, often well established, escapes. Flowers shaped like a narrow wine-glass, the six petals often spreading in sunshine, differing from *Colchicum* (**4**) in their three pale yellow stamens, much shorter than the feathery orange stigma. Leaves very narrow with a *whitish midrib*. Often abundant in churchyards.

1 Dutch Crocus *Crocus × stellaris*. The familiar garden crocus and much the most widespread escape. Flowers yellow, the petals often with brownish-purple stripes outside; March-April, with the leaves. Usually casual, occasionally well established.

2 Spring Crocus *Crocus vernus*. Flowers deep to pale purple, white with purple stripes or white, 30-55mm; March-April, with the leaves. Widely and often long naturalised, especially at Inkpen, Berkshire. The increasing **2a Early Crocus** *C. tommasinianus* has much slenderer and paler flowers, with a white tube; late February-early April; leaves narrower.

3 Autumn Crocus *Crocus nudiflorus*. Flowers pale lilac-purple, 30-60mm, on long (20-30mm) sprawling white stems; *Sept-Oct*, without the leaves, which appear in spring and wither in summer. Long naturalised (introduced by medieval monks) in grassy places, especially S Lancashire and around Huddersfield and Halifax, W Yorkshire. Also autumn-flowering, but much less frequent, is the shorter **3a Veined Autumn Crocus** *C. speciosus*, whose petals have darker purple veins.

~

4 Meadow Saffron *Colchicum autumnale*. Sometimes also called Autumn Crocus because of its late-flowering crocus-like flowers, but actually a member of the Lily Family (p. 308) and differing from true Autumn Crocus (**3**) in its *six stamens*, orange anthers and shorter white styles. Flowers pale pinkish-mauve, 30-45cm, on a long (5-20cm) sprawling white tube, whence folk-name Naked Ladies; August-Sept. Leaves broad lanceolate, bright green, appearing in confusingly flowerless tufts in *spring*, along with the egg-shaped fruits, and withering long before the flowers. Woods, especially in the Cotswolds, and damp meadows; occasionally naturalised elsewhere.

5 ***Sand Crocus *Romulea columnae*. Low, to 10cm. Flowers like a tiny Crocus (above), the six narrow pointed petals pale purple, purple-veined, yellow at the base and greenish outside, and anthers bright yellow, 10-12mm, *opening fully only in sunshine*; March-May. Leaves like curly green bristles, merging into the surrounding grass. Sandy places, only on Dawlish Warren, S Devon, and one site in Cornwall.

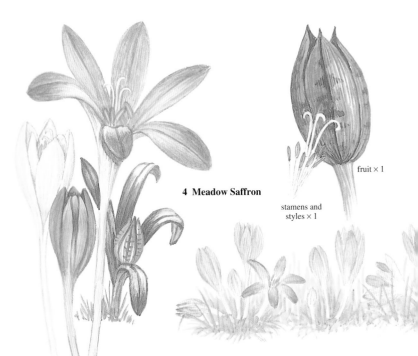

4 Meadow Saffron

fruit × 1

stamens and styles × 1

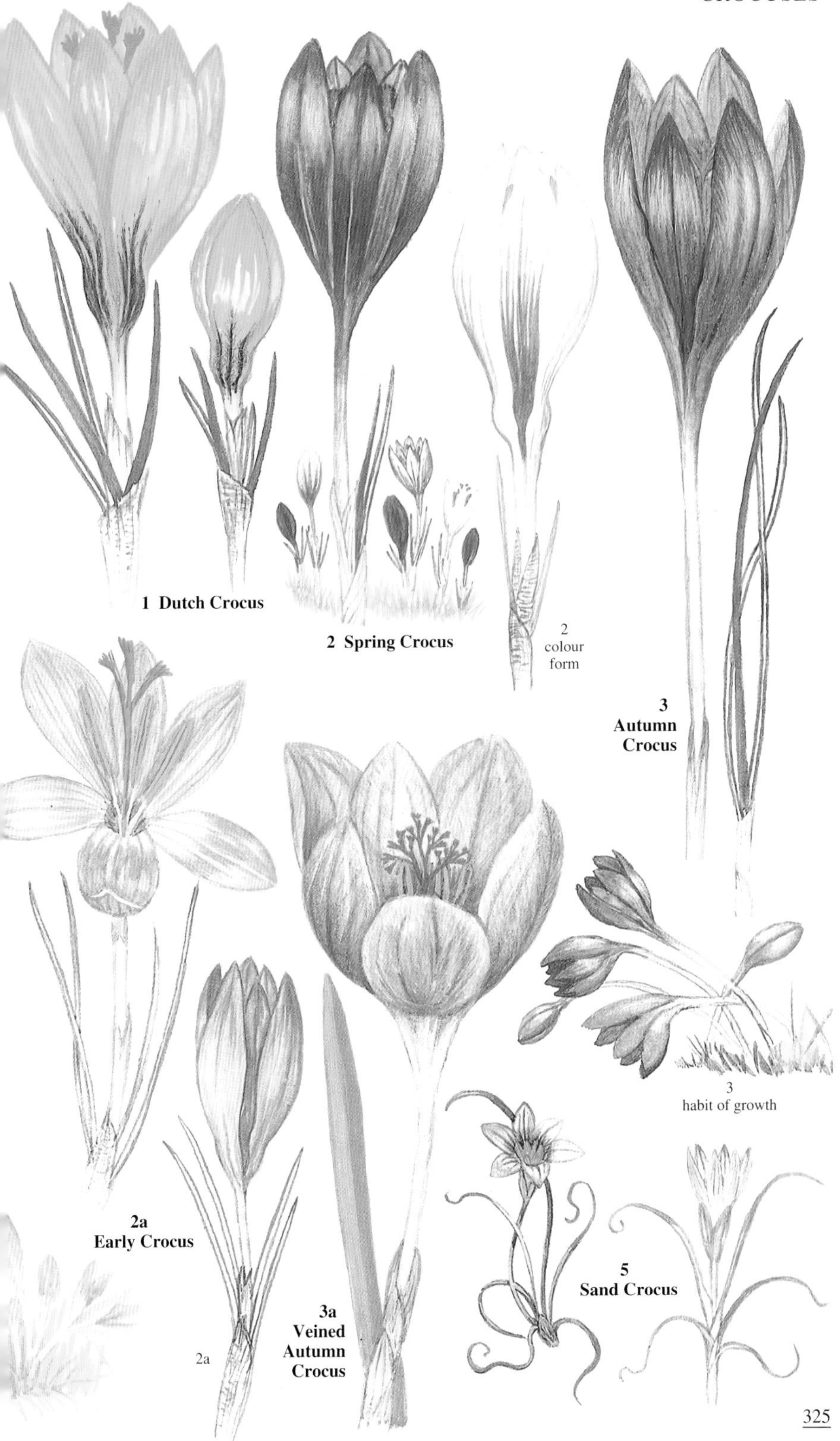

1 Dutch Crocus

2 Spring Crocus

2
colour
form

3
Autumn
Crocus

2a
Early Crocus

2a

3a
Veined
Autumn
Crocus

3
habit of growth

5
Sand Crocus

ORCHID FAMILY Orchidaceae

Unbranched perennials, virtually hairless, except for helleborines *Epipactis* (p. 334). Flowers of diverse shapes, but always *2-lipped*, with one extremely variable lower petal or lip, usually larger, sometimes much larger than the two upper ones and often grotesquely shaped and spurred behind; sepals three, sometimes the same colour as the two upper petals; in spikes, each with a leaf-like bract and the stamens and stigmas joined in a central column. Leaves undivided, untoothed. Fruit egg-shaped or cylindrical, the seeds minute and very numerous. Hybrids frequent.

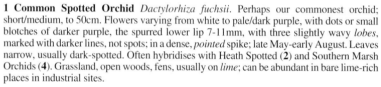

Lower lip with a conspicuous long spur:	Fragrant Orchid, Pyramidal Orchid, Butterfly Orchids
not spurred:	Musk, Bog, Fen, Bee, Fly, Spiders, Helleborines, Lady's Tresses's, Saprophytes, Tongue Orchids
not lobed:	Heath/Early/Southern/Northern Spotted Orchids, Butterfly Orchids, White/Narrow-leaved/Red Helleborines, Lady's Tresses's, Ghost Orchid
2-lobed:	Twayblades, Frog Orchid, Musk Orchid, Birdsnest Orchid
4-lobed (manikin):	Burnt-tip, Lady, Military, Monkey, Man, Fly
very long lobe:	Lizard
Leaves dark-spotted:	Spotted Orchids, Southern Marsh, var. *junialis*, Western/Lapland Marsh, Early Purple, Lizard, Dense-flowered

1 Common Spotted Orchid *Dactylorhiza fuchsii*. Perhaps our commonest orchid; short/medium, to 50cm. Flowers varying from white to pale/dark purple, with dots or small blotches of darker purple, the spurred lower lip 7-11mm, with three slightly wavy *lobes*, marked with darker lines, not spots; in a dense, *pointed* spike; late May-early August. Leaves narrow, usually dark-spotted. Often hybridises with Heath Spotted (**2**) and Southern Marsh Orchids (**4**). Grassland, open woods, fens, usually on *lime*; can be abundant in bare lime-rich places in industrial sites.

2 Heath Spotted Orchid *Dactylorhiza maculata*. Very like Common Spotted Orchid (**1**). Flowers similar but with a *short central tooth* on the more wavy *unlobed* lower lip, in a flatter, blunter spike. Heaths, moors and bogs on *acid* soils.

3 Early Marsh Orchid *Dactylorhiza incarnata*. Short, to 40cm. Flowers exceptionally variable, most often flesh-coloured, but also of many shades of pink, rose, mauve, purple, bright red (ssp. *coccinea*), brick-red (ssp. *pulchella*) and straw-yellow (ssp. *ochroleuca*); lip 5-7mm with neat double loops and a (sometimes obscure) central tooth, looking very narrow as the sides are soon *folded right back*; spur *straight*, tapering; May-July. Leaves yellowish-green, usually unspotted, hooded at tip. Marshes, wet meadows, fens, bogs, dune slacks, lough shores.

4 Southern Marsh Orchid *Dactylorhiza praetermissa*. Short/medium, to 50cm. Flowers usually dark rose-purple with the sepals spread like a bird's wings, the lip 9-14mm with darker spots and streaks and a (sometimes obscure) central tooth, concave with the edges curled up at first, later turned down; spur stout, *curved* with a blunt tip; late May-July. Leaves dark green, usually unspotted, scarcely hooded. Var. *junialis* has dark rings on the leaves and loops not spots on the lower lip; formerly confused with the hybrid between Southern Marsh and Common Spotted (**1**) Orchids. Marshes, wet meadows, fens, bogs, dune slacks, bare lime-rich places in industrial sites, exceptionally even in chalk grassland, the commonest marsh orchid in England.

5 Northern Marsh Orchid *Dactylorhiza purpurella*. Shorter, to 25cm, than Southern Marsh Orchid (**4**), with which it scarcely overlaps, and has flowers of a markedly redder purple, the lip 7-9mm with a central tooth, and a short stout spur. Leaves usually unspotted. Marshes, wet meadows, fens, dune slacks, the commonest marsh orchid in Scotland.

6 Western Marsh Orchid *Dactylorhiza majalis*. Differs from Northern Marsh Orchid (**5**) in the lower lip of its pale reddish-purple flowers having a more conspicuous central lobe, May-June, but especially in its leaves being *well spotted*, except in Ireland. Marshes, wet meadows, fens, dune slacks.

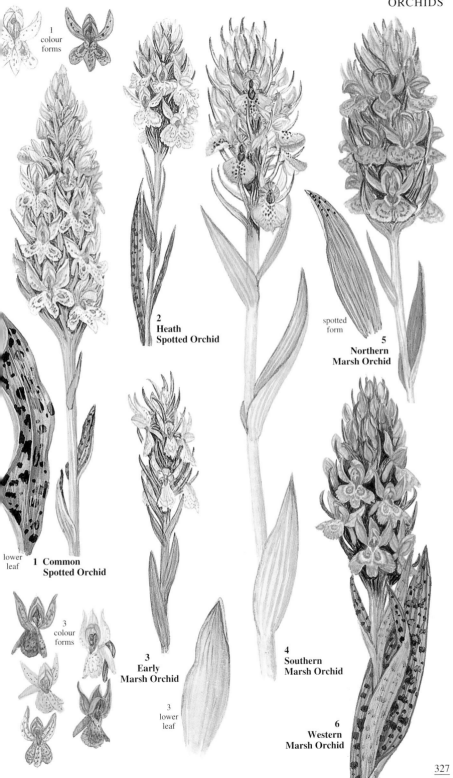

1
colour
forms

**2
Heath
Spotted Orchid**

spotted
form

**5
Northern
Marsh Orchid**

lower
leaf

**1 Common
Spotted Orchid**

3
colour
forms

**3
Early
Marsh Orchid**

3
lower
leaf

**4
Southern
Marsh Orchid**

**6
Western
Marsh Orchid**

1 *Narrow-leaved Marsh Orchid *Dactylorhiza traunsteineri*. Slenderer than other marsh orchids (p. 326), to 30cm. Flowers pale to deep red-purple, the lower lip 3-lobed or with central lobe; May-June. Leaves *narrow*, un- or faintly spotted. Damp grassy places, *fens on lime*.

2 **Lapland Marsh Orchid *Dactylorhiza lapponica*. Short, to 20cm. Flowers red-purple, the lower lip either 1- or 3-lobed, much more heavily marked than other marsh orchids (p. 326). Leaves well *blotched or spotted*. Flushes in hills in far western Scotland; not discovered till 1986.

3 Fragrant Orchid *Gymnadenia conopsea*. Short, to 40cm. Flowers pale pink-purple, very *fragrant*, 8-12mm with a 3-lobed lip and a *slender* spur, much *longer* (8-17mm) than all our other pink/purple orchids except Pyramidal (**4**); in a dense *elongated* spike; June-July. Leaves narrow, unspotted. Grassland and fens on lime; hill grassland in the N.

4 Pyramidal Orchid *Anacamptis pyramidalis*. Short, to 60cm. Flowers deep pink, either clove-scented or foxy-smelling, 10-12mm, with 3-lobed lip and a curved spur as long (12-14mm) and slender as Fragrant Orchid (**3**), but in a much *squatter*, almost pyramidal spike; June-early August. Leaves narrow, unspotted. Grassland, usually on lime, dunes.

5 Early Purple Orchid *Orchis mascula*. Short, to 40cm. Flowers usually some shade of purple, sometimes pinkish or white, with an unpleasant tom-cat smell; one sepal and two petals form a hood, the two other sepals erect and backing against each other, the 6-8mm lip slightly lobed, spurred; in a loose spike; *April*-June. Leaves usually *blotched* purplish-black. Woods, hedge-banks, grassland.

6 Green-winged Orchid *Anacamptis morio*. Distinctly shorter than Early Purple Orchid (**5**), to 20cm, and with a range of flower colour second only to Early Marsh Orchid (p. 326). Flowers fragrant, deep to pale purple, pink or white (the most often white of the purple-flowered orchids), readily told by the parallel *dark green veins* on the three purple sepals, which together form a hood, the spurred 8-10mm lip shallowly 3-lobed; in a loose spike; May-June. Leaves *unspotted*. Grassland, especially meadows; decreasing.

7 Musk Orchid *Herminium monorchis*. Slender, low, inconspicuous, to 15cm. Flowers yellowish-green, 6-8mm, misleadingly named as they smell of honey, not musk; the *unspurred* 3-4mm lip with two *short basal lobes*; in a small dense spike; June-July. Leaves broad, blunt, 2-3 near base of stem. Short turf on lime.

8 *Bog Orchid *Hammarbya paludosa*. Our smallest, very inconspicuous orchid; low, to 8cm. Flowers yellowish-green, with the 2mm unspurred lip twisted round to the top, 6-8mm; July-Sept. Leaves elliptical, fringed with *tiny bulbils*. On wet *Sphagnum* moss in *bogs*.

9 **Fen Orchid *Liparis loeselii*. Low/short, to 20cm. Flowers yellow, with the broad upright 4-5mm unspurred lip often twisted round to the top, 9-11mm; June-July. Leaves, an opposite basal pair, yellowish-green, shiny. Fens (E Anglia), dune slacks (S Wales).

10 Small White Orchid *Pseudorchis albida*. Low/short, to 20cm. Flowers fragrant, white, variously tinged creamy, yellowish or greenish, the short-spurred 2-3mm lip *3-lobed to a T-shape*; in a short spike; May-June. Leaves narrow, up the stem. Short turf on mountain ledges, often on lime.

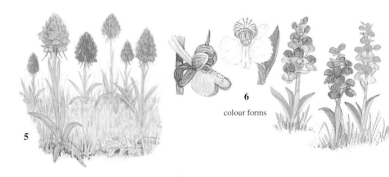

6
colour forms

5

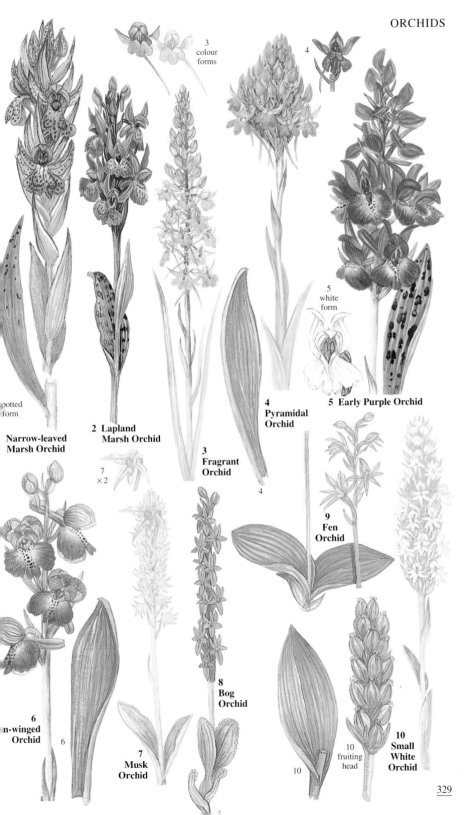

3
colour
forms

4

5
white
form

5 Early Purple Orchid

potted
form

4
Pyramidal
Orchid

2 Lapland
Marsh Orchid

Narrow-leaved
Marsh Orchid

7
× 2

3
Fragrant
Orchid

4

9
Fen
Orchid

6
n-winged
Orchid

6

7
Musk
Orchid

8
Bog
Orchid

10

10
fruiting
head

10
Small
White
Orchid

329

'Manikin' Orchids. The next five orchids have their spurred lip 4-lobed to mimic a manikin, whence most of their names; flowers in spikes. Leaves unspotted.

1 *Burnt-tip Orchid *Orchis ustulata*. One of our smallest and most distinctive orchids, low, to 15mm. Flowers heliotrope-scented, with the dark *maroon-purple* hooded sepals (the burnt tip) contrasting strongly with the pink-dotted white 4-8mm manikin lip; in a short dense spike; May-June. *Short turf on lime*, rarely in meadows.

2 *Lady Orchid *Orchis purpurea*. An outsize version of Burnt-tip Orchid (**1**), medium, to 50cm. Flowers perhaps the most beautiful of all our orchids, fragrant, with the *dark purplish-brown* hooded sepals contrasting exquisitely with the pale pink 10-15mm manikin lip; May-June. Woods and scrub on chalk.

3 ***Military Orchid *Orchis militaris*. Short, to 45cm. Flowers pale to dark pink-purple, the *paler* hooded sepals (the 'soldier's' helmet) contrasting with the darker 12-15mm manikin lip; May-June. Three wooded or scrubby sites, two in the Chilterns, one in W Suffolk.

4 ***Monkey Orchid *Orchis simia*. Short, to 30cm. Flowers like miniature Military Orchids (**3**), the hood greyish-white, faintly streaked with pink, the red-spotted pale pinkish 14-16mm manikin lip having *very narrow*, often *curled*, 'limbs'; May-June. Unlike all other orchids, the flowers open from the top downwards. Three sites on chalk turf, two in Kent, one in the Chilterns.

5 *Man Orchid *Orchis anthropophorum*. Short, to 40cm. The only manikin orchid with *yellow* flowers (but beware the 'armless' Common Twayblade, **8**), the 12-15mm lip, sometimes edged red-brown, with very narrow 'limbs'; late May-early July. Leaves lanceolate. Short turf on lime, especially on the North Downs in Kent.

~

6 Dense-flowered Orchid *Neotinea maculata*. Short, to 30cm. Flowers vanilla-scented, hooded, greenish-white, either unmarked with unspotted leaves or less often with purplish spots or streaks and spotted leaves; the 3-4mm lip *3-lobed* with a short blunt spur; May-early June, followed by conspicuous close-ranked fruiting capsules. Limestone pavements, dunes; W Ireland, one dune site on Man.

7 **Lizard Orchid *Himantoglossum hircinum*. Stout, greyish, medium, to 70cm. Flowers yellow-green tinged grey-purple, fancifully lizard-like by taking the manikin theme to an extreme; the long twisted straplike 30-50mm lips with a short spur and two short 'arms' form an untidy raggle-taggle spike, smelling of billy goat, especially if kept in a confined space; June-July. Leaves elliptic, sometimes mottled purple. Short turf and scrub on lime, dunes.

8 Common Twayblade *Listera ovata*. An unobtrusive all-green medium orchid, to 60cm. Flowers yellowish-green, with a long narrow forked unspurred 7-15mm lip, in a long spike; May-July. Leaves, a distinctive *single pair*, unstalked and low down on the stem, *broadly oval*; cf. butterfly orchids (p. 332). Woods, grassy places.

9 Lesser Twayblade *Listera cordata*. Slender, inconspicuous, low, 4-10cm. Flowers like a miniature Common Twayblade (**8**), *dull reddish-green*, more hooded, the purplish 3-4mm lip with two short lobes at the base; June-August. Leaves a single pair, glossy and *heart-shaped*. Moors, bogs, pinewoods, among moss and quite often hidden under heather.

10 Frog Orchid *Dactylorhiza viridis*. Low/short, often very inconspicuous, 5-20cm. Flowers, supposedly like a jumping frog, yellowish-green, edged and tinged *reddish*, hooded, the 6-8mm lip very short-spurred, straplike, *forked at the tip* with a tooth in the middle; in a short spike; June-August. Leaves lanceolate. Grassy places, short turf on lime in the S, elsewhere meadows, mountain ledges, dunes.

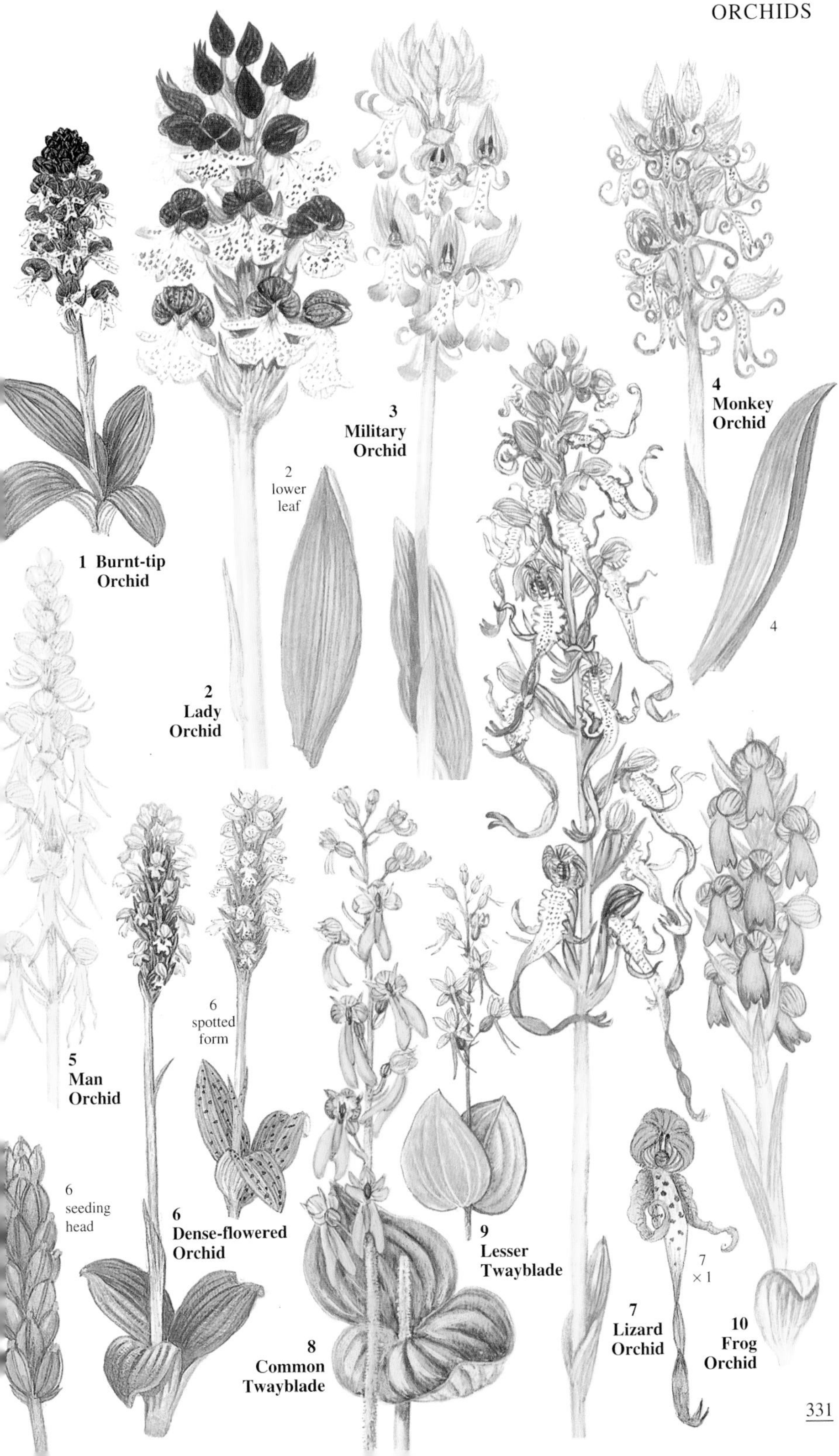

1 Burnt-tip Orchid

2 lower leaf

2 Lady Orchid

3 Military Orchid

4 Monkey Orchid

4

5 Man Orchid

6 spotted form

6 seeding head

6 Dense-flowered Orchid

8 Common Twayblade

9 Lesser Twayblade

7 × 1

7 Lizard Orchid

10 Frog Orchid

1 Greater Butterfly Orchid *Platanthera chlorantha*. Medium, to 60cm. Flowers slightly vanilla-scented, white, often tinged green, the sepals converging, two petals diverging at right-angles, the 8-12mm undivided green-tipped lip with a long 18-27mm, often well curved spur, the yellow pollen-masses *diverging*; in a loose spike; June-July. One pair of broadly elliptical root leaves (cf. Common Twayblade, p. 330), with narrower leaves up the stem. Woods, also grassland in the N, usually on lime.

2 Lesser Butterfly Orchid *Platanthera bifolia*. Generally smaller in all its parts than Greater Butterfly Orchid (**1**), but best separated by its *closely parallel* pollen-masses; also has a stronger vanilla scent and a longer (25-30mm), less curved spur. Woods, grassland (flowers usually white); moors, bogs (flowers greener).

3 Bee Orchid *Ophrys apifera*. Short, to 45cm. The most conspicuous part of the flower looks remarkably like the rear of a small bumblebee visiting it; this is the swollen 3-lobed 10-13mm lip, *warm brown* with *honey-coloured* markings, unspurred but with an append-age which is normally tucked right under it, but may project straight downwards; such plants, **3a** var. *trollii*, are called wasp orchids, but 'wasp' flowers can occur on the same plant as 'bees'. The three sepals are *pink*, broad and spreading, and the two inner petals narrow and *green*; June-July. Leaves narrowly oval, rather waxy, up the stem. Grassland and bare places on lime.

4 Fly Orchid *Ophrys insectifera*. Short/medium, slender, to 60cm. Flowers with a 9-10mm chocolate-brown unspurred *manikin* lip having two broad 'legs' and two tiny 'arms', the two inner petals dark brown and antenna-like (hence the 'fly') and the three se-pals lanceolate and green; May-June. Leaves rather glossy, mainly at the base. Woodland edges, scrub, grassy places, fens, mainly on lime.

5 **Early Spider Orchid *Ophrys sphegodes*. Like a rather large squat early-flowering (*March-May*) Bee Orchid (**3**); short, to 20cm. Flowers similar, but the lip larger, 10-12mm, with no appendage but a *notch* at the tip, and with a *bluish* mark like X, H or Greek Π (the 'spider'); the inner petals *yellowish-green*. Leaves mostly at the base. Short turf on lime.

6 **Late Spider Orchid *Ophrys fuciflora*. Intermediate between Bee (**3**) and Early Spi-der (**5**), resembling Bee in being short/medium, to 35cm, having sepals pinkish and flow-ering June-July; and Early Spider in the hieroglyphic on its lip and leaves mainly basal; but differing from both in its broader (11-15mm) lip with a short broad greenish appendage not turning back, and inner petals pinkish. Chalk turf, E Kent.

7 Autumn Lady's Tresses *Spiranthes spiralis*. Low, to 15cm. Flowers differing from all other white-flowered orchids, except Irish and Creeping Lady's Tresses (**8, 9**), in its 4-6mm flowers being arranged *spirally* up the stem; fragrant, green-centred within, not spurred; with small bracts; *August-Sept*. Leaves bluish-green, the basal ones withering be-fore the flowering stem, with a few small scale-like leaves, appears. Dry grassy places.

8 *Irish Lady's Tresses *Spiranthes romanzoffiana*. One of our most striking orchids, when the bright creamy white flowers rise starkly and unexpectedly out of the mundane grasses. Short, to 30cm. Flowers 10-14mm, unspurred, in 3 spirals, with green bracts; August-Sept. Leaves narrow, mainly up the stem. Wet grassy places, disued lazy beds, loch shores.

9 Creeping Lady's Tresses *Goodyera repens*. Differs from Autumn Lady's Tresses (**7**) especially in its creeping stems and *smaller* (3-4mm), rather sickly-smelling white flow-ers, in a single spiral, with more *conspicuous bracts*; July-August. Leaves pointed oval, net-veined, sometimes marbled, in non-flowering overwintering rosettes, two basal and scale-like ones up the stems. Pine- and birchwoods, dunes.

pollen masses
× 2

3a Wasp Orchid

1   2   9

developing fruit

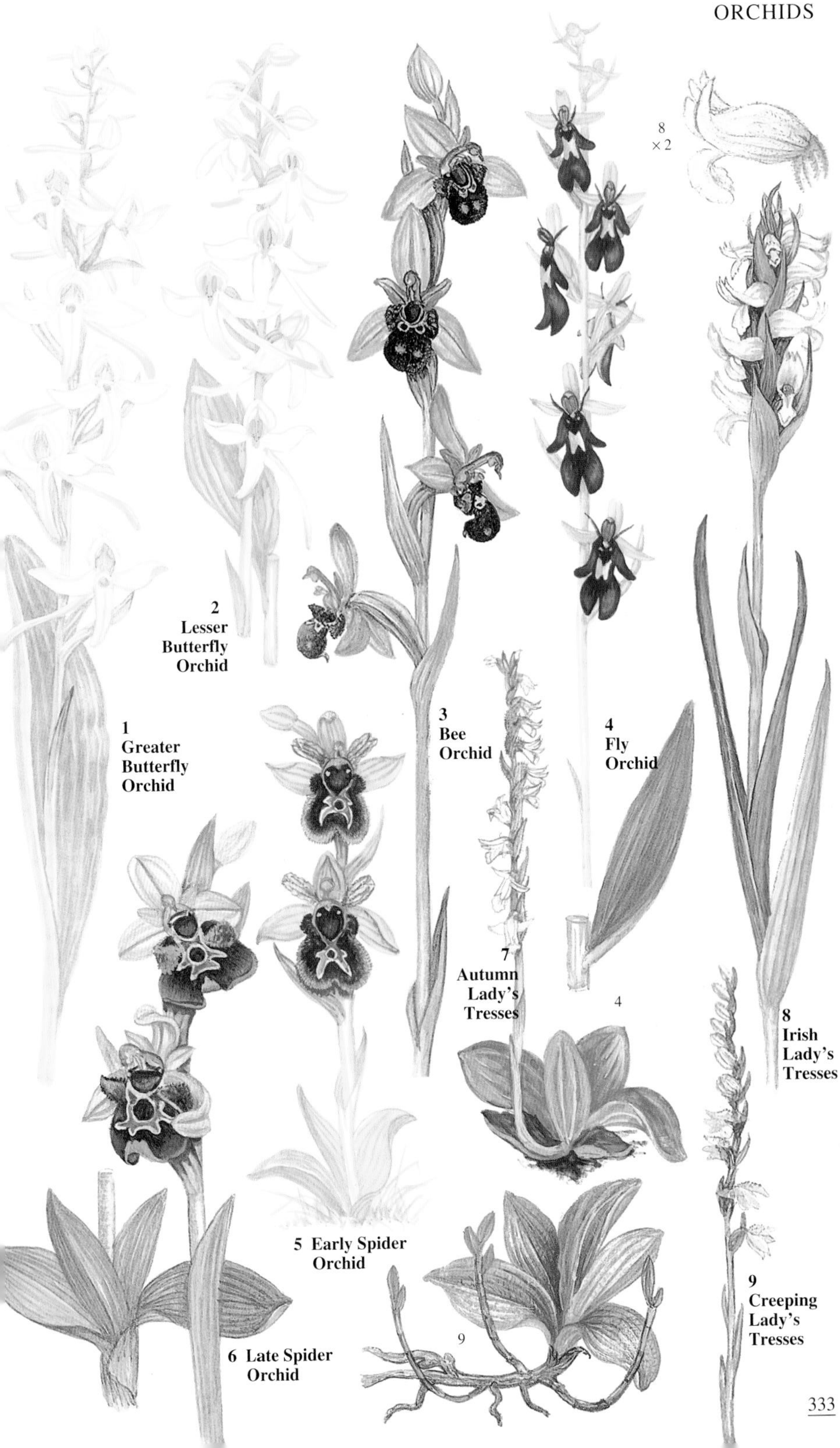

8
× 2

2
Lesser
Butterfly
Orchid

1
Greater
Butterfly
Orchid

3
Bee
Orchid

4
Fly
Orchid

7
Autumn
Lady's
Tresses

4

8
Irish
Lady's
Tresses

5 Early Spider
Orchid

9

9
Creeping
Lady's
Tresses

6 Late Spider
Orchid

Helleborines. Two quite distinct genera of orchids, *Cephalanthera* with flowers largely closed, so the unspurred lip may not be apparent, and *Epipactis*, with unspurred open flowers and an obvious lip. They are so named because the classical Greeks saw in one of them a likeness to the leaves of the Balkan plant we clumsily call White False Helleborine *Veratrum album*.

1 Marsh Helleborine *Epipactis palustris*. Medium, stem often purplish below, to 45cm. Flowers with a combination, unique in our flora, of petals mainly *crimson and white* both inside and out, and a long 2-jointed ll-13mm lip whose *frilly* white lower half has a yellow spot, the cup-shaped upper half with crimson streaks; the sepals purplish, tinged yellow inside and brown outside. July-August. Leaves narrow lanceolate. Fens, marshes, dune slacks.

2 Violet Helleborine *Epipactis purpurata*. Medium, the stems in a *clump*, to 60cm; the whole plant *suffused with purple*. Flowers pale greenish-white inside, purplish-green outside, the broad lip 8-10mm with its tip recurved, with long leafy bracts; in crowded spikes *late July*-Sept. Leaves narrow, parallel-sided, greyish above, purplish below. Woods, often in deep shade.

3 Broad-leaved Helleborine *Epipactis helleborine*. Generally our commonest helleborine; medium, stems *solitary*, often purplish below, to 80cm. Flowers greenish-yellow to purplish-pink (reddish on dunes at Kenfig, S Wales), fully open, the sepals pointed and the *broader-than-long* 9-10mm lip heart-shaped and eventually *curved back*; equalling the leafy bracts; and in a long 1-sided spike; July-Sept. Leaves sometimes tinged purplish, fairly broad, half-clasping, spirally up the stem. Woods, shady places. A curious plant found in Northumberland in 1976 has less open flowers with pink petals and green sepals edged pink or white and a 3-horned stigma; it may have originated as a hybrid with Green-flowered Helleborine (**5**) and has been described as **3a** ****Young's Helleborine** *E. youngiana*.

4 *Narrow-lipped Helleborine *Epipactis leptochila*. Medium, suffused *yellowish*, never purplish, to 60cm. Flowers pale *yellowish-green*, semi-nodding and often only half-open, with longer, more pointed petals than Broad-leaved Helleborine (**3**), the much-longer-than-broad 4-9mm lip with a whitish edge and some purple or white markings, and the pointed tip *not curved back*; equalling or shorter than the leafy bracts; July-Sept. Leaves narrowly elliptical, not oval, in two rows up the stem. Woods, especially on lime and in the Chilterns, stream-beds, dunes (4a var. *dunensis* has a broader lip, its tip curved back).

5 *Green-flowered Helleborine *Epipactis phyllanthes*. Short, to 40cm. Flowers *apple-green*, usually only partly opened and *hanging down* more markedly than our other helleborines, the lowest shorter than their leafy bracts; July-August. Leaves grass-green, longer than broad, 2-ranked up the stems. Woods on lime or sand, dunes.

6 *Dark Red Helleborine *Epipactis atrorubens*. Short, to 30cm. Flowers fully open, a distinctive *uniform* shade of *dark red*, slightly fragrant, the lip 5-6mm; June-July. Leaves oval, purplish, in two ranks up the stem. Limestone rocks, open ashwoods.

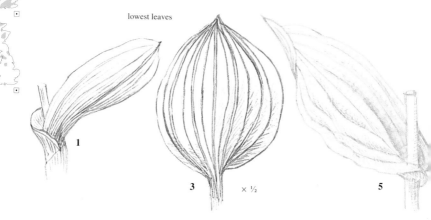

lowest leaves

1

3   × ½   5

3 Broad-leaved Helleborine

6 Dark Red Helleborine

2 Violet Helleborine

1 Marsh Helleborine

5 Green-flowered Helleborine

4 Narrow-lipped Helleborine

1 White Helleborine *Cephalanthera damasonium*. Medium, stem ridged, to 60cm. Flowers *creamy* white, rarely fully open, the base of the unspurred lip orange-yellow inside (whence folk name Poached-egg Plant), unstalked, all but the topmost shorter than their *conspicuous* leaflike bracts; May-July. Leaves slightly bluish-green, broad lanceolate, becoming narrower up the stem. Woods, usually of beech and on lime.

2 *Narrow-leaved Helleborine *Cephalanthera longifolia*, More graceful than White Helleborine (**1**), differing especially in its *pure white*, more widely open flowers with a much smaller orange spot on the lip, and more conspicuous because of their *tiny* bracts; May-June. Leaves darker green, longer, narrower, parallel-sided and drooping at the tip. Decreasing in beech and other woods, mainly on lime.

3 ***Red Helleborine *Cephalanthera rubra*. Short/medium, to 60cm. Flowers a most beautiful *purplish-pink*, the unspurred lip whitish, not usually opening widely, mostly longer than their bracts; June-July. Leaves tinged purple, narrow lanceolate, up the stems. Gaps in the canopy in beechwoods.

Saprophyte Orchids. The next three orchids are saprophytes, plants with no green colouring matter, *no leaves* but a few scales up the stem, and feeding on rotting vegetation with the aid of a fungus partner. The superficially similar broomrapes (p. 244) are root-parasites.

4 Birdsnest Orchid *Neottia nidus-avis*. Short/medium, *honey-coloured all over*, to 60cm. Flowers with a sickly fragrance, unspurred, the *2-lobed* 8-12mm lip distinguishing it both from the Broomrapes (lip 3-lobed) and from the smaller, unlobed but semantically confusing Yellow Birdsnest (p. 246). Named from the fancied likeness of its roots to a bird's nest. Woods, especially beechwoods, in deep shade.

5 Coralroot Orchid *Corallorhiza trifida*. Low/short, creeping, *yellowish all over*, but tinged brown or green, to 20cm; our only saprophyte orchid to have any green. Flowers *yellowish-green*, the shallowly slightly 3-lobed unspurred 4-6mm white lip marked with red; June-July. Moist peaty and mossy places in pine/birch woods, alder/willow scrub and dune slacks,

6 ***Ghost Orchid *Epipogium aphyllum*. Its erratic appearances and excellent camouflage make this perhaps our hardest wild plant to find; low, *pinkish-yellow all over*, to 25cm. Flowers with a sickly fragrance, very pale yellow, with a very pale mauve-pink 6-8mm *lip bent back* almost to touch the stout white upward-pointing spur; usually no more than 1-3 together; late May-early Oct. Beechwoods, in deep shade, now only in the S Chilterns, possibly extinct.

~

7 ***Lady's Slipper *Cypripedium calceolus*. Both the rarest and the most strikingly distinctive of our native orchids; short, to 30cm. Flowers solitary, at 30cm easily our largest orchid, with a billowing yellow unspurred lip, the other petals and sepals being narrowly lanceolate and maroon-purple; May-June. Leaves broad lanceolate, pale green. A single site in West Yorkshire, perhaps introduced elsewhere.

Tongue Orchids *Serapias*. Small spring-flowering S European orchids with red-brown flowers, the three sepals hooded, two of the petals narrowly pointed and an unspurred 3-lobed lip whose two upper lobes are rounded. Several species appear to be benefiting from global warming by appearing sporadically on either side of the English Channel.

The one with the greatest claim to be native, **8 Small-flowered Tongue Orchid** *Serapias parviflora*, has a narrow middle lip-lobe; in scrub in S Cornwall. **8a Heart-flowered Tongue Orchid** *S. cordigera* has its middle lobe shaped like an ace-of-spades (not hearts!); though seen in several recent years in a Kentish chalk-pit, its seed may have floated out of a nearby greenhouse. **8b Tongue Orchid** *S. lingua*, its middle lobe intermediate between the other two, has only appeared in Guernsey, and not since 1992.

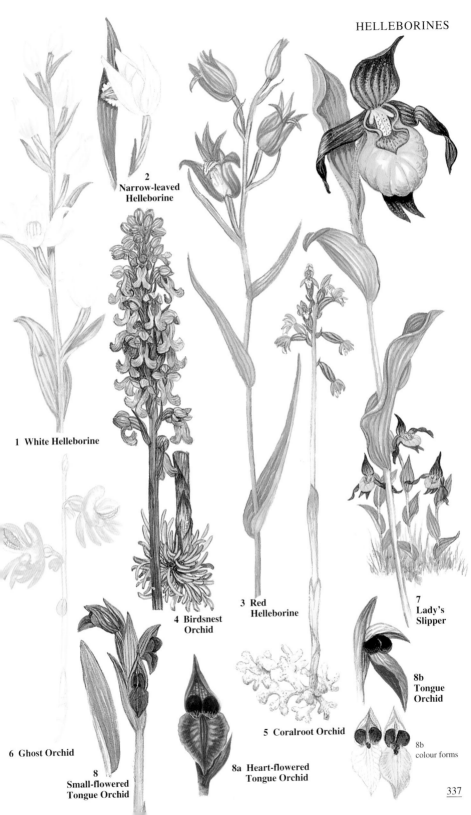

2 **Narrow-leaved Helleborine**

1 **White Helleborine**

4 **Birdsnest Orchid**

3 **Red Helleborine**

7 **Lady's Slipper**

8b **Tongue Orchid**

8b colour forms

5 **Coralroot Orchid**

6 **Ghost Orchid**

8 **Small-flowered Tongue Orchid**

8a **Heart-flowered Tongue Orchid**

FLOWERING-RUSH FAMILY Butomaceae

1 Flowering Rush *Butomus umbellatus*. Handsome aquatic plant, quite unrelated to the true Rushes (p. 412). A tall stout perennial, to 1.5m. Flowers with three *rose-pink* petals and three darker sepals, cup-shaped, 16-26mm, in large umbels; July-Sept. Leaves long, stiff, grass-like. Fruits purple. Fresh water.

WATER-PLANTAIN FAMILY Alismataceae

Aquatics. Flowers usually in whorls on leafless stems, with three petals and three sepals. Fruit a nutlet.

2 Water-plantain *Alisma plantago-aquatica*. A tall perennial, to 1m. Flowers pale lilac, 6-10mm; June-August, opening from midday to evening. Leaves broad lanceolate, slightly plantain-like, *rounded* at the base, long-stalked, all aerial and from the roots. Fruits in a close ring, a long beak (style) arising *at or below their middle*. In and by fresh water.

3 Narrow-leaved Water-plantain *Alisma lanceolata*. Differs from Water-plantain (**2**) mainly in its narrower leaves being *narrowed at the base, the pinker*, sometimes slightly larger flowers opening from morning to midday, and the fruits widest *near the middle* with the *straight* style arising in the *upper half* of the fruit. Especially on clay.

4 ***Ribbon-leaved Water-plantain *Alisma gramineum*. An often largely submerged perennial, to 30cm. Flowers *white* to pale lilac, 4-7mm; June-August. Leaves either submerged and ribbon-like or aerial and narrowly elliptic. Fruits widest *in upper half*, with a *recurved* style. Now only in one shallow pond near Droitwich, Worcestershire.

5 Lesser Water-plantain *Baldellia ranunculoides*. A low creeping and rooting perennial, to 20cm. Flowers pale lilac to white, 10-16mm; long-stalked; May-Sept. Leaves *coriander-scented* when crushed, strap-like when submerged, narrow lanceolate when aerial, with long stout stalks. Fruits green, in a buttercup-like *globular* head. Still, shallow, usually *peaty*, fresh water.

6 Floating Water-plantain *Luronium natans*. A slender creeping and rooting perennial, the aerial stems low. Flowers white to pale lilac, each petal with a large *yellow basal spot*, 12-18mm, often solitary; May-August. Leaves *unscented* when crushed and snapping off when folded; either submerged (often the only ones present, see p. 344) and strap-like, tapering to a pointed tip; or floating and oval, shiny and long-stalked. Fruits egg-shaped. Acid lakes in the hills, and both still and fresh water, especially canals, in the lowlands.

7 ***Starfruit *Damasonium alisma*. Low/short annual, to 30cm. Flowers white, petals three, each with a large *yellow basal spot*, 5-9mm; June-Sept. Leaves linear when submerged, long-stalked and narrow-oval when floating or aerial. Fruits in a distinctive 6-rayed *star-shape*. In and by muddy ponds, often those which dry out in summer.

8 Arrow-head *Sagittaria sagittifolia*. A tall perennial, to 1m. Flowers white, with a conspicuous *purple patch* at the base of each petal, anthers purple, 20-30cm; July-August. Aerial leaves broadly *arrow-shaped*, the submerged ones linear, translucent, especially in faster streams. Fruiting heads globular. Still and flowing shallow fresh water. Three N American species are very locally established: **8a Canadian Arrowhead** *S. rigida*, with flowers lacking the purple patch and the aerial leaves broad-elliptical, in the Exeter Canal, S Devon, since 1898; **Narrow-leaved Arrowhead** *S. subulata* with no aerial leaves but elliptical floating ones, in a Hampshire pond; and **8b Broad-leaved Arrowhead** or **Duck-potato** *S. latifolia* with arrow-shaped leaves but petals lacking the purple patch and anthers yellow, in several Surrey streams.

Water Plantain details

1
stem
section

2

3

4

5

6

7

all petals × 3

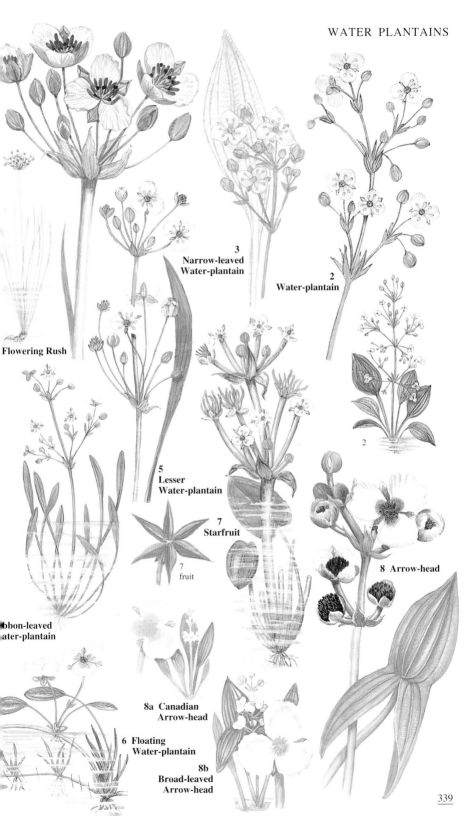

3 Narrow-leaved Water-plantain

2 Water-plantain

Flowering Rush

5 Lesser Water-plantain

2

7 Starfruit

7 fruit

Ribbon-leaved Water-plantain

8 Arrow-head

8a Canadian Arrow-head

6 Floating Water-plantain

8b Broad-leaved Arrow-head

FROGBIT FAMILY Hydrocharitaceae

Aquatic perennials with, unusually for monocots, male and female flowers on separate plants. For fully submerged species, see p. 344.

1 Frogbit *Hydrocharis morsus-ranae*. One of our two large-flowered *free-floating* aquatics. Flowers white, the three petals each with a large basal yellow spot, 20-30mm, solitary; July-August. Believed by the classical Greeks to have been eaten by frogs. *Still* fresh water.

2 Water Soldier *Stratiotes aloides*. A unique aquatic, normally fully submerged, either on the bottom or suspended in the water, but rising partly above the surface to flower; reproducing mainly from offsets at the end of its runners. Flowers white, 3-petalled, 30-40mm, 1-3 together; June-August. Leaves dark brownish-green, stiff, *sword-like* (whence its name), edged with spiny teeth, in a tuft. Native (see map) but often also introduced in *still* fresh water.

CAPE PONDWEED FAMILY Aponogetonaceae

3 Cape Pondweed *Aponogeton distachyos*. A low aquatic perennial, to 6cm above the surface. Flowers white, usually *2-petalled*, in *forked* spikes; August-Oct. Leaves floating, elliptical. Fruits egg-shaped. Much planted in ornamental and other lakes and ponds, and often more or less naturalised.

PONDWEED FAMILY Potamogetonaceae

Though several species have floating leaves and aerial flower-spikes, all are dealt with together for convenience (see p. 344).

DUCKWEED FAMILY Lemnaceae

Although only one species has submerged leaves, it seems more appropriate to describe the duckweeds on p. 354 with the other aquatic plants.

ARUM FAMILY Araceae

Perennials with a curious flower-design in which tiny flowers, the male above the female, are densely whorled around the base of a cylindrical *spadix*, which is usually backed by a large leaf-like *spathe*. Leaves usually large, broad and mostly from the roots. Fruit a berry. A dangerous family to try and eat.

Besides the four more frequent aliens described below, three others are widely scattered: **4 Dragon Arum** *Dracunculus vulgaris*, with dark purple spathe and spadix and large palmately lobed leaves; the well known decorative **5 Arum Lily** *Zantedeschia aethiopica* with white spathe, yellow spadix and long-stalked, broadly oval leaves; and **6 Mouseplant** *Arisarum proboscideum*, with an almost ludicrously long, to 15cm, 'mouse's tail' at the tip of the dark purplish-brown spathe, which hides the tiny spadix. Leaves arrow-shaped, prostrate.

7 P Lords-and-Ladies *Arum maculatum*. Low/short, to 20cm. Flowers with spadix either purple or yellow above, the large hooded spathe pale green, sometimes spotted darker, 20-25cm; April-June. Leaves broadly arrow-shaped, all-green (including the veins) or with purplish-black spots; not appearing until *late January*. Berries orange-red, in a spike, poisonous. Aka Cuckoo Pint. Shady places – woods, copses, hedge-banks.

8 P *Rare Lords-and-Ladies *Arum italicum*. Generally larger than Lords-and-Ladies (7), with the spadix *always yellow* and sometimes drooping at the tip, the spathe never spotted; May-June. Leaves with midrib and veins *paler*, less often spotted and appearing from *late September*. A quite frequent naturalised form has the leaves marbled with *creamy* veins and never spotted. The map shows ssp. *neglectum*; ssp. *italicum* with leaves marbled with creamy veins, and never spotted, is widely naturalised from gardens.

9 American Skunk-cabbage *Lysichiton americanus*. Tall perennial, to 1.5m, with creeping roots. Flowers with an *evil* smell, the spadix green and the spathe *yellow*, 10-35cm; April-May. Leaves large, oblong, short-stalked. Increasingly established in marshy places and by still water. Berries red. **Asian Skunk-cabbage** *L. camtschatcensis* with *unscented white* flowers is established in at least three places.

3 Cape Pondweed

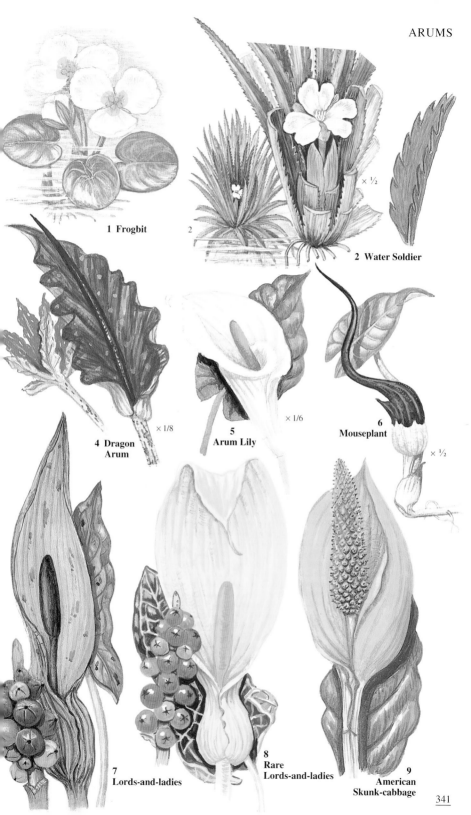

1 Frogbit

2

× ½

2 Water Soldier

× 1/8

4 Dragon Arum

× 1/6

5 Arum Lily

6 Mouseplant

× ½

7 Lords-and-ladies

8 Rare Lords-and-ladies

9 American Skunk-cabbage

1 Sweet Flag *Acorus calamus*. A tall stout waterside perennial, to 1.2m; smelling of both tangerines and vanilla when crushed. Spadix *green*, 5-90mm, projecting phallically upwards from the upper half of the stem; no spathe; June-July, but a shy flowerer. Leaves long, flat, sword-like, rather like Yellow Flag (p. 322), but the thicker midrib often not central and the edges *wrinkled* (cf. occasional narrower wrinkled leaves of Reed Sweet-grass, p. 406). No fruits develop. Established by still water for almost 400 years, for use as a sweet-smelling floor-covering. **Lesser Sweet Flag** *A. gramineus*, whose shorter leaves have no midrib, is established at Mytchett Lake, Surrey.

2 Bog Arum *Calla palustris*. Medium creeping perennial, to 45cm. Spathe *roundish, white* 30-80mm, not enfolding the more greenish-white spadix; June-August. Leaves roundish, long-stalked. Berries red. Established in scattered wet places.

BUR-REED FAMILY Sparganiaceae

Bur-reeds *Sparganium erectum*. Aquatic or waterside perennials. Flowers tiny, green, the male yellow from the soon-fading anthers, above the female always green from the stigmas, in *globular* heads; June-August. Leaves broad to narrow linear. Fruiting heads bur-like, with well beaked fruits.

3 Branched Bur-reed *Sparganium erectum*. The largest and tallest Bur-reed, to 1.5m. Flowerheads in a *branched* spike. Leaves broad, 10-15mm wide, iris-like, 3-sided, especially towards the sheathing base, the long veins translucent with *no dark border*, the cross-veins indistinct; floating leaves rare. Fruits variable. By fresh water.

4 Unbranched Bur-reed *Sparganium emersum*. Short/medium, to 60cm. Flowerheads many fewer than Branched Bur-reed (**3**), in an erect *unbranched* spike. Leaves usually *floating*, often conspicuous in parallel lines in rivers and streams; narrower (3-12mm) and keeled beneath, the translucent long veins with a *dark border* and the cross-veins conspicuous. Fruits with a slender beak. In, sometimes by, fresh water.

5 Floating Bur-reed *Sparganium angustifolium*. Stems and leaves usually floating, to 60cm. Flowerheads in a *spike*, the male usually *two*, and the female 2-4, the lowest with its stalk *shortly fused* to the stem and a bract *as long as* the spike. Leaves flat and grass-like, keeled and usually inflated at the base. Shallow acid peaty water.

6 Least Bur-reed *Sparganium natans*. Differs from Floating Bur-reed (**5**) in usually having only *one* male flowerhead and the lowest female with its stalk *not fused* to the stem and a bract scarcely as long as the spike. Stems to 30cm. Leaves narrower (2-6mm), scarcely inflated at base. Also in alkaline water.

BULRUSH FAMILY Typhaceae

Familiar tall aquatic perennials, which for many years shared the name Bulrush with the plant now known as Common Club-rush (p. 416), until in a judgment of Solomon it was awarded to *Typha*, hitherto alternatively known as Reedmace. The widespread American name Cattail must also have had an English folk origin.

7 Bulrush *Typha latifolia*. Stems and leaves very tall, to 3m. Flowers tiny, densely packed into conspicuous *sausage-shaped* 18-30mm spikes, the fluffy golden-brown soon-withering males usually *immediately* above the more numerous *chocolate-brown* females; June-August. Leaves greyish, fleshy, *8-24mm wide*, overtopping the flower-spikes. Fruits producing cottony down. In and by still fresh water, over which it may spread to create a scarcely penetrable swamp.

8 Lesser Bulrush *Typha angustifolia*. Has a slenderer, *paler brown*, milk-chocolate female flower-spike than Bulrush (**7**), separated from the male spike by a *3-8cm gap*, markedly longer than Bulrush's occasional small one. Leaves *narrower* (3-6mm) and paler green. Similar places, especially on the coast.

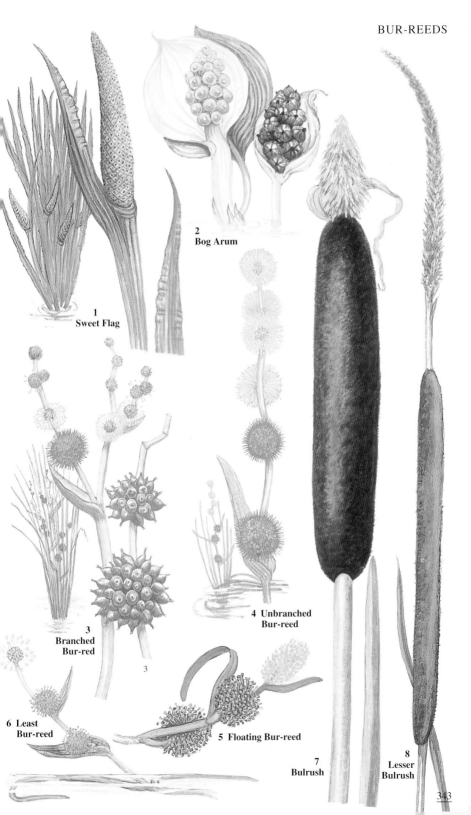

1
Sweet Flag

2
Bog Arum

3
Branched
Bur-red

3

4 Unbranched
Bur-reed

6 Least
Bur-reed

5 Floating Bur-reed

7
Bulrush

8
Lesser
Bulrush

AQUATIC PLANTS WITH ALL LEAVES SUBMERGED

1. Leaves in a basal rosette or tuft
2. Leaves on stem, undivided:

   2a. alternate, p. 346   2b. forked, p. 351   2c. pinnate, p. 350.

3. Leaves on stem, opposite or whorled, p. 352.
4. Leaves floating: several groups of aquatic plants can have both floating and submerged leaves:

   4a. Rooted on the bottom, including some pondweeds (p. 354) and some water starworts (p. 356)

   4b. Duckweeds (p. 354) entirely floating.

~

1. Leaves in a basal rosette or tuft, narrow; sometimes all aerial

1 Awlwort *Subularia aquatica*. (Cabbage Family, p. 82). The most uncabbagelike member of the Cabbage Family, a tiny 2-4-cm annual/biennial, nearly always completely submerged. Leaves in a tuft, pale green, cylindrical, finely pointed, shorter and slenderer than those of Shoreweed (**2**) and similar plants, which often grow with it. Its flowers, 2-3mm across with *4 narrow white petals*, are, however, quite distinctive; June-Sept. Pods egg-shaped. Gravelly and stony bottoms of shallow lochs/lakes in northern and western hill districts, sometimes among taller plants. An awl is a small narrow tool, now rarely used.

2 Shore-weed *Littorella uniflora*. (Plantain Family, p. 248). Low hairless perennial, often with long rooting runners, sometimes forming swards. Leaves usually *flat on one side*, rounded on the other, sheathing at the base, to 10cm. Flowers greenish, male and female separate, the male stalked, solitary with *prominent long stamens*, the female unstalked at the base of the same plant. In and by still, usually acid water; when submerged, flowers are rare and leaves much longer. Widespread.

3 *Mudwort *Limosella aquatica*. (Figwort Family, p. 228). A low small hairless annual, sometimes perennating by runners, often gregarious, to 10cm. Leaves dark green, narrowly elliptical, untoothed, *long-stalked*, in a rosette. Flowers white or pale mauve-pink, 5-petalled, 2-5mm, the *uncoloured* petal-tube *shorter* than the *pointed* sepal-teeth, stalked, solitary from the base of the leaves, not scented, opening only in sunshine; June-Sept. Fruits usually oval, on stalks curving downwards. Mud usually by, sometimes in, shallow fresh water, mainly in the Midlands. **3a **Welsh Mudwort** *L. australis*. Differs from Mudwort especially in its narrow, fresher green leaves having the stalk and blade *not differentiated*, the flowers always white with the *orange* petal-tube *longer* than the *blunt* sepal-teeth, with a longer style, scented and not closing in dull weather. Fruits almost globular, on stalks which arch and force them into the mud when ripe. Often also on estuarine mud. Wales only.

4 Water Lobelia *Lobelia dortmanna*. (Bellflower Family, p. 250). A short/medium perennial, with milky juice in its leafless flowering stems, to 70cm. Leaves linear, untoothed, in always submerged basal rosettes. Flowers very *pale lilac*, 2-lipped like the other Lobelias (p. 254). Shallow *acid* lakes in northern and western hill districts.

5 *Pipewort *Eriocaulon aquaticum* (Pipewort Family – Eriocaulaceae). Short/tall un-branched perennial, 20-150cm, depending on water level, recalling Water Horsetail (p. 452) at a distance. Leaves translucent, narrow, *tapering to a fine point*, in a short basal tuft. Flowers white, tiny, in *flat 5-15mm heads*; July-Sept. Fruit a capsule. Quiet shallow fresh water, waterlogged peaty places in Ireland; rare in Scotland.

6 Quillwort *Isoetes lacustris* (Quillwort Family – Isoetaceae). Not a flowering plant, but its always submerged tuft of dark green *cylindrical* pointed leaves can be confused with other aquatic plants with a basal rosette. Still water in northern and western hill districts. The smaller **6a Spring Quillwort** *I. echinospora* with paler green, more often spreading or recurved leaves, can be found in more acid waters and further south in the lowlands.

7 Floating Water-plantain *Luronium natans* (p. 338) has a non-flowering form, with all its tufts of pointed, strap-shaped leaves submerged, more frequent than the flowering form in many lowland districts. Mainly N Wales and adjacent England.

8 Water Soldier *Stratiotes aloides* (p. 340) is completely submerged until flowering time.

344

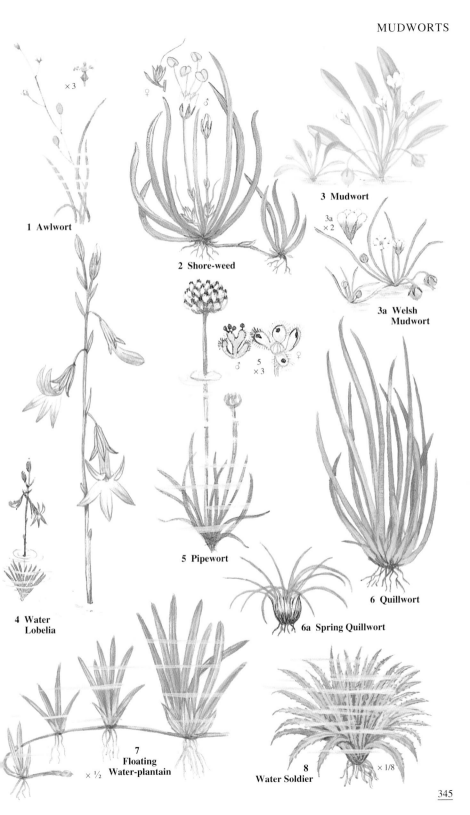

1 Awlwort

× 3

2 Shore-weed

3 Mudwort

3a Welsh Mudwort

3a × 2

5 Pipewort

♂ 5 × 3 ♀

4 Water Lobelia

6 Quillwort

6a Spring Quillwort

7 Floating Water-plantain × ½

8 Water Soldier × 1/8

2a. Leaves on stem: undivided: alternate

Pondweeds *Potamogeton* (Pondweed Family – Potamogetonaceae). Perennials, with usually translucent submerged leaves and some also with floating leaves (see p. 354 and Red Pondweed (**5**), *alternate* with stipules or sheaths at their base; leaf-shape often varying with the speed and depth of the water, e. g. Various-leaved Pondweed (p. 354) may have only submerged leaves in fast or deep water. Flowers small, with no petals but 4 green sepals, all, except sometimes Fennel and Slender-leaved Pondweeds (p. 348), in aerial spikes; May/June-Sept. Fruit with 4 nutlets. Hybrids are frequent; only *P × zizii* (see p. 354) regularly produces fruits. Fresh water, sometimes on muddy margins, when can look very different. The closely related *Groenlandia* (p. 352) has opposite leaves and flowers in pairs.

Pondweed leaves:

(i) wavy (ii) clasping the stem (iii) narrow lanceolate (iv) strap-like, stems flattened (v) thread-like, stems flattened (vi) bootlace-like, rounded.

(i) Leaves wavy

1 Curled Pondweed *Potamogeton crispus*. One of our most distinctive pondweeds, with its markedly *wavy*, distinctly toothed, narrow oblong leaves; cf. Opposite-leaved Pondweed (p. 352). Stipules and flower-spikes small. Avoids acid water. Widespread.

2 Long-stalked Pondweed *Potamogeton praelongus*. Our only wavy-leaved pondweed with stems often *zigzag*. Leaves lanceolate, blunt-tipped, net-veined and unstalked, with whitish stipules clasping the stem. Flower-spikes on stalks up to 20cm, not thickened at top. Fruits large, brownish. Often in limy water, especially deeper lakes and rivers. Scattered.

3 Shining Pondweed *Potamogeton lucens*. Our broadest-leaved pondweed with wavy leaves, which are usually *broad lanceolate*, net-veined, un- to very short-stalked, with stiff winged stipules. Flower-spikes on short stalks thickened at the top. Limy water in the lowlands. Mainly southern.

(ii) Leaves clasping the stem

4 Perfoliate Pondweed *Potamogeton perfoliatus*. Our only pondweed with the stem obviously *clasped* by the leaves, which are untoothed and variably green, and although usually broad oval can be much narrower. Flower-spike long-stalked. Usually in deeper water. Widespread.

(iii) Leaves narrow lanceolate

5 Red Pondweed *Potamogeton alpinus*. Leaves (sometimes also floating), narrow lanceolate, unstalked, *reddish*, especially when dried. Stems unbranched. Avoids limy water. Widespread.

(iv) Leaves strap-like; stems flattened

6 Blunt-leaved Pondweed *Potamogeton obtusifolius*. Leaves 2. 5-3. 5mm, blunt, sometimes with a minute awn, *obscurely* 5-veined, scarcely stalked, with conspicuous glands at the base and stipules always open. Cf. Small Pondweed (p. 348). Preferring shallower, more acid waters. Scattered.

7 *Flat-stalked Pondweed *Potamogeton friesii*. Has more conspicuously flattened stems than Blunt-leaved Pondweed (**6**) and narrower, rather more pointed leaves with a *more conspicuous awn*, more obviously 5-veined, unstalked; stipules closed when young. Still water only, usually limy. Mainly southern.

8 *Grass-wrack Pondweed *Potamogeton compressus*. Has broader (3-6mm) unstalked leaves than Blunt-leaved Pondweed (**6**), with both the 5 major veins and the awn more conspicuous and *no* glands at the base. Flower-stalks much longer. Canals and other still water. Mainly Midlands.

9 **Sharp-leaved Pondweed *Potamogeton acutifolius*. Our rarest strap-leaved pondweed, readily told from the other three by its conspicuously *pointed* unstalked 1.5-5. 5mm leaves, which have 3 main and many obscurer veins and no basal glands. Flower-stalks short. Now mainly in ditches on grazing marshes. South-eastern.

1   o   ■↓

2   oz   □↓

3   o   ■

4   oz   □

5   z   ■

6   □

7   oz   □↓

8   ■↓↓

9   □↓

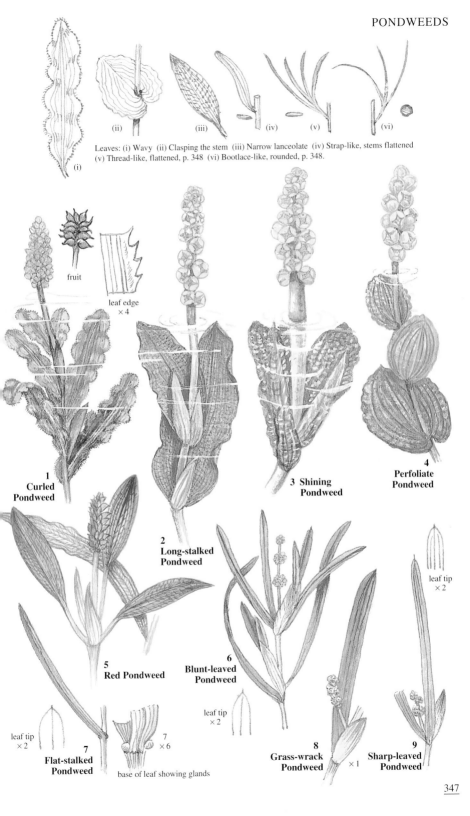

Leaves: (i) Wavy (ii) Clasping the stem (iii) Narrow lanceolate (iv) Strap-like, stems flattened
(v) Thread-like, flattened, p. 348 (vi) Bootlace-like, rounded, p. 348.

fruit

leaf edge
× 4

1
Curled
Pondweed

2
Long-stalked
Pondweed

3 Shining
Pondweed

4
Perfoliate
Pondweed

5
Red Pondweed

6
Blunt-leaved
Pondweed

leaf tip
× 2

leaf tip
× 2

leaf tip
× 2

7
Flat-stalked
Pondweed

7
× 6

base of leaf showing glands

8
Grass-wrack
Pondweed

× 1

9
Sharp-leaved
Pondweed

1 Small Pondweed *Potamogeton berchtoldii*. Stems slightly flattened. Leaves variable, dark to pale green, 1-2mm, 3-veined, *bluntly* pointed with a tiny awn and a conspicuous gland at the base; stipules small, open. Flower-spike small. Not in limy water.

2 Lesser Pondweed *Potamogeton pusillus*. Very like Small Pondweed (**1**), but leaves more *sharply* pointed, usually no basal glands and stipules closed when young. Not in acid, sometimes in brackish water, occasionally with Small Pondweed.

3 Hairlike Pondweed *Potamogeton trichoides*. Has still narrower leaves (rarely more than 1mm) than both Small (**1**) and and Lesser (**2**) Pondweeds, with the unawned tip *more sharply pointed* than Lesser, a more prominent midrib, and usually no glands; stipules open, longer. Lowland waters, often with Lesser Pondweed.

4 **Shetland Pondweed *Potamogeton rutilus*. More like Lesser Pondweed (**2**) than the two other Pondweeds (**1, 3**) with thread-like leaves, but has even *more sharply* pointed leaves than Hairlike (**3**), usually an obscure basal gland, and stipules, closed when young, that are strongly veined when dry. Our rarest pondweed, only in lochs or streams on or near limestone in N Scotland and the Isles.

Tasselweeds *Ruppia*, see p. 352. **Horned Pondweed** *Zannichellia palustris*, see p. 352

5 Fennel Pondweed *Potamogeton pectinatus*. Stems to more than 2m, with distinctive *long sheaths* below the leaves. Leaves up to 4mm and to more than 1m long, dark green, *pointed*, with no basal glands but open *white-edged* stipules. Spikes, usually submerged but sometimes aerial, compact in flower but spread out in fruit. Often in rivers; can cope with polluted and brackish waters better than most pondweeds. Widespread. Hybrids in the Rivers Tweed and Till on the Scottish Border have the Scandinavian *P. vaginatus* as their other parent.

6 Slender-leaved Pondweed *Potamogeton filiformis*. Smaller than Fennel Pondweed (**5**) and with flattened stems, narrower *blunt-tipped* leaves, often in tufts, stipules closed and not white-edged, and spikes spread out in flower. Shallow still water, often near the sea and in brackish water.

~

Waterweeds *Elodea*. (Frogbit Family, p. 340). Submerged aquatic plants, mostly introduced at various times between 1836 (**7**) and 1966 (**7a**), with leaves *in whorls, usually of 3*, and infrequent tiny whitish, very long-stalked flowers floating on the surface. Still fresh water.

Water Starworts *Callitriche*, see p. 356.

The commonest, and most widespread, since 1836, is **7 Canadian Waterweed** *Elodea canadensis*, with leaves varying from oval to narrowly oblong, the tips blunt to bluntly pointed, often slightly recurved. The rapidly spreading, but still mainly southern **7a Nuttall's Waterweed** *E. nuttallii*, now sometimes as frequent as **7**, has much narrower, often linear, more pointed leaves, often *strongly recurved or twisted*. The much rarer **7b South American Waterweed** *E. callitrichoides* has leaves like **7a**, but scarcely recurved or twisted and prefers artificially heated waters; mainly southern. Two similar species with leaves in *whorls of 4-5* are the very rare native (one lough in W Ireland and one loch in S Scotland) **7c ***Esthwaite Waterweed** *Hydrilla verticillata* with very narrow pointed leaves; and **7d Large-flowered Waterweed** *Egeria densa* with much broader, well pointed leaves and rarely large white flowers; mainly canals, N England. The not infrequent S. African, **7e Curly Waterweed** *Lagarosiphon major* differs from all the foregoing in its *large curly* toothed leaves being arranged *spirally* up the stem.

8 Six-stamened Waterwort *Elatine hexandra*. (Waterwort Family – Elatinaceae). A very small elusive, creeping annual, rooting at the nodes, to 10cm, often completely submerged (when it may not flower), sometimes in a thick mat, frequently reddening. Often all that shows above the mud is a row of short narrow oval to spoon-shaped fresh green opposite leaves, with the tiny stalked 3-petalled 6-stamened pink flowers, solitary at their base, not visible; July-August. In or by shallow, often peaty, fresh water. The scarcer **8a Eight-stamened Waterwort** *E. hydropiper* has flowers often un- or scarcely stalked, with 4 petals and 8 stamens.

8 sz ▫↓   **8a** ▫

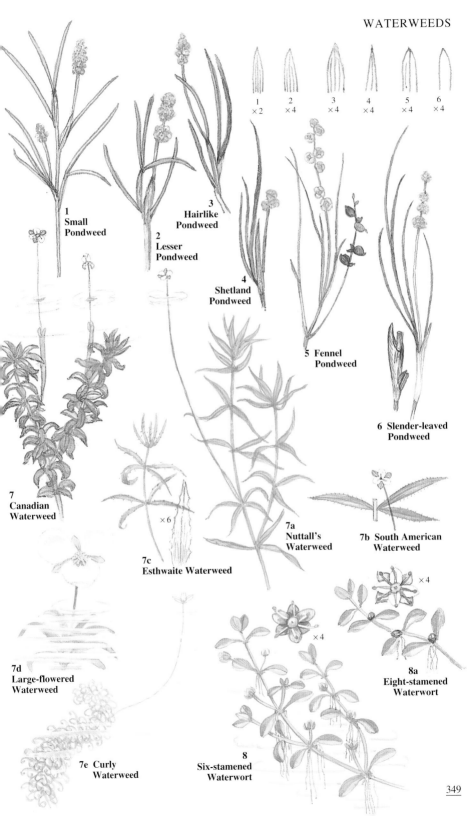

WATERWEEDS

1 ×2 2 ×4 3 ×4 4 ×4 5 ×4 6 ×4

1 Small Pondweed

2 Lesser Pondweed

3 Hairlike Pondweed

4 Shetland Pondweed

5 Fennel Pondweed

6 Slender-leaved Pondweed

7 Canadian Waterweed

7a Nuttall's Waterweed

7b South American Waterweed

7c Esthwaite Waterweed

7d Large-flowered Waterweed

7e Curly Waterweed

8 Six-stamened Waterwort

8a Eight-stamened Waterwort

1 Australian Swamp Stonecrop *Crassula helmsii*. (Stonecrop Family, p. 120). An aquarists' throw-out, aggressively invading our fresh still waters; a submerged perennial, sometimes stranded on mud, to 30cm. Leaves linear-lanceolate, up the stems. Flowers whitish, with 4 petals *longer than sepals*, 1-2mm, stalked at the base of the leaves; June-August. Aka New Zealand Pigmyweed. Ponds, ditches. Widespread, mainly southeastern.

Pigmyweed *Crassula aquatica*, see p. 122.

2 Tapegrass *Vallisneria spiralis*. Our only waterweed with all leaves long, ribbon-like and basal. Flowers whitish, very long-stalked, rare. Introduced from S Europe; northern canals, often warmed by mill effluents; mainly southern, including the Lea Navigation.

3 Marestail *Hippuris vulgaris*. (Marestail Family – Hippuridaceae). An unbranched perennial waterweed, erect to 1m or more, but largely submerged in streams. Leaves strap-shaped, soft, dark green, in whorls of *6-12* (unlike any of our other waterweeds except Curly Waterweed, p. 348) up the stem. Has been semantically confused with Horsetails (p. 452), which are non-flowering plants, whose longer and narrower whorls are hard and actually stems. Flowers tiny, pink, petalless, at base of leaves. Fruit a tiny greenish nut. Still and slow-flowing, often limy fresh water. Widespread.

Water Purslane *Lythrum portula*. See p. 114.

Eelgrasses *Zostera*. (Eelgrass Family – Zosteraceae). Not seaweeds (which are Algae) but our only flowering plants that grow *completely submerged by the sea*. Perennials, with parallel-sided grass-like leaves up and with sheaths fused into the stem (except Dwarf Eelgrass, **4b**). Flowers minute, green, petalless, male and female separate, in spikes more or less inside the leaf-sheath. Muddy, sandy and gravelly intertidal shores.

4 Eelgrass *Zostera marina* has leaves to 50cm long and *4-10mm* wide, blunt or pointed at the tip, with 5-11 parallel veins. Flower-spikes branched, terminal; June-Sept. Near and below spring low-water mark; widespread. **4a Narrow-leaved Eelgrass** *Z. angustifolia* has leaves up to 30cm long and *1-2mm* wide, 3—5-veined and notched at the tip when mature. Flower-spikes branched, terminal; June-Nov. Muddy tidal flats, mainly from half- to low-tide mark; widespread. **4b Dwarf Eelgrass** *Z. noltii* has leaves up to 20cm long and *c*. 1mm wide, 3-veined and slightly notched at the tip, and flower-spikes *unbranched* and up the stems; June-Oct. Muddy tidal flats, from half-tide to low-tide mark, but not below it; scattered.

2b. Leaves on stem: undivided: forked (see opposite)

2c. Leaves on stem: undivided: pinnate

Water Violet *Hottonia palustris*, see p. 112.

Water Milfoils *Myriophyllum* (Water-Milfoil Family – Haloragaceae). Perennial water-weeds whose stems bear submerged (except the alien Parrot's Feather p. 356) whorled leaves, pinnate with thread-like leaflets. Flowers 4-petalled, in whorls always above the surface, usually with stamens only, styles only and both all on the same spike. Fruit a nut. Still and slow fresh water.

6 Spiked Water Milfoil *Myriophyllum spicatum*. Stems to 2. 5m. Flowers in *almost leafless* spikes, always erect, with small narrow bracts at their base, the topmost red, with yellow anthers, the lowest green with styles, and 1-2 whorls in between with both; June-Sept. Leaves usually *four* in a whorl. Prefers *limy* water, sometimes brackish, mainly in the lowlands; widespread.

7 Alternate Water Milfoil *Myriophyllum alterniflorum*. Stems, slender, to 1m. Flowers like Spiked Water Milfoil (**6**), but spike *drooping* at first, the upper ones often alternate with petals yellow streaked red; May-August. Leaves similar but shorter. Preferring *acid* water, often in the uplands; mainly northern and western.

8 Whorled Water Milfoil *Myriophyllum verticillatum*. Stems to 3m. Flowers greenish, mostly *five* in a whorl, with *feathery leaf-like* bracts at their base; July-August. Leaves usually *five* in a whorl. Prefers *limy* water in the lowlands; mainly southern.

Lesser Marshwort *Apium inundatum*, p. 192. Often largely submerged.

River Water Dropwort *Oenanthe fluviatilis*, p. 188. Fully submerged until flowering time.

1   s   ■↑↑

3   oz   ■

4   soz   ■↓

4a

4b

5

5a

6   o

7   oz

8   □↓

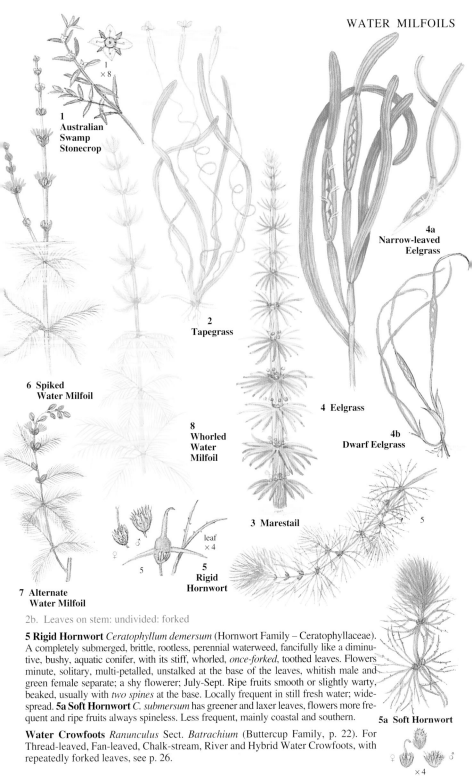

1
× 8

**1
Australian
Swamp
Stonecrop**

**4a
Narrow-leaved
Eelgrass**

**2
Tapegrass**

**6 Spiked
Water Milfoil**

**8
Whorled
Water
Milfoil**

4 Eelgrass

**4b
Dwarf Eelgrass**

♂

♀

5

leaf
× 4

**5
Rigid
Hornwort**

3 Marestail

5

**7 Alternate
Water Milfoil**

2b. Leaves on stem: undivided: forked

5 Rigid Hornwort *Ceratophyllum demersum* (Hornwort Family – Ceratophyllaceae). A completely submerged, brittle, rootless, perennial waterweed, fancifully like a diminutive, bushy, aquatic conifer, with its stiff, whorled, *once-forked*, toothed leaves. Flowers minute, solitary, multi-petalled, unstalked at the base of the leaves, whitish male and green female separate; a shy flowerer; July-Sept. Ripe fruits smooth or slightly warty, beaked, usually with *two spines* at the base. Locally frequent in still fresh water; widespread. **5a Soft Hornwort** *C. submersum* has greener and laxer leaves, flowers more frequent and ripe fruits always spineless. Less frequent, mainly coastal and southern.

5a Soft Hornwort

Water Crowfoots *Ranunculus* Sect. *Batrachium* (Buttercup Family, p. 22). For Thread-leaved, Fan-leaved, Chalk-stream, River and Hybrid Water Crowfoots, with repeatedly forked leaves, see p. 26.

♀ ♂
× 4

Bladderworts *Utricularia*. (Bladderwort Family, p. 250). Floating rootless insectivorous perennials, hard to separate in the field, especially as they are shy flowerers and thus often only identifiable with the aid of a microscope. Leaves with many thread-like green segments, with minute bristles and small bladders, which entrap tiny aquatic animals and in autumn fill with water and sink the plant to the bottom. Flowers *yellow*, 2-lipped, the mouth closed, with a blunt spur, in stalked spikes on leafless stems above the water. Fruit a capsule. Still or slow fresh water.

1 Greater Bladderwort *Utricularia vulgaris*. The largest and most frequent species, with all stems bearing both green leaves and bladders, flowers rich yellow, 10-15mm, the lower lip with *down-turned* margins, the spur 7-8mm on 10-20-cm stems; perhaps the most frequent flowerer; June-Sept. Preferring *limy* water; mainly southern. **1a Wavy Bladderwort** *U. australis* is its *acid*-water and much less frequent counterpart, differing in its stems being *wavy* when mature and the paler yellow flowers having margins *flat* or slightly upturned. Widespread.

2 Pale Bladderwort *Utricularia ochroleuca*. Has two kinds of stem, floating ones with green leaves and few bladders and submerged ones with a few non-green leaves and many bladders, often anchored (but not rooted) on the bottom. Flowers pale yellow, 7-14mm, the lower lip margins becoming down-turned, the spur 2-4mm; July-Sept. Shallow pools on *acid* soils. **2a Nordic Bladderwort** *U. stygia* differs especially in having flowers (when present) often red-tinged, the margins flat or slightly upturned. **2b Intermediate Bladderwort** *U. intermedia* never has bladders on its green-leaved stems; flowers yellow, but perhaps the shyest-flowering of all, the spur 8-l0mm, equalling the lower lip. All three are mainly in W Scotland and W Ireland.

3 Lesser Bladderwort *Utricularia minor*. The smallest and slenderest species, having some stems with both *bristle-less* green leaves and bladders, and sometimes others with bladders only. Flowers pale to greenish yellow, with a *very short* 1-2mm) blunt spur; June-Sept. Bog pools, fen ditches; mainly northern and western.

3. Leaves opposite or whorled: undivided

4 Opposite-leaved Pondweed *Groenlandia densa*. Differs from Curled Pondweed (p. 346) in its shorter wavy leaves being *opposite* and its small stalked flowers in heads. Mainly in limy water, especially chalk streams; mainly south-eastern.

Tasselweeds *Ruppia* (Tasselweed Family – Ruppiaceae). Two very similar slender perennials, differing from pondweeds (p. 346) with thread-like leaves especially in their leaves being either *opposite* or alternate. Flowers green, petalless, in short-stalked *pairs*, rising to the surface on long common stalks; July-Sept. Fruit pear-shaped. Brackish pools and ditches.

5 Beaked Tasselweed *Ruppia maritima* has bright green leaves and straight common flower-stalks. Widespread, dwarf forms, largely buried in mud, occur in Scotland. **5a Spiral Tasselweed** *R. cirrhosa* has darker green leaves in more inflated sheaths and the common flower-stalks *coiled*. In deeper water; mainly south-eastern.

~

6 Horned Pondweed *Zannichellia palustris*. (Horned-Pondweed Family – Zannichelliaceae). Variable slender perennial, differing from Pondweeds (p. 346) with thread-like leaves especially in its leaves being usually *opposite*. Flowers tiny, green, petalless, solitary, male (1 stamen) and female separate, short- or unstalked at base of leaves; May-August. Fruit beaked. Still or slow fresh or brackish water. Widespread, mainly south-eastern, e. g. the Round Pond, Kensington Gardens, London.

7 *Slender Naiad *Najas flexilis* (Naiad Family – Najadaceae). Slender perennial. Differs from thread-leaved Pondweeds (p. 346) in its rather short translucent leaves being in *whorls* of 2-3. Flowers small, green, 2-lipped, unstalked, male and female separate, *1-3 together* at base of leaves; August-Sept. Deep water in lakes, mainly W Scotland and W Ireland.

8 **Holly-leaved Naiad *Najas marina*. Both one of the most distinctive and one of the rarest of our submerged aquatic plants. Stems slightly and leaves *strongly toothed*. Flowers like Slender Naiad (**7**), July-August. Slightly brackish Norfolk Broads only.

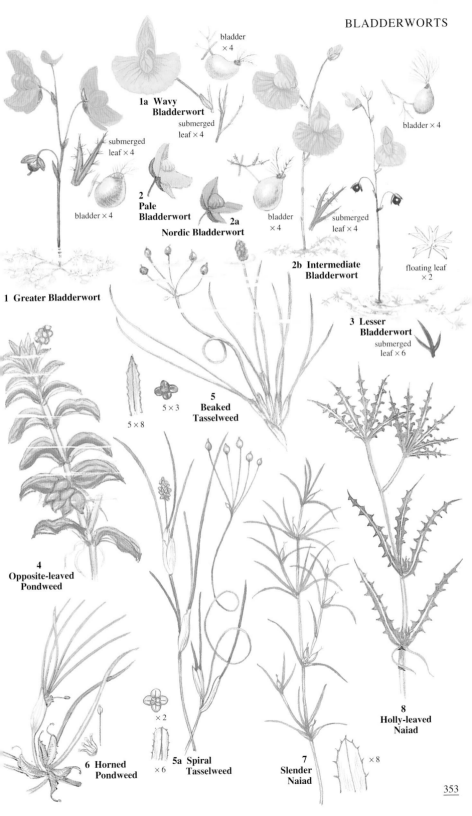

1a Wavy Bladderwort

bladder ×4

submerged leaf ×4

2 Pale Bladderwort

2a Nordic Bladderwort

bladder ×4

submerged leaf ×4

2b Intermediate Bladderwort

bladder ×4

submerged leaf ×4

floating leaf ×2

3 Lesser Bladderwort

submerged leaf ×6

submerged leaf ×4

bladder ×4

1 Greater Bladderwort

5 ×8

5 ×3

5 Beaked Tasselweed

4 Opposite-leaved Pondweed

8 Holly-leaved Naiad

×2

×6

6 Horned Pondweed

5a Spiral Tasselweed

7 Slender Naiad

×8

4a. Leaves floating and submerged: plant rooted on bottom (see also p. 356)

Pondweeds *Potamogeton*, other Pondweeds, see p. 346. **Water Starworts** *Callitriche*, p. 356.

1 Broad-leaved Pondweed *Potamogeton natans*. Generally the commonest pondweed. Floating leaves variably green, *broadly elliptical to oval*, opaque, pale-veined, to 120mm long, with conspicuous stipules; our only pondweed with leaves usually *apparently jointed* at junction with long stalk. Submerged leaves linear with no blade. Flower-stalks long, stout. Sometimes carpeting still water; rarely on dried-out mud. Widespread.

2 Bog Pondweed *Potamogeton polygonifolius*. The commonest pondweed of acid water. Floating (sometimes aerial, occasionally submerged) leaves often reddish, dark-veined and varying from broad oval (especially when aerial) to broad lanceolate. Submerged leaves *lanceolate*, stalked, untoothed. Fruits reddish. Bogs, flushes, shallow *acid* water.

3 *Fen Pondweed *Potamogeton coloratus*. The limy-water counterpart of Bog Pondweed (**2**). Floating leaves often reddish, broad oval to broad/narrower lanceolate, *translucent* and *net-veined*. Submerged leaves lanceolate to elliptical. Fruits green. Fens, shallow *limy* water; scattered.

4 **Loddon Pondweed *Potamogeton nodosus*. Floating leaves broad lanceolate, opaque and not net-veined. Submerged leaves longer, narrower and long-stalked. Only in three rivers, the Bristol Avon, the Berkshire Loddon, and the Dorset Stour.

5 Various-leaved Pondweed *Potamogeton gramineus*. Floating leaves very variable (sometimes none in fast or deep water), oval with conspicuous stipules. Submerged leaves narrow elliptical, sometimes recurved, minutely toothed and often minutely pointed, *unstalked*, with short stiff stipules. Flower-stalks thickened at top. A parent of the two commonest hybrids: *P.* × *nitens* × Perfoliate Pondweed. (p. 346) and *P.* × *zizii* × Shining Pondweed. (p. 346). Usually in shallow acid water, rarely in brackish.

Red Pondweed *Potamogeton alpinus*, p. 346. May have floating leaves.

6 *American Pondweed *Potamogeton epihydrus*. Floating leaves narrow oval on *flattened* stems; submerged leaves linear, much longer. Naturalised in a few canals near Halifax since 1907; native in three Outer Hebridean lochs.

4b. Leaves floating: plant not rooted on bottom

Duckweeds – Lemnaceae. Tiny annuals floating on the surface, except Ivy-leaved Duckweed (**9**), with no stems or leaves, but a frond or thallus. Flowers minute, without petals, rare; May-July. Still water, often making a complete green carpet.

7 Common Duckweed *Lemna minor*. Much the commonest and most widespread species. Frond shiny dark green, smooth, oval, 3-veined, 3-5mm; 1 root. The fast-spreading, since 1977, and smaller (1-3mm, but cf. immature Common Duckweed). N American **7a Least Duckweed** *L. minuta* has dull pale green fronds, faintly ridged, *elliptical* and 0-1 veined. **7b Fat Duckweed** *L. gibba* has fronds distinctly *swollen*. Also in brackish and polluted water.

8 Ivy-leaved Duckweed *Lemna trisulca*. Our only duckweed with submerged fronds, just below the surface, translucent, narrow lanceolate, 7-12mm, at right angles to each other; 1 root.

9 Greater Duckweed *Spirodela polyrhiza*. Has the largest fronds, 5-8mm, dark shiny green, *purplish beneath*, 5-11-veined, with a tuft of roots. (*L. turionifera*, with smaller red-tinged olive-green fronds might colonise us from C Europe in the next few years.) Mainly in England.

10 *Rootless Duckweed *Wolffia arrhiza*. Our smallest flowering plant, with minute 0.5-1mm rootless egg-shaped fronds, sometimes submerged. Never flowers.

11 Water Fern *Azolla filiculoides*, mistakable for a duckweed as it also carpets still fresh water, is actually a fern (Water Fern Family – Azollaceae) from subtropical America. Fronds like a large feathery duckweed, overlapping along the stems; bluish-green but reddening in autumn; carpeting still fresh water. Aka Fairy Fern.

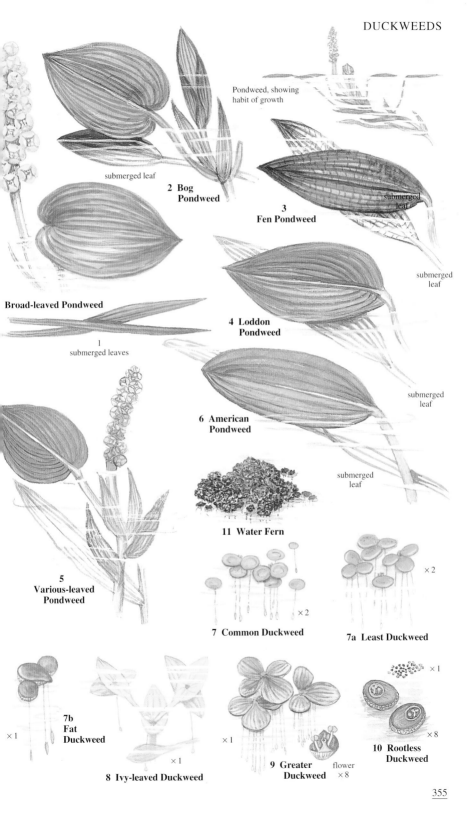

Pondweed, showing
habit of growth

submerged leaf

**2 Bog
Pondweed**

**3
Fen Pondweed**

submerged
leaf

submerged
leaf

Broad-leaved Pondweed

**4 Loddon
Pondweed**

1
submerged leaves

submerged
leaf

**6 American
Pondweed**

submerged
leaf

11 Water Fern

**5
Various-leaved
Pondweed**

× 2

7 Common Duckweed

× 2

7a Least Duckweed

**7b
Fat
Duckweed**

× 1

× 1

× 1

8 Ivy-leaved Duckweed

× 1

**9 Greater
Duckweed**

flower
× 8

× 1

× 8

**10 Rootless
Duckweed**

4a. Leaves floating and submerged: plant rooted on bottom (continued from p. 354)

Water Starworts *Callitriche* (Water Starwort Family – Callitrichaceae). One of the more difficult waterweed groups, with very variable leaf-shape and ripe fruits often elusive. Annuals/perennials with leaves aerial/floating/submerged, roundish/elliptical/linear, and opaque/translucent, joined at the base except Autumnal and Short-leaved Water Starworts; submerged leaves at least slightly notched at tip. Flowers tiny, green, petalless, solitary/paired at base of leaves, male and female separate, yellow anthers in aerial male flowers. Fruit four tiny green nutlets, usually winged. Still and slow-moving fresh water, wet mud. For leaf shape and fruit characters, see Key below.

LEAF SHAPE		
Aerial, in rosettes:	broadly elliptical/roundish:	Common W, Various-leaved W
Floating:	broadly diamond-shaped:	Blunt-fruited W
	broadly elliptical/roundish:	Common W, Marsh W
	elliptical:	Various-leaved W, Intermediate W
	narrowly elliptical:	Pedunculate W
Submerged (some):	elliptical:	Intermediate W (large spanner-shaped tip)
	narrowly elliptical:	Common W, Various-leaved W, Pedunculate W (spanner-shaped tip)
	linear:	Blunt-fruited W, Marsh W
Submerged (all):	linear: Autumnal W (tapering to tip), Short-leaved W (parallel-sided, darker)	
FRUITS		
Broadly winged:	Common W, Various-leaved W	
Narrowly winged:	Pedunculate W, Intermediate W, Autumnal W, Marsh W	
Unwinged:	Blunt-fruited W, Short-leaved W	

1 Common Water Starwort *Callitriche stagnalis*. Generally the commonest water starwort, with stems to 60cm in water and 15cm on mud. Aerial leaves fresh green. Male flowers with yellow anthers. Sometimes in woodland rides and on wet mud, occasionally fast streams, often on lime. Widespread.

2 Various-leaved Water Starwort *Callitriche platycarpa*. Stems to 1m. Aerial leaves often dull or slightly bluish-green. Male flowers with yellow anthers. Sometimes in brackish water. Scattered.

3 Blunt-fruited Water Starwort *Callitriche obtusangula*. Stems to 60cm. Leaves yellowish-green. Male flowers with yellow anthers. Still water only, often limy. Mainly south-eastern.

4 Pedunculate Water Starwort *Callitriche brutia*. Stems to 50cm or more. Leaf-tips horned like a small spanner. Often in pools shallow enough to dry out in summer. Mainly western. **4a Marsh Water Starwort** *Callitriche palustris* (see p. 462), is more delicate and fruits are winged only at the tip. Recently discovered.

5 Intermediate Water Starwort *Callitriche hamulata*. Stems to 50cm or more. Leaves dark green with tips larger and even more curved and spanner-like than Pedunculate Water Starwort (**4**), also resembling an earwig's pincers. Usually in acid water. Widespread.

6 Autumnal Water Starwort *Callitriche hermaphroditica*. Stems yellowish, to 50cm. All leaves submerged, yellowish-green, translucent, joined at the base. Northern and western.

7 Short-leaved Water Starwort *Callitriche truncata*. Often reddish, with stems to 20cm. All leaves submerged, translucent, bluish-green, joined at the base. Occurs largely to the S and E of Autumnal Water Starwort (**6**). Sometimes in brackish water. Very local away from E Midlands.

Other plants with both floating and submerged leaves include the water-lilies (p. 306), some water crowfoots (p. 26) and the introduced water milfoil called **8 Parrot's Feather** *Myriophyllum aquaticum*, an increasing aquarist's throw-out in the south, differing from the three native species (p. 350) in having conspicuous glandular *aerial* as well as submerged leaves, 4-6 in a whorl, and *whitish* female flowers only, 4-6 in a whorl. Ponds, usually near towns or villages.

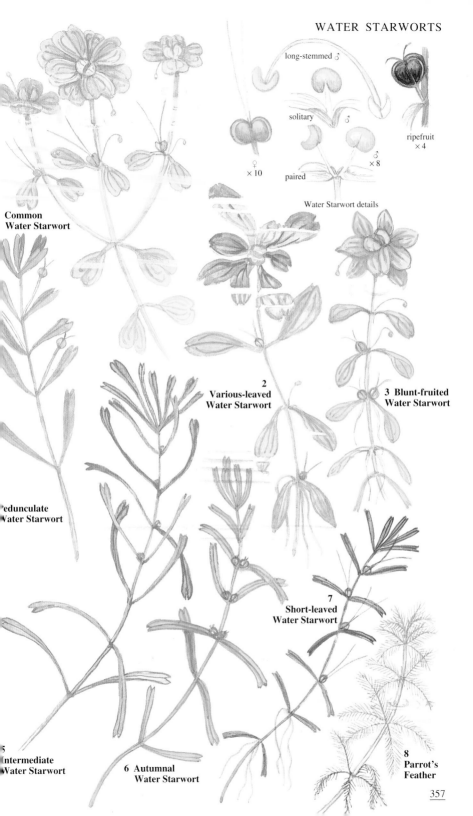

long-stemmed ♂

solitary
♂

ripefruit
× 4

♀
× 10

♂
× 8

paired

Water Starwort details

**Common
Water Starwort**

**2
Various-leaved
Water Starwort**

**3 Blunt-fruited
Water Starwort**

**edunculate
Water Starwort**

**7
Short-leaved
Water Starwort**

**5
Intermediate
Water Starwort**

**6 Autumnal
Water Starwort**

**8
Parrot's
Feather**

TREES AND TALL SHRUBS

more than 1m high (including Mistletoe and some woody climbers)

Leaf-shapes:

1. Roundish. 2. Ace-of-spades. 3. Oval/pointed oval (p. 362). 4. Lanceolate (p. 377).
5. Pinnate (p. 388). 6. Pinnately lobed (p. 390). 7. Trefoil (p. 394). 8. Palmate (p. 394).
9. Palmately lobed (p. 396). 10. Prickly (p. 398). 11. Linear/needle-like (p. 398).
12. Scale-like (p. 400).

Both the Rose (Rosaceae, p. 124) and Pea (Fabaceae, p. 140) Families contain many ornamental trees and shrubs, too many of which have become more or less naturalised in limited
areas for all to be included here. See p.18 for typical peaflower shape.

1. Leaves roundish

1 Hazel *Corylus avellana* (Hazel Family – Corylaceae) Tall shrub, to 6m, beloved for its
early 'lambstail' catkins; bark red-brown, smooth, peeling. Leaves almost roundish, 5-
12cm; often pale purple-brown when young, later sometimes with a chocolate-brown
blotch, turning yellow in autumn. Male catkins hanging, lemon-yellow, visible in bud
from October onwards; female flowers tiny, erect. bud-like, with bright red styles;
January-March, before the leaves. Fruit an edible nut, encased at first in a thick green, jaggedly toothed and lobed husk. Woods, often with oak and coppiced, scrub, hedges. Widespread, common.

2 Alder *Alnus glutinosa* (Birch Family – Betulaceae). Waterside tree to 22m, often quite
small and bushy, appearing dull purplish in late winter from its purplish leaf and catkin
buds; bark dark brown, rugged; twigs hairless. Leaves dark green, almost hairless, shallowly toothed, roundish, with a blunt or indented tip, 4-10cm; turning golden-yellow in
autumn. Male catkins yellowish, long, hanging; female purplish, short, erect and finally
cone-like, persisting for months; February-April, before the leaves. Fruit a narrowly
winged nut. By fresh water, forming small woods (carr) in swampy places. Widespread,
common.

Aspen *Populus tremula*, p. 362. **Grey Poplar** *Populus × canescens*, p. 362. **Eared Willow**
Salix aurita, p. 380. **Woolly Willow** *Salix lanata*, p. 380. **Net-leaved Willow** *S. reticulata*
and **Dwarf Willow** *S. herbacea*, p. 382.

3 *Dwarf Birch *Betula nana* (Birch Family). Sprawling shrub to 1m, rarely more, with
hairless twigs. Leaves small, 5-15mm, rounded, deeply toothed, downy when young.
Catkins (May-June) smaller than and fruits more narrowly winged than Silver/Downy
Birches (below). May hybridise with Downy Birch. On high moorland peat. Scottish
Highlands.

Common Elm *Ulmus procera*, p. 382. **Whitebeams** *Sorbus eminens, S. latifolia, S. hibernica*, p. 368. ***Welsh Cotoneaster** *Cotoneaster cambrensis*, p. 372.

2. Leaves ace-of-spades

4 Silver Birch *Betula pendula* (Birch Family – Betulaceae). An elegant tree, to 30m, easily told when mature by its peeling papery black and white bark (reddish in young trees)
with bosses at base of trunk; twigs shining brown, hairless, with whitish resinous dots.
Leaves very pointed oval, irregularly toothed; turning yellow in autumn. Flowers in yellowish catkins, the male longer and looser than the erect female; April-May, with the
leaves. Fruit a nut with two wings longer than the style. Woods, heaths, moors, especially
on sand and gravel. Widespread, common.

5 Downy Birch *Betula pubescens* has no bosses on the trunk; bark grey-brown; twigs
downy and scarcely shining; resinous dots, if present, brown; leaves less narrowly pointed,
downy at least on the veins beneath, with teeth more or less equal; and fruits with wings
narrower and shorter than the style. Often hybridises with Silver Birch (**4**), less often with
Dwarf Birch (**3**). Often grows with Silver Birch, though usually in wetter places. In the N
may be only a shrub. Widespread, common.

1
2
3
4
5
6

7
8
9
10
11
12

fruit
×1

2 Alder

♂

2

2 × ½

♀

1 Hazel

♂ winter

♀ spring

1

1 ripe fruit

unripe fruit

1
autumn leaf
× ½

♀

♂

**3
Dwarf Birch**

**4 Silver
Birch**

♂

5

edge of leaf

4
ripe catkins

seed

**5
Downy
Birch**

Poplars *Populus*. (Willow Family – Salicaceae). Tall deciduous trees with leaves broad, long-stalked and alternate; the spring leaves often differ from those on the frequent suckers and sometimes also from those produced by the tree in summer. Flowers tiny, with an often deeply divided scale at their base, in hanging catkins appearing before the leaves, the reddish male and the greenish female on separate trees. The fruiting catkins are white-woolly from the hairy seeds; when they fall they litter the ground so untidily that more male than female poplars are usually planted.

1 Hybrid Black Poplar *Populus* × *canadensis*. Generally our commonest black poplar, a very variable group of hybrids between native Black Poplar (**2**) and the **1a North American Cottonwood** *P. deltoides*; a lofty tree to 40m, with rugged blackish bark, *no bosses* on the trunk, usually with branches curving upwards to a fan-shaped crown, young twigs slightly angled and buds sticky; sometimes suckering. Leaves broad, ace-of-spades, with a clear translucent border and *unstalked warts* near the junction with the flattened stalks; appearing later than other poplars; turning yellow in autumn. Catkins April-May. Only male trees are known, so almost always planted. Widespread, frequent. Many other cultivar poplars with ace-of-spades leaves are planted and some may naturalise by suckering. One of the most frequent is the often suckering **1b Balm of Gilead** *P.* × *jackii* (female trees only) with very sticky buds. The **1c Railway Poplar** *P.* × *euramerica* cv. 'Regenerata', another female only clone with young leaves pale brown and no 'wool' until July, is especially frequent by urban main railway lines.

2 Black Poplar *Populus nigra* ssp. *betulifolia*. Less tall and more spreading than Hybrid Black Poplar (**1**), to 33m, and easily distinguished by the *large bosses on its trunk*; young twigs rounded, hairy. Leaves somewhat smaller with longer, much narrower points and *no warts*. Both male and female trees occur; catkins March-April. Local as native, usually by streams and ponds, but much planted in the Vale of Aylesbury, Bucks, and often elsewhere. **2a Cv. 'Italica'**, the Lombardy Poplar, narrowly fastigiate to 36m, is even more widely planted, and may spread by suckering.

3 Aspen *Populus tremula*. A smallish tree, to 20m, with smooth grey-brown bark; twigs and buds downy only when young. Tree leaves *roundish*, broadest about the middle, bluntly toothed, dark greyish-green (yellow in autumn), on stalks so thin and *flattened* that they tremble easily in the wind. Sucker leaves ovate/heart-shaped with rounded stalks and greyish down beneath. Catkins February-April. Damp woods, heaths and fens, the suckers often forming thickets; also on mountains. Widespread, frequent.

4 Grey Poplar *Populus* × *canescens*. The hybrid between Aspen (**3**) and the less frequent White Poplar (**5**), a tall tree, to 46m, with smooth grey bark, smooth at first but later ridged, and sometimes blackish gashes on the lower trunk; young twigs and buds whitely downy. Tree leaves less roundish and with larger coarse teeth than Aspen and *broadest above the middle*, dark green above, cottony greyish-white beneath when young, later almost hairless; stalks more rounded than Aspen but less so than White Poplar. Summer and sucker leaves more ovate. Flowers February-April; female trees and so woolly fruits uncommon. Widely planted, usually on stream banks or other damp places; perhaps rarely as a natural hybrid.

5 White Poplar *Populus alba*. A smallish tree, to 24m, with many black gashes on the smooth pale grey bark; young twigs and buds *densely cottony* with white down. Tree leaves similar to Grey Poplar, but *broadest below the middle*, more whitely cottony beneath and still downy in summer; leaf-stalks rounded. Summer and sucker leaves deeply *palmately lobed*. Catkins March-April. Widely planted and forming suckering thickets, mainly near the coast.

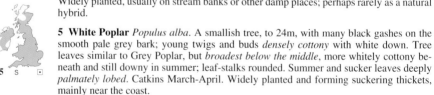

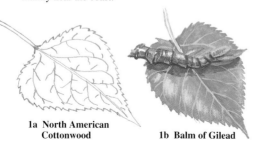

| 1a North American Cottonwood | 1b Balm of Gilead | 1c Railway Poplar |

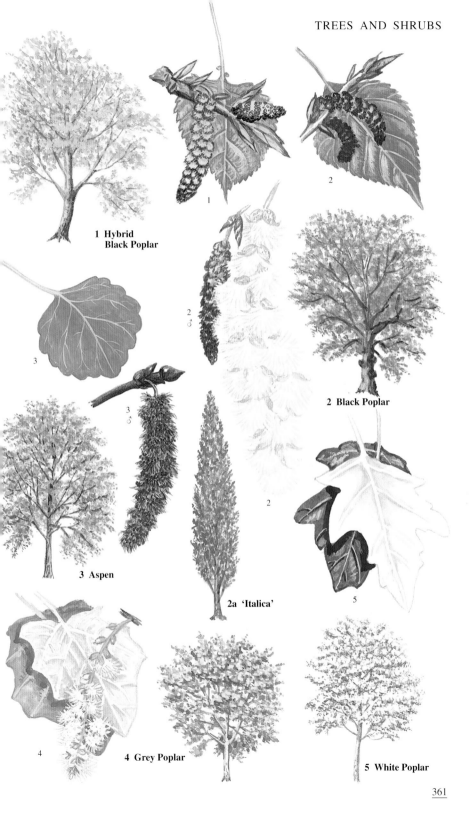

1 Hybrid Black Poplar

1

2

2 ♂

3

3 ♂

3 Aspen

2a 'Italica'

2

2 Black Poplar

5

4

4 Grey Poplar

5 White Poplar

Limes *Tilia*. (Lime Family – Tiliaceae). Tall deciduous trees with alternate, undivided, toothed, heart-shaped leaves. Flowers very pale yellow, very fragrant, 5-petalled, in small umbel-like clusters on a stalk half-joined to a distinctive oblong papery bracteole. Fruit a globular nut.

1 Common Lime *Tilia × europaea*. Much the commonest lime, the partially fertile hybrid between the two native limes (below); usually planted, occasionally a natural hybrid or self-sown. Tall, to 46m, with smooth dark brown bark and *bosses on the trunk*; very young twigs downy. Leaves 6-9cm, dark green, hairless above, paler below with a few *tufts of whitish hairs*, often covered with honey-dew from aphids. Flowers hanging down, usually 4-10 to a cluster, stamens equalling or slightly longer than petals; late June-July. Fruits downy, ribbed. Aka Linden. Widespread in rows or avenues in streets and parks, also in hedges.

2

2 Small-leaved Lime *Tilia cordata*. The commoner of our two native limes, to 38m. Has *smaller, rounder leaves* than Common Lime (**1**), 3-6cm, with less prominent veins and *tufts of reddish hairs* beneath; flower clusters half-erect above leaves, the stamens about equalling the petals; and fruits hardly ribbed. Formerly a dominant woodland tree, still frequent in many scattered woods, also on inland cliffs, especially on lime-rich soils. Mainly England and Wales.

3

3 *Large-leaved Lime *Tilia platyphyllos*. Shorter than Common Lime (**1**), to 34m, with *no bosses on the trunk* and young twigs usually downy. Leaves larger, 6-12cm, more abruptly pointed, *uniformly downy*, the veins beneath more prominent. Flowers larger and 2-4 to the cluster, stamens longer than petals and appearing slightly earlier in June. Fruits very downy and strongly ribbed. Woods, copses, inland cliffs, especially on lime-rich soils; most frequent, England/Wales borders, widely planted or naturalised.

leaf × ½

~

4 Lilac *Syringa vulgaris* (Olive Family – Oleaceae). Suckering and patch-forming shrub to 7m. Flowers lilac, purple or white, 4-petalled, in clusters; May-June. Fruit a capsule. Often naturalised in hedges and on railway banks.

4 Lilac

3. Leaves oval/pointed oval

5 Beech *Fagus sylvatica* (Beech Family – Fagaceae). Tall tree to 40m, with a massive trunk and smooth grey bark. Leaf-buds pointed, warm brown before leafing in May; leaves pointed oval, 4-9cm long; pale green and silky when young, later dark green and hairless, and a flaming orange-yellow in autumn. Flowers a greenish tassel; male stalked and hanging, female unstalked and erect; May. Fruit a warm brown 3-sided nut (mast) in a tough bristly husk. Native in woods in the S, e.g. Chilterns, Cotswolds and South Downs, but very widely planted elsewhere in parks and shelter-belts.

5

Common Elm *Ulmus procera*, p. 382.

6 Evergreen Oak *Quercus ilex*. (Beech Family – Betulaceae). Our largest evergreen tree, to 28m, with scaly greyish bark. Leaves pointed oval, often with holly-like spines, especially when young, dark green above, downy beneath. Catkins May-June. Acorns with scaly cup. Aka Holm Oak, Widely planted and naturalised, forming woods on the Isle of Wight and the Exmoor coast.

6

7 Grey Alder *Alnus incana* (Birch Family) has bark grey and smooth, and young twigs and sharply toothed pointed oval leaves downy at least when young. Catkins January-February. Cf. Alder (p. 358). Planted and self-sown, often in drier places.

7

8 Hornbeam *Carpinus betulus* (Hazel Family – Corylaceae). A smallish tree, to 30m; bark grey, fluted. Leaves pointed oval, toothed, 4-10cm long; turning yellow in autumn. Catkins greenish, loose, hanging, the female smaller with large leafy 3-lobed bracts hiding the small nut-like fruit; April-May, with the leaves. Woods (usually with oak, often coppiced, especially in Epping Forest, Essex), hedges, parkland; most frequent SE England.

8

9 Bog Myrtle *Myrica gale* (Bog-Myrtle Family – Myricaceae). Patch-forming shrub to 1.5m, aka Sweet Gale from the resinous smell of glands on twigs and leaves; twigs red-brown, shiny. Leaves greyish, narrow oval, 2-6cm. Flowers in catkins, orange male and red female on separate plants; April-May, before the leaves. Fruit a nut. Wet heaths, bogs; most frequent, W Scotland, W Ireland.

Aspen *Populus tremula* and **Grey Poplar** *P. × canescens*, p. 360. **Goat Willow** *Salix caprea* and **Grey Willow** *S. cinerea*, **Tea-leaved Willow** *S. phylicifolia* and **Dark-leaved Willow** *S. myrsinifolia*, **Downy Willow** *S. lapponum* and **Woolly Willow** *S. lanata*, p. 380. **Whortle-leaved Willow** *S. myrsinites* and **Mountain Willow** *S. arbuscula*, p. 382.

9

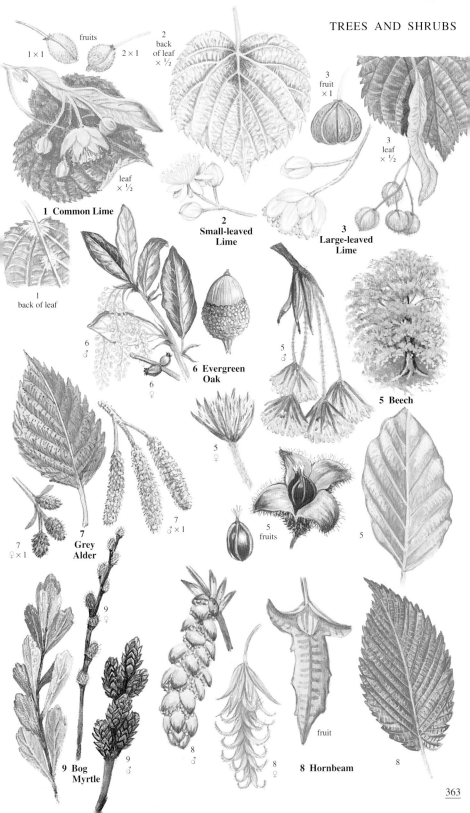

fruits
1×1
2×1

1 Common Lime

leaf × ½

1 back of leaf

2 back of leaf × ½

2 Small-leaved Lime

3 fruit × 1

3 leaf × ½

3 Large-leaved Lime

6 ♂

6 ♀

6 Evergreen Oak

5 ♂

5 ♀

5 fruits

5 Beech

5

7 ♀ × 1

7 ♂ × 1

7 Grey Alder

9 ♀

9 ♂

9 Bog Myrtle

8 ♂

8 ♀

fruit

8 Hornbeam

8

Cherries *Prunus* (Rose Family – Rosaceae). Trees or shrubs, usually deciduous. Flowers white (except sometimes Dwarf Cherry, **2**) 5-petalled. Leaves undivided, usually toothed. Fruit a succulent red or black berry, sometimes tasting very tart. The **Japanese Cherries** *P. serrulata* of gardens are almost always planted, while Peach, Apricot and Almond rarely get beyond the seedling stage on dumps.

(i) Flowers in loose heads or clusters

1 Wild Cherry *Prunus avium*. Tall tree, to 30m, with smooth shiny reddish-brown bark, peeling in strips. Flowers white, 15-25mm, the petals often slightly notched and the calyx tube *narrowed at the top*; late March-May, 'wearing white for Easter-tide'. Leaves pointed oval, slightly downy beneath, often coppery when young, turning pink or red in autumn. Fruit usually red, but sometimes black or yellow, like a pinched cultivated cherry, *sweet or tart*. Aka Gean. Beech and other woods, hedges. Widespread, frequent.

2 Dwarf Cherry *Prunus cerasus* is a suckering *shrub* or small tree to 8m. Flowers sometimes pale pink, smaller (12-18mm) than the much more frequent Wild Cherry (**1**) and with petals un- or scarcely notched and calyx-tube *not* narrowed at the top. Leaves thicker, glossy dark green above and almost hairless beneath. Fruit (Morello cherry) usually dark red and *always tart*. Bird-sown from gardens and orchards to hedges and scrub. Scattered, mainly England and Ireland.

3 Blackthorn *Prunus spinosa*. A stiffly thorny shrub, to 4m, suckering to form impenetrable thickets; young twigs downy. Flowers white, 10-15mm. appearing *before* the leaves, and so contrasting strongly with the blackish stems and twigs; *late March*-May, a fortnight after Cherry-plum (**4**) and a month before Hawthorn (p. 390). Leaves oval, matt. Fruit (sloe) a diminutive blackish plum, with a bluish bloom and and tongue-numbingly tart. Intermediates, perhaps hybrids, with Cherry-plum occur. Woods, scrub, hedges, often on sea cliffs. Widespread, common.

4 Cherry-plum *Prunus cerasifera*. All too often confused with Blackthorn (**3**), but it starts to flower in *February*, often with the leaves. Shrub or *small tree*, to 8m, usually *thornless*, the twigs *green*, shiny, hairless. Flowers larger, 15-20mm; February-April. Leaves ovate, pale glossy green. Fruit globular, *yellow or reddish*, only in hotter summers. Almost always planted, especially in hedges. Mainly south-eastern.

5 Wild Plum *Prunus domestica*. A small tree or tall shrub, to 8m or more, *very variable* because it encompasses a bird-sown mixture of Plums, Greengages, Damsons and Bullaces; twigs matt, sometimes thorny, downy when young. Flowers white, often tinged green, 15-25mm; April-May, with the oval leaves. Fruit egg-shaped, blue-black, purple, red or green. **5a** ssp. *insititia* with very downy, often thorny twigs, and smaller, usually purple-black fruits produces Bullaces and Damsons; and ssp. *italica* with rounder green fruits produces Greengages, but the whole group is so interbred that individual shrubs can often not be named. Hedges and scrub. Widespread, frequent.

(ii) Flowers in stalked spikes

6 Bird Cherry *Prunus padus*. A shrub or small tree, to 17m; bark purplish. Flowers quite different from Wild Cherry (**1**), being smaller (10-16mm), creamy-white and fragrant; May-June. Leaves similar but hairy only along the midrib beneath, yellowing in autumn. Fruit *black*, tart. Woods, scrub, mainly northern/western, usually planted in the S (except E Anglia), widely naturalised. **6a Rum Cherry** *P. serotina* has creamy white 5-10mm flowers in shorter flower-spikes, leaves with no or *brownish* hairs on leaf underside and *purplish*-black fruits. Now well established on some southern heaths, e.g. in Surrey. **6b St Lucie's Cherry** *P. mahaleb* has flowers 8-12mm, fragrant and in short spikes; glandular-hairy twigs; shorter, more roundish leaves; and tart black fruits. Established in a few woods.

5b Greengage

5a Damson

5a Bullace

2 Dwarf Cherry

1 Wild Cherry

3 Blackthorn

4 Cherry-plum

4

5 Wild Plum

6

6 Bird Cherry

6b St. Lucie's Cherry

6a Rum Cherry

1 Cherry Laurel *Prunus laurocerasus*. A very familiar spreading garden shrub or rarely a small tree, to 8m, easily told by its large (200mm x 60mm) bright green shiny leathery blunt *evergreen* leaves; twigs green. Flowers white, 7-9mm; late March-May. Fruit purple-black. Often planted or bird-sown; woods and scrub, mainly southern. The taller (to 12m) and less often bird-sown **1a Portugal Laurel** *P. lusitanica*, has quite different, darker green, thinner and *more pointed* leaves with dark red stalks, and more egg-shaped fruits.

2 Crab Apple *Malus sylvestris*. A small, often spiny tree, to 10m. Flowers pale pink, darker on the back, in small clusters, 30-40mm; April-May. Leaves pointed oval, *downy at first*. Fruit a small apple, yellow-green but often reddening, 20-30mm, extremely tart. Woods, scrub, hedges. Widespread, frequent, except N Scotland. **2a Cultivated Apple** *M. domestica* is very variable, having originated from apple cores of many varieties, but is generally larger and not spiny, with leaves remaining downy beneath and fruits much larger, to 120mm. Hedges, scrub, waste ground, much commoner around towns and villages.

3 Wild Pear *Pyrus pyraster*. A shrub or small tree, usually *spiny*, to 15m. Flowers white with *purple anthers*, 5-petalled, 22-34mm, in clusters; April-May. Leaves pointed oval. Fruit inedible, more or less rounded, occasionally pear-shaped, 13-35mm; sepals persisting. Woods, scrub, hedges; southern. **3a Cultivated Pear** *P. communis* is often scarcely distinguishable, but is always a *spineless tree*, to 20m, with edible *pear-shaped* fruits. Often spread from picnickers' throwaways.

4 ***Plymouth Pear *Pyrus cordata*. Perhaps our rarest native shrub, to 8m. Differs from Wild Pear (**3**) in being always *spiny* and having flowers sometimes *pale pink* on the back, 12-18mm, and *very much* smaller *blackthorn-sized* leaves and *haw-sized* fruits, the sepals falling early. Hedges near Plymouth, woods near Truro, Cornwall.

Other Fruit Trees. Two other fruit trees of the Rose Family are bird-sown (or planted) in similar places but much more rarely. Both are small trees with white or pink flowers, untoothed leaves and roundish fruits: **5 Quince** *Cydonia oblonga*, thornless with flowers, 40-50mm, pointed oblong leaves grey-downy below and *yellow* fruits; and **Medlar** (p. 384)

Whitebeams *Sorbus* (Rose Family – Rosaceae). Trees or shrubs with clusters of white, usually 5-petalled flowers, anthers cream or pink; May-June; leaves of varying shapes (the best identification clue, together with geography); and fruit a globular red or orange berry, much relished by thrushes in autumn. Most whitebeams are some shade of white beneath the leaves. Of the 20 native species only the Rowan (p. 388) is widespread and common (less so in the S), while Common Whitebeam (p. 368) is frequent as a native only on lime in the S. A few other species are widespread but scattered, but most are very localised; all except Rowan and the two Arran species (p. 370) are confined to *chalk and limestone*, though Wild Service Tree (p. 392) also grows on clay. Of the five bird-sown aliens, only Swedish Whitebeam (p. 392) is at all frequent. Occasional hybrids add to the identification problems. Aka Sorbs. *Sorbus* is Latin for berry, corrupted into service(-tree). Beam is Anglo-Saxon for tree.

SORBUS LEAVES	
Broadly ovate:	Common Whitebeam, *devoniensis, subcuneata, vexans, bristoliensis, wilmottiana, decipiens, croceocarpa, leyana, porrigentiformis, leptophylla, lancastriensis, pseudofennica*
Narrowly ovate/lanceolate:	Common Whitebeam, Rock Whitebeam, *anglica, minima, arranensis*
Rounded:	*eminens, latifolia, hibernica*
Lobed:	Swedish Whitebeam, Wild Service Tree, *leyana, pseudofennica*
Pinnate:	Rowan, Service Tree
Evenly toothed:	Rowan, Rock Whitebeam, *vexans, wilmottiana, eminens, porrigentiformis, lancastriensis, hibernica*
Large teeth/small lobes:	Common Whitebeam, *devoniensis, subcuneata, bristoliensis, croceocarpa, anglica, minima, arranensis*
Large, sharp teeth:	*decipiens, latifolia*
Silvery white beneath:	Common Whitebeam, Rock Whitebeam, *vexans*
Yellowish-white beneath:	Swedish Whitebeam
Green beneath:	Rowan, Wild Service Tree
Greenish-white beneath:	*wilmottiana, eminens, leptophylla, porrigentiformis,* Irish Whitebeam
Greyish-white beneath:	*devoniensis* (tinged greenish), *subcuneata, bristoliensis, anglica, lancastriensis, leyana, minima, pseudofennica, arranensis,*

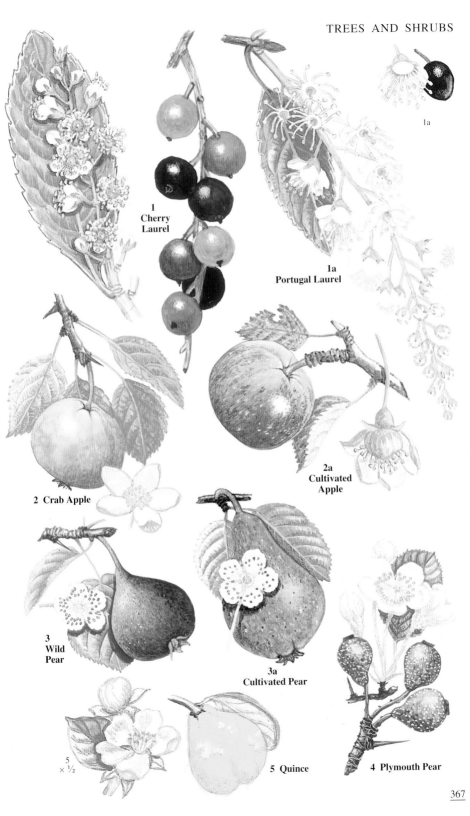

1
Cherry
Laurel

1a

1a
Portugal Laurel

2 Crab Apple

2a
Cultivated
Apple

3
Wild
Pear

3a
Cultivated Pear

5
× ½

5 Quince

4 Plymouth Pear

SORBUS BERRIES	
Orange:	*bristoliensis, decipiens*
Orange-red:	Rowan, Common Whitebeam, Swedish Whitebeams, *vexans, eminens, leptophylla, lancastriensis, pseudofennica*, Irish Whitebeam (tinged pink)
Red:	*leyana, mimima, arranensis*
Purplish-red:	Rock Whitebeam, *wilmottiana, anglica, porrigentiformis*
Yellow/orange-yellow:	*latifolia*
Orange-brown:	*devoniensis, subcuneata*
Brown:	Wild Service Tree, *devoniensis, subcuneata*

(i) Widespread species

Rowan, see p. 388.

1 Common Whitebeam *Sorbus aria*. By far the most frequent whitebeam, easily identified on the southern chalk by the silvery white undersides of its leaves waving in the wind; in spring whole hillsides can look silvery. A tall tree, to 25m. Leaves varying from broad to narrow ovate, jaggedly toothed, sometimes almost lobed. Flowers 10-15mm, anthers creamy or pinkish. Berries *orange-red*, 8-15mm. Woods, scrub and inland cliffs on southern chalk and limestone; bird-sown N of its native range.

2 *Rock Whitebeam *Sorbus rupicola*. The only other widespread native whitebeam, a *shrub* or small tree to 6m or more. Flowers 12-16mm, anthers cream or pinkish. Leaves narrowly oval, narrowing to an *untoothed base*, silvery white beneath. Berries 7-15mm, slightly *purplish-red*. Limestone cliffs and rocks; mainly N England.

Wild Service Tree, see p. 392. **Swedish Whitebeam**, see p. 392.

(ii) Localised species

Devon/Exmoor. **3** **S. devoniensis*, a tree to 15m, the leaves with large teeth/small lobes grey-green beneath, creamy anthers and berries orange-brown becoming brown, with a few lens-shaped glands, is widespread in Devon, marginal in Cornwall and Somerset. Confined to the Exmoor Coast are **4** ****S. subcuneata*, a tree to 10m, with narrowly oval, sharply pointed, large-toothed/small-lobed leaves, greyish beneath, anthers creamy and similar berries to *devoniensis* but with many lens-shaped glands; and **5** ****S. vexans*, so named by Dr. E.F. Warburg for being vexatiously hard to identify, a small tree to 6m with narrow oval, toothed leaves, untoothed at the base, white beneath, creamy anthers and orange-red berries with few lens-shaped glands. Also Rock Whitebeam (**2**).

Avon Gorge/Wye Valley The richest area for whitebeams, with 11 species, including Common and Rock Whitebeams (p. 368). Confined to the Avon Gorge are **6** ****S. bristoliensis* with oval leaves, jaggedly toothed/lobed, greyish beneath, pink anthers and orange berries, and **7** ****S. wilmottiana* with smaller, less jaggedly toothed leaves, greenish-white below, and purplish-red berries.

Common to both Gorge and Valley is **8** ****S. eminens*, perhaps the most distinctive whitebeam with its markedly rounded leaves, greenish-white beneath. pink anthers and orange-red berries. Also in both areas, but more frequent in Wales (p. 370), are *S. anglica*, p. 370, *S. porrigentiformis*, p. 370 and the Service Tree *S. domestica*, p. 388.

Just to add to the confusion at least three other whitebeams are naturalised in the Gorge (and elsewhere): **9** ****S. decipiens*, with very sharply toothed leaves and orange berries with lens-shaped glands; **10** ***S. croceocarpa* with broadly oval leaves and bright orange berries; and **11** ***S. latifolia* with almost rounded, sharply toothed leaves and yellow or orange-yellow berries.

1

2

3

4

5

6

7

8

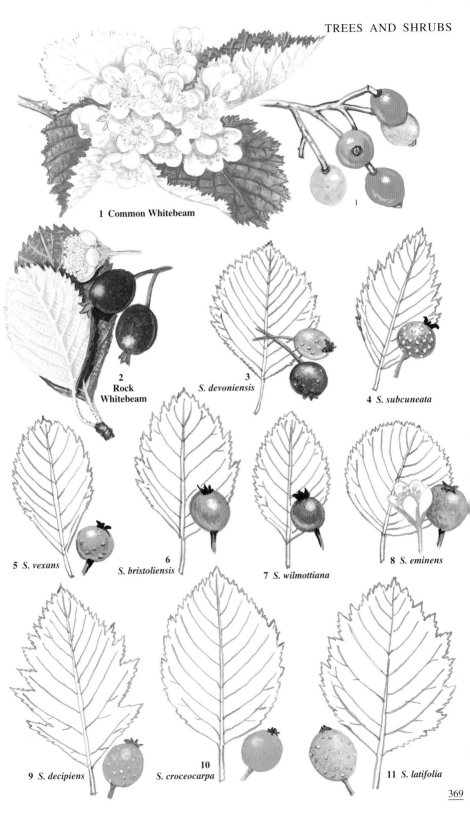

1 Common Whitebeam

2 Rock Whitebeam

3 S. devoniensis

4 S. subcuneata

5 S. vexans

6 S. bristoliensis

7 S. wilmottiana

8 S. eminens

9 S. decipiens

10 S. croceocarpa

11 S. latifolia

Wales. The widely distributed whitebeams are Rock Whitebeam (p. 368) and the somewhat misnamed **1** ***S. anglica**, a shrub with narrow oval leaves, large teeth/small lobes, greyish beneath, anthers pink and purplish-red berries with small lens-shaped glands. Over much of S Wales grows **2** *****S. porrigentiformis**, which may be a shrub, with broadly oval leaves, fairly evenly-toothed except for the untoothed base, greenish-white below, anthers pink and berries purplish-red. Also *****Service Tree, see p. 388. A smallish area of limestone cliffs and rocks in Breconshire has 3 highly localised *shrub* species: **3** ******S. leptophylla**, with broadly oval, fairly evenly toothed leaves, greenish-white beneath, cream or pinkish anthers and orange-red berries; **4** ******S. leyana**, sometimes a small tree, with hawthorn-like lobed leaves, greyish beneath, anthers pinkish and red berries; and **5** ******S. minima**, with almost lanceolate leaves, large teeth/small lobes, greyish beneath, creamy anthers and red berries.

Northern Limestone Rock Whitebeam (p. 368) is widespread on the Westmorland and Cartmel limestone. **6** ******S. lancastriensis**, a shrub or small tree with evenly toothed oval leaves, greyish beneath, and purplish-red berries is much more localised, e.g at Humphrey Head, S Cumbria.

Isle of Arran. Rowan (p. 388) is widespread on Arran, but Glen Catacol in the N has two endemics: **7** ******S. pseudofennica**, with deeply lobed pointed oval leaves greyish below, creamy anthers and orange-red berries, and **8** ******S. arranensis** with lanceolate leaves like *minima* (5), but more deeply lobed and greyish beneath, anthers cream or pink, and berries red.

Ireland. **9 Irish Whitebeam** *S. hibernica*, a tree to 6m, with almost roundish, evenly toothed leaves, greenish-white beneath, pinkish anthers and pinkish-orange berries is the most widespread whitebeam in Ireland. Common and Rock Whitebeams, with *anglica, devoniensis*, and *intermedia* are much more local.

~

10 Juneberry *Amelanchier lamarckii* (Rose Family – Rosaceae). Shrub or small tree, to 12m. Flowers white, 35-40mm, with five *narrow* petals, upright at first, anthers yellow, in loose clusters, appearing with the leaves; April-May. Leaves pointed oval, finely toothed, *purple* at first, then greyish, finally yellow or red in autumn. Fruit a berry, green, then red, finally purplish-black. Naturalised in woods and scrub and on heaths in the S, including, since the 1890s, the Hurtwood, Surrey.

11 Barberry *Berberis vulgaris* (Barberry Family – Berberidaceae*).* Deciduous shrub, to 3m, with usually 3-forked spines on the grooved twigs. Flowers small, yellow, in hanging clusters; March-May. Leaves oval, sharply toothed. Fruit an oblong red berry, edible. Hedges, scrub; widely scattered. Many planted species are self-sown, the most frequent being **11a Thunberg's Barberry** *B. thunbergii* with red-tinged flowers, pear-shaped, untoothed, often purplish leaves and brighter red berries; **11b Mrs Wilson's Barberry** *B. wilsoniae* with yellow flowers in short clusters, semi-evergreen, very narrow leaves and pinkish-red berries; and **11c Darwin's Barberry** *B. darwinii* with orange flowers, spiny evergreen leaves and blue-purple berries. One of its hybrids, **11d** *B. × stenophylla,* has narrower spiny evergreen leaves, yellower flowers and blue-black fruits.

12 Dogwood *Cornus sanguinea* (Dogwood Family – Cornaceae). Shrub to 4m, easily picked out in winter by its *red* twigs. Flowers creamy white, 4-petalled, 8-10mm, in a *flat-topped* head, faintly foetid; June-July, *and sporadically in autumn*. Leaves pointed oval, opposite, stalked, with *prominent veins*, reddening in autumn. Fruit a black berry. Woods, scrub, hedges, especially on lime; frequent in Midlands and South. **12a Red Osier Dogwood** *C. sericea* suckers vigorously and has deeper red twigs, yellower flowers, longer leaves with a *tapering point* and white berries. Widely planted and naturalised; not to be confused with the much less frequent **12b White Dogwood** *C. alba*, with abruptly pointed leaves. **12c Cornelian Cherry** *C. mas*. An early-flowering shrub, to 4m. Flowers yellow, 4-5mm, in small clusters with yellow-green bracts; Feb-March, *before* the pointed oval leaves. Fruit a red berry, rare in Britain. Woods, hedges; widely planted but naturalised only in a few places, as at Hargham, Norfolk.

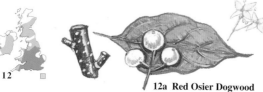

12a Red Osier Dogwood

**12b
White
Dogwood**

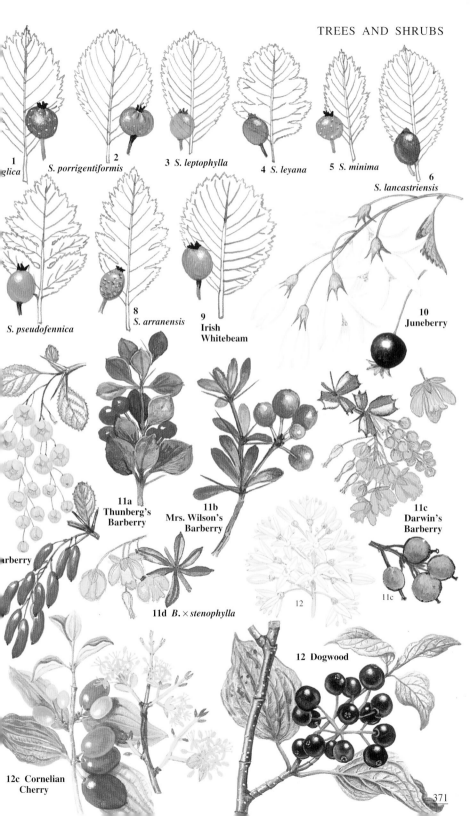

1 *S. anglica*

2 *S. porrigentiformis*

3 *S. leptophylla*

4 *S. leyana*

5 *S. minima*

6 *S. lancastriensis*

7 *S. pseudofennica*

8 *S. arranensis*

9 Irish Whitebeam

10 Juneberry

11a Thunberg's Barberry

11b Mrs. Wilson's Barberry

11c Darwin's Barberry

11c

Barberry

11d *B.* × *stenophylla*

12

12 Dogwood

12c Cornelian Cherry

Cotoneasters *Cotoneaster* (Rose Family – Rosaceae). Low to tall, usually deciduous shrubs. Flowers either pink with the five petals erect or white with them spreading, in clusters. Leaves undivided and untoothed. Fruit a berry, usually more or less globular. Only the very rare Welsh Cotoneaster (**4**) is native, but some 70 other species have been bird-sown from parks and gardens, of which only 11 are widespread and frequent enough to be described here, all with berries some shade of red.

(i) Tall shrubs, flowers pink, petals erect, anthers white, clusters usually small.

1 Himalayan Cotoneaster *Cotoneaster simonsii*. Tall, sometimes semi-evergreen, to 4m; twigs hairy. Flowers very pale pink with a distinctive *large rosy-red patch* on each petal, 7-8mm; May-July. Leaves pointed oval, shiny above, the veins indented, whitish downy beneath. Berry orange-red, oblong. Scrub, woods, especially on chalk in the S; the most frequent of the taller species.

2 Chinese Cotoneaster *Cotoneaster dielsianus*. Medium, to 2m; twigs downy at first, branches *drooping gracefully*. Flowers pink, anthers *white*, 3-7 in the cluster; June. Leaves broad pointed oval, veins prominent, grey-downy beneath at first, later *brownish*. Berry red to orange-red, globular to pear-shaped. Widely bird-sown. **2a** *C. franchetii* is taller and *ever-green*, with 5-15 flowers (May) to the cluster, *pale purple* anthers, narrower leaves, indented veins and orange-red ovoid berries. Less often bird-sown.

3 Blistered Cotoneaster *Cotoneaster rehderi*. Tall, to 5m. Flowers pink, the petals soon falling, in large clusters; May-June. Leaves dark green, shiny, *conspicuously blistered* above, somewhat downy beneath, 5-15cm. Berry bright red, 8-11mm. Often bird-sown. Can be mistaken for the less frequent **3a** *C. bullatus*, which has smaller (4-7cm) leaves only slightly blistered but downier beneath, and berries 6-8mm.

4 ***Welsh Cotoneaster *Cotoneaster cambricus*. Our only native species and one of the rarest. Medium, to 1-1.5m; young twigs downy. Flowers pale pink, 6-7mm; April-June. Leaves roundish but pointed, *matt* above, downy beneath. Berry red, *globular*. Scrub, Great Orme's Head, N Wales, where Himalayan Cotoneaster (**1**) also grows.

(ii) Tall shrubs, flowers white, petals spreading, anthers purplish, clusters large.

5 Tree Cotoneaster *Cotoneaster frigidus*. May be semi-evergreen and a tree, to 8m or more. Flowers 4-5mm; June. Leaves 6-15cm, *broad lanceolate*, downy beneath. Berries usually bright red, sometimes orange or yellow, 4-6mm. Widely bird-sown. **5a** *C. salicifolius* is a more or less evergreen shrub, to 5m, with much narrower, *willow-like* leaves, somewhat blistered above, and fruits always red, 4-5mm. **5b** *C.* × *watereri* is a widely grown and bird-sown hybrid between the two, intermediate especially in its leaves, but with berries often larger (5-8mm) than both parents.

6 Late Cotoneaster *Cotoneaster lacteus*. Evergreen, to 5m. Flowers June-July. Leaves large, broad oval, *cherry-like*, with veins indented; downy beneath. Berries bright red. A hedge plant in E Anglia, and widely bird-sown.

(iii) Low, sprawling shrubs

7 Wall Cotoneaster *Cotoneaster horizontalis*. Prostrate to upright (on walls), easily told by its *herring-bone* branching, to 2m or more. Flowers pink, 4-5mm, petals erect, anthers white; May-June. Leaves dark green above, paler beneath and shiny on both sides. Berry orange-red. The most frequent sprawling cotoneaster in the S.

8 Rock Cotoneaster *Cotoneaster integrifolius*. Usually more closely prostrate than Wall Cotoneaster (**7**) and with larger (10-12mm), often solitary, *white* flowers with *spreading* petals and purplish-black anthers, narrower, less pointed leaves, 7-15mm, and redder fruits, 8-10mm. The most frequent sprawling cotoneaster in the N and W, often on rocks in open country well away from gardens. Not to be confused with *C. microphyllus*, with flowers (5-7mm), leaves (5-8mm) and berries (5-8mm) all smaller and flowers rarely solitary, which may be being overlooked.

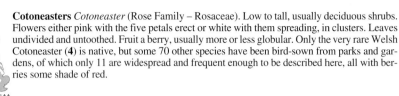

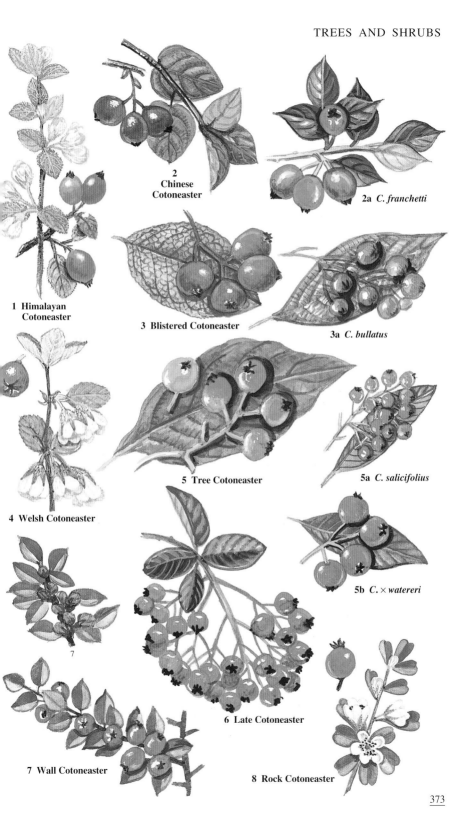

2 Chinese Cotoneaster

2a *C. franchetti*

1 Himalayan Cotoneaster

3 Blistered Cotoneaster

3a *C. bullatus*

5 Tree Cotoneaster

5a *C. salicifolius*

4 Welsh Cotoneaster

5b *C.* × *watereri*

7

6 Late Cotoneaster

7 Wall Cotoneaster

8 Rock Cotoneaster

1 Spindle *Euonymus europaeus* (Spindle Family – Celastraceae). Tall shrub, with green 4-sided twigs, to 5m or more, most noticeable in autumn, with its distinctive *bright coral-pink* berries and pinkish-red leaves. Leaves mid-green, lanceolate, opposite, slightly toothed, 3-8cm. Flowers greenish-white, 4-petalled, 8-10mm, in easily overlooked small stalked clusters; May-June. Seeds bright orange. Woods, scrub, hedges, especially on lime; mainly southern. **1a Large-leaved Spindle** *E. latifolius* has twigs less markedly 4-sided, larger (7-15cm), more abruptly pointed leaves and flowers 5-petalled. Bird-sown in several places.

2 Evergreen Spindle *Euonymus japonica*. Shrub or small tree, to 5m. Leaves *evergreen*, dark green, shiny, bluntly oval, relished by the black and white caterpillars of the magpie moth *Abraxas grossulariata*. Flowers and fruits like Spindle (**1**). Much planted near the sea and sometimes naturalised on cliffs and in woods.

3 **Box *Buxus sempervirens* (Box Family – Buxaceae). Shrub or tree, to 5m or more; bark grey, twigs green. Leaves *evergreen*, small, 1-2cm, oval, shiny, rather leathery. Flowers petalless, male and female on separate plants, the male with 4 sepals, greenish-white with *yellow stamens*, the female sepal-less, greenish. Fruit a horned green capsule. Native in woods and scrub, at Box Hill, Surrey, and a few other places on lime in the S; also widely planted in parks, gardens and churchyards. Widely naturalised.

4 Buckthorn *Rhamnus cathartica* (Buckthorn Family – Rhamnaceae). A dense deciduous shrub to 8m, with *thorns* on the twigs. Leaves pointed oval, finely *toothed*, turning yellow and brown in autumn. Flowers green, tiny (3-5mm), *4-petalled*, male and female on separate bushes, in dense unstalked clusters; May-June. Fruit a berry, green and then *purplish-black*, purging rapidly if eaten, whence aka Purging Buckthorn. Scrub, hedges, fens, especially on lime; mainly southern. **4a Mediterranean Buckthorn** *R. alaternus*, with no thorns, smaller evergreen leaves and 5 petals, is well naturalised around Llandudno, N Wales.

5 Alder Buckthorn *Frangula alnus*. Less thick-set than Buckthorn (**4**), and with *no thorns*, untoothed leaves turning yellow or red in autumn, flowers *5-petalled*, 2-4mm, with stamens and styles together, and berries green, then *red*, finally purplish-black. Damp woods, scrub, fens, usually on acid soils; mainly southern. Both species grow at Wicken Fen, N of Cambridge.

6 Wayfaring-tree *Viburnum lantana* (Honeysuckle Family – Caprifoliaceae). A downy shrub, never a tree, to 6m. Leaves opposite, *oval* wrinkled, minutely toothed. Flowers creamy white, *all alike*, with a sickly fragrance, in rather flat-topped umbel-like clusters; April-June. Fruit a berry, red then black. Scrub, especially on lime; southern only as native.

7 Snowberry *Symphoricarpos albus*. (Honeysuckle Family), little-branched suckering shrub, to 2m. Leaves opposite, oval, untoothed, sometimes deeply lobed. Flowers pink, bell-shaped, 5-8mm. Fruit a conspicuous *white* berry. Insidiously aggressive thicket-former in woods and scrub, also on waste ground; widespread. Two increasing escapes which spread by rooting at the stem-tips are **7a Coralberry** *S. orbiculatus* with all-pink berries and its hybrid with Snowberry, **7b** *S.* × *chenaultii* with berries pink on one side only.

8 Flowering Nutmeg *Leycesteria formosa*. Shrub with drooping branched stems to 2m. Leaves opposite, oval, very long-pointed. Flowers in a showy spike, the 5 creamy white to purple petals, encased in green bracts strongly tinged *red-purple*; June-Sept. Fruit a purple berry. Aka Himalayan Honeysuckle. Increasingly planted, often bird-sown in woods and

7 Snowberry

7b *S.* × *chenaultii*

7a Coralberry

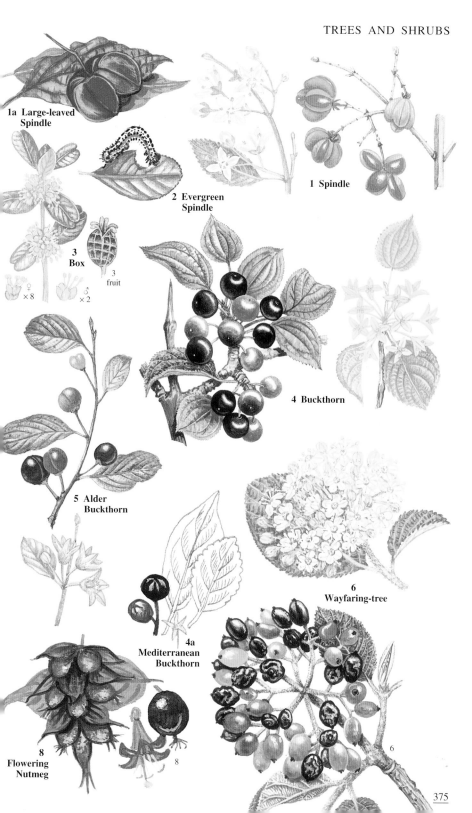

1a Large-leaved Spindle

1 Spindle

2 Evergreen Spindle

3 Box

3 fruit

♀ ×8   ♂ ×2

4 Buckthorn

5 Alder Buckthorn

6 Wayfaring-tree

4a Mediterranean Buckthorn

8 Flowering Nutmeg

8

6

1

1 **Fly Honeysuckle** *Lonicera xylosteum*. Erect shrub to 2m. Leaves oval, opposite, short-stalked. Flowers yellowish-cream, sometimes tinged pink or red, 2-lipped with a long tube, 8-15mm, in pairs at the base of the leaves; May-June. Fruit a red berry. Native in a few woods on the South Downs, occasionally naturalised elsewhere.

Introduced Honeysuckles. Four bird-sown or garden-escaped shrubby honeysuckles (for climbers, see p. 258): **2 Wilson's Honeysuckle** *Lonicera nitida* with small oval leaves, small creamy flowers and violet berries; **2a Box-leaved Honeysuckle** *L. pileata*, similar but with narrow lanceolate leaves; **Tartar Honeysuckle** *L. tatarica*, with red/pink/white flowers and red berries; and **2b Californian Honeysuckle** *L. involucrata*, mainly in Ireland (p. 461).

3 **Fuchsia** *Fuchsia magellanica* (Willowherb Family – Onagraceae). Shrub, to 3m. Flowers unique in British flora, with four conspicuous spreading *deep red sepals*, four much smaller erect dark purple petals, eight prominent red stamens and an even more prominent red style, three times as long; solitary, long-stalked, 4cm; June-Oct. Leaves pointed oval, toothed, opposite. Fruit an elongated black berry. Much planted in hedges, especially in Ireland and often naturalised, e.g. its large-flowered cultivar Corallina on Lundy I, Bristol Channel.

4 **Escallonia** *Escallonia macrantha* (Currant Family – Grossulariaceae). Evergreen shrub from Chile, to 3m. Leaves oval, toothed, with pale dots, aromatic. Flowers *pink or reddish-pink*, 5-petalled, semi-tubular. Fruit a capsule. A favourite hedge-plant near the sea in the W; sometimes naturalised on cliffs and elsewhere.

Holly, see p. 398. **Tutsans** *Hypericum* spp, see p. 74. **Hedge Veronicas** *Hebe*, see p. 386.

3 Fuchsia

1 Fly Honeysuckle

2 Wilson's Honeysuckle

2a Box-leaved Honeysuckle

4 Escallonia

2b Californian Honeysuckle

4

4. Leaves lanceolate

Willows, **Sallows** and **Osiers** *Salix* range from tall trees to prostrate undershrubs, all deciduous, mostly with alternate leaves, almost all growing in damper places. Willows have lanceolate leaves if trees, shorter broader leaves if low shrubs. Sallows are low trees or tall shrubs with broad leaves. Osiers are tall shrubs with long narrow leaves on long pliant branches or withies used in basket-work, for which they are often planted. Some tree willows are regularly pollarded (beheaded at 2-3 m from the ground) to produce a similar crop of withies.

All have their small flowers in catkins, each with two stamens and a rounded scale at the base. Catkins can be either long and hanging (tree willows) or short and erect, the male and female on different plants. Male catkins, often white and silky at first, whence the name Pussy Willow, are generally yellow from their anthers and called Palm when (mainly Goat and Grey Willows) used in processions on Palm Sunday. Female catkins are grey-green and less conspicuous, going silky in fruit. The two kinds of catkin can look so different, especially as they often appear before the leaves, as to be mistaken for different species.

All species hybridise very readily, some hybrids being as or more frequent than their parents. For detailed descriptions of the hybrids, see BSBI Handbook No 4 *Willows and Poplars of Great Britain and Ireland*, by R.D. Meikle (1984).

Several frequent species of willow are almost always planted. They include the well known Weeping Willow, usually a hybrid between the true *S. babylonica* and either Crack or White Willow; **Violet Willow** *S. daphnoides* with purplish twigs; and **Olive Willow** *S. elaeagnos* with reddish/yellowish twigs very narrow toothed leaves.

Trees:	Crack, White, Bay, Almond, Osier, Goat, Grey, Dark-leaved	
Tall shrubs:	Bay, Almond, Purple, Osier, Goat, Grey, Eared, Tea-leaved, Dark-leaved	
Low shrubs:	Creeping, Downy, Woolly, Whortle-leaved, Mountain, Net-veined, Dwarf	
Leaves broad lanceolate:	Bay	
narrow lanceolate:	Crack, White, Almond, Purple, Osier	
ovate:	Goat, Grey, Eared, Tea-leaved, Dark-leaved, Creeping, Downy, Whortle-leaved, Mountain	
roundish:	Woolly, Net-veined, Dwarf	

× 2

♂ flower

♂

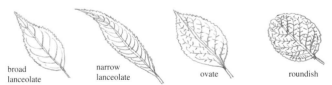

broad lanceolate
narrow lanceolate
ovate
roundish

× 2

♀ flower

Catkins with the leaves:	Crack, White, Bay, Almond, Tea-leaved, Downy, Woolly, Whortle-leaved, Mountain, Net-veined, Dwarf	
before the leaves:	Purple, Osier, Goat, Grey, Eared, Dark-leaved, Creeping	
long:	Crack, White, Almond	
short cylindrical:	Bay, Purple, Downy, Net-leaved, females of Goat, Grey, Osier, Tea-leaved, Dark-leaved, Whortle-leaved	
oval:	Eared, Creeping, Downy, Woolly, Mountain, Dwarf, males of Osier, Goat, Grey, Tea-leaved, Dark-leaved, Creeping, Whortle-leaved	

♀

catkins with leaves
before the leaves
long
short cylindrical
oval

1 Crack Willow *Salix fragilis*. A frequently pollarded riverside Willow, which if left alone becomes a tree to 25m, with wide-angled branches, grey fissured bark and hairless twigs that *break off easily*. Leaves variable, lanceolate, toothed, asymmetrical at tip, bright glossy green above, paler beneath, hairless when mature. Catkins slender, elongated, on short leafy stalks; April-May, with the leaves. Fruits stalked. By fresh water, usually planted; widespread, common; though certainly native, it is now hard to find a tree of an undoubtedly natural origin. Its hybrid with White Willow (**2**) is frequent.

2 White Willow *Salix alba*. Readily distinguished at a distance from Crack Willow (**1**) by its *silvery white leaves*, also when not pollarded by its more upright branches and narrower crown. Also differs in its rather smoother bark; twigs silky when young, not breaking off so easily; shorter, more finely toothed leaves, often symmetrical at the tip and covered, especially beneath, with silky white hairs; catkins appearing slightly later, in May; and unstalked fruits. In a much planted variety the twigs are orange. Habitat and native status like Crack Willow; widespread.

3 Bay Willow *Salix pentandra*. A shrub or small tree, to 10m, with hairless shiny twigs. Leaves *broad elliptical*, toothed, *glossy dark green*, paler beneath and sticky when young. Catkins slender, elongated, on short leafy stalks; our only willow with 5, or rarely more, stamens; May-June, with the leaves. Both young leaves and catkins are slightly fragrant, but of balsam rather than bay. Fruits short-stalked. By fresh water and on wet ground; northern.

4 Almond Willow *Salix triandra*. A tall shrub or small tree to 10m, with smooth *flaking cinnamon bark* and a smell of almonds; twigs ridged, glossy, hairless. Leaves lanceolate, rather broad at the base, hairless, dark green, shiny, paler beneath, with persistent stipules at their base; buds not sticky. Catkins elongated, on short leafy stalks, the males *conspicuously bright yellow*; our only willow with 3 stamens; April-May, with the leaves. Fruits long-stalked, hairless. Native but often planted as an osier; damper places, usually by fresh water; mainly south-eastern.

5 Purple Willow *Salix purpurea*. A tall hairless shrub, to 5m; twigs glossy, yellowish, often purplish at first. Leaves almost opposite. at least at the top of the twig, usually lanceolate, broad, often *slightly toothed at the tip*; dull and slightly bluish above, paler and greyish beneath; blackening when dried. Most attractive when its neat male catkins are out, with their golden pollen, reddish anthers and *dark purple-tipped scales*; our only willow with 2 stamens which are united to appear as one; often opposite, on short leafy stalks; March-April, before the leaves. Fruits unstalked, silky. Its hybrid with Osier (**6**) is quite frequent. Native in fens and by fresh water, but often planted as an osier; widely scattered.

6 Osier *Salix viminalis*. The true Osier is a tall shrub or small tree, to 6m; widely grown for its long flexible brown or yellowish-brown twigs (withies) used in basket-work. Leaves *long*, up to 15 or even 18cm, and *narrow*, 5-15mm, dark green and hairless, covered with *glistening white hairs beneath*, margins scarcely toothed, inrolled. Catkins hardly stalked, the male short, the female longer; March-April, before the leaves. By fresh water, marshy and damp places; often planted in withy-beds; widespread. Among the most frequent of its numerous hybrids, both with longer catkins, are **6a Holme Willow** *S.* × *calodendron*, a triple hybrid with Goat and Grey Willows (p. 380) with leaves broader and grey beneath, to 25mm; and **6b Green-leaved Willow** *S.* × *rubra*, a hybrid with Purple Willow (**5**) with leaves green beneath.

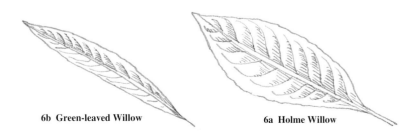

6b Green-leaved Willow   **6a Holme Willow**

1
pollarded
tree

1 Crack Willow

2
White
Willow

3 Bay Willow

4
Almond
Willow

4
fruit

5
Purple
Willow

♂ × 6

6
Osier

The next three broad-leaved species (**1**, **2**, **3**) are often called sallows or pussy willows.

1 Goat Willow *Salix caprea*. A tree or tall shrub, to 10 m or more; twigs *smooth under the bark*. Leaves short, broad, 5-12cm long and 3-8cm across. Both twigs and leaves are downy at first, becoming hairless, the leaves *soft to the touch*; in ssp. *sphacelata* (Scottish mountains only) both twigs and leaves keep their down longer. Catkins short, almost un-stalked, with black-brown scales; March-April, before the leaves. Aka Common Sallow. The hybrid with Grey Willow (**2**) is common. Woods, scrub and hedges, often on dry ground, also common in marshes and by fresh water; widespread.

2 Grey Willow *Salix cinerea* ssp. *oleifolia*. Generally less tall than Goat Willow and less often a small tree, with twigs *ridged under the bark* (best seen by peeling the bark off a 2-5-year-old twig) and often staying downy. Leaves smaller and narrowed towards the base, in-rolled at the edges and with *rust-coloured hairs* among the grey ones on the underside, never soft to the touch. **2a** ssp. *cinerea*, with downier twigs, no rust-coloured hairs and leaves soft to the touch grows mainly in fens in E England. Catkins as Goat Willow. Aka Grey Sallow. Much less often away from damp habitats.

3 Eared Willow *Salix aurita*. Generally smaller and more of a bush, to 2m, than Goat (**1**) and Grey Willows (**2**), with branches almost at right angles and twigs rather slender, hair-less when mature, and *ridges under the bark*. Leaves *rounded and markedly wrinkled*, un-derside pale silvery green, wavy and inrolled at the edges, with large and persistent stipules at their base. Catkins slender, with green scales; April-May, before the leaves. Aka Eared Sallow. Heaths, moors, damp woods, on acid soils, often by fresh water; most fre-quent, Scotland and Ireland.

~

4 Tea-leaved Willow *Salix phylicifolia*. A bush or tall shrub, to 4m; mature twigs shiny red-brown, *not downy*. Leaves rather thick, pointed oval to lanceolate, toothed, hairless, *bright shiny green above*, glaucous beneath; not blackening when dried; stipules small, soon falling. Catkins slender, male short, female longer, both sexes yellow; May-June, usually with the leaves. Fruits downy. Northern hill districts, usually on limestone and near water.

5 Dark-leaved Willow *Salix myrsinifolia*. Differs from Tea-leaved Willow (**4**) in being sometimes a small tree, in having dull brown or greenish, more or less downy twigs, thin-ner, *darker green leaves*, dull above, shiny beneath, and *blackening when dried*, stipules larger and persistent, catkins usually appearing before the leaves, and hairless fruits. Habi-tat similar, but commoner in Ireland.

6 Creeping Willow *Salix repens*. Very variable low shrub, our only lowland willow with a *creeping rootstock*; twigs finely ridged. Leaves very variable, usually almost untoothed. Catkins short; Apr-May, before the leaves. Three marked varieties: the commonest, var.*repens* has *sprawling stems* to c. 1m, downy only at first; and leaves pointed oval, downy on both sides at first, but soon hairless above; heaths and moors; hybridises with Dwarf Willow (p. 382). Var. *fusca* differs mainly in its erect stems, to 2m,; fens in E An-glia. **6a** var. *argentea* has erect stems, to 1.5m, with stems and both sides of its larger, more rounded leaves always silvery with down; dune slacks; widespread.

7 *Downy Willow *Salix lapponum*. A compact shrub, to 1m, covered with *grey down*; twigs becoming reddish-brown and hairless. Leaves pointed oval to lanceolate, downy be-neath, the *small stipules soon falling*. Catkins whitish, the male with anthers yellow or sometimes reddish; May-June, with the leaves. Damp mountain rock ledges, mainly Scot-land.

8 **Woolly Willow *Salix lanata*. The handsomest of the mountain willows in spring, when its large golden yellow catkins contrast with the silvery leaves. Even more thickly covered with *whiter down* than the much more frequent Downy Willow (**7**), with both the browner twigs and the buds stouter, *leaves broader*, sometimes almost rounded, the *larger stipules persistent* and the catkins having yellow hairs; May-June, with the leaves. Rocky mountain slopes and ledges, Scottish Highlands.

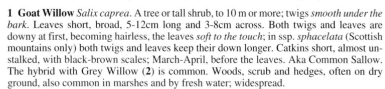

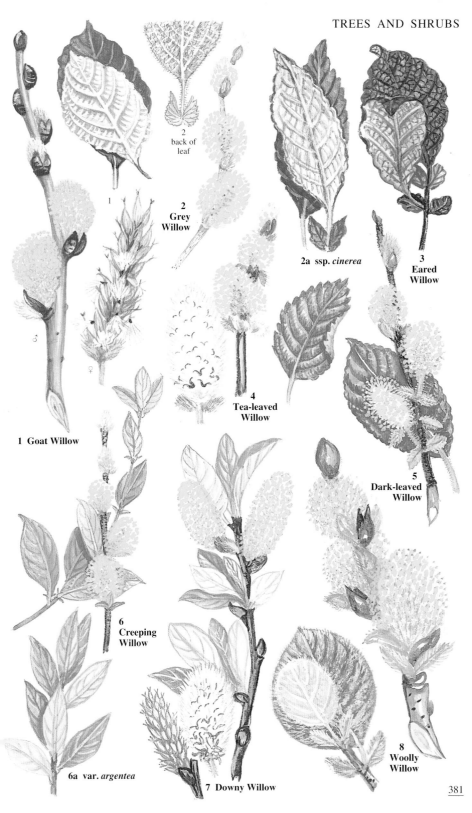

2
back of
leaf

**2
Grey
Willow**

2a ssp. *cinerea*

**3
Eared
Willow**

♂

♀

**4
Tea-leaved
Willow**

1 Goat Willow

**5
Dark-leaved
Willow**

**6
Creeping
Willow**

6a var. *argentea*

7 Downy Willow

**8
Woolly
Willow**

1 *Whortle-leaved Willow *Salix myrsinites*. A low spreading shrub, to 50cm, with twigs smooth under the bark and slightly downy at first, becoming hairless and shiny. Leaves pointed oval, not unlike Blaeberry (p. 106) – whence the ham-handed English name, for Scottish blaeberries are whortleberries in southern England, soon *bright green and glossy* on both sides, the dead ones often overwintering. Catkins on long leafy stalks, the male with *dark red-purple scales*, the female rather large; late May-June, with the leaves. Wettish rock ledges on Scottish mountains.

2 *Mountain Willow *Salix arbuscula*. Another unhelpfully named Willow, for there are six mountain willows, three of them more frequent; a low shrub, to 80cm, more erect than the more frequent Whortle-leaved Willow (**1**) and readily distinguished by its twigs being *ridged* under the bark, leaves *greyish* and downy beneath at first, and shorter-stalked catkins with *red-purple anthers*; late May-June, with the leaves. Damp, often rocky mountain slopes and ledges, Scotland.

3 *Net-leaved Willow *Salix reticulata*. A very low, to 20cm, prostrate mat-forming undershrub, with distinctive rounded untoothed long-stalked leaves that are delicately *net-veined and white beneath*, as well as dark green and wrinkled above. Male catkins small, bright yellow, the female rather large; late June-July, with the leaves. Wet rocks and ledges on Scottish mountains.

4 Dwarf Willow *Salix herbacea*. Our smallest willow, a tiny prostrate undershrub, often *no more than 5cm* high, but sometimes to 10cm; its thin spreading branches may creep just underground and form large open patches. Leaves *rounded, toothed*, shining green, slightly paler beneath, with prominent veins. Catkins sometimes tinged red; June-August, with the leaves. The confusing hybrid with Creeping Willow (p. 380) may occur where both parents grow. High bare and rocky ground and ledges, mainly in Scotland, down to 150 m in the far north.

Elms *Ulmus* (Elm Family – Ulmaceae). Tall deciduous trees to 38m, with rough bark and stalked, roughly downy toothed alternate leaves, ranging from almost roundish to broad pointed oval (Common Elm) through broad lanceolate (Wych Elm) to narrow lanceolate or narrow oval (Small-leaved and Plot's Elms), often asymmetrical; April-May, turning yellow in autumn. Leaves from suckers and the shoots on the trunk are often atypical. Flowers a tuft of reddish stamens on bare twigs, well before the leaves; March-April. Fruit a conspicuous pale green notched disc, *c.* 12mm wide, around the seed; shed in May. Since the Dutch Elm disease outbreak of the 1960s and 1970s, Wych Elm has been much the most likely elm to produce flowers and fruits, since the great majority of Common Elms are now only hedgerow suckers. Hybrids are frequent.

5 Wych Elm *Ulmus glabra*. Leaves broad lanceolate, 8-16cm long, rough above, narrowed to the shorter stalk, which is often hidden by the overlapping base of one side of the leaf; very rarely suckers; no shoots on trunk. Freely fertile with fruits shallowly notched, the seed in the centre. Woods, hedges. Widespread,

6 Common Elm *Ulmus procera*. Leaves broad pointed oval to roundish, rough above, 5-9cm long; twigs sometimes with corky wings; suckers and shoots on trunk numerous. Flowers and deeply notched fruits now rarely seen. Now quite scarce, except in E Sussex.

7 Small-leaved Elm *Ulmus minor*. Leaves variable, always smooth above, often narrowly oval, 4-10cm long. Mainly south-eastern. **7a** ssp. *cornubiensis* of southern coastal counties has lower branches at acute angle to trunk. **7b Plot's Elm** *U. plotii* has leaves narrow, 3-7cm, and branches drooping at tip. Very scattered.

~

8 Sweet Chestnut *Castanea sativa* (Beech Family). Spreading tree to 35m, with rugged grey-brown bark. Leaves broad lanceolate, sharply toothed, shiny, 15-20cm. Flowers pale yellow catkins, all-male or male with female at base, 25-32cm long; July. Fruit the well-known edible nut in an open green husk covered with long soft spines. Planted for timber, mainly as coppice in the SE, and for ornament more widely; self-sown on acid soil; mainly southern.

| 5 | 6 | 7 | 7a | 7b |

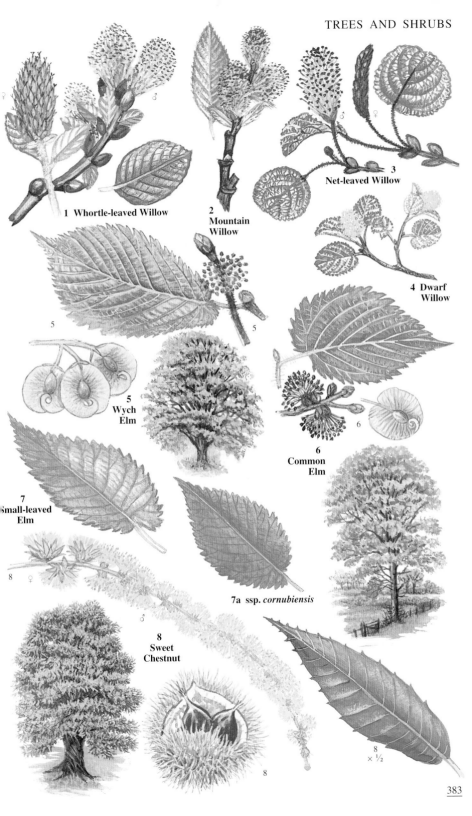

1 Whortle-leaved Willow

2 Mountain Willow

3 Net-leaved Willow

4 Dwarf Willow

5 Wych Elm

6 Common Elm

7 Small-leaved Elm

7a ssp. *cornubiensis*

8 Sweet Chestnut

8 × ½

1 Rhododendron *Rhododendron ponticum* (Heath Family – Ericaceae). Tall evergreen shrub to 5m, aggressively colonising woods, heaths and moors. Flowers unmistakably large and showy, bell-shaped, *mauve-purple*, 4-6cm; May-June. Leaves dark green, elliptic, untoothed, 6-20cm. Widespread. **1a Yellow Azalea** *R. luteum* is shorter, to 2m, with shorter *toothed* leaves but same-sized *yellow* flowers. Mainly bird-sown in woods at Burnham Beeches, Bucks, and elsewhere.

1 S

2 Strawberry Tree *Arbutus unedo*. A small evergreen tree or tall shrub, to 5m or more; bark red-brown. Leaves alternate, lanceolate, slightly toothed, dark green and shiny above. Flowers creamy white globular/bell-shaped, in drooping clusters, 7-9mm; August-Dec. Fruit a warty berry, 18-20mm, turning yellow and then red and strawberry-like as the next year's flowers open. Rocky woods; an Irish speciality.

2

Labrador Tea *Ledum palustre*, **Mountain-laurel** *Kalmia latifolia*, **Shallon** *Gaultheria shallon* and **Prickly Heath** *G. mucronata*, see p. 108.

Brideworts *Spiraea* (Rose Family – Rosaceae). Tall deciduous shrubs, usually *suckering* in small thickets, to 2m. Flowers pink or white, 7-9mm, in conspicuous dense clusters; June-August. Leaves broad to narrow, usually *lanceolate*, toothed; no stipules. Fruits dry.

At least 14 species or hybrids are established locally, the most frequent being **3 Willow-leaved Bridewort** *S. × pseudosalicifolia* with pink flowers in almost cylindrical panicles and leaves hairless beneath and slightly toothed in the upper half; **3a Steeplebush** *S. douglasii*, differing especially in its leaves being grey-downy below and untoothed in the basal half; and **Pale Bridewort** *S. alba* with flowers usually white in more conical panicles and leaves broader; especially frequent in the Isle of Man. Somewhat similar, but with white flowers and *pinnate* leaves is **3b Sorbaria** *Sorbaria sorbifolia*, the most frequent of three somewhat similar and sometimes established species. **3c Ninebark** *Physocarpus opulifolius*, with *much larger*, about 1cm, white or pale pink flowers, and leaves like Wild Guelder (p. 392), is a northern speciality, especially by the R. Conon in Easter Ross. **3d Oceanspray** *Holodiscus discolor* can be taller, to 4m, and has a more open spray of cream-coloured flowers and broader leaves, coarsely toothed or lobed; especially on rocks at Wetherby, W Yorks, and Kilmacolm, Renfrewshire.

Medlar *Mespilus germanica* (p. 366) is sometimes spiny, with flowers 25-36mm, broad lanceolate untoothed downy leaves and *brown*, scarcely edible fruits.

4 Firethorn *Pyracantha coccinea*. Thorny evergreen shrub, to 5m. Flowers white, 5-petalled, 7-9mm, in clusters; June. Leaves *lanceolate*, toothed, the stalks downy. Fruit an orange-red berry, sometimes yellow. Well known in gardens, increasingly bird-sown elsewhere. **4a Asian Firethorn** *P. rogersiana*, with smaller leaves on hairless stalks, is much less frequent, but also increasingly being recognised. **4b Stranvaesia** *Photinia davidiana*, with longer *red-stalked* leaves, is infrequently bird-sown in the S, but being widely planted on forest verges in Scotland may well soon be more often bird-sown in the N.

Tree Cotoneaster *Cotoneaster frigidus*, **Willow-leaved Cotoneaster** *C. salicifolius*, p. 372.

5 Wild Privet *Ligustrum vulgare* (Olive Family – Oleaceae). A half-evergreen shrub, to 3m. Leaves opposite, lanceolate, untoothed, rather leathery, often bronzing in winter. Flowers white, strong-smelling, the free part *equalling* the the joined part of the four petals, in short thick spikes; June-July. Fruit a conspicuous shiny *black* berry. Scrub, especially on lime; widespread, common. **5a Garden Privet** *L. ovalifolium*, the most frequent privet in garden hedges, has more elliptical leaves and the free part of the petals *longer* than the joined part. Widespread, usually as a garden relic.

5 S

4a Asian Firethorn

1 Rhododendron

2 Strawberry Tree

1a Yellow Azalea

3a Steeplebush

3d Oceanspray

3 Willow-leaved Bridewort

3b Sorbaria

4 Firethorn

3c Ninebark

4b Stranvaesia

5a Garden Privet

5 Wild Privet

1 Sea-buckthorn *Elaeagnus rhamnoides* (Sea-buckthorn Family – Elaeagnaceae). A thorny medium shrub, the stems silvery, to 3m; suckering and making thickets. Leaves narrow, untoothed, brown beneath, *silvery* when young. Flowers tiny, green, petalless, up the stems; April-June, before the leaves. Fruit an *orange berry*. Coastal dunes and cliffs, especially eastern; often planted inland.

2 Spurge-laurel *Daphne laureola* (Mezereon Family – Thymelaeaceae). Neither a Spurge nor a Laurel; an *evergreen* shrub, to 1.5m. Flowers yellow-green, slightly fragrant, petalless but with 4 sepals, 8-12mm, in clusters at base of *dark green* glossy laurel-like leaves; January-April. Fruit a black berry. Woods and scrub, especially on lime or clay; mainly southern.

3 *Mezereon *Daphne mezereum*. A deciduous shrub, to 2m. Flowers like Spurge-laurel (**2**), but *pink-purple*, strongly fragrant, appearing *before* the leaves, January-April. Leaves lanceolate, *pale green*. Fruit a red berry. Woods and scrub on lime; mainly southern; often bird-sown from gardens, to which too many wild plants have been removed.

4 Mistletoe *Viscum album* (Mistletoe Family – Viscaceae). An evergreen perennial, with rather woody stems to 1m; semi-parasitic on trees and shrubs. Usually grows so high up that its modest green 4-petalled flowers, male and female on separate plants, cannot be seen; most easily seen in apple orchards where grown as a crop; February-April. Leaves yellowish-green, leathery, elliptical, usually in pairs. Fruit a round sticky white berry, relished by mistle thrushes and other birds; not appearing till Nov-Dec. Most often on apple, lime, hawthorn and Hybrid Black Poplar, rarely on oak; mainly southern.

5 Mock Orange *Philadelphus coronarius* (Hydrangea Family – Hydrangeaceae). A well known deciduous garden shrub, to 7m. Leaves lanceolate to oval. Flowers white, *fragrant*, 4-petalled, 25-50mm, May-July. Fruit a capsule. Aka Syringa. Usually planted or originating from gardens, often as a hybrid, but sometimes in woods, scrub and hedges far from houses.

6 Shrubby Hare's-ear *Bupleurum fruticosum* (Carrot Family – Apiaceae). A half-evergreen shrub, to 2.5m, but, coming from S Europe, often cut right back by frost; twigs purple. Leaves narrow oblong. Flowers *yellow*, in a typical umbel (see p. 19), with both upper and lower bracts; July-August. Fruits ridged. Road and railway banks, notably at Malvern, Worcestershire, since 1909.

7 Duke of Argyll's Teaplant *Lycium barbarum* (Nightshade Family – Solanaceae). A bushy, somewhat spiny shrub, to nearly 3m, with flexuous arching stems, sometimes rooting at the tip. Leaves alternate, narrow lanceolate, *broadest near the middle*, untoothed, stalked. Flowers pale purple, with 5 joined petals divided to *about half-way* and a column of yellow anthers, 10-15mm; June-Sept. Fruit a small scarlet egg-shaped berry. Naturalised in hedges and on walls and waste ground; mainly southern. **7a Chinese Teaplant** *L. chinense* has leaves *broadest below the middle* and petals divided to *more than half-way*. Probably less frequent.

8 Butterfly Bush *Buddleja davidii* (Buddleja Family – Buddlejaceae). Tall shrub, to 8m, well known in gardens for the many butterflies attracted to its *long dense spikes* of strongly fragrant pale purple 4-petalled flowers; June-Sept. Leaves opposite, usually lanceolate, toothed, downy beneath. A cultivar developed in France in the 1890s, not the original wild Chinese plant; an increasing escape on bare and waste ground, especially in or near towns and suburbs, mainly in the S.

Hedge Veronicas *Hebe* (Figwort Family – Scrophulariaceae). Evergreen shrubs, mainly from New Zealand, with opposite untoothed leaves and showy flower-spikes like speedwells (p. 240) at the base of the leaves.

Much the most frequent is **9 Hedge Veronica** *Hebe × franciscana*, to 1.5m, with lanceolate to oval leaves, flowers violet-blue, occasionally pink-purple, rarely white, in shortish spikes to 8cm. Mainly near the sea, especially on cliffs and walls. **9a Koromiko** *H. salicifolia*, taller, to 2m, with narrower leaves and longer (10-20cm) spikes of white or lilac flowers, is more scattered. 10 other species are more rarely naturalised.

9a Koromiko

7a Chinese Teaplant

2 Spurge-laurel

1
1 Sea-buckthorn

4 Mistletoe

3 Mezereon

3

5 Mock Orange

6 Shrubby Hare's-ear

7 Duke of Argyll's Teap[lant

8
×1

8 Butterfly Bush

9 Hedge Veronica

5. Leaves pinnate

1 Ash *Fraxinus excelsior* (Olive Family – Oleaceae). A lofty tree, with grey bark smooth at first, to 37m. Our only native tree with *opposite* pinnate leaves, the leaflets dark green, lanceolate, toothed. Flowers petalless, with tufts of *purplish-black* stamens, turning greenish; late March-May, before the leaves. Fruits with a long narrow wing on one side of the seed, hanging together like a bunch of *keys*. Woods, hedges, especially on lime. Widespread, common.

2 Rowan *Sorbus aucuparia*, (p. 366). Tree or tall shrub, to 18m. Leaves *alternate* pinnate, the leaflets lanceolate and toothed, green and hairy beneath. Flowers foetid, anthers creamy, 8-10mm. Berries orange-red, 6-9mm. Aka Mountain Ash. Woods, moors, rocks, heaths on *acid soils*; widespread, common in the N; in towns and villages cultivars, some with yellow berries, may be bird-sown.

3 **Service Tree *Sorbus domestica* (p. 368) has pinnate leaves like Rowan (**2**) and highly distinctive greenish-brown oblong to *pear-shaped* fruits, a native tree recently discovered on sea and estuarine cliffs in the Bristol Channel and Severn & Wye estuaries

4 Elder *Sambucus nigra* (Honeysuckle Family – Caprifoliaceae). Strong-smelling shrub or small tree, to 10m; bark corky and fissured, *2nd-year twigs scaly*, with white pith inside. Leaves dark green, pinnate with *5 leaflets*. Flowers white, fragrant, small, in conspicuous *flat-topped* umbel-like clusters, the anthers *yellow*; May-August. Fruit a juicy edible purplish-black berry, rarely greenish. Cf. Dwarf Elder, p. 260. Woods, scrub, waste ground, often near rabbit warrens as rabbits do not eat it; widespread, common. **American Elder** *S. canadensis*, suckering, with 2nd-year twigs scarcely scaly, 7 leaflets and fruit rarely red, is naturalised on railway banks. **4a Red-berried Elder** *S. racemosa* has 5-7, more pointed, yellower-green leaflets, flowers creamier in a dense egg-shaped cluster, April-May, and berries red. Naturalised in woods, scrub and hedges, mainly in Scotland.

Roses *Rosa* and Brambles *Rubus* (Rose Family – Rosaceae), though some are quite tall scramblers, are all on pp. 124-6. *Sorbaria*, see p. 384.

5 Walnut *Juglans regia* (Walnut Family – Juglandaceae). Spreading tree to 23m; bark pale grey, smooth at first. Leaves pinnate, aromatic, 20-45cm. Fls yellow-green, male in hanging catkins, female in short erect spikes; Apr-May. Fruit a pale brown nut in a smooth green husk. Hedgerows; widely planted, often bird-sown, especially at Great Kimble, Bucks.

6 False Acacia *Robinia pseudacacia* (Pea Family – Fabaceae). Tall suckering tree to 25-30m; bark grey-brown, deeply furrowed; shoots *thorny*. Leaves pinnate, Flowers *white* peaflowers (p. 18) with reddish sepals, fragrant, 55-65mm, in drooping stalked spikes; June. Pods long, to 8cm. Woods, scrub, heaths, sometimes forming thickets; introduced.

7 Bladder Senna *Colutea arborescens*. Medium shrub, to 4m. Leaves alternate, the leaflets oval. Flowers yellow peaflowers (p. 18), often streaked red (if orange, may be a hybrid with *C. orientalis*), 55-65mm, in spikes of 2-6 on stalks shorter than the leaves; June-August. Pods *inflated*, papery, to 7cm. Naturalised in waste, often grassy places, especially railway banks near London.

young catkins

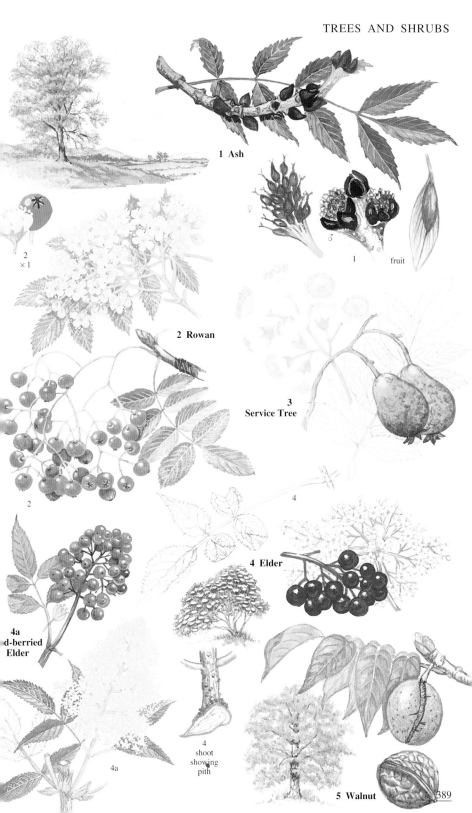

1 Ash

2
×1

♀

♂

1

fruit

2 Rowan

**3
Service Tree**

2

4

4 Elder

**4a
d-berried
Elder**

4a

4
shoot
showing
pith

5 Walnut

1 Oregon Grape *Mahonia aquifolium* (Barberry Family – Berberidaceae). Low evergreen shrub, to 1.5m high. Flowers yellow, fragrant, in erect clusters. Leaves pinnate, spine-toothed, bronzed in winter. Berries blue-black. Very widely planted and often bird-sown in hedges, shrubberies and shelter-belts. A hybrid *M.* × *decumbens* with sprawling stems may also occur.

2 Staghorn Sumach *Rhus typhina* (Sumach Family – Anacardiaceae). Suckering shrub to 5m; twigs downy. Leaves pinnate, to 12cm, the *11-15* leaflets lanceolate and toothed, turning bright red in autumn. Flowers tiny, greenish-white, 5-petalled, male and female on separate plants, in upright clusters that become bright red; July-August. Fruit a small deep red berry. Forms thickets on road and railway banks, where much planted, and elsewhere. Not to be confused with suckers or saplings of **2a Tree of Heaven** *Ailanthus altissima* (Simaroubaceae), which have much longer (to 90cm) leaves with up to 41 leaflets, and appear near the often planted *trees*, especially in and around London parks and gardens.

Ashleaf Maple *Acer negundo*, see p. 396.

6. Leaves pinnately lobed

Oaks *Quercus*. (Beech Family) Tall trees, usually deciduous, with flowers in greenish-yellow hanging catkins, male and shorter female separate on the same tree; May. Fruit a nut (acorn) in a cup. **3** and **4** often hybridise.

3 Pedunculate Oak *Quercus robur*. Perhaps our best known tree, with its massive rugged grey-brown trunk and broad crown, to 40m. Leaves oblong, usually broader at the base, lobed, the basal lobes sometimes overlapping the very short stalk, 10-12cm long; turning golden-brown in autumn. Catkins yellow-green, with the leaves. Acorn cup scaly, with common stalks 2-3cm long. Aka English Oak. Woods, especially on lime, hedges, parkland; native but widely planted. **3a Turkey Oak** *Q. cerris*. has twigs downy when young, distinctive longer (9-20cm), narrower, more pointed and *more deeply jagged* leaves, slightly downy below, and short-stalked *bristly* acorn cups. Planted and widely naturalised, especially on acid soils. **3b American Red Oak** *Q. rubra*, often planted and sometimes self-sown, has *dark red twigs* and much larger leaves, 12-22cm, bright yellow when young and turning red in autumn.

4 Sessile Oak. *Quercus petraea* differs from Pedunculate Oak (**3**) in having leaves tapering to the unlobed base, on longer stalks and with more hairs beneath when mature, and acorns almost unstalked (sessile). Aka Durmast Oak. Prefers more acid soils; commoner in the W; less often planted.

Hawthorns *Crataegus* (Rose Family – Rosaceae). Shrubs or small trees, to 10-15m, with small clusters of white or pink 5-petalled flowers, well lobed leaves and reddish berries (haws). Some 21 species are planted or bird-sown, but not many are found away from parks and gardens and most of those look planted.

5 Hawthorn *Crataegus monogyna*, the commoner of our two native species, has flowers white, fragrant, 8-15mm, with pink or purple anthers, only *one style* and becoming deep pink as they fade; *late April*-June. Leaves with *3-5 deeply cut* lobes, scarcely shiny above; leafing in April, but the *non-British* form widely planted in roadside hedges often leafs and even flowers in *February-March*. Haw with *one stone*. Hedges, scrub, woodland margins. Widespread, common.

6 Midland Hawthorn *Crataegus laevigata* has flowers 9-12mm, not fading pink, May-June, much shinier leaves with only *3, shallower*, lobes, and styles and haw stones *2-3*. Hybridises freely with Hawthorn. so that many individual shrubs are hard to identify. More often in woods, south-eastern; occasionally naturalised elsewhere.

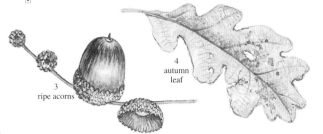

3
ripe acorns

4
autumn
leaf

Midl.
Hawth.

1 Oregon Grape

2 Staghorn Sumach

2a Tree of Heaven

3 Pedunculate Oak

3b American Red Oak

3a Turkey Oak

4 Sessile Oak

5 Hawthorn

1 Wild Service Tree *Sorbus torminalis* (p. 368). Forest tree to 27m. Flowers with creamy anthers, 10-15mm. Leaves rather maple-like, sharply *lobed* and toothed, green and hairless *on both sides*. Anthers creamy. Berries *brown*, egg-shaped to almost pear-shaped. Hybridises with Common Whitebeam (p. 368), especially in the W. Woods, scrub, hedges, on limy or clay soils; southern.

2 Swedish Whitebeam *Sorbus intermedia* (p. 368). A tree to 10 m or more, but usually seen as a bird-sown sapling. Flowers dull white, anthers cream, 12-20mm. Leaves pointed oval, *deeply lobed*, yellowish-green above, *yellowish*-grey beneath. Berries orange-red, oblong, 12-18mm. Widely planted and increasingly bird-sown, e.g on Hampstead Heath, London, and Askham Bog, near York.

Currants *Ribes* (Currant Family – Grossulariaceae) are deciduous shrubs with alternate leaves and small greenish 5-petalled flowers; fruit a berry. Gooseberry and Red and Black Currants are familiar garden fruits and some aliens are grown for ornament; all are probably native and often bird-sown.

3 Gooseberry *Ribes uva-crispa*. A *spiny* bush with spreading branches, to 1.5m. Leaves 3-lobed, blunt-toothed, downy. Flowers drooping, green but often red-tinged, 6-12mm, the petals turned back, *1-2 together* on short stalks; late March-May. Fruit green, egg-shaped, often hairy and sometimes tinged red or yellow. Woods, scrub, hedges, often bird-sown; widespread, frequent.

4 Red Currant *Ribes rubrum*. Erect and fairly tall, to 2m. Leaves 3-lobed, 3-5-lobed, blunt-toothed, often hairless, *not* aromatic. Flowers yellow-green, purple-edged, 4-6mm, in hanging clusters; April-May. Berry *red*, rarely white. Woods, scrub, stream-sides, fens, often bird-sown; most frequent in the S.

5 *Downy Currant *Ribes spicatum* is usually downy and has the receptacle at the base of the flower *cup-shaped* not saucer-shaped, with the anther lobes *close together* not apart. Native on northern limestone, rare elsewhere; not cultivated.

6 Black Currant *Ribes nigrum*. Readily distinguished from Red Currant (**4**) by its slightly larger and sticky *aromatic* leaves, larger flowers (10-15mm) and *purple-black* berries. May be native in fens and wet woods, also often bird sown in drier woods and scrub; widespread, frequent.

7 *Mountain Currant *Ribes alpinum*. An often thick-set, much branched shrub, to 2m. Leaves smaller and more deeply toothed than Red Currant (**4**). Flowers greenish-yellow, 2-3mm, in *erect* clusters, male and female on *separate plants*; April-May. Berry red. Woods, cliffs, rocks and walls on limestone in the N, e.g. Fountains, Rievaulx and Roche Abbeys, Yorkshire, occasionally bird-sown elsewhere.

8 Flowering Currant *Ribes sanguineum*. A popular garden shrub, to 2.5m. Leaves bluntly lobed, downy beneath, *aromatic*. Flowers *reddish-pink*, in hanging clusters, 6-10cm; March-May. Berry purple-black. Scrub, woods, pollard willows, often bird-sown.

9 Guelder-rose *Viburnum opulus* (Honeysuckle Family – Caprifoliaceae). An almost hairless shrub or small tree, to 4m. Leaves palmately *3-5-lobed*, downy on the veins beneath, reddening in autumn. Flowers bright white, slightly fragrant, in flattish umbel-like clusters. the outer ones sterile, with *5 showy petals*, much larger than the inner ones; May-July. Fruit a shiny red berry. Dry and damp scrub, hedges, fens.

Ninebark *Physocarpus opulifolius*, p. 384. **Oceanspray** *Holodiscus discolor*, p. 384.

♂ × 3

7
Mountain
Currant

4

6

♀

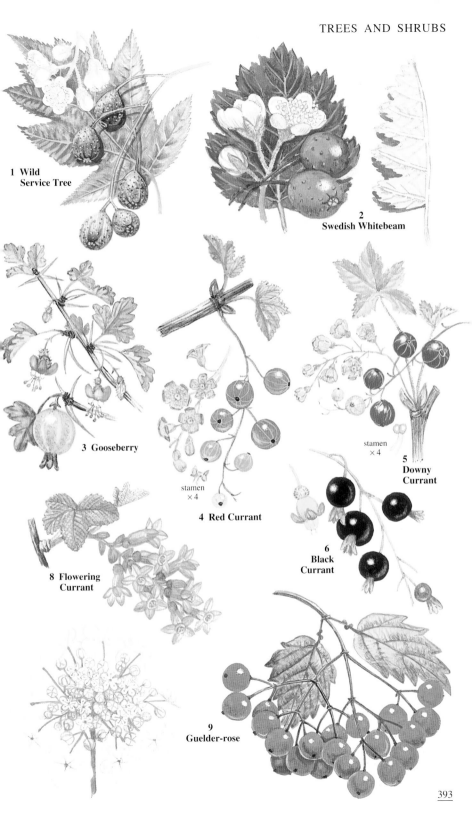

1 Wild
Service Tree

2
Swedish Whitebeam

3 Gooseberry

4 Red Currant

stamen
×4

5
Downy
Currant

stamen
×4

6
Black
Currant

8 Flowering
Currant

9
Guelder-rose

7. Leaves trefoil

1 Broom *Cytisus scoparius*. (Pea Family – Fabaceae). An almost hairless shrub, to 2.5m, *deciduous*, but the leaves are so small and fall so early and the 5-ridged stems are so green in winter that it might be thought evergreen; young twigs silky hairy. Flowers rich yellow peaflowers (see p. 18), sometimes marked reddish (as accentuated in some garden forms), joined sepals *hairless*, 15-20mm, scattered up the stems; April-June. Leaves trefoil below, lanceolate above. Pods flattened, black, hairy-edged, 25-40mm. Heaths, sandy and gravelly ground. Widespread, frequent. Ssp. *maritimus* is prostrate to sprawling, with young branches more silkily hairy, on cliffs by the sea. **1a Hairy-fruited Broom** *C. striatus*, increasingly planted and bird-sown on road banks, has 10-ridged stems, slightly smaller and paler flowers with joined sepals *downy*, and pods *whitely* hairy all over. A Broom in flower July-Sept, usually on a road or railway bank, is likely to be planted or bird-sown **1b Spanish Broom** *Spartium junceum*, with twigs not angled, leaves never trefoil, flowers with joined sepals closely sheathing the harder yellow petals, spikes leafless, and pods hairy all round. Two more locally established bird-sown Brooms are **1c Black Broom** *C. nigricans* with flowers in leafless spikes (June-July) and all leaves trefoil, and the white-flowered **White Broom** *C. multiflorus*.

2 Laburnum *Laburnum anagyroides*. One of the most often bird-sown of ornamental trees, to 8m; twigs and most other parts silvery-downy, especially when young. Flowers bright yellow peaflowers (p. 18), 17-23mm, in *hanging* spikes; May-June. Leaves trefoil, downy beneath. Pods 40-60mm, blackish-brown. Waysides, woodland edges; along with **Scottish Laburnum** *L. alpinum* (less downy, flower-spikes more open, pods winged) and their hybrid, formerly used for hedging.

Brambles *Rubus*, see p. 126.

8. Leaves palmate

3 Horse Chestnut *Aesculus hippocastanum* (Horse Chestnut Family – Hippocastanaceae). A familiar tall, to 40m, ornamental tree. Flowers *white*, with a yellow to pink spot, 4-5-petalled, in striking 'candles' to 30cm; May-June. Leaves palmate, with 5-7 leaflets. In winter can be told from the quite unrelated Sweet Chestnut (p. 382), by its smooth bark, and in early spring by its *sticky* buds. Fruit, the much prized 'conker', a large warm brown nut inside a thick fleshy green case covered with soft spines much thicker than those of Sweet Chestnut. Self-sown seedlings are common, but do not often become trees or even saplings. **3a Indian Horse Chestnut** *Ae. indica*, with flowers tinged red, pink or yellow, leaflets narrower, buds not sticky and nutcases spineless, is occasionally naturalised, e.g. in Highgate Woods, N London. **3b Red Horse Chestnut** *Ae. carnea*, with deep pink or red flowers, buds scarcely sticky and nutcases with only a few bumps is equally rarely naturalised.

4 Tree Lupin *Lupinus arboreus* (Pea Family – Fabaceae). Another misnamed plant, being not a tree, but an *evergreen shrub* to 2m. Flowers *sulphur-yellow*, sometimes whitish or tinged blue or purple, 14-17mm, in a spike; May-August. Leaves palmate, with 7-11 lanceolate leaflets, hairless above, silky beneath. Pods hairy, 40-80mm. Widely naturalised on waste ground, most often on coastal sand and shingle; mainly southern.

Virginia Creepers, see Vine Family, p. 396.

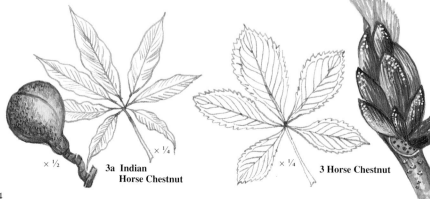

× ½   × ¼

3a Indian Horse Chestnut

× ¼   **3 Horse Chestnut**

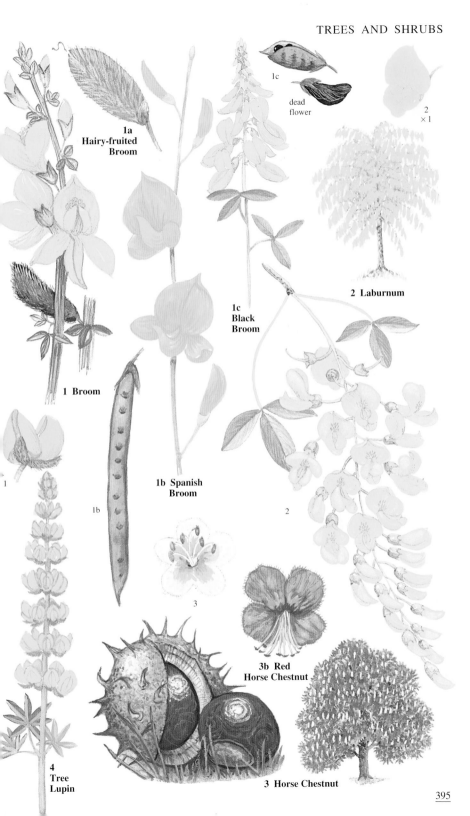

1c

dead
flower

2
×1

**1a Hairy-fruited
Broom**

2 Laburnum

**1c
Black
Broom**

1 Broom

1

1b

**1b Spanish
Broom**

2

3

**3b Red
Horse Chestnut**

**4
Tree
Lupin**

3 Horse Chestnut

9. Leaves palmately lobed

Maples *Acer* (Maple Family – Aceraceae). Deciduous trees with leaves opposite and usually palmately lobed. Flowers yellowish-green, petalless, with five sepals, male and female in separate erect clusters on same tree. Fruits with long wing (key) on one side.

Besides those described below, a dozen other Maples can be self-sown or suckering, the most frequent being **1 Cappadocian Maple** *Acer cappadocicum* with leaves sharply palmately lobed but untoothed, and **1a Ashleaf Maple** *A. negundo* with leaves pinnate like Ash (p. 388).

2 Sycamore *Acer pseudoplatanus*. Familiar wayside tree to 35m; bark smooth, flaking in old age. Leaves *opposite*, palmately lobed with rather blunt teeth, often black-spotted from the fungus *Rhytisma acerinum*. Flowers yellowish-green, in *hanging* clusters; May-June, *after* the leaves. Keys hairless, in right-angled pairs. Cf. London Plane (**5**); in Scotland Sycamore is often confusingly called Plane. Parks, hedges, woods, producing many saplings; widespread, common.

2　SOZ　■

3 Norway Maple *Acer platanoides*. Tree to 30m. Leaves as sharply palmately lobed and toothed as London Plane (**5**), but smaller. Flowers bright yellow-green, in erect clusters; very conspicuous on leafless twigs, late March-early May. Keys in opposite pairs. Increasingly planted and self-sown in parks, gardens, woods and hedges.

3　□↑

4 Field Maple *Acer campestre*. Tree to 25m, but often trimmed to make a hedgerow shrub; twigs often corky. Leaves much smaller than Sycamore (**2**) or Norway Maple (**3**), rather *bluntly* lobed, untoothed, the young shoots in hedges conspicuously red, autumn leaves fading purple. Flowers yellowish-green, in erect clusters; May-June, *after* the leaves. Keys, downy, in opposite pairs. Woods, hedges; frequent in England and E Wales, uncommon elsewhere.

4　□

5 London Plane *Platanus* × *hispanica* (Plane Family – Platanaceae). The hybrid between Oriental (*orientalis*) and American (*occidentalis*) Planes, known in Britain for more than 300 years. Spreading tree to 44m, with smooth grey bark, constantly *flaking off*. Leaves *alternate*, sharply palmately lobed and toothed. Flowers (and fruits) in roundish heads, male green, female crimson; May-June. Widely planted, especially in towns; self-sown seedlings especially frequent in London.

6 Ivy *Hedera helix* (Ivy Family – Araliaceae). A familiar evergreen woody climber, carpeting the ground or climbing up trees and walls by tiny roots, to 30m; hairs *whitish*. Leaves very variable, dark green or, especially in winter, purplish, often *marbled paler*, shiny, leathery; of the well known 5-lobed ivy-shape on non-flowering shoots, but on flowering branches often larger and pointed, but not lobed. Flowers green with yellow anthers, 7-9mm, in erect umbels; Sept-Nov. Fruit a black berry. **6a** ssp. *hibernica* has pale yellowish-brown hairs and leaves usually not marbled. Woods, hedges, rocks, walls; widespread, common. Two often naturalised cultivated forms are cv. Hibernica with very large hairless glossy leaves, usually along the ground; and **Persian Ivy** *H. colchica* with roundish matt leaves, often unlobed, and orange-brown hairs

6　SO　■

7 Fig *Ficus carica* (Mulberry Family – Moraceae). Spreading shrub or small tree to 10m. Leaves palmate with large blunt lobes, 10-20cm. Flowers small, green, in pear-shaped receptacles that turn into figs. Self-sown on walls and disturbed ground, forming urban woodland in Sheffield, Yorkshire.

Vine Family – Vitaceae. Woody climbers, to 10 or even 20m, climbing with tendrils. Flowers small, red or green, 5-petalled, in small clusters up the stems. Fruits like small grapes.

Five species more or less naturalised in various places: **8 Grape Vine** *Vitis vinifera*; **Crimson Glory Vine** *V. coignetiae* with red-brown hairs; **9 Virginia Creeper** *Parthenocissus quinquefolia*, **False Virginia Creeper** *P. inserta* and **Boston Ivy** *P. tricuspidata*.

Tendrils ending in a disc:	Virginia Creeper, Boston Ivy
not ending in a disc:	Grape Vine, Crimson Glory Vine, False Virginia Creeper
Leaves undivided:	Grape Vine (palmately lobed), Crimson Glory Vine (scarcely lobed), Boston Ivy (un-or 3-lobed)
palmate:	Virginia Creeper (5 leaflets), False V C (5 leaflets, more sharply toothed), Boston Ivy (sometimes 3 leaflets)

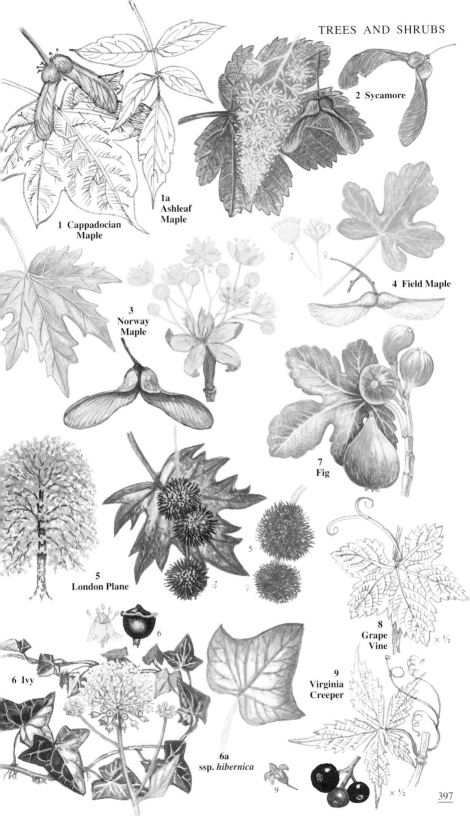

1 Cappadocian Maple

1a Ashleaf Maple

2 Sycamore

3 Norway Maple

4 Field Maple

♂   ♀

5 London Plane

♂   ♀

5

7 Fig

6

6 Ivy

6a ssp. *hibernica*

9

8 Grape Vine × ½

9 Virginia Creeper

9

× ½

10. Leaves prickly

1 SO

1 Holly *Ilex aquifolium* (Holly Family – Aquifoliaceae). Perhaps our most distinctive native tree or shrub, and the only one with *evergreen* prickly leaves; attaining 23m, but usually much shorter. Leaves dark green, glossy, wavy and sometimes without prickles. Flowers white, sometimes tinged purple, 4-petalled, 5-7mm. in close clusters, male and female often on different trees; May-August, occasionally again in autumn. Fruit the familiar Yuletide red berry. Woods, scrub, hedges; widespread, frequent.

Darwin's Barberry *Berberis darwinii*, see p. 370.

2 S

2 New Zealand Holly *Olearia macrodonta* (Daisy Family – Asteraceae). The most frequent of five evergreen New Zealand species established in warmer areas; a shrub to 3m or more. Leaves alternate, ovate, toothed like *miniature Holly* (**1**) leaves, dark glossy green above, white-downy beneath. Flowers daisy-like with *short white rays* and a few reddish disc florets, 6-8mm; in flattish clusters, June-July. Widely grown and often naturalised in our western fringes. The next most frequent is **2a Daisy Bush** *O.* × *haastii* with flat untoothed leaves and yellow disc florets. See also p. 458.

Evergreen Oak *Quercus ilex*, see p. 362.

11. Leaves linear or needles

Gorses *Ulex* (Pea Family – Fabaceae). Evergreen shrubs, with yellow flowers and leaves reduced to *spines*. Pods audibly bursting. Usually on acid soils.

3 SO

3 Gorse *Ulex europaeus*. A familiar, impenetrably thicket-forming *sharply spiny* shrub, to 3m; stems furrowed, downy when young. Flowers rich golden yellow peaflowers (p. 18), almond-scented, *wings longer than keel,* the joined sepals yellow with *spreading* hairs and more than half as long as petals, 15-20mm; bracts *c.* 6mm; throughout the year, but at its best April-June. Spines furrowed, ferociously rigid. Pods hairy, black, bursting loudly on hot summer days. Aka Furze, Whin. Grassland, heaths, moors, scrub, open woods, acid or neutral cappings on chalk downs, often on sand or peat; widespread, common.

4 S

4 Western Gorse *Ulex gallii*. Generally shorter, to 1.5m, compacter and more spreading than Gorse (**3**), with which it hybridises, the hybrid flowering Oct-March. Flowers smaller (8-10mm), narrower, less fragrant and of a harder, less golden yellow, the sepals with few *appressed* hairs, and much smaller bracts; *July-Oct.* Spines less deeply furrowed. Pods burst in spring. Habitat as Gorse, but most frequent on heaths and moors on acid soils in the W, but rare in Scotland and NW Ireland.

5

5 Dwarf Gorse *Ulex minor*. The eastern counterpart of Western Gorse (**4**) distinguished chiefly by its shorter, *weaker* spines; a lower, still more spreading shrub, to 1m. Flowers *paler* yellow, fewer, smaller (8-15mm), with wings *shorter* than keel, the sepals less downy and *almost equalling* petals; July-Oct. Heaths, mainly S of the Thames.

Conifers are non-flowering trees or shrubs with needle-like, linear or scale-like, evergreen (except Larches, p. 400) leaves and usually conical fruits (cones), produced from flower-like organs, here called flowers.

6

6 Scots Pine *Pinus sylvestris* (Pine Family – Pinaceae). Our only native (in Scotland) pine, to 35m, with flaking grey and reddish bark. Needles in pairs, often twisted, grey-green, 10-14cm when young, half as long when mature; buds resinous, sticky. Male flowers yellow, female pink to purple; May-June. Cones green in first year, then grey-brown, pointed oval, 5-8cm. Woods, heaths, also widely planted and naturalised. **6a Maritime Pine** *Pinus pinaster*. Our our only other well naturalised conifer (mainly in Dorset), with the scales of the buds curved at the tip, paler and longer needles, both twisted, 15-20cm, and longer (10cm), prickly, shiny brown cones. **6b Austrian Pine** *P. nigra* ssp. *nigra*, to 42m, has blackish bark, needles blackish, spiny, scarcely twisted, stiff, but curved when older, 7-10cm, and cones dark grey, minutely prickly, 4-6cm. **6c Corsican Pine** *P. nigra* ssp. *laricio* has greyer bark, needles slenderer, laxer and greyer, much twisted when young. Both subspecies are widely planted and often self-sown. Other widely planted pines are rarely self-sown.

1 Holly

1 ♂
♀

2 New Zealand Holly

3 Gorse

4 Western Gorse

5 Dwarf Gorse

2a Daisy Bush

♀
6
♂
6

6a Maritime Pine

6c Corsican Pine

Scots Pine

× ½

6a × ½

6b Austrian Pine

6

6b

6c

Several other conifers are often planted and self-sown; all except Norway Spruce have two white or pale stripes beneath their single flattened leaves, and all except Silver and Giant Firs and Western Hemlock have hanging cylindrical cones. They include **1 Norway Spruce** *Picea abies*, the familiar Christmas tree, distinctive with its glossy green, 4-sided needles on persistent peg-like bases, and 12-15-cm cones; **1a Sitka Spruce** *P. sitchensis* with its flattened needles sharply pointed and cones 6-10cm; **1b Silver Fir** *Abies alba* with non-resinous buds and untoothed bracts projecting from its erect cylindric 15-20-cm cones; **1c Giant Fir** *A. grandis* with grapefruit-scented resinous buds and bracts not projecting; **1d Douglas Fir** *Pseudotsuga menziesii* with needles strongly aromatic, variably green, 20-35mm, and 50-80mm cones with projecting 3-toothed bracts; and **1e Western Hemlock** *Tsuga heterophylla*, with distinct stalks to the shiny dark green leaves, and distinctive small egg-shaped 20-30mm cones.

2 European Larch *Larix decidua*. Larches are our only deciduous conifers, tall trees, to 46m, with rough grey-brown bark. Needles pale green, yellow in autumn, 2-3cm long. Flowers small, March-April; males whitish with purple edges, then yellow, appearing after the females, pink, then purple, then green, Cones 2-3cm tall, pale brown, often surviving on trees for years. A popular introduced forestry tree, fast-growing and often self-sown. Also widely planted and often self-sown are **2a Japanese Larch** *L. kaempferi* with bark, young shoots and twigs red-brown, leaves broader and grey-green, male flowers yellow, female flowers often yellowish or greenish and ripe cones with scales turned back, to resemble a flower; and the hybrid between the two.

3 Yew *Taxus baccata* (Yew Family – Taxaceae). Our third native conifer besides Scots Pine (p. 398) and and Juniper (**4**). Evergreen tree or shrub to 20m, with flaking red-brown bark. Leaves linear, pointed, dark green, often shiny, in two rows. Flowers green, the male with yellow spores; February-April. Fruit in a conspicuous fleshy dark pink cup. Woods, scrub, screes, downs, often on lime; widely planted or naturalised.

4 Juniper *Juniperus communis* (Cypress Family – Cupressaceae). The smallest of our three native conifers, an evergreen shrub (rarely a small tree), usually less than 7m high, either spreading and bushy or narrowly conical. Leaves needle-like, 4-20mm, grey-green with a white stripe on the upper surface, spine-tipped. Flowers small, yellow, male and female usually on separate shrubs; May-June. Cones berry-like, green in first year, then blue-black. On low western coastal cliffs ssp. *hemisphaerica* is lower and more compact. A prostrate northern hill form (ssp. *nana*) has shorter, greyer, broader, overlapping, scarcely prickly leaves. Chalk and limestone hills, heaths, moors, birch- and pinewoods. Common in the Scottish Highlands, the Lake District, W Ireland and SE England; scarce elsewhere.

Osier, p. 378. **Mrs Wilson's Barberry**, p. 370. **Spanish Broom**, p. 394.

12. Leaves scale-like

5 Lawson's Cypress *Chamaecyparis lawsoniana* (Cypress Family – Cupressaceae). Columnar resinous evergreen coniferous tree, to 65m, with red-brown bark. Leaves scale-like, whitish beneath, parsley-scented, opposite. closely pressed to flattened stems, the leading shoots drooping. Male flowers blackish, edged white or red; female flowers grey-blue; March-April. Cones purplish, globular, 6-8mm. Widely planted and often self-sown, sometimes on old walls. **5a Leyland Cypress** × *Cupressocyparis leylandii*, now even more often planted and increasingly self-sown near buildings, has erecter leading shoots, leaves not whitish and larger cones with a conical wart on each scale.

6 Tamarisk *Tamarix gallica* (Tamarisk Family – Tamaricaceae). A graceful evergreen or deciduous shrub, to 3m, with reddish twigs and pale grey-green feathery foliage, the tiny *scale-like leaves* overlapping and, unlike the Cypresses (**5**), alternate. Flowers small, in stalked spikes, the five *pink petals* persisting in fruit; July onwards. Widely planted by the sea, but rarely self-sown.

3

4   oz

6

6 Tamarisk

♀ **4** ♂

5a
Leyland Cypress

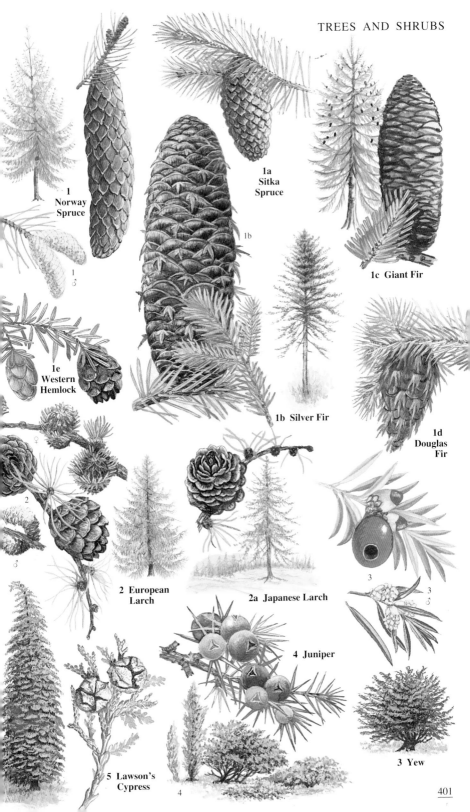

1a
Sitka
Spruce

1
Norway
Spruce

1
♂

1c Giant Fir

1b

1e
Western
Hemlock

1b Silver Fir

1d
Douglas
Fir

2

♂

2 European
Larch

2a Japanese Larch

3

3
♂

4 Juniper

3 Yew

5 Lawson's
Cypress

4

GRASSES, SEDGES AND RUSHES

These three groups are described here much more briefly than the plants in the main text, and some of the less frequent species are either aggregated (agg.) with similar species or omitted. Only a handful of the most widespread and frequent introduced species are included – 580 such grasses have been recorded (Ryves, Clement and Foster *Alien Grasses of the British Isles*, 1996). The accurate identification of many species calls for the help of a hand lens.

Leaves are narrow and 'grass-like', though some sedges and rushes are leafless. Sedges and rushes are tufted, except where stated. In grasses the small membranous *ligules* where the leaves join the stems are often important clues to identity. Wood-rushes are easily told by their long white hairs.

Grass flowers are either in branched, often pyramidal, panicles or in spikes. The individual flowers are fairly complex, arranged in *spikelets*, which consist of one or more flowers. Each individual flower consists of two petal-like scales, enclosing the stamens and styles. The outer scale (*lemma*) is more important than the inner (palea) in identification. Enfolding these are two sepal-like scales (*glumes*). Any or none of these scales may be tipped with *awns*, often tiny but sometimes long and conspicuous. Flowering periods are given for first appearance of clusters, not when (easily overlooked) anthers appear. See *Grasses*, by C.E. Hubbard, 1984

Sedge flowers are extremely simple, the male spikelets consisting just of a glume and 2-3 stamens, and the female of a glume, the embryo seed and 2-3 styles. The spikelets may be solitary, e. g. Deer-grass (p. 438), or in heads or spikes, and, especially in the true sedges (*Carex*), the two sexes may be on separate spikes. Male catkins are often conspicuous with their yellow anthers. Sedges flower in May/June, except where stated. Sedges can be told from grasses by their *solid stems*. See Jermy, Chater and David, *Sedges of the British Isles*, 1982.

Rush and **Wood-rush flowers** all consist of six petals/sepals (*tepals*), surrounding the stamens and styles. They are in clusters above leafy stems or in heads on leafless stems.

1. Flowers in spreading branched clusters (p. 404)

(i) Spikelets unawned p. 404   *(ii) Spikelets awned* p. 408

1a Grasses p. 404   1b Rushes p. 412

2. Flowers in erect branched clusters (p. 414)

2a Grasses p. 414   2b Sedges p. 416

(i) Spikelets unawned p. 414 *(ii) Spikelets awned* p. 414   *(i) Clusters simple* p. 416   *(ii) Clusters compound* p. 4

2c Rushes p. 418   2d Wood-rushes p. 418

3. Flowers in erect *stout* spikes (p. 420)

3a Grasses p. 420

(i) Spikelets unawned p. 420   *(ii) Spikelets awned* p. 420

3b Sedges p. 422

4. Flowers in erect *slender* spikes (p. 424)

4a Grasses p. 424

(i) Spikelets unawned p. 424   *(ii) Spikelets awned* p. 424

4b Sedges p. 426

5. Flowers in catkin-like spikes (p. 428)

5a Grasses, *erect* p. 428   *(i) Erect* p. 428   *(i) Erect or drooping* p. 430   *(i) Drooping* p. 432

5b Sedges p. 428

6. Flowers in clusters of tight rounded/egg-shaped heads (p. 432)

6a Grasses p. 432   6b Sedges p. 432   6c Rushes p. 434   6d Wood-rushes p. 434

7. Flowers in solitary rounded/egg-shaped heads (p. 436)

7a Grasses p. 436   7b Sedges p. 436   7c Rushes p. 436

8. Flowers in solitary elongated heads (p. 438)

Sedges p. 438

1a. Flowers in spreading branched clusters: Grasses

Four species are always (Viviparous Fescue, p. 408), partly, on mountains (Tufted Hair-grass, p. 412), usually (Alpine Meadow-grass **6**) or often (Bulbous Meadowgrass **5**) viviparous, i.e. have their spikelets replaced by green shoots.

(i) Spikelets unawned

1 Annual Meadow-grass *Poa annua*. Our commonest and most familiar grass of *bare and disturbed ground*. Low. Spikelets crowded along outer half of branches; Jan-Dec. Leaves pale green with a bluntly pointed ligule. Widespread. **1a *Early Meadow-grass** *P. infirma* has stems more compressed, spikelets spread out along whole length of branches, March-May, and leaves yellowish-green, with a blunter ligule. Usually near the sea in the S. **1b Flattened Meadow-grass** *P. compressa* has markedly *flattened* stems, greyer leaves, with a shorter, rounded ligule, and smaller narrower clusters with spikelets along whole length of branches, which are more erect in fruit. Often on walls.

2 Smooth Meadow-grass *Poa pratensis*. Medium, creeping, stems usually grouped. Leaves mid-green, 2-4mm wide, with *smooth* sheaths and a short blunt ligule. April-June. Grassy places, walls. Widespread. **2a Narrow-leaved Meadow-grass** *P. angustifolia* has narrower (1-2mm) wiry, slightly greyish leaves. May-June. Dry, usually limy grassland, mainly southern. **2b Spreading Meadow-grass** *P. humilis* is shorter, with stems usually single, the sheaths usually slightly hairy at base, ligule broader and glumes more sharply pointed; May-June. Damper grassland, mainly northern.

3 Rough Meadow-grass *Poa trivialis*. Differs from Smooth Meadow-grass (**2**) especially in its paler green leaves with *slightly rough* sheaths and much longer ligules. May-July. Shadier places; widespread.

4 Wood Meadow-grass *Poa nemoralis*. Medium. Spikelets well separated, May-July. Leaves almost *at right angles to* stem. Woods, mountain rocks.

5 *Bulbous Meadow-grass *Poa bulbosa*. Short, stems bulbous at base, ligule pointed. Spikelets along whole length of branches, often viviparous (above); March-May. Bare sandy places, usually by the sea.

6 *Alpine Meadow-grass *Poa alpina*. The most frequent of three mainly Scottish mountain meadow-grasses (cf. also **4**), and the only one with almost always viviparous (above) flowers; June-August. Short. Ligules long, blunt. **6a *Glaucous Meadow-grass** *P. glauca* has stems and leaves usually glaucous with shorter ligules; July-August. **6b **Wavy Meadow-grass** *P. flexuosa* has narrower leaves with short blunt ligules and spikelets on slightly wavy stalks.

7 Meadow Fescue *Festuca pratensis*. Medium/tall. Cluster branches in pairs, one of which usually has only a single spikelet; spikelets 11-12mm; June-July. Leaves 4mm across with green basal auricles. Cf. Tall Fescue (**8**). Hybridises with Rye-grass (p. 424). Grassland.

8 Tall Fescue *Festuca arundinacea*. Tall, to 2m, in tussocks. Spikelets 10-18mm, sometimes shortly awned, several on all branches; May-July. Leaves broad, to 10mm, with conspicuous basal auricles. Cf. Meadow Fescue (**7**). Grassy places, often on road verges.

9 Wood Fescue *Festuca altissima*. Tall, to 1.2m; hairless. Spikelets 5-8mm; June-July. Leaves broad, to 10mm, smooth, with 5mm ligules. Woods, shady rocks, often by streams.

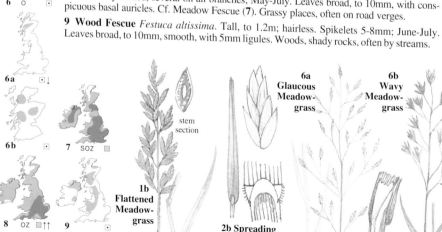

6a
Glaucous Meadow-grass

6b
Wavy Meadow-grass

stem section

1b Flattened Meadow-grass

2b Spreading Meadow-grass

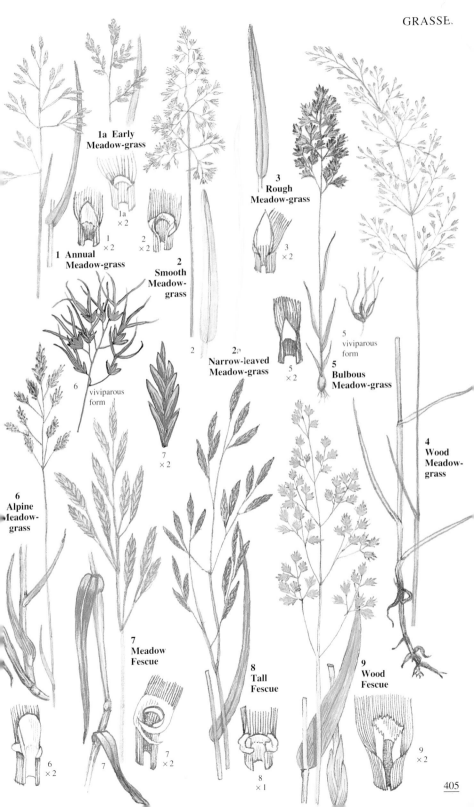

1a Early Meadow-grass

1a ×2

1 ×2

2 ×2

3 Rough Meadow-grass

3 ×2

1 Annual Meadow-grass

2 Smooth Meadow-grass

2

2a Narrow-leaved Meadow-grass

5 viviparous form

5 ×2

5 Bulbous Meadow-grass

6 viviparous form

7 ×2

4 Wood Meadow-grass

6 Alpine Meadow-grass

7 Meadow Fescue

7 ×2

7

8 Tall Fescue

8 ×1

9 Wood Fescue

9 ×2

6 ×2

1 Creeping Bent *Agrostis stolonifera*. Medium/tall, to 1m, with creeping runners to 2m. Clusters spreading in flower, contracted in fruit, the usually unawned, sometimes purplish spikelets with only one floret; June-August. Leaves flat, with *long pointed* ligules. (Its hybrid with Annual Beard-grass (p. 422) has denser clusters.) Dry to wet grassland and bare ground. Widespread. **1a Common Bent** *A. capillaris* creeps much less far and has clusters spreading in fruit and *short blunt* ligules. Cf. Velvet and Brown Bents (p. 410). Heaths and grassland on acid soils. Widespread. **1b Black Bent** *A. gigantea* is taller than Common Bent (**1a**), to 1.5m, and has broader leaves, to 6mm, and longer ligules on non-flowering shoots. A weed of cultivation and waste ground.

2 Quaking Grass *Briza media*. Short/medium, to 50cm. Spikelets usually purplish, most distinctive, *flattened*, ovoid to broadly triangular, dancing in the wind on slender stalks; May-August. Grassland, especially on lime. **2a *Lesser Quaking Grass** B. minor*, with smaller green spikelets and a longer ligule is a weed of bare and disturbed ground; south coast.

3 Wood Melick *Melica uniflora*. Short/medium, to 60cm. Cluster very open, the spikelets with one floret and purplish-brown glumes, singly on long stalks; May-July. Leaves pale green, with a bristle at the top of the sheath behind the short ligule. Beech and other woods, shady banks.

4 Whorl Grass *Catabrosa aquatica*. Short/medium, to 70cm, creeping. Clusters with branches in distinctive *alternate half-whorls*, the purplish spikelets with two florets (only one by the sea); May-July. Leaves broad, to 10mm, soft, blunt-tipped, sweet-tasting. In or by shallow fresh water.

5 Reed Canary-grass *Phalaris arundinacea*. A tall, to 2m, stout, patch-forming water-side grass. Panicle lobed, the spikelets 2-3-flowered, pale purple, white or pale yellow; June-August. Leaves broad, to 2cm, *rough-edged*, persisting dead through winter; ligules blunt, often torn. By fresh water, damp grassy places; fens.

6 **Holy Grass *Hierochloe odorata*. Medium, to 60cm; *aromatic*. Spikelets rounded in flower (less so in fruit), sometimes with a very short bent awn; late March to June. Leaves bright green. By fresh water, wet peaty grassland.

7 **Cut Grass *Leersia oryzoides*. Medium/tall, to 1m; stems downy at leaf-junctions. Leaves pale yellowish-green, with inflated sheaths *enfolding* the flower cluster. Spikelets with one floret on wavy branches, the cluster not spreading till freed (sometimes never or only partly) from the leaf-sheath; August-Oct. By fresh water, sometimes scrambling over other plants.

8 Common Reed *Phragmites australis*. Very tall, to 3.5m, stout and creeping, making extensive reed-beds, the hard cane-like stems lasting through the winter. Spikelets purple, with long silky hairs on their common stalk; August-Oct. Leaves greyish, to 5cm broad, with a ring of hairs as ligule. Marshes, swamps, fens, by fresh/brackish water, also on damp clayey slopes.

9 Reed Sweet-grass *Glyceria maxima*. A tall, to 2m, waterside grass, forming less extensive patches than Common Reed (**8**). Spikelets green; June-August. Leaves narrower, to 18mm, bright green, with short, sharply pointed ligules and a brown mark at the stem-junction. By fresh water, marshes.

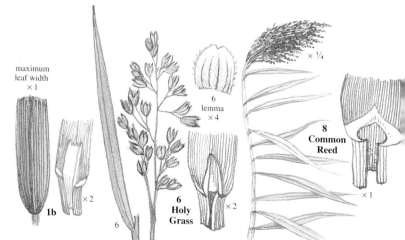

maximum
leaf width
× 1

6
lemma
× 4

× ¼

**8
Common
Reed**

× 2

6
**Holy
Grass**

× 2

1b

× 2

6

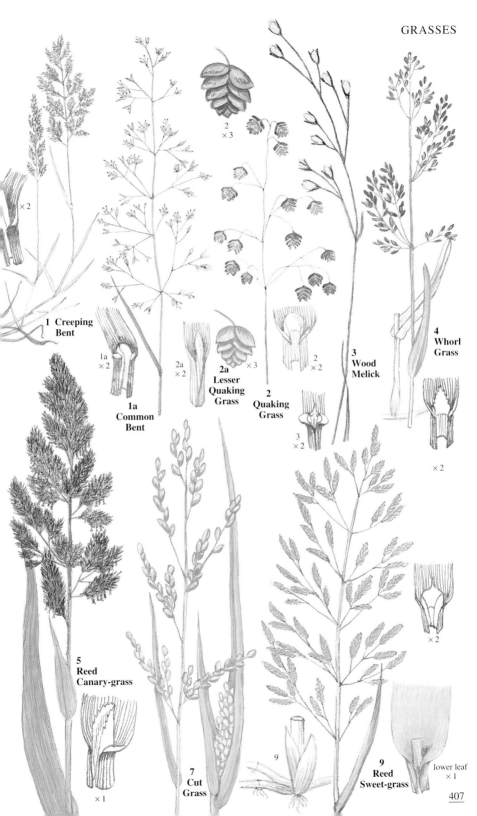

1 Creeping Bent

2
× 3

1a
× 2

1a
Common
Bent

2a
× 2

2a
Lesser
Quaking
Grass × 3

2
Quaking
Grass

2
× 2

3
× 2

3
Wood
Melick

4
Whorl
Grass

× 2

5
Reed
Canary-grass

7
Cut
Grass

× 1

× 2

9

9
Reed
Sweet-grass

lower leaf
× 1

1 Wood Millet *Milium effusum.* Tall. to 1.8m. Spikelets pale green, with one floret; May-July. Leaves pale green, to 15mm broad. Damp woods.

Saltmarsh Grasses *Puccinellia.* Short/medium, to 85mm, often half-prostrate. Clusters with (often purplish) spikelets usually all along the branches; June-July. Leaves greyish, usually flat, with short blunt ligules. Coastal. Only **2 Common Saltmarsh Grass** *Puccinellia maritima* ever forms a sward. Cluster branches erect to half-spreading. Wetter saltmarshes. **2a Reflexed Saltmarsh Grass** *P. distans* has spikelets only on the outer half of the branches, which are spreading but turn down in fruit; in the N reflexing much weaker and leaves often folded. Drier saltmarshes and bare ground. **2b Borrer's Saltmarsh Grass** *P. fasciculata* has rather stiff one-sided erect clusters, the branches erect and only the longer ones with no spikelets at the base. Drier places. **2c Stiff Saltmarsh Grass** *P. rupestris* is often prostrate, with rather stiff, one-sided erect clusters. Bare ground.

Fern Grass *Catapodium rigidum*, see p. 424; **Fine-leaved Sheep's Fescue (4a)**; **California Brome** *Ceratochloa carinata*, see p. 410.

(ii) Spikelets awned

3 Red Fescue *Festuca rubra.* Short/medium, loosely tufted to shortly creeping, very variable. Basal leaves thread-like, flat or folded, the sheaths *completely closed* when young, sometimes glaucous or bluish, especially near the sea, sometimes hairy. May-July. Grassy places, dunes, saltmarshes, much sown on road verges. Widespread. **3a Rush-leaved Fescue** *F. arenaria* has long creeping runners, and thick, always folded leaves. Mobile coastal dunes.

4 Sheep's Fescue *Festuca ovina* agg. is more strongly tufted than Red Fescue (**3**), with leaf-sheaths *always split* to more than half-way. June-July. Downs, heaths, moors. Widespread. (Includes *F. lemanii*). **4a Fine-leaved Sheep's Fescue** *F. filiformis* has sheaths split to the base and spikelets very often unawned, Widespread on acid soils. Southern. **4b Blue Fescue** *F. longifolia*, a Breckland speciality, has very bluish leaves, but is not to be confused with the widely sown **Hard Fescue** *F. brevipila*, which often has slightly bluish leaves.

5 Viviparous Fescue *Festuca vivipara* is like Sheep's Fescue (**4**), but has spikelets always viviparous (p. 404). Northern moors.

Tall Fescue *Festuca arundinacea*, see p.404.

6 Giant Fescue *Festuca gigantea.* Tall, to 1.5m; *hairless.* Clusters drooping, conspicuously long-awned 8-13mm spikelets; July-August. Leaves broad, to 18mm, dark shiny green, with conspicuous basal auricles and dark *purplish* stem-junctions. Cf. Hairy Brome (p. 410). Woods, hedge-banks, shady places.

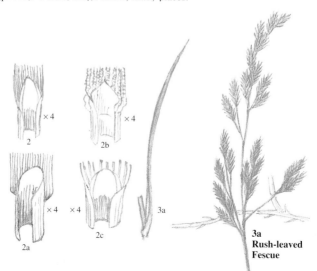

3a
3a Rush-leaved Fescue

4b Blue Fescue

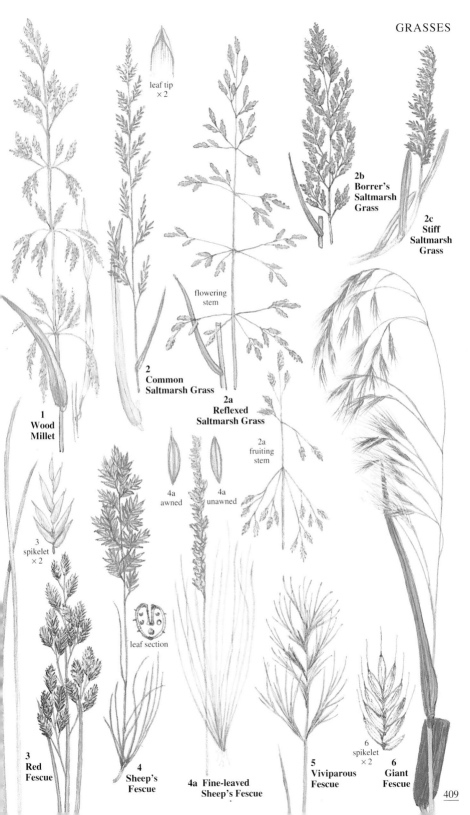

leaf tip
× 2

2b
Borrer's
Saltmarsh
Grass

2c
Stiff
Saltmarsh
Grass

flowering
stem

2
Common
Saltmarsh Grass

2a
Reflexed
Saltmarsh Grass

2a
fruiting
stem

1
Wood
Millet

3
spikelet
× 2

4a
awned

4a
unawned

leaf section

3
Red
Fescue

4
Sheep's
Fescue

4a Fine-leaved
Sheep's Fescue

5
Viviparous
Fescue

6
spikelet
× 2

6
Giant
Fescue

1 Hairy Brome *Bromopsis ramosa*. Tall, *to 2m*. Clusters *conspicuously* drooping, with a hairy scale at the base and long-awned, often purplish spikelets; July-August. Leaves broad, to 15mm, the sheaths with long white hairs – cf. the hairless Giant Fescue (p. 408). Woods and other shady places. **1a Lesser Hairy Brome** *B. benekenii* has much less spreading and drooping clusters, more like False Brome (p. 426), with a hairless scale at the base, and leaf-sheaths with shorter hairs, the topmost often hairless. Beech and other woods on lime, also rock-ledges.

2 Upright Brome *Bromopsis erecta*. Much the commonest tall grass of limy grassland, to 1.2m. Clusters *erect*, the spikelets often purplish with 3-8mm awns; May-July. Lower leaves often inrolled. **2a California Brome** *Ceratochloa carinata*, with broader leaves, to 1cm, and short or no awns, is locally frequent in grassy places by the Thames and elsewhere. More widespread but less frequent is **2b Rescue Grass** *C. cathartica* with much longer awns, to 1cm.

3 Barren Brome *Anisantha sterilis*. One of the commonest weedy grasses. Medium/tall, stems hairless, to 80cm. Clusters *nodding*, the spikelets long-awned (15-30mm), usually only one (20-35mm) on each branch; May-July. **3a Great Brome** *A. diandra* has stems hairy at the top and longer (50-70mm) spikelets and awns (35-65mm). Well naturalised in the Breckland and the Scilly Isles, spreading elsewhere. **3b Drooping Brome** *A. tectorum* has up to four 10-20mm spikelets per branch, the awns 10-18mm. Another Breckland speciality, scattered elsewhere.

4 Compact Brome *Anisantha madritensis*. Differs from Barren Brome (**3**) especially in its dense *erect* cluster of 30-50mm single or paired spikelets, with awns 12-20mm; May-July. Dry rocky banks, old walls, bare places, perhaps native on the Bristol limestone, introduced and scattered elsewhere. **4a Stiff Brome** *A. rigida* has stems downy at the top, spikelets 25-35mm and longer (30-50mm) awns. Increasing, especially on sandy ground on the S coast.

5 Soft Brome *Bromus hordeaceus*. Very variable, medium/tall, to 1m, but much shorter on dunes (ssp. *thominei*) and sea-cliffs (ssp. *ferronii*). Leaf-sheaths hairy. Clusters erect to drooping, spikelets rather plump, short-awned, usually downy, the bluntly-angled lemmas with a narrow pale margin; May-July. Grassy and bare places, waysides, meadows. Widespread. If spikelets hairless, may be either *thominei* or **5a Slender Brome** *B. lepidus*, whose lemmas are sharply angled with a broad pale margin; or **5b Smooth Brome** *B. racemosus* (incl. Meadow Brome *B. commutatus*) which has clusters more often nodding, with spikelets often hairless, lemmas angled or not and *upper leaf-sheaths hairless*. Damp meadows and other grassy places

6 Velvet Bent *Agrostis canina*. Medium, to 70cm, with short leafy runners. Clusters spreading in flower but contracted in fruit, with florets always awned, only one in each purplish spikelet; June-August. Leaves very narrow, with a long pointed jagged ligule. *Damp* grassy places. **6a Brown Bent** *A. vinealis* has no runners, a denser cluster and ligules often blunter. Drier ground, especially heaths and moors.

Creeping, **Common** and **Black Bents**, see p. 406.

7 Loose Silky Bent *Apera spica-venti*. Medium/tall annual, to 1m. Cluster with *spreading* branches, the spikelets each with one floret and a very long awn; June-July. Leaves roughish, variable, to 10mm, the sheaths often purplish and the ligules bluntly pointed. Bare sandy ground, a Breckland speciality. **Dense Silky Bent** *A. interrupta*, see p. 416.

Yorkshire Fog *Holcus lanatus*, see p. 414.

8 False Oat-grass *Arrhenatherum elatius*. Tall, to 2m, stems sometimes swollen at the base. Spikelets shining, with two florets and a long *straight* awn; May-Sept. Leaves with a blunt ligule. Grassy and waste places. Widespread, common.

9 Wild Oat *Avena fatua* (incl. Winter Wild Oat *A. sterilis*). Tall, to 1m. Spikelets dull, with two florets, a tuft of *tawny* hairs at the base and a long *bent* awn; June-August. Ligule bluntly pointed. Cornfields, bare ground. Mainly southern. **9a Cultivated Oat** *A. sativa* differs especially in having no tawny hairs and often a straight awn.

10 Yellow Oat-grass *Trisetum flavescens*. Medium/tall, to 80cm. Spikelets *yellowish*, with 2-4 florets and a bent awn, the cluster not spreading widely; June-July. Grassland, especially on lime. **Downy** and **Meadow Oat-grasses**, see p. 414.

leaf section   2a   2b   5a   5b

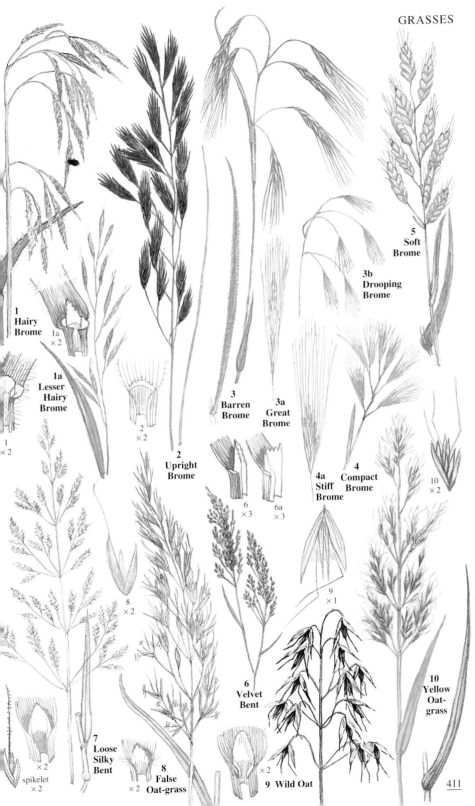

1 Hairy Brome

1a × 2

1a Lesser Hairy Brome

1 × 2

2 × 2

2 Upright Brome

3 Barren Brome

3a Great Brome

6 × 3

6a × 3

8 × 2

spikelet × 2

7 Loose Silky Bent

8 False Oat-grass × 2

6 Velvet Bent

9 × 1

9 Wild Oat

× 2

3b Drooping Brome

5 Soft Brome

4a Stiff Brome

4 Compact Brome

10 × 2

10 Yellow Oat-grass

2 oz ☐

2a z ☐

3 soz ☐↓

4 oz ☐↓

4a soz ☐↓

4b ☐↓

4c ☐↓

1 Tufted Hair-grass *Deschampsia cespitosa*. Tall, to 2m, and conspicuously tuf Spikelets silvery/purplish with a straight awn, on mountains largely replaced by gr shoots; June-August. Leaves dark green, rough-edged. Damp woods and grassla marshes, mountains. Widespread.

2 Wavy Hair-grass *Deschampsia flexuosa*. Medium/tall, to 1m. Spikelets shining, p plish/silvery, with a long bent awn; May-July. Leaves thread-like with short blunt ligu Dry heaths, moors, woods, on acid soils. **2a Bog Hair-grass** *D. setacea* has long poir ligules. Bogs, peaty pools on wet heaths.

3 Silver Hair-grass *Aira caryophyllea*. Short/medium, to 50cm. Spikelets silvery/p plish, shortly awned; May-July. Leaves channelled with roughish sheaths. Dry bare pla on sand and gravel.

Holy Grass *Hierochloe odorata*, see p. 406.

1b. Flowers in spreading branched clusters: Rushes

4 Sharp-flowered Rush *Juncus acutiflorus*. Medium/tall, to 1m. Flowers green brown with sharply pointed tepals; July-August. Leaves rounded, straight. Fruits wa brown, gradually narrowed to a small point. Wet grassy places, usually on acid so **4a Jointed Rush** *J. articulatus* is shorter with browner flowers, only the outer tep pointed; leaves curved, flattened and often sprawling, and fruits abruptly narrowed t small beak. Widespread. **4b Blunt-flowered Rush** *J. subnodulosus* has paler flowers w all tepals blunt and 3-sided fruits. Marshes, fens, preferring limy soils. **4c *Alpine Rus** *alpinoarticulatus* has darker flowers with all tepals blunt and fruits blunt but minu pointed. Bare wet places, usually on mountains.

5 Toad Rush *Juncus bufonius* agg. Low/medium tufted annual, to 60cm. Flow greenish-white, singly with several short bracts as well as longer ones at base of clus May-Sept. Leaves mostly basal. Fruits brown, blunt or pointed. Bare damp places. Wi spread. Incl. **5a** *J. foliosus* (flowers dark brown, leaves broader), *J. minutulus* (low, to 5c leaves narrower) and **5b** *J. ambiguus* (outer tepals with broad pale margin).

6 Bulbous Rush *Juncus bulbosus*. Very variable, low/short to 30cm or floating to 100c Flowers green or brown, often replaced by green shoots, in a forking cluster; June-Se Leaves usually narrow, often jointed, sometimes slightly flattened, often bronzy w floating. Fruits 3-sided, brown. Bogs, wet heaths, often in flooded ruts, on acid soils.

7 Sea Rush *Juncus maritimus*. Tall, stems greyish, to 1m. Flowers yellowish, surmoun by a long, sharply pointed bract. Leaves sharply pointed. Fruits brown, bluntly pointed. the sea. **7a *Sharp Rush** *J. acutus* forms much taller (to 1.5m), stouter clumps, with r brown flowers and spiny tips noticeably sharper. Fruits rounded.

Soft Rush *Juncus effusus*, see p. 436.

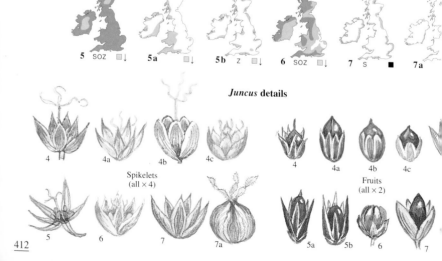

5 soz ☐↓   **5a** ☐↓   **5b** z ☐↓   **6** soz ☐↓   **7** s ■   **7a**

Juncus **details**

4   4a   4b   4c   4   4a   4b   4c

Spikelets   Fruits
(all × 4)   (all × 2)

5   6   7   7a   5a   5b   6   7

412

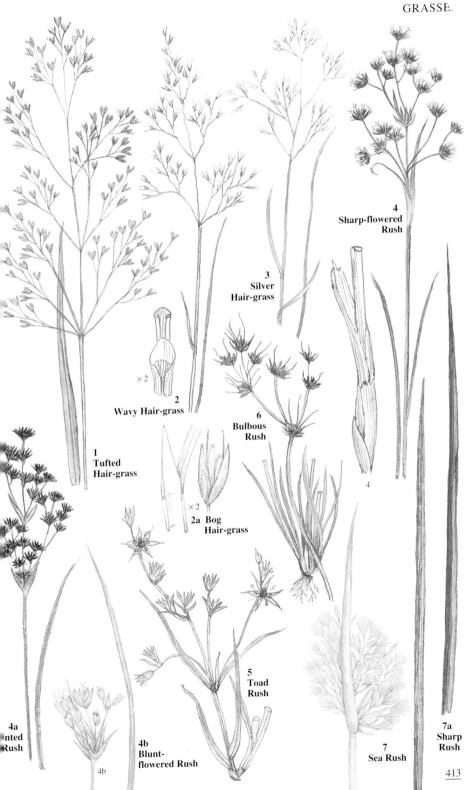

4
Sharp-flowered Rush

3
Silver Hair-grass

×2

2
Wavy Hair-grass

6
Bulbous Rush

4

1
Tufted Hair-grass

×2

2a Bog Hair-grass

5
Toad Rush

4a
nted Rush

4b
Blunt-flowered Rush

4b

7
Sea Rush

7a
Sharp Rush

2a. Flowers in erect branched clusters: Grasses

(i) Spikelets unawned

1 Floating Sweet-grass *Glyceria fluitans*. The commonest of the smaller sweet-grasses, medium/tall, to 1.2m. Clusters nodding, with elongated spikelets, the lemmas *pointed*; late May-August. Leaves sweet-tasting, green/glaucous, often *floating*; ligule long, acutely pointed. Its hybrid with Plicate Sweet-grass (**1a**) is frequent. In and by still and slow-flowing fresh water. Widespread. **1a Plicate Sweet-grass** *G. notata* is shorter, to 80cm, with a more spreading cluster, lemmas bluntly pointed and ligules oblong. **1b Small Sweet-grass** *G. declinata* is still shorter, to 50cm, the stems often curved, the cluster narrower, the lemmas minutely toothed and the ligules shorter.

2 Purple Moor-grass *Molinia caerulea*. Medium/tall, to 90cm, with conspicuous tussocks of greyish leaves; ligule a ring of hairs. Clusters narrow, the 1-4-flowered spikelets usually purple, less often yellowish or green; anthers purple-brown; July-Sept. Wet heaths and moors on acid soils.

3 Heath Grass *Danthonia decumbens*. Low/medium, to 60cm, but often almost prostrate. Spikelets 4-6-flowered, almost globular; June-August. Leaves pale green, ligule a ring of hairs. Heaths, dry acid grassland.

Fern Grass *Catapodium rigidum*, see p. 424.

(ii) Spikelets awned

4 Yorkshire Fog *Holcus lanatus*. One of our commonest grasses, medium, to 1m, softly grey-downy all over, except on stem joints. Cluster narrow/spreading, the spikelets pink-purple to white, with short *hooked* awns; May-August. Grassland, waste ground, sometimes in fog-like swards. Widespread. **4a Creeping Soft-grass** *H. mollis* creeps and has greener leaves. *bearded* stem-joints, usually narrower clusters and longer *bent* awns; June-August. Open woods, hedge-banks, heaths, bare sandy ground, preferring acid soils.

5 Downy Oat-grass *Helictotrichon pubescens*. Medium/tall, to 1m. Spikelets silvery, with a *bent* awn; May-July. Leaves green, hairy with hairy sheaths; ligules pointed. Limy grassland. **5a Meadow Oat-grass** *H. pratense* has a narrower cluster, appearing a little later, and glaucous leaves and sheaths both *hairless*. Also in other dry grassland.

Small-reeds *Calamagrostis*. Tall, tufted, with 1-flowered spikelets purplish, greenish or silvery, the glumes narrow lanceolate, except Narrow Small-reed (**6c**), the lemmas with a tuft of hairs at the base; June-August. Leaves flat, hairless except Purple Small-reed (**6a**). Hybrids occur. Damp/wet woods, fens, marshes. Much the most frequent is **6 Wood Small-reed** *Calamagrostis epigeios*, to 2m, with narrow lanceolate glumes, lemmas 3-veined; and leaves to 20mm wide, the ligules jagged. For its hybrid with Marram, see p. 420. Often on clay. **6a Purple Small-reed** *C. canescens* has stems often *branched*, to 1.5m, lemmas 5-veined, cleft at the tip and with a much shorter awn, and leaves downy, to 8mm, with bluntly pointed ligules. The recently discovered **6b **Scandinavian Small-reed** *C. purpurea* has longer awns and hairless leaves; S to the Lake District. **6c **Narrow Small-reed** *C. stricta*, to 1m, has a narrower cluster, broad lanceolate glumes, stems all hairless and leaves to 5mm with a short blunt ligule. Readily hybridises with **6d ***Scottish Small-reed** *C. scotica*, which has glumes less sharply pointed and stems usually rough just below the cluster.

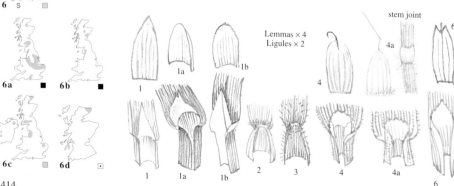

stem joint

Lemmas × 4
Ligules × 2

414

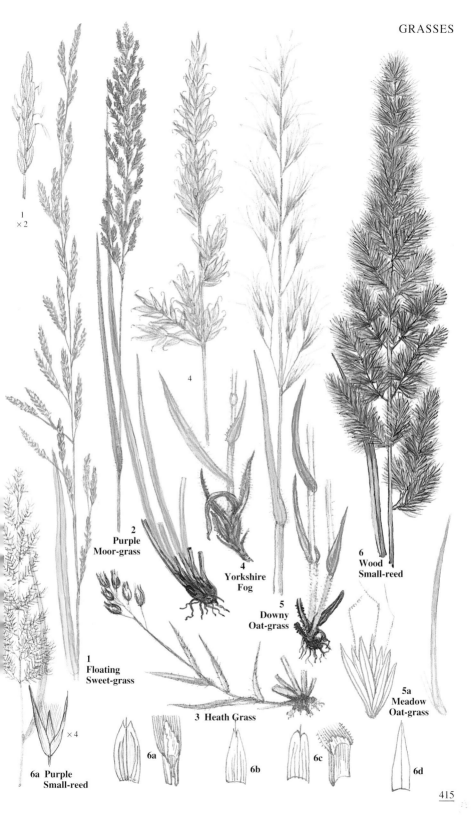

1
×2

2
Purple
Moor-grass

4
Yorkshire
Fog

6
Wood
Small-reed

5
Downy
Oat-grass

1
Floating
Sweet-grass

3 Heath Grass

5a
Meadow
Oat-grass

6a Purple
Small-reed

×4

6a

6b

6c

6d

Fescues *Vulpia*. Low/short, to 65cm. Spikelets on one side of stem, in either narrow clusters or, (except Squirrel-tail Fescue (**1**), stalked spikes (and see p. 402), the glumes unequal and long-awned; May-July. Dry bare places. **1 Squirrel-tail Fescue** *Vulpia bromoides*. The most frequent species, the cluster well above the upper leaf-sheath and the lower glume at least half as long as the upper. **1a Ratstail Fescue** *V. myuros*. The tallest species, with clusters drooping, usually partly within the upper leaf-sheath, the lower glume less than half as long as the upper. **1b Bearded Fescue** *V. ciliata*, has clusters well above the upper leaf-sheath, and with the tiny lower glume much shorter than the upper, which is unawned; gradually reddening. Often on coastal sand/shingle. **1c Dune Fescue** *V. fasciculata* has clusters often almost or partly within the inflated upper leaf-sheath, glumes like Bearded Fescue (**1b**), but with two very long awns, to 12mm; becoming orange-brown in fruit. Mainly coastal dunes.

2 Bristle Bent *Agrostis curtisii*. Short/medium, to 60cm. Spikelets yellow-green; June-August. Leaves hair-like, often greyish, conspicuously tufted. Unlike Creeping Bent (p. 406), always clusters contracted. Dry south-western heaths and moors.

3 Dense Silky Bent *Apera interrupta* has a much narrower cluster than Loose Silky Bent (p. 410), appearing interrupted from the space between the branches, and narrower leaves with a more pointed ligule. A Breckland speciality.

4 Grey Hair-grass *Corynephorus canescens*. Noticeably tufted, short/medium, to 60cm. Spikelets purplish, 2-flowered, with an awn thickened at the tip; June-July. Leaves hair-like, glaucous, with purple-pink sheaths. Coastal dunes, one site inland.

5 Cockspur *Echinochloa crus-galli* Tall, to 1.2m. Clusters thick, to 25cm, the spikelets 2-flowered, either shortly awned or sharply pointed; August-Oct. No ligules. The most frequent of a group of rubbish-dump aliens.

2b. Flowers in erect branched clusters: Sedges

(i) Clusters simple

6 Common Club-rush *Schoenoplectus lacustris*. Very tall, with leafless green stems to 3m. Spikelets egg-shaped, red-brown, with 3 styles and a leaflike bract shorter than the cluster; June-August. Leaves strap-like, all submerged. Still widely known as Bulrush; cf. Bulrush, p. 342. Still and slow-moving fresh water. **6a Grey Club-rush** *S. tabernaemontani* has greyish stems, red-dotted glumes and 2styles. Also in marshes and on tidal rivers. **6b **Triangular Club-rush** *S. triqueter* has 3-sided stems and much smaller clusters. Now confined to the tidal Tamar and Shannon, but its hybrid with Grey Club-rush (**6a**) survives on tidal parts of the Sussex Arun and Kentish Medway as well as the Devon Tamar.

7 Great Fen Sedge *Cladium mariscus*. Patch-forming, with stout hollow stems to 2.5m. Spikelets short-stalked in long-stalked umbels up the stem, egg-shaped, pale brown; July-August. Leaves glaucous, stiff, saw-edged, 10-15mm, to 2m, but usually bent in a V-shape. Fens, by fresh, usually limy, water; 'sedge' in E Anglia, still cut for litter.

8 Wood Club-rush *Scirpus sylvaticus*. Medium/tall, stems bluntly 3-sided, leafy, to 1.2m. Spikelets egg-shaped, brown with olive-green glumes, leaf-like bracts about as long as the forking cluster; May-July. Leaves rough-edged, to 20mm. Cf. Galingale (**11**). Wet woods, fens, marshes.

9 **Brown Galingale *Cyperus fuscus*. Low/short, to 30cm. Spikelets in a (sometimes compound) umbel, red-brown, with bracts much longer than the umbel; July-Sept. Dried-up ponds and other bare mud.

10 *Gingerbread Sedge *Carex elongata*. Loose tussocks, medium, to 80cm. Flowerheads branched, the flowers dark red-brown. Leaves yellow-green, reddening in autumn, with a long pointed ligule. Damp meadows, fens, by fresh water.

(ii) Clusters compound

11 Galingale *Cyperus longus*. Medium/tall, stems 3-sided, to 1.5m. Clusters compound (unlike Wood Club-rush, **8**), with up to 10 rays, each with 4-25 spikelets, glumes red-brown, the outer bract longer than the whole cluster; August-Oct. Leaves rough-edged, to 10mm. Damp places, by fresh water, native but widely introduced. **11a American Galingale** *C. eragrostis* is smaller with green spikelets. Scattered. **Brown Galingale** *Cyperus fuscus*, see above (**9**).

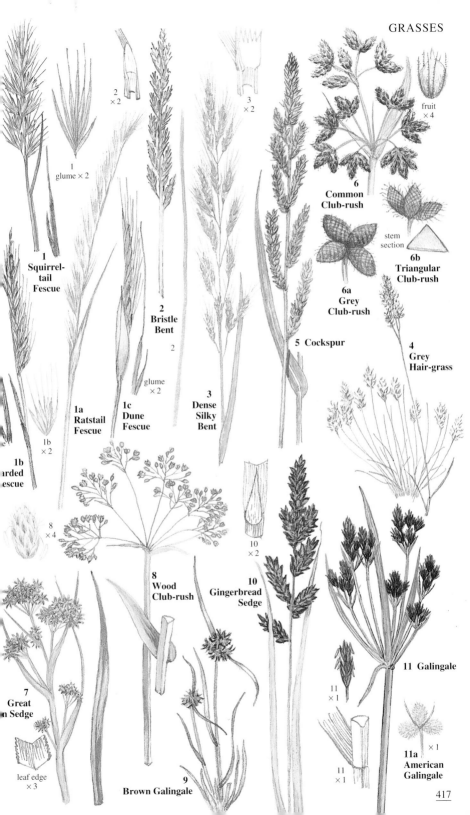

1 Squirrel-tail Fescue

1 glume × 2

2 × 2

3 × 2

fruit × 4

6 Common Club-rush

6a Grey Club-rush

stem section

6b Triangular Club-rush

2 Bristle Bent

2

glume × 2

1a Ratstail Fescue

1c Dune Fescue

3 Dense Silky Bent

5 Cockspur

4 Grey Hair-grass

1b × 2

1b arded escue

e

8 × 4

10 × 2

8 Wood Club-rush

10 Gingerbread Sedge

11 Galingale

11 × 1

7 Great n Sedge

leaf edge × 3

11 × 1

11 × 1

9 Brown Galingale

11a American Galingale

× 1

2c. Flowers in erect branched clusters: Rushes

1 Hard Rush *Juncus inflexus*. One of our two commonest rushes. Medium/tall, to 1.2m. Flowers brown, in a cluster with unequal stalks, near the top of the hard greyish ridged leaf-less stems with interrupted pith; May-July. Fruits brown, egg-shaped. Damp grassy places, especially on lime and clay. **1a Baltic Rush** *J. balticus* has a much smaller flower cluster and is best told by its long creeping rows of smooth greyish stems with continuous pith and its sandy habitat, usually by the sea but also by rivers inland. **1b *Thread Rush** *J. filiformis* has slightly larger flower clusters than Baltic Rush, but its rows of stems are slender, green and ridged. Lake and reservoir shores.

2 Heath Rush *Juncus squarrosus*. Short/medium, tufted, stems very stiff, usually leaf-less, to 50cm. Flowers dark brown, pale-edged; June-July. Leaves wiry, in a basal rosette. Fruits egg-shaped, brown. Heaths, moors, on acid soils.

3 Slender Rush *Juncus tenuis*. Short/tall, tufted, to 80cm. Flowers greenish/yellowish, in a rather sparse cluster, with very long bracts; June-Sept. Leaves very narrow, pale green, with long whitish auricles at base. Fruits egg-shaped, grey-brown. Widely introduced on sandy ground, especially by tracks, on acid soils.

4 Round-fruited Rush *Juncus compressus*. Short, stems usually flattened, to 40cm. Flowers pale brown, the lowest bract usually longer than the cluster; June-July. Leaves very narrow, glaucous. Fruits dark brown. Fens, marshes, damp grassland, on limy soils. **4a Saltmarsh Rush** *J. gerardi* is its coastal counterpart, more patch-forming, with flowers dark brown, the lowest bract usually shorter than the cluster, dark green leaves and paler brown fruits. Saltmarshes, also brackish.

2d. Flowers in erect branched clusters: Wood-rushes

Tufted; leaves with long white hairs.

5 Great Wood-rush *Luzula sylvatica*. By far our largest wood-rush, medium/tall, to 80cm. Flowers brown, in a wide-spreading forking cluster; April-June. Leaves glossy, to 20mm across. Fruits egg-shaped, brown. Woods, rocky places, mainly on acid soils. Two smaller naturalised wood-rushes are **5a White Wood-rush** *L. luzuloides* with off-white flowers and **5b Snowy Wood-rush** *L. nivea* with pure white flowers.

6 Heath Wood-rush *Luzula multiflora*. Short, to 30cm; no runners. Heads stalked, the flowers red-brown, with anthers about as long as their stalks; May-June. Leaves green. Fruits brown, globular. Heathy places on acid soils. Cf. Congested Wood-rush, p. 434. **6a ***Fen Wood-rush** *L. pallidula* has pale yellow-brown flowers, the central cluster scarcely stalked and pale or yellow-green leaves. Perhaps now extinct in two fens N of Huntingdon.

7 Hairy Wood-rush *Luzula pilosa*. Low/short, to 30cm. Flowers dark brown, singly in a forking cluster on very unequal stalks, which turn down in fruit; March-May. Leaves to 10mm across. Fruits yellow-green, 3-sided, abruptly narrowing to a short beak. Woods, shady places. **7a Southern Wood-rush** *L. forsteri* has flower-stalks erecter and remaining so in fruit and fruits narrowing more gradually to a longer beak.

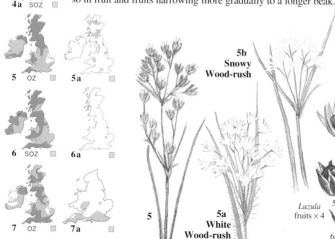

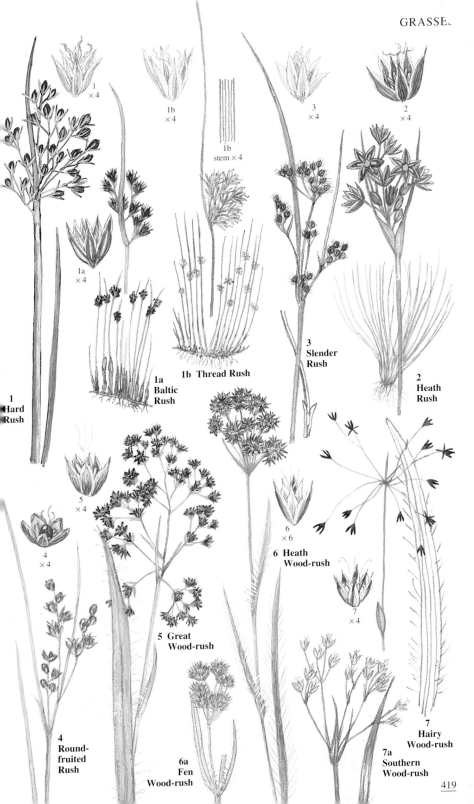

1
× 4

1b
× 4

3
× 4

2
× 4

1b
stem × 4

1a
× 4

1b Thread Rush

3
Slender
Rush

1a
Baltic
Rush

2
Heath
Rush

1
Hard
Rush

5
× 4

6
× 6

4
× 4

6 Heath
Wood-rush

5 Great
Wood-rush

7
× 4

7
Hairy
Wood-rush

4
Round-
fruited
Rush

6a
Fen
Wood-rush

7a
Southern
Wood-rush

3a. Flowers in erect *stout* spikes: Grasses

(i) Spikelets unawned

1 Crested Hair-grass *Koeleria macrantha*. Short, to 40cm. Spike often incipiently branched, the spikelets green, brown or purplish and narrowly silvery-edged, the glumes pointed with a tiny awn-like bristle; June-July. Leaves flat, often glaucous. Grassland, especially on lime, dunes. **1a **Somerset Hair-grass** *K. vallesiana* is woody at the base with a mass of old fibres, the glumes with a broad silvery edge, and leaves often hair-like. Short limestone turf, Somerset only.

2 Marram *Ammophila arenaria*. Tall, stout, to 1.2mm, binding its sand-dune habitat together with its tough rootstock. Spike long, with straw-coloured one-flowered spikelets; June-August. Leaves grey-green, sharply pointed, the margins inrolled. Hybridises with Wood Small-reed, see p. 414. Widespread on coast.

3 Lyme Grass *Leymus arenarius*. Tall, stout and bluish-grey, to 1.5m. Spikelets in unstalked pairs up the stem; June-August. Leaves broad, to 15mm. Dunes, bare coastal sand.

Nit Grass, see p. 422. **Bread Wheat**, see p. 422.

(ii) Spikelets awned

Foxtails *Alopecurus*. Spikelets one-flowered with glumes unawned and lemmas usually awned. Cf. Catstails (below). **4 Meadow Foxtail** *Alopecurus pratensis*, the commonest and tallest, to 1.1m, has long cylindrical spikes, to 9cm, with glumes and lemmas both pointed, conspicuous awns and anthers orange or purplish; *April*-June. Grassland. Widespread. **4a Black Grass** *A. myosuroides*, medium/tall, to 85cm, has narrower tapering spikes with blunt long-awned lemmas; May-August. A tiresome arable weed. **4b Marsh Foxtail** *A. geniculatus* is short, to 45cm, with stems creeping and rooting or floating and often bent, shorter spikes, to 6cm, glumes and lemmas blunt, awns short and anthers yellow or purplish; June-August. Ligules blunt. Wet grassy places, shallow still water. **4c *Orange Foxtail** *A. aequalis* differs from Marsh Foxtail (**4b**) in its paler and more shining glumes, obscure awns not projecting beyond lemma tip and more pointed ligules. Especially on drying mud. **4d *Bulbous Foxtail** *A. bulbosus* has erecter stems than Marsh Foxtail (**4b**), bulbous at the base and not rooting, and pointed glumes; June-July; grassy places and saltmarshes *by the sea*. **Alpine Foxtail**, see p. 436.

Catstails *Phleum*. Spikelets often purplish, one-flowered with glumes shortly awned and lemmas unawned. **5 Timothy** *Phleum pratense*, the commonest and tallest, to 1.5m, has long cylindrical spikes, to 15cm or more, with awns 1-2mm; June-August. Ligules blunt. Grassy places, often sown. Widespread. **5a Smaller Catstail** *P. bertolonii* is shorter, to 70cm, with shorter spikes, to 8cm, shorter awns, and ligules pointed. Grassland, especially on lime. **5b **Purple-stem Catstail** *P. phleoides* is medium, to 90cm, with spikes to 10cm, slender and tapering, the glumes abruptly narrowed to a very short awn. Ligules blunt. Sandy grassland, a Breckland speciality. **5c Sand Catstail** *P. arenarium* is short, to 35cm, with a short spike, to 5cm, and glumes gradually narrowing to the awn; May-June. Ligules bluntly pointed. Coastal sand and shingle, rare inland. Alpine Catstail, see p. 436.

N.B. Several species of **5d Bristle-grass** *Setaria*, confusingly like foxtails and catstails, often occur on rubbish tips.

6 Sweet Vernal Grass *Anthoxanthum odoratum*. Short, to 50cm; smelling of new-mown hay when dried. Spikelets with a *bent* awn; April-July. Grassland. Widespread.

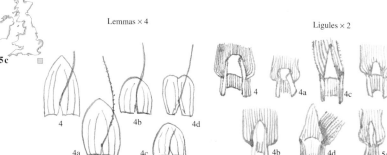

Lemmas × 4   Ligules × 2

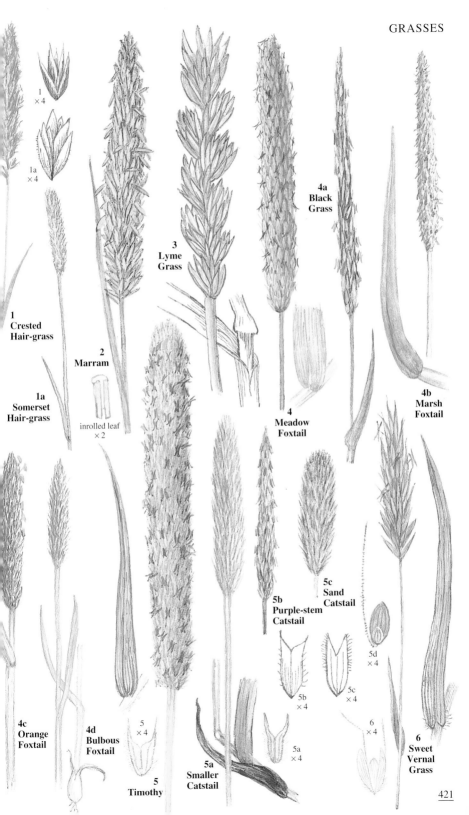

1
× 4

1a
× 4

1
Crested
Hair-grass

1a
Somerset
Hair-grass

2
Marram

inrolled leaf
× 2

3
Lyme
Grass

4a
Black
Grass

4
Meadow
Foxtail

4b
Marsh
Foxtail

4c
Orange
Foxtail

4d
Bulbous
Foxtail

5
× 4

5
Timothy

5a
Smaller
Catstail

5a
× 4

5b
Purple-stem
Catstail

5b
× 4

5c
Sand
Catstail

5c
× 4

5d
× 4

6
× 4

6
Sweet
Vernal
Grass

Barleys *Hordeum*. Spikelets 1-flowered, conspicuously long-awned, in dense triplets up the stem. **1 Wall Barley** *Hordeum murinum*, the commonest, is short, to 50cm, with awns to 30mm; May-Nov. Leaves with long basal auricles. Waste ground, waysides, often at the foot of walls. **1a Meadow Barley** *H. secalinum* has shorter spikes, and awns to 12mm; June-July. Grassland on heavier soils. **1b *Sea Barley** *H. marinum* has still shorter spikes, awns to 25mm and glaucous leaves. By the sea. **1c Four-rowed Barley** *H. distichon*, the commonest crop relic, is taller, to 1.3cm, with awns varying up to 90mm. (The equally common relic **1d Bread Wheat** *Triticum aestivum* has no or quite short awns.) **1e Foxtail Barley** *H. jubatum*, increasing on roadsides, especially roundabouts, has very distinctive long white awns, to 100mm.

2 *Wood Barley *Hordelymus europaeus* differs from the true Barleys (above) especially in growing in woods, especially beechwoods, on lime. Tall, to 1.1m, with downy leaf-junctions, hairy leaf-sheaths and awns to 25mm.

3 *Annual Beard-grass *Polypogon monspeliensis*. Medium/tall, to 90cm. Spike long, to 16cm, with dense one-flowered spikelets, appearing white from the long silky awns, to 7mm; June-August. Ligules long, pointed. For Perennial Beard-grass, its hybrid with Creeping Bent, see p. 410. Bare and sparsely grassy places, especially near the sea, casual elsewhere.

4 **Nit Grass *Gastridium ventricosum*. Medium, to 60cm. Spike tapering to tip, spikelets one-flowered, yellowish-green, shiny, the glumes swollen at the base and supposedly like nits, bent-awned and unawned lemmas often in same spike; June-August. Ligules bluntly pointed. Bare and sparsely grassy places, especially near the sea.

5 Hybrid Marram × *Calammophila baltica*, the hybrid between Marram (p. 420) and Wood Small-reed (p. 414), is often planted with Marram as a sand-binder, differing especially in its more open spike, awned lemmas and flat leaves.

Blue Moor-grass, see p. 436. **Crested Hair-grass**, see p. 420.

3b. Flowers in erect *stout* spikes: Sedges

6 Sand Sedge *Carex arenaria*. Unique for its far-creeping, rooting stems, to 1m or more, with green shoots at intervals. Flowerhead brownish, slightly triangular, on short stems, to 90cm. Leaves often inrolled. Widespread on sand by the sea, rare inland. **6a Brown Sedge** *C. disticha*, its taller inland counterpart, sometimes overlapping in dune slacks, but usually in damp grassland and fens. Flowerhead narrower, brown/red-brown.

7 False Fox Sedge *Carex otrubae*. Stems with 3 flat sides, unwinged, medium, to 1m. Flowerhead greenish/brownish, 3-7cm, often with a long lower bract. Leaves 4-10mm wide, with pointed ligules and basal auricles. Damp grassy places. The stouter **7a **True Fox Sedge** *C. vulpina* has sharply angled winged concave stems, flowers red-brown and leaves with short blunt ligules and no auricles.

8 Greater Tussock Sedge *Carex paniculata*. Very large overwintering tussocks, the thickset base of brownish fibrous stems to 1m tall and 1m wide. Flowers brown, 5-15cm, on stems tall, to 1.5m, rough, with 3 flat sides and dark brown scales at the base. Leaves to 1.2m, rough, fens, wet woods, on peat. **8a *Fibrous Tussock Sedge** *C. appropinquata*, medium, to 80cm, has blackish scales at the stem-base, red-brown flowers and 1-2mm yellowish green leaves. **8b Lesser Tussock Sedge** *C. diandra*, medium, to 60cm, has dark brown flowers on convex stems with basal sheaths sometimes greyish, and leaves greyish-green, 1-2mm.

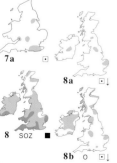

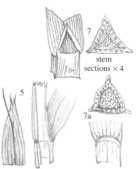

stem sections × 4

lemma × 4

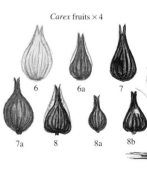

Carex fruits × 4

1b Sea Barley

1a Meadow Barley

1d Bread Wheat

unawned

1b

awned

5 Hybrid Marram

1 Wall Barley

1e Foxtail Barley

4 ×4

2 Wood Barley

3 Annual Beard-grass

4 Nit Grass

1c Four-rowed Barley

5

8 ♀×4

7 False Fox Sedge

7a True Fox Sedge

8 Greater Tussock Sedge

6a Brown Sedge

8b leaf tip ×4

8b ♀×4

8a ♀×4

8a Fibrous Tussock

8b Lesser Tussock Sedge

nd Sedge

Oval Sedge *Carex ovalis*, see p. 432.

1 Pale Sedge *Carex pallescens*. Short/medium, to 60cm. Glumes pale brown, the lowest bract ridged and twisted at the base, longer than the top spike. Leaves often hairy beneath. Fruits green. Open woods, damp grassy places, often on clay.

2 White Sedge *Carex curta*. Stems short, to 50cm, sharply 3-sided. Flowerhead short, the female glumes whitish. Leaves pale green. Wet heaths and mires on acid soils, often on mountains. **2a **Haresfoot Sedge** *C. lachenalii* has bluntly 3-sided stems and a shorter, narrower flowerhead, the female glumes red-brown. Central Highlands of Scotland.

3 *Russet Sedge *Carex saxatilis*. Low/short, stems sometimes curved, to 40cm. Female spikes rounded, glumes purple-brown, the lowest bract shorter than the top spike. Leaves folded or grooved. Fruits abruptly contracted to the short beak, spreading when ripe. Wet places on mountains.

4a. Flowers in erect *slender* spikes: Grasses *(i) Spikelets unawned*

4 Perennial Ryegrass *Lolium perenne*. One of our commonest, most distinctive and most widely sown grasses; short/medium, to 90cm. Spikelets unstalked; May-Nov. Widespread on cultivated land. Cf. Italian Ryegrass (p. 426), with which it hybridises.

Couches *Elytrigia*. Spikelets solitary, unstalked, alternating up the stem. Hybrids not infrequent. **5 Common Couch** *Elytrigia repens*. Tiresome creeping weed, medium/tall, to 1.2m. Spikelets pointed, glumes/lemmas sometimes awned; June-August. Leaves green, flat, with scattered white hairs above. Cultivated/waste ground. Widespread. **5a Sea Couch** *E. atherica* has spikes usually shorter, spikelets pointed, glumes sometimes awned and leaves *glaucous* and usually tightly inrolled. By the sea. **5b Sand Couch** *E. juncea* is shorter, to 60cm, with thicker, blunter spikelets, always unawned, and glaucous leaves usually slightly inrolled. Coastal sand all round coast, seaward of Sea Couch.

6 Common Cord-grass *Spartina anglica*. A sward-making grass derived from the hybrid between the native Small Cord-grass (**6a**) and the North American **Smooth Cord-grass** *S. alternifolia*, often planted in estuaries and on mudflats to stabilise wet mud. Medium/tall, to 1.3m. Spikelets one-flowered, in clusters of 3-6 erect narrow spikes, the stem ending in a long bristle above the topmost spike; July-Nov. Leaves yellowish-green, with the ligule a ring of hairs. **6a Small Cord-grass** *S. maritima*, to 70cm, has only 2-3 shorter spikes, July-Sept, a shorter bristle and narrower green or purplish leaves, with a much shorter ring of hairs. Saltmarshes, on drier mud.

7 Early Hair-grass *Aira praecox*. Low/short annual, spikes narrow with awned lemmas, but plant most obvious before flowering (April-June) when spikes hidden by silvery sheaths. Dry bare ground, often on acid sands.

8 Fern Grass *Catapodium rigidum*. Low stiff stems, to 15cm. Spike, sometimes partly spreading, with stalked spikelets, the lemma twice as long as broad; May-July. Leaves often purplish. Dry bare or sparsely grassy places, often on chalk or sand. **8a Sea Fern Grass** *C. marinum* has spike tighter and never spreading, the lemma nearly as broad as long and greener and fleshier leaves. By the sea.

9 Mountain Melick *Melica nutans*. Medium, to 60cm. Spikelets stalked, in a one-sided spike, with distinctive purplish-brown glumes; May-July. Dry open woods.

10 Hard Grass *Parapholis strigosa*. Short stiff *straight* stems, to 40cm. Spike very slender, the one-flowered spikelets *sunk into the stem*, often detectable only by their anthers; June-August. Ligules very short. Bare and grassy places by the sea. **10a *Curved Hard Grass** *P. incurva* is usually shorter, to 10cm, with the topmost leaf-sheath inflated, the spikes curved and the anthers even tinier.

11 **Early Sand-grass *Mibora minima*. Perhaps our smallest grass, low, 2-15cm. Spikelets one-flowered, in one-sided stalked spikes on thread-like stems; February-May. Leaves often greyish. Dunes and sandy ground by the sea, rare away from Anglesey.

(ii) Spikelets awned

12 Crested Dogstail *Cynosurus cristatus*. One of our commoner grasses, medium, to 60cm. Spikelets shortly awned, in a one-sided stalked spike; June-August. Meadows, pastures. Widespread.

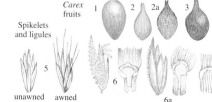

Carex fruits

Spikelets and ligules

unawned   awned

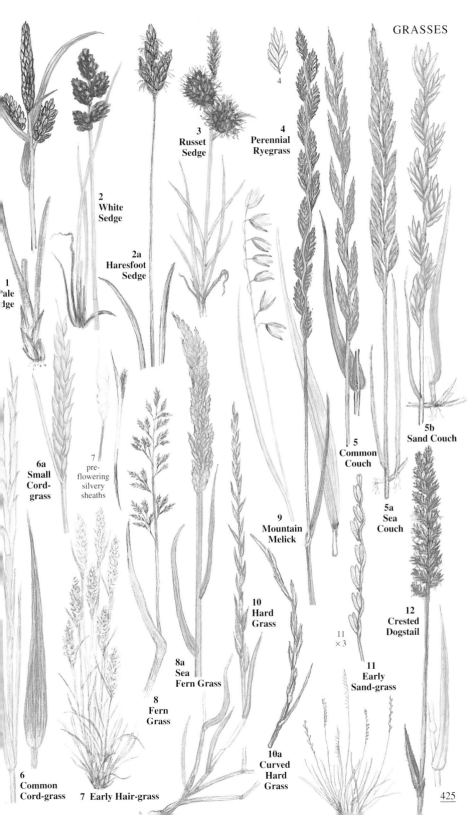

GRASSES

1 Pale Sedge

2 White Sedge

2a Haresfoot Sedge

3 Russet Sedge

4 Perennial Ryegrass

5 Common Couch

5a Sea Couch

5b Sand Couch

6 Common Cord-grass

6a Small Cord-grass

7 pre-flowering silvery sheaths

7 Early Hair-grass

8 Fern Grass

8a Sea Fern Grass

9 Mountain Melick

10 Hard Grass

10a Curved Hard Grass

11 Early Sand-grass

11 × 3

12 Crested Dogstail

425

1 Italian Ryegrass *Lolium multiflorum*. Like Perennial Ryegrass (p. 424) but with awned spikelets; June-July. Widespread, now less frequent than formerly.

2 False Brome *Brachypodium sylvaticum*. A common woodland grass, medium/tall, to 1m. Spikelets stalked, multi-flowered, long-awned to 15mm, in a nodding spike; July-August. Leaves green to yellowish-green, drooping, with their sheaths usually hairy. Cf. Bearded Couch (**4**). Woods, scrub, hedge-banks. Widespread and abundant.

3 Tor Grass *Brachypodium rupestre*. Aggressively patch-forming, medium/tall, stems stiff, to 1.2m. Spikelets stalked, long, short-awned, in an erect spike; June-August. Leaves yellowish-green, often inrolled, the sheaths usually hairless. Grassland on lime. **3a Drooping Tor Grass** *B. pinnatum* is much more downy, has spike slightly drooping and likes shadier habitats, often on clay.

4 Bearded Couch *Elymus caninus*. Medium/tall, to 1.1m, usually downy at the leaf-junctions. Spike slightly nodding, spikelets solitary, unstalked alternating up the stem, very long-awned, to 18mm, glumes narrowly pale-edged; June-August. Cf. False Brome (**2**). Woods, hedge-banks, shady rocks. **Common Couch** and **Sea Couch** (p. 424) may have awned spikelets.

5 Mat Grass *Nardus stricta*. Low, to 20cm. Spike one-sided, the spikelets one-flowered, the lemmas shortly awned; June-August. Leaves greyish, wiry. Heaths, moors, mountains, on very infertile soils.

6 *Mat-grass Fescue *Vulpia unilateralis*. Low/short, to 20cm. Spike tight, the spikelets stalked, short-awned, the lower glume more than half as long as the upper; May-June. Chalk grassland, including anthills, railway tracks, spoilheaps and other bare ground. Other *Vulpia*, see p. 416.

7 French Oat *Gaudinia fragilis*. Medium/tall, to 1.2m. Spike rather long, to 35cm, spikelets solitary, alternating up the stem, with a short *bent* awn; May-July. Leaves downy with downy sheaths. Grassy and bare places, hedge-banks.

4b. Flowers in erect *slender* spikes: Sedges

8 Spring Sedge *Carex caryophyllea*. Low, to 30cm. Glumes red-brown, the female with a short green awn and the lowest bract usually shorter than its spike; *April*-May. Leaves *c.* 2mm, dark green. Fruits green, downy. (**8c**). Dry grassland, mainly on lime; also in mountain flushes. The slightly taller **8a *Heath Sedge** *C. ericetorum* has pale-edged purple-brown glumes, the female awnless, leaves 2-4mm and a very short lowest bract. Also on heaths, not on mountains. The shorter **8b Dwarf Sedge** *C. humilis* is the earliest Sedge to flower, *March*-April, with pale green, often curved leaves, much longer than the stems. Limy grassland. **8c Pill Sedge** *Carex pilulifera* differs from Spring Sedge in having stems often curved, the female glumes unawned, the lowest bract longer than its spike, flowering May-June, the leaves paler green, and especially in growing on acid soils. The taller and more tufted **8d *Soft-leaved Sedge** *C. montana* has female glumes and fruits blackish and softly hairy leaves turning yellow with bright red basal sheaths. Often on lime.

9 Remote Sedge *Carex remota*. Short/medium, to 60cm. Flowerheads with short spikes well separated up the stem, with very long leaf-like bracts. Leaves narrow, pale green. Moist woods and shady places.

10 Spiked Sedge *Carex spicata*. Medium, to 1m, the basal sheaths tinged purple. Flowerheads greenish/brownish, 2-3cm, the glumes awned. Leaves with long pointed ligules and bases and bracts often tinged wine-red. Fruits narrowing gradually to the beak. Grassy places, mainly on lime. **10a Prickly Sedge** *C. muricata* has no red or purple tinge, shorter, blunter ligules and fruit narrowing more abruptly to the beak.

11 Grey Sedge *Carex divulsa*. Medium, to 75cm. Flowerhead with short spikes widely scattered up to 15cm along the stem. Leaves with broad blunt ligules. Fruit blackish or red-brown, fairly abruptly narrowed to the beak.

Carex fruits × 2

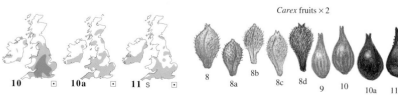

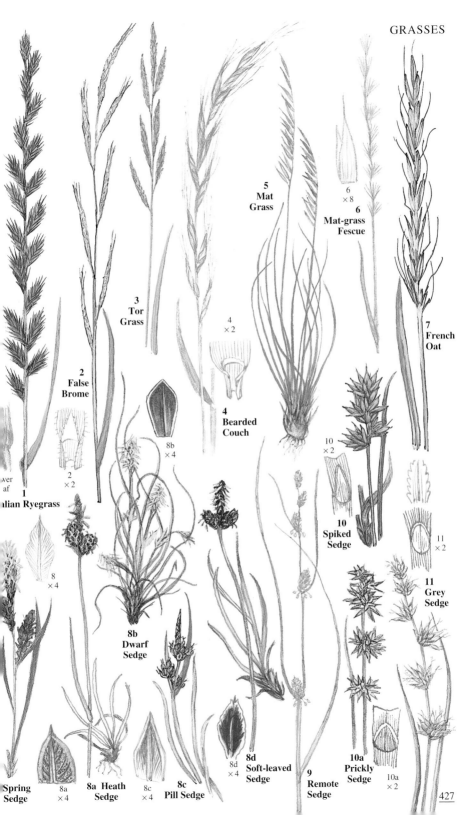

GRASSES

1
Italian Ryegrass

flower
leaf

2
False Brome

2
×2

3
Tor Grass

4
Bearded Couch

4
×2

5
Mat Grass

6
×8

6
Mat-grass Fescue

7
French Oat

8b
×4

8b
Dwarf Sedge

8a
×4

8
×4

8a Heath Sedge

8c
×4

8c
Pill Sedge

8d
×4

8d
Soft-leaved Sedge

9
Remote Sedge

Spring Sedge

10
×2

10
Spiked Sedge

10a
Prickly Sedge

10a
×2

11
×2

11
Grey Sedge

427

1 Star Sedge *Carex echinata*. Short, to 40cm. Flower-spikes short, distinctly separated, greenish/red-brown; the glumes spreading star-like in fruit. Leaves narrow. Wet heaths, marshes, bogs, on acid soils.

2 ***Starved Wood Sedge *Carex depauperata*. Medium, to 1m. Flowerhead with one slender male spike above 3-6 short females at intervals down the stem; bracts very long, leaf-like. Leaves green/yellow-green. Dry open woods and scrub, often on lime; Somerset and Surrey only.

3 Flat Sedge *Blysmus compressus*. Low/medium, to 45cm. Spikelets in a flattened spike, glumes tinged yellow or red; June-July. Leaves roughish. Fruit dark brown, shiny, with long brown bristles. Inland marshes and damp grassland, bare ground by the sea. **3a Salt-marsh Flat Sedge** *B. rufus* has smaller heads, leaves smooth with inrolled margins and fruit yellowish, sometimes with shorter white bristles. Coastal saltmarshes.

5a. Flowers in catkin-like spikes: Grasses, erect

4 Bermuda Grass *Cynodon dactylon*. Short, creeping, to 30cm. Spikes 2-5cm, 3-6 in a fan, spikelets one-flowered, purplish, unawned; July-Sept. Ligule a ring of hairs. Bare, often sandy, ground, usually near the sea. Two species of **Finger-grass** *Digitaria* with spikelets 2-flowered and normal ligules are also locally frequent or established: **4a Hairy Finger-grass** *D. sanguinalis*, taller, to 60cm, with 4-16 spikes to 20cm, and leaf-sheaths hairy; and **4b Smooth Finger-grass** *D. ischaemum*, to 40cm, with 2-8 spikes to 8cm, *not fanlike*, and sheaths hairless.

5b. Flowers in catkin-like spikes: Sedges

Male catkins slenderer and always above females.

(i) Erect

5 Hairy Sedge *Carex hirta*. Easily identified by its hairy leaves. Short/medium, to 70cm. Female catkins greenish with long bracts, well spaced out. Fruits green, hairy. Grassy places.

6 Carnation Sedge *Carex panicea*. Not unlike Glaucous Sedge (p. 430), but has only a single male catkin, markedly shorter female catkins and leaves glaucous on both sides. Damp or wet places on moors and in mires. **6a *Sheathed Sedge** *C. vaginata* has warm brown female glumes and green/yellow-green leaves. Wet ledges and grassland on mountains.

7 Green-ribbed Sedge *Carex binervis*. Short/tall, to 1.5m. One male catkin above several females spaced out down stem, glumes purple-brown, upper bracts short. Leaves dark green, often blotched reddish; ligules very short. Fruit purple-brown with two green ribs. Drier moors, heath, grassland, on acid soils. **7a Tawny Sedge** *Carex hostiana* has shorter catkins and yellowish-green leaves 3-sided at the top. Damper places. **7b Distant Sedge** *C. distans* has catkins at top of stem at first but well spaced out in fruit, glumes red-brown, leaves greyish and fruits green, not ribbed. Mostly by the sea, marshes inland. **7c Dotted Sedge** *C. punctata* has red-brown glumes, at least one bract overtopping the male catkin, short pointed ligules and pale green fruits, dotted red-brown and markedly ribbed, looking spiky when ripe. By the sea.

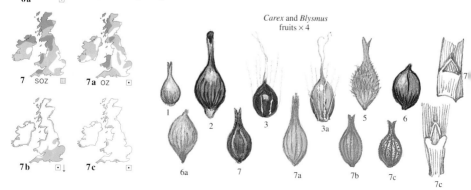

Carex and *Blysmus*
fruits × 4

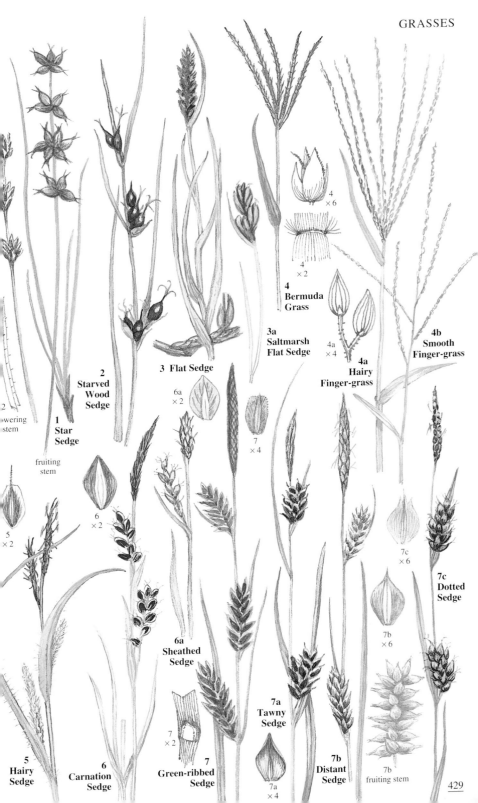

4
×6

4
×2

4 Bermuda Grass

3a Saltmarsh Flat Sedge

4a
×4

4a Hairy Finger-grass

4b Smooth Finger-grass

3 Flat Sedge

6a
×2

7
×4

2 Starved Wood Sedge

1 Star Sedge

flowering stem

fruiting stem

5
×2

6
×2

7c
×6

7c Dotted Sedge

6a Sheathed Sedge

7b
×6

7
×2

7 Green-ribbed Sedge

6 Carnation Sedge

5 Hairy Sedge

7a Tawny Sedge

7a
×4

7b Distant Sedge

7b
fruiting stem

1 Common Sedge *Carex nigra*. Short/medium, sometimes forming small tussocks, to 70cm. Female catkins overlapping, the glumes blackish, styles 2; lowest bract usually about equalling the whole spike. Leaves glaucous. Fruits usually partly blackish. Marshes, dune slacks and other wet grassy places. **1a Tufted Sedge** *C. elata*, forms much larger tussocks, the stems medium/tall, to 1m. Lowest bract much shorter than the whole spike. Fruits greyish, often partly reddish. Fens, swamps, in and by fresh water. **1b Stiff Sedge** *C. bigelowii* is low/short, with stiff, sharply 3-sided stems to 30cm, female glumes purple-black with a short lowest bract and fruits green, usually tinged purple-black. Rather bare places on mountains.

2 Slender Tufted Sedge *Carex acuta*. Tall, stems sharply 3-sided, to 1.2m. Female glumes blackish-brown, usually pointed, *2-styled*, cf. the 3-styled Pond Sedges (**8, 8a**); the lowest bract overtopping the male catkins. Leaves glaucous. Fruits green. Marshes, by fresh water. **2a Water Sedge** *C. aquatilis* has bluntly 3-sided stems, female glumes blunt, and leaves glaucous above, bright green beneath. Also on mountains, much smaller, with brown fruits. **2b **Estuarine Sedge** *C. recta* has flat-faced stems, female glumes with a minute point, and yellowish-green leaves. Far N Scotland.

3 Bottle Sedge *Carex rostrata*. Tall, extensively patch-forming, stems bluntly 3-sided, to 1m. Female glumes purple-brown, bluntly pointed. Leaves greyish above, sometimes in-rolled, ligules short, blunt. Fruits roundish. Cf. Bladder Sedge (**9**). Swamps, in and by lakes, on acid soils.

4 Smooth-stalked Sedge *Carex laevigata*. Tall, stems sharply 3-sided, to 1.2cm. Glumes brown, the lowest bract shorter than the top male catkin. Leaves green with long ligules. Fruits reddish-green or green with reddish dots. Damp woods. **4a Slender Sedge** *C. lasio-carpa* has more purplish glumes, the lowest bract longer than the top male catkin, leaves greyish and inrolled with short blunt ligules, and greyish downy fruits. Reedswamps and other very wet places.

5 Thin-spiked Wood Sedge *Carex strigosa*. Not unlike the much commoner Wood Sedge (p. 432), but has very much shorter catkin-stalks, green female glumes, broader leaves with pointed ligules and much shorter-beaked fruits. Damp spots in woods, often on lime.

6 Fingered Sedge *Carex digitata*. Low, to 30cm. Flowerhead with 2-3 finger-like red-brown female spikes overtopping the thin male one; *April*-May. Leaves narrow, often sparsely hairy, with purplish basal sheaths. Fruit pale brown. Dry, often rocky grassland, mainly on lime. The smaller **6a Birdsfoot Sedge** *C. ornithopoda* has shorter, more spreading flower-spikes, supposedly like a bird's foot, and hairless leaves; May-June.

(ii) Erect or drooping

7 Glaucous Sedge *Carex flacca*. Short/medium, stems bluntly 3-sided, to 60cm. Male catkins usually 2-3; female glumes broadly blunt, purple-brown; *April*-May. Leaves con-spicuously glaucous beneath. Cf. Carnation Sedge (p. 428). Much the commonest sedge of grassland on lime, also in fens and dune slacks.

8 Greater Pond Sedge *Carex riparia*. Tall, patch-forming, stems sharply 3-sided, to 1.3m. Mature catkins often drooping; male glumes dark brown, sharply pointed. Leaves broad, 6-15mm, glaucous when young. Fruits gradually narrowed to the beak; cf. 2-styled Slender Tufted Sedge (**2**). Wet meadows, swamps, by fresh water. **8a Lesser Pond Sedge** *C. acutiformis* has the male glumes bluntly pointed, leaves to 10mm and fruits abruptly narrowed to the beak.

9 Bladder Sedge *Carex vesicaria*. Not unlike Bottle Sedge (**3**) but has stems sharply 3-sided, female glumes long and pointed, and fruits more elongated.

1b
base of plant

Carex fruits
×2

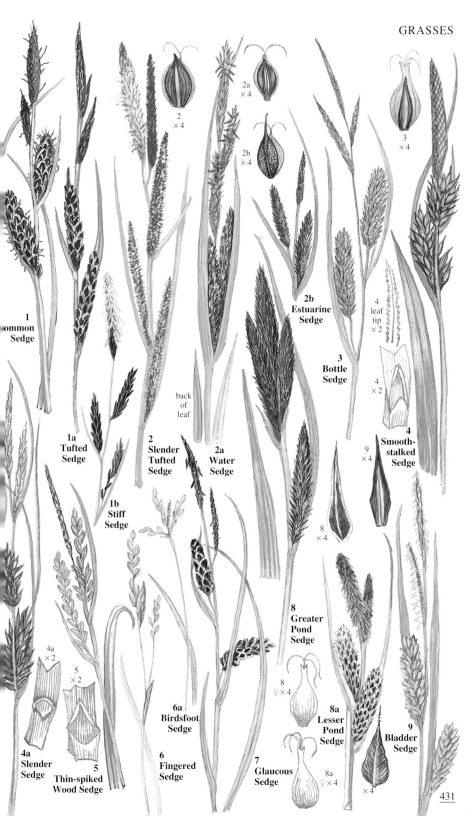

1 Common Sedge

1a Tufted Sedge

1b Stiff Sedge

2 ×4

2a ×4

2b ×4

2b Estuarine Sedge

2 Slender Tufted Sedge

2a Water Sedge

3 ×4

3 Bottle Sedge

4 leaf tip ×2

4 ×2

4 Smooth-stalked Sedge

back of leaf

4a ×2

5 ×2

4a Slender Sedge

5 Thin-spiked Wood Sedge

6a Birdsfoot Sedge

6 Fingered Sedge

7 Glaucous Sedge

8 Greater Pond Sedge

8 ♀ ×4

8a Lesser Pond Sedge

8a ♀ ×4

9 ×4

8 ×4

9 Bladder Sedge

×4

(iii) Drooping

1 Wood Sedge *Carex sylvatica.* Short/medium, to 60cm. Female catkins long-stalked, the glumes usually pale yellow. Leaves to 6mm wide, shiny, green/yellowish-green; ligules blunt. Fruit long-beaked. Cf. Thin-spiked Wood Sedge (p. 430). The commonest woodland sedge.

2 Pendulous Sedge *Carex pendula.* Tall, clump-forming, with bluntly 3-sided stems to 2m or more. Catkins conspicuously drooping. Leaves to 2cm wide, green/yellowish-green above, glaucous beneath. Damp woods and stream-sides, especially on clayey soils.

3 Hop Sedge *Carex pseudocyperus.* Stems medium/tall, sharply 3-sided, to 90cm. Female spikes stout, pale green, markedly drooping, the glumes long-awned. Leaves yellow-green, taller than stems. Fruits gradually narrowed to the beak. In and by fresh water, swamps.

4 *Hair Sedge *Carex capillaris.* Short, slender, to 40cm. Female catkins very short, on long hair-like stalks. Leaves very narrow, greyish. Fruit scarcely beaked. Wet places on hillsides, often on lime, occasionally in bogs.

6a. Flowers in clusters of tight roundish/egg-shaped heads: Grasses

5 Cocksfoot *Dactylis glomerata.* Perhaps the most distinctive of all our grasses, medium/tall, to 80cm. Spikelets shortly awned, in long-stalked oval heads, visible throughout mild winters, but anthers only late April-Nov. Leaves stout, flat, with long ligules, in tufts easily recognisable in winter. Very common, grassy places.

6b. Flowers in clusters of tight roundish/egg-shaped heads: Sedges

6 Yellow Sedge *Carex viridula.* Very variable, short/medium, stems 3-sided, to 75cm. Female heads rounded, mostly clustered at the top, but the lowest often well down the stem, the glumes brown, often tinged yellow or orange; lowest bract usually longer than the usually single erect male catkin. Leaves sometimes recurved. Fruits yellowish, usually abruptly narrowed to the beak, the lower usually down-turned when ripe. Damp and wet places, fens, bogs, dune slacks, on heaths, moors and mountains, on both acid and limy soils. **6a ***Large Yellow Sedge** *C. flava* has orange-brown female glumes, broader, bright yellow-green leaves and larger, yellower fruits; Roudsea Wood, Cumbria, only.

7 Oval Sedge *Carex ovalis.* Stems short, to 60cm, often curved. Flowerhead pale/reddish brown, compact. Leaves narrow, rough-edged. Heaths, moors, damp grassland, open woods, on acid soils. **7a Divided Sedge** *C. divisa* has smaller clusters with purple-brown glumes, usually with a long bract. Damp grassy places, often near the sea. **7b ***String Sedge** *C. chordorrhiza* is far-creeping with still shorter clusters and yellowish fruits. Three Highland bogs.

8 Long-bracted Sedge *Carex extensa.* Short, to 40cm. Female heads usually clustered at the top, but often one down the stem, glumes red-brown; the bracts very long, often spreading or curved downwards. Leaves greyish. Fruits grey-green or brown. By the sea, especially saltmarshes.

9 **Downy-fruited Sedge *Carex filiformis.* Short/medium, stems creeping, to 50cm. Male and female heads both 1-2, the female, mostly unstalked, slightly apart, glumes purple-brown. Leaves glaucous. Fruits green, downy. Damp or dry limy grassland.

10 Bog Sedge *Carex limosa.* Short, stems sharply 3-sided, to 40cm. Female heads long-stalked, drooping, the glumes reddish-brown; the lowest bract not longer than the male spike. Leaves glaucous. Fruits glaucous, abruptly narrowed to a very short beak. Wet bogs, peaty lake shores. **10a *Tall Bog Sedge** *C. magellanica* has bluntly 3-sided stems, the lowest bract usually longer than the male spike, pale green leaves, and blue-green fruits gradually narrowed to the beak and broader than their glume. Upland bogs with running water, valley mires. **10b **Mountain Bog Sedge** *C. rariflora* is shorter than Tall Bog Sedge (**10a**) with the lowest bract shorter than the male spike and fruits ribbed, scarcely beaked and not broader than their glume. Wet peaty mountain slopes, often with White (p. 424) and Water (p. 430) Sedges.

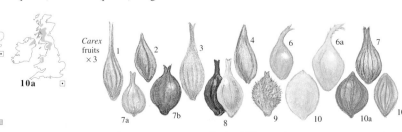

Carex fruits × 3

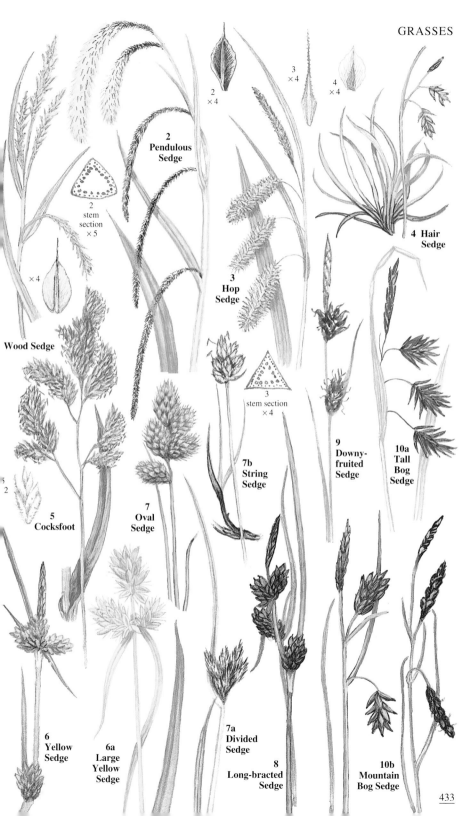

2
Pendulous
Sedge

2
× 4

3
× 4

4
× 4

2
stem
section
× 5

× 4

3
Hop
Sedge

4 Hair
Sedge

Wood Sedge

3
stem section
× 4

7b
String
Sedge

9
Downy-
fruited
Sedge

10a
Tall
Bog
Sedge

5
2

5
Cocksfoot

7
Oval
Sedge

6
Yellow
Sedge

6a
Large
Yellow
Sedge

7a
Divided
Sedge

8
Long-bracted
Sedge

10b
Mountain
Bog Sedge

1 *Black Alpine Sedge *Carex atrata*. Short/medium, to 60cm. Heads blackish, egg-shaped, slightly nodding, more or less clustered at the top of the sharply 3-sided stem. Leaves glaucous or pale green. Fruits yellowish, often marked purple, gradually narrowed to the beak. Grassy places, rocks, mainly on mountains. **1a **Scorched Alpine Sedge** *C. atrofusca* has stems bluntly 3-sided, heads more obviously nodding, glumes more purplish, leaves mid-green and fruits dark purple, abruptly narrowed to the beak. Stony flushes on mountains.

2 **Close-headed Alpine Sedge *Carex norvegica*. Medium, stems sharply 3-sided, to 60cm. Heads closely clustered at top of stem, glumes purplish-black. Leaves green. Fruits greenish-to greyish-brown, blackish at tip. Wet ledges and rocky slopes on mountains. **2a ***Club Sedge** *Carex buxbaumii* has heads more spread out, the top one club-shaped, glumes red-brown, leaves glaucous with inrolled margins and green fruits. Two Highland fens.

Cotton-grasses *Eriophorum*. The bright yellow anthers of the flowers in April-May are strikingly different from the long white cottony hairs of the fruiting heads in May-July. Short/medium, stems 3-sided, rough (smooth in Common Cotton-grass), to 75cm. Spikelets in drooping clusters, except Harestail Cotton-grass (p. 436), with long rough stalks (short and smooth in Common Cotton-grass). Aka Bog Cotton. Bogs, wet peat, on acid soils, except Broad-leaved Cotton-grass. **3 Common Cotton-grass** *Eriophorum angustifolium*, much the commonest, often whitening the ground, has stems 3-sided only at the top, and 3-5mm leaves, with a long 3-sided tip and a short ligule. **3a Broad-leaved Cotton-grass** *E. latifolium* has spikelets with rough 3-sided stalks, and 3-8mm leaves with a short 3-sided tip and no ligule. Fens and other wet peat on lime. **3b **Slender Cotton-grass** *E. gracile* has very narrow, 1-2mm leaves with a short ligule.

4 Sea Club-rush *Bolboschoenus maritimus*. Medium/tall, stems sharply 3-sided, to 1.2m. Spikelets egg-shaped, unstalked, brown with red-brown glumes, with leaf-like bracts much longer than the flowerhead; June-August. Leaves keeled, often rough-edged. Brackish water, usually near the sea, rarely in fresh water, as at Brent Reservoir, NW London.

5 **Round-headed Club-rush *Scirpoides holoschoenus*. Medium/tall, stems rounded, to 1.5m. Spikelets pale brown, in long-stalked *globular* heads with a very long leaflike bract at the base of the cluster; June-Sept. Leaves short, strap-like, near the base. Damp sand by the sea, especially Braunton Burrows, N Devon.

6c. Flowers in clusters of tight roundish/egg-shaped heads: Rushes

6 Three-leaved Rush *Juncus trifidus*. Low/medium, with tufts of slender stems, to 40cm. Flowers dark brown, in small heads, each with 2-3 very long bracts; June-August. Leaves rather short, in a basal tuft. Fruits shortly beaked. Bare places on mountains.

6d. Flowers in clusters of tight roundish/egg-shaped heads: Wood-rushes

Tufted; leaves with long white hairs.

7 Field Wood-rush *Luzula campestris*. Low/short, with short runners, to 30cm. Heads in a close cluster, warm brown with conspicuous bright yellow anthers, much longer than their stalks; *April*-May. Fruit globular, brown, shorter than petals. Grassland, avoiding acid soils. Widespread. **7a Congested Wood-rush** *L. congesta* is taller with no runners and has a much tighter cluster; May-June. Peaty soils; distribution not fully known. Cf. Heath Wood-rush, p. 418.

8 Spiked Wood-rush *Luzula spicata*. Low, to 25cm. Heads in an elongated cluster, chestnut-brown; June-July. Leaves grooved, slightly curved. Fruits dark brown. Rocky and stony places on mountains.

9 Curved Wood-rush *Luzula arcuata*. Low/short, tufted, to 25cm. Heads mostly on drooping stalks, flowers warm brown; June-July. Leaves grooved, sometimes hairless and slightly curved. Fruits brown. Wet stony places on mountains.

1   1a   2   2a

4   6   7   8   9

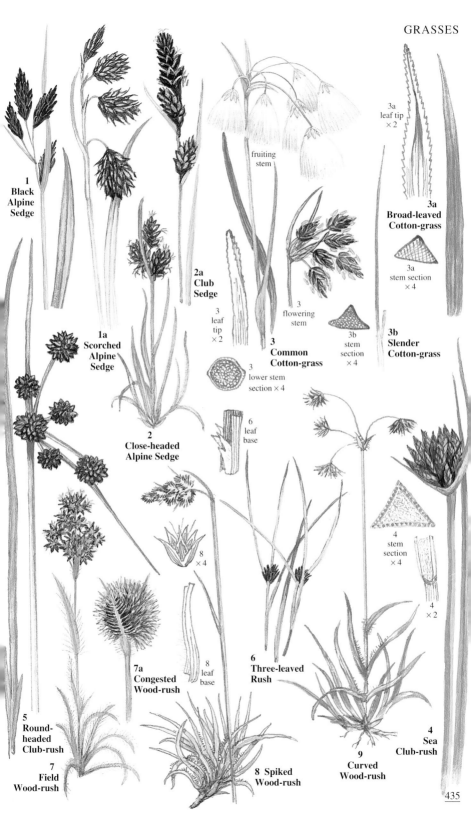

1 Black Alpine Sedge

1a Scorched Alpine Sedge

2 Close-headed Alpine Sedge

2a Club Sedge

3 leaf tip × 2

3 flowering stem

fruiting stem

3 Common Cotton-grass

3 lower stem section × 4

3a leaf tip × 2

3a Broad-leaved Cotton-grass

3a stem section × 4

3b stem section × 4

3b Slender Cotton-grass

6 leaf base

5 Round-headed Club-rush

7 Field Wood-rush

7a Congested Wood-rush

8 × 4

8 leaf base

8 Spiked Wood-rush

6 Three-leaved Rush

4 stem section × 4

4 × 2

4 Sea Club-rush

9 Curved Wood-rush

1 Blue Moor-grass *Sesleria caerulea*. Short/medium, to 45cm. Spikelets bluish-purple to greenish-white, minutely awned, in a tight, more or less ovoid, head; April-June. Leaves green/greyish. Limestone grassland.

2 Harestail Grass *Lagurus ovatus*. Short/medium, to 50cm. Spikelets in a very distinctive soft white woolly oval head, with long white bent awns; June-August. Leaves with inflated sheaths. Bare ground by the sea, waste ground inland; introduced.

3 Canary Grass *Phalaris canariensis*. Short/medium, to 1.2m. Spikelets on an egg-shaped head, 2-3-flowered, unawned; June-Sept. The most frequent of several alien grasses found in places where wild birds are fed, and on rubbish dumps.

4 Alpine Catstail *Phleum alpinum*. Short, to 50cm. Spike egg-shaped, usually purplish, the blunt glumes shortly awned and the lemmas unawned; July-August. Cf. Alpine Foxtail (**5**). Wet places on mountains.

5 Alpine Foxtail *Alopecurus borealis*. Short, to 30cm. Spike egg-shaped, the glumes pointed and unawned and lemmas with or without a short awn; June-August. Wet places on mountains.

6 Curved Sedge *Carex maritima*. Low, far-creeping, to 20cm. Flowerhead almost globular, female glumes dark brown. Leaves very narrow, often well curved. Fruit blackish-brown, gone by late July.

7 Black Bog-rush *Schoenus nigricans*. Medium, to 60cm. Spikelets blackish-brown, the lower bract longer than the head; May-July. Leaves 1-2mm, with inrolled margins, greyish with sheaths blackish. Fens, bogs, dune slacks, usually on lime. **7a ***Brown Bog-rush** *S. ferrugineus* has brown spikelets, the lower bract equalling the narrower head; June-July. Leaf-sheaths red-brown. Flushes, wet peat, Perthshire.

8 White Beak-sedge *Rhynchospora alba*. Short, to 40cm. Spikelets *whitish* to pale brown, in a flattish cluster; June-Sept. Leaves 1-2mm, often with bulbils at the base. Bogs, moors, wet heaths on acid soils.

9 Brown Beak-sedge *Rhynchospora fusca*. Short, to 40cm. Spikelets red-brown, the upper bract much longer than the head; May-July. Leaves thread-like. Bog pools, wet heaths, on acid soils.

10 Harestail Cotton-grass *Eriophorum vaginatum*. The only cottongrass (p. 434) with a single, erect head. Acid soils.

11 Bristle Club-rush *Isolepis setacea*. Low/short, tufted, to 30cm. Spikelets 1-4 in an egg-shaped head, purple-brown, at the top of the leafless stem with with a pin-like bract beyond it; May-July. Leaves thread-like, paired at the stem-base. Ripe nut blackish. Damp sandy places, often by fresh water. **11a Slender Club-rush** *I. cernua* has the bract equalling or shorter than the usually solitary spikelet, with green or whitish glumes and a red-brown nut. Usually coastal.

12 Floating Club-rush *Eleogiton fluitans*. Easily confused with Pondweeds (p. 354). Stems floating, to 50cm or more. Leaves very narrow, flat, fresh green, in tufts up the stem, usually submerged. Flowers in a single long-stalked *aerial* spikelet (see p. 402) and lacking the sepal-like petals of Pondweeds; May-July. Still and slow-moving, usually acid, fresh water.

13 Soft Rush *Juncus effusus*. One of our two commonest rushes. Medium/tall, tufted, to l.5cm. Stems smooth or faintly ridged. Flowers greenish-brown, in a tight or sometimes rather looser head near the top of the leafless stem, which has continuous pith; June-July. Fruits brown, egg-shaped, usually shorter than the tepals. Damp, usually grassy and especially overgrazed places. Widespread. **13a Compact Rush** *J. conglomeratus* usually has tight clusters, but sometimes looser, differing especially in its conspicuously ridged stems, darker brown flowers and fruits as long as tepals, also in avoiding limy soils.

| 11 soz ■ | 11a s ■ | 12 oz ■ | 13 soz ■ | 13a oz ■ |

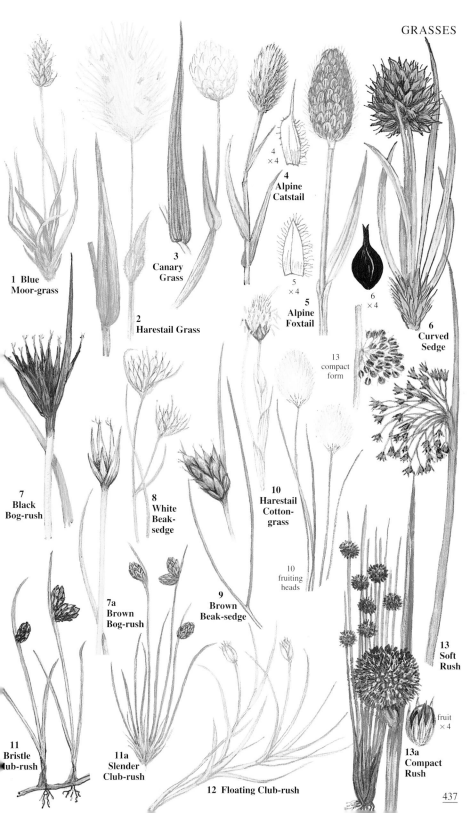

1 Blue Moor-grass

2 Harestail Grass

3 Canary Grass

4 Alpine Catstail

4 ×4

5 ×4

5 Alpine Foxtail

6 ×4

6 Curved Sedge

7 Black Bog-rush

7a Brown Bog-rush

8 White Beak-sedge

9 Brown Beak-sedge

10 Harestail Cotton-grass

10 fruiting heads

11 Bristle Club-rush

11a Slender Club-rush

12 Floating Club-rush

13 compact form

13 Soft Rush

13a Compact Rush

fruit ×4

1 Chestnut Rush *Juncus castaneus*. Low/short, to 30cm. Flowers blackish- to chestnut-brown in a tight cluster of 1-3 heads; June-July. Leaves almost all basal. Fruits red-brown, glossy. Wet places on mountains.

2 **Dwarf Rush *Juncus capitatus*. Low tufted annual. Flowers in a tight cluster of 1-4, greenish becoming red-brown, the inner ones colourless; two unequal bracts, one much longer than the flowerhead; April-June. Fruit much shorter than tepals, whose tips curve downwards. Leaves all basal, very narrow. Damp bare heaths. Lizard and Anglesey only. **2a **Pygmy Rush** *J. pygmaeus* has prominent pointed auricles, sometimes one stem-leaf, both bracts shorter than the flowerhead, which may have up to 15 all-greenish flowers, May-June, (cf. a small starved Toad Rush, p. 412), and tepals spreading in fruit. Whole plant may turn pinkish-red. Lizard only, especially on old cart tracks.

3 Three-flowered Rush *Juncus triglumis*. Low/short, stem with one leaf, to 20cm. Flowers pale brown or yellowish, 3 in a head, with bracts shorter than the head; June-July. Leaves thread-like, basal. Fruits pointed. Wet acid places on mountains. **3a *Two-flowered Rush** *J. biglumis* has leafless stems, the head with 2 flowers and shorter than its bract, and blunt fruits. Prefers limy soils.

8. Flowers in solitary elongated heads: Sedges

Spike-rushes *Eleocharis*. Low/medium, more or less tufted, mostly to 30cm, with usually brownish sheaths on the completely leafless stems, cf. Deergrass (**5**). Sheaths truncated evenly in Common, Slender and Needle, obliquely in Many-stalked, Few-flowered and Dwarf. Spikelets pointed, usually brown, single, at the top of the stem, the lowest glume(s) barren (except sometimes Few-flowered and Needle) and encircling the base. **4 Common Spike-rush** *Eleocharis palustris* agg., much the commonest, has stems to 75cm, the top sheath yellowish, the lower reddish, the two lowest glumes each half-encircling the spikelet base; May-August. Marshes, wet grassland, shallow fresh water. Incl. *E. austriaca*. **4a Many-stalked Spike-rush** *E. multicaulis* has the top sheath pointed, the lower sheaths yellowish, the florets often viviparous (see p. 404), the lowest glume usually *c*.1/4 as long as the spikelet; June-August. Wet heaths, bog pools, on acid soils. **4b Few-flowered Spike-rush** *E. quinqueflora* has the lowest glume more than half as long as the spikelet; June-July. Bare places in fens and marshes. The three less frequent species are: **4c Slender Spike-rush** *E. uniglumis*, to 60cm, with the lower sheaths purplish-red; lowest glumes like Common Spike-rush (**4**); May-August; marshes, sometimes brackish; **4d Needle Spike-rush** *E. acicularis*, with 4-angled stems, the lowest glume less than half as long as the spikelet; June-Oct; shallow water, often submerged, and nearby mud; and **4e **Dwarf Spike-rush** *E. parvula* with roots ending in whitish tubers, stems thread-like, sometimes barren, to 8cm; and spikelets green; August-Sept; tidal mud.

5 Deergrass *Trichophorum cespitosum*. Low/short, tussock-forming, stems rounded, to 35cm, leafless except for a single short strap; cf. the Spike-rushes (above). Spikelet egg-shaped, solitary at the top of the stem; glumes red-brown to yellowish; May-June. Acid heaths, moors and bogs, often abundant.

6 Dioecious Sedge *Carex dioica*. Short, stems rounded, creeping, to 40cm. Distinctive in having male and shorter, stouter female flowers on separate plants; glumes red-brown. Leaves very narrow. Fruits red-brown, abruptly narrowing to a short beak. Marshes on lime.

7 Flea Sedge *Carex pulicaris*. Short, stems rounded, to 30cm. Flower-spike 10-25mm, glumes red-brown. Leaves very narrow. Fruits dark brown, shiny, down-turned after glumes have fallen. Fens, flushes, on lime. **7a Few-flowered Sedge** *C. pauciflora* has bluntly 3-sided stems, flower-spike 3-8mm and straw-yellow fruits. Bogs. **7b **Bristle Sedge** *C. microglochin* differs from Few-flowered Sedge (**7a**) in its rounded stems, the bristle on its fruit and its habitat in flushes high on mountains.

8 *Rock Sedge *Carex rupestris*. Low, stems bluntly 3-sided, to 20cm. Female glumes red-brown, pale-edged with a short bristle; a shy flowerer. Leaves curly, very narrow. Fruits greenish-brown. Bare ground and ledges on high mountains.

9 False Sedge *Kobresia simpliciuscula*. Low, stems stiff, 3-sided, to 20cm. Spikelets red-brown, 1-flowered, in an elongated head, male above female; June-July. Leaves thread-like, grooved, the sheaths warm brown. Damp, often bare places on lime in the hills.

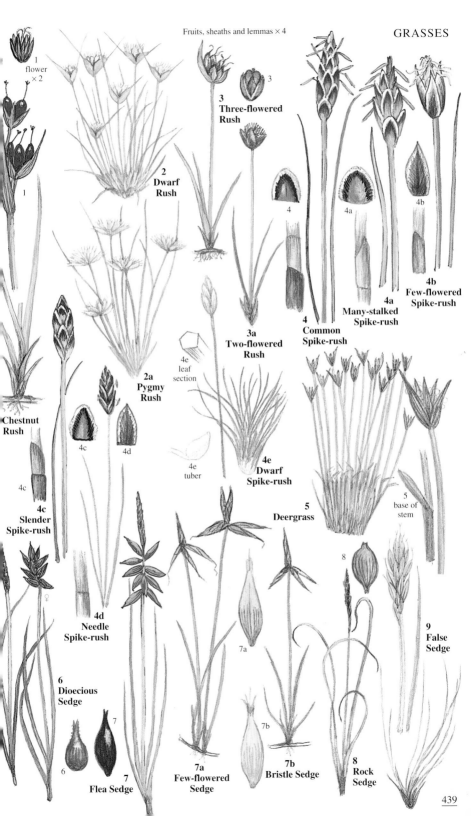

Fruits, sheaths and lemmas × 4

1
flower
× 2

1

2 Dwarf Rush

3 Three-flowered Rush

3

3a Two-flowered Rush

4

4 Common Spike-rush

4a

4a Many-stalked Spike-rush

4b

4b Few-flowered Spike-rush

Chestnut Rush

4c

4d

2a Pygmy Rush

4c

4c Slender Spike-rush

4e leaf section

4e tuber

4e Dwarf Spike-rush

5 Deergrass

5 base of stem

8

4d Needle Spike-rush

♀

6 Dioecious Sedge

6

7

7a

7b

9 False Sedge

7 Flea Sedge

7a Few-flowered Sedge

7b Bristle Sedge

8 Rock Sedge

Our **Ferns** (Pteropsida) are almost all perennials, with hairy or scaly stems and usually well divided leaves (fronds), Instead of flowers they have spores, carried in spore-cases (sporangia) beneath the leaves and usually covered by an indusium. The exceptions, whose spore-cases are borne separately in spikes like flowering plants, are Royal Fern (p. 446) and Sensitive Fern (p. 450) together with the annual adderstongues (below) and Moonwort (below). Lime-loving species may occur in acid districts on lime-mortar in walls. Ferns are here arranged by their leaf-shape.

(i) Leaves undivided

1 Hartstongue *Phyllitis scolopendrium*. Our only fern with tufts of evergreen *strap-shaped* leaves, 10-60cm long and 3-6cm across. Spore-cases in diagonal rows, the spores ripening August-March. Rocks, walls, woods, hedge-banks. Widespread, but commonest in the W.

Adderstongues *Ophioglossum*. Annuals with single leaves near the stem-base and spore-cases in a green plantain-like spike. barren shoots frequent. **2 Adderstongue** *Ophioglossum vulgatum*. Stems *single*, short, to 30cm. Leaves May-Nov; spores ripe June-August. Grassy places, dune slacks, on lime. Widespread in the S. **2a *Small Adderstongue** *O. azoricum* has stems shorter, to 8cm, and *2-3 together*, leaves narrower May-Sept and spores ripening July-August. Much less frequent, coastal short turf and bare ground, especially on islands in the W. **2b ***Least Adderstongue** *O. lusitanicum* is smaller still (search for on hands and knees) with tiny strap-like leaves less than 1cm that have been compared in size with a rabbit dropping, and most shoots barren. Leaves *Oct-May*, spores ripe April. Bare ground, Scilly only. **2c Pillwort** *Pilularia globulifera* is the most un-fern-like of ferns with thread-like, upright, yellowish leaves, forming a curly turf on wet mud and sand.

(ii) Leaves forked

3 *Forked Spleenwort *Asplenium septentrionale*. A most distinctive small fern, with long stalks dark at the base and bearing *narrow* dark green wintergreen leaves, 4-15cm, each usually *forked twice* and toothed at the tip. Spores ripe August-Sept. Its rare hybrid with Maidenhair Spleenwort (p. 442) is more like this parent. Rocks, walls, uncommon in the N and W, especially N Wales. The only similar fern but with unforked leaves is Pillwort (**2c**).

Filmy Ferns *Hymenophyllum*. Small creeping, somewhat *moss-like*, with thin *translucent* overwintering leaves, 2-12cm, forming mats among mosses on damp rocks and tree-trunks on *acid* soils. Spores in stalked pouches near the leaf-tip, ripe June-July. **4 Tunbridge Filmy Fern** *Hymenophyllum tunbrigense* has dull green, somewhat flattened leaves, forked several times, the veins *not reaching the tips*. Mainly in the W, but still in the Sussex Weald near Tunbridge Wells. **4a Wilson's Filmy Fern** *H. wilsonii* has leaves darker green, not flattened and less forked but with longer lobes whose veins *reach the tip*. Spore-pouches longer-stalked.

(iii) Leaves pinnately lobed

5 Rusty-back *Ceterach officinarum*. Another distinctive small fern, whose tufts of mid-green wintergreen leaves, 3-25cm, are encrusted beneath with rust-coloured scales, which partly hide the spore-cases, ripening May-August. Rocks, walls, mainly on lime. Widespread but commoner in the S and W.

(iv) Leaves 1-pinnate

6 Hard Fern *Blechnum spicant*. Has an overwintering tuft of tough lanceolate leaves, mid-green but darkening later, 10-40cm. Spores only on inner leaves, ripening August-Nov. Woods, heaths, moors, mainly on acid soils. Widespread and common, but less frequent in S and E England.

7 Moonwort *Botrychium lunaria*. Stems low/short, to 30cm. Leaves unstalked, oblong, with 3-9 pairs of *fan-shaped* or half-moon-shaped leaflets, May-August. Spores in a 2-pinnate spike, June-August. All kinds of dry grassy places, including dunes and rock ledges. Widespread, mainly in the N and W.

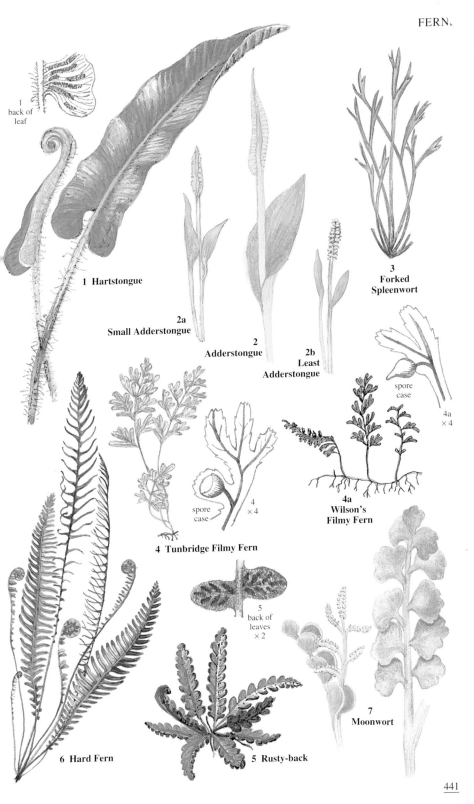

1
back of
leaf

1 **Hartstongue**

2a
Small Adderstongue

2
Adderstongue

2b
**Least
Adderstongue**

3
**Forked
Spleenwort**

spore
case

4a
× 4

4a
**Wilson's
Filmy Fern**

spore
case

4
× 4

4 **Tunbridge Filmy Fern**

5
back of
leaves
× 2

6 **Hard Fern**

5 **Rusty-back**

7
Moonwort

Polypodies *Polypodium*. Rootstock creeping, covered with brown scales. Leaves overwintering, leathery and mid-green, both except **1b**, with the leaflets more or less joined at the base, their tips pointed, except **1**. Woods, often on trees, walls, rocks. Preferring limy soils, except **1**. All three frequently interbreed. Widespread, mainly in the W. **1 Common Polypody** *Polypodium vulgare* has *blunt* leaflets, mostly more or less equal in length, the lowest pair usually projecting *sideways*, making leaf-base rectangular. Spores ripe August-March. Preferring acid soils. **1a Western Polypody** *P. interjectum* is badly named as it is the most frequent of the three in the E. Lowest leaflets projecting *forwards*. Spores ripe Sept-February. **1b Southern Polypody** *P. cambricum* is also misleadingly named, being less frequent than **1a** in the S. Leaves yellowish-green and not leathery, the lowest pair often held *upwards*, making the leaf appear narrowly triangular. Spores ripe Dec-May

2 Maidenhair Spleenwort *Asplenium trichomanes*. Small, with a tuft of long narrow overwintering leaves, 5-20cm, oval/oblong, slightly toothed, leaflets; stalks and midribs *blackish*. Scales on rootstock with a *dark central stripe*. Spores ripe Sept-Oct. Walls, rocks. Widespread, but mainly in the W.

3 Green Spleenwort *Asplenium viride*. Somewhat smaller than **2** and with more distinctly toothed leaflets, the leaf-stalks, midribs and upper part of main stalk *green*. Rootstock scales *not* striped. Spores ripe August-Nov. Walls, rocks, limestone pavements, mainly in the NW. not in S and E England.

4 Sea Spleenwort *Asplenium marinum*. Our only fern almost confined, except in SW Ireland, to cliffs, caves, rocks and walls *exposed to sea-spray*. Tufted, with rather leathery, bright shiny green, overwintering leaves, 15-20cm, midrib green. Spores almost always ripe, except mid-July to mid-August.

5 Holly Fern *Polystichum lonchitis*. Medium, with a tuft of overwintering leathery leaves, 15-60cm, the leaflets with *many spiny teeth*. Spores ripe August-April. Rocks, mainly on limestone, in hill country in the NW, S to N Wales.

(v) Leaves 1/2-pinnate (pinnately-lobed/2-pinnate)

6 Beech Fern *Phegopteris connectilis*. Smallish, 8-20 or even 30cm and graceful, with a creeping rootstock. Leaves soft, pale green, triangular, the two lowest leaflets *bent downwards*; May-Oct. Woods, shady rocks, despite its name rarely associated with Beeches, and avoiding both very acid and very limy soils. Mainly in the W, especially Scotland, and absent from E Anglia and the Midlands.

7 Hard Shield Fern *Polystichum aculeatum*. Medium/tall, tufted, 30-90cm. Not unlike a smaller, narrower dark green Male Fern (p. 444), but leaves markedly *leathery*, overwintering, on stalks with red-brown scales and either pinnate or pinnately lobed, these secondary leaflets being pointed and either un- or very shortly stalked, *narrowing down* on to the midrib of the main leaflet. Spores ripe July-February. Cf. Soft Shield Fern (p. 444), with which it hybridises. Widespread but commoner in the N.

8 **Crested Buckler Fern *Dryopteris cristata*. Medium/tall, 30-90cm, creeping and tufted. Leaves *narrow* lanceolate/parallel-sided, pale green, the stalks with pale brown scales, the leaflets short and sharply toothed; June-Dec. Spores, on inner leaves only, ripe August-Sept. *Fens*, whence aka Fen Buckler Fern, mainly in E Anglia; cf. Marsh Fern p. 446).

Male Fern *Dryopteris filix-mas*, p. 444.

Pinnules showing spores

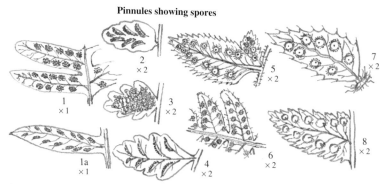

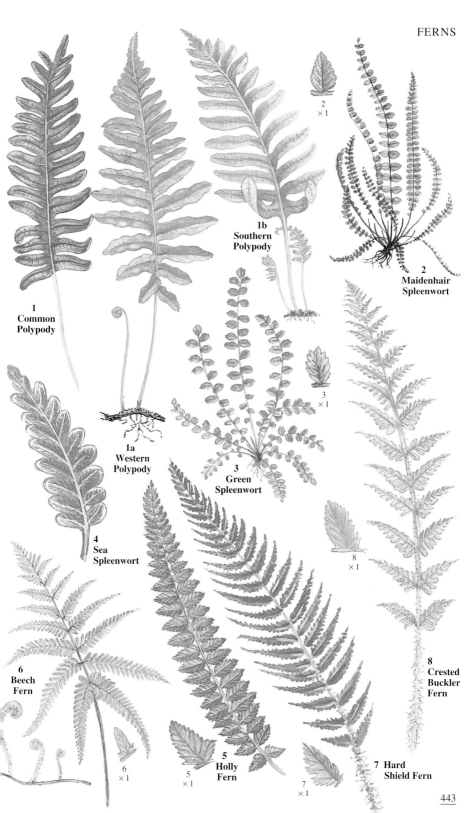

1 Common Polypody

1b Southern Polypody

1a Western Polypody

2 ×1

2 Maidenhair Spleenwort

3 ×1

3 Green Spleenwort

4 Sea Spleenwort

6 Beech Fern

6 ×1

5 ×1

5 Holly Fern

7 ×1

7 Hard Shield Fern

8 ×1

8 Crested Buckler Fern

Woodsias *Woodsia*. Low, to 8cm, rarely up to 30cm. Leaves in rosettes, overwintering, with pinnately lobed leaflets, Rounded spore-cases help to distinguish them from young ferns of other species. Mountain cliffs and rocks. **1 **Alpine Woodsia** *Woodsia alpina* is pale green, the leaves with sparse long zigzag hairs and a few scales beneath the midrib, tapering to the base, their *triangular* leaflets scarcely opposite, with 1-4 pairs of lobes. Spores ripe July-August. Scottish Highlands with an outpost in N Wales. The rarer **1a Oblong Woodsia** *W. silvensis* is usually larger and darker green and not unlike a dwarfed Brittle Bladder Fern (p. 446). Leaves not tapering to the base, the undersides and midrib very hairy and the leaflets opposite, the lower *oblong* with 4-8 pairs of lobes. Spores ripe July-Sept. Prefers basic rocks. Widely scattered from Inverness-shire S to N Wales.

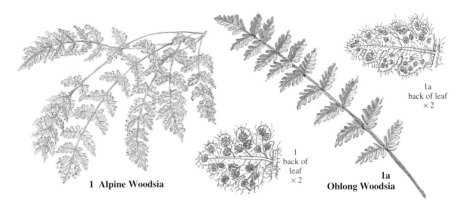

1 Alpine Woodsia

1
back of leaf
×2

1a
back of leaf
×2

1a
Oblong Woodsia

(vi) Leaves 2-pinnate

Male Ferns and **Buckler Ferns** *Dryopteris*. Differ from shield ferns, *Polystichum* (p. 442), in having no bristles at the tip of the leaflets. May hybridise with each other.

2 Male Fern *Dryopteris filix-mas*. One of our commonest ferns, usually medium/tall and robust, 30-130cm; each rootstock usually with only one crown; leaf-stalks with pale brown scales. Leaves sometimes overwintering, new ones appearing in April, mid-green, tapering at both ends, the leaflets usually pinnate, occasionally pinnately lobed, the secondary leaflets or lobes *flat*, toothed and *blunt*. Spores ripe August-Nov, *near midrib*. Woods, hedge-banks, rocks, screes. Widespread. **2a Golden-scaled Male Fern** *D. affinis* has golden-brown scales on the stalks and leaves yellowish-green, shinier, with a *blackish spot* where the leaflets meet the midrib and the secondary leaflets *convex* and toothed only at the tip. Spores ripe August-Sept. Aka Scaly Male Fern. Mainly on acid soils. Less frequent in the SE.

3 Mountain Male Fern *Dryopteris oreades*. Like a miniature Male Fern (**2**), 40-50cm, but with *several crowns* on each rootstock, the leaf-stalks yellowish with a blackish base and pale brown scales. Leaves slightly fragrant when crushed, the leaflets concave. Spores ripe August-Oct. *Mountain* rocks and screes, S Wales northwards.

4 Narrow Buckler Fern *Dryopteris carthusiana*. Tufted, medium, 40-80cm, with leaf-stalk scales *uniformly pale brown*. Leaves *narrowly* lanceolate, pale to yellowish-green, May-Oct. Spores ripe August-Sept. Damp and wet woods, bogs. Widespread. Cf. Broad Buckler Fern, p. 448.

5 Soft Shield Fern *Polystichum setiferum*. Tufted, medium/tall, 30-150cm; leaf-stalks with golden brown scales. Leaves rather pale green, *soft to the touch*, often overwintering, the leaflets distinctly stalked near the base and not narrowing down to the midrib, and the secondary leaflets blunter and more *softly spiny* than Hard Shield Fern (p. 442). Woods, hedge-banks, rocks. mainly in the W and S of the Thames.

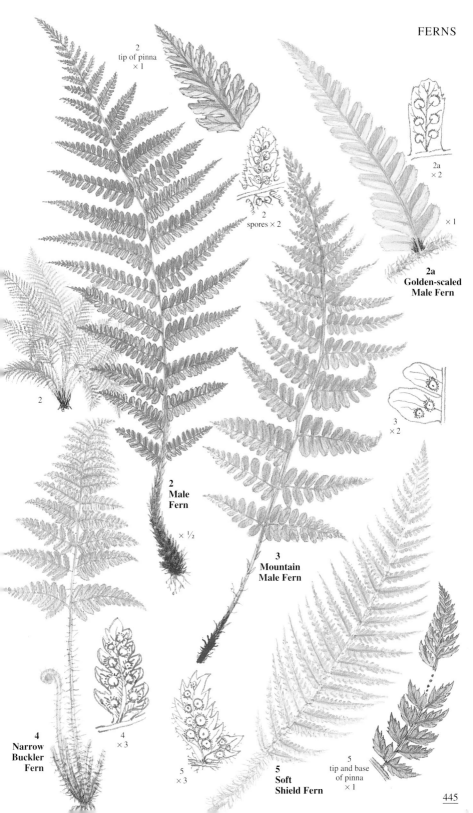

2
tip of pinna
× 1

2a
× 2

× 1

2a
**Golden-scaled
Male Fern**

2
spores × 2

3
× 2

2
**Male
Fern**

× ½

3
**Mountain
Male Fern**

2

4
× 3

5
× 3

4
**Narrow
Buckler
Fern**

5
**Soft
Shield Fern**

5
tip and base
of pinna
× 1

1 Lady Fern *Athyrium filix-femina*. Tall and tufted, to 150cm, differing from Male Fern (p. 444) especially in its paler green, more graceful leaves (April-Nov), the secondary leaflets *pointed* and much more *deeply toothed*. Spores ripe August-Nov. Damp woods, rocks and hedge-banks, streamsides, mountains, mainly on acid soils. Widespread, much commoner in the N and W. **1a** *****Alpine Lady Fern** *A. distentifolium* is a smaller montane species, usually 20-30 but up to 70cm, only certainly distinguishable by its *rounded* (not curved) spore-cases, whose covering flap falls off quite early. Spores ripe July-August. Screes in the Scottish Highlands. The much rarer **1b** ****Scottish Lady Fern** *A. flexile* has much shorter stalks than **1a** (with which it usually grows) *bent right back* so that the almost parallel-sided leaves are almost horizontal.

2 Lemon-scented Fern *Oreopteris limbosperma*. Medium/tall, 30-90cm, tufted like Male Fern (p. 444), but differing both in its lemony scent when crushed and in its yellowish-green leaves (May-Oct) being more narrowly tapered at each end. Spores, black when ripe (August-Sept) and with no spore-cases, are near the margins (not the midrib) of the secondary leaflets. Woods, heaths, screes, stream banks, on acid soils mainly in the N and W

3 *****Marsh Fern *Thelypteris palustris*. Our least rare fern of really wet and marshy habitats (cf. the tufted Crested Buckler Fern, p. 442), the more delicate, soft pale green leaves (June-Oct), arising *singly* on hairless stalks from a creeping rootstock, the fertile ones to 80cm, the infertile to 150cm. Spores ripe August-Sept. Mainly in the S, especially E Anglia.

4 Royal Fern *Osmunda regalis*. Our most majestic fern, usually 60-120cm, but can be 3 or even 4m. Leaves (April-Nov), in a large tuft with oblong leaflets. Spores golden-brown, in *flower-like spikes* on the inner leaves, June-August. Wet woods, fens, usually on acid soils. Widespread, but mainly in the W.

5 Wall-rue *Asplenium ruta-muraria*. One of our most distinctive small tufted ferns, often only 2-6cm, but sometimes to 15cm. Leaves overwintering, the leaflets *fan-shaped*. Spores ripe June-August. Walls, rocks, limestone pavements, especially in limy districts. Widespread and frequent.

6 *****Lanceolate Spleenwort *Asplenium obovatum*. Tufted, 15-30cm, with bright green overwintering leaves on red-brown stalks, not tapering at the base, the lowest pair of leaflets sometimes shorter and *turned down*, the secondary leaflets toothed. Spores ripe July-Oct. Rocks, walls, hedge-banks, old mine-shafts, usually near the sea in the W, very rare N of N Wales.

(vii) Leaves 2/3-pinnate

7 Brittle Bladder Fern *Cystopteris fragilis*. Tufted, with leaf-stalks green, blackish at the base and with few scales. Leaves (April-Nov) *delicate*, lanceolate, 5-45cm. Spores black when ripe (June-Sept), the cases whitish. Rocks, walls, mainly in limy districts. Widespread, mainly in the N and W. **7a** ****Dickie's Fern** *C. dickieana* has shorter stalks and broader, more crowded leaflets, but is only certainly distinguishable by the absence of microscopic spines on the spores. Caves, rocks and ravines, Four sites on the coast S of Aberdeen and three more recently found inland in the Highlands.

1
×2

3
×2

5
×2

6
×2

1a
×2

2
×2

4   autumn

7
×2

7a
×2

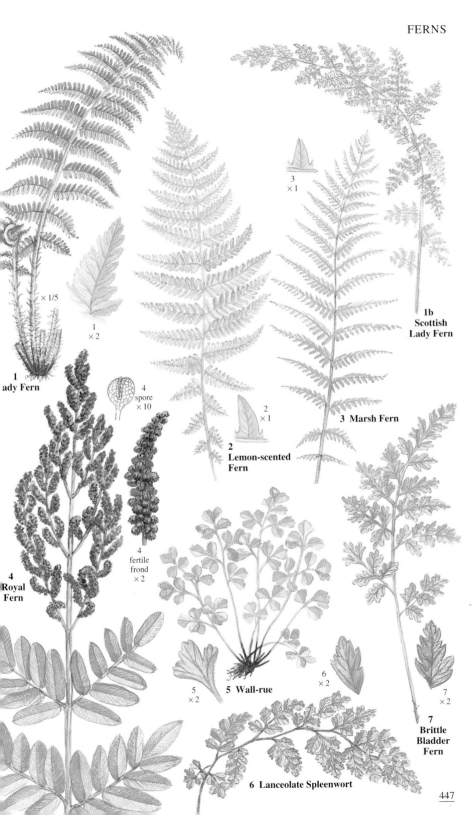

1b
Scottish Lady Fern

3
× 1

3 Marsh Fern

2
× 1

2 Lemon-scented Fern

× 1/5

1
× 2

1
ady Fern

4
spore
× 10

4
fertile frond
× 2

4
Royal Fern

5
× 2

5 Wall-rue

6
× 2

7
× 2

7
Brittle Bladder Fern

6 Lanceolate Spleenwort

1 Hay-scented Buckler Fern *Dryopteris aemula*. Tufted, with few pale orange-brown scales on the dark brown stalks, 15-60cm. Leaves overwintering, *hay-scented* when freshly dried, broadly triangular, with the secondary leaflets crisped, the lowest on the lowest leaflet as least half as long as the leaflet. Spores ripe August-Oct, Woods, hedge-banks, shady rocks. Mainly near the sea in the W, absent between N Yorks and S Devon.

2 *Limestone Buckler Fern *Dryopteris submontana*. Medium, 20-60cm, the yellowish stalks with a blackish base and pale brown scales. Leaves (May-Nov) *stiff*, narrowly triangular, greyish mealy, usually with many yellowish hairs, balsam-scented, the secondary leaflets with pointed teeth. Spores ripe July-Sept. Aka Rigid Buckler Fern. Only on *limestone* rocks and pavements. Rare away from NW England.

3 Oak Fern *Gymnocarpium dryopteris*. Short/medium, 10-40cm, stems dark purple-brown with few pale brown scales. Leaves (May-Sept), growing *singly* from a creeping rootstock, *triangular* because the lowest leaflet pair often as long as the rest of the leaf; in bud the leaves are rolled into three balls. Spores ripe July-August. Cf. Limestone Oak Fern (**4**). Damp, often oak, woods, shady rocks, screes, only on acid soils. N and Mid Wales northwards.

4 *Limestone Oak Fern *Gymnocarpium robertianum*. The limestone counterpart of Oak Fern (**3**), but often taller, to 60cm, and more upright, with larger, duller green leaves, which with their stalks are slightly hairy, fragrant when bruised, and when young rolled into one ball. *Limestone* pavements and screes. Local or rare away from the York-shire/Westmorland limestone.

5 Black Spleenwort *Asplenium adiantum-nigrum*. Short/medium, 10-50cm, with red-brown stalks. Leaves overwintering, *shiny dark green*, the secondary leaflets pointed and toothed, but blunt at the base. Spores ripe, July-Nov. Rocks, walls, hedge-banks. Wide-spread, but most frequent in the W. **5a Irish Spleenwort** *Asplenium onopteris* has longer stalks, red-brown extending on to midrib, and more delicate, narrower yellow-green leaves, the secondary leaflets narrowly pointed throughout. Aka Acute-leaved Spleenwort, Western Black Spleenwort. Limestone rocks, Ireland.

6 *Maidenhair Fern *Adiantum capillus-veneris*. One of our most distinctive ferns due to its *fan-shaped* secondary leaflets. Low/short, to 15 or even 40cm, stalks blackish. Leaves March-Oct. Spores ripe May-August. Limestone rocks by the sea, mainly from S Wales to Torbay, but scattered elsewhere; also introduced on walls and rocks inland in the S.

(viii) Leaves 3-pinnate

7 Northern Buckler Fern *Dryopteris expansa*. Differs from Broad Buckler Fern (**8**), with which it hybridises, in its rufous scales, paler, yellower-green and more broadly triangular leaves (May-Nov), with the lowest secondary leaflet of the lowest leaflet at least half as long as the leaflet – in **8** it is usually less than half as long. Spores ripen August-Sept. Hills and mountains from S Wales northwards, mainly in the Highlands.

8 Broad Buckler Fern *Dryopteris dilatata*. One of our three commonest larger ferns, short/tall, 10-150cm, with scales on the stalk all dark or dark-centred (cf. Narrow Buckler Fern, p. 444). Leaves April-Nov, dark green, spreading, isoceles-triangular. Spores ripe July-August. Woods, hedge-banks, heaths, hillsides, preferring drier and acid soils.

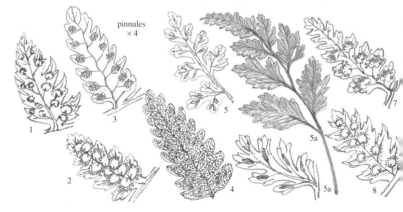

pinnules
× 4

1 pores
× 6

3
× 1

4
× 1

3
Oak
Fern

4
Limestone
Oak Fern

1
ay-scented
ckler Fern

2
tip of
frond

5
Black
Spleenwort

1
1

2
Limestone
Buckler
Fern

6
× 1

2
base

8
× 1

8 Broad
Buckler Fern

spore
× 6

scale
× 2

6
aidenhair
Fern

7
Northern
Buckler Fern

1 Bracken *Pteridium aquilinum.* Perhaps our commonest fern and the only one with pest status when its extensive, often closed, communities cover hillsides. Stems 1-4m, from a creeping rootstock. Leaves appearing at first as a 'shepherd's crook', April-Oct, and persisting dead and copper-brown through the winter. Spores ripe August-Oct. Drier heaths and moors, open woods.

2 Parsley Fern *Cryptogramma crispa.* Short, 15-30cm, distinctive with its bright green tuft of well crisped leaves (May-Nov). Spores only on inner leaves, ripe July-August. Walls and rocks mainly in the hills in the W, most frequent in the Lake District and N Wales.

3 **Mountain Bladder Fern *Cystopteris montana.* Differs from the much commoner Brittle Bladder Fern (p. 446) especially in its more triangular 3-pinnate leaves (May-Sept) arising *singly* from its creeping rootstock. Spores ripe August-Sept. Mountain rocks and woods on limestone in the Scottish Highlands.

4 **Killarney Fern *Trichomanes speciosum.* Our only fern with delicate *translucent 3-4-pinnate* overwintering leaves, 20-25cm, the creeping rootstock with blackish hairs. Spores ripe July-August. Damp or wet rocks, wells. This sporophyte form is rare and mainly in Ireland and W Britain (see map). The more primitive moss-like gametophyte form, which for some reason does not develop into the sporophyte form, has recently been discovered to be quite widespread in Britain.

Introduced Ferns

Leaves 1-pinnate

The tall, to 150cm, tufted **5 Ostrich Fern** *Matteucia struthiopteris* has bright green lanceolate outer leaves with pinnately lobed leaflets that die back, with the spores (ripe June-August) borne on much smaller brown inner overwintering leaves. Moist woods and other damp places.

Two overwintering ferns on walls are **6 Ribbon Fern** *Pteris cretica*, to 40cm, from Crete with 4-7 pairs of linear leaflets, the lowest sometimes forked and spores ripe April-May; and the larger **6a Ladder Brake** *P. vittata* with 10 or more pairs of leaflets, the lowest never forked.

Leaves 2-pinnate

7 Sensitive Fern *Onoclea sensibilis.* Medium, to 50cm, with a creeping rootstock has triangular green leaves that die back, and the spores (ripe June-Oct) in blackish berry-like globules on overwintering spikes. Established in a few damp shady places.

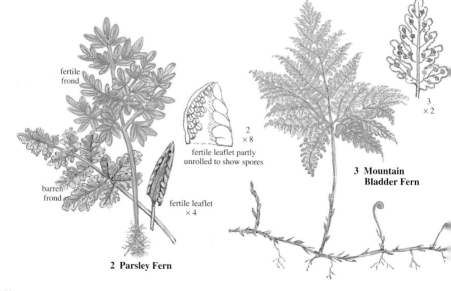

fertile frond

barren frond

2 ×8
fertile leaflet partly unrolled to show spores

fertile leaflet ×4

2 Parsley Fern

3 ×2

3 Mountain Bladder Fern

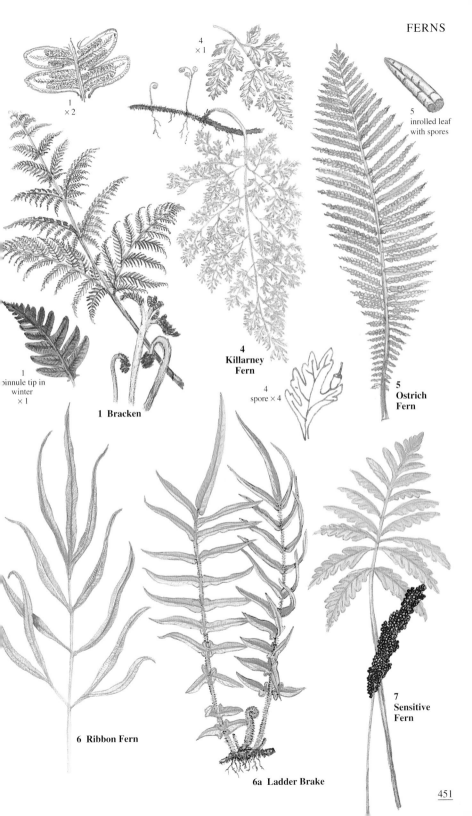

1
× 2

4
× 1

5
inrolled leaf
with spores

1
pinnule tip in
winter
× 1

1 Bracken

**4
Killarney
Fern**

4
spore × 4

**5
Ostrich
Fern**

6 Ribbon Fern

6a Ladder Brake

**7
Sensitive
Fern**

451

HORSETAILS Equisetaceae

Leafless non-flowering perennials with stems hollow, ridged, roughish and jointed, the joints covered by toothed sheaths and mostly bearing whorls of branches that are linear, ribbed and jointed. Spores in cones: at tip of some green stems in Marsh, Water, Rough, Variegated and Boston Horsetails; or at tip of special stouter unbranched paler or whitish stems in Field, Shade, Wood and Great Horsetails. Hybrids are frequent. N.B. Marestail (p. 350) is often miscalled horsetail.

(i) Branches none

1 Water Horsetail *Equisetum fluviatile*. The most aquatic horsetail, often growing *right in the water*. Stems (May-Nov) medium/tall, to 150cm, usually little or *unbranched*, the central hollow wide, smooth, yellow-green, often tinged orange, the teeth whitish with a black midrib; ridges obscure, 10-30. Sheaths tight, green, the teeth short. black, pale-edged. Cones blunt, spores ripe June. Its hybrid with Field Horsetail (**4**) is frequent. Often fringing lakes and ponds, also in swamps and carr. Widespread, commonest in NW Scotland. Cf. Marsh Horsetail (**6**).

2 Rough Horsetail *Equisetum hyemale*. Stems medium/tall, to 1m, *stiff*, dark green, inflated between the joints, overwintering; ridges 10-30. Sheaths black with a green or whitish central band, *untoothed*. Cones pointed, spores ripe January-April. Hybridises with Variegated (**3**) and Boston (**8**) Horsetails. Aka Dutch Rush. Forms colonies in damp shady places, often on clayey river banks. Scattered, mainly in the N.

3 *Variegated Horsetail *Equisetum variegatum*. Stems dark green, overwintering, short/tall, to 80cm, erect/*prostrate*, often curly, sometimes *branching from base*, dark green; ridges 4-10, sheaths black above, green below, sometimes tinged *orange*, the teeth *whitish* with a black midrib. Cones pointed, spores ripe March-June. Hybridises with Rough Horsetail (**2**). Damp places, often dune slacks, by fresh water, often in mountain flushes and on limy soils. Widely scattered, very rare in the S.

(ii) Branches simple

4 Field Horsetail *Equisetum arvense*. Generally our commonest horsetail. Short/tall green sterile stems (April-Oct), to 80cm, or sometimes *sprawling*, forming patches, with 6-9 ridges; sheaths green with *spreading* green teeth; usually with several whorls of rather thick simple branches. Fertile stems whitish or *pinkish*, unbranched, April-May, usually before the sterile ones. Hybridises with Water Horsetail (**1**). Much the most frequent horsetail in *drier* grassy and waste places, often a tiresome weed.

5 Great Horsetail *Equisetum telmateia*. Much the largest Horsetail, the *very tall* whitish sterile stems (April-Nov) sometimes reaching 2m, the numerous branches simple, ridges 20-40; sheaths green, tight, with pale-edged brown teeth. Fertile stems *whitish*, April, usually before the sterile stems. Forms large patches in damp places, especially on clay soils, often near a limy spring. Widespread, but mainly in the S.

6 Marsh Horsetail *Equisetum palustre*. Stems (May-Oct) short/medium, to 50cm, the central hollow very small, ridges 8-10. with loose sheaths, the teeth black with *broad white edges*. Branches usually present, their sheath-teeth green with black tips. Cones pointed, spores ripe June-July. Marshes, damp grassland. Widespread and common.

7 *Shade Horsetail *Equisetum pratense*. Sterile stems (April-Nov) patch-forming, *short*, to 30cm, rather stiff, slender, with whorls of thin simple branches, often *drooping* at the tip, ridges 8-20; sheaths green, the slender brown teeth with a *darker midrib*. Fertile stems rarely produced, May, unbranched at first. Damp grassy places in the N, especially river banks.

8 Boston Horsetail *Equisetum ramosissimum*. An introduced rarity on the bank of the R.Witham near Boston, Lincs. Stems to 1m, sometimes overwintering, with numerous branches and green sheaths, turning brown with a *black band* at the base, the teeth *blackish*, pale-edged and very finely pointed. Spores ripe August-Sept.

Cf. **Water Horsetail** (**1**) and **Variegated Horsetail** (**3**)

(iii) 2-Branched

9 Wood Horsetail *Equisetum sylvaticum*. Our most graceful horsetail, like a tiny pale green Christmas tree, the sterile stems (April-Nov) short/medium, to 50cm, the many branches finely branched and drooping at the tip; ridges 10-18, obscure; sheaths loose, green, with 3-6 *rufous brown* teeth. Fertile stems paler, unbranched at first, May. Forms colonies in woods and on moors and banks. Widespread, but much commoner in the N.

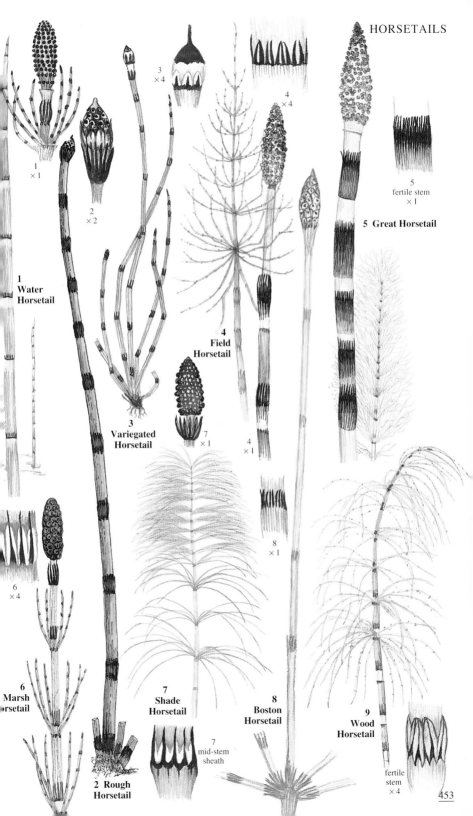

HORSETAILS

1
×1

1
Water
Horsetail

2
×2

3
×4

3
Variegated
Horsetail

4
×4

4
Field
Horsetail

7
×1

4
×1

5
fertile stem
×1

5 Great Horsetail

6
×4

6
Marsh
rsetail

7
Shade
Horsetail

7
mid-stem
sheath

8
×1

8
Boston
Horsetail

2 Rough
Horsetail

9
Wood
Horsetail

fertile
stem
×4

453

CLUBMOSSES Lycopodiopsida

Low, often prostrate, overwintering evergreen perennials, somewhat like large mosses. Unlike all mosses, however, they have both true roots and true vascular tissue in their stems and so are much stouter and stiffer. Their small pointed leaves have either no veins or just a midrib and overlap along the stems. Spores usually in erect cigar-shaped cones. All except Marsh Clubmoss (**4**) are commoner in the N, and only Stagshorn Clubmoss (**3**) is really widespread.

(i) Stems erect

1 Fir Clubmoss *Huperzia selago*. Our stoutest clubmoss, with stems stiff, low, to 10cm, *forking*. Leaves spreading, untoothed, rather sharp. Cones solitary, *unstalked*, near the top of the stems, spores ripe August. *Dry* grassland on heaths, moors and mountains. **1a *Interrupted Clubmoss** *Lycopodiella annotina* has long creeping stems ending in erect stems, distinctively *constricted* at intervals, the leaves minutely toothed, the spores ripe August-Sept.

2 Lesser Clubmoss *Selaginella selaginoides*. Stems rather weakly erect, to 16cm, slender and soft to the touch. Leaves finely toothed, with a *tiny ligule*, unlike true Mosses. Cones yellowish, July-August. Damp grassy places, dune slacks, on limy soils.

(ii) Stems sprawling or creeping, leaves spreading

3 Stagshorn Clubmoss *Lycopodium clavatum*. Far-creeping, its long, branched stems trailing *up to 1m* or more. Leaves bright green, incurved, ending in a *long whitish hair*. Cones long-stalked (in the far N almost unstalked); spores ripe July-August. Heaths, moors, mountains.

4 *Marsh Clubmoss *Lycopodiella inundata*. Stems shortly creeping, to 20cm, little-branched. Leaves bright green, only semi-evergreen, *untoothed*. Cones solitary, *unstalked*, spores ripe August. Wet heaths and moors, also dune slacks, especially on acid soils.

5 Mossy Clubmoss *Selaginella kraussiana*. Stems flattened, trailing to 30cm or more. Leaves in *four rows*, two appressed and two longer and spreading. Cones unstalked. A greenhouse escape, established in milder districts.

(iii) Stems sprawling or creeping, leaves appressed

6 Alpine Clubmoss *Diphasiastrum alpinum*. Our most distinctive clubmoss, with the *closely appressed*, slightly glaucous leaves on its creeping, slightly *flattened* stems, to 50cm. Cones unstalked, greyer than leaves, spores ripe August. Its hybrid **6a** with the European *D. complanatum* is very rare. Upland heaths, moors, mountains.

See also **Pillwort** *Pilularia globulifera* (Marsileaceae) p. 440, **Quillworts** (Isoetaceae), p. 344 and **Water Fern** *Azolla*, p. 354.

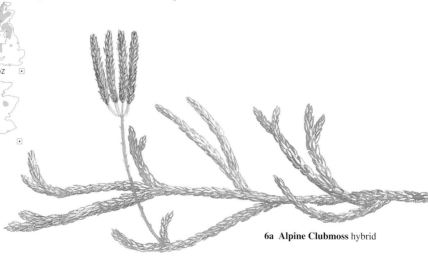

6a Alpine Clubmoss hybrid

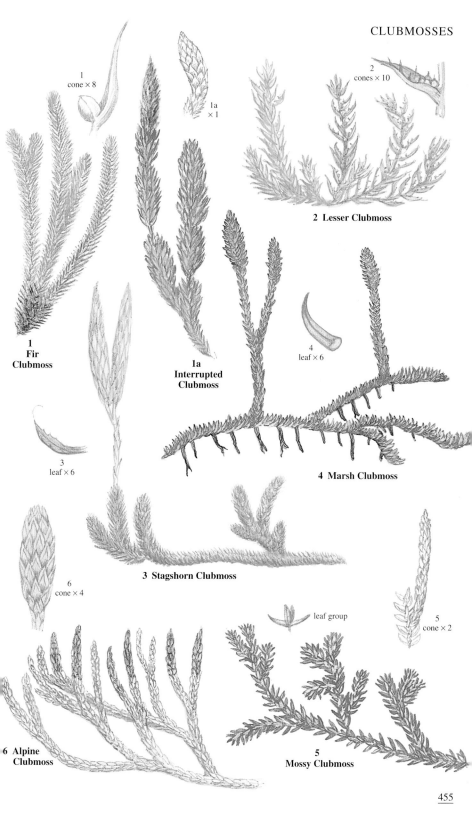

1
cone × 8

1a
× 1

2
cones × 10

2 Lesser Clubmoss

**1
Fir
Clubmoss**

**1a
Interrupted
Clubmoss**

4
leaf × 6

3
leaf × 6

4 Marsh Clubmoss

6
cone × 4

3 Stagshorn Clubmoss

leaf group

5
cone × 2

**6 Alpine
Clubmoss**

**5
Mossy Clubmoss**

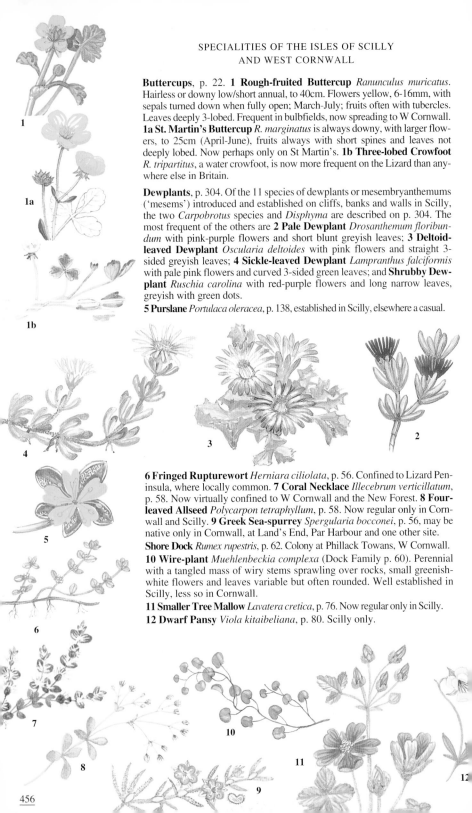

Buttercups, p. 22. **1 Rough-fruited Buttercup** *Ranunculus muricatus*. Hairless or downy low/short annual, to 40cm. Flowers yellow, 6-16mm, with sepals turned down when fully open; March-July; fruits often with tubercles. Leaves deeply 3-lobed. Frequent in bulbfields, now spreading to W Cornwall. **1a St. Martin's Buttercup** *R. marginatus* is always downy, with larger flowers, to 25cm (April-June), fruits always with short spines and leaves not deeply lobed. Now perhaps only on St Martin's. **1b Three-lobed Crowfoot** *R. tripartitus*, a water crowfoot, is now more frequent on the Lizard than anywhere else in Britain.

Dewplants, p. 304. Of the 11 species of dewplants or mesembryanthemums ('mesems') introduced and established on cliffs, banks and walls in Scilly, the two *Carpobrotus* species and *Disphyma* are described on p. 304. The most frequent of the others are **2 Pale Dewplant** *Drosanthemum floribundum* with pink-purple flowers and short blunt greyish leaves; **3 Deltoid-leaved Dewplant** *Oscularia deltoides* with pink flowers and straight 3-sided greyish leaves; **4 Sickle-leaved Dewplant** *Lampranthus falciformis* with pale pink flowers and curved 3-sided green leaves; and **Shrubby Dewplant** *Ruschia carolina* with red-purple flowers and long narrow leaves, greyish with green dots.

5 Purslane *Portulaca oleracea*, p. 138, established in Scilly, elsewhere a casual.

6 Fringed Rupturewort *Herniara ciliolata*, p. 56. Confined to Lizard Peninsula, where locally common. **7 Coral Necklace** *Illecebrum verticillatum*, p. 58. Now virtually confined to W Cornwall and the New Forest. **8 Four-leaved Allseed** *Polycarpon tetraphyllum*, p. 58. Now regular only in Cornwall and Scilly. **9 Greek Sea-spurrey** *Spergularia bocconei*, p. 56, may be native only in Cornwall, at Land's End, Par Harbour and one other site.

Shore Dock *Rumex rupestris*, p. 62. Colony at Phillack Towans, W Cornwall.

10 Wire-plant *Muehlenbeckia complexa* (Dock Family p. 60). Perennial with a tangled mass of wiry stems sprawling over rocks, small greenish-white flowers and leaves variable but often rounded. Well established in Scilly, less so in Cornwall.

11 Smaller Tree Mallow *Lavatera cretica*, p. 76. Now regular only in Scilly.
12 Dwarf Pansy *Viola kitaibeliana*, p. 80. Scilly only.

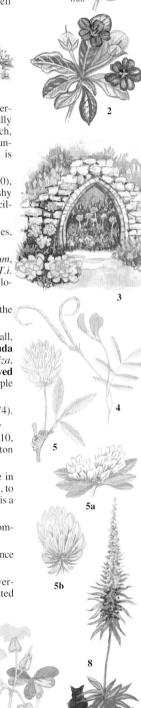

2
fruit

Three **Heaths** *Erica*, p. 104, are naturalised: **Tree Heath** *E. arborea* in Abbey Wood, Tresco, Scilly, and **Lusitanian Heath** *E. lusitanica*, as well as the well known garden early-flowerer *E.* × *darleyensis* in Cornwall.

Cornish Heath

1 Cornish Heath, p. 104. Abundant on the Lizard Peninsula.

2 Karo *Pittosporum crassifolium* (Karo Family *Pittosporaceae*). An evergreen New Zealand shrub or small tree, well naturalised in Scilly, especially on Tresco, less so in W Cornwall. Flowers dark red; February-March, Leaves dark green, downy white below, with inrolled margins. Fruit a roundish capsule. **Kohuhu** *P. tenuifolium*, with narrower all-green leaves, is much less frequent.

3 Pastel del Risco [Cliff Pasty] *Aeonium* spp. (Stonecrop Family, p. 120), Perennials from the Canary Islands with pasty-like rosettes of large fleshy leaves and many-petalled yellow flowers, naturalised in parts of the Scillies, notably *Ae. arboreum* on the walls of Tresco Abbey Garden.

4 Orange Birdsfoot *Ornithopus pinnatus*, p. 142. Confined to the Scillies, especially Bryher and Tresco.

Three rare Clovers, p. 150: **5 Upright Clover** *Trifolium strictum*, **5a Twin-headed Clover** *T. bocconei* and **5b Long-headed Clover** *T.i.* ssp. *molinerii* are all confined to the Lizard Peninsula, though Upright Clover has also occurred sporadically at Stanner Rocks, Radnorshire.

Wood Spurge *Euphorbia amygdaloides*, p. 166, in Scilly grows in the open with Heather.

Several **Wood-sorrels**, p. 172, are naturalised in Scilly and W Cornwall, and three are Scilly specialities: the widespread and abundant **Bermuda Buttercup** *Oxalis pes-caprae*; **6 Fleshy Yellow Sorrel** *O. megalorrhiza*, with thick stems and leaves and bright yellow flowers; and **6a Four-leaved Pink Sorrel** *O. tetraphylla*, with bulbils on creeping stems, pink-purple flowers and four leaflets.

7 Giant Herb Robert *Geranium maderense* (Cranesbill Family, p. 174). Like an outsize Herb Robert, to 1m. Well naturalised on cliffs, Tresco.

Yellow Alkanet *Anchusa ochroleuca* and **Alkanet** *A. officinalis*, p. 210, have been established since 1918 at a former army camp on dunes at Upton Towans, near Hayle, but Alkanet may now have gone.

Purple Viper's Bugloss *Echium plantagineum*, p. 214, now very rare in both W Cornwall and Scilly. **8 Giant Viper's Bugloss** *E. pininana*, a tall, to 4m, single-stemmed shrub with large lanceolate leaves and blue flowers, is a more frequent escape in Scilly than elsewhere on the S and W coasts.

Balm-leaved Figwort *Scrophularia scorodonia*, p. 228, is much the commonest figwort in Scilly.

Bearsbreech *Acanthus mollis*, p. 246, has been naturalised on St Agnes since at least 1800.

9 Tree Bedstraw *Coprosma repens* (Bedstraw Family, p. 254). An evergreen New Zealand shrub with opposite glossy oval leaves, much planted in the Scillies and often self-sown.

9   7   6a   6   8

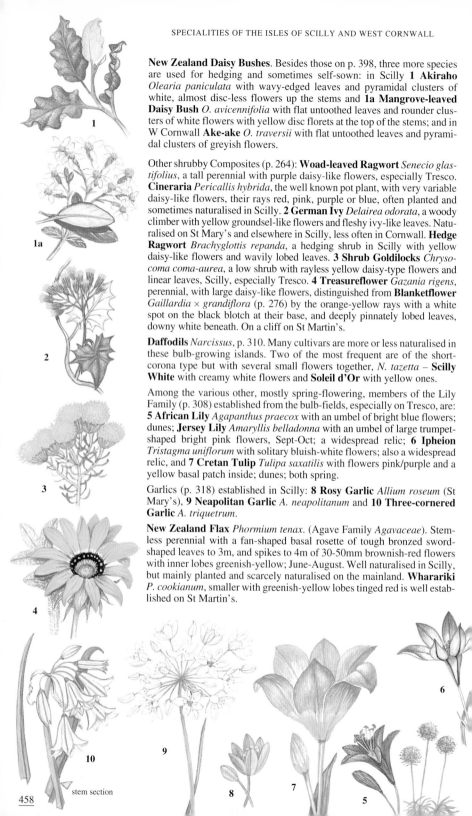

New Zealand Daisy Bushes. Besides those on p. 398, three more species are used for hedging and sometimes self-sown: in Scilly **1 Akiraho** *Olearia paniculata* with wavy-edged leaves and pyramidal clusters of white, almost disc-less flowers up the stems and **1a Mangrove-leaved Daisy Bush** *O. avicennifolia* with flat untoothed leaves and rounder clusters of white flowers with yellow disc florets at the top of the stems; and in W Cornwall **Ake-ake** *O. traversii* with flat untoothed leaves and pyramidal clusters of greyish flowers.

Other shrubby Composites (p. 264): **Woad-leaved Ragwort** *Senecio glastifolius*, a tall perennial with purple daisy-like flowers, especially Tresco. **Cineraria** *Pericallis hybrida*, the well known pot plant, with very variable daisy-like flowers, their rays red, pink, purple or blue, often planted and sometimes naturalised in Scilly. **2 German Ivy** *Delairea odorata*, a woody climber with yellow groundsel-like flowers and fleshy ivy-like leaves. Naturalised on St Mary's and elsewhere in Scilly, less often in Cornwall. **Hedge Ragwort** *Brachyglottis repanda*, a hedging shrub in Scilly with yellow daisy-like flowers and wavily lobed leaves. **3 Shrub Goldilocks** *Chrysocoma coma-aurea*, a low shrub with rayless yellow daisy-type flowers and linear leaves, Scilly, especially Tresco. **4 Treasureflower** *Gazania rigens*, perennial, with large daisy-like flowers, distinguished from **Blanketflower** *Gaillardia* × *grandiflora* (p. 276) by the orange-yellow rays with a white spot on the black blotch at their base, and deeply pinnately lobed leaves, downy white beneath. On a cliff on St Martin's.

Daffodils *Narcissus*, p. 310. Many cultivars are more or less naturalised in these bulb-growing islands. Two of the most frequent are of the short-corona type but with several small flowers together, *N. tazetta* – **Scilly White** with creamy white flowers and **Soleil d'Or** with yellow ones.

Among the various other, mostly spring-flowering, members of the Lily Family (p. 308) established from the bulb-fields, especially on Tresco, are: **5 African Lily** *Agapanthus praecox* with an umbel of bright blue flowers; dunes; **Jersey Lily** *Amaryllis belladonna* with an umbel of large trumpet-shaped bright pink flowers, Sept-Oct; a widespread relic; **6 Ipheion** *Tristagma uniflorum* with solitary bluish-white flowers; also a widespread relic, and **7 Cretan Tulip** *Tulipa saxatilis* with flowers pink/purple and a yellow basal patch inside; dunes; both spring.

Garlics (p. 318) established in Scilly: **8 Rosy Garlic** *Allium roseum* (St Mary's), **9 Neapolitan Garlic** *A. neapolitanum* and **10 Three-cornered Garlic** *A. triquetrum*.

New Zealand Flax *Phormium tenax*. (Agave Family *Agavaceae*). Stemless perennial with a fan-shaped basal rosette of tough bronzed sword-shaped leaves to 3m, and spikes to 4m of 30-50mm brownish-red flowers with inner lobes greenish-yellow; June-August. Well naturalised in Scilly, but mainly planted and scarcely naturalised on the mainland. **Wharariki** *P. cookianum*, smaller with greenish-yellow lobes tinged red is well established on St Martin's.

stem section

Ten members of the Iris Family (p. 320), nine with flowers in spikes, and eight from S Africa, are more or less naturalised in Scilly, especially around the bulb fields: **1 Chilean Iris** *Libertia formosa*, tufted with white flowers, also in W Cornwall; **2 Blue Corn-lily** *Aristea ecklonii* with small clusters of blue flowers, Tresco; **3 Bugle Lily** *Watsonia borbonica* with white flowers, Appletree Banks, Tresco; **4 Red Corn-lily** *Ixia campanulata* with red flowers streaked white or yellow; **4a Tubular Corn-lily** *I. paniculata* with pale yellow flowers tinged red, St Mary's; **5 Spanish Iris** *Iris xiphium* with flowers bluish-violet with a yellow patch; **6 Harlequin Flower** *Sparaxis grandiflora* with red flowers, often striped white and with yellow at the base; **7 Freesia** *Freesia refracta* with fragrant flowers of various colours; **Chasmanthe** *Chasmanthe bicolor* with petals orange above and yellow below, especially Tresco; and **African Tulip** *Homeria collina* with fragrant pale yellow or pink flowers, a weed in Tresco Abbey Garden.

8 Dwarf Rush *Juncus capitatus* and **8a Pygmy Rush** *Juncus pygmaeus*, p. 438. Two tiny annual May-June-flowering rushes, confined to damp heaths in W Cornwall and often growing together, have tight few-flowered clusters of greenish flowers, Dwarf with a bract longer and Pigmy with bracts shorter than the head.

The tiny **Land Quillwort** *Isoetes histrix* is confined to the Lizard Peninsula. The equally tiny **Least Adderstongue** *Ophioglossum lusitanicum* (see p. 440) grows only under one large rock on St Agnes.

Tresco Abbey Woodlands. A number of woody southern-hemisphere species, mainly evergreens, are readily self-sowing and becoming naturalised in the woodlands on the hill above the Abbey. They include:

Myrtle Family *Myrtaceae*: two **Gum-trees** *Eucalyptus* with alternate lanceolate leaves, blue-grey when young, *E. globulus* with dark green, usually curved leaves and *E. pulchella* with narrower, almost linear, straight leaves; two **Tea-trees** *Leptospermum,* with alternate leaves, *L. scoparium* with sharply pointed, and *L. lanigerum* with abruptly pointed leaves; and **Chilean Myrtle** *Luma apiculata* with narrow opposite leaves.

Tasmanian Fuchsia *Correa backhousiana*. (Rue Family *Rutaceae*). An evergreen shrub to 2m, with undivided leaves, glossy above and downy below, and yellowish-green fuchsia-like flowers, February-March.

9 Mint-scented Geranium *Pelargonium tomentosum* (Cranesbill Family, p. 174): woody-based perennial, smelling of peppermint, with large heads of pale pink flowers.

Some common Scilly Bulbfield Weeds: Rough-fruited Buttercup, p. 22; Hairy Birdsfoot Trefoil, p. 146; Bermuda Buttercup, p. 172; Musk Storksbill, p. 178; Ipheion, p. 458; and Hairy Finger-grass, p. 428.

IRISH SPECIALITIES

Lusitanian plants are found mainly in Spain and Portugal, but also in W Ireland and SW England. * = Irish Red Data Book. $ = Confined to Ireland

1 *Arctic Sandwort *Arenaria norvegica*, p. 54, Burren only. **1a** $*Fringed Sandwort *A. ciliata*, p. 54, Ben Bulben, Co. Sligo, only. **1b** *Recurved Sandwort *Minuartia recurva*, p. 54, Co. Cork only.

2 Red Bistort *Persicaria amplexicaulis* and **Lesser Knotweed** *P. campanulata* (p. 68) are both more frequent in Ireland than in Great Britain. **American Tear-thumb** *P. sagittata*, with prickly stems, was long established in Kerry, but is now probably extinct.

3 Lax-flowered Sea-lavender *Limonium humile*, p. 70, is commoner on the Irish than on the British coast.

4 $*Irish St John's Wort *Hypericum canadense*, p. 74, by L. Mask, Mayo. A N American plant first found in Ireland in 1954; now considered probably native.

Pitcherplant *Sarracenia purpurea*, p. 306. Well naturalised since 1906 in bogs in Roscommon and neighbouring counties.

5 *Common Rockrose *Helianthemum nummularium* and **5a** *Hoary Rock-rose *H. oelandicum*, p. 70, reverse their British status in Ireland, where Common is confined to one locality on the limestone near Ballintra, Donegal, and Hoary is common around Galway Bay.

6 *Fen Violet *Viola persicifolia*, p. 80, is commoner in the turloughs (shallow depressions) of the limestone in C and W Ireland than anywhere in Britain.

7 *Tea-leaved Willow *Salix phylicifolia*, p. 380, is confined to Sligo and Leitrim. No recent records of Dark-leaved Willow.

8 Hairy Rock-cress *Arabis hirsuta* p. 92. A small variant, on dunes in W Ireland, with hairs confined to the edges of the leaves, has been described as *A. h.* var. *brownii*.

8a *Northern Rock-cress *Arabis petraea*, p. 92. In Ireland only on Galtee Mts, Tipperary, and Glenade Mts, Leitrim.

9 $*Strawberry Tree *Arbutus unedo*, p. 384. A Lusitanian plant confined to Cork, Kerry and Sligo.

10 $*Irish Heath *Erica erigena*, p. 104, endemic in Galway and Mayo. **10a** $*Mackay's Heath *E. mackaiana*, p. 104, a Lusitanian plant from Connemara. **10b** $$St Dabeoc's Heath *Daboecia cantabrica*, p. 104, a Lusitanian plant confined to Connemara, where it is locally common. **10c** *Cornish Heath *E. vagans*, p. 104, one site in Fermanagh. **10d** *Dorset Heath *E. ciliaris*, p. 104, one site, Roundstone, Galway, where perhaps planted. **Corsican Heath** *E. terminalis*, a Mediterranean plant naturalised for 100 years on Magilligan Dunes, Co. Derry.

1 White Stonecrop *Sedum album* and **1a Thick-leaved Stonecrop** *S. dasyphyllum*, p. 122, are both established on limestone rocks near Cork, White as a probable native, Thick-leaved as an escape.

2 *Irish Saxifrage** *Saxifraga rosacea*, p. 116, is almost confined to Ireland, especially the Burren, with the stouter $ssp. *hartii* only on Arranmore Island, Donegal. **2a** $St Patrick's Cabbage** *S. spathularis* is especially frequent in SW Ireland. **2b** $Kidney Saxifrage** *S. hirsuta* is less widespread. Their hybrid may occur in the absence of Kidney Saxifrage.

2b

2a

2

3 $Irish Whitebeam** *Sorbus hibernica*, p. 370. The only Whitebeam endemic to Ireland.

4 Fuchsia *Fuchsia magellanica*, p. 376, is well naturalised in most coastal districts.

5 Irish Spurge *Euphorbia hyberna*, p. 166. Much commoner in Ireland than elsewhere.

Ivy, p. 396. *Hedera helix* ssp. *hibernica*, the common subspecies in Ireland, has pale yellowish-brown hairs.

Hedge Bindweed *Calystegia sepium*, p. 204. The pink-flowered Bindweed seen in many parts of Ireland is a form of this species.

6 Water Germander *Teucrium scordium*, p. 224, is frequent on shores of the Shannon loughs, Derg and Ree.

7 Corsican Mint *Mentha requienii*. Well naturalised, N slope of Slieve Gullion, Armagh, and head of Killary Harbour, Galway.

Lousewort *Pedicularis sylvatica*, p. 234. The flower-stalks and joined sepals of the Irish ssp. *hibernica* are downy.

8 $Eyebright** *Euphrasia salisburgensis* is found only in Ireland. Other Irish species are starred on p. 236.

9 $Irish Butterwort** *Pinguicula grandiflora*, p. 250, is confined as a native to SW Ireland.

10 Californian Honeysuckle *Lonicera involucrata* (Honeysuckle Family, p. 258). Shrub to 2m, with branches often arching, leaves pointed oval, pale yellow flowers often tinged red, and berry black with purple bracts, often in old hedges.

11 $*Irish Fleabane** *Inula salicina*, p. 274. Now one of the rarest Irish plants, confined to a very few sites on L. Derg, Tipperary.

12 $*Cottonweed** *Otanthus maritimus*, p. 278. Now only one site in Britain/Ireland, Lady's Island Lake, Wexford.

Hawkweeds, p. 300. Ironically, the commonest hawkweed in Ireland is named *Hieracium anglicum*.

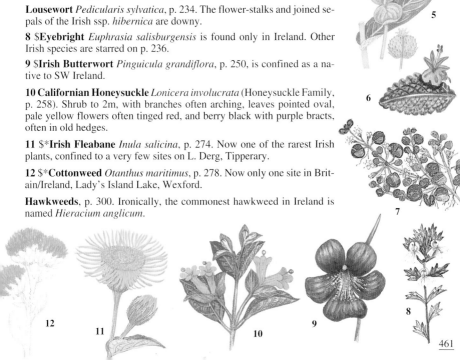

461

1 $Kerry Lily *Simethis planifolia*, p. 312. A Lusitanian plant, confined to gorse-covered rocky heaths around Derrynane, Co. Kerry.

Crow Garlic *Allium vineale*, p. 318, may have blue flowers in Kerry.

2 Common Spotted Orchid *Dactylorhiza fuchsii*, p. 326, has a pure white form $ssp. *o'kellyi* in W Ireland. **Western Marsh Orchid** *D. majalis*, p. 326, usually has unspotted leaves in Ireland. **2a $Dense-flowered Orchid** *Neotinea maculata*, p. 330, is confined to the Burren and other limestone areas in the W.

3 Irish Lady's Tresses *Spiranthes romanzoffiana*, p. 332, is scattered in coastal districts, with several sites around L. Neagh.

4 *Slender Cotton-grass *Eriophorum gracile*, p. 434, is more frequent in Ireland than in Great Britain.

5 Grass-leaved Rush *Juncus planifolius* (Rush Family, p. 418). Flowers dark brown in tight stalked heads. Leaves grass-like, shiny. Fruits warm brown glossy. By tracks and loughs, especially around Carna, Galway; introduced from Australia.

6 Slender Naiad *Najas flexilis*, p. 352, is more frequent and **Pipewort** *Eriocaulon aquaticum*, p. 344, much more frequent in Ireland than in Great Britain.

7 *Esthwaite Waterweed *Hydrilla verticillata* p. 348. Now confined to a small lough in W Galway, but recently found in Galloway; formerly also in Esthwaite Water, Cumbria.

8 $Marsh Water Starwort *Callitriche palustris*, frequently misreported as a British/Irish plant, was discovered in July 1999 on the dried bed of a turlough in W Ireland and more recently in Scotland. It differs from other semi-terrestrial water starworts (p. 356) especially in the fruits being distinctly longer than wide, narrower at the base than at the tip and with wings broad at the tip but absent at the base.

Creeping Raspwort *Haloragis micrantha* (Water-milfoil Family, p. 350). An often tiny mat-forming plant, to 1m, with obscure greenish 4-petalled flowers (August-Oct) and opposite, rounded, un- or scarcely toothed leaves, naturalised on bare wet peat in a bog in Galway.

Specialities of the Burren, Clare, a region of limestone hills and pavements surrounding the Burren Hills: a fine spring display of Bloody Cranesbill, p. 174, Early Purple Orchid, p. 328, Hoary Rock-rose, p. 70, Mountain Avens, p. 134, and Spring Gentian, p. 198. Less conspicuous are Shrubby Cinquefoil, p. 132, Fen Violet, p. 80, Pyramidal Bugle, p. 224, Dense-flowered Orchid, p. 330, Dark Red Helleborine, p. 334, the endemic ssp. *o'kellyi* of the Common Spotted Orchid, p. 326, Irish Saxifrage, p. 116, Mountain Sandwort, p. 54, Maidenhair Fern, p. 448, and Irish Eyebright, p. 236.

Specialities of the Killarney District, Kerry*: Strawberry Tree, p. 384, St. Patrick's Cabbage, Kidney Saxifrage and their hybrid, p. 116, Great and Pale Butterworts, p. 250, Blue-eyed Grass, p. 322, Kerry Lily p. 312, near Derrynane, Tunbridge and Wilson's Filmy Ferns, p. 440, the increasingly rare Killarney Fern, p. 450, and Irish Spleenwort, p. 448.

Specialities of Connemara and Galway: Irish, Mackay's and St Dabeoc's Heaths, p. 104, Pipewort, p. 344, the only Irish sites for *Callitriche palustris*, above, Esthwaite Waterweed, p. 348, Grass-leaved Rush, and Creeping Raspwort, above.

1 Creeping Spearwort *Ranunculus reptans* (Buttercup Family, p. 22). Frequently reported extinct, but reappears from time to time; exact number of current localities uncertain. **2 Pheasant's Eye** *Adonis annua*. A long-established red-flowered arable weed, now virtually extinct except as a rare casual, and in one area of Salisbury Plain.

3 Jagged Chickweed *Holosteum umbellatum* (Pink Family, p. 44). White-flowered annual, dry sandy places, walls. Extinct since 1930. **Boyd's Pearl-wort** *Sagina boydii*. Presumed discovered in Aberdeenshire in 1878; never seen in the wild since, but perpetuated in cultivation. **4 Corn-cockle** *Agrostemma githago*. Extinct, except as casual or sown.

5 Arctic Bramble *Rubus arcticus* (Rose Family, p. 144). Pink-flowered. Scottish moors. Extinct for well over 100 years.

6 Black Pea *Lathyrus niger* (Pea Family, p. 124). Flowers purple. Long extinct as a native at Killiekrankie and elsewhere in Scotland; now only on a railway bank at Tunbridge Wells, Kent, otherwise a rare casual.

7 Hairy Spurge *Euphorbia villosa* (Spurge Family, p. 166). Known in a coppiced wood and hedge-bank near Bath, Somerset, from 1576 to 1941, dying out when coppicing ceased.

8 Sussex Yellow Sorrel *Oxalis dillenii* (Wood-sorrel Family, p. 172). Established near Pulborough, Sussex, for 34 years to 1984.

9 Sickle Hare's-ear *Bupleurum falcatum* (Carrot Family, p. 180). Known (perhaps native) in Essex from 1831 till the site was destroyed in 1962; reintroduced in several sites in the county and may yet return. Our only Hare's-ear to look like a conventional (yellow) umbellifer. **10 Thorow-wax** *B. rotundifolium*, which looked like False Thorow-wax (p. 196), was an arable weed which became extinct by the 1980s.

Broad-leaved Centaury *Centaurium latifolium* (Gentian Family, p. 198). Probably a variant of Common Centaury (p. 200), found on the Lancashire coast but now extinct.

1 Flax Dodder *Cuscuta epilinum* (Dodder Family, p. 200). Formerly a pest of flax fields, became extinct in 1968, but should perhaps be looked for again in the increasingly Europe-funded flax fields of today.

2 Downy Hemp-Nettle *Galeopsis segetum* (Dead-nettle Family, p. 216). Only ever considered native in a few fields in Caernarfonshire, where it is now virtually extinct. Otherwise rare casual. Like Red Hemp-Nettle (p. 218), but with yellow flowers.

3 Hemp Broomrape *Orobanche ramosa* (Broomrape Family, p. 244). Often branched, was a pest of Hemp (p. 36) fields until 1928, but thanks to European grants might well return.

4 Alpine Butterwort *Pinguicula alpina* (Butterworts p. 250). Flowers white. Extinct in Easter Ross since *c.* 1900.

5 Marsh Fleawort *Tephroseris palustris* (Daisy Family, p. 264). A fen plant with daisy-type yellow flowers, extinct since 1899. **6 Swine's Succory** *Arnoseris minima*. A plant of sandy fields in E Britain with tiny dandelion-type yellow flowers, extinct since 1971. Succory is an old name for Chicory.

7 Summer Lady's Tresses *Spiranthes aestivalis* (Orchid Family, p. 326). Our only extinct Orchid, with larger flowers and longer bracts than Autumn Lady's Tresses (p. 332), has not been seen in its only British site, the New Forest, since 1959.

8 Interrupted Brome *Bromus interruptus* (Grasses, see p. 402), an endemic British grass, a former weed of Sainfoin (p. 154) fields, became in 1972 extinct world-wide.

9 Sharp Club-rush *Schoenoplectus pungens* (Sedges, see p. 402) became extinct in its only British site on the Lancashire coast, but has been reintroduced; stems 3-sided. **Alpine Deergrass** *Trichophorum hudsonianum* became extinct when its sole site, a bog in Angus, was drained in 1813. **Bath Sedge** *Carex davalliana*, like Dioecious Sedge (p. 438) but forming tussocks, became extinct in Somerset *c.* 1845. **Rannoch-rush** *Scheuchzeria palustris*, p. 248, was found in Offaly in 1951, but is apparently now extinct.

INDEX OF
SCIENTIFIC NAMES

INDEX OF
ENGLISH NAMES